Level I

Paradigm
PUBLISHING

Microsoft®

Word

2007

BENCHMARK SERIES

Nita Rutkosky
Pierce College at Puyallup
Puyallup, Washington

Audrey Rutkosky Roggenkamp
Pierce College at Puyallup
Puyallup, Washington

Managing Editor	Sonja Brown
Production Editor	Donna Mears
Cover and Text Designer	Leslie Anderson
Copy Editor	Susan Capecchi
Desktop Production	John Valo, Desktop Solutions
Proofreader	Laura Nelson
Indexer	Nancy Fulton

Acknowledgments: The authors and editors wish to thank the following individuals for their technical and academic contributions.

- Catherine Caldwell, a technical writer and consultant from Memphis, Tennessee, tested the instruction and exercises for accuracy.
- Madlyn Huber, Instructor, Bridgerland Applied Technology College, Logan, Utah, tested exercises for accuracy and prepared annotated model answers.
- Pamela J. Silvers, Chairperson, Business Computer Technologies, Asheville-Buncombe Technical Community College, Asheville, North Carolina, tested the instruction and exercises for accuracy.

Care has been taken to verify the accuracy of information presented in this book. However, the authors, editors, and publisher cannot accept responsibility for Web, e-mail, newsgroup, or chat room subject matter or content, or for consequences from application of the information in this book, and make no warranty, expressed or implied, with respect to its content.

Photo Credits: Introduction page 1 (clockwise from top), Lexmark International, Inc., courtesy of Dell Inc., all rights Hewlett-Packard Company, Logitech, Micron Technology, Inc.; Word Level 1 page 3, Asia Images Group/AsiaPix/Getty Images, page 4, © Corbis; photos in Student Resources CD, courtesy of Kelly Rutkosky and Michael Rutkosky.

Trademarks: Microsoft is a trademark or registered trademark of Microsoft Corporation in the United States and/or other countries. Some of the product names and company names included in this book have been used for identification purposes only and may be trademarks or registered trade names of their respective manufacturers and sellers. The authors, editors, and publisher disclaim any affiliation, association, or connection with, or sponsorship or endorsement by, such owners.

We have made every effort to trace the ownership of all copyrighted material and to secure permission from copyright holders. In the event of any question arising as to the use of any material, we will be pleased to make the necessary corrections in future printings. Thanks are due to the aforementioned authors, publishers, and agents for permission to use the materials indicated.

ISBN 978-0-76382-984-1 (Text)
ISBN 978-0-76383-000-7 (Text + CD)

CONTENTS

Unit 2 Enhancing and Customizing Documents — 151

Chapter 5 Applying Formatting and Inserting Objects — 153

Chapter 6 Maintaining Documents — 193

Benchmark Microsoft Word 2007 is designed for students who want to learn how to use this powerful word processing program to create professional-looking documents for workplace, school, and personal communication needs. No prior knowledge of word processing is required. After successfully completing a course using this textbook, students will be able to

- Create and edit memos, letters, and reports of varying complexity
- Apply appropriate formatting elements and styles to a range of document types
- Add graphics and other visual elements to enhance written communication
- Plan, research, write, revise, and publish documents to meet specific information needs
- Given a workplace scenario requiring a written solution, assess the communication purpose and then prepare the materials that achieve the goal efficiently and effectively

In addition to mastering Word skills, students will learn the essential features and functions of computer hardware, the Windows XP operating system, and Internet Explorer 7.0. Upon completing the text, they can expect to be proficient in using Word to organize, analyze, and present information.

Achieving Proficiency in Word 2007

Since its inception several Office versions ago, the Benchmark Series has served as a standard of excellence in software instruction. Elements of the book function individually and collectively to create an inviting, comprehensive learning environment that produces successful computer users.

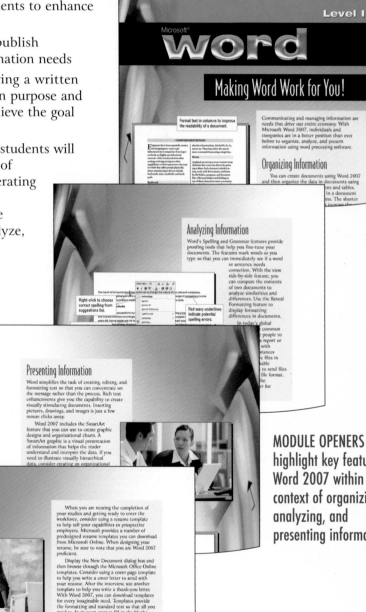

MODULE OPENERS highlight key features of Word 2007 within the context of organizing, analyzing, and presenting information.

Level 1

Microsoft®
word

Unit 2: Enhancing and Customizing Documents

➤ Applying Formatting and Inserting Objects

➤ Maintaining Documents

➤ Creating Tables and SmartArt

➤ Merging Documents

UNIT OPENERS display the unit's four chapter titles. Each level has two units, which conclude with a comprehensive unit performance assessment.

CHAPTER
5

Applying Formatting and Inserting Objects

CHAPTER OPENERS present the Performance Objectives and an overview of the skills taught.

PERFORMANCE OBJECTIVES

Upon successful completion of Chapter 5, you will be able to:

- Insert section breaks
- Create and format text in columns
- Hyphenate words automatically and manually
- Create a drop cap
- Insert symbols, special characters, and the date and time
- Use the Click and Type feature
- Vertically align text
- Insert, format, and customize pictures, clip art images, text boxes, shapes, and WordArt

word Chapter 5

SNAP

Tutorial 5.1
Creating Presentable Documents
Tutorial 5.2
Using Additional Features

CD icon identifies a folder of data files to be copied to the student's storage medium.

The SNAP icon alerts students to corresponding SNAP tutorial titles.

To apply page or document formatting to only a portion of the document, insert a section break. You can insert a continuous section break or a section break that begins a new page. A section break is useful when formatting text in columns. The hyphenation feature hyphenates words at the end of lines, creating a less ragged margin. Use buttons in the Text and Symbols groups in the Insert tab to insert symbols, special characters, and the date and time. With the Click and Type feature, you can position the insertion point at various locations in the document and change the paragraph alignment. Use the *Vertical alignment* option at the Page Setup dialog box with the Layout tab selected to align text vertically on the page. Along with these features, you will also learn how to increase the visual appeal of a document by inserting and customizing images such as pictures, clip art, text boxes, shapes, and WordArt.

Note: Before beginning computer projects, copy to your storage medium the Word2007L1C5 subfolder from the Word2007L1 folder on the CD that accompanies this textbook and then make Word2007L1C5 the active folder.

New! PROJECT APPROACH organizes instruction and practice into projects that focus on related program features.

roject **1** **Format a Document on Computer Input Devices**
You will format into columns text in a document on computer input devices, improve the readability of the document by hyphenating long words, and improve the visual appeal by inserting a drop cap.

Project overview identifies tasks to accomplish and the features to use in completing the work.

word Level 1
Applying Formatting and Inserting Objects **153**

PROJECT APPROACH: Builds Skill Mastery within Realistic Context

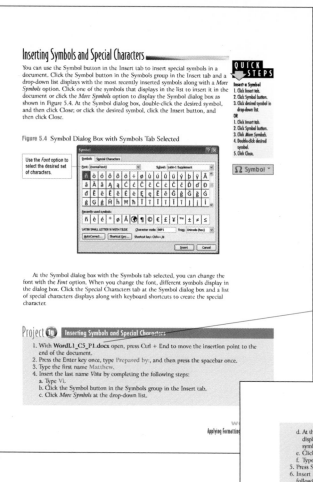

Following each project part, the text presents instruction on the features and skills necessary to accomplish the next section of the project.

Typically, a file remains open throughout all parts of the project. Students save their work incrementally.

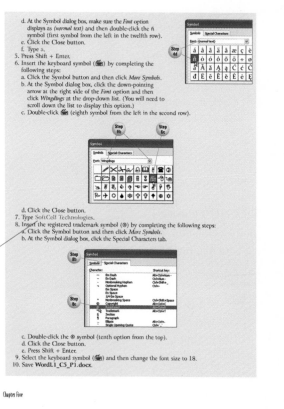

Each project exercise guides students step by step to a successful conclusion. Screen captures illustrate what the screen should look like at key points.

Text in magenta identifies material to type.

At the end of the project, students print their work. Locked, watermarked model answers in PDF format on the Student Resources CD allow students to check their work. This option rewards careful effort and ensures software mastery.

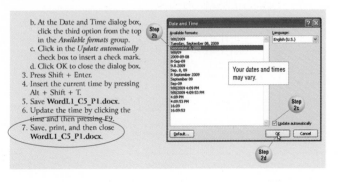

b. At the Date and Time dialog box, click the third option from the top in the *Available formats* group.
c. Click in the *Update automatically* check box to insert a check mark.
d. Click OK to close the dialog box.
3. Press Shift + Enter.
4. Insert the current time by pressing Alt + Shift + T.
5. Save **WordL1_C5_P1.docx**.
6. Update the time by clicking the time and then pressing F9.
7. Save, print, and then close **WordL1_C5_P1.docx**.

Project 2 Create an Announcement about Supervisory Training

You will create an announcement about upcoming supervisory training and use the click and type feature to center and right align text. You will vertically center the text on the page and insert and format a picture to add visual appeal to the announcement.

QUICK STEPS

Use Click and Type
1. Hover mouse at left margin, between left and right margin, or at right margin.
2. Double-click left mouse button.

QUICK STEPS

Use Click and Type
1. Hover mouse at left margin, between left and right margin, or at right margin.
2. Double-click left mouse button.

Using the Click and Type Feature

Word contains a click and type feature you can use to position the insertion point at a specific location and alignment in the document. This feature allows you to position one or more lines of text as you write (type), rather than typing the text and then selecting and reformatting the text, which requires multiple steps.

To use click and type, make sure the document displays in Print Layout view and then hover the mouse pointer at the location where you want the insertion point positioned. As you move the mouse pointer, you will notice that the pointer displays with varying horizontal lines representing the alignment. Double-click the mouse button and the insertion point is positioned at the location of the mouse pointer. Turn off the click and type feature by clicking the Office button and then clicking Word Options. Click the Advanced option in the left pane, click the *Enable click and type* check box to remove the check mark, and then click OK.

QUICK STEPS provide feature summaries for reference and review.

CHAPTER REVIEW ACTIVITIES: A Hierarchy of Learning Assessments

CHAPTER summary

- Insert a section break in a document to apply formatting to a portion of a document. You can insert a continuous section break or a section break that begins a new page. View a section break in Draft view since section breaks are not visible in Print Layout view.
- Set text in columns to improve readability of documents such as newsletters or reports. Format text in columns using the Columns button in the Page Setup group in the Page Layout tab or with options at the Columns dialog box.
- Remove column formatting with the Columns button in the Page Layout tab or at the Columns dialog box. Balance column text on the last page of a document by inserting a continuous section break at the end of the text.
- Improve the display of text lines by hyphenating long words that fall at the end of the line. You can automatically or manually hyphenate words in a document.
- To enhance the appearance of text, use drop caps to identify the beginning of major sections or parts of a paragraph. Create drop caps with the Drop Cap button in the Text group in the Insert tab.
- Insert symbols with options at the Symbol dialog box with the Symbols tab selected and insert special characters with options at the Symbol dialog box with the Special Characters [...]
- Click the Date & Time bu[...] the Date and Time dialog [...] dialog box or with keyboard [...] update the field with the [...]
- Use the click and type fea[...]
- Vertically align text in a d[...] Setup dialog box with the [...]
- Insert an image such as a [...] group in the Insert tab.
- Customize and format an [...] Format tab. Size an image [...] Picture Tools Format tab [...] selected image.
- Move an image with optio[...] in the Picture Tools Forma[...] moving the image by drag[...]
- To insert a picture, click t[...] desired folder at the Inser[...]
- To insert a clip art image, [...] then click the desired ima[...]
- Insert a pull quote in a d[...] tab, clicking the Text Box [...] box at the drop-down list. [...]

CHAPTER SUMMARY captures the purpose and execution of key features.

186 Chapter Five

COMMANDS review

FEATURE	RIBBON TAB, GROUP	BUTTON	OPTION	KEYBOARD SHORTCUT
Continuous section break	Page Layout, Page Setup	Breaks	Continuous	
Columns dialog box	Page Layout, Page Setup	Columns	More Columns	
Columns	Page Layout, Page Setup	Columns		
Hyphenate words automatically	Page Layout, Page Setup	Hyphenation	Automatic	
Manual Hyphenation dialog box	Page Layout, Page Setup	Hyphenation	Manual	
Drop cap	Insert, Text	Drop Cap		
Symbol dialog box	Insert, Symbols	Symbol		
Date and Time dialog box	Insert, Text	Date & Time		
Insert date				Alt + Shift + D
Insert time				
Update field				
Page Setup dialog box	Page Layout, Page Setup			
Insert Picture dialog box	Insert, Illustrations			
Clip Art task pane	Insert, Illustrations			
Pull quote (Built-in text box)	Insert, Text			
Shapes	Insert, Illustrations			
Text box	Insert, Text			
Link text box	Text Box Tools Format, Text			
Select objects	Home, Editing			
WordArt	Insert, Text			

COMMANDS REVIEW summarizes visually the major features and alternative methods of access.

188 Chapter Five

CONCEPTS check

Test Your Knowledge

Completion: On a blank sheet of paper, indicate the correct term, symbol, or command for each item.

1. View a section break in this view.

2. Format text into columns with the Columns button located in this group in the Page Layout tab.

3. Balance column text on the last page of a document by inserting this type of break at the end of the text.

4. The first letter of the first word of a paragraph that is set into a paragraph is called this.

5. The Symbol button is located in this tab.

6. This is the keyboard shortcut to insert the current date.

7. Use this feature to position the insertion point at a specific location and alignment in a document.

8. Vertically align text with the *Vertical alignment* option at the Page Setup dialog box with this tab selected.

9. Insert an image in a document with buttons in this group in the Insert tab.

10. Customize and format an image with options and buttons in this tab.

11. Size an image with the sizing handles that display around the selected image or with these boxes in the Picture Tools Format tab.

12. Click the Picture button in the Insert tab and this dialog box displays.

13. Click the Clip Art button in the Insert tab and this displays at the right side of the screen.

14. This is the term for a quote that is enlarged and positioned in an attractive location on the page.

15. Format text boxes with options and buttons in this tab.

16. The Shapes button is located in this tab.

CONCEPTS CHECK questions assess knowledge recall.

word Level 1
Applying Formatting and Inserting Objects 189

17. To copy a selected shape, hold down this key while dragging the shape.

18. Link text boxes using this button in the Text group.

19. To select multiple objects in a document, click the Select button in the Editing group in the Home tab and then click this option.

20. Use this feature to distort or modify text to conform to a variety of shapes.

SKILLS check
Demonstrate Your Proficiency

Assessment

1 ADD VISUAL APPEAL TO A REPORT ON THE FUTURE OF THE INTERNET

1. Open **WordReport02.docx** and then save the document and name it **WordL1_C5_A1**.
2. Remove the first line indent by selecting text from the beginning of the first paragraph of text to the end of the document and then dragging the First Line Indent marker on the horizontal ruler to the 0″ mark.
3. Apply the Heading 1 style to the title of the report and apply the Heading 2 style to the headings in the report.
4. Change the Quick Styles set to *Formal*.
5. Format the text from the first paragraph to the end of the document into two columns with 0.4 inches between columns.
6. Select the title *FUTURE OF THE INTERNET* and then change the font size to 16 points, increase the spacing after the title to 12 points and, if necessary center-align the title.
7. Balance the text on the second page.
8. Insert a clip art image related to *satellite*. (Choose the clip art image that is available with Word and does not require downloading. This clip art image is blue and black and contains a satellite and a person holding a telephone and a briefcase.)
9. Make the following customizations to the clip art image:
   a. Change the height to 1.3″.
   b. Apply tight text wrapping.
   c. Recolor the clip art image to Accent color 6 Dark.
   d. Change the brightness to +10%.
   e. Drag the image so it is positioned at the left margin in the *Satellite Internet Connections* section.
10. Insert the *Alphabet Quote* built-in text box and then make the following customizations:
   a. Type the following text in the text box: "A remedy for the traffic clogging the information highway is Internet2."

SKILLS CHECK exercises ask students to create a variety of documents using multiple features without how-to directions.

CASE study
Apply Your Skills

Part 1
You work for Honoré Financial Services and have been asked by the office manager, Jason Monroe, to prepare an information newsletter. Mr. Monroe has asked you open the document named **WordBudget.docx** and then format it into columns. You determine the number of columns and any additional enhancements to the columns. He also wants you to proofread the document and correct any spelling and grammatical errors. Save the completed newsletter and name it **WordL1_C5_CS_P1** and then print the newsletter. When Mr. Monroe reviews the newsletter, he decides that it needs additional visual appeal. He wants you to insert visual elements in the newsletter such as WordArt, clip art, a built-in text box, and/or a drop cap. Save **WordL1_C5_CS_P1.docx** and then print and close the document.

Part 2
Honoré Financial Services will be offering a free workshop on Planning for Financial Success. Mr. Monroe has asked you to prepare an announcement containing information on the workshop. You determine what to include in the announcement such as the date, time, location, and so forth. Enhance the announcement by inserting a picture or clip art and by applying formatting such as font, paragraph alignment, and borders. Save the completed document and name it **WordL1_C5_CS_P2**. Print and then close the document.

Part 3
Honoré Financial Services has adopted a new slogan and Mr. Monroe has asked you to create a shape with the new slogan inside. Experiment with the shadow and 3-D effects available at the Text Box Tools Format tab and then create a shape and enhance the shape with shadow and/or 3-D effects. Insert the new Honoré Financial Services slogan "Retirement Planning Made Easy" in the shape. Include any additional enhancements to improve the visual appeal of the shape and slogan. Save the completed document and name it **WordL1_C5_CS_P3**. Print and then close the document.

Part 4
Mr. Monroe has asked you to prepare a document containing information on teaching children how to budget. Use the Internet to find Web sites and articles that provide information on how to teach children to budget their money. Write a synopsis of the information you find and include at least four suggestions on how to teach children to manage their money. Format the text in the document into newspaper columns. Add additional enhancements to improve the appearance of the document. Save the completed newsletter and name it **WordL1_C5_CS_P4**. Print and then close the document.

The chapter CASE STUDY requires planning and executing multi-part workplace projects.

Students search the Web and/or use the program's Help feature to locate information.

UNIT PERFORMANCE ASSESSMENT: Cross-Disciplinary, Comprehensive Evaluation

Unit 2
Enhancing and Customizing Documents

ASSESSING proficiency

In this unit, you have learned to format text into columns; insert, format, and customize objects to enhance the visual appeal of a document; manage files, print envelopes and labels, and create documents using templates; create and edit tables; visually represent data in SmartArt diagrams and organizational charts; and use Mail Merge to create letters, envelopes, labels, and directions.

Note: Before beginning unit assessments, delete the Word2007L1C8 folder from your storage medium. Next, copy to your storage medium the Word2007L1U2 subfolder from the Word2007L1 folder on the CD that accompanies this textbook and then make Word2007L1U2 the active folder.

Assessment 1 Format a Technology Occupations Document
1. Open WordReport09.docx and then save the document and name it WordL1_U2_A1.
2. Move the insertion point to the beginning of the heading *Telecommuting* and then insert the file named **WordDocument19.docx**.
3. Apply the Heading 1 style to the title and the Heading 2 style to the headings in the document.
4. Change the Quick Styles set to *Formal*.
5. Insert a continuous section break at the beginning of the first paragraph of text (the paragraph that begins *The march of computer technology . . .*).
6. Format the text below the section break into two newspaper columns.
7. Balance the columns on the second page.
8. Insert a pull quote of your choosing on the first page of the document that includes the text *"As the future of wireless unfolds, many new jobs will emerge as well."*
9. Create a drop cap with the first letter of the first word *The* that begins the first paragraph of text and make the drop cap two lines in height.
10. Manually hyphenate words in the document.
11. Insert page numbering that prints at the bottom of each page (you determine the page number formatting).
12. Save, print, and then close **WordL1_U2_A1.docx**.

Assessment 2 Create a Workshop Flyer
1. Create the flyer shown in Figure U2.1 with the following specifications:
   a. Insert the WordArt shape with WordArt style 15 and then customize the WordArt by changing the shadow effect to Shadow Style 1, the shape to Deflate Bottom, and increasing the width of the WordArt to 6.5" and the height to 1".

ASSESSING PROFICIENCY
checks mastery of features.

WRITING ACTIVITIES involve applying program skills in a communication context.

WRITING activities
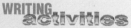

The following activities give you the opportunity to practice your writing skills along with demonstrating an understanding of some of the important Word features you have mastered in this unit. Use correct grammar, appropriate word choices, and clear sentence constructions.

Activity 1 Compose a Letter to Volunteers
You are an employee for the City of Greenwater and are responsible for coordinating volunteers for the city's Safe Night program. Compose a letter to the volunteers listed below and include the following information in the letter:
- Safe Night event scheduled for Saturday, June 19, 2010.
- Volunteer orientation scheduled for Thursday, May 20, 2010, at 7:30 p.m. At the orientation, participants will learn about the types of volunteer positions available and the work schedule.

Include any additional information in the letter, including a thank you to the volunteers. Use the Mail Merge feature to create a data source with the names [...] main document, which is the letter to the [...] WordL1_U2_Act01 and then print the [...]

Mr. Matthew Klein
7408 Ryan Road
Greenwater, OR 99034

Mr. Brian McDonald
8980 Union Street
Greenwater, OR 99034

Mrs. Nola Alverez
598 McBride Street
Greenwater, OR 99034

[...]ead

[...] shipping business and need letterhead [...] company in a header and/or footer. Use [...]ating a header that only displays and prints [...] in a header that displays and prints only on [...] the following: clip art image, a picture, a [...]de the following information in the header:

[...]e it WordL1_U2_Act02. Print and then

INTERNET research

Create a Flyer on an Incentive Program
The owner of Evergreen Travel is offering an incentive to motivate travel consultants to increase travel bookings. The incentive is a sales contest with a grand prize of a one-week paid vacation to Cancun, Mexico. The owner has asked you to create a flyer that will be posted on the office bulletin board that includes information about the incentive program and some information about Cancun. Create this flyer using information about Cancun that you find on the Internet. Include a photo you find on a Web site (make sure it is not copyrighted) or include a clip art image representing travel. Include any other information or object to add visual appeal to the flyer. Save the completed flyer and name it **WordL1_U2_InternetResearch**. Print and then close the document.

INTERNET RESEARCH project reinforces research, writing, and word processing skills.

JOB study

Develop Recycling Program Communications
The Chief Operating Officer of Harrington Engineering has just approved your draft of the company's new recycling policy (see the file named **WordRecyclingPolicy.docx** located in the Word2007L1U2 folder) with a note that you need to add some statistics on national average costs of recycling, which you can locate on the Internet. Edit the draft and prepare a final copy of the policy along with a memorandum to all employees describing the new guidelines. To support the company's energy resources conservation effort, you will send hard copies of the new policy to the Somerset Recycling Program president and to directors of Somerset Chamber of Commerce.

Using the concepts and techniques you learned in this unit, prepare the following documents:
- Format the recycling policy manual, including a cover page, appropriate headers and footers, and page numbers. Add at least one graphic and one diagram where appropriate. Format the document using a Quick Styles set and styles. Save the manual and name it **WordL1_U2_JobStudyManual**. Print the manual.
- Download a memo template from the Microsoft Online Web site and then create a memo from Susan Gerhardt, Chief Operating Officer of Harrington Engineering to all employees introducing the new recycling program. Copy the *Procedure* section of the recycling policy manual into the memo where appropriate. Include a table listing five employees who will act as Recycling Coordinators at Harrington Engineering (make up the names). Add columns for the employees' department names and their telephone extensions. Save the memo and name it **WordL1_U2_JobStudyMemo**. Print the memo.
- Write a letter to the President of the Somerset Recycling Program, William Elizondo, enclosing a copy of the recycling policy manual. Add a notation

JOB STUDY presents a capstone assessment requiring critical thinking and problem solving.

Student Courseware

Student Resources CD Each Benchmark Series textbook is packaged with a Student Resources CD containing the data files required for completing the projects and assessments. A CD icon and folder name displayed on the opening page of chapters reminds students to copy a folder of files from the CD to the desired storage medium before beginning the project exercises. Directions for copying folders are printed on the inside back cover. The Student Resources CD also contains the model answers in PDF format for the project exercises within chapters. Files are locked and watermarked, but students can compare their completed documents with the PDF files, either on screen or in hard copy (printed) format.

Internet Resource Center Additional learning tools and reference materials are available at the book-specific Web site at www.emcp.net/BenchmarkWord07XP. Students can access the same resources that are on the Student Resources CD along with study aids, Web links, and tips for using computers effectively in academic and workplace settings.

SNAP Training and Assessment SNAP is a Web-based program that provides hands-on instruction, practice, and testing for learning Microsoft Office 2007 and Windows. SNAP course work simulates operations of Office 2007. The program is comprised of a Web-based learning management system, multimedia tutorials, performance skill items, a concept test bank, and online grade book and course planning tools. A CD-based set of tutorials teaching the basics of Office and Windows is also available for additional practice not requiring Internet access.

Class Connections Available for both WebCT and Blackboard e-learning platforms, Paradigm's Class Connection provides self-quizzes and study aids and facilitates communication among students and instructors via e-mail and e-discussion.

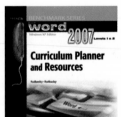

Instructor Resources

Curriculum Planner and Resources Instructor support for the Benchmark Series has been expanded to include a *Curriculum Planner and Resources* binder with CD. This all-in-one print resource includes planning resources such as Lesson Blueprints and sample course syllabi; presentation resources such as teaching hints and handouts; and assessment resources including an overview of assessment venues, model answers for intrachapter projects, and annotated model answers for end-of-chapter and end-of-unit assessments. Contents of the *Curriculum Planner and Resources* binder are also available on the Instructor's CD and on the password-protected Instructor's section of the Internet Resource Center for this title at www.emcp.com.

Computerized Test Generator Instructors can use ExamView test generating software and the provided bank of multiple-choice items to create customized Web-based or print tests.

System Requirements

This text is designed for the student to complete projects and assessments on a computer running a standard installation of Microsoft Office 2007, Professional Edition, and the Microsoft Windows XP operating system with Service Pack 2 or later. To effectively run this suite and operating system, your computer should be outfitted with the following:

- 500 MHz processor or higher; 256 MB RAM or higher
- DVD drive
- 2 GB of available hard-disk space
- CD-ROM drive
- 800 by 600 minimum monitor resolution; 1024 by 768 recommended
  Note: Screen captures in this book were created using 1024 by 768 resolution; screens with higher resolution may look different.
- Computer mouse or compatible pointing device

About the Authors

Nita Rutkosky began teaching business education courses at Pierce College in Puyallup, Washington, in 1978. Since then she has taught a variety of software applications to students in postsecondary Information Technology certificate and degree programs. In addition to co-authoring texts in the *Benchmark Office 2007 Series*, she has co-authored *Signature Word 2007*, *Marquee Office 2007*, and *Using Computers in the Medical Office: Microsoft Word, Excel, and PowerPoint 2003*. Other textbooks she has written for Paradigm Publishing include books on previous versions of Microsoft Office along with WordPerfect, desktop publishing, keyboarding, and voice recognition.

    Audrey Rutkosky Roggenkamp has been teaching courses in the Business Information Technology department at Pierce College in Puyallup including keyboarding, skill building, and Microsoft Office programs. In addition to titles in the *Benchmark Office 2007 Series*, she has co-authored *Using Computers in the Medical Office*, *Marquee Office 2007*, and *Signature Word 2007*.

Microsoft® word

Making Word Work for You!

Format text in columns to improve the readability of a document.

COMPUTER INPUT DEVICES

Engineers have been especially creative in designing new ways to get information into computers. Some input methods are highly specialized and unusual, while common devices often undergo redesign to improve their capabilities or their ergonomics, the ways in which they affect people physically. Some common input devices include keyboards, mice, trackballs, and touch pads.

Keyboard

A keyboard can be an external device that is attached by means of a cable, or it can

also have function keys, labeled F1, F2, F3, and so on. These keys allow the user to issue commands by pressing a single key.

Mouse

Graphical operating systems contain many elements that a user can choose by pointing at them. Such elements include buttons, tools, pull-down menus, and icons for file folders, programs, and document files. Often pointing to and clicking on one of these elements is more convenient than using the cursor or arrow keys on the keyboard. This pointing and clicking can be done by using a mouse. The mouse is

Organize text in tables to help readers interpret information more quickly.

TRI-STATE PRODUCTS		
Computer Technology Department Microsoft® Office 2007 Training		
Application	# Enrolled	# Completed
Access 2007	20	15
Excel 2007	62	56
PowerPoint 2007	40	33
Word 2007	80	72
Total	202	176

Communicating and managing information are needs that drive our entire economy. With Microsoft Word 2007, individuals and companies are in a better position than ever before to organize, analyze, and present information using word processing software.

Organizing Information

You can create documents using Word 2007 and then organize the data in documents using a variety of tools such as columns and tables. Improve the readability of text in a document by organizing the text in columns. The shorter line length of column text helps increase the ease with which a person can read the text. Organizing text in tables can help readers interpret complex information much more quickly. For example, which is easier to understand: paragraphs of text identifying various stocks, their type, and their prices—or a table of the same information with columns for stock, stock type, and price? With Word's Table feature, you can create tables or convert existing data into a table.

To help organize personal or company documents, apply a theme to provide a uniform and consistent appearance and help "brand" documents. Apply a Word theme to customize the fonts, colors, and effects applied to data in a document.

Analyzing Information

Word's Spelling and Grammar features provide proofing tools that help you fine-tune your documents. The features mark words as you type so that you can immediately see if a word or sentence needs correction. With the view side-by-side feature, you can compare the contents of two documents to analyze similarities and differences. Use the Reveal Formatting feature to display formatting differences in documents.

In today's global workplace, it is common for two or more people to collaborate on a report or proposal, often with geographical distances between them. Word's ability to save files in different formats, such as PDF (Portable Document Format), allows a person to send files to other collaborators in a common file format. Each person can add comments to the document and return it to the sender for preparing a final version.

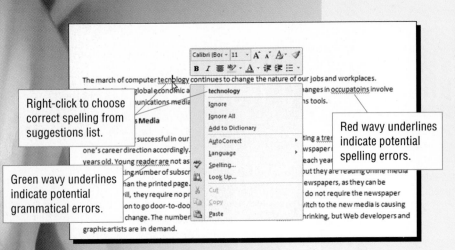

Right-click to choose correct spelling from suggestions list.

Green wavy underlines indicate potential grammatical errors.

Red wavy underlines indicate potential spelling errors.

When sending files to other collaborators, consider saving a document in a universal file format such as PDF.

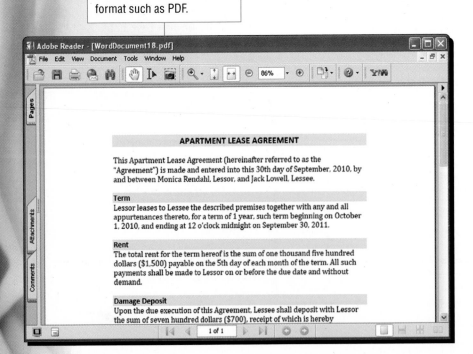

Presenting Information

Word simplifies the task of creating, editing, and formatting text so that you can concentrate on the message rather than the process. Rich text enhancements give you the capability to create visually stimulating documents. Inserting pictures, drawings, and images is just a few mouse clicks away.

Word 2007 includes the SmartArt feature that you can use to create graphic designs and organizational charts. A SmartArt graphic is a visual presentation of information that helps the reader understand and interpret the data. If you need to illustrate visually hierarchical data, consider creating an organizational chart with the SmartArt feature.

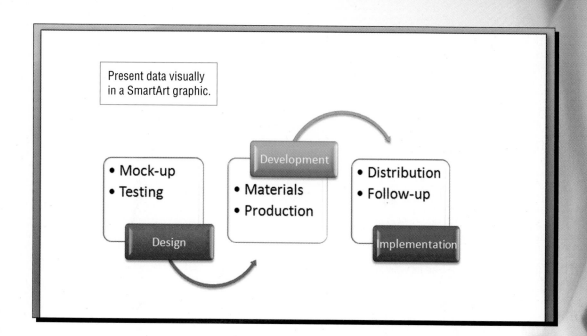

Present data visually in a SmartArt graphic.

When you are nearing the completion of your studies and getting ready to enter the workforce, consider using a resume template to help sell your capabilities to prospective employers. Microsoft provides a number of predesigned resume templates you can download from Microsoft Online. When designing your resume, be sure to note that you are Word 2007 proficient.

Display the New Document dialog box and then browse through the Microsoft Office Online templates. Consider using a cover page template to help you write a cover letter to send with your resume. After the interview, use another template to help you write a thank-you letter. With Word 2007, you can download templates for every imaginable need. Templates provide the formatting and standard text so that all you need to do in most cases is fill in the blanks.

Learning Word is an essential skill for today's employee. Microsoft Word 2007 is an easy-to-use program that will have you creating, editing, and formatting documents in no time—like a pro. You have our word.

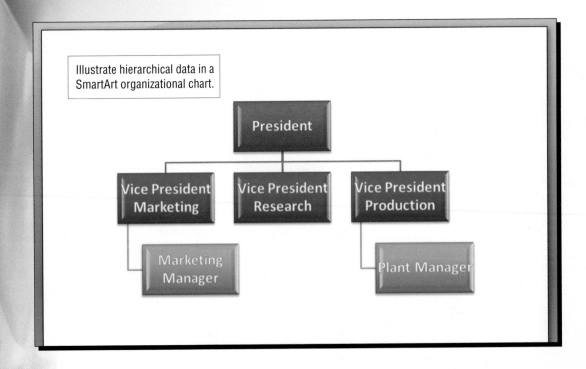

Illustrate hierarchical data in a SmartArt organizational chart.

Level 1

Microsoft® Word

Unit 1: Editing and Formatting Documents

- ➤ Preparing Documents
- ➤ Formatting Characters and Paragraphs
- ➤ Customizing Paragraphs
- ➤ Formatting Pages

Benchmark Microsoft® Word 2007 Level 1

Microsoft Certified Application Specialist Skills—Unit 1

Reference No.	Skill	Pages
1	**Creating and Customizing Documents**	
1.1	Create and format documents	
1.1.2	Apply styles from a Quick Styles set	45-46
1.1.3	Apply themes to documents	47-48
1.1.4	Modify themes	47-48
1.1.5	Format page backgrounds	125-128
1.1.6	Add a blank page or a cover page	115-118, 116-118
1.2	Lay out documents	
1.2.1	Change page format	103-139, 109-118
1.2.2	Insert and edit headers and footers (not using Quick Parts)	120-125, 124, 125
2	**Formatting Content**	
2.1	Format text and paragraphs	
2.1.1	Format with Format Painter	57-58
2.1.3	Change typestyles, fonts, and font effects	36-44
2.1.4	Customize paragraph formats	48-56, 69-97
2.1.5	Manipulate tabs	82-85
2.2	Manipulate text	
2.2.1	Cut, move, copy, and paste text	88-93
2.2.2	Use Find and Replace	129-136
2.3	Control pagination	
2.3.1	Insert and remove page breaks	114-115
3	**Working with Visual Content**	
3.2	Format illustrations	
3.2.3	Use Quick Styles	45-46
5	**Reviewing Documents**	
5.1	Navigate documents	106-108
5.1.1	Locate and move to locations in a document; use Find and Go To	17-19
5.1.2	Switch to a different window view	104-109

Note: The Level 1 and Level 2 texts each address approximately half of the Microsoft Certified Application Specialist skills. Complete coverage of the skills is offered in the combined Level 1 and Level 2 text titled *Benchmark Series Microsoft® Word 2007: Levels 1 and 2,* which has been approved as certified courseware and which displays the Microsoft Certified Application Specialist logo on the cover.

Preparing Documents

PERFORMANCE OBJECTIVES

Upon successful completion of Chapter 1, you will be able to:

- **Open Microsoft Word**
- **Create, save, name, print, open, and close a Word document**
- **Exit Word and Windows**
- **Edit a document**
- **Move the insertion point within a document**
- **Scroll within a document**
- **Select text in a document**
- **Use the Undo and Redo buttons**
- **Check spelling and grammar in a document**
- **Use the Help feature**

Tutorial 1.1
Creating a Document

In this chapter, you will learn to create, save, name, print, open, close, and edit a Word document as well as complete a spelling and grammar check. You will also learn about the Help feature, which is an on-screen reference manual providing information on features and commands for each program in the Office suite. Before continuing, make sure you read the *Getting Started* section presented at the beginning of this book. This section contains information about computer hardware and software, using the mouse, executing commands, and exploring Help files.

Note: Before beginning computer projects, copy to your storage medium the Word2007L1C1 subfolder from the Word2007L1 folder on the CD that accompanies this textbook. Steps on how to copy a folder are presented on the inside of the back cover of this textbook. Do this every time you start a chapter's projects.

Project Prepare a Word Document

You will create a short document containing information on computers and then save, print, and close the document.

Opening Microsoft Word

QUICK STEPS

Open Word
1. Click Start button.
2. Point to *All Programs, Microsoft Office.*
3. Click *Microsoft Office Word 2007.*

Microsoft Office 2007 contains a word processing program named Word that you can use to create, save, edit, and print documents. The steps to open Word may vary depending on your system setup. Generally, to open Word, you would click the Start button on the Taskbar at the Windows desktop, point to *All Programs*, point to *Microsoft Office*, and then click *Microsoft Office Word 2007*.

Creating, Saving, Printing, and Closing a Document

HINT

To avoid opening the same program twice, use the Taskbar to see which programs are open.

When Microsoft Word is open, a blank document displays as shown in Figure 1.1. The features of the document screen are described in Table 1.1.

At a blank document, type information to create a document. A document is any information you choose—for instance, a letter, report, term paper, table, and so on. Some things to consider when typing text are:

- **Word Wrap:** As you type text to create a document, you do not need to press the Enter key at the end of each line because Word wraps text to the next line. A word is wrapped to the next line if it begins before the right margin and continues past the right margin. The only times you need to press Enter are to end a paragraph, create a blank line, or end a short line.

Figure 1.1 Blank Document

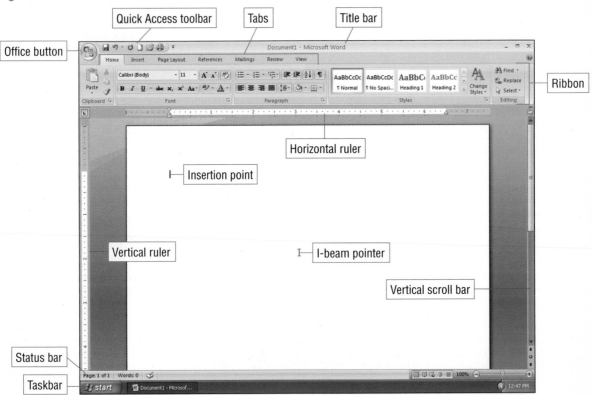

Table 1.1 Microsoft Word Screen Features

Feature	Description
Office button	Displays as a Microsoft Office logo and, when clicked, displays a list of options along with the most recently opened documents
Quick Access toolbar	Contains buttons for commonly used commands
Title bar	Displays document name followed by program name
Tabs	Contains commands and features organized into groups
Ribbon	Area containing the tabs and commands divided into groups
Horizontal ruler	Used to set margins, indents, and tabs
Vertical ruler	Used to set top and bottom margins
I-beam pointer	Used to move the insertion point or to select text
Insertion point	Indicates location of next character entered at the keyboard
Vertical scroll bar	Used to view various parts of the document
Status bar	Displays number of pages and words, View buttons, and the Zoom slider bar

- **AutoCorrect:** Word contains a feature that automatically corrects certain words as you type them. For example, if you type the word *adn* instead of *and*, Word automatically corrects it when you press the spacebar after the word. AutoCorrect will also superscript the letters that follow an ordinal number. For example, if you type *2nd* and then press the spacebar or Enter key, Word will convert this ordinal number to 2nd.

- **Automatic Spell Checker:** By default, Word will automatically insert a red wavy line below words that are not contained in the Spelling dictionary or automatically corrected by AutoCorrect. This may include misspelled words, proper names, some terminology, and some foreign words. If you type a word not recognized by the Spelling dictionary, leave it as written if the word is correct. However, if the word is incorrect, you have two choices—you can delete the word and then type it correctly, or you can position the I-beam pointer on the word, click the right mouse button, and then click the correct spelling in the pop-up list.

- **Automatic Grammar Checker:** Word includes an automatic grammar checker. If the grammar checker detects a sentence containing a grammatical error, a green wavy line is inserted below the sentence. You can leave the sentence as written or position the mouse I-beam pointer on the sentence, click the *right* mouse button, and a pop-up list will display with possible corrections.

- **Spacing Punctuation:** Typically, Word uses Calibri as the default typeface, which is a proportional typeface. (You will learn more about typefaces in Chapter 2.) When typing text in a proportional typeface, space once (rather than twice) after end-of-sentence punctuation such as a period, question mark, or exclamation

HINT

A book icon displays in the Status bar. A check mark on the book indicates no spelling errors detected in the document by the spell checker, while an X in the book indicates errors. Double-click the book icon to move to the next error. If the book icon is not visible, right-click the Status bar and then click the *Spelling and Grammar Check* option at the pop-up list.

point, and after a colon. Proportional typeface is set closer together, and extra white space at the end of a sentence or after a colon is not needed.

- **Option Buttons:** As you insert and edit text in a document, you may notice an option button popping up in your text. The name and appearance of this option button varies depending on the action. If a word you type is corrected by AutoCorrect, if you create an automatic list, or if autoformatting is applied to text, the AutoCorrect Options button appears. Click this button to undo the specific automatic action. If you paste text in a document, the Paste Options button appears near the text. Click this button to display options for controlling how the pasted text is formatted.

- **AutoComplete:** Microsoft Word and other Office applications include an AutoComplete feature that inserts an entire item when you type a few identifying characters. For example, type the letters *Mond* and *Monday* displays in a ScreenTip above the letters. Press the Enter key or press F3 and Word inserts *Monday* in the document.

Using the New Line Command

A Word document is based on a template that applies default formatting. Some basic formatting includes 1.15 line spacing and 10 points of spacing after a paragraph. Each time you press the Enter key, a new paragraph begins and 10 points of spacing is inserted after the paragraph. If you want to move the insertion point down to the next line without including the additional 10 points of spacing, use the New Line command, Shift + Enter.

Project **1a** **Creating a Document**

1. Follow the instructions in this chapter to open Microsoft Word or check with your instructor for specific instructions.
2. At a blank document, type the information shown in Figure 1.2 with the following specifications:
   a. Correct any errors highlighted by the spell checker as they occur.
   b. Space once after end-of-sentence punctuation.
   c. After typing *Created:* press Shift + Enter to move the insertion point to the next line without adding 10 points of additional spacing.
   d. To insert the word *Thursday* located towards the end of the document, type **Thur** and then press F3. (This is an example of the AutoComplete feature.)
   e. To insert the word *December*, type **Dece** and then press the Enter key. (This is another example of the AutoComplete feature.)
   f. Press Shift + Enter after typing *December 9, 2010*.
   g. When typing the last line (the line containing the ordinal numbers), type the ordinal number text and AutoCorrect will automatically convert the letters in the ordinal numbers to superscript.
3. When you are finished typing the text, press the Enter key once.

Saving a Document

Save a document if you want to use it in the future. You can use a variety of methods to save a document such as clicking the Save button on the Quick Access toolbar, clicking the Office button and then clicking *Save As* at the drop-down menu, or using the keyboard shortcut Ctrl + S. To save a document, click the Save button on the Quick Access toolbar. At the Save As dialog box shown in Figure 1.3, type the name of the document and then press Enter or click the Save button located in the lower right corner of the dialog box.

Save a Document
1. Click Save button.
2. Type document name.
3. Click Save button.

HINT
Save a document approximately every 15 minutes or when interrupted.

Save

Figure 1.3 Save As Dialog Box

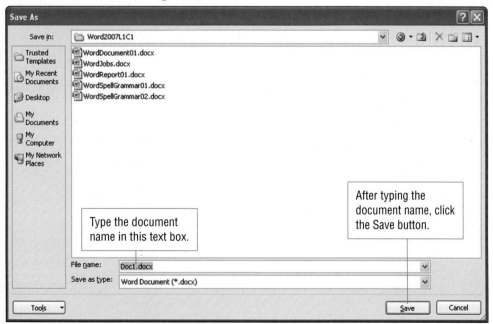

After typing the document name, click the Save button.

Type the document name in this text box.

Office button

Quick Print

Naming a Document

Document names created in Word and other applications in the Office suite can be up to 255 characters in length, including drive letter and any folder names, and may include spaces. File names cannot include any of the following characters:

forward slash (/)	question mark (?)
backslash (\)	quotation mark (")
greater than sign (>)	colon (:)
less than sign (<)	semicolon (;)
asterisk (*)	pipe symbol (|)

Printing a Document

Many of the computer exercises you will be creating will need to be printed. A printing of a document on paper is referred to as *hard copy* and a document displayed in the screen is referred to as *soft copy*. Send a document to the printer by clicking the Quick Print button on the Quick Access toolbar. This sends the document immediately to the printer. (If the Quick Print button does not display on the Quick Access toolbar, click the Customize Quick Access Toolbar button that displays at the right side of the toolbar and then click *Quick Print* at the drop-down list.) You can also print by clicking the Office button and then clicking *Print* at the drop-down list or by pressing the keyboard shortcut, Ctrl + P. This displays the Print dialog box. At this dialog box, click OK to send the document to the printer.

Closing a Document

When you save a document it is saved on your storage medium and remains in the document screen. To remove the document from the screen, click the Office button and then click *Close* at the drop-down list or use the keyboard shortcut, Ctrl + F4. When you close a document, the document is removed and a blank screen displays. At this screen, you can open a previously saved document, create a new document, or exit the Word program.

Project **1b** | **Saving, Printing, and Closing a Document**

1. Save the document you created for Project 1a and name it **WordL1_C1_P1** (for Word Level 1, Chapter 1, Project 1) by completing the following steps:
   a. Click the Save button on the Quick Access toolbar.

Step 1a

b. At the Save As dialog box, type WordL1_C1_P1 and then press Enter.

2. Print the document by clicking the Quick Print button on the Quick Access toolbar.

3. Close the document by clicking the Office button and then clicking *Close* at the drop-down list.

Step 2

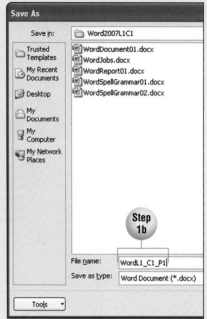

Step 1b

Project ② **Save and Edit a Word Document**

You will open a document located in the Word2007L1C1 folder on your storage medium, add text to the document, and then save the document with a new name.

Creating a New Document

When you close a document, a blank screen displays. If you want to create a new document, display a blank document. To do this, click the New button on the Quick Access toolbar or click the Office button and then click *New*. (If the New button does not display on the Quick Access toolbar, click the Customize Quick Access Toolbar button that displays at the right side of the toolbar and then click *New* at the drop-down list.) At the New Document dialog box, double-click the *Blank document* option. You can also open a new document using the keyboard shortcut, Ctrl + N.

New

Opening a Document

After you save and close a document, you can open it at the Open dialog box shown in Figure 1.4. To display this dialog box, click the Open button on the Quick Access toolbar, click the Office button and then click *Open*, or use the keyboard shortcut, Ctrl + O. (If the Open button does not display on the Quick Access toolbar, click

QUICK STEPS

Open a Document
1. Click Office button.
2. Click *Open*.
3. Double-click document name.

Open

the Customize Quick Access Toolbar button that displays at the right side of the toolbar and then click *Open* at the drop-down list.) At the Open dialog box, double-click the document name. The most recently opened documents display in a list at the right side of the Office button drop-down menu. Click a document in the list to open the document.

Figure 1.4 Open Dialog Box

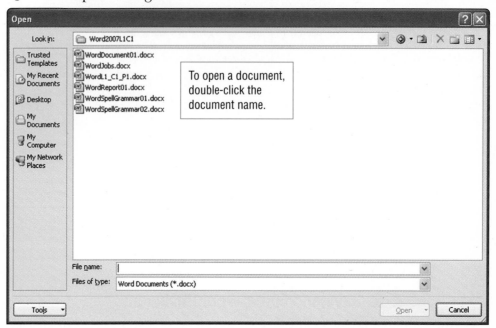

Project **2a** **Opening a Document**

1. Open the **WordJobs.docx** document by completing the following steps:
   a. Click the Open button on the Quick Access toolbar.
   b. At the Open dialog box, make sure the Word2007L1C1 folder on your storage medium is the active folder.
   c. Double-click *WordJobs.docx*.
2. With the insertion point positioned at the beginning of the document, type the text shown in Figure 1.5.

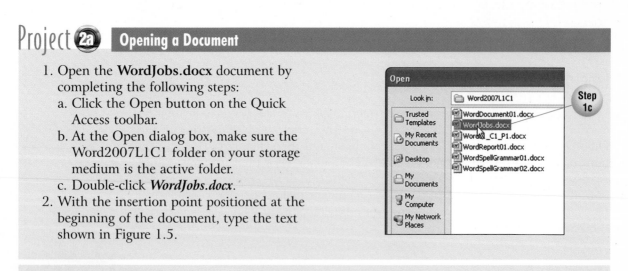

Figure 1.5 Project 2a

The majority of new jobs being created in the United States today involve daily work with computers. Computer-related careers include technical support jobs, sales and training, programming and applications development, network and database administration, and computer engineering.

Saving a Document with Save As

If you open a previously saved document and want to give it a new name, use the *Save As* option from the Office button drop-down list rather than the *Save* option. When you click *Save As*, the Save As dialog box displays. At this dialog box, type the new name for the document and then press Enter.

Exiting Word

When you are finished working with Word and have saved all necessary information, exit Word by clicking the Office button and then clicking the Exit Word button (located at the bottom right side of the drop-down list). You can also exit the Word program by clicking the Close button located in the upper right corner of the screen.

QUICK STEPS

Save a Document with Save As
1. Click Office button.
2. Click *Save As*.
3. Navigate to desired folder.
4. Type document name.
5. Click Save button.

Exit Word
1. Click Office button.
2. Click Exit Word.
OR
Click Close button.

HINT
Save any open documents before exiting Word.

✕ E**x**it Word

Project 2b Saving a Document with Save As

1. With **WordJobs.docx** open, save the document with a new name by completing the following steps:
   a. Click the Office button and then click *Save As*.
   b. At the Save As dialog box, type WordL1_C1_P2.
   c. Press Enter.
2. Print the document by clicking the Quick Print button on the Quick Access toolbar.
3. Close the document by pressing Ctrl + F4.

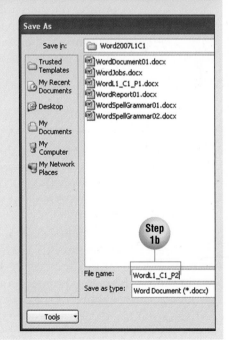

Project ③ Scroll and Browse in a Document

You will open a previously created document, save it with a new name, and then use scrolling and browsing techniques to move the insertion point to specific locations in the document.

Editing a Document

When editing a document, you may decide to insert or delete text. To edit a document, use the mouse, the keyboard, or the mouse combined with the keyboard to move the insertion point to specific locations in the document. To move the insertion point using the mouse, position the I-beam pointer where you want the insertion point located and then click the left mouse button.

You can also scroll in a document, which changes the text display but does not move the insertion point. Use the mouse with the *vertical scroll bar*, located at the right side of the screen, to scroll through text in a document. Click the up scroll arrow at the top of the vertical scroll bar to scroll up through the document and click the down scroll arrow to scroll down through the document. The scroll bar contains a scroll box that indicates the location of the text in the document screen in relation to the remainder of the document. To scroll up one screen at a time, position the arrow pointer above the scroll box (but below the up scroll arrow) and then click the left mouse button. Position the arrow pointer below the scroll box and click the left button to scroll down a screen. If you hold down the left mouse button, the action becomes continuous. You can also position the arrow pointer on the scroll box, hold down the left mouse button, and then drag the scroll box along the scroll bar to reposition text in the document screen. As you drag the scroll box along the vertical scroll bar in a longer document, page numbers display in a box at the right side of the document screen.

Project ③a Scrolling in a Document

1. Open **WordReport01.docx** and then press the Enter key once. (This document is located in the Word2007L1C1 folder you copied to your storage medium.)
2. Save the document with Save As and name it **WordL1_C1_P3**.
3. Position the I-beam pointer at the beginning of the first paragraph and then click the left mouse button.
4. Click the down scroll arrow on the vertical scroll bar several times. (This scrolls down lines of text in the document.) With the mouse pointer on the down scroll arrow, hold down the left mouse button and keep it down until the end of the document displays.
5. Position the mouse pointer on the up scroll arrow and hold down the left mouse button until the beginning of the document displays.
6. Position the mouse pointer below the scroll box and then click the left mouse button. Continue clicking the mouse button (with the mouse pointer positioned below the scroll box) until the end of the document displays.

7. Position the mouse pointer on the scroll box in the vertical scroll bar. Hold down the left mouse button, drag the scroll box to the top of the vertical scroll bar, and then release the mouse button. (Notice that the document page numbers display in a box at the right side of the document screen.)
8. Click on the title at the beginning of the document. (This moves the insertion point to the location of the mouse pointer.)

Moving the Insertion Point to a Specific Page

Along with scrolling options, Word also contains navigation buttons for moving the insertion point to specific locations. Navigation buttons display toward the bottom of the vertical scroll bar and include the Previous button, the Select Browse Object button, and the Next button. The full names of and the tasks completed by the Previous and Next buttons vary depending on the last navigation completed. Click the Select Browse Object button and a palette of browsing choices displays. You will learn more about the Select Browse Object button in the next section.

Previous

Next

Word includes a Go To option you can use to move the insertion point to a specific page within a document. To move the insertion point to a specific page, click the Find button arrow located in the Editing group in the Home tab and then click *Go To* at the drop-down list. At the Find and Replace dialog box with the Go To tab selected, type the page number in the *Enter page number* text box and then press Enter. Click the Close button to close the dialog box.

Browsing in a Document

The Select Browse Object button located toward the bottom of the vertical scroll bar contains options for browsing through a document. Click this button and a palette of browsing choices displays. Use the options on the palette to move the insertion point to various features in a Word document. Position the arrow pointer on an option in the palette and the option name displays below the options. The options on the palette and the location of the options vary depending on the last function performed.

Select
Browse Object

Moving the Insertion Point with the Keyboard

To move the insertion point with the keyboard, use the arrow keys located to the right of the regular keyboard. You can also use the arrow keys on the numeric keypad. If you use these keys, make sure Num Lock is off. Use the arrow keys together with other keys to move the insertion point to various locations in the document as shown in Table 1.2.

When moving the insertion point, Word considers a word to be any series of characters between spaces. A paragraph is any text that is followed by a stroke of the Enter key. A page is text that is separated by a soft or hard page break. If you open a previously saved document, you can move the insertion point to where the insertion point was last located when the document was closed by pressing Shift + F5.

Table 1.2 Insertion Point Movement Commands

To move insertion point	Press
One character left	Left Arrow
One character right	Right Arrow
One line up	Up Arrow
One line down	Down Arrow
One word to the left	Ctrl + Left Arrow
One word to the right	Ctrl + Right Arrow
To end of a line	End
To beginning of a line	Home
To beginning of current paragraph	Ctrl + Up Arrow
To beginning of next paragraph	Ctrl + Down Arrow
Up one screen	Page Up
Down one screen	Page Down
To top of previous page	Ctrl + Page Up
To top of next page	Ctrl + Page Down
To beginning of document	Ctrl + Home
To end of document	Ctrl + End

Project 3b Moving the Insertion Point and Browsing in a Document

1. With **WordL1_C1_P3.docx** open, move the insertion point to page 3 by completing the following steps:
   a. Click the Find button arrow located in the Editing group in the Home tab and then click *Go To* at the drop-down list.
   b. At the Find and Replace dialog box with the Go To tab selected, type 3 in the *Enter page number* text box and then press Enter.
   c. Click the Close button to close the Find and Replace dialog box.
2. Click the Previous Page button located immediately above the Select Browse Object button on the vertical scroll bar. (This moves the insertion point to page 2.)

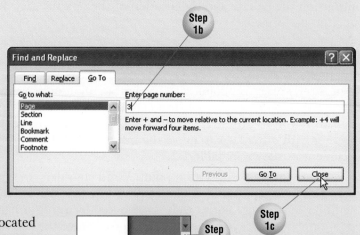

Step 1b

Step 1c

Step 2

3. Click the Previous Page button again. (This moves the insertion point to page 1.)
4. Click the Next Page button located immediately below the Select Browse Object button on the vertical scroll bar. (This moves the insertion point to the beginning of page 2.)

Step 4

5. Move to the beginning of page 3 by completing the following steps:
   a. Click the Select Browse Object button.
   b. At the palette of browsing choices, click the last choice in the bottom row (*Browse by Page*). (This moves the insertion point to page 3.)

Step 5b

Step 5a

6. Press Ctrl + Home to move the insertion point to the beginning of the document.
7. Practice using the keyboard commands shown in Table 1.2 to move the insertion point within the document.
8. Close **WordL1_C1_P3.docx**.

Project ④ Insert and Delete Text

You will open a previously created document, save it with a new name, and then make editing changes to the document. The editing changes include selecting, inserting, and deleting text.

Inserting and Deleting Text

Editing a document may include inserting and/or deleting text. To insert text in a document, position the insertion point in the desired location and then type the text. Existing characters move to the right as you type the text. A number of options are available for deleting text. Some deletion commands are shown in Table 1.3.

Table 1.3 Deletion Commands

To delete	Press
Character right of insertion point	Delete key
Character left of insertion point	Backspace key
Text from insertion point to beginning of word	Ctrl + Backspace
Text from insertion point to end of word	Ctrl + Delete

By default, text you type in a document is inserted in the document and existing text is moved to the right. If you want to type over something, you need to turn on the Overtype mode. With the Overtype mode on, anything you type will replace existing text. To turn on the Overtype mode, click the Office button and then click the Word Options button located toward the bottom of the drop-down list. At the Word Options dialog box, click *Advanced* in the left panel. In the *Advanced options for working with Word.* section, insert a check mark in the *Use Overtype mode* check box if you want the Overtype mode always on in the document. Or, insert a check mark in the *Use the Insert key to control Overtype mode* check box if you want to use the Insert key to turn Overtype mode on and off. After making your selection, click the OK button located in the lower right corner of the dialog box.

Selecting Text

You can use the mouse and/or keyboard to select a specific amount of text. Once selected, you can delete the text or perform other Word functions involving the selected text. When text is selected, it displays with a blue background as shown in Figure 1.6 and the Mini toolbar displays in a dimmed fashion and contains options for common tasks. Move the mouse pointer over the Mini toolbar and it becomes active. (You will learn more about the Mini toolbar in Chapter 2.)

Figure 1.6 Selected Text and Mini Toolbar

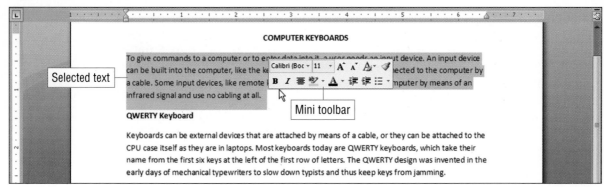

Selecting Text with the Mouse

Use the mouse to select a word, line, sentence, paragraph, or the entire document. Table 1.4 indicates the steps to follow to select various amounts of text. To select a specific amount of text such as a line or a paragraph, the instructions in the table tell you to click in the selection bar. The selection bar is the space located toward the left side of the document screen between the left edge of the page and the text. When the mouse pointer is positioned in the selection bar, the pointer turns into an arrow pointing up and to the right (instead of to the left).

To select an amount of text other than a word, sentence, or paragraph, position the I-beam pointer on the first character of the text to be selected, hold down the left mouse button, drag the I-beam pointer to the last character of the text to be selected, and then release the mouse button. You can also select all text between the current insertion point and the I-beam pointer. To do this, position the insertion point where you want the selection to begin, hold down the Shift key, click the I-beam pointer at the end of the selection, and then release the Shift key. To cancel a selection using the mouse, click anywhere in the document screen outside the selected text.

HINT
To select text vertically, hold down the Alt key while dragging the mouse.

Table 1.4 Selecting with the Mouse

To select	Complete these steps using the mouse
A word	Double-click the word.
A line of text	Click in the selection bar to the left of the line.
Multiple lines of text	Drag in the selection bar to the left of the lines.
A sentence	Hold down the Ctrl key, then click anywhere in the sentence.
A paragraph	Double-click in the selection bar next to the paragraph or triple-click anywhere in the paragraph.
Multiple paragraphs	Drag in the selection bar.
An entire document	Triple-click in the selection bar.

Selecting Text with the Keyboard

To select a specific amount of text using the keyboard, turn on the Selection Mode by pressing the F8 function key. With the Selection Mode activated, use the arrow keys to select the desired text. If you want to cancel the selection, press the Esc key and then press any arrow key. You can customize the Status bar to display text indicating that the Selection Mode is activated. To do this, right-click any blank location on the Status bar and then click *Selection Mode* at the pop-up list. When you press F8 to turn on the Selection Mode, the words *Selection Mode* display on the Status bar. You can also select text with the commands shown in Table 1.5.

HINT
If text is selected, any character you type replaces the selected text.

Project **4a** **Editing a Document**

1. Open **WordDocument01.docx**. (This document is located in the Word2007L1C1 folder you copied to your storage medium.)
2. Save the document with Save As and name it **WordL1_C1_P4**.
3. Change the word *give* in the first sentence of the first paragraph to *enter*.
4. Change the second *to* in the first sentence to *into*.
5. Delete the words *means of* in the first sentence in the *QWERTY Keyboard* section.
6. Select the words *and use no cabling at all* and the period that follows located at the end of the last sentence in the first paragraph, and then press the Delete key.
7. Insert a period immediately following the word *signal*.

Step 3

COMPUTER KEYBOARDS

To enter commands to a computer or to enter data into it, a user can be built into the computer, like the keyboard in a laptop, or it a cable. Some input devices, like remote keyboards, send directio infrared signal and use no cabling at all.

8. Delete the heading line containing the text *QWERTY Keyboard* using the Selection Mode by completing the following steps:
   a. Position the insertion point immediately before the *Q* in *QWERTY*.
   b. Press F8 to turn on the Selection Mode.
   c. Press the Down Arrow key.
   d. Press the Delete key.
9. Complete steps similar to those in Step 8 to delete the heading line containing the text *DVORAK Keyboard*.
10. Begin a new paragraph with the sentence that reads *Keyboards have different physical appearances.* by completing the following steps:
    a. Position the insertion point immediately left of the *K* in *Keyboards* (the first word of the fifth sentence in the last paragraph).
    b. Press the Enter key.
11. Save **WordL1_C1_P4.docx**.

Steps 8a–8c

To enter commands into a computer device can be built into the computer computer by a cable. Some input dev means of an infrared signal.

QWERTY Keyboard

Keyboards can be external devices tha itself as they are in laptops. Most key the first six keys at the left of the first of mechanical typewriters to slow do

Steps 10a–10b

To enter commands into a computer or device can be built into the computer, li computer by a cable. Some input device means of an infrared signal.

Keyboards can be external devices that itself as they are in laptops. Most keybo the first six keys at the left of the first ro of mechanical typewriters to slow down

The DVORAK keyboard is an alternative commonly used keys are placed close to install software on a QWERTY keyboard keyboards is convenient especially whe

Keyboards have different physical appe that of a calculator, containing numbers "broken" into two pieces to reduce stra change the symbol or characters entere

Table 1.5 Selecting with the Keyboard

To select	Press
One character to right	Shift + Right Arrow
One character to left	Shift + Left Arrow
To end of word	Ctrl + Shift + Right Arrow
To beginning of word	Ctrl + Shift + Left Arrow
To end of line	Shift + End
To beginning of line	Shift + Home
One line up	Shift + Up Arrow
One line down	Shift + Down Arrow
To beginning of paragraph	Ctrl + Shift + Up Arrow
To end of paragraph	Ctrl + Shift + Down Arrow
One screen up	Shift + Page Up
One screen down	Shift + Page Down
To end of document	Ctrl + Shift + End
To beginning of document	Ctrl + Shift + Home
Entire document	Ctrl + A or click Select button in Editing group and then Select All

Using the Undo and Redo Buttons

If you make a mistake and delete text that you did not intend to, or if you change your mind after deleting text and want to retrieve it, you can use the Undo or Redo buttons on the Quick Access toolbar. For example, if you type text and then click the Undo button, the text will be removed. You can undo text or commands. For example, if you add formatting such as bolding to text and then click the Undo button, the bolding is removed.

If you use the Undo button and then decide you do not want to reverse the original action, click the Redo button. For example, if you select and underline text and then decide to remove underlining, click the Undo button. If you then decide you want the underlining back on, click the Redo button. Many Word actions can be undone or redone. Some actions, however, such as printing and saving, cannot be undone or redone.

Word maintains actions in temporary memory. If you want to undo an action performed earlier, click the Undo button arrow. This causes a drop-down list to display. To make a selection from this drop-down list, click the desired action and the action, along with any actions listed above it in the drop-down list, is undone.

Undo

Redo

Project 4b Undoing and Redoing Deletions

1. With **WordL1_C1_P4.docx** open, delete the last sentence in the last paragraph using the mouse by completing the following steps:
   a. Position the I-beam pointer anywhere in the sentence that begins *All keyboards have modifier keys . . . .*
   b. Hold down the Ctrl key and then click the left mouse button.

   > install software on a QWERTY keyboard that emulates a DVORAK keyboard. The ability to emulate other keyboards is convenient especially when working with foreign languages.
   >
   > Keyboards have different physical appearances. Many keyboards have a separate numeric keypad, like that of a calculator, containing numbers and mathematical operators. Some keyboards are sloped and "broken" into two pieces to reduce strain. All keyboards have modifier keys that enable the user to change the symbol or characters entered when a given key is pressed.

   Steps 1a–1b

   c. Press the Delete key.
2. Delete the last paragraph by completing the following steps:
   a. Position the I-beam pointer anywhere in the last paragraph (the paragraph that reads *Keyboards have different physical appearances.*).
   b. Triple-click the left mouse button.
   c. Press the Delete key.
3. Undo the deletion by clicking the Undo button on the Quick Access toolbar.
4. Redo the deletion by clicking the Redo button on the Quick Access toolbar.
5. Select the first sentence in the second paragraph and then delete it.
6. Select the first paragraph in the document and then delete it.

7. Undo the two deletions by completing the following steps:
   a. Click the Undo button arrow.
   b. Click the *second* Clear listed in the drop-down list. (This will redisplay the first sentence in the second paragraph as well as displaying the first paragraph. The sentence will be selected.)
8. Click outside the sentence to deselect it.
9. Save, print, and then close **WordL1_C1_P4.docx**.

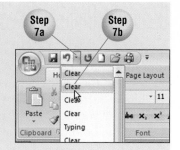

Project 5 Complete a Spelling and Grammar Check

You will open a previously created document, save it with a new name, and then check the spelling and grammar in the document.

Checking the Spelling and Grammar in a Document

Check Spelling and Grammar
1. Click Review tab.
2. Click Spelling & Grammar button.
3. Change or ignore error.
4. Click OK.

HINT

Complete a spelling and grammar check on a portion of a document by selecting the text first and then clicking the Spelling & Grammar button.

Spelling &
Grammar

Two tools for creating thoughtful and well-written documents include a spelling checker and a grammar checker. The spelling checker finds misspelled words and offers replacement words. It also finds duplicate words and irregular capitalizations. When you spell check a document, the spelling checker compares the words in your document with the words in its dictionary. If the spelling checker finds a match, it passes over the word. If a match is not found for the word, the spelling checker will stop, select the word, and offer replacements.

The grammar checker will search a document for errors in grammar, punctuation, and word usage. The spelling checker and the grammar check can help you create a well-written document, but do not replace the need for proofreading. To complete a spelling and grammar check, click the Review tab and then click the Spelling & Grammar button in the Proofing group. You can also begin spelling and grammar checking by pressing the keyboard shortcut, F7. As the spelling and grammar checker selects text, make a choice from some of the options in the Spelling and Grammar dialog box as shown in Table 1.6.

By default, a spelling and grammar check are both completed on a document. If you want to check only the spelling in a document and not the grammar, remove the check mark from the *Check grammar* check box located in the lower left corner of the Spelling and Grammar dialog box. When spell checking a document, you can temporarily leave the Spelling and Grammar dialog box, make corrections in the document, and then resume spell checking by clicking the Resume button.

Table 1.6 Spelling and Grammar Dialog Box Buttons

Button	Function
Ignore Once	During spell checking, skips that occurrence of the word; in grammar checking, leaves currently selected text as written
Ignore All	During spell checking, skips that occurrence of the word and all other occurrences of the word in the document
Ignore Rule	During grammar checking, leaves currently selected text as written and ignores the current rule for remainder of the grammar check
Add to Dictionary	Adds selected word to the main spelling check dictionary
Change	Replaces selected word in sentence with selected word in *Suggestions* list box
Change All	Replaces selected word in sentence with selected word in *Suggestions* list box and all other occurrences of the word
AutoCorrect	Inserts selected word and correct spelling of word in AutoCorrect dialog box
Explain	During grammar checking, displays grammar rule information about the selected text
Undo	Reverses most recent spelling and grammar action
Next Sentence	Accepts manual changes made to sentence and then continues grammar checking
Options	Displays a dialog box with options for customizing a spelling and grammar check

Project 5 Checking the Spelling and Grammar in a Document

1. Open **WordSpellGrammar01.docx**.
2. Save the document with Save As and name it **WordL1_C1_P5**.
3. Click the Review tab.
4. Click the Spelling & Grammar button in the Proofing group.

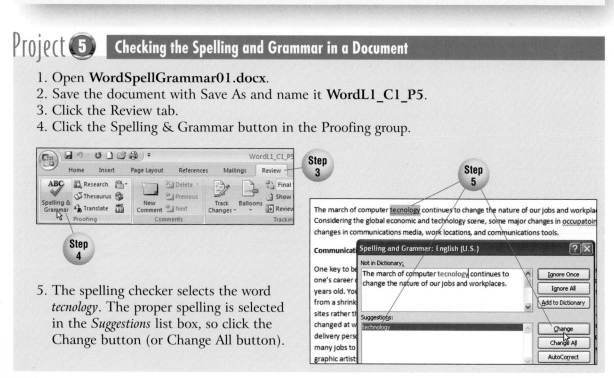

5. The spelling checker selects the word *tecnology*. The proper spelling is selected in the *Suggestions* list box, so click the Change button (or Change All button).

6. The spelling checker selects the word *occupatoins*. The proper spelling of the word is selected in the *Suggestions* list box, so click the Change button (or Change All button).

7. The grammar checker selects the sentence that begins *One key to being successful . . .* and displays *trends* and *a trend* in the *Suggestions* list box. Click *a trend* in the *Suggestions* list box and then click the Change button.

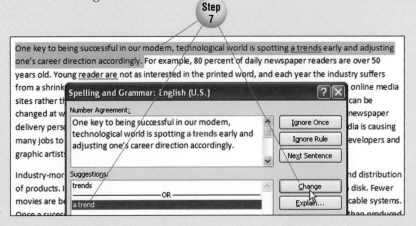

Step 7

8. The grammar checker selects the sentence that begins *Young reader are not as interested . . .* and displays *reader is* and *readers are* in the *Suggestions* text box. Click the Explain button, read the information about subject-verb agreement that displays in the Word Help window, and then click the Close button located in the upper right corner of the Word Help window.

9. Click *readers are* in the *Suggestions* text box and then click the Change button.

10. The spelling checker selects *excelent*. The proper spelling is selected in the *Suggestions* list box, so click the Change button.

11. The grammar checker selects the sentence that begins *The number of printing and lithography job's is shrinking . . . .* Click the Explain button, read the information about plural or possessive that displays in the Word Help window, and then click the Close button located in the upper right corner of the Word Help window.

12. With *jobs* selected in the *Suggestions* list box, click the Change button.

13. The spelling checker selects the word *successful* and offers *successful* in the *Suggestions* text box. Since this word is misspelled in another location in the document, click the Change All button.

14. The spelling checker selects the word *telework*. This word is correct so click the Ingore All button.

15. The spelling checker selects the word *are* that is repeated twice. Click the Delete button to delete the word.

16. When the message displays telling you that the spelling and grammar check is complete, click the OK button.

17. Save, print, and then close **WordL1_C1_P5.docx**.

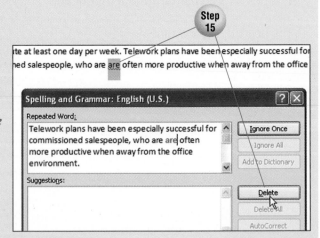

Step 15

Project ⑥ Use the Help Feature

You need to learn more about selecting text and saving a document so you decide to use Help to research these features.

Using Help

Word's Help feature is an on-screen reference manual containing information about all Word features and commands. Word's Help feature is similar to the Windows Help and the Help features in Excel, PowerPoint, and Access. Get help by clicking the Microsoft Office Word Help button located in the upper right corner of the screen (a question mark in a circle) or by pressing the keyboard shortcut, F1. This displays the Word Help window. In this window, type a topic, feature, or question in the *Search* text box and then press Enter. Topics related to the search text display in the Help window. Click a topic that interests you. If the topic window contains a Show All hyperlink in the upper right corner, click this hyperlink and the information expands to show all help information related to the topic. When you click the Show All hyperlink, it becomes the Hide All hyperlink.

Project ⑥a Using the Help Feature

1. At a blank document, click the Microsoft Office Word Help button located in the upper right corner of the screen.
2. At the Word Help window, type selecting text in the *Search* text box.

Step 1

Step 2

3. Press the Enter key.
4. When the list of topics displays, click the Select text hyperlink.

Step 4

5. Click the <u>Show All</u> hyperlink that displays in the upper right corner of the window.
6. Read the information about selecting text.
7. Print the information by clicking the Print button located toward the top of the Word Help window.
8. At the Print dialog box, click the Print button.
9. Click the Close button to close the Word Help window.

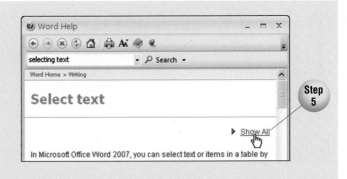

Getting Help in a Dialog Box

Dialog boxes contain a Help button you can click to display the Word Help window that is specific to the dialog box. This button is located in the upper right corner of the dialog box and displays as a question mark inside a square. Click this button and the Word Help window displays with topics related to the dialog box.

Project **6b**   **Getting Help in a Dialog Box**

1. At a blank document, click the Office button and then click *Save As* at the drop-down list.
2. At the Save As dialog box, click the Help button located in the upper right corner of the dialog box.
3. At the Word Help window, click the <u>Save As</u> hyperlink.
4. In the Save As list box, click *Microsoft Office Word*.
5. Read the information that displays about saving in Word and then click the Close button to close the Word Help window.
6. Close the Save As dialog box.

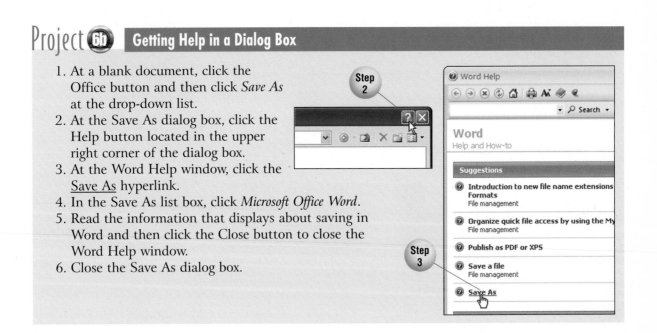

CHAPTER summary

- Open Microsoft Word by clicking the Start button on the Taskbar, pointing to *All Programs*, pointing to *Microsoft Office*, and then clicking *Microsoft Office Word 2007*.

- The Office button displays as a Microsoft Office logo and, when clicked, displays a list of options and most recently opened documents.

- The Quick Access toolbar is located to the right of the Office button and contains buttons for commonly used commands.

- The Title bar is located to the right of the Quick Access toolbar and displays the document name followed by the program name.

- The ribbon area contains tabs with commands and options divided into groups.

- The insertion point displays as a blinking vertical line and indicates the position of the next character to be entered in the document.

- The mouse displays in the screen as an I-beam pointer or as an arrow pointing up and to the left.

- Use the vertical scroll bar to view various parts of the document.

- The Status bar displays the number of pages and words, View buttons, and the Zoom slider bar.

- Word automatically wraps text to the next line as you type information. Press the Enter key only to end a paragraph, create a blank line, or end a short line.

- Word contains a feature named AutoCorrect that automatically corrects certain words as they are typed.

- When typing text, the automatic spell checker feature inserts a red wavy line below words not contained in the Spelling dictionary, and the automatic grammar checker inserts a green wavy line below a sentence containing a grammatical error.

- The AutoComplete feature inserts an entire item when you type a few identifying characters and then press Enter or F3.

- Document names can contain a maximum of 255 characters, including the drive letter and folder names, and may include spaces.

- The insertion point can be moved throughout the document without interfering with text by using the mouse, the keyboard, or the mouse combined with the keyboard.

- You can move the insertion point by character, word, screen, or page, and from the first to the last character in a document. Refer to Table 1.2 for keyboard insertion point movement commands.

- The scroll box on the vertical scroll bar indicates the location of the text in the document in relation to the remainder of the document.

- Click the Select Browse Object button located at the bottom of the vertical scroll bar to display options for browsing through a document.

- You can delete text by character, word, line, several lines, or partial page using specific keys or by selecting text using the mouse or the keyboard.

- You can select a specific amount of text using the mouse or the keyboard. Refer to Table 1.4 for information on selecting with the mouse and refer to Table 1.5 for information on selecting with the keyboard.

- Use the Undo button on the Quick Access toolbar if you change your mind after typing, deleting, or formatting text and want to undo the action. Use the Redo button to redo something that had been undone with the Undo button.

- The spelling checker matches the words in your document with the words in its dictionary. If a match is not found, the word is selected and possible corrections are suggested. The grammar checker searches a document for errors in grammar, style, punctuation, and word usage. When a grammar error is detected, display information about the error by clicking the Explain button at the Spelling & Grammar dialog box.

- Word's Help feature is an on-screen reference manual containing information about all Word features and commands.

- Click the Microsoft Office Word Help button or press F1 to display the Word Help window. At this window, type a topic and then press Enter.

- Dialog boxes contain a Help button you can click to display the Word Help window with information specific to the dialog box.

COMMANDS review

FEATURE	RIBBON TAB, GROUP	BUTTON	QUICK ACCESS TOOLBAR	OFFICE BUTTON DROP-DOWN LIST	KEYBOARD SHORTCUT
Close document				Close	Ctrl + F4
Exit Word		⊠		Exit Word	
Find and Replace dialog box with Go To tab selected	Home, Editing	🔍 Find ▾ , Go To			Ctrl + G
New blank document			📄	New, Blank document	Ctrl + N
Open dialog box			📂	Open	Ctrl + O
Print dialog box				Print	Ctrl + P
Print document			🖨	Print, Quick Print	
Save document			💾	Save	Ctrl + S
Select document	Home, Editing	▸ Select ▾			Ctrl + A
Spelling and Grammar dialog box	Review, Proofing	🔠 ABC			F7
Word Help window		❓			F1

CONCEPTS check

Test Your Knowledge

Completion: In the space provided at the right, indicate the correct term, symbol, or command.

1. This toolbar contains the Save button. _____

2. This button displays in the upper left corner of the screen and displays with the Microsoft logo. _____

3. This is the area located toward the top of the screen that contains tabs with commands and options divided into groups. _____

4. This bar, located toward the bottom of the screen, displays number of pages and words, View buttons, and the Zoom slider bar. _____

5. This tab is selected by default. _____

6. This feature automatically corrects certain words as you type them. _____

7. This feature inserts an entire item when you type a few identifying characters and then press Enter or F3. _____

8. This is the keyboard shortcut to display the Print dialog box. _____

9. This is the keyboard shortcut to close a document. _____

10. This is the keyboard shortcut to display a new blank document. _____

11. Use this keyboard shortcut to move the insertion point to the beginning of the previous page. _____

12. Use this keyboard shortcut to move the insertion point to the end of the document. _____

13. Press this key on the keyboard to delete the character left of the insertion point. _____

14. Using the mouse, do this to select one word. _____

15. To select various amounts of text using the mouse, you can click in this bar. _____

16. Click this tab to display the Spelling & Grammar button in the Proofing group. _____

17. This is the keyboard shortcut to display the Word Help window. _____

SKILLS check
Demonstrate Your Proficiency

Assessment

1 TYPE AND EDIT A DOCUMENT ON FUZZY LOGIC

1. Open Word and then type the text in Figure 1.7. Correct any errors highlighted by the spell checker and space once after end-of-sentence punctuation.
2. Make the following changes to the document:
   a. Delete *AI* in the first sentence of the first paragraph and then insert *artificial intelligence*.
   b. Insert the words *for approximations and* between the words *allowing* and *incomplete* located in the first sentence of the first paragraph.
   c. Insert the words *or numerical* between the words *yes/no* and *information* in the second sentence of the first paragraph.
   d. Delete the words *hard to come by* in the last sentence of the first paragraph and replace with the word *rare*.
   e. Insert the letters *SQL* between the words *logic* and *database* in the last sentence of the second paragraph.
   f. Move the insertion point immediately left of the period at the end of the last sentence of the last paragraph, type a comma, and then insert the words *and trade shares on the Tokyo Stock Exchange*. Delete the word *and* before the words *automobile transmissions* in the last sentence.
   g. Join the first and second paragraphs.
   h. Delete the name *Marie Solberg* and then type your first and last names.
3. Save the document and name it **WordL1_C1_A1**.
4. Print and then close **WordL1_C1_A1.docx**.

Assessment

2 CHECK THE SPELLING AND GRAMMAR OF A COMPUTER SOFTWARE DOCUMENT

1. Open **WordSpellGrammar02.docx**.
2. Save the document with Save As and name it **WordL1_C1_A2**.
3. Complete a spelling and grammar check on the document. You determine what to change and what to leave as written.
4. Insert the sentence *Wizards are small programs designed to assist users by automating tasks.* between the third and fourth sentences in the *User-Friendly System Software* section.
5. Move the insertion point to the end of the document, type your first and last names, press Shift + Enter, and then type the current date.
6. Save, print, and then close **WordL1_C1_A2.docx**.

Figure 1.7 Assessment 1

Fuzzy Logic

The fuzzy logic branch of AI attempts to model human reasoning by allowing incomplete input data. Instead of demanding precise yes/no information, fuzzy logic systems allow users to input "fuzzy" data. The terminology used by the system is deliberately vague and includes terms such as very probable, somewhat decreased, reasonable, or very slight. This is an attempt to simulate real-world conditions, where precise answers are hard to come by.

A fuzzy logic system attempts to work more naturally with the user by piecing together an answer in a manner similar to that used by a traditional expert system. Fuzzy logic database queries seem significantly more human than traditional queries.

Fuzzy logic systems are much more common in Japan than they are in the United States, where traditional expert systems and neural networks tend to be favored. In Japan, microprocessors specially designed by Toshiba and Hitachi to use fuzzy logic operate subways, consumer electronics, and automobile transmissions.

Created by Marie Solberg
Monday, September 27, 2010
Note: Please insert this information between the 4th and 5th sections.

Assessment

3 CREATE A DOCUMENT DESCRIBING KEYBOARD SHORTCUTS

1. Click the Microsoft Office Word Help button, type keyboard shortcuts, and then press Enter.
2. At the Word Help window, click the <u>Keyboard shortcuts for Microsoft Office Word</u> hyperlink.
3. At the keyboard shortcut window, click the <u>Show All</u> hyperlink.
4. Read through the information in the Word Help window.
5. Create a document describing four keyboard shortcuts.
6. Save the document and name it **WordL1_C1_A3**.
7. Print and then close **WordL1_C1_A3.docx**.

CASE study
Apply Your Skills

Part 1

You are the assistant to Paul Brewster, the training coordinator at a medium-sized service-oriented business. You have been asked by Mr. Brewster to prepare a document for Microsoft Word users within the company explaining how to use the Save As command when saving a document rather than the Save command. Save the document and name it **WordL1_C1_CS_P1**. Print and then close the document.

Part 2

Mr. Brewster would like a document containing a brief summary of some basic Word commands for use in Microsoft Word training classes. He has asked you to prepare a document containing the following information:

- A brief explanation on how to move the insertion point to a specific page
- Keyboard shortcuts to move the insertion point to the beginning and end of a text line and beginning and end of a document
- Commands to delete text from the insertion point to the beginning of the word and from the insertion point to the end of the word
- Steps to select a word, a sentence, a paragraph, and an entire document using the mouse.
- • Keyboard shortcut to select the entire document

Save the document and name it **WordL1_C1_CS_P2**. Print and then close the document.

Part 3

According to Mr. Brewster, the company is considering updating the Resources Department computers to Microsoft Office 2007. He has asked you to use the Internet to go to the Microsoft home page at www.microsoft.com and then use the search feature to find information on the system requirements for Office Professional Edition 2007. When you find the information, type a document that contains the Office Professional Edition 2007 system requirements for the computer and processor, memory, hard disk space, drives, and operating system. Save the document and name it **WordL1_C1_CS_P3**. Print and then close the document.

CHAPTER 2

Formatting Characters and Paragraphs

PERFORMANCE OBJECTIVES

Upon successful completion of Chapter 2, you will be able to:

- Change the font and font effects
- Format selected text with buttons on the Mini toolbar
- Apply styles from Quick Styles sets
- Apply themes
- Change the alignment of text in paragraphs
- Indent text in paragraphs
- Increase and decrease spacing before and after paragraphs
- Repeat the last action
- Automate formatting with Format Painter
- Change line spacing in a document
- Reveal and compare formatting

word Chapter 2

Tutorial 2.1
Modifying Text Format
Tutorial 2.2
Other Formatting Features
Tutorial 2.3
Modifying and Comparing Text
  Formatting

A Word document is based on a template that applies default formatting. Some of the default formats include 11-point Calibri, line spacing of 1.15, 10 points of spacing after each paragraph, and left-aligned text. The appearance of a document in the document screen and how it looks when printed is called the *format*. In this chapter, you will learn about character formatting that can include such elements as changing the typeface, type size, and typestyle as well as applying font effects such as bolding and italicizing. The Paragraph group in the Home tab includes buttons for applying formatting to paragraphs of text. In Word, a paragraph is any amount of text followed by the press of the Enter key. In this chapter, you will learn to apply paragraph formatting to text such as changing text alignment, indenting text, applying formatting with Format Painter, and changing line spacing.

Note: Before beginning computer projects, copy to your storage medium the Word2007L1C2 subfolder from the Word2007L1 folder on the CD that accompanies this textbook and then make Word2007L1C2 the active folder.

Project 1 Apply Character Formatting

Project ① **Apply Character Formatting**

You will open a document containing a glossary of terms, add additional text, and then format the document by applying character formatting.

Changing Fonts

Clear Formatting

The Font group shown in Figure 2.1 contains a number of buttons you can use to apply character formatting to text in a document. The top row contains buttons for changing the font and font size as well as buttons for increasing and decreasing the size of the font. The bottom row contains buttons for applying typestyles such as bold, italics, underlining, superscript, and subscript. You can remove character formatting (as well as paragraph formatting) applied to text by clicking the Clear Formatting button in the Font group. Remove only character formatting from selected text by pressing the keyboard shortcut, Ctrl + spacebar.

Figure 2.1 Font Group Buttons

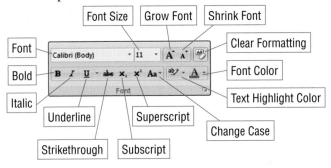

HINT
Change the default font by selecting the desired font at the Font dialog box, clicking the Default button, and then clicking Yes.

HINT
Use a serif typeface for text-intensive documents.

A Word document is based on a template that formats text in 11-point Calibri. You may want to change this default to some other font for such reasons as changing the mood of the document, enhancing the visual appeal, and increasing the readability of the text. A font consists of three elements—typeface, type size, and typestyle.

A typeface is a set of characters with a common design and shape and can be decorative or plain and either monospaced or proportional. Word refers to typeface as *font*. A monospaced typeface allots the same amount of horizontal space for each character while a proportional typeface allots a varying amount of space for each character. Proportional typefaces are divided into two main categories: *serif* and *sans serif*. A serif is a small line at the end of a character stroke. Consider using a serif typeface for text-intensive documents because the serifs help move the reader's eyes across the page. Use a sans serif typeface for headings, headlines, and advertisements.

Microsoft Word 2007 includes six new typefaces designed for extended on-screen reading. These typefaces include the default, Calibri, as well as Cambria, Candara, Consolas, Constantia, and Corbel. Calibri, Candara, and Corbel are sans serif typefaces; Cambria and Constantia are serif typefaces; and Consolas is monospaced. These six typefaces as well as some other popular typefaces are shown in Table 2.1.

Table 2.1 Serif and Sans Serif Typefaces

Serif Typefaces	Sans Serif Typefaces	Monospaced Typefaces
Cambria	Calibri	Consolas
Constantia	Candara	Courier
Times New Roman	Corbel	Letter Gothic
Bookman Old Style	Arial	

Type size is generally set in proportional size. The size of proportional type is measured vertically in units called *points*. A point is approximately ¹⁄₇₂ of an inch—the higher the point size, the larger the characters. Within a typeface, characters may have a varying style. Type styles are divided into four main categories: regular, bold, italic, and bold italic.

You can use the Font button in the Font group to change the font and the Font Size button to change the size. When you select text and then click the Font button arrow, a drop-down gallery displays of font options. Hover your mouse pointer over a font option and the selected text in the document displays with the font applied. You can continue hovering your mouse pointer over different font options to see how the selected text displays in the specified font. The Font button drop-down gallery is an example of the *live preview* feature, which allows you to see how the font formatting affects your text without having to return to the document. The live preview feature is also available when you click the Font Size button arrow.

Project ⓐ Changing the Font

1. Open **WordDocument02.docx**.
2. Save the document with Save As and name it **WordL1_C2_P1**.
3. Change the typeface to Cambria by completing the following steps:
   a. Select the entire document by pressing Ctrl + A. (You can also select all text in the document by clicking the Select button in the Editing group and then clicking *Select All* at the drop-down list.)
   b. Click the Font button arrow, scroll down the Font drop-down gallery until *Cambria* displays, and then hover the mouse pointer over *Cambria*. This displays a live preview of the text set in Cambria.
   c. Click the mouse button on *Cambria*.

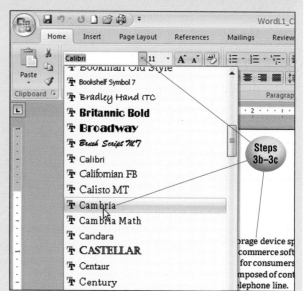

4. Change the type size to 14 by completing the following steps:
   a. With the text in the document still selected, click the Font Size button arrow.
   b. At the drop-down gallery that displays, hover the mouse pointer on *14* and look at the live preview of the text with 14 points applied.
   c. Click the left mouse button on *14*.
5. At the document screen, deselect the text by clicking anywhere in the document screen outside the selected text.
6. Change the type size and typeface by completing the following steps:
   a. Press Ctrl + A to select the entire document.
   b. Click three times on the Shrink Font button in the Font group. (This decreases the size to 10 points.)
   c. Click twice on the Grow Font button. (This increases the size of the font to 12 points.)
   d. Click the Font button arrow, scroll down the drop-down gallery, and then click *Constantia*. (The most recently used fonts display at the beginning of the document, followed by a listing of all fonts.)
7. Save **WordL1_C2_P1.docx**.

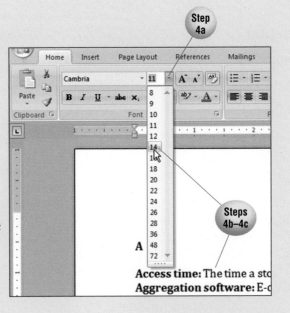

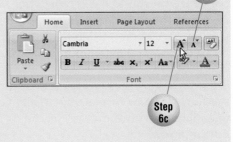

Bold

Italic

Underline

Choosing a Typestyle

Apply a particular typestyle to text with the Bold, Italic, or Underline buttons in the bottom row in the Font group. You can apply more than one style to text. For example, you can bold and italicize the same text or apply all three styles to the same text.

Each of the three styles has traditional uses that you may find appropriate in your documents. Bold is often used to draw the reader's attention to important words to remember. In this text, for example, bold is used for file names in exercises. Italics typically are used to emphasize certain words or phrases within a sentence. In biology texts, they are used for genus and species names. In this text, you may have noticed italics are used to set apart the names of features in drop-down galleries. Underlining also serves to emphasize and set apart words or phrases, although most style manuals recommend using italics instead of underlines.

1. With **WordL1_C2_P1.docx** open, press Ctrl + Home to move the insertion point to the beginning of the document.
2. Type a heading for the document by completing the following steps:
   a. Press the Caps Lock key.
   b. Click the Bold button in the Font group. (This turns on bold.)
   c. Click the Underline button in the Font group. (This turns on underline.)
   d. Type GLOSSARY OF TERMS.

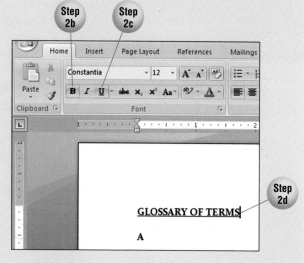

3. Press Ctrl + End to move the insertion point to the end of the document.
4. Type the text shown in Figure 2.2 with the following specifications:
   a. While typing the document, make the appropriate text bold as shown in the figure by completing the following steps:
      1) Click the Bold button in the Font group. (This turns on bold.)
      2) Type the text.
      3) Click the Bold button in the Font group. (This turns off bold.)
   b. While typing the document, italicize the appropriate text as shown in the figure by completing the following steps:
      1) Click the Italic button in the Font group.
      2) Type the text.
      3) Click the Italic button in the Font group.
5. After typing the text, press the Enter key twice.
6. Remove underlining from the title by selecting _GLOSSARY OF TERMS_ and then clicking the Underline button in the Font group.
7. With the title _GLOSSARY OF TERMS_ selected, change the font size to 14 points.
8. Save **WordL1_C2_P1.docx**.

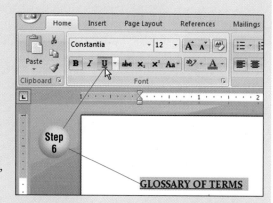

Figure 2.2 **Project 1b**

C

Chip: A thin wafer of _silicon_ containing electronic circuitry that performs various functions, such as mathematical calculations, storage, or controlling computer devices.

Cluster: A group of two or more _sectors_ on a disk, which is the smallest unit of storage space used to store data.

Coding: A term used by programmers to refer to the act of writing source code.

Crackers: A term coined by computer hackers for those who intentionally enter (or hack) computer systems to damage them.

Choosing a Font Effect

Strikethrough

Subscript

Superscript

Change Case

Text Highlight Color

Font Color

Apply font effects with some of the buttons in the bottom row in the Font group. Use the Strikethrough button to draw a line through selected text. This has a practical application in some legal documents in which deleted text must be retained in the document. Use the Subscript button to create text that is lowered slightly below the line such as the chemical formula H_2O. Use the Superscript button to create text that is raised slightly above the text line such as the mathematical equation four to the third power (written as 4^3).

Change the case of text with the Change Case button drop-down list. Click the Change Case button and a drop-down list displays with the options *Sentence case*, *lowercase*, *UPPERCASE*, *Capitalize Each Word*, and *tOGGLE cASE*. You can also change the case of selected text with the keyboard shortcut, Shift + F3. Each time you press Shift + F3, selected text cycles through the case options.

The bottom row in the Font group contains two additional buttons—the Text Highlight Color button and the Font Color button. Use the Text Highlight Color button to highlight specific text in a document and use the Font Color button to change the color of text.

Using Keyboard Shortcuts

Several of the buttons in the Font group have keyboard shortcuts. For example, you can press Ctrl + B to turn on bold or press Ctrl + I to turn on italics. Position the mouse pointer on a button and an enhanced ScreenTip displays with the name of the button; the keyboard shortcut, if any; a description of the action performed by the button; and sometimes access to the Word Help window. Table 2.2 identifies the keyboard shortcuts available for buttons in the Font group.

Table 2.2 Font Button Keyboard Shortcuts

Font Group Button	Keyboard Shortcut
Font	Ctrl + Shift + F
Font Size	Ctrl + Shift + P
Grow Font	Ctrl + Shift + >
Shrink Font	Ctrl + Shift + <
Bold	Ctrl + B
Italic	Ctrl + I
Underline	Ctrl + U
Subscript	Ctrl + =
Superscript	Ctrl + Shift + +
Change Case	Shift + F3

Formatting with the Mini Toolbar

When you select text, the Mini toolbar displays in a dimmed fashion above the selected text. Hover the mouse pointer over the Mini toolbar and it becomes active. Click a button on the Mini toolbar to apply formatting to selected text.

Project 1C Applying Font Effects

1. With **WordL1_C2_P1.docx** open, move the insertion point to the beginning of the term *Chip*, press the Enter key, and then press the Up Arrow key. Type the text shown in Figure 2.3. Create the superscript numbers by clicking the Superscript button, typing the number, and then clicking the Superscript button.
2. Change the case of text by completing the following steps:
   a. Select the title *GLOSSARY OF TERMS*.
   b. Click the Change Case button in the Font group and then click *Capitalize Each Word* at the drop-down list.
3. Strike through text by completing the following steps:
   a. Select the words and parentheses *(or hack)* in the *Crackers* definition.
   b. Click the Strikethrough button in the Font group.

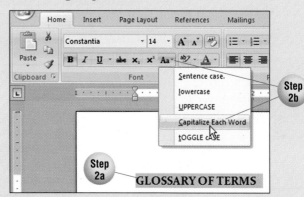

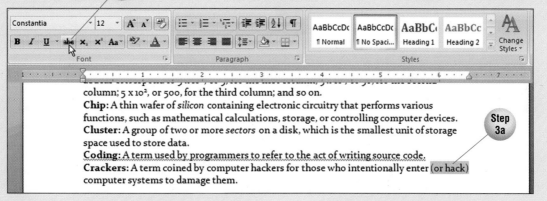

4. Change the font color by completing the following steps:
   a. Press Ctrl + A to select the entire document.
   b. Click the Font Color button arrow.
   c. Click the Dark Blue color (second color from *right* in the *Standard Colors* section) at the drop-down gallery.
   d. Click outside the selected area to deselect text.

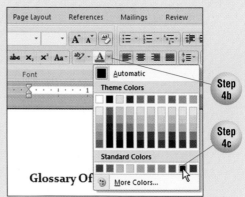

5. Highlight text in the document by completing the following steps:
   a. Click the Text Highlight Color button in the Font group. (This causes the mouse pointer to display as an I-beam pointer with a pen attached.)
   b. Select the term *Beta-testing* and the definition that follows.

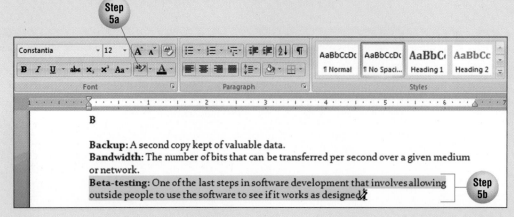

c. Click the Text Highlight Color button arrow and then click a green color (you decide which green).
   d. Select the term *Cluster* and the definition that follows.
   e. Click the Text Highlight Color button arrow and then click the yellow color that displays in the upper left corner of the drop-down gallery.
   f. Click the Text Highlight Color button to turn off highlighting.
6. Change the case of the title by selecting *Glossary Of Terms* and then pressing Shift + F3. (This changes the case of the title text to uppercase.)
7. Apply italic formatting using the Mini toolbar by completing the following steps:
   a. Select the text *one-stop shopping* located in the definition for the term *Aggregation software*. (When you select the text, the Mini toolbar displays.)
   b. Click the Italic button on the Mini toolbar.
   c. Select the word *bits* located in the definition for the term *Bandwidth* and then click the Italic button on the Mini toolbar.
8. Save **WordL1_C2_P1.docx**.

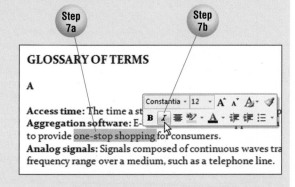

Figure 2.3 Project 1c

Chinese abacus: Pebbles strung on a rod inside a frame. Pebbles in the upper part of an abacus correspond to 5×10^0, or 5, for the first column; 5×10^1, or 50, for the second column; 5×10^2, or 500, for the third column; and so on.

Changing Fonts at the Font Dialog Box

In addition to buttons in the Font group, you can use options at the Font dialog box shown in Figure 2.4 to change the typeface, type size, and typestyle of text as well as apply font effects. Display the Font dialog box by clicking the Font group dialog box launcher. The dialog box launcher is a small square containing a diagonal-pointing arrow that displays in the lower right corner of the Font group.

QUICK STEPS

Change Font and Apply Effects
1. Click Font group dialog box launcher.
2. Choose desired options at dialog box.
3. Click OK.

Figure 2.4 Font Dialog Box

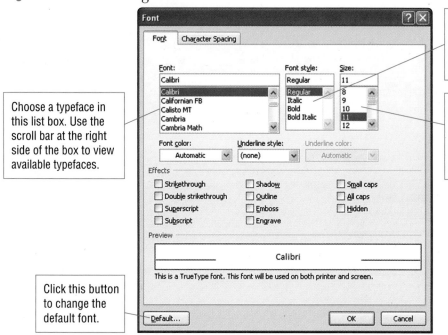

Choose a typeface in this list box. Use the scroll bar at the right side of the box to view available typefaces.

Choose a typestyle in this list box. The options in the box may vary depending on the selected typeface.

Choose a type size in this list box, or select the current measurement in the top box and then type the desired measurement.

Click this button to change the default font.

Project 1d   **Changing the Font at the Font Dialog Box**

1. With **WordL1_C2_P1.docx** open, press Ctrl + End to move the insertion point to the end of the document. (Make sure the insertion point is positioned a double space below the last line of text.)
2. Type **Created by Susan Ashby** and then press the Enter key.
3. Type **Wednesday, February 17, 2010**.
4. Change the font to 13-point Times New Roman and the color to dark red by completing the following steps:
   a. Press Ctrl + A to select the entire document.
   b. Click the Font group dialog box launcher.

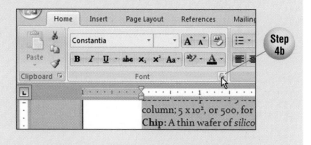

Step 4b

c. At the Font dialog box, click the down-pointing arrow at the right side of the *Font* list box to scroll down the list box and then click *Times New Roman*.

d. Click in the *Size* text box and then type 13.

e. Click the down-pointing arrow at the right side of the *Font color* list box and then click a dark red color of your choosing at the color gallery.

f. Click OK to close the dialog box.

5. Double underline text by completing the following steps:

a. Select *Wednesday, February 17, 2010*.

b. Click the Font group dialog box launcher.

c. At the Font dialog box, click the down-pointing arrow at the right side of the *Underline style* option box and then click the double-line option at the drop-down list.

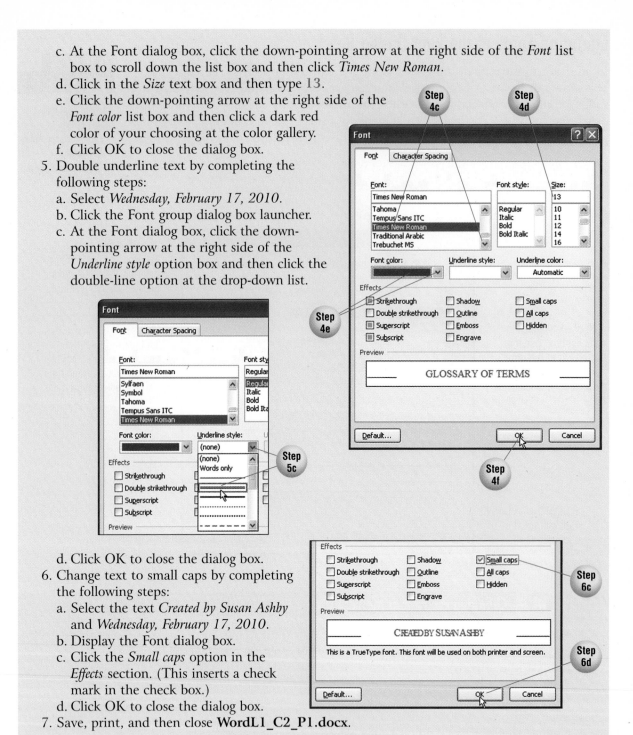

d. Click OK to close the dialog box.

6. Change text to small caps by completing the following steps:

a. Select the text *Created by Susan Ashby* and *Wednesday, February 17, 2010*.

b. Display the Font dialog box.

c. Click the *Small caps* option in the *Effects* section. (This inserts a check mark in the check box.)

d. Click OK to close the dialog box.

7. Save, print, and then close **WordL1_C2_P1.docx**.

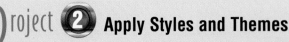 roject ② **Apply Styles and Themes**

You will open a document containing information on the life cycle of software, apply styles to text, and then change the Quick Styles set. You will also apply a theme and then change the theme colors and fonts.

Applying Styles from a Quick Styles Set

A Word document contains a number of predesigned formats grouped into style sets called Quick Styles. Four of the styles in the default Quick Styles set display in the Styles group in the Home tab. Display additional styles by clicking the More button that displays at the right side of the four styles. This displays a drop-down gallery of style choices. To apply a style, position the insertion point in the paragraph of text to which you want the style applied, click the More button at the right side of the styles in the Styles group, and then click the desired style at the drop-down gallery.

A Word document contains some default formatting including 10 points of spacing after paragraphs and a line spacing of 1.15. (You will learn more about these formatting options later in this chapter.) You can remove this default formatting as well as any character formatting applied to text in your document by applying the No Spacing style to your text. This style is located in the Styles group.

Changing the Quick Styles Set

Word contains a number of Quick Styles sets containing styles you can use to apply formatting to a document. To change to a different Quick Styles set, click the Change Styles button in the Styles group in the Home tab and then point to Style Set. This displays a side menu with Quick Styles sets. Click the desired set and the style formatting changes for the styles in the set.

QUICK STEPS

Apply a Style
1. Position insertion point in paragraph of desired text.
2. Click More button in Styles group.
3. Click desired style.

Change Quick Style Set
1. Click Change Style button.
2. Point to Style Set.
3. Click desired set.

More

Change Styles

Project 2a   Applying Quick Styles

1. Open **WordDocument05.docx**.
2. Save the document with Save As and name it **WordL1_C2_P2**.
3. Remove the 10 points of spacing after paragraphs and change the line spacing to 1 by completing the following steps:
   a. Press Ctrl + A to select the entire document.
   b. Click the No Spacing style in the Styles group in the Home tab.

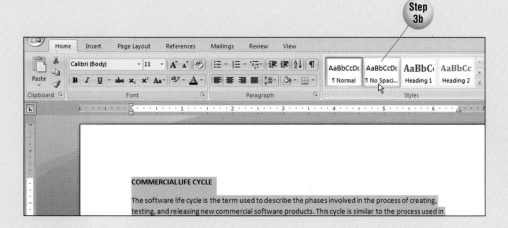

Step 3b

4. Position the insertion point on any character in the title *COMMERCIAL LIFE CYCLE* and then click the Heading 1 style that displays in the Styles group.

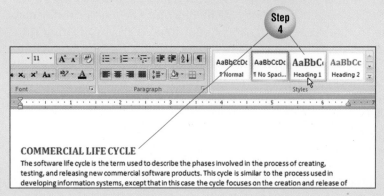

5. Position the insertion point on any character in the heading *Proposal and Planning* and then click the Heading 2 style that displays in the Styles group.

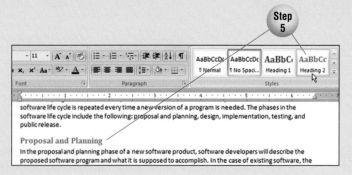

6. Position the insertion point on any character in the heading *Design* and then click the Heading 2 style in the Styles group.
7. Apply the Heading 2 style to the remaining headings (*Implementation*, *Testing*, and *Public Release and Support*).
8. Click the Change Styles button in the Styles group, point to *Style Set*, and then click *Modern*. (Notice how the Heading 1 and Heading 2 formatting changes.)

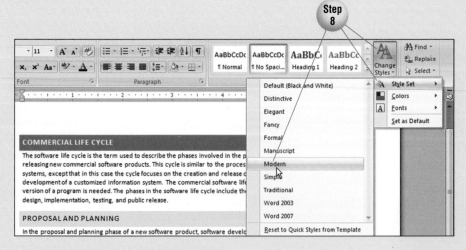

9. Save and then print **WordL1_C2_P2.docx**.

Applying a Theme

Word provides a number of themes you can use to format text in your document. A theme is a set of formatting choices that include a color theme (a set of colors), a font theme (a set of heading and body text fonts), and an effects theme (a set of lines and fill effects). To apply a theme, click the Page Layout tab and then click the Themes button in the Themes group. At the drop-down gallery that displays, click the desired theme. You can hover the mouse pointer over a theme and the live preview feature will display your document with the theme formatting applied. With the live preview feature you can see how the theme formatting affects your document before you make your final choice. Applying a theme is an easy way to give your document a professional look.

Project 2b Applying a Theme to Text in a Document

1. With **WordL1_C2_P2.docx** open, click the Page Layout tab and then click the Themes button in the Themes group.
2. At the drop-down gallery, hover your mouse pointer over each theme and notice how the text formatting changes in your document.
3. Click the *Module* theme.
4. Save and then print **WordL1_C2_P2.docx**.

Changing Themes

You can change a theme with the three buttons that display at the right side of the Themes button. A theme contains specific color formatting, which you can change with options from the Theme Colors button in the Themes group. Click this button and a drop-down gallery displays with named color schemes. The names of the color schemes correspond to the names of the themes. Each theme applies specific fonts, which you can change with options from the Theme Fonts button in the Themes group. Click this button and a drop-down gallery displays with font choices. Each font group in the drop-down gallery contains two choices. The first choice in the group is the font that is applied to headings and the second choice is the font that is applied to body text in the document. If you are formatting a document containing graphics with lines and fills, you can apply a specific theme effect with options at the Theme Effects drop-down gallery.

1. With **WordL1_C2_P2.docx** open, click the Theme Colors button in the Themes group and then click *Foundry* at the drop-down gallery. (Notice how the colors in the title and headings change.)
2. Click the Theme Fonts button and then click the *Civic* option. (Notice how the document text font changes.)

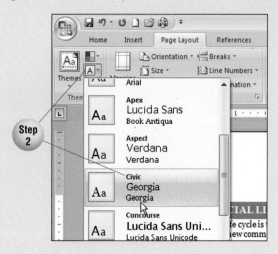

Step 2

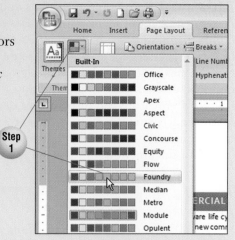

Step 1

3. Save, print, and then close **WordL1_C2_P2.docx**.

Project ③ Apply Paragraph Formatting and Use Format Painter

You will open a report on intellectual property and fair use issues and then format the report by changing the alignment of text in paragraphs, applying spacing before and after paragraphs of text, and repeating the last formatting action.

Changing Paragraph Alignment

By default, paragraphs in a Word document are aligned at the left margin and ragged at the right margin. Change this default alignment with buttons in the Paragraph group in the Home tab or with keyboard shortcuts as shown in Table 2.3.

You can change the alignment of text in paragraphs before you type the text or you can change the alignment of existing text. If you change the alignment before typing text, the alignment formatting is inserted in the paragraph mark. As you type text and press Enter, the paragraph formatting is continued. For example, if you click the Center button in the Paragraph group, type text for the first paragraph, and then press the Enter key, the center alignment formatting is still active and the insertion point displays centered between the left and right margins. To display the paragraph symbols in a document, click the Show/Hide ¶ button in the Paragraph

Center

Show/Hide

Table 2.3 Paragraph Alignment Buttons and Keyboard Shortcuts

To align text	Paragraph Group Button	Keyboard Shortcut
At the left margin		Ctrl + L
Between margins		Ctrl + E
At the right margin		Ctrl + R
At the left and right margins		Ctrl + J

group. With the Show/Hide ¶ button active (displays with an orange background), nonprinting formatting symbols display such as the paragraph symbol ¶ indicating a press of the Enter key or a dot indicating a press of the spacebar.

To return paragraph alignment to the default (left-aligned), click the Align Text Left button in the Paragraph group. You can also return all paragraph formatting to the default with the keyboard shortcut, Ctrl + Q. This keyboard shortcut removes paragraph formatting from selected text. If you want to remove all formatting from selected text including character and paragraph formatting, click the Clear Formatting button in the Font group.

To change the alignment of existing text in a paragraph, position the insertion point anywhere within the paragraph. You do not need to select the entire paragraph. To change the alignment of several adjacent paragraphs in a document, select a portion of the first paragraph through a portion of the last paragraph. You do not need to select all of the text in the paragraphs.

Align Text Left

HINT

Align text in a document so the message of the document can be followed and the page is attractive.

Project 3a   Changing Paragraph Alignment

1. Open **WordReport03.docx**. (Some of the default formatting in this document has been changed.)
2. Save the document with Save As and name it **WordL1_C2_P3**.
3. Click the Show/Hide ¶ button in the Paragraph group in the Home tab to turn on the display of nonprinting characters.

Step 3

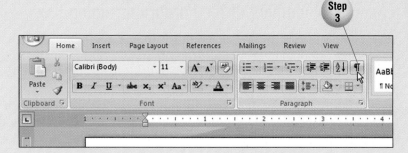

4. Press Ctrl + A to select the entire document and then change the alignment to Justify by clicking the Justify button in the Paragraph group in the Home tab.

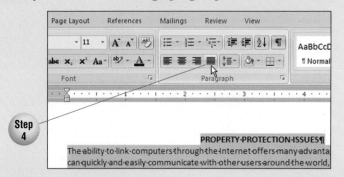

5. Press Ctrl + End to move the insertion point to the end of the document.
6. Press the Enter key once.
7. Press Ctrl + E to move the insertion point to the middle of the page.
8. Type **Prepared by Clarissa Markham**.
9. Press Shift + Enter and then type **Edited by Joshua Streeter**.

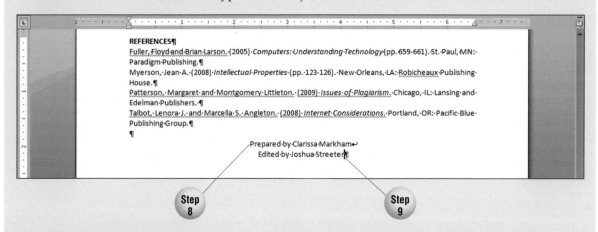

10. Click the Show/Hide ¶ button in the Paragraph group in the Home tab to turn off the display of nonprinting characters.
11. Save **WordL1_C2_P3.docx**.

QUICK STEPS

Change Paragraph Alignment
Click desired alignment button in Paragraph group.
OR
1. Click Paragraph group dialog box launcher.
2. Click *Alignment* option down-pointing arrow.
3. Click desired alignment.
4. Click OK.

Changing Alignment at the Paragraph Dialog Box

Along with buttons in the Paragraph group and keyboard shortcuts, you can also change paragraph alignment with the Alignment option at the Paragraph dialog box shown in Figure 2.5. Display this dialog box by clicking the Paragraph group dialog box launcher. At the Paragraph dialog box, click the down-pointing arrow at the right side of the *Alignment* option box. At the drop-down list that displays, click the desired alignment option and then click OK to close the dialog box.

Figure 2.5 Paragraph Dialog Box with Alignment Options

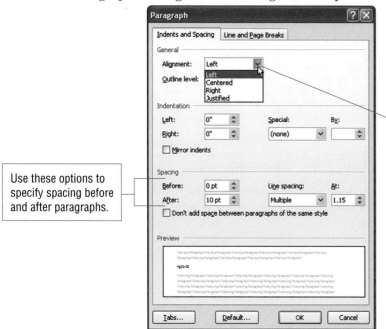

Change paragraph alignment by clicking this down-pointing arrow and then clicking the desired alignment at the drop-down list.

Use these options to specify spacing before and after paragraphs.

Project ③b — Changing Paragraph Alignment at the Paragraph Dialog Box

1. With **WordL1_C2_P3.docx** open, change paragraph alignment by completing the following steps:
   a. Select the entire document.
   b. Click the Paragraph group dialog box launcher.
   c. At the Paragraph dialog box with the Indents and Spacing tab selected, click the down-pointing arrow at the right of the *Alignment* list box and then click *Left*.
   d. Click OK to close the dialog box.
   e. Deselect the text.
2. Change paragraph alignment by completing the following steps:
   a. Press Ctrl + End to move the insertion point to the end of the document.
   b. Position the insertion point on any character in the text *Prepared by Clarissa Markham*.
   c. Click the Paragraph group dialog box launcher.
   d. At the Paragraph dialog box with the Indents and Spacing tab selected, click the down-pointing arrow at the right of the *Alignment* list box and then click *Right*.

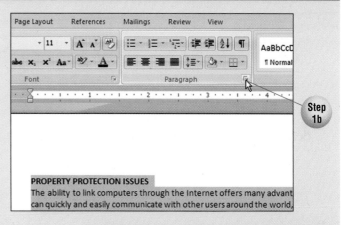

Step 1b

PROPERTY PROTECTION ISSUES
The ability to link computers through the Internet offers many advant can quickly and easily communicate with other users around the world,

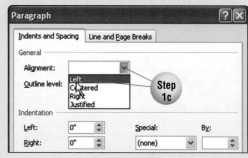

Step 1c

e. Click OK. (The line of text containing the name *Clarissa Markham* and the line of text containing the name *Joshua Streeter* are both aligned at the right since you used the New Line command, Shift + End, to separate the lines of text without creating a new paragraph.)

3. Save and then print **WordL1_C2_P3.docx**.

Indenting Text in Paragraphs

QUICK STEPS

Indent Text in Paragraph

Drag indent marker(s) on Ruler.

OR

Press keyboard shortcut keys.

OR

1. Click Paragraph group dialog box launcher.
2. Insert measurement in *Left, Right,* and/or *By* text box.
3. Click OK.

View Ruler

By now you are familiar with the word wrap feature of Word, which ends lines and wraps the insertion point to the next line. To indent text from the left margin, the right margin, or both, use indent buttons in the Paragraph group, in the Page Layout tab, keyboard shortcuts, options from the Paragraph dialog box, markers on the Ruler, or use the Alignment button on the Ruler. Figure 2.6 identifies indent markers and the Alignment button on the Ruler. Refer to Table 2.4 for methods for indenting text in a document. To display the Ruler, click the View Ruler button located at the top of the vertical scroll bar.

One situation that may call for indented text is the use of a lengthy passage of quoted material. Suppose you are writing a report in which you quote a paragraph of text from a well known expert's book. Rather than using quotation marks to set off the paragraph, consider indenting it from both margins. This option creates a block of text that the reader recognizes instantly as being separate from the body of the report and therefore "new" or "different."

Another type of indent is a negative indent, which is referred to as an "outdent" because it moves the text out into the left margin. A negative indent is an additional option for highlighting, or calling special attention to, a section of writing.

Figure 2.6 Ruler and Indent Markers

Alignment Button   First Line Indent Marker

Left Indent Marker   Hanging Indent Marker   Right Indent Marker

Table 2.4 Methods for Indenting Text

Indent	*Methods for Indenting*
First line of paragraph	• Press the Tab key. • Display Paragraph dialog box, click the down-pointing arrow to the right of the *Special* list box, click *First line*, and then click OK. • Drag the First Line Indent marker on the Ruler. • Click the Alignment button located at the left side of the Ruler until the First Line Indent button displays and then click on the Ruler at the desired location.
Text from left margin	• Click the Increase Indent button in the Paragraph group in the Home tab to increase the indent or click the Decrease Indent button to decrease the indent. • Insert a measurement in the *Indent Left* measurement button in the Paragraph group in the Page Layout tab. • Press Ctrl + M to increase the indent or press Ctrl + Shift + M to decrease the indent. • Display the Paragraph dialog box, type the desired indent measurement in the *Left* measurement box, and then click OK. • Drag the left indent marker on the Ruler.
Text from right margin	• Insert a measurement in the *Indent Right* measurement button in the Paragraph group in the Page Layout tab. • Display the Paragraph dialog box, type the desired indent measurement in the *Right* measurement box, and then click OK. • Drag the right indent marker on the Ruler.
All lines of text except the first (called a hanging indent)	• Press Ctrl + T. (Press Ctrl + Shift + T to remove hanging indent.) • Display the Paragraph dialog box, click the down-pointing arrow to the right of the *Special* list box, click *Hanging*, and then click OK. • Click the Alignment button located at the left side of the Ruler until the Hanging Indent button displays and then click on the Ruler at the desired location.
Text from both left and right margins	• Display the Paragraph dialog box, type the desired indent measurement in the *Left* measurement box, type the desired measurement in the *Right* measurement box, and then click OK. • Insert a measurement in the *Indent Right* and *Indent Left* measurement buttons in the Paragraph group in the Page Layout tab. • Drag the left indent marker on the Ruler; then drag the right indent marker on the Ruler.

1. With **WordL1_C2_P3.docx** open, indent the first line of text in paragraphs by completing the following steps:

   a. Select the first two paragraphs of text in the document (the text after the title *PROPERTY PROTECTION ISSUES* and before the heading *Intellectual Property*.

   b. Position the mouse pointer on the First Line Indent marker on the Ruler, hold down the left mouse button, drag the marker to the 0.5-inch mark, and then release the mouse button.

   c. Select the paragraphs of text in the *Intellectual Property* section and then drag the First Line Indent marker on the Ruler to the 0.5-inch mark.

   d. Select the paragraphs of text in the *Fair Use* section, click the Alignment button located at the left side of the Ruler until the First Line Indent button displays, and then click on the Ruler at the 0.5-inch mark.

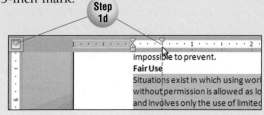

   e. Position the insertion point on any character in the paragraph of text below the *Intellectual Property Protection* heading, make sure the First Line Indent button displays in the Alignment button, and then click at the 0.5-inch mark on the Ruler.

2. Since the text in the second paragraph in the *Fair Use* section is a quote, you need to indent the text from the left and right margins by completing the following steps:

   a. Position the insertion point anywhere within the second paragraph in the *Fair Use* section (the paragraph that begins *[A] copyrighted work, including such . . .*).

   b. Click the Paragraph group dialog box launcher.

   c. At the Paragraph dialog box, with the Indents and Spacing tab selected, select the current measurement in the *Left* measurement box and then type 0.5.

   d. Select the current measurement in the *Right* measurement box and then type 0.5.

   e. Click the down-pointing arrow at the right side of the *Special* list box and then click *(none)* at the drop-down list.

   f. Click OK or press Enter.

3. Create a hanging indent for the first paragraph in the *REFERENCES* section by positioning the insertion point anywhere in the first paragraph below *REFERENCES* and then pressing Ctrl + T.

4. Create a hanging indent for the second paragraph in the *REFERENCES* section by completing the following steps:

   a. Position the insertion point anywhere in the second paragraph in the *REFERENCES* section.

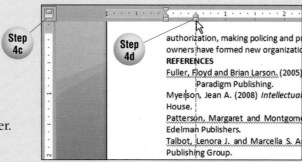

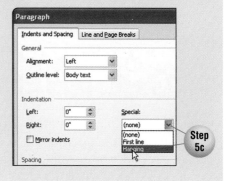

b. Make sure the Ruler is displayed. (If not, click the View Ruler button located at the top of the vertical scroll bar.)

c. Click the Alignment button located at the left side of the Ruler until the Hanging Indent button displays.

d. Click on the 0.5-inch mark on the Ruler.

5. Create a hanging indent for the third and fourth paragraphs by completing the following steps:

a. Select a portion of the third and fourth paragraphs.

b. Click the Paragraph group dialog box launcher.

c. At the Paragraph dialog box with the Indents and Spacing tab selected, click the down-pointing arrow at the right side of the *Special* list box and then click *Hanging* at the drop-down list.

d. Click OK or press Enter.

6. Save **WordL1_C2_P3.docx**.

Spacing Before and After Paragraphs

By default, Word applies 10 points of additional spacing after a paragraph. You can remove this spacing, increase or decrease the spacing, and insert spacing above the paragraph. To change spacing before or after a paragraph, use the Spacing Before and Spacing After measurement boxes located in the Paragraph group in the Page Layout tab, or the *Before* and/or *After* options at the Paragraph dialog box with the Indents and Spacing tab selected.

Spacing before or after a paragraph is part of the paragraph and will be moved, copied, or deleted with the paragraph. If a paragraph, such as a heading, contains spacing before it, and the paragraph falls at the top of a page, Word ignores the spacing.

Spacing before or after paragraphs is added in points and a vertical inch contains approximately 72 points. To add spacing before or after a paragraph you would click the Page Layout tab, select the current measurement in the *Spacing Before* or the *Spacing After* measurement box, and then type the desired number of points. You can also click the up- or down-pointing arrows at the right side of the *Spacing Before* and *Spacing After* measurement boxes to increase or decrease the amount of spacing.

HINT

Line spacing determines the amount of vertical space between lines while paragraph spacing determines the amount of space above or below paragraphs of text.

Repeating the Last Action

If you apply formatting to text and then want to apply the same formatting to other text in the document, consider using the Repeat command. To use this command, apply the desired formatting, move the insertion point to the next location where you want the formatting applied, and then press the F4 function key or press Ctrl + Y.

QUICK STEPS

Repeat Last Action
Press F4
OR
Press Ctrl + Y

1. With **WordL1_C2_P3.docx** open, add 6 points of spacing before and after each paragraph in the document by completing the following steps:
   a. Select the entire document.
   b. Click the Page Layout tab.
   c. Click once on the up-pointing arrow at the right side of the *Spacing Before* measurement box in the Paragraph group (this inserts *6 pt* in the box).
   d. Click once on the up-pointing arrow at the right side of the *Spacing After* measurement box in the Paragraph group (this inserts *6 pt* in the text box).

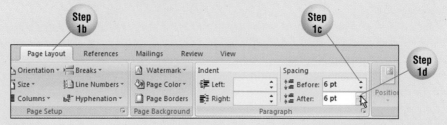

Step
1b

Step
1c

Step
1d

2. Add an additional 6 points of spacing above the headings by completing the following steps:
   a. Position the insertion point on any character in the heading *Intellectual Property* and then click once on the up-pointing arrow at the right side of the *Spacing Before* measurement box (this changes the measurement to *12 pt*).

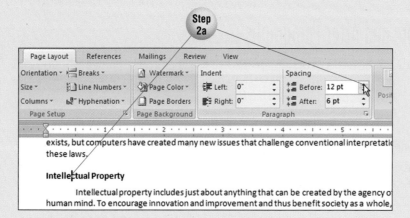

Step
2a

   b. Position the insertion point on any character in the heading *Fair Use* and then press F4 (this is the Repeat command).
   c. Position the insertion point on any character in the heading *Intellectual Property Protection* and then press F4.
   d. Position the insertion point on any character in the heading *REFERENCES* and then press Ctrl + Y (this is also the Repeat command).
3. Save **WordL1_C2_P3.docx**.

Formatting with Format Painter

The Clipboard group in the Home tab contains a button for copying formatting and displays in the Clipboard group as a paintbrush. To use the Format Painter button, position the insertion point on a character containing the desired formatting, click the Format Painter button, and then select text to which you want the formatting applied. When you click the Format Painter button, the mouse I-beam pointer displays with a paintbrush attached. If you want to apply formatting a single time, click the Format Painter button once. If you want to apply the formatting in more than one location in the document, double-click the Format Painter button and then select text to which you want formatting applied. When you are finished, click the Format Painter button to turn it off. You can also turn off Format Painter by pressing the Esc key.

Format with Format Painter
1. Format text.
2. Double-click Format Painter button.
3. Select text.
4. Click Format Painter button.

Format Painter

Project **3e** **Formatting Headings with the Format Painter**

1. With **WordL1_C2_P3.docx** open, click the Home tab.
2. Select the entire document and then change the font to 12-point Cambria.
3. Select the title *PROPERTY PROTECTION ISSUES*, click the Center button in the Paragraph group, and then change the font to 16-point Candara bold.
4. Apply 16-point Candara bold formatting to the *REFERENCES* heading by completing the following steps:
   a. Click on any character in the title *PROPERTY PROTECTION ISSUES*.
   b. Click once on the Format Painter button in the Clipboard group.

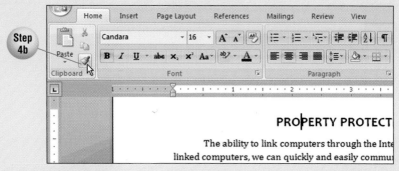

   c. Press Ctrl + End to move the insertion point to the end of the document and then select the heading *REFERENCES*. (This applies the 16-point Candara bold formatting and centers the text.)
5. With the insertion point positioned on any character in the heading *REFERENCES*, add an additional 6 points of spacing before the heading.
6. Select the heading *Intellectual Property* and then change the font to 14-point Candara bold.
7. Use the Format Painter button and apply 14-point Candara bold formatting to the other headings by completing the following steps:
   a. Position the insertion point on any character in the heading *Intellectual Property*.
   b. Double-click the Format Painter button in the Clipboard group.
   c. Using the mouse, select the heading *Fair Use*.

d. Using the mouse, select the heading *Intellectual Property Protection*.

e. Click once on the Format Painter button in the Clipboard group. (This turns off the feature.)

f. Deselect the heading.

8. Save **WordL1_C2_P3.docx**.

QUICK STEPS

Change Line Spacing
Click Line Spacing button in Paragraph group, then click desired option at drop-down list.
OR
Press shortcut command keys.
OR
1. Click Paragraph group dialog box launcher.
2. Click *Line Spacing* option down-pointing arrow.
3. Click desired line spacing option.
4. Click OK.
OR
1. Click Paragraph group dialog box launcher.
2. Type line measurement in *At* text box.
3. Click OK.

Line Spacing

Changing Line Spacing

The default line spacing for a document is 1.15. (The line spacing for the **WordReport03.docx** document, which you opened at the beginning of Project 3, had been changed to single.) In certain situations, Word automatically adjusts the line spacing. For example, if you insert a large character or object such as a graphic, Word increases the line spacing of that specific line. But you also may sometimes encounter a writing situation in which you decide to change the line spacing for a section or for the entire document.

Change line spacing using the Line Spacing button in the Paragraph group in the Home tab, with keyboard shortcuts, or with options from the Paragraph dialog box. Table 2.5 displays the keyboard shortcuts to change line spacing.

Table 2.5 Line Spacing Keyboard Shortcuts

Press	*To change line spacing to*
Ctrl + 1	single spacing
Ctrl + 2	double spacing
Ctrl + 5	1.5 line spacing

You can also change line spacing at the Paragraph dialog box with the *Line spacing* option or the *At* option. If you click the down-pointing arrow at the right side of the *Line spacing* option, a drop-down list displays with a variety of spacing options. For example, to change the line spacing to double you would click *Double* at the drop-down list. You can type a specific line spacing measurement in the *At* text box. For example, to change the line spacing to 1.75, type 1.75 in the *At* text box.

1. With **WordL1_C2_P3.docx** open, change the line spacing for all paragraphs to double spacing by completing the following steps:
   a. Select the entire document.
   b. Click the Line Spacing button located in the Paragraph group in the Home tab.
   c. Click *2.0* at the drop-down list.
2. With the entire document still selected, press Ctrl + 5. (This changes the line spacing to 1.5 line spacing.)
3. Change the line spacing to 1.3 using the Paragraph dialog box by completing the following steps:
   a. With the document still selected, click the Paragraph group dialog box launcher.
   b. At the Paragraph dialog box, make sure the Indents and Spacing tab is selected, click inside the *At* text box, and then type 1.3. (This text box is located to the right of the *Line spacing* list box.)
   c. Click OK or press Enter.
   d. Deselect the text.
4. Save, print, and then close **WordL1_C2_P3.docx**.

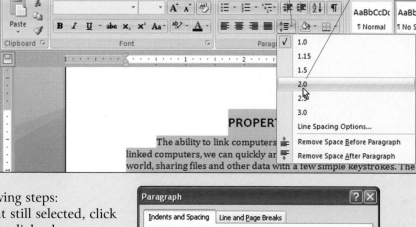

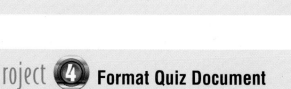

Project 4 **Format Quiz Document**

You will open a document containing two problems to solve, reveal the formatting, compare the formatting, and make formatting changes.

Revealing Formatting

Display formatting applied to specific text in a document at the Reveal Formatting task pane. The Reveal Formatting task pane displays font, paragraph, and section formatting applied to text where the insertion point is positioned or to selected text. Display the Reveal Formatting task pane with the keyboard shortcut Shift + F1.

Generally, a minus symbol precedes *Font* and *Paragraph* and a plus symbol precedes *Section* in the *Formatting of selected text* section of the Reveal Formatting task pane. Click the minus symbol to hide any items below a heading and click the plus symbol to reveal items. Some of the items below headings in the *Formatting of selected text* section are hyperlinks. Click a hyperlink and a dialog box displays with the specific option.

Figure 2.7 Reveal Formatting Task Pane

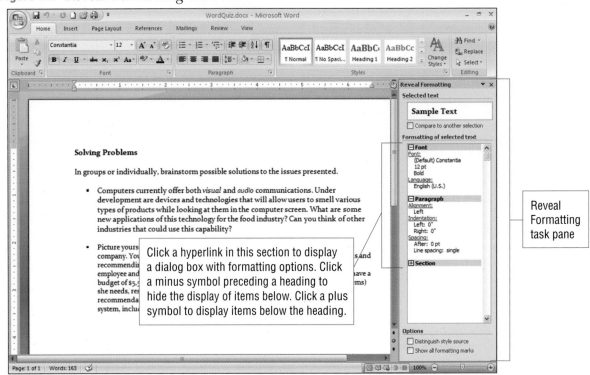

Click a hyperlink in this section to display a dialog box with formatting options. Click a minus symbol preceding a heading to hide the display of items below. Click a plus symbol to display items below the heading.

Reveal Formatting task pane

Project 4a Revealing Formatting

1. Open **WordQuiz.docx**.
2. Save the document with Save As and name it **WordL1_C2_P4**.
3. Press Shift + F1 to display the Reveal Formatting task pane.
4. Click anywhere in the heading *Solving Problems* and then notice the formatting information that displays in the Reveal Formatting task pane.
5. Click in the bulleted paragraph and notice the formatting information thast displays in the Reveal Formatting task pane.

Comparing Formatting

Along with displaying formatting applied to text, you can use the Reveal Formatting task pane to compare formatting of two text selections to determine what formatting is different. To compare formatting, select the first instance of formatting to be compared, click the *Compare to another selection* check box, and then select the second instance of formatting to compare. Any differences between the two selections display in the *Formatting differences* list box.

QUICK STEPS

Compare Formatting
1. Display Reveal Formatting task pane.
2. Click or select text.
3. Click *Compare to another selection* check box.
4. Click or select text.

Project 4b   Comparing Formatting

1. With **WordL1_C2_P4.docx** open, make sure the Reveal Formatting task pane displays. If it does not, turn it on by pressing Shift + F1.
2. Select the first bulleted paragraph (the paragraph that begins *Computers currently offer both . . .*).
3. Click the *Compare to another selection* check box to insert a check mark.
4. Select the second bulleted paragraph (the paragraph that begins *Picture yourself working in the . . .*).
5. Determine the formatting differences by reading the information in the *Formatting differences* list box. (The list box displays *12 pt -> 11 pt* below the Font: hyperlink, indicating that the difference is point size.)
6. Format the second bulleted paragraph so it is set in 12-point size.
7. Click the *Compare to another selection* check box to remove the check mark.
8. Select the word *visual* that displays in the first sentence in the first bulleted paragraph.
9. Click the *Compare to another selection* check box to insert a check mark.
10. Select the word *audio* that displays in the first sentence of the first bulleted paragraph.
11. Determine the formatting differences by reading the information in the *Formatting differences* list box.
12. Format the word *audio* so it matches the formatting of the word *visual*.
13. Click the *Compare to another selection* check box to remove the check mark.
14. Close the Reveal Formatting task pane by clicking the Close button (contains an X) that displays in the upper right corner of the task pane.
15. Save, print, and then close **WordL1_C2_P4.docx**.

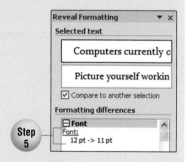

Step 5

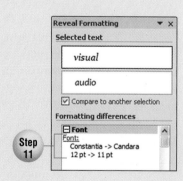

Step 11

CHAPTER summary

- The appearance of a document in the document screen and how it looks when printed is called the format.
- The top row in the Font group in the Home tab contains buttons for changing the font and font size. The bottom row contains buttons for applying typestyles and effects.
- A font consists of three parts: typeface, type size, and typestyle.
- A typeface (font) is a set of characters with a common design and shape. Typefaces are either monospaced, allotting the same amount of horizontal space to each character, or proportional, allotting a varying amount of space for each character. Proportional typefaces are divided into two main categories: serif and sans serif.
- Type size is measured in point size—the higher the point size, the larger the characters.
- A typestyle is a variation of style within a certain typeface. You can apply typestyle formatting with some of the buttons in the Font group.
- With some of the buttons in the Font group, you can apply font effects such as superscript, subscript, and strikethrough.
- Some buttons in the Font group contain keyboard shortcuts. Refer to Table 2.2 for a list of these shortcuts.
- The Mini toolbar automatically displays above selected text. Use buttons on this toolbar to apply formatting to selected text.
- With options at the Font dialog box, you can change the font, font size, and font style and apply specific effects. Display this dialog box by clicking the Font group dialog box launcher.
- A Word document contains a number of predesigned formats grouped into style sets called Quick Styles. Change to a different Quick Styles set by clicking the Change Styles button in the Styles group in the Home tab, pointing to Style Set, and then clicking the desired set.
- Word provides a number of themes, which are a set of formatting choices that include a color theme (a set of colors), a font theme (a set of heading and body text fonts), and an effects theme (a set of lines and fill effects). Apply a theme and change theme colors, fonts, and effects with buttons in the Themes group in the Page Layout tab.
- In Word, a paragraph is any amount of text followed by a paragraph mark (a stroke of the Enter key). Word inserts into the paragraph mark any paragraph formatting that is turned on.
- By default, paragraphs in a Word document are aligned at the left margin and ragged at the right margin. Change this default alignment with buttons in the Paragraph group, at the Paragraph dialog box, or with keyboard shortcuts.
- To turn on or off the display of nonprinting characters such as paragraph marks, click the Show/Hide ¶ button in the Paragraph group.

- Indent text in paragraphs with indent buttons in the Paragraph group in the Home tab, buttons in the Paragraph group in the Page Layout tab, keyboard shortcuts, options from the Paragraph dialog box, markers on the Ruler, or use the Alignment button on the Ruler. Refer to Table 2.4 for a description of the various indenting options.

- Increase and/or decrease spacing before and after paragraphs using the *Spacing Before* and *Spacing After* measurement boxes in the Paragraph group in the Page Layout tab, or using the *Before* and/or *After* options at the Paragraph dialog box.

- Repeat the last action by pressing the F4 function key or pressing Ctrl + Y.

- Use the Format Painter button in the Clipboard group in the Home tab to copy formatting already applied to text to different locations in the document.

- Change line spacing with the Line Spacing button in the Paragraph group in the Home tab, keyboard shortcuts, or options from the Paragraph dialog box.

- Display the Reveal Formatting task pane to display formatting applied to text. Use the *Compare to another selection* option in the task pane to compare formatting of two text selections to determine what formatting is different.

COMMANDS review

FEATURE	RIBBON TAB, GROUP	BUTTON	KEYBOARD SHORTCUT
Bold text	Home, Font	**B**	Ctrl + B
Center-align text	Home, Paragraph	≣	Ctrl + E
Change case of text	Home, Font	Aa ▾	Shift + F3
Change Quick Styles set	Home, Styles	AA	
Clear all formatting	Home, Font		
Clear character formatting			Ctrl + spacebar
Clear paragraph formatting			Ctrl + Q
Decrease font size	Home, Font	A ▾	Ctrl + <
Display nonprinting characters	Home, Paragraph	¶	Ctrl + *
Font	Home, Font	Calibri (Body) ▾	
Font color	Home, Font	A ▾	
Font dialog box	Home, Font		Ctrl + Shift + F
Format Painter	Home, Clipboard		Ctrl + Shift + C

continued

FEATURE	RIBBON TAB, GROUP	BUTTON	KEYBOARD SHORTCUT
Highlight text	Home, Font	ab✐ ▾	
Increase font size	Home, Font	A▲	Ctrl + >
Italicize text	Home, Font	I	Ctrl + I
Justify-align text	Home, Paragraph	☰	Ctrl + J
Left-align text	Home, Paragraph	☰	Ctrl + L
Line spacing	Home, Paragraph	☰ ▾	Ctrl + 1 (single) Ctrl + 2 (double) Ctrl + 5 (1.5)
Paragraph dialog box	Home, Paragraph	⌐	
Repeat last action			F4 or Ctrl + Y
Reveal Formatting task pane			Shift + F1
Right-align text	Home, Paragraph	☰	Ctrl + R
Spacing after paragraph	Page Layout, Paragraph	After: 0 pt	
Spacing before paragraph	Page Layout, Paragraph	Before: 0 pt	
Strikethrough text	Home, Font	abc	
Subscript text	Home, Font	X₂	Ctrl + =
Superscript text	Home, Font	X²	Ctrl + Shift + +
Theme Colors	Page Layout, Themes	▣ ▾	
Theme Fonts	Page Layout, Themes	A ▾	
Themes	Page Layout, Themes	Aa	
Underline text	Home, Font	U ▾	Ctrl + U

CONCEPTS check

Test Your Knowledge

Completion: In the space provided at the right, indicate the correct term, symbol, or command.

1. The Bold button is located in this group in the Home tab. _____

2. Click this button in the Font group to remove all formatting from selected text. _____

3. Proportional typefaces are divided into two main categories, serif and this.

_____

4. This is the keyboard shortcut to italicize selected text.

_____

5. This term refers to text that is raised slightly above the regular text line.

_____

6. This automatically displays above selected text.

_____

7. Click this to display the Font dialog box.

_____

8. A Word document contains a number of predesigned formats grouped into style sets called this.

_____

9. Apply a theme and change theme colors, fonts, and effects with buttons in the Themes group in this tab.

_____

10. This is the default paragraph alignment.

_____

11. Click this button in the Paragraph group to turn on the display of nonprinting characters.

_____

12. Return all paragraph formatting to normal with this keyboard shortcut.

_____

13. Click this button in the Paragraph group in the Home tab to align text at the right margin.

_____

14. In this type of paragraph, the first line of text remains at the left margin and the remaining lines of text are indented to the first tab.

_____

15. Repeat the last action by pressing F4 or with this keyboard shortcut.

_____

16. Use this button in the Clipboard group in the Home tab to copy formatting already applied to text to different locations in the document.

_____

17. Change line spacing to 1.5 with this keyboard shortcut.

_____

18. Press these keys to display the Reveal Formatting task pane.

_____

SKILLS check

Demonstrate Your Proficiency

1 APPLY CHARACTER FORMATTING TO A LEASE AGREEMENT DOCUMENT

1. Open **WordDocument03.docx**.
2. Save the document with Save As and name it **WordL1_C2_A1**.
3. Press Ctrl + End to move the insertion point to the end of the document and then type the text shown in Figure 2.8. Bold, italicize, and underline text as shown.
4. Select the entire document and then change the font to 12-point Candara.
5. Select and then bold *THIS LEASE AGREEMENT* located in the first paragraph.
6. Select and then bold *DOLLARS* located in the *Rent* section.
7. Select and then bold *DOLLARS* located in the *Damage Deposit* section.
8. Select and then italicize *12 o'clock midnight* in the *Term* section.
9. Select the title *LEASE AGREEMENT* and then change the font to 18-point Corbel and the font color to dark blue. (Make sure the title retains the bold formatting.)
10. Select the heading *Term*, change the font to 14-point Corbel, and apply small caps formatting. (Make sure the heading retains the bold formatting.)
11. Use Format Painter to change the formatting to small caps in 14-point Corbel for the remaining headings (*Rent, Damage Deposit, Use of Premises, Condition of Premises, Alterations and Improvements, Damage to Premises, Inspection of Premises, Default*, and *Late Charge*).
12. Save, print, and then close **WordL1_C2_A1.docx**.

Figure 2.8 Assessment 1

Inspection of Premises

Lessor shall have the right at all reasonable times during the term of this Agreement to exhibit the Premises and to display the usual *for sale*, *for rent*, or *vacancy* signs on the Premises at any time within <u>forty-five</u> days before the expiration of this Lease.

Default

If Lessee fails to pay rent when due and the default continues for <u>seven</u> days thereafter, Lessor may declare the entire balance immediately due and payable and may exercise any and all rights and remedies available to Lessor.

Late Charge

In the event that any payment required to be paid by Lessee is not made by the 10th day of the month, Lessee shall pay to Lessor a *late fee* in the amount of **$50**.

Assessment

2 APPLY STYLES, A QUICK STYLES SET, AND A THEME TO A HARDWARE TECHNOLOGY DOCUMENT

1. Open **WordDocument06.docx**.
2. Save the document with Save As and name it **WordL1_C2_A2**.
3. Apply the Heading 1 style to the title *ON THE HORIZON*.
4. Apply the Heading 2 style to the headings in the document (*Increased Optical Disk Storage Capacity, Improved Monitors, Holographic Storage,* and *Electronic Paper*).
5. Change the Quick Styles set to *Fancy*.
6. Apply the *Foundry* theme.
7. Change the theme colors to *Aspect*.
8. Change the theme fonts to *Flow*.
9. Highlight the second sentence in the *Increased Optical Disk Storage Capacity* section.
10. Highlight the second sentence in the *Holographic Storage* section.
11. Save, print, and then close **WordL1_C2_A2.docx**.

Assessment

3 APPLY CHARACTER AND PARAGRAPH FORMATTING TO AN EMPLOYEE PRIVACY DOCUMENT

1. Open **WordDocument04.docx**.
2. Save the document with Save As and name it **WordL1_C2_A3**.
3. Move the insertion point to the beginning of the document and then type WORKPLACE PRIVACY centered.
4. Select text from the beginning of the first paragraph to the end of the document and then make the following changes:
   a. Change the line spacing to 1.5.
   b. Change the spacing after to 0 points.
   c. Indent the first line of each paragraph 0.5 inch.
   d. Change the alignment to Justify.
5. Move the insertion point to the end of the document and, if necessary, drag the First Line Indent marker on the Ruler back to 0". Type the text shown in Figure 2.9. (Hang indent text as shown in Figure 2.9.)
6. Select the entire document and then change the font to Constantia.
7. Select the title *WORKPLACE PRIVACY* and then change the font to 14-point Calibri bold and the font color to dark red.
8. Apply the same formatting to the title *BIBLIOGRAPHY* that you applied to the title *WORKPLACE PRIVACY*.
9. Save, print, and then close **WordL1_C2_A3.docx**.

Figure 2.9 Assessment 3

BIBLIOGRAPHY

Amaral, Howard G. (2009). *Privacy in the Workplace*, 2nd edition (pp. 103-

112). Denver, CO: Goodwin Publishing Group.

Cuevas, Roxanne A. (2007). *Employer and Employee Rights* (pp. 18-35). Los

Angeles, CA: North Ridge, Inc.

Forsyth, Stuart M. (2010). *Protecting Your Privacy* (pp. 23-31). San Francisco,

CA: Roosevelt & Carson Publishing.

CASE study
Apply Your Skills

Part 1

You work for your local chamber of commerce and are responsible for assisting the Office Manager, Teresa Alexander. Ms. Alexander would like to maintain consistency in articles submitted for publication in the monthly chamber newsletter. She wants you to explore various handwriting, decorative, and plain fonts. She would like you to choose two handwriting fonts, two decorative fonts, and two plain fonts and then prepare a document containing an illustration of each of these fonts. Save the document and name it **WordL1_C2_CS_P1**. Print and then close the document.

Part 2

Ms. Alexander has asked you to write a short article for the upcoming chamber newsletter. In the article, she would like you to describe an upcoming event at your school, a local college or university, or your local community. Effectively use at least two of the fonts you wrote about in the document you prepared for Case Study Part 1. Save the document and name it **WordL1_C2_CS_P2**. Print and then close the document.

Part 3

Help

When preparing the monthly newsletter, additional fonts may be necessary. Ms. Alexander has asked you to research the steps needed to install new fonts on your computer. Use the Help feature to research the steps and then prepare a document listing the steps. Format the document with appropriate headings and fonts. Save the document and name it **WordL1_C2_CS_P3**. Print and then close the document.

CHAPTER 3

Customizing Paragraphs

PERFORMANCE OBJECTIVES

Upon successful completion of Chapter 3, you will be able to:

- Apply numbering and bulleting formatting to text
- Insert paragraph borders and shading
- Apply custom borders and shading
- Sort paragraph text
- Set, clear, and move tabs on the Ruler and at the Tabs dialog box
- Cut, copy, and paste text in a document
- Copy and paste text between documents

word Chapter 3

Tutorial 3.1
Using Formatting Features
Tutorial 3.2
Copying and Moving Text

As you learned in Chapter 2, Word contains a variety of options for formatting text in paragraphs. In this chapter you will learn how to insert numbers and bullets in a document, how to apply borders and shading to paragraphs of text in a document, how to sort paragraphs of text, and how to manipulate tabs on the Ruler and at the Tabs dialog box. Editing some documents might include selecting and then deleting, moving, or copying text. You can perform this type of editing with buttons in the Clipboard group in the Home tab or with keyboard shortcuts.

Note: Before beginning computer projects, copy to your storage medium the Word2007L1C3 subfolder from the Word2007L1 folder on the CD that accompanies this textbook and then make Word2007L1C3 the active folder.

Project ① Format a Document on Computer Technology

You will open a document containing information on computer technology, type numbered text in the document, and apply numbering and bullet formatting to paragraphs in the document.

Applying Numbering and Bullets

Automatically number paragraphs or insert bullets before paragraphs using buttons in the Paragraph group. Use the Bullets button to insert bullets before specific paragraphs and use the Numbering button to insert numbers.

Numbering Paragraphs

If you type 1., press the spacebar, type a paragraph of text, and then press the Enter key, Word indents the number approximately 0.25 inch and then hang indents the text in the paragraph approximately 0.5 inch from the left margin. Additionally, *2.* is inserted 0.25 inch from the left margin at the beginning of the next paragraph. Continue typing items and Word inserts the next number in the list. To turn off numbering, press the Enter key twice or click the Numbering button in the Paragraph group. (You can also remove all paragraph formatting from a paragraph, including automatic numbering, with the keyboard shortcut, Ctrl + Q. Remove all formatting including character and paragraph formatting from selected text by clicking the Clear Formatting button in the Font group.)

If you press the Enter key twice between numbered paragraphs, the automatic number is removed. To turn it back on, type the next number in the list (and the period) followed by a space, type the paragraph of text, and then press Enter. Word will automatically indent the number and hang indent the text.

When the AutoFormat feature inserts numbering and indents text, the AutoCorrect Options button displays. Click this button and a drop-down list displays with options for undoing and/or stopping the automatic numbering. An AutoCorrect Options button also displays when AutoFormat inserts automatic bulleting in a document. If you want to insert a line break without inserting a bullet or number, you do not need to turn off the automatic numbering/bulleting and then turn it back on again. Instead, simply press Shift + Enter to insert the line break.

QUICK STEPS

Type Numbered Paragraphs
1. Type 1.
2. Press spacebar.
3. Type text.
4. Press Enter.

HINT
Define new numbering by clicking the Numbering button arrow and then clicking Define New Number Format.

Bullets

Numbering

Project 1a Typing Numbered Paragraphs

1. Open **WordDocument12.docx**.
2. Save the document with Save As and name it **WordL1_C3_P1**.
3. Press Ctrl + End to move the insertion point to the end of the document and then type the text shown in Figure 3.1. Bold and center the title *Technology Career Questions*. When typing the numbered paragraphs, complete the following steps:
   a. Type 1. and then press the spacebar.
   b. Type the paragraph of text and then press the Enter key. (This moves the insertion point down to the next line, inserts *2.* indented 0.25 inch from the left margin, and also indents the first paragraph of text approximately 0.5 inch from the left margin. Also, the AutoCorrect Options button displays. Use this button if you want to undo or stop automatic numbering.)
   c. Continue typing the remaining text. (Remember, you do not need to type the paragraph number and period—these are automatically inserted.)
   d. After typing the last question, press the Enter key twice. (This turns off paragraph numbering.)
4. Save **WordL1_C3_P1.docx**.

Figure 3.1 Project 1a

Technology Career Questions

1. What is your ideal technical job?
2. Which job suits your personality?
3. Which is your first-choice certificate?
4. How does the technical job market look in your state right now? Is the job market wide open or are the information technology career positions limited?

If you do not want automatic numbering in a document, turn off the feature at the AutoCorrect dialog box with the AutoFormat As You Type tab selected as shown in Figure 3.2. To display this dialog box, click the Office button and then click the Word Options button that displays toward the bottom of the drop-down list. At the Word Options dialog box, click the *Proofing* option located in the left panel and then click the AutoCorrect Options button that displays in the *AutoCorrect options* section of the dialog box. At the AutoCorrect dialog box, click the AutoFormat As You Type tab and then click the *Automatic numbered lists* check box to remove the check mark. Click OK to close the AutoCorrect dialog box and then click OK to close the Word Options dialog box.

Figure 3.2 AutoCorrect Dialog Box with AutoFormat As You Type Tab Selected

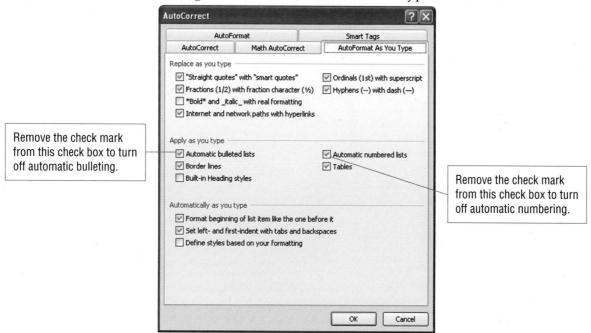

Remove the check mark from this check box to turn off automatic bulleting.

Remove the check mark from this check box to turn off automatic numbering.

You can also automate the creation of numbered paragraphs with the Numbering button in the Paragraph group. To use this button, type the text (do not type the number) for each paragraph to be numbered, select the paragraphs to be numbered, and then click the Numbering button in the Paragraph group. You can insert or delete numbered paragraphs in a document.

Project 1b Inserting Paragraph Numbering

1. With **WordL1_C3_P1.docx** open, apply numbers to paragraphs by completing the following steps:
   a. Select the five paragraphs of text in the *Technology Information Questions* section.
   b. Click the Numbering button in the Paragraph group.
2. Add the paragraph shown in Figure 3.3 between paragraphs 4 and 5 in the *Technology Information Questions* section by completing the following steps:
   a. Position the insertion point immediately to the right of the question mark at the end of the fourth paragraph.
   b. Press Enter.
   c. Type the paragraph shown in Figure 3.3.
3. Delete the second question (paragraph) in the *Technology Information Questions* section by completing the following steps:
   a. Select the text of the second paragraph (you will not be able to select the number).
   b. Press the Delete key.
4. Save **WordL1_C3_P1.docx**.

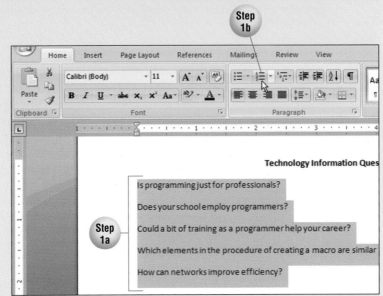

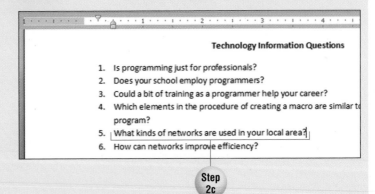

Figure 3.3 Project 1b

What kinds of networks are used in your local area?

Bulleting Paragraphs

In addition to automatically numbering paragraphs, Word's AutoFormat feature will create bulleted paragraphs. You can also create bulleted paragraphs with the Bullets button in the Paragraph group. Figure 3.4 shows an example of bulleted paragraphs. Bulleted lists with hanging indents are automatically created when a paragraph begins with the symbol *, >, or -. Type one of the symbols, press the spacebar, type text, and then press Enter. The AutoFormat feature inserts a bullet approximately 0.25 inch from the left margin and indents the text following the bullet another 0.25 inch. The type of bullet inserted depends on the type of character entered. For example, if you use the asterisk (*) symbol, a round bullet is inserted and an arrow bullet is inserted if you type the greater than symbol (>). Like the numbering feature, you can turn off the automatic bulleting feature at the AutoCorrect dialog box with the AutoFormat As You Type tab selected.

QUICK STEPS

Type Bulleted Paragraphs
1. Type *, >, or - symbol.
2. Press spacebar.
3. Type text.
4. Press Enter.

HINT
Define new bullets by clicking the Bullets button arrow and then clicking Define New Bullet.

Figure 3.4 Bulleted Paragraphs

- This is a paragraph preceded by a bullet. A bullet indicates a list of items or topics.

- This is another paragraph preceded by a bullet. You can easily create bulleted paragraphs by typing certain symbols before the text or with the Bullets button in the Paragraph group.

Project 1c Typing Bulleted Paragraphs

1. With **WordL1_C3_P1.docx** open, press Ctrl + End to move the insertion point to the end of the document and then press the Enter key once.
2. Type the text shown in Figure 3.5. Bold and center the title *Technology Timeline: Computer Design*. Create the bulleted paragraphs by completing the following steps:
   a. With the insertion point positioned at the left margin of the first paragraph to contain a bullet, type the greater than symbol (>).
   b. Press the spacebar once.
   c. Type the text of the first bulleted paragraph.
   d. Press the Enter key once and then continue typing the text after the bullets.
3. After typing the last bulleted paragraph, press the Enter key twice (this turns off bullets).
4. Save **WordL1_C3_P1.docx**.

Figure 3.5 Project 1c

Technology Timeline: Computer Design

➢ 1937: Dr. John Atanasoff and Clifford Berry design and build the first electronic digital computer.

➢ 1958: Jack Kilby, an engineer at Texas Instruments, invents the integrated circuit, thereby laying the foundation for fast computers and large-capacity memory.

➢ 1981: IBM enters the personal computer field by introducing the IBM-PC.

➢ 2004: Wireless computer devices, including keyboards, mice, and wireless home networks, become widely accepted among users.

QUICK STEPS

Create Bulleted Paragraphs
1. Select text.
2. Click Bullets button.

You can also create bulleted paragraphs with the Bullets button in the Paragraph group. To create bulleted paragraphs using the Bullets button, type the text (do not type the bullet) of the paragraphs, select the paragraphs, and then click the Bullets button in the Paragraph group.

Project 1d   Inserting Bullets Using the Bullets Button

1. With **WordL1_C3_P1.docx** open, insert bullets before the paragraphs of text in the *Technology Timeline: Computers in the Workplace* section by completing the following steps:
   a. Select the paragraphs of text in the *Technology Timeline: Computers in the Workplace* section.
   b. Click the Bullets button in the Paragraph group. (Word will insert the same arrow bullets that you inserted in Project 1c. Word keeps the same bullet formatting until you choose a different bullet.)

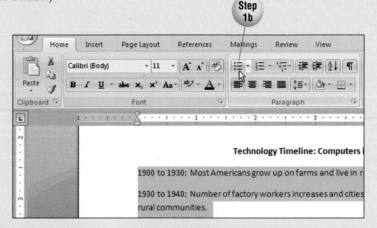

2. Save and then print **WordL1_C3_P1.docx**. (This document will print on two pages.)

Inserting Paragraph Borders and Shading

Every paragraph you create in Word contains an invisible frame. You can apply a border to the frame around the paragraph. You can apply a border to specific sides of the paragraph or to all sides, you can customize the type of border lines, and you can add shading and fill to the border. Add borders and shading to paragraphs in a document using the Borders and Shading buttons in the Paragraph group or options from the Borders and Shading dialog box.

Borders

Shading

Inserting Paragraph Borders

When a border is added to a paragraph of text, the border expands and contracts as text is inserted or deleted from the paragraph. You can create a border around a single paragraph or a border around selected paragraphs. One method for creating a border is to use options from the Borders button in the Paragraph group. Click the Borders button arrow and a drop-down list displays as shown in Figure 3.6.

Figure 3.6 Borders Drop-down List

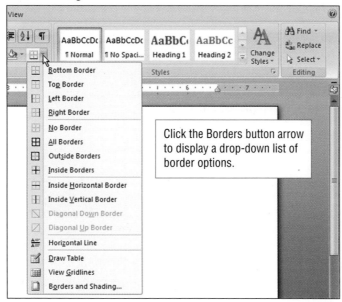

Click the Borders button arrow to display a drop-down list of border options.

At the drop-down list, click the option that will insert the desired border. For example, to insert a border at the bottom of the paragraph, click the *Bottom Border* option. Clicking an option will add the border to the paragraph where the insertion point is located. To add a border to more than one paragraph, select the paragraphs first and then click the desired option.

Apply Border
1. Select text.
2. Click Borders button.

1. With **WordL1_C3_P1.docx** open, select text from the beginning of the title *Technology Timeline: Computer Design* through the four bulleted paragraphs of text below and then press the Delete key.

2. Insert an outside border to specific text by completing the following steps:

   a. Select text from the title *Technology Information Questions* through the five numbered paragraphs of text.

   b. In the Paragraph group, click the Borders button arrow.

   c. At the Borders drop-down list, click the *Outside Borders* option.

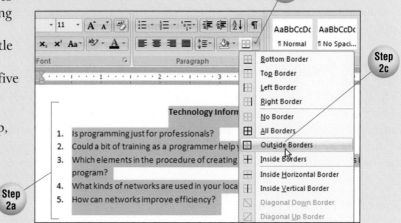

3. Select text from the title *Technology Timeline: Computers in the Workplace* through the six bulleted paragraphs of text and then click the Borders button in the Paragraph group. (The button will apply the border option that was previously selected.)

4. Select text from the title *Technology Career Questions* through the four numbered paragraphs of text below and then click the Borders button in the Paragraph group.

5. Save and then print **WordL1_C3_P1.docx**.

Adding Paragraph Shading

Apply Shading
1. Select text.
2. Click Shading button.

With the Shading button in the Paragraph group you can add shading to text in a document. Select text you want to shade and then click the Shading button. This applies a background color behind the text. Click the Shading button arrow and a Shading drop-down gallery displays as shown in Figure 3.7.

Figure 3.7 Shading Gallery

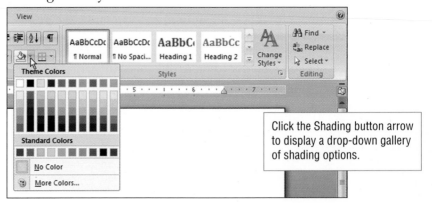

Click the Shading button arrow to display a drop-down gallery of shading options.

Paragraph shading colors display in themes in the drop-down gallery. Use one of the theme colors or click one of the standard colors that displays at the bottom of the gallery. Click the *More Colors* option and the Colors dialog box displays. At the Colors dialog box with the Standard tab selected, click the desired color or click the Custom tab and then specify a custom color.

Project ⑪ Applying Shading to Paragraphs

1. With **WordL1_C3_P1.docx** open, apply paragraph shading and change border lines by completing the following steps:
    a. Position the insertion point on any character in the title *Technology Information Questions*.
    b. Click the Borders button arrow and then click *No Border* at the drop-down list.
    c. Click the Borders button arrow and then click *Bottom Border* at the drop-down list.
    d. Click the Shading button arrow and then click the *Purple, Accent 4, Lighter 60%* option.

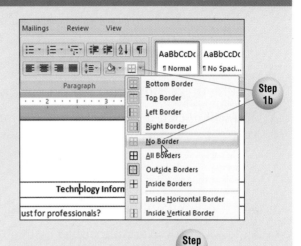

2. Apply the same formatting to the other titles by completing the following steps:
    a. With the insertion point positioned on any character in the title *Technology Information Questions*, double-click the Format Painter button in the Clipboard group.
    b. Select the title *Technology Timeline: Computers in the Workplace*.
    c. Select the title *Technology Career Questions*.
    d. Click the Format Painter button in the Clipboard group.

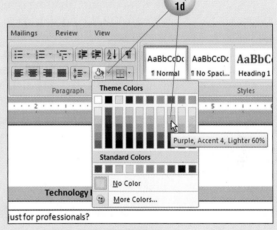

3. Remove the paragraph border and apply shading to paragraphs by completing the following steps:
    a. Select the numbered paragraphs of text below the *Technology Information Questions* title.
    b. Click the Borders button arrow and then click *No Border* at the drop-down list.
    c. Click the Shading button arrow and then click the *Purple, Accent 4, Lighter 80%* option.

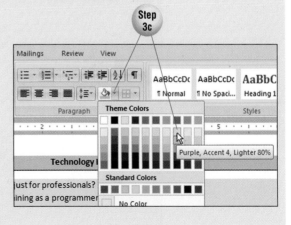

4. Select the bulleted paragraphs of text below the *Technology Timeline: Computers in the Workplace* title, click the Borders button, and then click the Shading button. (Clicking the Borders button will apply the previous border option, which was no border. Clicking the Shading button will apply the previous shading option, which was *Purple, Accent 4, Lighter 80%*.)
5. Select the numbered paragraphs of text below the *Technology Career Questions* title, click the Borders button, and then click the Shading button.
6. Save, print, and then close **WordL1_C3_P1.docx**.

Project ② Customize a Document on Online Shopping

You will open a document containing information on online shopping, apply and customize borders and shading, and then sort text in the document.

Customizing Borders and Shading

If you want to further customize paragraph borders and shading, use options at the Borders and Shading dialog box. Click the Borders tab and options display for customizing the border; click the Shading tab and shading options display. As you learned in a previous section, you can add borders to a paragraph with the Borders button in the Paragraph group. If you want to further customize borders, use options at the Borders and Shading dialog box with the Borders tab selected as shown in Figure 3.8. Display this dialog box by clicking the Borders button arrow and then clicking *Borders and Shading* at the drop-down list. At the Borders and Shading dialog box, specify the desired border, style, color, and width. Click the Shading tab and the dialog box displays with shading options as shown in Figure 3.9.

Figure 3.8 Borders and Shading Dialog Box with the Borders Tab Selected

Click the sides, top, or bottom of this preview area to insert or remove a border.

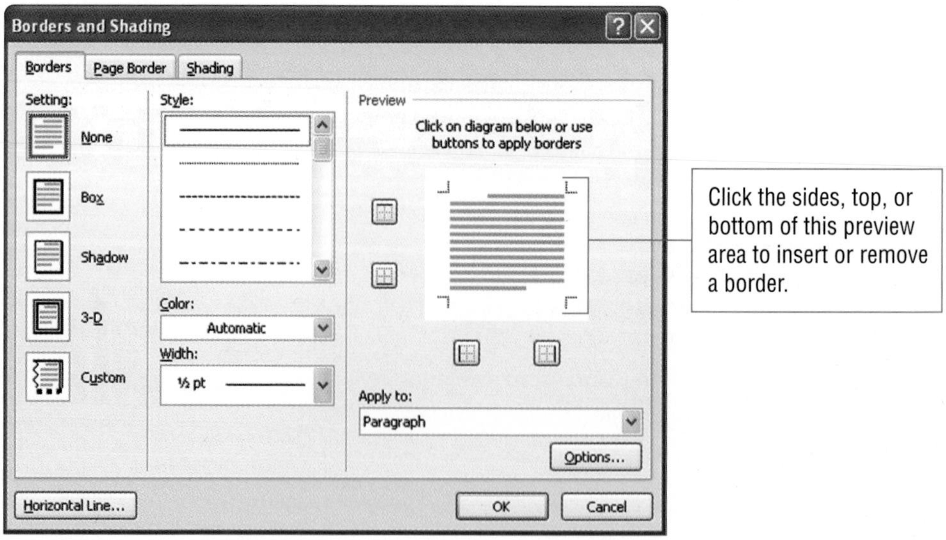

Figure 3.9 Borders and Shading Dialog Box with the Shading Tab Selected

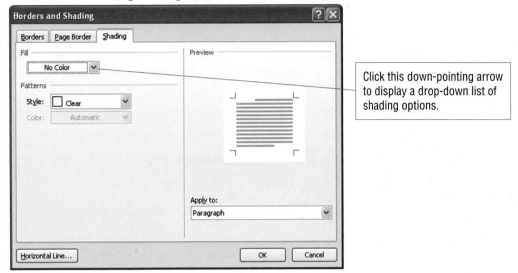

Click this down-pointing arrow to display a drop-down list of shading options.

Project 2a · Adding Customized Border and Shading to a Document

1. Open **WordDocument13.docx**.
2. Save the document with Save As and name it **WordL1_C3_P2**.
3. Make the following changes to the document:
   a. Insert 12 points of space before and 6 points of space after the headings *Online Shopping, Advantages of Online Shopping, Online Shopping Venues, Online Shopping Safety Tips,* and *REFERENCES*. (Do this with the *Spacing Before* and *Spacing After* measurement boxes in the Page Layout tab.)
   b. Center the *REFERENCES* title.
4. Insert a custom border and add shading to a heading by completing the following steps:
   a. Move the insertion point to any character in the heading *Online Shopping*.
   b. Click the Borders button arrow and then click *Borders and Shading* at the drop-down list.
   c. At the Borders and Shading dialog box with the Borders tab selected, click the down-pointing arrow at the right side of the *Color* option box and then click the *Dark Blue* color in the *Standard Colors* section.

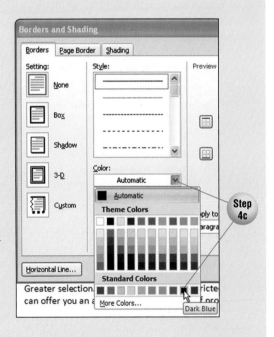

Step 4c

d. Click the down-pointing arrow at the right of the *Width* option box and then click *1 pt* at the drop-down list.
e. Click the top border of the box in the *Preview* section of the dialog box.
f. Click the down scroll arrow in the *Style* list box and then click the first thick/thin line.
g. Click the down-pointing arrow at the right side of the *Color* option box and then click the *Dark Blue* color in the *Standard Colors* section.
h. Click the bottom border of the box in the *Preview* section of the dialog box.
i. Click the Shading tab.
j. Click the down-pointing arrow at the right side of the *Fill* option box and then click *Olive Green, Accent 3, Lighter 60%*.
k. Click OK to close the dialog box.

5. Use Format Painter to apply the same border and shading formatting to the remaining headings by completing the following steps:
   a. Position the insertion point on any character in the heading *Online Shopping*.
   b. Double-click the Format Painter button in the Clipboard group in the Home tab.
   c. Select the heading *Advantages of Online Shopping*.
   d. Select the heading *Online Shopping Venues*.
   e. Select the heading *Online Shopping Safety Tips*.
   f. Click the Format Painter button once.

6. Move the insertion point to any character in the heading *Online Shopping* and then remove the 12 points of spacing above.

7. Save **WordL1_C3_P2.docx**.

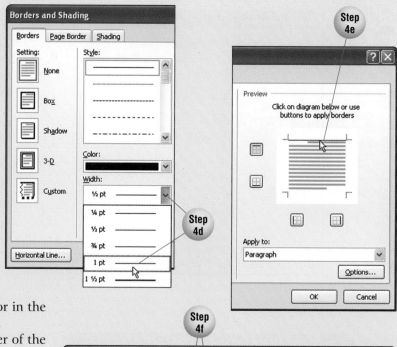

Step 4e

Step 4d

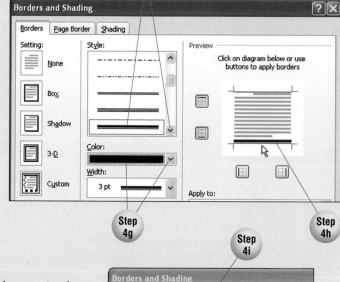

Step 4f

Step 4g

Step 4h

Step 4i

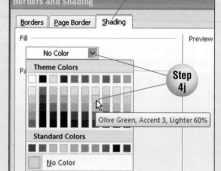

Step 4j

Olive Green, Accent 3, Lighter 60%

Sorting Text in Paragraphs

You can sort text arranged in paragraphs alphabetically by the first character. This character can be a number, symbol (such as $ or #), or letter. Type paragraphs you want to sort at the left margin or indented to a tab stop. Unless you select specific paragraphs for sorting, Word sorts the entire document.

To sort text in paragraphs, open the document. If the document contains text you do not want sorted, select the specific paragraphs. Click the Sort button in the Paragraph group and the Sort Text dialog box displays as shown in Figure 3.10. At this dialog box, click OK. If you select text and then display the dialog box the *Sort by* option is set at *Paragraph*. If the text you select is numbers, then *Numbers* displays in the Sort Text dialog box.

QUICK STEPS

Sort Paragraphs of Text
1. Click Sort button.
2. Make any needed changes at Sort Text dialog box.
3. Click OK.

Sort

Figure 3.10 Sort Text Dialog Box

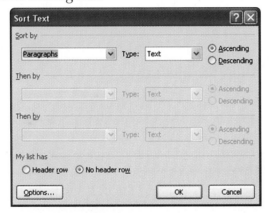

Project 2b Sorting Paragraphs Alphabetically

1. With **WordL1_C3_P2.docx** open, sort the bulleted text alphabetically by completing the following steps:
   a. Select the bulleted paragraphs in the *Advantages of Online Shopping* section.
   b. Click the Sort button in the Paragraph group.
   c. At the Sort Text dialog box, make sure *Paragraphs* displays in the *Sort by* option box and the *Ascending* option is selected.
   d. Click OK.

Step 1c

Step 1d

2. Sort the numbered paragraphs by completing the following steps:
   a. Select the numbered paragraphs in the *Online Shopping Safety Tips* section.
   b. Click the Sort button in the Paragraph group.
   c. Click OK at the Sort Text dialog box.
3. Follow steps similar to those in Step 1 or Step 2 to sort alphabetically the three paragraphs of text below the *REFERENCES* title.
4. Save, print, and then close **WordL1_C3_P2.docx**.

Project ③ Prepare a Document on Workshops and Training Dates

You will set and move tabs on the Ruler and at the Tabs dialog box and type tabbed text about workshops, training dates, and a table of contents.

Manipulating Tabs on the Ruler

When you work with a document, Word offers a variety of default settings such as margins and line spacing. One of these defaults is a left tab set every 0.5 inch. In some situations, these default tabs are appropriate; in others, you may want to create your own. Two methods exist for setting tabs. Tabs can be set on the Ruler or at the Tabs dialog box.

Use the Ruler to set, move, and delete tabs. If the Ruler is not visible, click the View Ruler button located at the top of the vertical scroll bar. The Ruler displays left tabs set every 0.5 inch. These default tabs are indicated by tiny vertical lines along the bottom of the Ruler. With a left tab, text aligns at the left edge of the tab. The other types of tabs that can be set on the Ruler are center, right, decimal, and bar. Use the Alignment button that displays at the left side of the Ruler to specify tabs. Each time you click the Alignment button, a different tab or paragraph alignment symbol displays. Table 3.1 shows the tab alignment button and what type of tab each will set.

Table 3.1 Tab Alignment Symbols

Alignment Button	Type of Tab
L	Left tab
⊥	Center tab
⌐	Right tab
⊥·	Decimal tab
I	Bar tab

Setting Tabs

To set a left tab on the Ruler, make sure the left alignment symbol (see Table 3.1) displays in the Alignment button. Position the arrow pointer just below the tick mark (the marks on the Ruler) where you want the tab symbol to appear and then click the left mouse button. When you set a tab on the Ruler, any default tabs to the left are automatically deleted by Word. Set a center, right, decimal, or bar tab on the Ruler in a similar manner.

Before setting a tab on the Ruler, click the Alignment button at the left side of the Ruler until the appropriate tab symbol displays and then set the tab. If you change the tab symbol in the Alignment button, the symbol remains until you change it again or you exit Word. If you exit and then reenter Word, the tab symbol returns to the default of left tab.

If you want to set a tab at a specific measurement on the Ruler, hold down the Alt key, position the arrow pointer at the desired position, and then hold down the left mouse button. This displays two measurements on the Ruler. The first measurement displays the location of the arrow pointer on the Ruler in relation to the left margin. The second measurement is the distance from the location of the arrow pointer on the Ruler to the right margin. With the left mouse button held down, position the tab symbol at the desired location and then release the mouse button and the Alt key.

If you change tab settings and then create columns of text using the New Line command, Shift + Enter, the tab formatting is stored in the paragraph mark at the end of the columns. If you want to make changes to the tab settings for text in the columns, position the insertion point anywhere within the columns (all of the text in the columns does not have to be selected) and then make the changes.

Project 3a — Setting Left, Center, and Right Tabs on the Ruler

1. At a new blank document, type WORKSHOPS centered and bolded as shown in Figure 3.11.
2. Press the Enter key and then return the paragraph alignment back to left and turn off bold.
3. Set a left tab at the 0.5-inch mark, a center tab at the 3.25-inch mark, and a right tab at the 6-inch mark by completing the following steps:
   a. Click the Show/Hide ¶ button in the Paragraph group in the Home tab to turn on the display of nonprinting characters.
   b. Make sure the Ruler is displayed. (If not, click the View Ruler button located at the top of the vertical scroll bar.)
   c. Make sure the left tab symbol displays in the Alignment button at the left side of the Ruler.
   d. Position the arrow pointer on the 0.5-inch mark on the Ruler and then click the left mouse button.

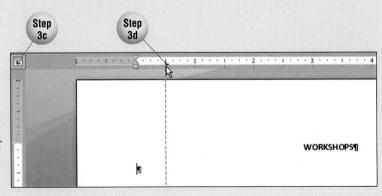

e. Position the arrow pointer on the Alignment button at the left side of the Ruler and then click the left mouse button until the center tab symbol displays (see Table 3.1).

f. Position the arrow pointer below the 3.25-inch mark on the Ruler. Hold down the Alt key and then the left mouse button. Make sure the first measurement on the Ruler displays as *3.25"* and then release the mouse button and the Alt key.

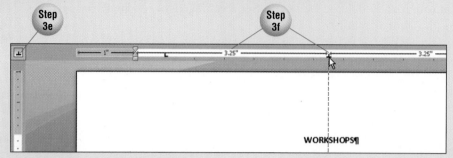

g. Position the arrow pointer on the Alignment button at the left side of the Ruler and then click the left mouse button until the right tab symbol displays (see Table 3.1).

h. Position the arrow pointer below the 6-inch mark on the Ruler. Hold down the Alt key and then the left mouse button. Make sure the first measurement on the Ruler displays as *6"* and then release the mouse button and the Alt key.

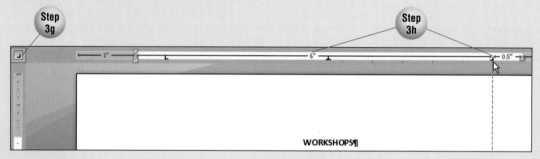

4. Type the text in columns as shown in Figure 3.11. Press the Tab key before typing each column entry and press Shift + Enter after typing the text in the third column.

5. After typing the last column entry, press the Enter key twice.

6. Press Ctrl + Q to remove paragraph formatting (tab settings).

7. Click the Show/Hide ¶ button to turn off the display of nonprinting characters.

8. Save the document and name it **WordL1_C3_P3**.

Figure 3.11 Project 3a

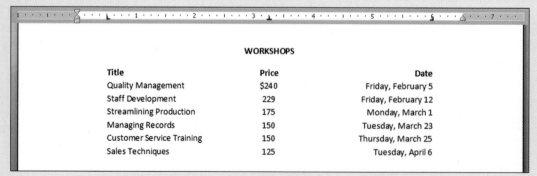

Title	Price	Date
Quality Management	$240	Friday, February 5
Staff Development	229	Friday, February 12
Streamlining Production	175	Monday, March 1
Managing Records	150	Tuesday, March 23
Customer Service Training	150	Thursday, March 25
Sales Techniques	125	Tuesday, April 6

Moving Tabs

After a tab has been set on the Ruler, it can be moved to a new location. To move a tab, position the arrow pointer on the tab symbol on the Ruler, hold down the left mouse button, drag the symbol to the new location on the Ruler, and then release the mouse button.

Deleting Tabs

To delete a tab from the Ruler, position the arrow pointer on the tab symbol you want deleted, hold down the left mouse button, drag the symbol down into the document, and then release the mouse button.

Project 3b Moving Tabs

1. With **WordL1_C3_P3.docx** open, position the insertion point on any character in the first entry in the tabbed text.
2. Position the arrow pointer on the left tab symbol at the 0.5-inch mark, hold down the left mouse button, drag the left tab symbol to the 1-inch mark on the Ruler, and then release the mouse button. *Hint: Use the Alt key to help you precisely position the tab symbol.*

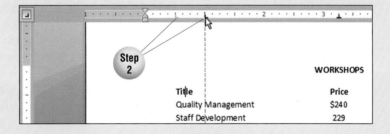

3. Position the arrow pointer on the right tab symbol at the 6-inch mark, hold down the left mouse button, drag the right tab symbol to the 5.5-inch mark on the Ruler, and then release the mouse button. *Hint: Use the Alt key to help you precisely position the tab symbol.*
4. Save **WordL1_C3_P3.docx**.

Manipulating Tabs at the Tabs Dialog Box

Use the Tabs dialog box shown in Figure 3.12 to set tabs at a specific measurement. You can also use the Tabs dialog box to set tabs with preceding leaders and clear one tab or all tabs. To display the Tabs dialog box, click the Paragraph group dialog box launcher. At the Paragraph dialog box, click the Tabs button located in the bottom left corner of the dialog box.

QUICK STEPS

Set Tabs at Tabs Dialog Box
1. Click Paragraph group dialog box launcher.
2. Click Tabs button.
3. Specify tab positions, alignments, and leader options.
4. Click OK.

Figure 3.12 Tabs Dialog Box

Type a tab measurement in this text box.

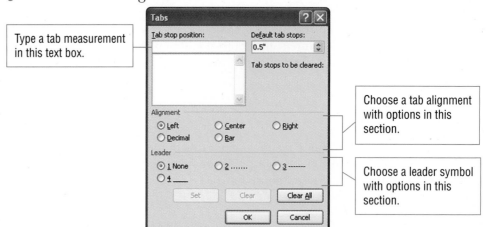

Choose a tab alignment with options in this section.

Choose a leader symbol with options in this section.

Clearing Tabs

At the Tabs dialog box, you can clear an individual tab or all tabs. To clear all tabs, click the Clear All button. To clear an individual tab, specify the tab position, and then click the Clear button.

Setting Tabs

At the Tabs dialog box, you can set a left, right, center, or decimal tab as well as a bar. (For an example of a bar tab, refer to Figure 3.13.) You can also set a left, right, center, or decimal tab with preceding leaders. To change the type of tab at the Tabs dialog box, display the dialog box and then click the desired tab in the *Alignment* section. Type the desired measurement for the tab in the *Tab stop position* text box.

Project **3C** **Setting Left Tabs and a Bar Tab at the Tabs Dialog Box**

1. With **WordL1_C3_P3.docx** open, press Ctrl + End to move the insertion point to the end of the document.
2. Type the title TRAINING DATES bolded and centered as shown in Figure 3.13, press the Enter key, return the paragraph alignment back to left, and then turn off bold.
3. Display the Tabs dialog box and then set left tabs and a bar tab by completing the following steps:
   a. Click the Paragraph group dialog box launcher.
   b. At the Paragraph dialog box, click the Tabs button located in the lower left corner of the dialog box.
   c. Make sure *Left* is selected in the *Alignment* section of the dialog box.
   d. Type 1.75 in the *Tab stop position* text box.
   e. Click the Set button.
   f. Type 4 in the *Tab stop position* text box and then click the Set button.
   g. Type 3.25 in the *Tab stop position* text box, click *Bar* in the *Alignment* section, and then click the Set button.
   h. Click OK to close the Tabs dialog box.

Step 3g

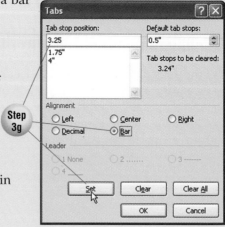

4. Type the text in columns as shown in Figure 3.13. Press the Tab key before typing each column entry and press Shift + Enter to end each line.
5. After typing *February 23*, complete the following steps:
   a. Press the Enter key.
   b. Clear tabs by displaying the Tabs dialog box, clicking the Clear All button, and then clicking OK.
   c. Press the Enter key.
6. Remove the 10 points of spacing after the last entry in the text by completing the following steps:
   a. Position the insertion point on any character in the *January 18* entry.
   b. Click the Page Layout tab.
   c. Click twice on the down-pointing arrow at the right side of the *Spacing After* measurement box. (This changes the measurement to *0 pt*.)
7. Save **WordL1_C3_P3.docx**.

Figure 3.13 Project 3c

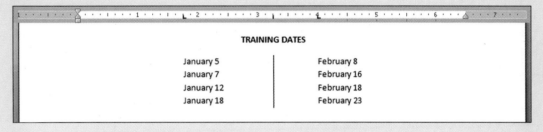

Setting Leader Tabs

The four types of tabs can also be set with leaders. Leaders are useful in a table of contents or other material where you want to direct the reader's eyes across the page. Figure 3.14 shows an example of leaders. Leaders can be periods (.), hyphens (-), or underlines (_). To add leaders to a tab, click the type of leader desired in the *Leader* section of the Tabs dialog box.

Project **3d** **Setting a Left Tab and a Right Tab with Dot Leaders**

1. With **WordL1_C3_P3.docx** open, press Ctrl + End to move the insertion point to the end of the document.
2. Type the title TABLE OF CONTENTS bolded and centered as shown in Figure 3.14.
3. Press the Enter key and then return the paragraph alignment back to left and turn off bold.
4. Set a left tab and a right tab with dot leaders by completing the following steps:
   a. Click the Paragraph group dialog box launcher.
   b. Click the Tabs button located in the lower left corner of the Paragraph dialog box.
   c. At the Tabs dialog box, make sure *Left* is selected in the *Alignment* section of the dialog box.
   d. With the insertion point positioned in the *Tab stop position* text box, type 1 and then click the Set button.

e. Type 5.5 in the *Tab stop position* text box.
f. Click *Right* in the *Alignment* section of the dialog box.
g. Click *2 ......* in the *Leader* section of the dialog box and then click the Set button.
h. Click OK to close the dialog box.
5. Type the text in columns as shown in Figure 3.14. Press the Tab key before typing each column entry and press Shift + Enter to end each line.
6. Save, print, and then close **WordL1_C3_P3.docx**.

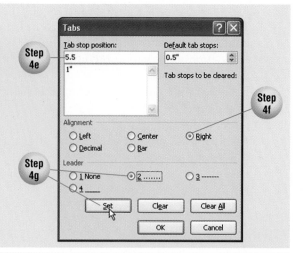

Step 4e
Step 4f
Step 4g

Figure 3.14 Project 3d

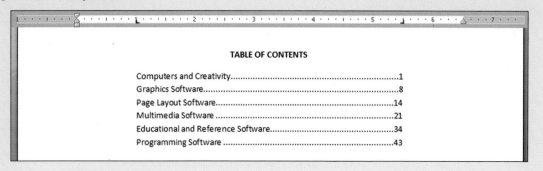

TABLE OF CONTENTS

Project 4 Move and Copy Text in a Document on Online Shopping Tips

You will open a document containing information on online shopping safety tips and then cut, copy, and paste text in the document.

Cutting, Copying, and Pasting Text

When editing a document, you may need to delete specific text, move text to a different location in the document, and/or copy text to various locations in the document. You can complete these activities using buttons in the Clipboard group in the Home tab.

Deleting Selected Text

Cut

Word offers different methods for deleting text from a document. To delete a single character, you can use either the Delete key or the Backspace key. To delete more than a single character, select the text, and then press the Delete key on the keyboard or click the Cut button in the Clipboard group. If you press the Delete key, the text is deleted permanently. (You can restore deleted text with the Undo button on the Quick Access toolbar.) The Cut button in the Clipboard group will remove the selected text from the document and insert it in the ***Clipboard***. Word's Clipboard is a temporary area of memory. The Clipboard holds text while it is being moved or copied to a new location in the document or to a different document.

Cutting and Pasting Text

To move text to a different location in the document, select the text, click the Cut button in the Clipboard group, position the insertion point at the location where you want the text inserted, and then click the Paste button in the Clipboard group.

You can also move selected text with a shortcut menu. To do this, select the text and then position the insertion point inside the selected text until it turns into an arrow pointer. Click the *right* mouse button and then click *Cut* at the shortcut menu. Position the insertion point where you want the text inserted, click the *right* mouse button, and then click *Paste* at the shortcut menu. Keyboard shortcuts are also available for cutting and pasting text. Use Ctrl + X to cut text and Ctrl + V to insert text.

When selected text is cut from a document and inserted in the Clipboard, it stays in the Clipboard until other text is inserted in the Clipboard. For this reason, you can paste text from the Clipboard more than just once. For example, if you cut text to the Clipboard, you can paste this text in different locations within the document or other documents as many times as desired.

HINT
The Clipboard contents are deleted when the computer is turned off. Text you want to save permanently should be saved as a separate document.

QUICK STEPS

Move Selected Text
1. Select text.
2. Click Cut button.
3. Move to desired location.
4. Click Paste button.

Project 4a Moving Selected Text

1. Open **WordDocument10.docx**.
2. Save the document with Save As and name it **WordL1_C3_P4**.
3. Move a paragraph by completing the following steps:
   a. Select the paragraph that begins with *Only buy at secure sites.* including the blank line below the paragraph.
   b. Click the Cut button in the Clipboard group in the Home tab.
   c. Position the insertion point at the beginning of the paragraph that begins with *Look for sites that follow . . . .*
   d. Click the Paste button in the Clipboard group. (If the first and second paragraphs are not separated by a blank line, press the Enter key once.)
4. Following steps similar to those in Step 3, move the paragraph that begins with *Never provide your social security number.* so it is positioned before the paragraph that begins *Look for sites that follow privacy . . .* and after the paragraph that begins *Only buy at secure sites.*.
5. Save **WordL1_C3_P4.docx**.

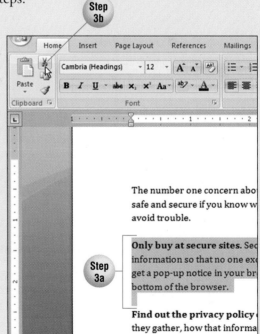

QUICK STEPS

Move Text with Mouse
1. Select text.
2. Position mouse pointer in selected text.
3. Hold down left mouse button and drag to desired location.

Moving Text by Dragging with the Mouse

You can also use the mouse to move text. To do this, select text to be moved and then position the I-beam pointer inside the selected text until it turns into an arrow pointer. Hold down the left mouse button, drag the arrow pointer (displays with a gray box attached) to the location where you want the selected text inserted, and then release the button. If you drag and then drop selected text in the wrong location, immediately click the Undo button.

Project **4h** | **Moving Text by Dragging with the Mouse**

1. With **WordL1_C3_P4.docx** open, use the mouse to select the paragraph that begins with *Keep current with the latest Internet scams.* including the blank line below the paragraph.
2. Move the I-beam pointer inside the selected text until it becomes an arrow pointer.
3. Hold down the left mouse button, drag the arrow pointer (displays with a small gray box attached) so that the insertion point, which displays as a grayed vertical bar, is positioned at the beginning of the paragraph that begins with *Never provide your social security number.*, and then release the mouse button.

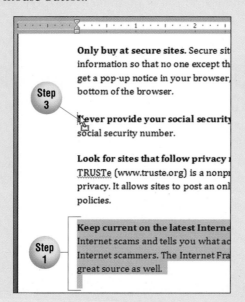

4. Deselect the text.
5. Save **WordL1_C3_P4.docx**.

Using the Paste Options Button

Paste Options

When selected text is pasted, the Paste Options button displays in the lower right corner of the text. Click this button and a drop-down list displays as shown in Figure 3.15. Use options from this drop-down list to specify how you want information pasted in the document. By default, pasted text retains the formatting of the selected text. You can choose to match the formatting of the pasted text with the formatting where the text is pasted, paste only the text without retaining formatting, or apply a style to pasted text.

Figure 3.15 Paste Options Button Drop-down List

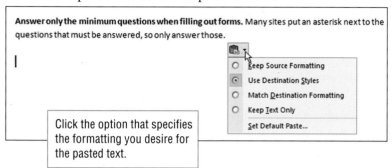

Click the option that specifies the formatting you desire for the pasted text.

Project 4C   Using the Paste Options Button

1. With **WordL1_C3_P4.docx** open, open **WordParagraph01.docx**.
2. Select the paragraph of text in the document including the blank line below the paragraph and then click the Copy button in the Clipboard group.
3. Close **WordParagraph01.docx**.
4. Move the insertion point to the end of the document.
5. Click the Paste button in the Clipboard group.
6. Click the Paste Options button that displays at the end of the paragraph and then click the *Match Destination Formatting* option. (This changes the font so it matches the formatting of the other paragraphs in the document.)

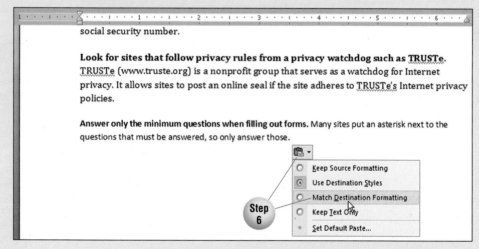

7. Save, print, and then close **WordL1_C3_P4.docx**.

P roject ⑤ Copy Text in a Staff Meeting Announcement

You will copy and paste text in a document announcing a staff meeting for the Technical Support Team.

QUICK STEPS

Copy Selected Text
1. Select text.
2. Click Copy button.
3. Move to desired location.
4. Click Paste button.

Copy

Copying and Pasting Text

Copying selected text can be useful in documents that contain repetitive portions of text. You can use this function to insert duplicate portions of text in a document instead of retyping the text. After you have selected text, copy the text to a different location with the Copy and Paste buttons in the Clipboard group in the Home tab or using the mouse. You can also use the keyboard shortcut, Ctrl + C, to copy text.

To use the mouse to copy text, select the text and then position the I-beam pointer inside the selected text until it becomes an arrow pointer. Hold down the left mouse button and hold down the Ctrl key. Drag the arrow pointer (displays with a small gray box and a box containing a plus symbol) to the location where you want the copied text inserted (make sure the insertion point, which displays as a grayed vertical bar, is positioned in the desired location) and then release the mouse button and then the Ctrl key.

P roject ⑤ₐ 　Copying Text

1. Open **WordBlock01.docx**.
2. Save the document with Save As and name it **WordL1_C3_P5**.
3. Copy the text in the document to the end of the document by completing the following steps:
   a. Select all of the text in the document and include one blank line below the text. *Hint: Click the Show/Hide ¶ button to turn on the display of nonprinting characters. When you select the text, select one of the paragraph markers below the text.*
   b. Click the Copy button in the Clipboard group.
   c. Move the insertion point to the end of the document.
   d. Click the Paste button in the Clipboard group.
4. Copy the text again at the end of the document. To do this, position the insertion point at the end of the document, and then click the Paste button in the Clipboard group. (This inserts a copy of the text from the Clipboard.)
5. Save **WordL1_C3_P5.docx**.

1. With **WordL1_C3_P5.docx** open, select all of the text in the document using the mouse and include one blank line below the text. (Consider turning on the display of nonprinting characters.)
2. Move the I-beam pointer inside the selected text until it becomes an arrow pointer.
3. Hold down the Ctrl key and then the left mouse button. Drag the arrow pointer (displays with a box with a plus symbol inside) to the end of the document, release the mouse button, and then release the Ctrl key.

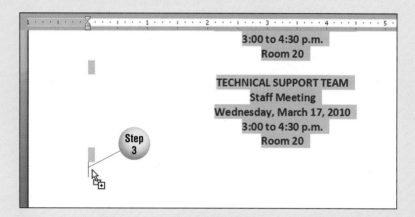

4. Deselect the text.
5. Make sure all text fits on one page. If not, consider deleting any extra blank lines.
6. Save, print, and then close **WordL1_C3_P5.docx**.

Project **6** Create a Contract Negotiations Document

You will use the Clipboard to copy and paste paragraphs to and from paragraphs in separate documents to create a contract negotiations document. You will also use the Paste Special dialog box to paste text in the contract negotiation document as unformatted text.

Using the Clipboard

Use the Clipboard to collect and paste multiple items. You can collect up to 24 different items and then paste them in various locations. To display the Clipboard task pane, click the Clipboard group dialog box launcher located in the lower right corner of the Clipboard group. The Clipboard task pane displays at the left side of the screen in a manner similar to what you see in Figure 3.16.

QUICK STEPS

Use Clipboard
1. Click Clipboard group dialog box launcher.
2. Select and copy desired text.
3. Move to desired location.
4. Click desired option in Clipboard task pane.

Figure 3.16 Clipboard Task Pane

Click this button to paste all of the Clipboard items into the document.

Click this button to clear all items from the Clipboard.

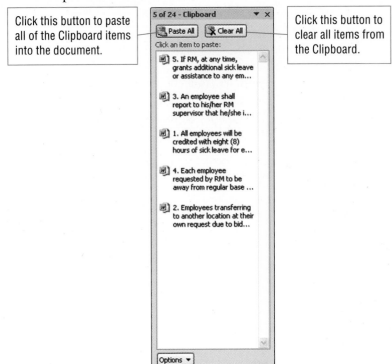

HINT

You can copy items to the Clipboard from various Office applications and then paste them into any Office file.

Select text or an object you want to copy and then click the Copy button in the Clipboard group. Continue selecting text or items and clicking the Copy button. To insert an item, position the insertion point in the desired location and then click the option in the Clipboard task pane representing the item. Click the Paste All button to paste all of the items in the Clipboard into the document. If the copied item is text, the first 50 characters display beside the button on the Clipboard task pane. When all desired items are inserted, click the Clear All button to remove any remaining items.

Project 6a Collecting and Pasting Paragraphs of Text

1. Open **WordContItems01.docx**.
2. Turn on the display of the Clipboard task pane by clicking the Clipboard group dialog box launcher. (If the Clipboard task pane list box contains any text, click the Clear All button located toward the top of the task pane.)
3. Select paragraph 1 in the document (the 1. is not selected) and then click the Copy button in the Clipboard group.
4. Select paragraph 3 in the document (the 3. is not selected) and then click the Copy button in the Clipboard group.
5. Close **WordContItems01.docx**.

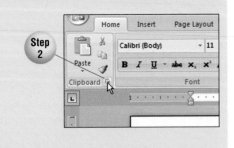

Step 2

6. Paste the paragraphs by completing the following steps:
   a. Press Ctrl + N to display a new blank document. (If the Clipboard task pane does not display, click the Clipboard group dialog box launcher.)
   b. Type **CONTRACT NEGOTIATION ITEMS** centered and bolded.
   c. Press the Enter key, turn off bold, and return the paragraph alignment back to left.
   d. Click the Paste All button in the Clipboard task pane to paste both paragraphs in the document.
   e. Click the Clear All button in the Clipboard task pane.
7. Open **WordContract01.docx**.
8. Select and then copy each of the following paragraphs:
   a. Paragraph 2 in the *Transfers and Moving Expenses* section.
   b. Paragraph 4 in the *Transfers and Moving Expenses* section.
   c. Paragraph 1 in the *Sick Leave* section.
   d. Paragraph 3 in the *Sick Leave* section.
   e. Paragraph 5 in the *Sick Leave* section.
9. Close **WordContract01.docx**.
10. Make sure the insertion point is positioned at the end of the document and then paste the paragraphs by completing the following steps:
    a. Click the button in the Clipboard task pane representing paragraph 2. (When the paragraph is inserted in the document, the paragraph number changes to 3.)
    b. Click the button in the Clipboard task pane representing paragraph 4.
    c. Click the button in the Clipboard task pane representing paragraph 3.
    d. Click the button in the Clipboard task pane representing paragraph 5.
11. Click the Clear All button located toward the top of the Clipboard task pane.
12. Close the Clipboard task pane.
13. Save the document and name it **WordL1_C3_P6**.
14. Print and then close **WordL1_C3_P6.docx**.

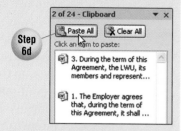

Step 6d

Step 10a

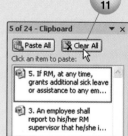

Step 11

CHAPTER summary

- Number paragraphs with the Numbering button in the Paragraph group in the Home tab and insert bullets before paragraphs with the Bullets button.

- Remove all paragraph formatting from a paragraph by pressing the keyboard shortcut, Ctrl + Q, and remove all character and paragraph formatting by clicking the Clear Formatting button in the Font group.

- The AutoCorrect Options button displays when the AutoFormat feature inserts numbers. Click this button to display options for undoing and/or stopping automatic numbering.

- Bulleted lists with hanging indents are automatically created when a paragraph begins with *, >, or -. The type of bullet inserted depends on the type of character entered.

- You can turn off automatic numbering and bullets at the AutoCorrect dialog box with the AutoFormat As You Type tab selected.

- A paragraph created in Word contains an invisible frame and you can insert a border around this frame. Click the Border button arrow to display a drop-down list of border choices.

- Apply shading to text by clicking the Shading button arrow and then clicking the desired color at the drop-down gallery.

- Use options at the Borders and Shading dialog box with the Borders tab selected to add a customized border to a paragraph or selected paragraphs and use options with Shading tab selected to add shading or a pattern to a paragraph or selected paragraphs.

- With the Sort button in the Paragraph group in the Home tab, you can sort text arranged in paragraphs alphabetically by the first character, which includes numbers, symbols, or letters.

- By default, tabs are set every 0.5 inch. These settings can be changed on the Ruler or at the Tabs dialog box.

- Use the Alignment button at the left side of the Ruler to select a left, right, center, or decimal tab. When you set a tab on the Ruler, any default tabs to the left are automatically deleted.

- After a tab has been set on the Ruler, it can be moved or deleted using the mouse pointer.

- At the Tabs dialog box, you can set any of the four types of tabs as well as a bar tab at a specific measurement. You can also set tabs with preceding leaders and clear one tab or all tabs. Preceding leaders can be periods, hyphens, or underlines.

- Cut, copy, and paste text using buttons in the Clipboard group or with keyboard shortcuts.

- When selected text is pasted, the Paste Options button displays in the lower right corner of the text with options for specifying how you want information pasted in the document.

- With the Office Clipboard, you can collect up to 24 items and then paste them in various locations in a document.

COMMANDS review

FEATURE	RIBBON TAB, GROUP	BUTTON, OPTION	KEYBOARD SHORTCUT
Borders	Home, Paragraph		
Borders and Shading dialog box	Home, Paragraph	, Borders and Shading	
Bullets	Home, Paragraph		
Clear character and paragraph formatting	Home, Font		
Clear paragraph formatting			Ctrl + Q
Clipboard task pane	Home, Clipboard		
Copy text	Home, Clipboard		Ctrl + C
Cut text	Home, Clipboard		Ctrl + X
New Line command			Shift + Enter
Numbering	Home, Paragraph		
Paragraph dialog box	Home, Paragraph		
Paste text	Home, Clipboard		Ctrl + V
Shading	Home, Paragraph		
Sort Text dialog box	Home, Paragraph		
Tabs dialog box	Home, Paragraph	, Tabs	

CONCEPTS check

Test Your Knowledge

Completion: In the space provided at the right, indicate the correct term, symbol, or command.

1. The Numbering button is located in this group in the Home tab. _____

2. Automate the creation of bulleted paragraphs with this button in the Home tab. _____

3. This button displays when the AutoFormat feature inserts numbers. _____

4. You can turn off automatic numbering and bullets at the AutoCorrect dialog box with this tab selected. _____

5. Bulleted lists with hanging indents are automatically created when you begin a paragraph with the asterisk symbol (*), the hyphen (-), or this symbol. _____

6. The Borders button is located in this group in the Home tab. _____

7. Use options at this dialog box with the Borders tab selected to add a customized border to a paragraph or selected paragraphs. _____

8. Sort text arranged in paragraphs alphabetically by the first character, which includes numbers, symbols, or this. _____

9. By default, each tab is set apart from the other by this measurement. _____

10. This is the default tab type. _____

11. When setting tabs on the Ruler, choose the tab type with this button. _____

12. Tabs can be set on the Ruler or here. _____

13. This group in the Home tab contains the Cut, Copy, and Paste buttons. _____

14. To copy selected text with the mouse, hold down this key while dragging selected text. _____

15. With this task pane, you can collect up to 24 items and then paste the items in various locations in the document. _____

SKILLS check
Demonstrate Your Proficiency

Assessment

1 APPLY PARAGRAPH FORMATTING TO A COMPUTER ETHICS DOCUMENT

1. Open **WordDocument07.docx**.
2. Save the document with Save As and name it **WordL1_C3_A1**.
3. Move the insertion point to the end of the document and then type the text shown in Figure 3.17.
4. Change the Quick Styles set to *Formal*.
5. Apply the Heading 1 style to the three headings in the document.
6. Apply the Paper theme.

7. Select the paragraphs of text in the *Computer Ethics* section and then apply numbering formatting.
8. Select the paragraphs of text in the *Technology Timeline* section and then apply bullet formatting.
9. Insert the following paragraph of text between paragraphs 2 and 3 in the *Computer Ethics* section: **Find sources relating to the latest federal and/or state legislation on privacy protection.**
10. Apply Blue-Gray, Accent 6, Lighter 60% paragraph shading to the three headings in the document.
11. Apply Blue-Gray, Accent 6, Lighter 80% paragraph shading to the numbered paragraphs in the *Computer Ethics* section and the bulleted paragraphs in the *Technology Timeline* and *ACLU Fair Electronic Monitoring Policy* sections.
12. Save, print, and then close **WordL1_C3_A1.docx**.

Figure 3.17 Assessment 1

ACLU Fair Electronic Monitoring Policy

➢ Notice to employees of the company's electronic monitoring practices

➢ Use of a signal to let an employee know he or she is being monitored

➢ Employee access to all personal data collected through monitoring

➢ No monitoring of areas designed for the health or comfort of employees

➢ The right to dispute and delete inaccurate data

➢ A ban on the collection of data unrelated to work performance

➢ Restrictions on the disclosure of personal data to others without the employee's consent

Assessment

2 TYPE TABBED TEXT AND APPLY FORMATTING TO A COMPUTER SOFTWARE DOCUMENT

1. Open **WordDocument14.docx**.
2. Save the document with Save As and name it **WordL1_C3_A2**.
3. Move the insertion point to the end of the document and then type the tabbed text as shown in Figure 3.18. Before typing the text in columns, set left tabs at the 0.75-inch, 2.75-inch, and 4.5-inch marks on the Ruler.
4. Apply the Heading 1 style to the three headings in the document (*Productivity Software, Personal-Use Software,* and *Software Training Schedule*).
5. Change the Quick Styles set to *Distinctive*.
6. Apply the Opulent theme.
7. Select the productivity software categories in the *Productivity Software* section (from *Word processing* through *Computer-aided design*) and then sort the text alphabetically.
8. With the text still selected, apply bullet formatting.
9. Select the personal-use software categories in the *Personal-Use Software* section (from *Personal finance software* through *Games and entertainment software*) and then sort the text alphabetically.

10. With the text still selected, apply bullet formatting.
11. Apply a single-line border to the top and a double-line border to the bottom of the three headings in the document and then apply paragraph shading of your choosing to each heading.
12. Select the text in columns and then move the tab symbols on the Ruler as follows:
    a. Move the tab at the 0.75-inch mark to the 1-inch mark.
    b. Move the tab at the 4.5-inch mark to the 4-inch mark.
13. Save, print, and then close **WordL1_C3_A2.docx**.

Figure 3.18 Assessment 2

Software Training Schedule		
Word	April 12	8:30 to 11:30 a.m.
PowerPoint	April 14	1:00 to 3:30 p.m.
Excel	May 11	8:30 to 11:30 a.m.
Access	May 13	1:00 to 3:30 p.m.
Outlook	May 18	8:30 to 11:30 a.m.
Vista	May 20	1:00 to 3:30 p.m.

Assessment

3 TYPE AND FORMAT A TABLE OF CONTENTS DOCUMENT

1. At a new blank document, type the document shown in Figure 3.19 with the following specifications:
   a. Change the font to 11-point Cambria.
   b. Bold and center the title as shown.
   c. Before typing the text in columns, display the Tabs dialog box and then set left tabs at the 1-inch mark and the 1.5-inch mark, and a right tab with dot leaders at the 5.5-inch mark.
2. Save the document and name it **WordL1_C3_A3**.
3. Print **WordL1_C3_A3.docx**.
4. Select the text in columns and then move the tab symbols on the Ruler as follows:
   a. Delete the left tab symbol that displays at the 1.5-inch mark.
   b. Set a new left tab at the 0.5-inch mark.
   c. Move the right tab at the 5.5-inch mark to the 6-inch mark.
5. Apply paragraph borders and shading of your choosing to enhance the visual appeal of the document.
6. Save, print, and then close **WordL1_C3_A3.docx**.

Figure 3.19 Assessment 3

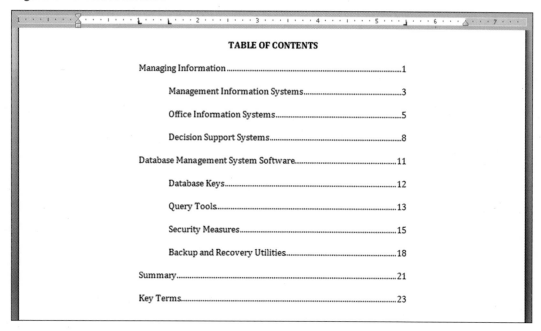

Assessment

4 FORMAT A BUILDING CONSTRUCTION AGREEMENT DOCUMENT

1. Open **WordAgreement02.docx**.
2. Save the document with Save As and name it **WordL1_C3_A4**.
3. Select and then delete the paragraph that begins *Supervision of Work*.
4. Select and then delete the paragraph that begins *Exclusions*.
5. Move the paragraph that begins *Financing Arrangements* above the paragraph that begins *Start of Construction*.
6. Open **WordDocument11.docx**.
7. Turn on the display of the Clipboard.
8. Select and then copy the first paragraph.
9. Select and then copy the second paragraph.
10. Select and then copy the third paragraph.
11. Close **WordDocument11.docx** without saving the changes.
12. With **WordL1_C3_A4.docx** open, paste the *Supervision* paragraph above the *Changes and Alterations* paragraph and match the destination formatting.
13. Paste the *Pay Review* paragraph above the *Possession of Residence* paragraph and match the destination formatting.
14. Clear all items from the Clipboard and then close the Clipboard.
15. Save, print, and then close **WordL1_C3_A4.docx**.

Assessment

5 HYPHENATE WORDS IN A REPORT

1. In some Word documents, especially documents with left and right margins wider than 1 inch, the right margin may appear quite ragged. If the paragraph alignment is changed to justified, the right margin will appear even, but there

will be extra space added throughout the line. In these situations, hyphenating long words that fall at the end of the text line provides the document with a more balanced look. Use Word's Help feature to learn how to automatically hyphenate words in a document.

2. Open **WordReport01.docx**.
3. Save the document with Save As and name it **WordL1_C3_A5**.
4. Automatically hyphenate words in the document, limiting the consecutive hyphens to 2. *Hint: Specify the number of consecutive hyphens at the* ***Hyphenation dialog box.***
5. Save, print, and then close **WordL1_C3_A5.docx**.

CASE study
Apply Your Skills

Part 1

You are the assistant to Gina Coletti, manager of La Dolce Vita, an Italian restaurant. She has been working on updating and formatting the lunch menu. She has asked you to complete the menu by opening the **WordMenu.docx** document (located in the Word2007L1C3 folder), determining how the appetizer section is formatted, and then applying the same formatting to the *Soup and Salad*; *Sandwiches, Calzones and Burgers*; and *Individual Pizzas* sections. Save the document and name it **WordL1_C3_CS_P1**. Print and then close the document.

Part 2

Ms. Coletti has reviewed the completed menu and is pleased with the menu but wants to add a page border around the entire page to increase visual interest. Open **WordL1_C3_CS_P1.docx** and then save the document and name it **WordL1_C3_CS_P2**. Display the Borders and Shading dialog box with the Page Border tab selected and then experiment with the options available. Apply an appropriate page border to the menu (consider applying an art page border). Save, print, and then close **WordL1_C3_CS_P2.docx**.

Part 3

Each week, the restaurant offers daily specials. Ms. Coletti has asked you to open and format the text in the **WordMenuSpecials.docx** document. She has asked you to format the specials menu in a similar manner as the main menu but to make some changes to make it unique from the main menu. Apply the same page border to the specials menu document that you applied to the main menu document. Save the document and name it **WordL1_C3_CS_P3**. Print and then close the document.

Part 4

You have been asked by the head chef to research a new recipe for an Italian dish. Using the Internet, find a recipe that interests you and then prepare a Word document containing the recipe and ingredients. Use bullets before each ingredient and use numbering for each step in the recipe preparation. Save the document and name it **WordL1_C3_CS_P4**. Print and then close the document.

Formatting Pages

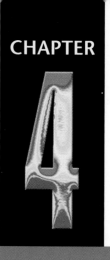

CHAPTER

4

PERFORMANCE OBJECTIVES

Upon successful completion of Chapter 4, you will be able to:

- **Change document views**
- **Navigate in a document with Document Map and Thumbnails**
- **Change margins, page orientation, and paper size in a document**
- **Format pages at the Page Setup dialog box**
- **Insert a page break, blank page, and cover page**
- **Insert page numbering**
- **Insert and edit predesigned headers and footers**
- **Insert a watermark, page color, and page border**
- **Find and replace text and formatting**

word Chapter 4

SNAP

Tutorial 4.1
Organizing Documents
Tutorial 4.2
Enhancing Documents
Tutorial 4.3
Searching within a Document

A document generally displays in Print Layout view. You can change this default view with buttons in the View area on the Status bar or with options in the View tab. Use the Document Map and Thumbnails features to navigate in a document. A Word document, by default, contains 1-inch top, bottom, left, and right margins. You can change these default margins with the Margins button in the Page Setup group in the Page Layout tab or with options at the Page Setup dialog box. You can insert a variety of features in a Word document including a page break, blank page, and cover page as well as page numbers, headers, footers, a watermark, page color, and page border. Use options at the Find and Replace dialog box to search for specific text or formatting and replace with other text or formatting.

Note: Before beginning computer projects, copy to your storage medium the Word2007L1C4 subfolder from the Word2007L1 folder on the CD that accompanies this textbook and then make Word2007L1C4 the active folder.

Project **1** **Navigate in a Report on Computer Input and Output Devices**

You will open a document containing information on computer input and output devices, change document views, navigate in the document using Document Map and Thumbnails, and show and hide white space at the top and bottom of pages.

Changing the View

HINT

Double-click the 100% that displays at the left side of the Zoom slider bar to display the Zoom dialog box.

By default a Word document displays in Print Layout view. This view displays the document on the screen as it will appear when printed. Other views are available such as Draft and Full Screen Reading. Change views with buttons in the View area on the Status bar or with options in the View tab. The buttons in the View area on the Status bar are identified in Figure 4.1. Along with the View buttons, the Status bar also contains a Zoom slider bar as shown in Figure 4.1. Drag the button on the Zoom slider bar to increase or decrease the size of display, or click the Zoom Out button to decrease size and click the Zoom In to increase size.

Figure 4.1 Viewing Buttons and Zoom Slider Bar

Zoom Out

Zoom In

Displaying a Document in Draft View

Draft

Change to Draft view and the document displays in a format for efficient editing and formatting. At this view, margins and other features such as headers and footers do not display on the screen. Change to Draft view by clicking the Draft button in the View section on the Status bar or click the View tab and then click the Draft button in the Document Views group.

Displaying a Document in Full Screen Reading View

Full Screen Reading

The Full Screen Reading view displays a document in a format for easy viewing and reading. Change to Full Screen Reading view by clicking the Full Screen Reading button in the View section on the Status bar or by clicking the View tab and then clicking the Full Screen Reading button in the Document Views group.

Navigate in Full Screen Reading view using the keys on the keyboard as shown in Table 4.1. You can also navigate in Full Screen Reading view with options from the View Options button that displays toward the top right side of the screen or with the Next Screen and Previous Screen buttons located at the top of the window and also located at the bottom of each page.

You can customize the Full Screen Reading view with some of the options from the View Options drop-down list. Display this list by clicking the View Options button located in the upper right corner of the Full Screen Reading window.

Table 4.1 Keyboard Commands in Full Screen Reading View

Press this key	To complete this action
Page Down key or spacebar	Move to the next page or section
Page Up key or Backspace key	Move to the previous page or section
Right Arrow key	Move to next page
Left Arrow key	Move to previous page
Home	Move to first page in document
End	Move to last page in document
Esc	Return to previous view

Project ⓐ Changing Views

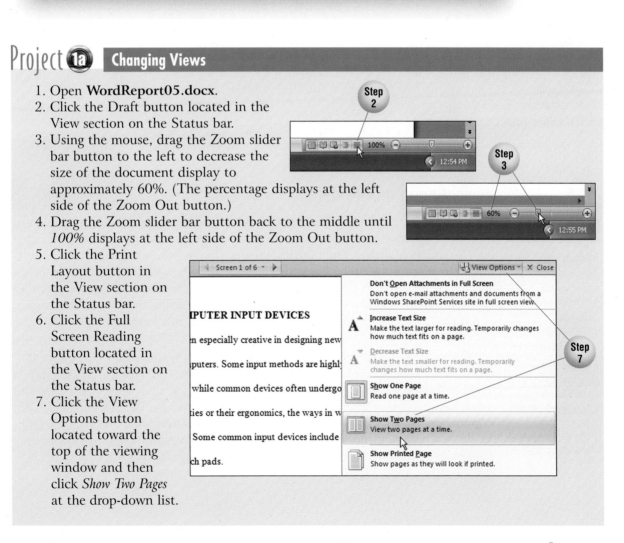

1. Open **WordReport05.docx**.
2. Click the Draft button located in the View section on the Status bar.
3. Using the mouse, drag the Zoom slider bar button to the left to decrease the size of the document display to approximately 60%. (The percentage displays at the left side of the Zoom Out button.)
4. Drag the Zoom slider bar button back to the middle until *100%* displays at the left side of the Zoom Out button.
5. Click the Print Layout button in the View section on the Status bar.
6. Click the Full Screen Reading button located in the View section on the Status bar.
7. Click the View Options button located toward the top of the viewing window and then click *Show Two Pages* at the drop-down list.

8. Click the Next Screen button to display the next two pages in the viewing window.

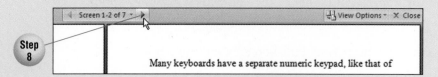

9. Click the Previous Screen button to display the previous two pages.
10. Click the View Options button located toward the top of the viewing window and then click *Show One Page* at the drop-down list.
11. Practice navigating using the actions shown in Table 4.1. (Try all of the actions in Table 4.1 except pressing the Esc key since that action will close Full Screen Reading view.)
12. Increase the size of the text by clicking the View Options button and then clicking the *Increase Text Size* option.

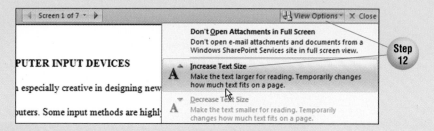

13. Press the Home key to display the first viewing page.
14. Decrease the size of the text by clicking the View Options button and then clicking the *Decrease Text Size* option.
15. Click the Close button located in the upper right corner of the screen.

Navigating in a Document

Navigate with Document Map
1. Click View tab.
2. Click *Document Map* check box.
3. Click desired heading in navigation pane.

Navigate with Thumbnails
1. Click View tab.
2. Click *Thumbnails* check box.
3. Click desired thumbnail in navigation pane.

Word includes a number of features you can use to navigate in a document. Along with the navigating features you have already learned, you can also navigate using the Document Map and Thumbnails features. To navigate using the Document Map feature, click the View tab and then click the *Document Map* check box in the Show/Hide group. This displays a navigation pane at the left side of the screen as shown in Figure 4.2. Document Map displays any headings formatted with styles or text that looks like headings, such as short lines set in a larger type size. Navigate to a specific location in the document by clicking the heading in the navigation pane.

To navigate in a document using the Thumbnails feature, click the View tab and then click the Thumbnails check box in the Show/Hide group. This displays a thumbnail of each page in the navigation pane at the left side of the screen. You can switch between Thumbnails and Document Map by clicking the Switch Navigation Window button that displays at the top of the navigation pane and then clicking the desired option at the drop-down list. Close the navigation pane by clicking the *Thumbnails* check box to remove the check mark or by clicking the Close button located in the upper right corner of the pane.

Figure 4.2 Navigation Pane

Switch Navigation Window button

Navigation pane

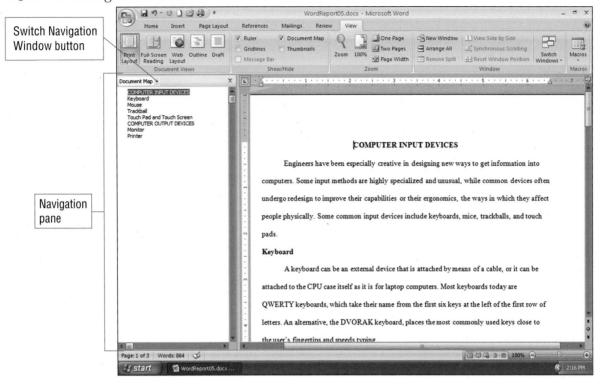

Project 1b Navigating Using Document Map

1. With **WordReport05.docx** open, click the View tab and then click the *Document Map* check box.
2. Click the *COMPUTER OUTPUT DEVICES* title that displays in the navigation pane.

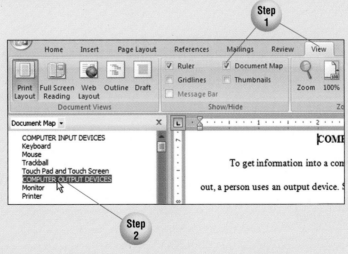

Step 1

Step 2

3. Click the *Keyboard* heading that displays in the navigation pane.
4. Click the *Document Map* check box to remove the check mark.

5. Click the *Thumbnails* check box in the Show/Hide group in the View tab.
6. Click the number 3 thumbnail in the navigation pane.
7. Click the number 1 thumbnail in the navigation pane.
8. Close the navigation pane by clicking the Close button located in the upper right corner of the navigation pane.

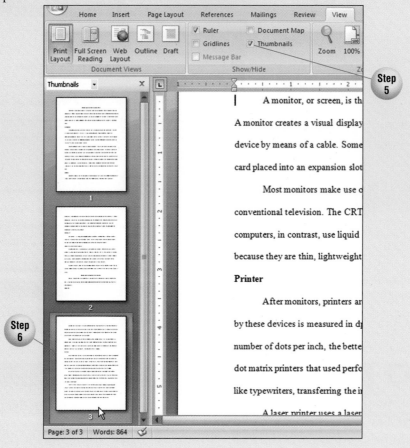

QUICK STEPS

Hiding/Showing White Space in Print Layout View

Hide White Space
1. Position mouse pointer at top of page until pointer displays as *Hide White Space* icon.
2. Double-click left mouse button.

Show White Space
1. Position mouse pointer on thin line separating pages until pointer displays as *Show White Space* icon.
2. Double-click left mouse button.

In Print Layout view, a page displays as it will appear when printed including the white space at the top and bottom of the page representing the default margins. To save space on the screen in Print Layout view, you can remove the white space by positioning the mouse pointer at the top edge or bottom edge of a page or between pages until the pointer displays as the *Hide White Space* icon and then double-clicking the left mouse button. To redisplay the white space, position the mouse pointer on the thin, black line separating pages until the pointer turns into the *Show White Space* icon and then double-click the left mouse button.

1. With **WordReport05.docx** open, make sure the document displays in Print Layout view.
2. Press Ctrl + Home to move the insertion point to the beginning of the document.
3. Hide the white spaces at the top and bottom of pages by positioning the mouse pointer at the top edge of the page until the pointer turns into the *Hide White Space* icon and then double-clicking the left mouse button.
4. Scroll through the document and notice the display of pages.
5. Redisplay the white spaces at the top and bottom of pages by positioning the mouse pointer on any thin, black, horizontal line separating pages until the pointer turns into the *Show White Space* icon and then double-clicking the left mouse button.

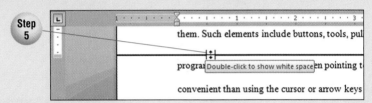

6. Close **WordReport05.docx**.

P**roject** **2** **Format a Document on Online Etiquette Guidelines**

You will open a document containing information on guidelines for online etiquette and then change the margins, page orientation, and page size.

Changing Page Setup

The Page Setup group in the Page Layout tab contains a number of options for affecting pages in a document. With options in the group you can perform such actions as changing margins, orientation, and page size and inserting page breaks. The Pages group in the Insert tab contains three buttons for inserting a page break, blank page, and cover page.

Changing Margins

Change page margins with options at the Margins drop-down list as shown in Figure 4.3. To display this list, click the Page Layout tab and then click the Margins button in the Page Setup group. To change the margins, click one of the preset margins that display in the drop-down list. Be aware that most printers contain a required margin (between one-quarter and three-eighths inch) because printers cannot print to the edge of the page.

QUICK STEPS

Change Margins
1. Click Page Layout tab.
2. Click Margins button.
3. Click desired margin option.

Margins

Figure 4.3 Margins Drop-down List

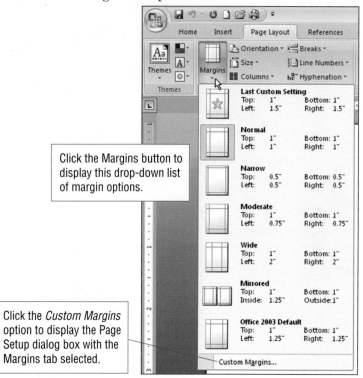

Click the Margins button to display this drop-down list of margin options.

Click the *Custom Margins* option to display the Page Setup dialog box with the Margins tab selected.

Project 2a — Changing Margins

1. Open **WordNetiquette.docx**.
2. Save the document with Save As and name it **WordL1_C4_P2**.
3. Click the Page Layout tab.
4. Click the Margins button in the Page Setup group and then click the *Office 2003 Default* option.
5. Save **WordL1_C4_P2.docx**.

Step 3

Step 4

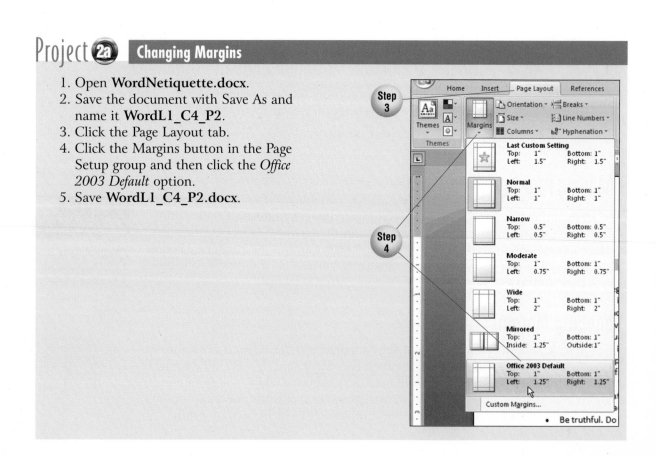

Changing Page Orientation

Click the Orientation button in the Page Setup group in the Page Layout tab and two options display—*Portrait* and *Landscape*. At the portrait orientation, which is the default, the page is 11 inches tall and 8.5 inches wide. At the landscape orientation, the page is 8.5 inches tall and 11 inches wide. Change the page orientation and the page margins automatically change.

Can you picture some instances in which you might use a landscape orientation? Suppose you are preparing a company's annual report and you need to include a couple of tables that have several columns of text. If you use the default portrait orientation, the columns would need to be quite narrow, possibly so narrow that reading becomes difficult. Changing the orientation to landscape results in three more inches of usable space. Also, you are not committed to using landscape orientation for the entire document. You can use portrait and landscape in the same document. To do this, select the text, display the Page Setup dialog box, click the desired orientation, and change the *Apply to* option box to *Selected text*.

Change Page Orientation
1. Click Page Layout tab.
2. Click Orientation button.
3. Click desired orientation.

Project **2b**   **Changing Page Orientation**

1. With **WordL1_C4_P2.docx** open, make sure the Page Layout tab is selected.
2. Click the Orientation button in the Page Setup group.
3. Click *Landscape* at the drop-down list.
4. Scroll through the document and notice how the text displays on the page in landscape orientation.
5. Save **WordL1_C4_P2.docx**.

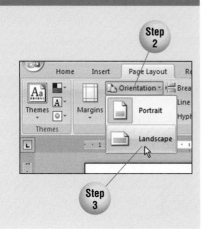

Changing Page Size

By default, Word uses a page size of 8.5 inches wide and 11 inches tall. You can change this default setting with options at the Size drop-down list shown in Figure 4.4. Display this drop-down list by clicking the Size button in the Page Setup group in the Page Layout tab.

Change Page Size
1. Click Page Layout tab.
2. Click Size button.
3. Click desired size option.

Size ▾

Figure 4.4 Size Drop-down List

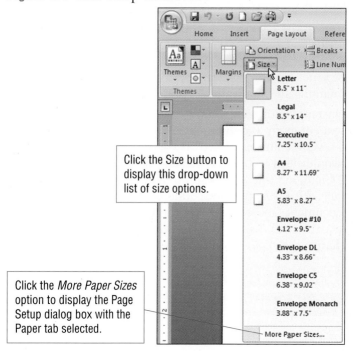

Click the Size button to display this drop-down list of size options.

Click the *More Paper Sizes* option to display the Page Setup dialog box with the Paper tab selected.

Project **2c** **Changing Page Size**

1. With **WordL1_C4_P2.docx** open, make sure the Page Layout tab is selected.
2. Click the Orientation button in the Page Setup group and then click *Portrait* at the drop-down list. (This changes the orientation back to the default.)
3. Click the Size button in the Page Setup group.
4. Click the A5 option (displays with *5.83″ × 8.27″* below *A5*). If this option is not available, choose an option with a similar size.
5. Scroll through the document and notice how the text displays on the page.
6. Click the Size button and then click *Legal* (displays with *8.5″ × 14″* below *Legal*).
7. Scroll through the document and notice how the text displays on the page.
8. Click the Size button and then click *Letter* (displays with *8.5″ × 11″* below *Letter*). (This returns the size back to the default.)
9. Save **WordL1_C4_P2.docx**.

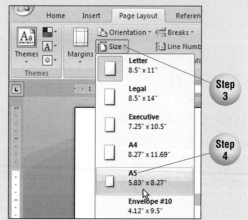

Changing Margins at the Page Setup Dialog Box

The Margins button in the Page Setup group provides you with a number of preset margins. If these margins do not fit your needs, you can set specific margins at the Page Setup dialog box with the Margins tab selected as shown in Figure 4.5. Display this dialog box by clicking the Page Setup group dialog box launcher or by clicking the Margins button and then clicking *Custom Margins* at the bottom of the drop-down list.

To change margins, select the current measurement in the *Top, Bottom, Left,* or *Right* text box, and then type the new measurement. You can also increase a measurement by clicking the up-pointing arrow at the right side of the text box. Decrease a measurement by clicking the down-pointing arrow. As you make changes to the margin measurements at the Page Setup dialog box, the sample page in the *Preview* section illustrates the effects of the margin changes.

QUICK STEPS

Change Margins at Page Setup Dialog Box
1. Click Page Layout tab.
2. Click Page Setup group dialog box launcher.
3. Specify desired margins.
4. Click OK.

Change Page Size at Page Setup Dialog Box
1. Click Page Layout tab.
2. Click Size button.
3. Click *More Paper Sizes* at drop-down list.
4. Specify desired size.
5. Click OK.

Figure 4.5 Page Setup Dialog Box with Margins Tab Selected

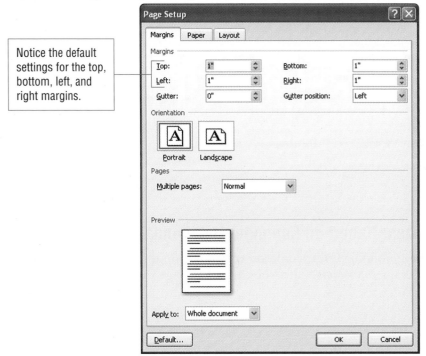

Notice the default settings for the top, bottom, left, and right margins.

Changing Paper Size at the Page Setup Dialog Box

The Size button drop-down list contains a number of preset page sizes. If these sizes do not fit your needs, you can specify page size at the Page Setup dialog box with the Paper tab selected. Display this dialog box by clicking the Size button in the Page Setup group and then clicking *More Paper Sizes* that displays at the bottom of the drop-down list.

1. With **WordL1_C4_P2.docx** open, make sure the Page Layout tab is selected.
2. Click the Page Setup group dialog box launcher.
3. At the Page Setup dialog box with the Margins tab selected, click the down-pointing arrow at the right side of the *Top* text box until *0.5"* displays.
4. Click the down-pointing arrow at the right side of the *Bottom* text box until *0.5"* displays.
5. Select the current measurement in the *Left* text box and then type 0.75.
6. Select the current measurement in the *Right* text box and then type 0.75.
7. Click OK to close the dialog box.
8. Click the Size button in the Page Setup group and then click *More Paper Sizes* at the drop-down list.
9. At the Page Setup dialog box with the Paper tab selected, click the down-pointing arrow at the right side of the *Paper size* option and then click *A4* at the drop-down list.
10. Click OK to close the dialog box.
11. Scroll through the document and notice how the text displays on the page.
12. Click the Size button in the Page Setup group and then click *Letter* at the drop-down list.
13. Save, print, and then close **WordL1_C4_P2.docx**.

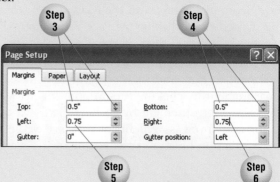

Project **3** **Customize a Report on Computer Input and Output Devices**

You will open a document containing information on computer input and output devices and then insert page breaks, a blank page, a cover page, and page numbering.

Inserting a Page Break

Insert Page Break
1. Click Insert tab.
2. Click Page Break button.
OR
Press Ctrl + Enter.

With the default top and bottom margins of one inch, approximately nine inches of text print on the page. At approximately the ten-inch mark, Word automatically inserts a page break. You can insert your own page break in a document with the keyboard shortcut, Ctrl + Enter, or with the Page Break button in the Pages group in the Insert tab.

A page break inserted by Word is considered a *soft* page break and a page break inserted by you is considered a *hard* page break. Soft page breaks automatically adjust if you add or delete text from a document. A hard page break does not adjust and is therefore less flexible than a soft page break. If you add or delete text from a document with a hard page break, check the break to determine whether it is still in a desirable location. In Draft view, a hard page break displays as a row of dots with the words Page Break in the center. To delete a page break, position the insertion point immediately below the page break and then press the Backspace key or change to Draft view, position the insertion point on the page break, and then press the Delete key.

Project 3a   Inserting Page Breaks

1. Open **WordReport05.docx**.
2. Save the document with Save As and name it **WordL1_C4_P3**.
3. Change the top margin by completing the following steps:
   a. Click the Page Layout tab.
   b. Click the Page Setup group dialog box launcher.
   c. At the Page Setup dialog box, click the Margins tab and then type 1.5 in the *Top* text box.
   d. Click OK to close the dialog box.
4. Insert a page break at the beginning of the heading *Mouse* by completing the following steps:
   a. Position the insertion point at the beginning of the heading *Mouse* (located toward the bottom of page 1).
   b. Click the Insert tab and then click the Page Break button in the Pages group.
5. Move the insertion point to the beginning of the title *COMPUTER OUTPUT DEVICES* (located at the bottom of page 2) and then insert a page break by pressing Ctrl + Enter.
6. Move the insertion point to the beginning of the heading *Printer* and then press Ctrl + Enter to insert a page break.
7. Delete the page break by completing the following steps:
   a. Click the Draft button in the view area on the Status bar.
   b. With the insertion point positioned at the beginning of the heading *Printer*, press the Backspace key. (This displays the page break in the document.)
   c. Press the Backspace key again to delete the page break.
   d. Click the Print Layout button in the view area of the Status bar.
8. Save **WordL1_C4_P3.docx**.

Inserting a Blank Page

Click the Blank Page button in the Pages group in the Insert tab to insert a blank page at the position of the insertion point. This might be useful in a document where you want to insert a blank page for an illustration, graphic, or figure.

Insert Blank Page
1. Click Insert tab.
2. Click Blank Page button.

Inserting a Cover Page

QUICK STEPS

Insert Cover Page
1. Click Insert tab.
2. Click Cover Page button.
3. Click desired cover page at drop-down list.

HINT

A cover page provides a polished and professional look to a document.

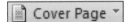

If you are preparing a document for distribution to others or you want to simply improve the visual appeal of your document, consider inserting a cover page. With the Cover Page button in the Pages group in the Insert tab, you can insert a predesigned and formatted cover page and then type personalized text in specific locations on the page. Click the Cover Page button and a drop-down list displays similar to the one shown in Figure 4.6. The drop-down list provides a visual representation of the cover page. Scroll through the list and then click the desired cover page.

A predesigned cover page contains location placeholders where you can enter specific information. For example, a cover page might contain the placeholder *[Type the document title]*. Click anywhere in the placeholder text and the placeholder text is selected. With the placeholder text selected, type the desired text. You can delete a placeholder by clicking anywhere in the placeholder text, clicking the placeholder tab, and then pressing the Delete key.

Figure 4.6 Cover Page Drop-down List

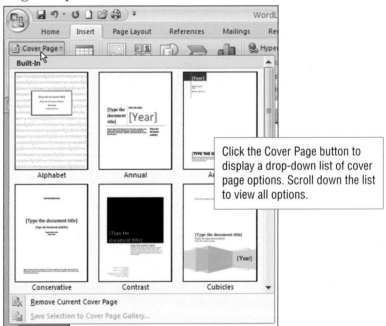

Click the Cover Page button to display a drop-down list of cover page options. Scroll down the list to view all options.

Project 3b   Inserting a Blank Page and a Cover Page

1. With **WordL1_C4_P3.docx** open, create a blank page by completing the following steps:
   a. Move the insertion point to the beginning of the heading *Touch Pad and Touch Screen* located on the second page.
   b. Click the Insert tab.
   c. Click the Blank Page button in the Pages group.
2. Insert a cover page by completing the following steps:
   a. Press Ctrl + Home to move the insertion point to the beginning of the document.
   b. Click the Cover Page button in the Pages group.
   c. At the drop-down list, scroll down and then click the *Motion* cover page.
   d. Click anywhere in the placeholder text *[Type the document title]* and then type **Computer Devices**.

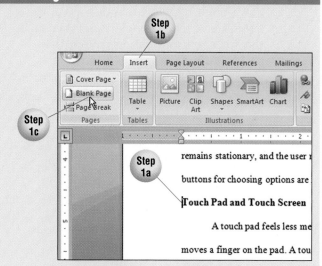

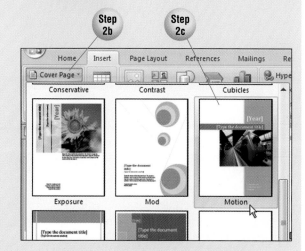

e. Click the placeholder text *[Year]*. Click the down-pointing arrow that displays at the right side of the placeholder and then click the Today button that displays at the bottom of the drop-down calendar.

f. Click anywhere in the placeholder text *[Type the company name]* and then type **Drake Computing**.

Step 2e

Step 2f

g. Click anywhere in the placeholder text *[Type the author name]* and then type your first and last names.

3. Remove the blank page you created in Step 1 by completing the following steps:

a. Move the insertion point to the beginning of page 5 immediately left of the heading *Touch Pad and Touch Screen*.

b. Click the Draft button in the View section on the Status bar.

c. Press the Backspace key until the heading *Touch Pad and Touch Screen* displays a double-space below the previous paragraph of text.

Step 3c

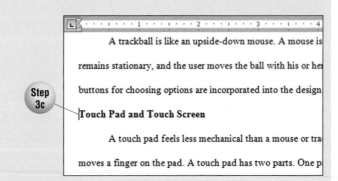

d. Click the Print Layout button in the View section on the Status bar.

4. Save **WordL1_C4_P3.docx**.

Inserting Predesigned Page Numbering

Word, by default, does not print page numbers on a page. If you want to insert page numbering in a document, use the Page Number button in the Header & Footer group in the Insert tab. When you click the Page Number button, a drop-down list displays with options for specifying the page number location. Point to an option at this list and a drop-down list displays of predesigned page number formats. Scroll through the options in the drop-down list and then click the desired option. If you want to change the format of page numbering in a document, double-click the page number, select the page number text, and then apply the desired formatting. You can remove page numbering from a document by clicking the Page Number button and then clicking *Remove Page Numbers* at the drop-down list.

Insert Page Numbering
1. Click Insert tab.
2. Click Page Number button.
3. Click desired option at drop-down list.

Project **3c**   **Inserting Predesigned Page Numbering**

1. With **WordL1_C4_P3.docx** open, insert page numbering by completing the following steps:
   a. Move the insertion point so it is positioned on any character in the title *COMPUTER INPUT DEVICES*.
   b. Click the Insert tab.
   c. Click the Page Number button in the Header & Footer group and then point to *Top of Page*.
   d. Scroll through the drop-down list and then click the *Brackets 2* option.

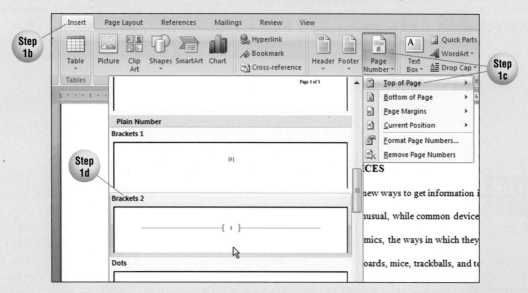

2. Double-click the document to make it active and then scroll through the document and notice the page numbering that displays at the top of each page except the cover page. (The cover page and text are divided by a section break, which you will learn more about in Chapter 5. Word considers the cover page as page 1 but does not include the numbering on the page.)
3. Remove the page numbering by clicking the Insert tab, clicking the Page Number button, and then clicking *Remove Page Numbers* at the drop-down list.

4. Click the Page Number button, point to *Bottom of Page*, scroll down the drop-down list and then click the *Circle* option.

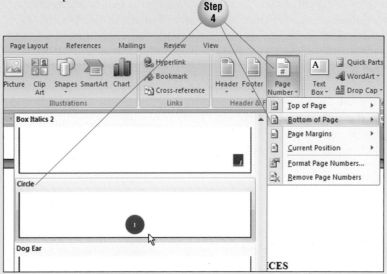

Step 4

5. Save, print, and then close **WordL1_C4_P3.docx**.

P roject ④ **Add Elements to a Report on the Future of the Internet**

You will open a document containing information on the future of the Internet, insert a predesigned header and footer in the document, remove a header, and format and delete header and footer elements.

Inserting Predesigned Headers and Footers

Insert Predesigned Header
1. Click Insert tab.
2. Click Header button.
3. Click desired option at drop-down list.
4. Type text in specific placeholders in header.

Header

Text that appears at the top of every page is called a *header* and text that appears at the bottom of every page is referred to as a *footer*. Headers and footers are common in manuscripts, textbooks, reports, and other publications. Insert a predesigned header in a document by clicking the Insert tab and then clicking the Header button in the Header & Footer group. This displays the Header drop-down list as shown in Figure 4.7. At this list, click the desired predesigned header option and the header is inserted in the document. The header is visible in Print Layout view but not Draft view.

A predesigned header or footer may contain location placeholders where you can enter specific information. For example, a header might contain the placeholder *[Type the document title]*. Click anywhere in the placeholder text and all of the placeholder text is selected. With the placeholder text selected, type the desired text. You can delete a placeholder by clicking anywhere in the placeholder text, clicking the placeholder tab, and then pressing the Delete key.

Figure 4.7 Header Drop-down List

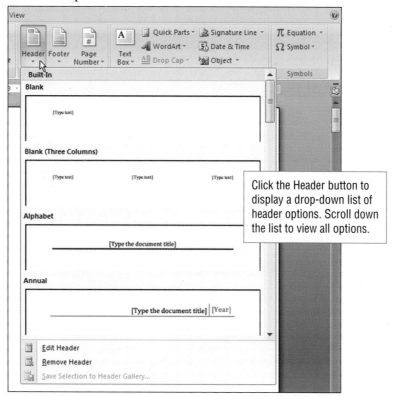

Click the Header button to display a drop-down list of header options. Scroll down the list to view all options.

Project 4a **Inserting a Predesigned Header in a Document**

1. Open **WordReport02.docx**.
2. Save the document with Save As and name it **WordL1_C4_P4**.
3. Make the following changes to the document:
   a. Select the entire document, change the line spacing to *2*, and then deselect the document.
   b. Change the Quick Styles set to *Formal*. (*Hint: Use the Changes Styles button in the Styles group in the Home tab.*)
   c. Apply the *Heading 1* style to the title *FUTURE OF THE INTERNET*.
   d. Apply the *Heading 2* style to the headings *Satellite Internet Connections*, *Second Internet*, *Internet Services for a Fee*, and *Internet in 2030*.
   e. Move the insertion point to the beginning of the heading *INTERNET IN 2030* (located at the bottom of page 2) and then insert a page break by clicking the Insert tab and then clicking the Page Break button in the Pages group.

4. Press Ctrl + Home to move the insertion point to the beginning of the document and then insert a header by completing the following steps:
   a. If necessary, click the Insert tab.
   b. Click the Header button in the Header & Footer group.
   c. Scroll to the bottom of the drop-down list that displays and then click *Tiles*.

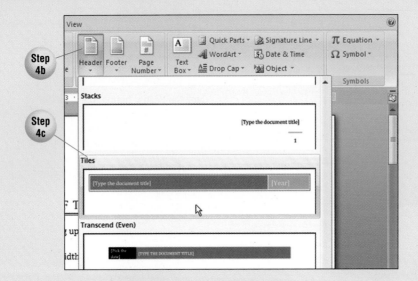

   d. Click anywhere in the placeholder text *[Type the document title]* and then type Future of the Internet.
   e. Click anywhere in the placeholder text *[Year]* and then type the current year.
   f. Double-click in the document text. (This makes the document text active and dims the header.)

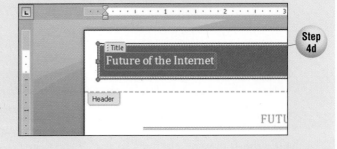

5. Scroll through the document to see how the header will print.
6. Save and then print **WordL1_C4_P4.docx**.

Insert Predesigned Footer
1. Click Insert tab.
2. Click Footer button.
3. Click desired option at drop-down list.
5. Type text in specific placeholders in footer.

Insert a predesigned footer in the same manner as inserting a header. Click the Footer button in the Header & Footer group in the Insert tab and a drop-down list displays similar to the Header drop-down list shown in Figure 4.7. Click the desired footer and the predesigned footer formatting is applied to the document.

Removing a Header or Footer

Remove a header from a document by clicking the Insert tab and then clicking the Header button in the Header & Footer group. At the drop-down list that displays, click the *Remove Header* option. Complete similar steps to remove a footer.

1. With **WordL1_C4_P4.docx** open, press Ctrl + Home to move the insertion point to the beginning of the document.
2. Remove the header by clicking the Insert tab, clicking the Header button in the Header & Footer group, and then clicking the *Remove Header* option at the drop-down menu.

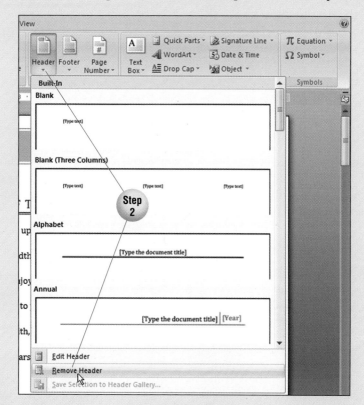

3. Insert a footer in the document by completing the following steps:
   a. Click the Footer button in the Header & Footer group.
   b. Click *Alphabet* at the drop-down list.

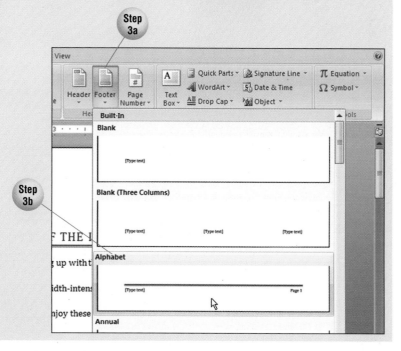

c. Click anywhere in the placeholder text *[Type text]* and then type Future of the Internet.

d. Double-click in the document text. (This makes the document text active and dims the footer.)

4. Scroll through the document to see how the footer will print.

5. Save and then print **WordL1_C4_P4.docx**.

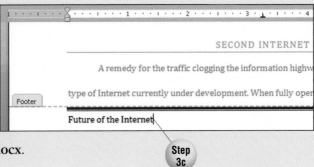

Step 3c

Editing a Predesigned Header or Footer

Predesigned headers and footers contain elements such as page numbers and a title. You can change the formatting of the element by clicking the desired element and then applying the desired formatting. You can also select and then delete an item.

Project **4C** **Formatting and Deleting Header and Footer Elements**

1. With **WordL1_C4_P4.docx** open, remove the footer by clicking the Insert tab, clicking the Footer button, and then clicking *Remove Footer* at the drop-down list.

2. Insert and then format a header by completing the following steps:

a. Click the Header button in the Header & Footer group in the Insert tab, scroll in the drop-down list, and then click *Motion (Odd Page)*. (This header inserts the document title as well as the page number.)

Step 2a

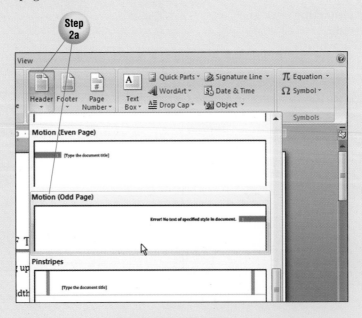

b. Delete the document title from the header by clicking anywhere in the text *FUTURE OF THE INTERNET*, selecting the text, and then pressing the Delete key.

c. Double-click in the document text.

3. Insert and then format a footer by completing the following steps:

a. Click the Insert tab.

b. Click the Footer button, scroll down the drop-down list, and then click *Motion (Odd Page)*.

c. Click on any character in the date that displays in the footer, select the date, and then type the current date.

d. Select the date, turn on bold, and then change the font size to 12.

e. Double-click in the document text.

4. Scroll through the document to see how the header and footer will print.

5. Save, print, and then close **WordL1_C4_P4.docx**.

Project ⑤ Format a Report on Robots

You will open a document containing information on the difficulties of creating a humanlike robot and then insert a watermark, change page background color, and insert a page border.

Formatting the Page Background

The Page Background group in the Page Layout tab contains three buttons for customizing a page background. Click the Watermark button and choose a predesigned watermark from a drop-down list. If a document is going to be viewed on-screen or on the Web, consider adding a page color. In Chapter 3, you learned how to apply borders and shading to text at the Borders and Shading dialog box. This dialog box also contains options for inserting a page border.

Inserting a Watermark

A watermark is a lightened image that displays behind text in a document. Using watermarks is an excellent way to add visual appeal to a document. Word provides a number of predesigned watermarks you can insert in a document. Display these watermarks by clicking the Watermark button in the Page Background group in the Page Layout tab. Scroll through the list of watermarks and then click the desired option.

Changing Page Color

Use the Page Color button in the Page Background group to apply background color to a document. This background color is intended for viewing a document on-screen or on the Web. The color is visible on the screen but does not print. Insert a page color by clicking the Page Color button and then clicking the desired color at the color palette.

QUICK STEPS

Insert Watermark
1. Click Page Layout tab.
2. Click Watermark button.
3. Click desired option at drop-down list.

Change Page Color
1. Click Page Layout tab.
2. Click Page Color button.
3. Click desired option at color palette.

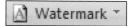 Watermark ⁻

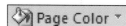 Page Color ⁻

1. Open **WordReport07.docx** and then save the document and name it **WordL1_C4_P5**.
2. Apply the Heading 1 style to the title *ROBOTS AS ANDROIDS* and the Heading 2 style to the five headings in the document.
3. Change the Quick Styles set to *Formal*.
4. Insert a page break at the beginning of the heading *Tactile Perception*.
5. Insert a watermark by completing the following steps:
   a. Move the insertion point to the beginning of the document.
   b. Click the Page Layout tab.
   c. Click the Watermark button in the Page Background group.
   d. At the drop-down list, click the *CONFIDENTIAL 1* option.

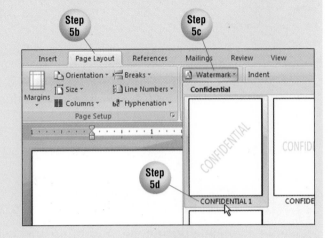

6. Scroll through the document and notice how the watermark displays behind the text.
7. Remove the watermark and insert a different one by completing the following steps:
   a. Click the Watermark button in the Page Background group and then click *Remove Watermark* at the drop-down list.
   b. Click the Watermark button and then click *DO NOT COPY 1* at the drop-down list.

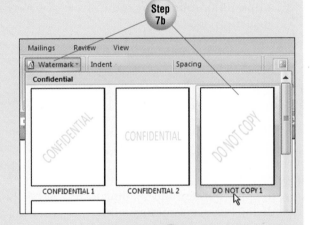

8. Scroll through the document and notice how the watermark displays.
9. Move the insertion point to the beginning of the document.
10. Click the Page Color button in the Page Background group and then click *Aqua, Accent 5, Lighter 80%* at the color palette.
11. Save **WordL1_C4_P5.docx**.

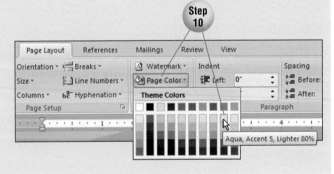

Inserting a Page Border

To improve the visual appeal of a document, consider inserting a page border. When you insert a page border in a multiple-page document, the border prints on each page. To insert a page border, click the Page Borders button in the Page Background group in the Page Layout tab. This displays the Borders and Shading dialog box with the Page Border tab selected as shown in Figure 4.8. At this dialog box, you can specify the border style, color, and width.

The dialog box contains an option for inserting a page border containing an image. To display the images available, click the down-pointing arrow at the right side of the *Art* list box. Scroll down the drop-down list and then click the desired image. (This feature may need to be installed the first time you use it.)

Insert Page Border
1. Click Page Layout tab.
2. Click Page Borders button.
3. Specify desired options at dialog box.

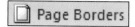

Figure 4.8 Borders and Shading Dialog Box with Page Border Tab Selected

Click this down-pointing arrow to scroll through a list of page border styles.

Preview the page border in this section.

Click this down-pointing arrow to display a palette of page border colors.

Click this down-pointing arrow to display a list of art border images.

Click this down-pointing arrow to display a list of width points.

1. With **WordL1_C4_P5.docx** open, remove the page color by clicking the Page Color button in the Page Background group and then clicking *No Color* at the color palette.
2. Insert a page border by completing the following steps:
   a. Click the Page Borders button in the Page Background group in the Page Layout tab.
   b. Click the *Box* option in the *Setting* section.
   c. Scroll down the list of line styles in the *Style* list box until the end of the list displays and then click the third line from the end.
   d. Click the down-pointing arrow at the right of the *Color* list box and then click *Red, Accent 2, Darker 25%* at the color palette.
   e. Click OK to close the dialog box.

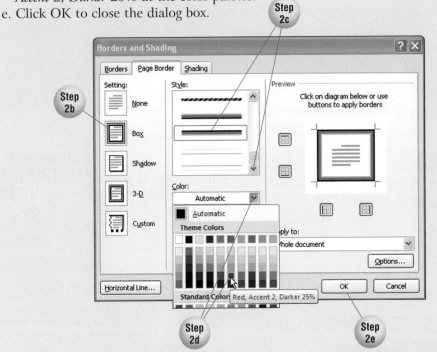

3. Save and then print **WordL1_C4_P5**.
4. Insert an image page border by completing the following steps:
   a. Click the Page Borders button in the Page Background group.
   b. Click the down-pointing arrow at the right side of the *Art* list box and then click the border image shown at the right.
   c. Click OK to close the dialog box.
5. Save, print, and then close **WordL1_C4_P5.docx**.

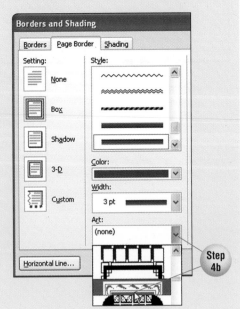

Project **6** **Format a Lease Agreement Document**

You will open a lease agreement document, search for specific text and replace it with other text, and then search for specific formatting and replace it with other formatting.

Finding and Replacing Text and Formatting

With Word's Find feature you can search for specific characters or formatting. With the Find and Replace feature, you can search for specific characters or formatting and replace them with other characters or formatting. The Find button and the Replace button are located in the Editing group in the Home tab.

Finding Text

With the Find feature, you can search a document for specific text. To use the Find feature, click the Find button in the Editing group in the Home tab or use the keyboard shortcut, Ctrl + F. This displays the Find and Replace dialog box with the Find tab selected as shown in Figure 4.9. Type the text you want to find in the *Find what* text box. Click the Find Next button and Word searches for and selects the first occurrence of the text in the document. Make corrections to the text if needed and then search for the next occurrence by clicking the Find Next button again. Click the Cancel button to close the Find and Replace dialog box.

QUICK STEPS

Find Text
1. Click Find button in Home tab.
2. Type search text.
3. Click Find Next button.

Figure 4.9 Find and Replace Dialog Box with Find Tab Selected

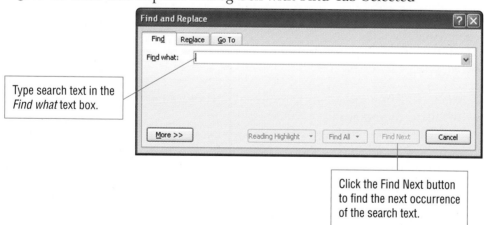

Type search text in the *Find what* text box.

Click the Find Next button to find the next occurrence of the search text.

word Level 1

Formatting Pages   **129**

Highlighting Find Text

You can use the Find feature to highlight specific text in a document. This can help you easily scan a document for every occurrence of the specific text. To find and highlight text, click the Find button, type the text you want highlighted in the *Find what* text box, click the Reading Highlight button, and then click *Highlight All* at the drop-down list. All occurrences of the text in the document are highlighted. To remove highlighting, click the Reading Highlight button and then click *Clear Highlighting* at the drop-down list.

Project 6a — Finding Text and Finding and Highlighting Text

1. Open **WordAgreement01.docx** and then save the document and name it **WordL1_C4_P6**.
2. Find all occurrences of *lease* by completing the following steps:
   a. Click the Find button in the Editing group in the Home tab.
   b. At the Find and Replace dialog box with the Find tab selected, type lease in the *Find what* text box.
   c. Click the Find Next button.

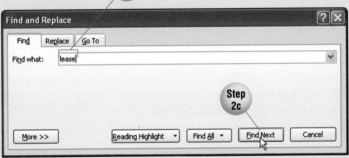

   d. Continue clicking the Find Next button until a message displays telling you that Word has finished searching the document. At this message, click OK.
3. Highlight all occurrences of *Premises* in the document by completing the following steps:
   a. At the Find and Replace dialog box with the Find tab selected, select the text in the *Find what* text box and then type Premises.
   b. Click the Reading Highlight button and then click *Highlight All* at the drop-down list.
   c. Click in the document to make it active and then scroll through the document and notice the occurrences of highlighted text.
   d. Click in the dialog box to make it active.
   e. Click the Reading Highlight button and then click *Clear Highlighting* at the drop-down list.

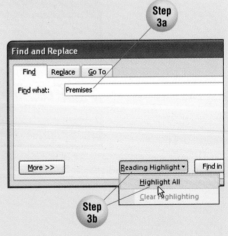

4. Click the Close button to close the Find and Replace dialog box.

Finding and Replacing Text

To find and replace text, click the Replace button in the Editing group in the Home tab or use the keyboard shortcut, Ctrl + H. This displays the Find and Replace dialog box with the Replace tab selected as shown in Figure 4.10. Type the text you want to find in the *Find what* text box, press the Tab key, and then type the replacement text.

Figure 4.10 Find and Replace Dialog Box with the Replace Tab Selected

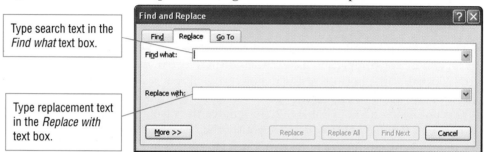

Type search text in the *Find what* text box.

Type replacement text in the *Replace with* text box.

QUICK STEPS

Find and Replace Text
1. Click Replace button in Home tab.
2. Type search text.
3. Press Tab key.
4. Type replace text.
5. Click Replace or Replace All button.

HINT
If the Find and Replace dialog box is in the way of specific text, drag the dialog box to a different location.

The Find and Replace dialog box contains several command buttons. Click the Find Next button to tell Word to find the next occurrence of the characters. Click the Replace button to replace the characters and find the next occurrence. If you know that you want all occurrences of the characters in the *Find what* text box replaced with the characters in the *Replace with* text box, click the Replace All button. This replaces every occurrence from the location of the insertion point to the beginning or end of the document (depending on the search direction). Click the Cancel button to close the Find and Replace dialog box.

Project 6b   Finding and Replacing Text

1. With **WordL1_C4_P6.docx** open, make sure the insertion point is positioned at the beginning of the document.
2. Find all occurrences of *Lessor* and replace with *Tracy Hartford* by completing the following steps:
   a. Click the Replace button in the Editing group in the Home tab.
   b. At the Find and Replace dialog box with the Replace tab selected, type Lessor in the *Find what* text box.
   c. Press the Tab key to move the insertion point to the *Replace with* text box.
   d. Type Tracy Hartford.
   e. Click the Replace All button.

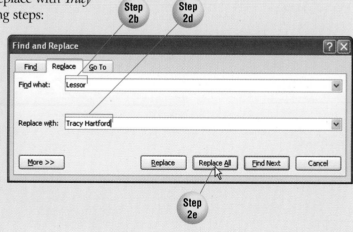

f. At the message *Word has completed its search of the document and has made 11 replacements*, click OK. (Do not close the Find and Replace dialog box.)
3. With the Find and Replace dialog box still open, complete steps similar to those in Step 2 to find all occurrences of *Lessee* and replace with *Michael Iwami*.
4. Close the Find and Replace dialog box.
5. Save **WordL1_C4_P6.docx**.

Choosing Check Box Options

The Find and Replace dialog box contains a variety of check boxes with options you can choose for completing a search. To display these options, click the More button located at the bottom of the dialog box. This causes the Find and Replace dialog box to expand as shown in Figure 4.11. Each option and what will occur if it is selected is described in Table 4.2. To remove the display of options, click the Less button. (The Less button was previously the More button.) Note that if you make a mistake when replacing text, you can close the Find and Replace dialog box and then click the Undo button on the Quick Access toolbar.

Figure 4.11 Expanded Find and Replace Dialog Box

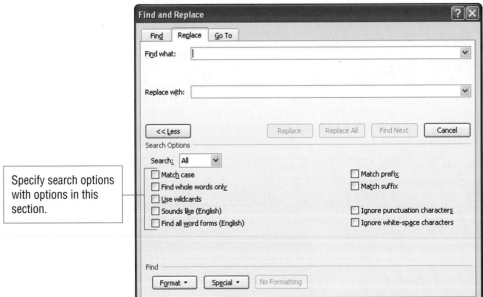

Specify search options with options in this section.

Table 4.2 Options at the Expanded Find and Replace Dialog Box

Choose this option	*To*
Match case	Exactly match the case of the search text. For example, if you search for *Book* and select the *Match case* option, Word will stop at *Book* but not *book* or *BOOK*.
Find whole words only	Find a whole word, not a part of a word. For example, if you search for *her* and did not select *Find whole words only*, Word would stop at *there*, *here*, *hers*, etc.
Use wildcards	Search for wildcards, special characters, or special search operators.
Sounds like	Match words that sound alike but are spelled differently such as *know* and *no*.
Find all word forms	Find all forms of the word entered in the *Find what* text box. For example, if you enter *hold*, Word will stop at *held* and *holding*.
Match prefix	Find only those words that begin with the letters in the *Find what* text box. For example, if you enter *per*, Word will stop at words such as *perform* and *perfect* but skip words such as *super* and *hyperlink*.
Match suffix	Find only those words that end with the letters in the *Find what* text box. For example, if you enter *ly*, Word will stop at words such as *accurately* and *quietly* but skip over words such as *catalyst* and *lyre*.
Ignore punctuation characters	Ignore punctuation within characters. For example, if you enter *US* in the *Find what* text box, Word will stop at *U.S.*
Ignore white space characters	Ignore spaces between letters. For example, if you enter *F B I* in the *Find what* text box, Word will stop at FBI.

1. With **WordL1_C4_P6.docx** open, make sure the insertion point is positioned at the beginning of the document.
2. Find all word forms of the word *lease* and replace with *rent* by completing the following steps:
   a. Click the Replace button in the Editing group in the Home tab.
   b. At the Find and Replace dialog box with the Replace tab selected, type lease in the *Find what* text box.
   c. Press the Tab key and then type rent in the *Replace with* text box.
   d. Click the More button.
   e. Click the *Find all word forms* option. (This inserts a check mark in the check box.)
   f. Click the Replace All button.
   g. At the message telling you that Replace All is not recommended with Find All Word Forms, click OK.
   h. At the message *Word has completed its search of the document and has made 6 replacements*, click OK.
   i. Click the *Find all word forms* option to remove the check mark.

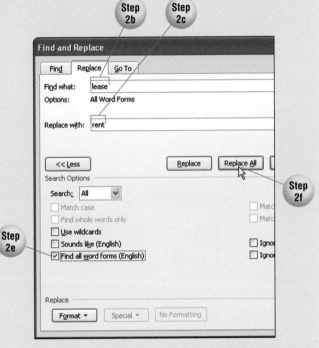

3. Find the word *less* and replace with the word *minus* and specify that you want Word to find only those words that end in *less* by completing the following steps:
   a. At the expanded Find and Replace dialog box, select the text in the *Find what* text box and then type less.
   b. Select the text in the *Replace with* text box and then type minus.
   c. Click the *Match suffix* check box to insert a check mark and tell Word to find only words that end in *less*.
   d. Click the Replace All button.
   e. At the message telling you that 2 replacements were made, click OK.
   f. Click the *Match suffix* check box to remove the check mark.
   g. Click the Less button.
   h. Close the Find and Replace dialog box.
4. Save **WordL1_C4_P6.docx**.

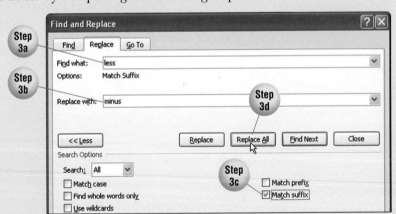

Finding and Replacing Formatting

With options at the Find and Replace dialog box with the Replace tab selected, you can search for characters containing specific formatting and replace them with other characters or formatting. To specify formatting in the Find and Replace dialog box, click the More button and then click the Format button that displays toward the bottom of the dialog box. At the pop-up list that displays, identify the type of formatting you want to find.

Project 6d   Finding and Replacing Fonts

1. With **WordL1_C4_P6.docx** open, move the insertion point to the beginning of the document.
2. Find text set in 12-point Candara bold dark red and replace it with text set in 14-point Calibri bold dark blue by completing the following steps:
   a. Click the Replace button in the Editing group.
   b. At the Find and Replace dialog box, press the Delete key. (This deletes any text that displays in the *Find what* text box.)
   c. Click the More button. (If a check mark displays in any of the check boxes, click the option to remove the check mark.)
   d. With the insertion point positioned in the *Find what* text box, click the Format button located toward the bottom of the dialog box and then click *Font* at the pop-up list.
   e. At the Find Font dialog box, change the Font to *Candara*, the Font style to *Bold*, the Size to *12*, and the Font color to *Dark Red* (first color option from the left in the *Standard Colors* section).
   f. Click OK to close the Find Font dialog box.
   g. At the Find and Replace dialog box, click inside the *Replace with* text box and then delete any text that displays.
   h. Click the Format button located toward the bottom of the dialog box and then click *Font* at the pop-up list.

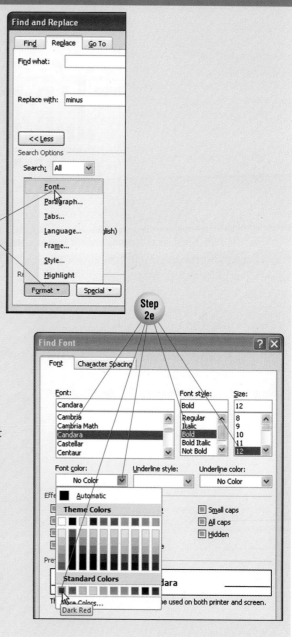

i. At the Replace Font dialog box, change the Font to *Calibri*, the Font style to *Bold*, the Size to *14*, and the Font color to *Dark Blue* (second color option from the right in the *Standard Colors* section).

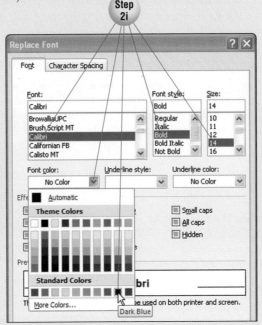

j. Click OK to close the Replace Font dialog box.
k. At the Find and Replace dialog box, click the Replace All button.
l. At the message telling you that the search of the document is complete and eight replacements were made, click OK.
m. Click in the *Find what* text box and then click the No Formatting button.
n. Click in the *Replace with* text box and then click the No Formatting button.
o. Click the Less button.
p. Close the Find and Replace dialog box.
3. Save, print, and then close **WordL1_C4_P6.docx**.

CHAPTER summary

- You can change the document view with buttons in the View section on the Status bar or with options in the View tab.
- Print Layout is the default view, which can be changed to other views such as Draft view or Full Screen Reading view.
- The Draft view displays the document in a format for efficient editing and formatting.
- Use the Zoom slider bar to change the percentage of the display.
- Full Screen Reading view displays a document in a format for easy viewing and reading.
- Navigate in Full Screen Reading view using keys on the keyboard or with the Next and Previous buttons.
- Navigate in a document using the Document Map or Thumbnails features. Click the *Document Map* check box in the View tab or the *Thumbnails* check box and a navigation pane displays at the left side of the screen.
- In Print Layout view, you can remove the white space at the top and bottom of pages.
- By default, a Word document contains 1-inch top, bottom, left, and right margins. Change margins with preset margin settings at the Margins drop-down list or with options at the Page Setup dialog box with the Margins tab selected.
- The default page orientation is portrait, which can be changed to landscape with the Orientation button in the Page Setup group in the Page Layout tab.
- The default page size is 8.5 by 11 inches, which can be changed with options at the Size drop-down list or options at the Page Setup dialog box with the Paper tab selected.
- The page break that Word inserts automatically is a soft page break. A page break that you insert is a hard page break. Insert a page break with the Page Break button in the Pages group in the Insert tab or by pressing Ctrl + Enter.
- Insert a blank page in a document by clicking the Blank Page button in the Pages group in the Insert tab.
- Insert a predesigned and formatted cover page by clicking the Cover Page button in the Pages group in the Insert tab and then clicking the desired option at the drop-down list.
- Insert predesigned and formatted page numbering by clicking the Page Number button in the Header & Footer group in the Insert tab, specifying the desired location of page numbers, and then clicking the desired page numbering option.
- Text that appears at the top of every page is called a header and text that appears at the bottom of every page is called a footer.
- You can insert predesigned headers and footers in a document with the Header button and the Footer button in the Header & Footer group in the Insert tab.
- A header or footer displays in Print Layout view but will not display in Draft view.
- You can remove and/or edit predesigned headers and footers.

- A watermark is a lightened image that displays behind text in a document. Use the Watermark button in the Page Background group in the Page Layout tab to insert a watermark.

- Insert page color in a document with the Page Color button in the Page Background group. Page color is designed for viewing a document on-screen and does not print.

- Click the Page Borders button in the Page Background group and the Borders and Shading dialog box with the Page Border tab selected displays. Use options at this dialog box to insert a page border or an image page border in a document.

- Use the Find feature to search for specific characters or formatting. Use the Find and Replace feature to search for specific characters or formatting and replace with other characters or formatting.

- At the Find and Replace dialog box, click the Find Next button to find the next occurrence of the characters and/or formatting. Click the Replace button to replace the characters or formatting and find the next occurrence, or click the Replace All button to replace all occurrences of the characters or formatting.

- Click the More button at the Find and Replace dialog box to display additional options for completing a search.

COMMANDS review

FEATURE	RIBBON TAB, GROUP	BUTTON	KEYBOARD SHORTCUT
Blank page	Insert, Pages	Blank Page	
Borders and Shading dialog box with Page Border tab selected	Page Layout, Page Background	Page Borders	
Cover page	Insert, Pages	Cover Page	
Document Map	View, Show/Hide	☑ Document Map	
Draft view	View, Document Views		
Find and Replace dialog box with Find tab selected	Home, Editing	Find	Ctrl + F
Find and Replace dialog box with Replace tab selected	Home, Editing	Replace	Ctrl + H
Footer	Insert, Header & Footer		
Full Screen Reading view	View, Document Views		
Header	Insert, Header & Footer		
Margins	Page Layout, Page Setup		
Orientation	Page Layout, Page Setup	Orientation	
Page break	Insert, Pages	Page Break	Ctrl + Enter
Page color	Page Layout, Page Background	Page Color	
Page numbering	Insert, Header & Footer		
Page Setup dialog box with Margins tab selected	Page Layout, Page Setup	, *Custom Margins;* or Page Setup group dialog box launcher	
Page Setup dialog box with Paper tab selected	Page Layout, Page Setup	Size , *More Paper Sizes*	
Page size	Page Layout, Page Setup	Size	
Print Layout view	View, Document Views		
Thumbnails	View, Show/Hide	☑ Thumbnails	
Watermark	Page Layout, Page Background	Watermark	

CONCEPTS check

Test Your Knowledge

Completion: In the space provided at the right, indicate the correct term, symbol, or command.

1. This is the default measurement for the top, bottom, left, and right margins. _____

2. This view displays a document in a format for efficient editing and formatting. _____

3. This view displays a document in a format for easy viewing and reading. _____

4. The Document Map check box is located in this group in the View tab. _____

5. Insert a check mark in the *Document Map* or *Thumbnails* check box and this displays at the left side of the screen. _____

6. To remove white space, double-click this icon. _____

7. This is the default page orientation. _____

8. Set specific margins at this dialog box with the Margins tab selected. _____

9. Press these keys on the keyboard to insert a page break. _____

10. The Cover Page button is located in the Pages group in this tab. _____

11. Text that appears at the top of every page is called this. _____

12. A footer displays in Print Layout view, but not this view. _____

13. A lightened image that displays behind text in a document is called this. _____

14. The Page Borders button displays in this group in the Page Layout tab. _____

15. If you want to replace every occurrence of what you are searching for in a document, click this button at the Find and Replace dialog box. _____

16. Click this option at the Find and Replace dialog box if you are searching for a word and all of its forms. _____

SKILLS check
Demonstrate Your Proficiency

Assessment

1 FORMAT A SOFTWARE LIFE CYCLE DOCUMENT AND CREATE A COVER PAGE

1. Open **WordDocument05.docx** and then save the document and name it **WordL1_C4_A1**.
2. Select the entire document, change the line spacing to 2, and then deselect the document.
3. Apply the Heading 1 style to the title of the document and apply the Heading 2 style to the headings in the document.
4. Change the Quick Styles set to *Fancy*.
5. Change the theme colors to *Flow*.
6. Insert a page break at the beginning of the heading *Testing*.
7. Move the insertion point to the beginning of the document and then insert the *Austere* cover page.
8. Insert the following text in the specified fields:
   a. Insert the current year in the *[Year]* placeholder.
   b. Insert your school's name in the *[Type the company name]* placeholder.
   c. If a name displays below your school's name, select the name and then type your first and last names.
   d. Insert *software life cycle* in the *[TYPE THE DOCUMENT TITLE]* placeholder (the placeholder will convert the text you type to all uppercase letters).
   e. Click the text below the document title, click the Abstract tab, and then press the Delete key twice.
9. Move the insertion point to any character in the title *COMMERCIAL LIFE CYCLE* and then insert the Box Italics 2 page numbering at the bottom of the pages (the page numbering will not appear on the cover page).
10. Save, print, and then close **WordL1_C4_A1.docx**.

Assessment

2 FORMAT AN INTELLECTUAL PROPERTY REPORT AND INSERT HEADERS AND FOOTERS

1. Open **WordReport03.docx** and then save the document and name it **WordL1_C4_A2**.
2. Select the entire document and then change the line spacing to 2 and the font to 12-point Constantia.
3. Select text from the beginning of the first paragraph of text to just above the *REFERENCES* title located toward the end of the document and then indent the first line to 0.25 inch.
4. Apply the Heading 1 style to the titles *PROPERTY PROTECTION ISSUES* and *REFERENCES* (located toward the end of the document).
5. Apply the Heading 2 style to the headings in the document.
6. Change the Quick Styles set to *Distinctive*.
7. Center the *PROPERTY PROTECTION ISSUES* and *REFERENCES* titles.
8. Select and then hang indent the paragraphs below the *REFERENCES* title.

9. Insert a page break at the beginning of the *REFERENCES* title.
10. Move the insertion point to the beginning of the document and then insert the Exposure header. Type Property Protection Issues in the *[Type the document title]* placeholder and, if necessary, insert the current date in the *[Pick the date]* placeholder.
11. Insert the Pinstripes footer and type your first and last names in the *[Type text]* placeholder.
12. Save and then print **WordL1_C4_A2.docx**.
13. Remove the header and footer.
14. Insert the *Austere (Odd Page)* footer and then make the following changes:
    a. Delete the *[Type the company name]* placeholder.
    b. Select the text and page number in the footer and then change the font to 10-point Constantia bold.
15. Insert the DRAFT 1 watermark in the document.
16. Insert a page border of your choosing to the document.
17. Save, print, and then close **WordL1_C4_A2.docx**.

Assessment

3 FORMAT A REAL ESTATE AGREEMENT

1. Open **WordContract02.docx** and then save the document and name it **WordL1_C4_A3**.
2. Find all occurrences of *BUYER* (matching the case) and replace with *James Berman*.
3. Find all occurrences of *SELLER* (matching the case) and replace with *Mona Trammell*.
4. Find all word forms of the word *buy* and replace with *purchase*.
5. Search for 14-point Tahoma bold formatting in dark red and replace with 12-point Times New Roman bold formatting in black.
6. Insert page numbers at the bottom of each page.
7. Save, print, and then close **WordL1_C4_A3.docx**.

CASE study

Apply Your Skills

Part 1

Help

You work for Citizens for Consumer Safety, a non-profit organization providing information on household safety. Your supervisor, Melinda Johansson, has asked you to attractively format a document on smoke detectors. She will be using the document as an informational handout during a presentation on smoke detectors. Open the document named **WordSmokeDetectors.docx** and then save the document and name it **WordL1_C4_CS_P1**. Apply a theme to the document and apply appropriate styles to the title and headings. Ms. Johansson has asked you to change the page orientation and then change the left and right margins to 1.5 inches. She wants the extra space at the left and right margins so audience members can write notes in the margins. Use the Help feature or experiment with the options in the Header & Footer Tools Design tab and figure out how to number pages on every page but the first page. Insert page numbering in the document that prints at the top right side of every page except the first page. Save, print, and then close **WordL1_C4_CS_P1.docx**.

Part 2

Help

After reviewing the formatted document on smoke detectors, Ms. Johansson has decided that she wants the document to print in the default orientation and she is not happy with the theme and style choices. She also noticed that the term "smoke alarm" should be replaced with "smoke detector." She has asked you to open and then format the original document. Open **WordSmokeDetectors.docx** and then save the document and name it **WordL1_C4_CS_P2**. Apply a theme to the document (other than the one you chose for Part 1) and apply styles to the title and headings. Search for all occurrences of *smoke alarm* and replace with *smoke detector*. Insert a cover page of your choosing and insert the appropriate information in the page. Use the Help feature or experiment with the options in the Header & Footer Tools Design tab and figure out how to insert an odd-page and even-page footer in a document. Insert an odd-page footer that prints the page number at the right margin and insert an even-page footer that prints the page number at the left margin. You do not want the footer to print on the cover page so make sure you position the insertion point below the cover page before inserting the footers. After inserting the footers in the document, you decide that they need to be moved down the page to create more space between the last line of text on a page and the footer. Use the Help feature or experiment with the options in the Header & Footer Tools Design tab to figure out how to move the footers down and then edit each footer so they display 0.3″ from the bottom of the page. Save, print, and then close **WordL1_C4_CS_P2.docx**.

Ms. Johansson has asked you to prepare a document on infant car seats and car seat safety. She wants this informational car seat safety document available for distribution at a local community center. Use the Internet to find Web sites that provide information on child and infant car seats and car seat safety. Write a report on the information you find that includes at least the following information:

- Description of the types of car seats (such as rear-facing, convertible, forward-facing, built-in, and booster)
- Safety rules and guidelines
- Installation information
- Specific child and infant seat models
- Sites on the Internet that sell car seats
- Price ranges
- Internet sites providing safety information

Format the report using a theme and styles and include a cover page and headers and/or footers. Save the completed document and name it **WordL1_C4_CS_P3**. Print and then close the document.

Editing and Formatting Documents

ASSESSING proficiency

In this unit, you have learned to create, edit, save, and print Word documents. You also learned to format characters, paragraphs, and pages.

word Unit 1

Note: Before beginning unit assessments, copy to your storage medium the Word2007L1U1 subfolder from the Word2007L1 folder on the CD that accompanies this textbook and then make Word2007L1U1 the active folder.

Assessment 1 Format *Designing an Effective Web Site* Document

1. Open **WordDocument08.docx** and then save the document and name it **WordL1_U1_A1**.
2. Complete a spelling and grammar check.
3. Select from the paragraph that begins *Make your home page work for you.* through the end of the document and then apply bullet formatting.
4. Select and then bold the first sentence of each bulleted paragraph.
5. Apply paragraph border and shading to the document title.
6. Save and then print **WordL1_U1_A1.docx**.
7. Change the top, left, and right margins to 1.5 inches.
8. Select the bulleted paragraphs, change the paragraph alignment to justified, and then insert numbering.
9. Select the entire document and then change the font to 12-point Constantia.
10. Insert the text shown in Figure U1.1 after paragraph number 2. (The number 3. should be inserted preceding the text you type.)
11. Save, print, and then close **WordL1_U1_A1.docx**.

Figure U1.1 Assessment 1

Avoid a cluttered look. In design, less is more. Strive for a clean look to your pages, using ample margins and white space.

Assessment 2 Format *Accumulated Returns* Document

1. Open **WordDocument09.docx** and then save the document and name it **WordL1_U1_A2**.
2. Select the entire document and then make the following changes:
   a. Click the No Spacing style.
   b. Change the line spacing to 1.5.
   c. Change the font to 12-point Cambria.
   d. Apply 6 points of spacing after paragraphs.

3. Select the title *TOTAL RETURN CHARTS*, change the font to 14-point Corbel bold, change the alignment to center, and apply paragraph shading of your choosing.
4. Bold the following text that appears at the beginning of the second through the fifth paragraphs:
   Average annual total return:
   Annual total return:
   Accumulation units:
   Accumulative rates:
5. Select the paragraphs of text in the body of the document (all paragraphs except the title) and then change the paragraph alignment to justified.
6. Select the paragraphs that begin with the bolded words, sort the paragraphs, and then indent the text 0.5 inch from the left margin.
7. Insert a watermark that prints *DRAFT* diagonally across the page.
8. Save, print, and then close **WordL1_U1_A2.docx**.

Assessment 3 Format Computer Ethics Report

1. Open **WordReport04.docx** and then save the document and name it **WordL1_U1_A3**.
2. Apply the *Foundry* theme to the document.
3. Apply the Heading 1 style to the titles *FUTURE OF COMPUTER ETHICS* and *REFERENCES*.
4. Apply the Heading 2 style to the headings in the document.
5. Change the Quick Styles set to *Modern*.
6. Change the theme colors to *Opulent*.
7. Center the two titles (*FUTURE OF COMPUTER ETHICS* and *REFERENCES*).
8. Hang indent the paragraphs of text below the *REFERENCES* title.
9. Insert page numbering that prints at the bottom of each page.
10. Save, print, and then close **WordL1_U1_A3.docx**.

Assessment 4 Set Tabs and Type Division Income Text in Columns

1. At a new blank document, type the text shown in Figure U1.2 with the following specifications:
   a. Bold and center the title as shown.
   b. You determine the tab settings for the text in columns.
   c. Select the entire document and then change the font to 12-point Arial.
2. Save the document and name it **WordL1_U1_A4**.
3. Print and then close **WordL1_U1_A4.docx**.

Figure U1.2 Assessment 4

INCOME BY DIVISION

	2007	2008	2009
Public Relations	$14,375	$16,340	$16,200
Database Services	9,205	15,055	13,725
Graphic Design	18,400	21,790	19,600
Technical Support	5,780	7,325	9,600

Assessment 5 Set Tabs and Type Table of Contents Text

1. At a new blank document, type the text shown in Figure U1.3 with the following specifications:
   a. Bold and center the title as shown.
   b. You determine the tab settings for the text in columns.
   c. Select the entire document, change the font to 12-point Bookman Old Style (or a similar serif typeface), and then change the line spacing to 1.5.
2. Save the document and name it **WordL1_U1_A5**.
3. Print and then close **WordL1_U1_A5.docx**.

Figure U1.3 Assessment 5

TABLE OF CONTENTS

Online Shopping.. 2

Online Services... 4

Peer-to-Peer Online Transactions............................... 5

Transaction Payment Methods..................................... 8

Transaction Security and Encryption........................ 11

Establishing a Web Site..14

Assessment 6 Format Union Agreement Contract

1. Open **WordContract01.docx** and then save the document and name it **WordL1_U1_A6**.
2. Find all occurrences of *REINBERG MANUFACTURING* and replace with *MILLWOOD ENTERPRISES*.
3. Find all occurrences of *RM* and replace with *ME*.
4. Find all occurrences of *LABOR WORKER'S UNION* and replace with *SERVICE EMPLOYEE'S UNION*.
5. Find all occurrences of *LWU* and replace with *SEU*.
6. Select the entire document and then change the font to 12-point Cambria and the line spacing to double.
7. Select the numbered paragraphs in the *Transfers and Moving Expenses* section and change to bullets.
8. Select the numbered paragraphs in the *Sick Leave* section and change to bullets.
9. Change the page orientation to landscape and the top margin to 1.5".
10. Save and then print **WordL1_U1_A6.docx**.
11. Change the page orientation to portrait and the left margin (previously the top margin) back to 1".
12. Insert a footer that prints *Union Agreement* at the left margin and the page number at the right margin.

13. Insert a cover page of your choosing and insert *UNION AGREEMENT* as the document name and *Millwood Enterprises* as the company name. Include any additional information required by the cover page.
14. Save, print, and then close **WordL1_U1_A6.docx**.

Assessment 7 Copy and Paste Text in Health Plan Document

1. Open **WordKeyLifePlan.docx** and then save the document and name it **WordL1_U1_A7**.
2. Open **WordDocument15.docx** and then turn on the display of the Clipboard task pane. Make sure the Clipboard is empty.
3. Copy to the Clipboard the heading *Plan Highlights* and the six paragraphs of text below the heading.
4. Copy to the Clipboard the heading *Plan Options* and the two paragraphs of text below the heading.
5. Copy to the Clipboard the heading *Quality Assessment* and the six paragraphs of text below the heading.
6. Close **WordDocument15.docx**.
7. With **WordL1_U1_A7.docx** open, display the Clipboard task pane.
8. Move the insertion point to the beginning of the *Provider Network* heading, paste the *Plan Options* item from the Clipboard, and match the destination formatting.
9. With the insertion point positioned at the beginning of the *Provider Network* heading, paste the *Plan Highlights* item from the Clipboard, and match the destination formatting.
10. Move the insertion point to the end of the document, paste the *Quality Assessment* item from the Clipboard, and match the destination formatting.
11. Clear the Clipboard and then close it.
12. Apply the Heading 1 style to the title, *KEY LIFE HEALTH PLAN*.
13. Apply the Heading 2 style to the headings in the document.
14. Change to a Quick Styles set of your choosing (other than the default).
15. Change to a theme of your choosing (other than the default).
16. Insert a page border of your choosing in the document.
17. Insert a header or footer of your choosing in the document.
18. Add a cover page of your choosing to the document.
19. Save, print, and then close **WordL1_U1_A7.docx**.

WRITING activities

The following activities give you the opportunity to practice your writing skills along with demonstrating an understanding of some of the important Word features you have mastered in this unit. Use correct grammar, appropriate word choices, and clear sentence constructions. Follow the steps explained below to improve your writing skills.

The Writing Process

Plan: Gather ideas, select which information to include, and choose the order in which to present the information.

Checkpoints

What is the purpose?

What information do the readers need in order to reach your intended conclusion?

Write: Following the information plan and keeping the reader in mind, draft the document using clear, direct sentences that say what you mean.

Checkpoints

What are the subpoints for each main thought?

How can you connect paragraphs so the reader moves smoothly from one idea to the next?

Revise: Improve what is written by changing, deleting, rearranging, or adding words, sentences, and paragraphs.

Checkpoints

Is the meaning clear?

Do the ideas follow a logical order?

Have you included any unnecessary information?

Have you built your sentences around strong nouns and verbs?

Edit: Check spelling, sentence construction, word use, punctuation, and capitalization.

Checkpoints

Can you spot any redundancies or clichés?

Can you reduce any phrases to an effective word (for example, change *the fact that* to *because*)?

Have you used commas only where there is a strong reason for doing so?

Did you proofread the document for errors that your spell checker cannot identify?

Publish: Prepare a final copy that could be reproduced and shared with others.

Checkpoints

Which design elements, for example, bolding and different fonts, would help highlight important ideas or sections?

Would charts or other graphics help clarify meaning?

Activity 1 Write Hyphenation Steps and Hyphenate Computer Text in Health Plan Document

Use Word's Help feature to learn about hyphenating text in a document. Learn how to hyphenate text automatically as well as manually. Create a document that contains the following:

1. Include an appropriate title that is bolded and centered.
2. Write the steps required to automatically hyphenate text in a document.
3. Write the steps required to manually hyphenate text in a document.

Save the document and name it **WordL1_U1_Hyphen**. Print and then close **WordL1_U1_Hyphen.docx**. Open **WordL1_U1_A3.docx** and then save the document and name it **WordL1_U1_Act01**. Manually hyphenate text in the document. Save, print, and then close **WordL1_U1_Act01.docx**.

Activity 2 Write Information on Customizing Spelling and Grammar

Use Word's Help feature to learn about grammar and style options. Learn about grammar options and what they detect and style options and what they detect. Also, learn how to set rules for grammar and style. Once you have determined this information, create a document describing at least two grammar options and at least two style options. Also include in this document the steps required to change the writing style from grammar only to grammar and style. Save the completed document and name it **WordL1_U1_Act02**. Print and then close **WordL1_U1_Act02.docx**.

Research Business Desktop Computer Systems

You hold a part-time job at a local newspaper, *The Daily Chronicle*, where you conduct Internet research for the staff writers. Mr. Woods, the editor, has decided to purchase nine new desktop computers for the staff. He has asked you to identify at least three Macintosh PCs that can be purchased directly over the Internet, and he requests that you put your research and recommendations in writing. Mr. Woods is looking for solid, reliable, economical, and powerful desktop computers with good warranties and service plans. He has given you a budget of $1,300 per unit.

Search the Internet for three desktop Macintosh computer systems from three different manufacturers. Consider price, specifications (processor speed, amount of RAM, hard drive space, and monitor type and size), performance, warranties, and service plans when making your choice of systems. Print your research findings and include them with your report. (For helpful information on choosing a PC, read the article "Factors to Consider When Buying a PC," which is available in the Computer Concepts Resource Center at EMC/Paradigm's Web site. Go to www.emcp.com; click College Division and then click Resource Center for either *Computer Technology* or *Computers: Exploring Concepts*. Choose Student and then select the article under "Practical Tips for Computer Users.")

Using Word, write a brief report in which you summarize the capabilities and qualities of each of the three computer systems you recommend. Include a final paragraph detailing which system you suggest for purchase and why. If possible, incorporate user opinions and/or reviews about this system to support your decision. At the end of your report, include a table comparing the computer system. Format your report using the concepts and techniques you learned in Unit 1. Save the report and name it **WordL1_U1_InternetResearch**. Print and then close the file.

Level 1

Microsoft®

word

Unit 2: Enhancing and Customizing Documents

- ➤ Applying Formatting and Inserting Objects
- ➤ Maintaining Documents
- ➤ Creating Tables and SmartArt
- ➤ Merging Documents

Benchmark Microsoft® Word 2007 Level 1

Microsoft Certified Application Specialist Skills—Unit 2

Reference No.	Skill	Pages
1	**Creating and Customizing Documents**	
1.1	Create and format documents	
1.1.1	Use document templates	216-217
1.2	Lay out documents	
1.2.3	Create and design the appearance of columns	155-159
2	**Formatting Content**	
2.3	Control pagination	
2.3.2	Create and revise sections	154-155, 155-159
3	**Working with Visual Content**	
3.1	Insert illustrations	
3.1.1	Create SmartArt graphics	251-259
3.1.2	Add pictures from files and clip art	169-174
3.1.3	Add shapes to a document	177-184
3.2	Format illustrations	
3.2.1	Change text wrapping style	170-174
3.2.2	Size, crop, scale, and rotate images	170-174
3.2.4	Apply contrast, brightness, and coloration	169-172
3.2.5	Include text in SmartArt graphics and shapes	257-259
3.2.6	Reduce picture file size	169-172
3.3	Format text graphically	
3.3.1	Add and edit WordArt	184-185
3.3.2	Create Pull Quotes	175-177
3.3.3	Create and revise drop caps	162
3.4	Insert and modify text boxes	
3.4.1	Create text boxes	180-181
3.4.2	Design the appearance of text boxes	180-181
3.4.3	Connect text boxes with a link	182-183
4	**Organizing Content**	
4.2	Use tables and lists to organize content	225-229
4.2.1	Convert text to tables and lists and convert tables to text	247
4.2.2	Sort text	248
4.3	Modify tables	
4.3.1	Format tables with Quick Styles	229-230
4.3.2	Change table properties and options	234-236
4.3.3	Combine and split table cells	236-238
4.3.4	Calculate numbers in tables	249-251
4.3.5	Modify cell contents direction and position	243-244
4.5	Merge documents and data sources	
4.5.1	Create a data source and a main document	272-274, 275-276
4.5.2	Complete a merge with form letters	277, 283-285, 285-288
4.5.3	Merge envelopes and labels	278-280, 280-281
5	**Reviewing Documents**	
5.1	Navigate documents	
5.1.2	Change window views	201-205
6	**Sharing and Securing Content**	
6.1	Prepare documents for sharing	
6.1.1	Save a document in different formats	199-201

Note: The Level 1 and Level 2 texts each address approximately half of the Microsoft Certified Application Specialist skills. Complete coverage of the skills is offered in the combined Level 1 and Level 2 text titled *Benchmark Series Microsoft® Word 2007: Levels 1 and 2,* which has been approved as certified courseware and which displays the Microsoft Certified Application Specialist logo on the cover.

CHAPTER 5

Applying Formatting and Inserting Objects

PERFORMANCE OBJECTIVES

Upon successful completion of Chapter 5, you will be able to:

- Insert section breaks
- Create and format text in columns
- Hyphenate words automatically and manually
- Create a drop cap
- Insert symbols, special characters, and the date and time
- Use the Click and Type feature
- Vertically align text
- Insert, format, and customize pictures, clip art images, text boxes, shapes, and WordArt

Tutorial 5.1
Creating Presentable Documents
Tutorial 5.2
Using Additional Features

To apply page or document formatting to only a portion of the document, insert a section break. You can insert a continuous section break or a section break that begins a new page. A section break is useful when formatting text in columns. The hyphenation feature hyphenates words at the end of lines, creating a less ragged margin. Use buttons in the Text and Symbols groups in the Insert tab to insert symbols, special characters, and the date and time. With the Click and Type feature, you can position the insertion point at various locations in the document and change the paragraph alignment. Use the *Vertical alignment* option at the Page Setup dialog box with the Layout tab selected to align text vertically on the page. Along with these features, you will also learn how to increase the visual appeal of a document by inserting and customizing images such as pictures, clip art, text boxes, shapes, and WordArt.

Note: Before beginning computer projects, copy to your storage medium the Word2007L1C5 subfolder from the Word2007L1 folder on the CD that accompanies this textbook and then make Word2007L1C5 the active folder.

Project 1 Format a Document on Computer Input Devices

You will format into columns text in a document on computer input devices, improve the readability of the document by hyphenating long words, and improve the visual appeal by inserting a drop cap.

Inserting a Section Break

You can change the layout and formatting of specific portions of a document by inserting section breaks. For example, you can insert section breaks and then change margins for the text between the section breaks. If you want to format specific text in a document into columns, insert a section break.

Insert a section break in a document by clicking the Page Layout tab, clicking the Breaks button in the Page Setup group, and then clicking the desired option in the *Section Breaks* section of the drop-down list shown in Figure 5.1. You can insert a section break that begins a new page or a continuous section break that does not begin a new page. A continuous section break separates the document into sections but does not insert a page break. Click one of the other three options in the *Section Breaks* section of the Breaks drop-down list if you want to insert a section break that begins a new page.

Figure 5.1 Breaks Button Drop-down List

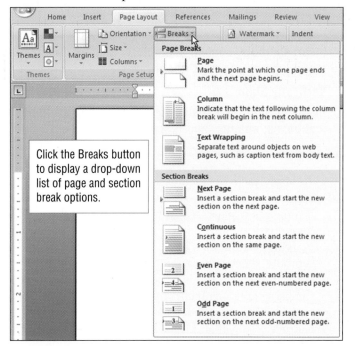

Click the Breaks button to display a drop-down list of page and section break options.

A section break inserted in a document is not visible in Print Layout view. Click the Draft button and a section break displays in the document as a double row of dots with the words *Section Break* in the middle. Depending on the type of section break you insert, text follows *Section Break*. For example, if you insert a continuous section break, the words *Section Break (Continuous)* display in the middle of the row of dots. To delete a section break, change to Draft view, position the insertion point on the section break, and then press the Delete key.

Project 1a — Inserting a Continuous Section Break

1. Open **WordDocument16.docx** and then save it and name it **WordL1_C5_P1**.
2. Insert a continuous section break by completing the following steps:
   a. Move the insertion point to the beginning of the *Keyboard* heading.
   b. Click the Page Layout tab.
   c. Click the Breaks button in the Page Setup group and then click *Continuous* in the *Section Breaks* section of the drop-down list.
3. Click the Draft button in the view area on the Status bar and then notice the section break that displays across the screen.
4. Click the Print Layout button in the view area on the Status bar.
5. With the insertion point positioned at the beginning of the *Keyboard* heading, change the left and right margins to 1.5 inches. (The margin changes affect only the text after the continuous section break.)
6. Save and then print **WordL1_C5_P1.docx**.

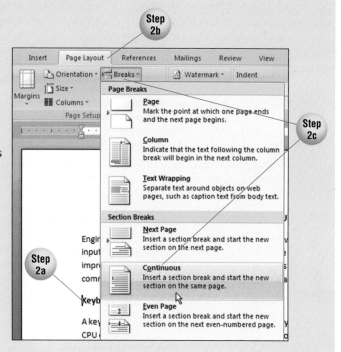

Step 2b

Step 2c

Step 2a

Creating Columns

When preparing a document containing text, an important point to consider is the readability of the document. Readability refers to the ease with which a person can read and understand groups of words. The line length of text in a document can enhance or detract from the readability of text. If the line length is too long, the reader may lose his or her place on the line and have a difficult time moving to the next line below. To improve the readability of some documents such as newsletters or reports, you may want to set the text in columns. One common type of column is newspaper, which is typically used for text in newspapers, newsletters, and magazines. Newspaper columns contain text that flows up and down in the document.

Create newspaper columns with the Columns button in the Page Setup group in the Page Layout tab or with options from the Columns dialog box. The Columns button creates columns of equal width. Use the Columns dialog box to create columns with varying widths. A document can include as many columns as room available on the page. Word determines how many columns can be included on the page based on the page width, the margin widths, and the size and spacing of the columns. Columns must be at least one-half inch in width. Changes in columns affect the entire document or the section of the document in which the insertion point is positioned.

QUICK STEPS

Create Columns
1. Click Page Layout tab.
2. Click Columns button.
3. Click on desired number of columns.

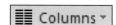

1. With **WordL1_C5_P1.docx** open, make sure the insertion point is positioned below the section break and then return the left and right margins to 1 inch.
2. Delete the section break by completing the following steps:
   a. Click the Draft button in the view area on the Status bar.
   b. Position the insertion point on the section break.

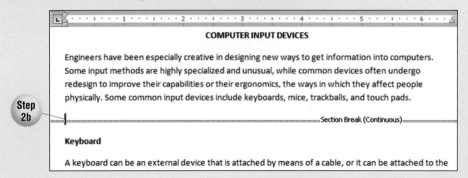

COMPUTER INPUT DEVICES

Engineers have been especially creative in designing new ways to get information into computers. Some input methods are highly specialized and unusual, while common devices often undergo redesign to improve their capabilities or their ergonomics, the ways in which they affect people physically. Some common input devices include keyboards, mice, trackballs, and touch pads.

Step 2b

———————————————— Section Break (Continuous) ————————————————

Keyboard

A keyboard can be an external device that is attached by means of a cable, or it can be attached to the

   c. Press the Delete key.
   d. Click the Print Layout button in the view area on the Status bar.
3. Move the insertion point to the beginning of the first paragraph of text in the document and then insert a continuous section break.
4. Format the text into columns by completing the following steps:
   a. Make sure the insertion point is positioned below the section break.
   b. Click the Page Layout tab.
   c. Click the Columns button in the Page Setup group.
   d. Click *Two* at the drop-down list.
5. Save **WordL1_C5_P1.docx**.

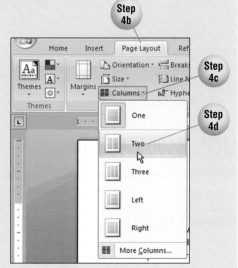

QUICK STEPS

Create Columns with Columns Dialog Box
1. Click Page Layout tab.
2. Click Columns button.
3. Click *More Columns* at the drop-down list.
4. Specify column options.
5. Click OK.

Creating Columns with the Columns Dialog Box

You can use the Columns dialog box to create newspaper columns that are equal or unequal in width. To display the Columns dialog box shown in Figure 5.2, click the Columns button in the Page Setup group of the Page Layout tab and then click *More Columns* at the drop-down list.

Figure 5.2 Columns Dialog Box

Choose the number of columns in this group or with this option.

Specify column width and spacing with options in this section.

Use this option to apply column formatting to the whole document or from the insertion point to the end of the document.

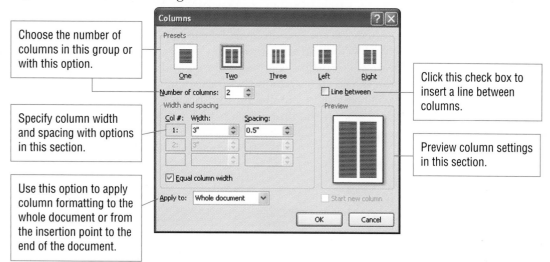

Click this check box to insert a line between columns.

Preview column settings in this section.

With options at the Columns dialog box you can specify the style and number of columns, enter your own column measurements, and create unequal columns. You can also insert a line between columns. By default, column formatting is applied to the whole document. With the *Apply to* option at the bottom of the Columns dialog box, you can change this from *Whole document* to *This point forward*. At the *This point forward* option, a section break is inserted and the column formatting is applied to text from the location of the insertion point to the end of the document or until other column formatting is encountered. The *Preview* section of the dialog box displays an example of how the columns will appear in your document.

Removing Column Formatting

To remove column formatting using the Columns button, position the insertion point in the section containing columns, click the Page Layout tab, click the Columns button, and then click *One* at the drop-down list. You can also remove column formatting at the Columns dialog box by selecting the *One* option in the *Presets* section.

Inserting a Column Break

When formatting text into columns, Word automatically breaks the columns to fit the page. At times, column breaks may appear in an undesirable location. You can insert a column break by positioning the insertion point where you want the column to end, clicking the Page Layout tab, clicking the Breaks button, and then clicking *Column* at the drop-down list.

HINT
You can also insert a column break with the keyboard shortcut, Ctrl + Shift + Enter.

1. With **WordL1_C5_P1.docx** open, delete the section break by completing the following steps:
   a. Click the Draft button in the view area on the Status bar.
   b. Position the insertion point on the section break and then press the Delete key.
   c. Click the Print Layout button in the view area on the Status bar.
2. Remove column formatting by clicking the Columns button in the Page Setup group in the Page Layout tab and then clicking *One* at the drop-down list.
3. Format text in columns by completing the following steps:
   a. Position the insertion point at the beginning of the first paragraph of text in the document.
   b. Click the Columns button in the Page Setup group and then click *More Columns* at the drop-down list.
   c. At the Columns dialog box, click *Two* in the *Presets* section.
   d. Click the down-pointing arrow at the right of the *Spacing* option box until 0.3" displays.
   e. Click the *Line between* check box to insert a check mark.
   f. Click the down-pointing arrow at the right side of the *Apply to* option box and then click *This point forward* at the drop-down list.
   g. Click OK to close the dialog box.
4. Insert a column break by completing the following steps:
   a. Position the insertion point at the beginning of the *Mouse* heading.
   b. Click the Breaks button in the Page Setup group and then click *Column* at the drop-down list.

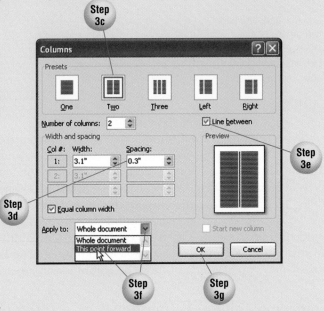

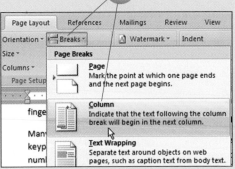

5. Save and then print **WordL1_C5_P1.docx**.

Balancing Columns on a Page

In a document containing text formatted into columns, Word automatically lines up (balances) the last line of text at the bottom of each column, except the last page. Text in the first column of the last page may flow to the end of the page, while the text in the second column may end far short of the end of the page. You can balance columns by inserting a continuous section break at the end of the text.

Project 1d Formatting and Balancing Columns of Text

1. With **WordL1_C5_P1.docx** open, delete the column break by completing the following steps:
   a. Position the insertion point at the beginning of the *Mouse* heading.
   b. Click the Draft button in the view area on the Status bar.
   c. Position the insertion point on the column break.

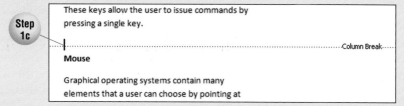

   d. Press the Delete key.
   e. Click the Print Layout button in the view area on the Status bar.
2. Select the entire document and then change the font to 12-point Constantia.
3. Move the insertion point to the end of the document and then balance the columns by clicking the Page Layout tab, clicking the Breaks button, and then clicking *Continuous* at the drop-down list.
4. Apply the Aqua, Accent 5, Lighter 60% paragraph shading to the title *COMPUTER INPUT DEVICES*.
5. Apply the Aqua, Accent 5, Lighter 80% paragraph shading to each of the headings in the document.
6. Insert page numbering that prints at the bottom of each page.
7. Save **WordL1_C5_P1.docx**.

Hyphenating Words

In some Word documents, especially documents with left and right margins wider than 1 inch, or text set in columns, the right margin may appear quite ragged. To improve the display of text lines by making line lengths more uniform, consider hyphenating long words that fall at the end of a text line. When using the hyphenation feature, you can tell Word to hyphenate words automatically in a document or you can manually insert hyphens.

Automatically Hyphenating Words

QUICK STEPS

Automatic Hyphenation
1. Click Page Layout tab.
2. Click Hyphenation button.
3. Click *Automatic* at drop-down list.

Manual Hyphenation
1. Click Page Layout tab.
2. Click Hyphenation button.
3. Click *Manual* at drop-down list.
4. Click Yes or No to hyphenate indicated words.
5. When complete, click OK.

To automatically hyphenate words in a document, click the Page Layout tab, click the Hyphenation button in the Page Setup group, and then click *Automatic* at the drop-down list. Scroll through the document and check to see if hyphens display in appropriate locations within the words. If, after hyphenating words in a document, you want to remove all hyphens, immediately click the Undo button on the Quick Access toolbar. This must be done immediately after hyphenating since the Undo feature undoes only the last function.

Manually Hyphenating Words

If you want to control where a hyphen appears in a word during hyphenation, choose manual hyphenation. To do this, click the Page Layout tab, click the Hyphenation button in the Page Setup group, and then click *Manual* at the drop-down list. This displays the Manual Hyphenation dialog box as shown in Figure 5.3. (The word in the *Hyphenate at* text box will vary.) At this dialog box, click Yes to hyphenate the word as indicated in the *Hyphenate at* text box; click No if you do not want the word hyphenated; or click Cancel to cancel hyphenation. You can also reposition the hyphen in the *Hyphenate at* text box. Word displays the word with syllable breaks indicated by a hyphen. The position where the word will be hyphenated displays as a blinking black bar. If you want to hyphenate at a different location in the word, position the blinking black bar where you want the hyphen and then click Yes. Continue clicking Yes or No at the Manual Hyphenation dialog box. Be careful with words ending in *-ed*. Several two-syllable words can be divided before that final syllable, for example, *noted*. However, one-syllable words ending in *-ed* should not be divided. An example is *served*. Watch for this type of occurrence and click No to cancel the hyphenation. At the hyphenation complete message, click OK.

HINT
Avoid dividing words at the ends of more than two consecutive lines.

bᵃ꞉ Hyphenation ▾

Figure 5.3 Manual Hyphenation Dialog Box

Click Yes to hyphenate the word at this location or move to a different syllable break and then click Yes.

Project 1e **Automatically and Manually Hyphenating Words**

1. With **WordL1_C5_P1.docx** open, hyphenate words automatically by completing the following steps:
   a. Press Ctrl + Home and then click the Page Layout tab.
   b. Click the Hyphenation button in the Page Setup group and then click *Automatic* at the drop-down list.

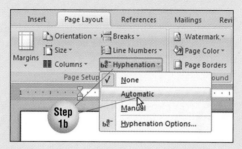

Step 1b

2. Scroll through the document and notice the automatic hyphenations.
3. Click the Undo button to remove the hyphens.
4. Manually hyphenate words by completing the following steps:
   a. Click the Hyphenation button in the Page Setup group and then click *Manual* at the drop-down list.

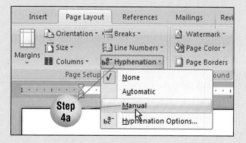

Step 4a

   b. At the Manual Hyphenation dialog box, make one of the following choices:
      • Click Yes to hyphenate the word as indicated in the *Hyphenate at* text box.
      • Move the hyphen in the word to a more desirable location, and then click Yes.
      • Click No if you do not want the word hyphenated.
   c. Continue clicking Yes or No at the Manual Hyphenation dialog box.
   d. At the hyphenation complete message, click OK.
5. Save **WordL1_C5_P1.docx**.

If you want to remove all hyphens in a document, immediately click the Undo button on the Quick Access toolbar. To delete a few, but not all, of the optional hyphens inserted during hyphenation, use the Find and Replace dialog box. To do this, you would display the Find and Replace dialog box with the Replace tab selected, insert an optional hyphen symbol in the *Find what* text box (to do this, click the More button, click the Special button and then click *Optional Hyphen* at the pop-up list), and make sure the *Replace with* text box is empty. Complete the find and replace, clicking the Replace button to replace the hyphen with nothing or clicking the Find Next button to leave the hyphen in the document.

Creating a Drop Cap

Create Drop Cap
1. Click Insert tab.
2. Click Drop Cap button.
3. Click desired type in drop-down list.

A≡ Drop Cap ▾

Use a drop cap to enhance the appearance of text. A drop cap is the first letter of the first word of a paragraph that is set into a paragraph, as shown below. Drop caps identify the beginning of major sections or parts of a document. Create a drop cap with the Drop Cap button in the Text group in the Insert tab. You can choose to set the drop cap in the paragraph or in the margin. At the Drop Cap dialog box, you can specify a font, the numbers of lines you want the letter to drop, and the distance you want the letter positioned from the text of the paragraph. You can drop cap the first word by selecting the word first and then clicking the Drop Cap button.

Drop caps look best when set in a paragraph containing text set in a proportional font. Here is an example of a drop cap.

Project ⑪ Inserting Drop Caps

1. With **WordL1_C5_P1.docx** open, create a drop cap by completing the following steps:
   a. Position the insertion point on the first word of the first paragraph of text (*Engineers*).
   b. Click the Insert tab.
   c. Click the Drop Cap button in the Text group.
   d. Click *In margin* at the drop-down gallery.
2. Looking at the drop cap, you decide that you do not like it in the margin and want it to be a little smaller. To change the drop cap, complete the following steps:
   a. With the E in the word *Engineers* selected, click the Drop Cap button in the Text group and then click *None* at the drop-down gallery.
   b. Click the Drop Cap button and then click *Drop Cap Options* at the drop-down gallery.
   c. At the Drop Cap dialog box, click *Dropped* in the *Position* section.
   d. Change the font to Times New Roman.
   e. Change the *Lines to drop* option to *2*.
   f. Click OK to close the dialog box.
   g. Click outside the drop cap to deselect it.
3. Save **WordL1_C5_P1.docx**.

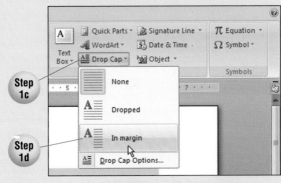

Step 1c

Step 1d

Step 2c

Step 2d

Step 2e

Step 2f

Inserting Symbols and Special Characters

You can use the Symbol button in the Insert tab to insert special symbols in a document. Click the Symbol button in the Symbols group in the Insert tab and a drop-down list displays with the most recently inserted symbols along with a *More Symbols* option. Click one of the symbols that displays in the list to insert it in the document or click the *More Symbols* option to display the Symbol dialog box as shown in Figure 5.4. At the Symbol dialog box, double-click the desired symbol, and then click Close; or click the desired symbol, click the Insert button, and then click Close.

QUICK STEPS

Insert a Symbol
1. Click Insert tab.
2. Click Symbol button.
3. Click desired symbol in drop-down list.
OR
1. Click Insert tab.
2. Click Symbol button.
3. Click *More Symbols*.
4. Double-click desired symbol.
5. Click Close.

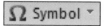
Ω Symbol ▾

Figure 5.4 Symbol Dialog Box with Symbols Tab Selected

Use the *Font* option to select the desired set of characters.

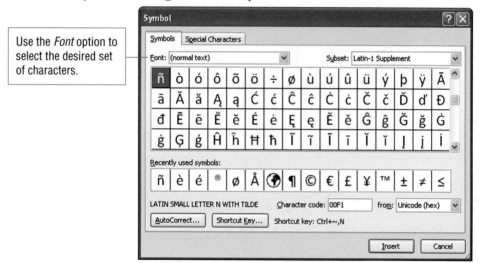

At the Symbol dialog box with the Symbols tab selected, you can change the font with the *Font* option. When you change the font, different symbols display in the dialog box. Click the Special Characters tab at the Symbol dialog box and a list of special characters displays along with keyboard shortcuts to create the special character.

Project 1g   Inserting Symbols and Special Characters

1. With **WordL1_C5_P1.docx** open, press Ctrl + End to move the insertion point to the end of the document.
2. Press the Enter key once, type Prepared by:, and then press the spacebar once.
3. Type the first name Matthew.
4. Insert the last name *Viña* by completing the following steps:
   a. Type Vi.
   b. Click the Symbol button in the Symbols group in the Insert tab.
   c. Click *More Symbols* at the drop-down list.

d. At the Symbol dialog box, make sure the *Font* option displays as *(normal text)* and then double-click the ñ symbol (first symbol from the left in the twelfth row).

e. Click the Close button.

f. Type a.

5. Press Shift + Enter.

6. Insert the keyboard symbol (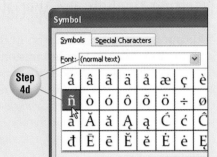) by completing the following steps:

a. Click the Symbol button and then click *More Symbols*.

b. At the Symbol dialog box, click the down-pointing arrow at the right side of the *Font* option and then click *Wingdings* at the drop-down list. (You will need to scroll down the list to display this option.)

c. Double-click 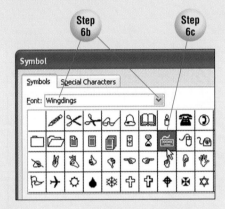 (eighth symbol from the left in the second row).

d. Click the Close button.

7. Type SoftCell Technologies.

8. Insert the registered trademark symbol (®) by completing the following steps:

a. Click the Symbol button and then click *More Symbols*.

b. At the Symbol dialog box, click the Special Characters tab.

c. Double-click the ® symbol (tenth option from the top).

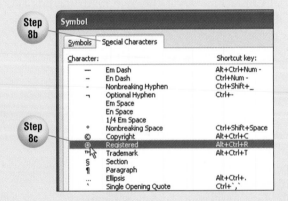

d. Click the Close button.

e. Press Shift + Enter.

9. Select the keyboard symbol (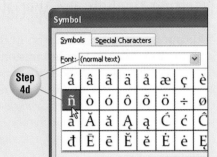) and then change the font size to 18.

10. Save **WordL1_C5_P1.docx**.

Inserting the Date and Time

Use the Date & Time button in the Text group in the Insert tab to insert the current date and time in a document. Click this button and the Date and Time dialog box displays as shown in Figure 5.5 (your date will vary from what you see in the figure). At the Date and Time dialog box, click the desired date and/or time format in the *Available formats* list box.

QUICK STEPS

Insert Date and Time
1. Click Insert tab.
2. Click Date and Time button.
3. Click option in list box.
4. Click OK.

Figure 5.5 Date and Time Dialog Box

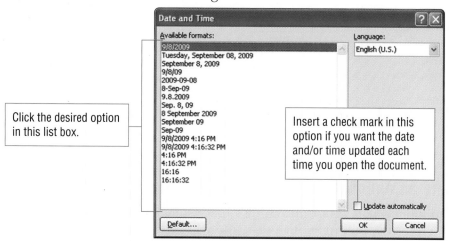

Click the desired option in this list box.

Insert a check mark in this option if you want the date and/or time updated each time you open the document.

If the *Update automatically* check box does not contain a check mark, the date and/or time are inserted in the document as normal text that you can edit in the normal manner. You can also insert the date and/or time as a field. The advantage to inserting the date or time as a field is that the field can be updated with the Update Field keyboard shortcut, F9. Insert a check mark in the *Update automatically* check box to insert the data and/or time as a field. You can also insert the date as a field using the keyboard shortcut Alt + Shift + D, and insert the time as a field with the keyboard shortcut Alt + Shift + T.

Project 1h   Inserting the Date and Time

1. With **WordL1_C5_P1.docx** open, press Ctrl + End and make sure the insertion point is positioned below the company name.
2. Insert the current date by completing the following steps:
   a. Click the Date & Time button in the Text group in the Insert tab.

b. At the Date and Time dialog box, click the third option from the top in the *Available formats* group.

c. Click in the *Update automatically* check box to insert a check mark.

d. Click OK to close the dialog box.

3. Press Shift + Enter.

4. Insert the current time by pressing Alt + Shift + T.

5. Save **WordL1_C5_P1.docx**.

6. Update the time by clicking the time and then pressing F9.

7. Save, print, and then close **WordL1_C5_P1.docx**.

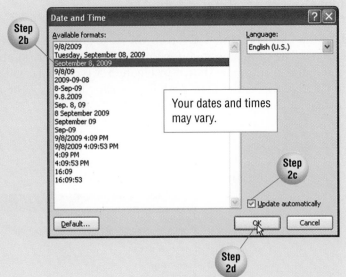

Step 2b

Step 2c

Step 2d

Your dates and times may vary.

Project 2 Create an Announcement about Supervisory Training

You will create an announcement about upcoming supervisory training and use the click and type feature to center and right align text. You will vertically center the text on the page and insert and format a picture to add visual appeal to the announcement.

Using the Click and Type Feature

QUICK STEPS

Use Click and Type
1. Hover mouse at left margin, between left and right margin, or at right margin.
2. Double-click left mouse button.

Word contains a click and type feature you can use to position the insertion point at a specific location and alignment in the document. This feature allows you to position one or more lines of text as you write (type), rather than typing the text and then selecting and reformatting the text, which requires multiple steps.

To use click and type, make sure the document displays in Print Layout view and then hover the mouse pointer at the location where you want the insertion point positioned. As you move the mouse pointer, you will notice that the pointer displays with varying horizontal lines representing the alignment. Double-click the mouse button and the insertion point is positioned at the location of the mouse pointer. Turn off the click and type feature by clicking the Office button and then clicking Word Options. Click the Advanced option in the left panel, click the *Enable click and type* check box to remove the check mark, and then click OK.

If the horizontal lines do not display next to the mouse pointer when you double-click the mouse button, a left tab is set at the position of the insertion point. If you want to change the alignment and not set a tab, make sure the horizontal lines display near the mouse pointer before double-clicking the mouse.

Project 2a Using Click and Type

1. At a blank document, create the centered text shown in Figure 5.6 by completing the following steps:
   a. Position the I-beam pointer between the left and right margins at about the 3.25-inch mark on the horizontal ruler and the top of the vertical ruler.
   b. When the center alignment lines display below the I-beam pointer, double-click the left mouse button.

Step 1b

   c. Type the centered text shown in Figure 5.6. Press Shift + Enter to end each text line.
2. Change to right alignment by completing the following steps:
   a. Position the I-beam pointer near the right margin at approximately the 1.5-inch mark on the vertical ruler until the right alignment lines display at the left side of the I-beam pointer.
   b. Double-click the left mouse button.
   c. Type the right-aligned text shown in Figure 5.6. Press Shift + Enter to end the text line.
3. Select the centered text and then change the font to 14-point Candara bold and the line spacing to double.
4. Select the right-aligned text, change the font to 10-point Candara bold, and then deselect the text.
5. Save the document and name it **WordL1_C5_P2**.

Figure 5.6 Project 2a

SUPERVISORY TRAINING
Maximizing Employee Potential
Wednesday, February 10, 2010
Training Center
9:00 a.m. to 3:30 p.m.

Sponsored by
Cell Systems

Vertically Aligning Text

Text in a Word document is aligned at the top of the page by default. You can change this alignment with the *Vertical alignment* option at the Page Setup dialog box with the Layout tab selected as shown in Figure 5.7. Display this dialog box by clicking the Page Layout tab, clicking the Page Setup group dialog box launcher, and then clicking the Layout tab at the Page Setup dialog box.

Figure 5.7 Page Setup Dialog Box with Layout Tab Selected

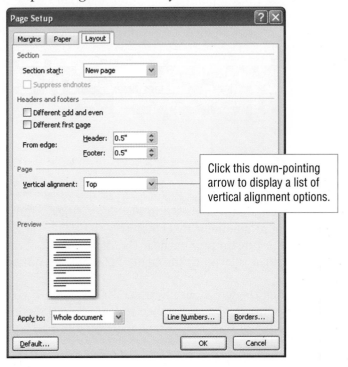

Click this down-pointing arrow to display a list of vertical alignment options.

Vertically Align Text
1. Click Page Layout tab.
2. Click Page Setup dialog box launcher.
3. Click Layout tab.
4. Click desired alignment.
5. Click OK.

The *Vertical alignment* option from the Page Setup dialog box contains four choices—*Top*, *Center*, *Justified*, and *Bottom*. The default setting is *Top*, which aligns text at the top of the page. Choose *Center* if you want text centered vertically on the page. The *Justified* option will align text between the top and the bottom margins. The *Center* option positions text in the middle of the page vertically, while the *Justified* option adds space between paragraphs of text (not within) to fill the page from the top to bottom margins. If you center or justify text, the text does not display centered or justified on the screen in the Draft view, but it does display centered or justified in the Print Layout view. Choose the *Bottom* option to align text in the document vertically along the bottom of the page.

1. With **WordL1_C5_P2.docx** open, click the Page Layout tab and then click the Page Setup group dialog box launcher.
2. At the Page Setup dialog box, click the Layout tab.
3. Click the down-pointing arrow at the right side of the *Vertical alignment* option box and then click *Center* at the drop-down list.
4. Click OK to close the dialog box.
5. Save and then print **WordL1_C5_P2.docx**.

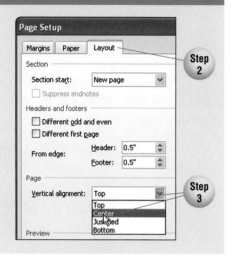

Inserting an Image

You can insert an image such as a picture or clip art in a Word document with buttons in the Illustrations group in the Insert tab. Click the Picture button to display the Insert Picture dialog box where you can specify the desired picture file or click the Clip Art button and then choose from a variety of images available at the Clip Art task pane. When you insert a picture or a clip art image in a document, the Picture Tools Format Tab displays as shown in Figure 5.8.

Figure 5.8 Picture Tools Format Tab

Customizing and Formatting an Image

With options in the Adjust group in the Picture Tools Format tab you can recolor the picture or clip art image and change the brightness and contrast of the image. You can also reset the picture or clip art back to its original color or change to a different image. Use the Compress Pictures button to compress the size of the image file. Word provides predesigned styles you can apply to your image. These styles are available in the Picture Styles group along with buttons for changing the image border and applying effects to the image. Use options in the Arrange group to position the image on the page, specify text wrapping in relation to the image, align the image with other objects in the document, and rotate the image. Use the Crop button in the Size group to remove any unnecessary parts of the image and specify the image size with the *Shape Height* and *Shape Width* measurement boxes.

Sizing an Image

You can change the size of an image with the *Shape Height* and *Shape Width* measurement boxes in the Size group in the Picture Tools Format tab or with the sizing handles that display around the selected image. To change size with a sizing handle, position the mouse pointer on a sizing handle until the pointer turns into a double-headed arrow and then hold down the left mouse button. Drag the sizing handle in or out to decrease or increase the size of the image and then release the mouse button. Use the middle sizing handles at the left or right side of the image to make the image wider or thinner. Use the middle sizing handles at the top or bottom of the image to make the image taller or shorter. Use the sizing handles at the corners of the image to change both the width and height at the same time.

Moving an Image

Move an image to a specific location on the page with options from the Position button drop-down gallery. The Position button is located in the Arrange group in the Picture Tools Format tab. When you choose an option at the Position button drop-down gallery, the image is moved to the specified location on the page and square text wrapping is applied to the image.

You can also move the image by dragging it to the desired location. Before dragging an image, you must first choose a text wrapping style by clicking the Text Wrapping button in the Arrange group and then clicking the desired wrapping style at the drop-down list. After choosing a wrapping style, move the image by positioning the mouse pointer on the image border until the arrow pointer turns into a four-headed arrow. Hold down the left mouse button, drag the image to the desired position, and then release the mouse button. To help precisely position an image, consider turning on gridlines. Do this by clicking the Align button in the Arrange group in the Picture Tools Format tab and then clicking *Show Gridlines*.

Rotate the image by positioning the mouse pointer on the green, round rotation handle until the pointer displays as a circular arrow. Hold down the left mouse button, drag in the desired direction, and then release the mouse button.

Inserting a Picture

Insert Picture
1. Click Insert tab.
2. Click Picture button.
3. Double-click desired picture in Insert Picture dialog box.

To insert a picture in a document, click the Insert tab and then click the Picture button in the Illustrations group. At the Insert Picture dialog box, navigate to the folder containing the desired picture and then double-click the picture. Use buttons in the Picture Tools Format tab to format and customize the picture. You can insert a picture from a Web page by opening the Web page, opening a Word document, and then dragging the picture from the Web page to the document. If the picture is linked, the link (rather than the image) will display in your document.

Project 2c Inserting and Customizing a Picture

1. With **WordL1_C5_P2.docx** open, return the vertical alignment back to *Top* by completing the following steps:
   a. Click the Page Layout tab.
   b. Click the Page Setup group dialog box launcher.
   c. At the Page Setup dialog box, click the Layout tab.
   d. Click the down-pointing arrow at the right side of the *Vertical alignment* option box and then click *Top* at the drop-down list.
   e. Click OK to close the dialog box.
2. Select and then delete the text *Sponsored by* and the text *Cell Systems*.
3. Select the remaining text and change the line spacing to single.
4. Move the insertion point to the beginning of the document and then press the Enter key until the first line of text displays at approximately the 3-inch mark on the vertical ruler.
5. Insert a picture by completing the following steps:
   a. Click the Insert tab.
   b. Click the Picture button in the Illustrations group.
   c. At the Insert Picture dialog box, navigate to your Word2007L1C5 folder.
   d. Double-click *Mountain.jpg* in the list box.
6. Crop the picture by completing the following steps:
   a. Click the Crop button in the Size group.
   b. Position the mouse pointer on the bottom, middle crop handle (displays as a short black line) until the pointer turns into the crop tool (displays as a small, black T).
   c. Hold down the left mouse button, drag up to just below the mountain as shown at the right, and then release the mouse button.
   d. Click the Crop button in the Size group to turn off the feature.

Step 6c

Maximizing Employee

7. Increase the size of the picture by clicking in the *Shape Width* measurement box, typing 5, and then pressing Enter.
8. Move the picture behind the text by clicking the Text Wrapping button in the Arrange group and then clicking *Behind Text* at the drop-down list.

Step 8

9. Rotate the image by clicking the Rotate button in the Arrange group and then clicking *Flip Horizontal* at the drop-down list.

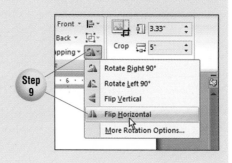

Step 9

10. Change the picture color by clicking the Recolor button in the Adjust group and then clicking the second option from the left in the Light Variations section (*Accent color 1 Light*).
11. After looking at the coloring you decide to return to the original color by clicking the Recolor button in the Adjust group and then clicking the option in the *No Recolor* section.
12. Click the Brightness button in the Adjust group and then click *+10%* at the drop-down gallery.
13. Click the Contrast button in the Adjust group and then click *-10%* at the drop-down gallery.
14. Apply a picture style by clicking the More button at the right side of the picture styles and then clicking *Soft Edge Rectangle* (first image from the left in the second row).

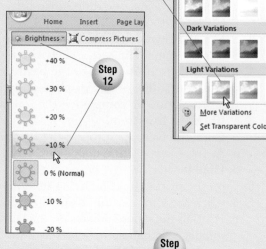

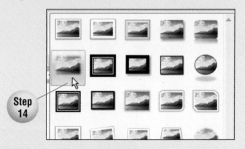

15. Compress the picture by completing the following steps:
    a. Click the Compress Pictures button in the Adjust group.
    b. At the Compress Pictures dialog box, click the *Apply to selected pictures only* check box to insert a check mark.
    c. Click OK.

16. Position the mouse pointer on the border of the selected picture until the pointer turns into a four-headed arrow and then drag the picture so it is positioned behind the text.
17. Click outside the picture to deselect it.
18. Save, print, and then close **WordL1_C5_P2.docx**.

 **roject 3 Customize a Report on Robots**

You will open a report on robots and then add visual appeal to the report by inserting and formatting a clip art image and a built-in text box.

Inserting a Clip Art Image

Microsoft Office includes a gallery of media images you can insert in a document such as clip art, photographs, and movie images, as well as sound clips. To insert an image in a Word document, click the Insert tab and then click the Clip Art button in the Illustrations group. This displays the Clip Art task pane at the right side of the screen as shown in Figure 5.9.

Figure 5.9 Clip Art Task Pane

Type the search word or topic in this text box.

Use this option to specify where to search.

Use this option to specify the type of files for which you are searching.

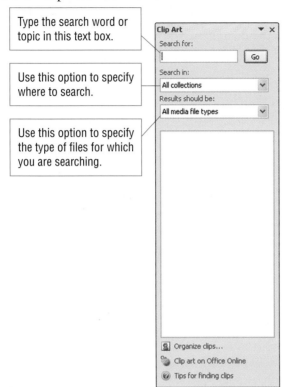

To view all picture, sound, and motion files, make sure the *Search for* text box in the Clip Art task pane does not contain any text and then click the Go button. When the desired image is visible, click the image to insert it in the document. Use buttons in the Picture Tools Format tab shown in Figure 5.8 to format and customize the clip art image.

By default (unless it has been customized), the Clip Art task pane looks for all media images and sound clips found in all locations. You can narrow the search to specific locations and to specific images. The *Search in* option at the Clip Art task pane has a default setting of *All collections*. This can be changed to *My Collections*, *Office Collections*, and *Web Collections*. The *Results should be* option has a default setting of *All media file types*. Click the down-pointing arrow at the right side of this option to display media types. To search for a specific media type, remove the check mark before all options at the drop-down list but the desired type. For example, if you are searching only for photograph images, remove the check mark before Clip Art, Movies, and Sounds.

If you are searching for specific images, click in the *Search for* text box, type the desired topic, and then click the Go button. For example, if you want to find images related to business, click in the *Search for* text box, type business, and then click the Go button. Clip art images related to *business* display in the viewing area of the task pane. If you are connected to the Internet, Word will search for images at the Office Online Web site matching the topic.

QUICK STEPS

Insert Clip Art Image
1. Click Insert tab.
2. Click Clip Art button.
3. Type search word or topic.
4. Press Enter.
5. Click desired image.

HINT
You can drag a clip art image from the Clip Art task pane to your document.

1. Open **WordReport07.docx** and then save the document and name it **WordL1_C5_P3**.
2. Apply the Heading 1 style to the title *ROBOTS AS ANDROIDS* and apply the Heading 2 style to the headings in the document.
3. Change the Quick Styles set to *Modern*. **Hint: Do this with the Change Styles button in the Styles group in the Home tab.**
4. Insert a clip art image by completing the following steps:
   a. Move the insertion point so it is positioned at the beginning of the first paragraph of text (the sentence that begins *Robotic factories are increasingly . . .*).
   b. Click the Insert tab.
   c. Click the Clip Art button in the Illustrations group.
   d. At the Clip Art task pane, select any text that displays in the *Search for* text box, type computer, and then press Enter.
   e. Click the computer image in the list box as shown at the right.
   f. Close the Clip Art task pane by clicking the Close button (contains an X) located in the upper right corner of the task pane.

Step 4d

Step 4e

5. Crop the clip art image by completing the following steps:
   a. Click the Crop button in the Size group.
   b. Position the mouse pointer on the top middle crop handle (displays as a short black line) until the pointer turns into the crop tool.
   c. Hold down the left mouse button, drag down to just above the top of the computer as shown at the right, and then release the mouse button.
   d. Click the Crop button in the Size group to turn off the feature.
6. Decrease the size of the picture by clicking in the *Shape Height* measurement box, typing 1.3, and then pressing Enter.
7. Change the text wrapping by clicking the Text Wrapping button in the Arrange group and then clicking *Square* at the drop-down list.
8. Rotate the image by clicking the Rotate button in the Arrange group and then clicking *Flip Horizontal* at the drop-down list.
9. Change the picture color by clicking the Recolor button in the Adjust group and then clicking the second option from the left in the Light Variations section (*Accent color 1 Light*).

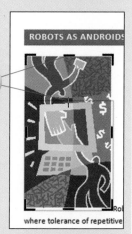

Step 5c

ROBOTS AS ANDROID

where tolerance of repetitive

10. Click the Picture Effects button in the Picture Styles group, point to *Shadow*, and then click the *Offset Diagonal Bottom Left* option (last option in the top row of the *Outer* section).
11. Position the mouse pointer on the border of the selected picture until the pointer turns into a four-headed arrow and then drag the picture so it is positioned as shown at the right.
12. Click outside the clip art image to deselect it.
13. Save **WordL1_C5_P3.docx**.

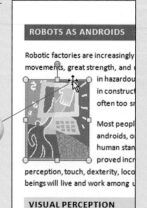

Step 11

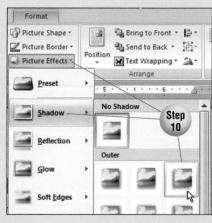

Step 10

Inserting and Customizing a Pull Quote

Use a pull quote in a document such as an article to attract attention. A pull quote is a quote from an article that is "pulled out" and enlarged and positioned in an attractive location on the page. Some advantages of pull quotes are that they reinforce important concepts, summarize your message, and break up text blocks to make them easier to read. If you use multiple pull quotes in a document, keep them in order to ensure clear comprehension for readers.

You can insert a pull quote in a document with a predesigned built-in text box. Display the available pull quote built-in text boxes by clicking the Insert tab and then clicking the Text Box button in the Text group. Click the desired pull quote from the drop-down list that displays and the built-in text box is inserted in the document. Type the quote inside the text box and then format the text and/or customize the text box. Use buttons in the Text Box Tools Format tab shown in Figure 5.10 to format and customize the built-in text box.

Inserting Pull Quote
1. Click Insert tab.
2. Click Text Box button.
3. Click desired pull quote.

Figure 5.10 Text Box Tools Format Tab

With options in the Text group in the Text Box Tools Format tab, you can draw a text box, change text direction in a text box, and link text boxes. Apply predesigned styles to a text box with options in the Text Box Styles group. You can also change the shape, shape fill, and shape outline. Add and customize shadows and 3-D effects with options in the Shadow Effects and 3-D Effects groups. Use options in the Arrange group to position the text box on the page, specify text wrapping in relation to the text box, align the text box with other objects in the document, and rotate the text box. Specify the image size with the *Shape Height* and *Shape Width* measurement boxes in the Size group.

Project 3b Inserting a Built-in Text Box

1. With **WordL1_C5_P3.docx** open, click the Insert tab.
2. Click the Text Box button in the Text group.
3. Scroll down the drop-down list and then click the *Contrast Quote* option.

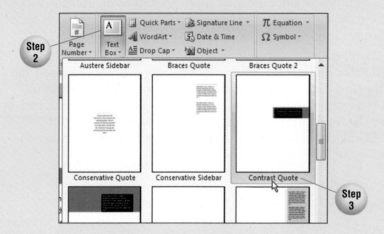

Step 2

Step 3

4. Type the following text in the text box: "The task of creating a humanlike body has proved incredibly difficult."
5. Click the More button at the right side of the Text Box Styles group.

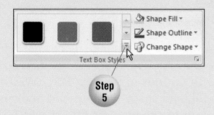

Step 5

6. Click the blue *Diagonal Gradient - Accent 1* option at the drop-down gallery (second option from the left in the sixth row).
7. Click the Shadow Effects button in the Shadow Effects group and then click the *Shadow Style 5* option in the *Drop Shadow* section (first option from the left in the second row).

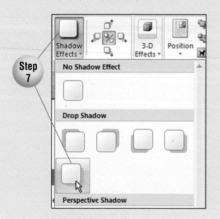

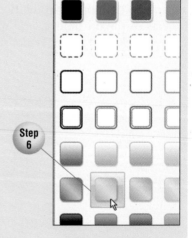

Step 7

Step 6

8. Position the mouse pointer on the border of the selected text box until the pointer turns into a four-headed arrow and then drag the text box so it is positioned as shown below.

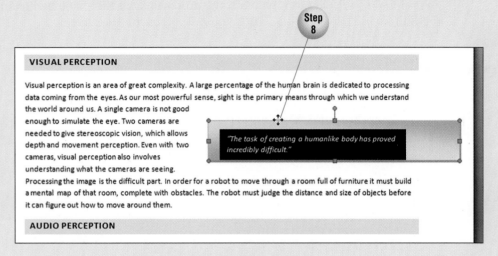

9. Save, print, and then close **WordL1_C5_P3.docx**.

Project ④ Prepare a Company Flyer

You will prepare a company flyer by inserting and customizing shapes, text boxes, and WordArt.

Drawing Shapes

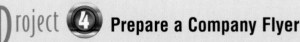

Use the Shapes button in the Insert tab to draw shapes in a document including lines, basic shapes, block arrows, flow chart shapes, callouts, stars, and banners. Click a shape and the mouse pointer displays as crosshairs (plus sign). Position the crosshairs where you want the shape to begin, hold down the left mouse button, drag to create the shape, and then release the mouse button. This inserts the shape in the document and also displays the Drawing Tools Format tab shown in Figure 5.11. Use buttons in this tab to change the shape, apply a style to the shape, arrange the shape, and change the size of the shape. This tab contains many of the same options and buttons as the Picture Tools Format tab and the Text Box Tools Format tab.

Draw a Shape
1. Click Insert tab.
2. Click Shapes button.
3. Click desired shape at drop-down list.
4. Drag in document screen to create shape.

Figure 5.11 Drawing Tools Format Tab

If you choose a shape in the *Lines* section of the drop-down list, the shape you draw is considered a **line drawing**. If you choose an option in the other sections of the drop-down list, the shape you draw is considered an **enclosed object**. When drawing an enclosed object, you can maintain the proportions of the shape by holding down the Shift key while dragging with the mouse to create the shape.

Copying Shapes

To copy a shape, select the shape and then click the Copy button in the Clipboard group in the Home tab. Position the insertion point at the location where you want the copied image and then click the Paste button. You can also copy a selected shape by holding down the Ctrl key while dragging the shape to the desired location.

Project 4a Drawing Arrow Shapes

1. At a blank document, press the Enter key twice and then draw an arrow shape by completing the following steps:
   a. Click the Insert tab.
   b. Click the Shapes button in the Illustrations group and then click the *Striped Right Arrow* shape in the *Block Arrows* section.

Step 1b

   c. Position the mouse pointer (displays as crosshairs) in the document at approximately the 1-inch mark on the horizontal ruler and the 0.5-inch mark on the vertical ruler.
   d. Hold down the Shift key and the left mouse button, drag to the right until the tip of the arrow is positioned at approximately the 5.5-inch mark on the horizontal ruler, and then release the mouse button and the Shift key.
2. Format the arrow by completing the following steps:
   a. Click in the *Shape Height* measurement box in the Size group, type 2.4, and then press Enter.
   b. Click in the *Shape Width* measurement box in the Size group, type 4.5, and then press Enter.

c. Click the More button at the right side of the Shape Styles group and then click the green *Linear Up Gradient - Accent 3* option at the drop-down gallery (fourth option from the left in the fifth row).

d. Click the 3-D Effects button in the 3-D Effects group and then click *3-D Style 6* in the *Perspective* section.

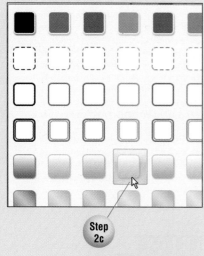

Step 2c

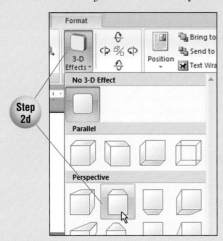

Step 2d

e. Click the 3-D Effects button, point to *3-D Color*, and then click the *Olive Green, Accent 3, Darker 50%* color.

3. Copy the arrow by completing the following steps:

a. With the insertion point positioned in the arrow (mouse pointer displays with four-headed arrow attached), hold down the Ctrl key.

b. Drag down until the outline of the copied arrow displays just below the top arrow, release the mouse button, and then release the Ctrl key.

c. Copy the arrow again by holding down the Ctrl key and then dragging the outline of the copied arrow just below the second arrow.

4. Flip the middle arrow by completing the following steps:

a. Click the middle arrow to select it.

b. Click the Rotate button in the Arrange group and then click *Flip Horizontal* at the drop-down gallery.

5. Insert text in the top arrow by completing the following steps:

a. Click the top arrow.

b. Click the Edit Text button in the Insert Shapes group in the Drawing Tools Format tab.

c. Click the Home tab.

d. Change the font size to 16, turn on bold, and then change the font color to Olive Green, Accent 3, Darker 50%.

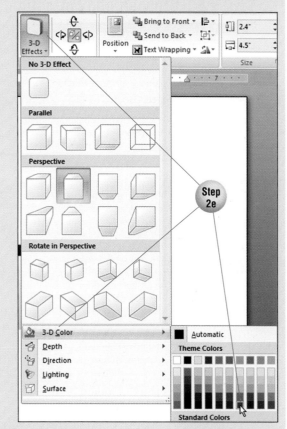

Step 2e

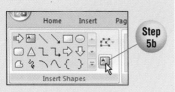

Step 5b

e. Click the Center button in the Paragraph group.
f. Type Financial.
g. Click the Text Box Tools Format tab.
h. Click the Text Direction button in the Text group.

6. Complete steps similar to those in Step 5 to insert the word *Direction* in the middle arrow. (Click twice on the Text Direction button to insert *Direction* in the tip of the arrow.)

7. Complete steps similar to those in Step 5 to insert the word *Retirement* in the bottom arrow.

8. Save the document and name it **WordL1_C5_P4**.

9. Print the document.

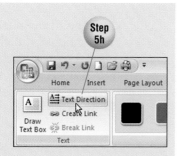

Step
5h

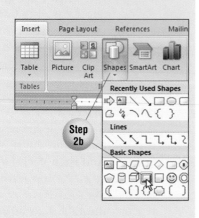

QUICK STEPS

Drawing and Formatting a Text Box

Draw a Text Box
1. Click Insert tab.
2. Click Text Box button in Text group.
3. Click *Draw Text Box.*
4. Drag in document screen to create box.

You can use the built-in text boxes provided by Word or you can draw your own text box. To draw a text box, click the Insert tab, click the Text Box button in the Text group, and then click *Draw Text Box* at the drop-down list. The mouse pointer displays as crosshairs. Position the crosshairs in the document and then drag to create the text box. When a text box is selected, the Text Box Tools Format tab displays as shown in Figure 5.11. Use buttons in this tab to format text boxes in the same manner as formatting built-in text boxes.

Project ❹b   Inserting a Text Box in a Shape

1. With **WordL1_C5_P4.docx** open, delete the bottom arrow by completing the following steps:
   a. Click the bottom arrow. (This displays a border around the arrow.)
   b. Position the mouse pointer on the border (displays with four-headed arrow attached) and then click the left mouse button.
   c. Press the Delete key.

2. Insert a shape below the two arrows by completing the following steps:
   a. Click the Insert tab.
   b. Click the Shapes button in the Illustrations group and then click the *Bevel* shape in the *Basic Shapes* section.
   c. Scroll down the document to display the blank space below the bottom arrow.
   d. Position the mouse pointer (displays as crosshairs) in the document at approximately the 1-inch mark on the horizontal ruler and the 6.5-inch mark on the vertical ruler and then click the left mouse button. (This inserts a bevel shape in the document.)

Step
2b

3. Format the shape by completing the following steps:
   a. Click in the *Shape Height* measurement box in the Size group, type 1.7, and then press Enter.
   b. Click in the *Shape Width* measurement box in the Size group, type 4.5, and then press Enter.
   c. Click the More button at the right side of the Shape Styles group and then click the *Linear Up Gradient - Accent 3* option at the drop-down gallery (fourth option from the left in the fifth row).
   d. Click the Shape Outline button arrow in the Shape Styles group and then click the *Olive Green, Accent 3, Darker 50%* color at the drop-down gallery.

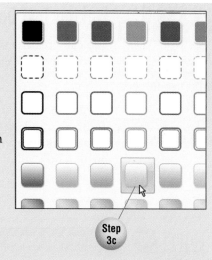

Step 3c

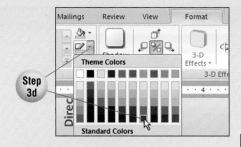

Step 3d

4. Insert a text box inside the shape by completing the following steps:
   a. Click the Insert tab.
   b. Click the Text Box button in the Text group and then click *Draw Text Box* at the drop-down list.
   c. Click inside the bevel shape.

Step 4c

5. Format the text box by completing the following steps:
   a. Click in the *Shape Width* measurement box in the Size group, type 3.5, and then press Enter.
   b. Drag the text box so it is centered inside the bevel shape.
   c. Click the Shape Fill button arrow in the Text Box Styles group and then click *No Fill* at the drop-down gallery.
   d. Click the Shape Outline button arrow in the Text Box Styles group and then click *No Outline* at the drop-down gallery.

6. Insert text inside the text box by completing the following steps:
   a. With the text box selected, click the Home tab.
   b. Change the font size to 24 points, turn on bold, and change the font color to Olive Green, Accent 3, Darker 50%.
   c. Click the Center button in the Paragraph group.
   d. Change the line spacing to 1.
   e. Type Retirement Financial Consulting. (Your shape and text box should appear as shown at the right.)

Step 6e

7. Save and then print **WordL1_C5_P4.docx**.

Linking Text Boxes

You can create several text boxes and then have text flow from one text box to another by linking the text boxes. To do this, draw the desired text boxes and then select the first text box you want in the link. Click the Create Link button in the Text group in the Text Box Tools Format tab and the mouse pointer displays with a link image attached. Click an empty text box to link it with the selected text box. To break a link between two boxes, select the first text box in the link, click the Break Link button in the Text group, and then click the linked text box. When you break a link, all of the text is placed in the selected text box.

Project ④C Linking Text Boxes

1. With **WordL1_C5_P4.docx** open, delete the text in the arrow shapes by completing the following steps:
   a. Click *Financial* located in the top arrow.
   b. Drag through *Financial* to select it. (You will need to drag down to select the word since the word displays vertically rather than horizontally.)
   c. Press the Delete key.
   d. Click *Direction* in the bottom arrow.
   e. Select *Direction* and then press the Delete key.
2. Draw a text box inside the top arrow by completing the following steps:
   a. Click the Insert tab.
   b. Click the Text Box button in the Text group and then click *Draw Text Box* at the drop-down list.
   c. Draw a text box inside the top arrow.

Step
1b

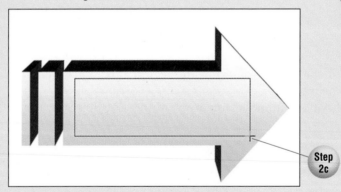

Step
2c

3. Format the text box by completing the following steps:
   a. Change the height measurement to *1"* and the width measurement to *3"*.
   b. Click the Shape Fill button arrow and then click *No Fill*.
   c. Click the Shape Outline button arrow and then click *No Outline*.
   d. Make sure the text box is centered in the arrow.
4. Copy the text box to the bottom arrow.
5. Click the text box in the top arrow to select it.

6. Link the top text box with the text box in the second arrow by clicking the Create Link button in the Text group and then clicking the text box in the second arrow.

7. With the top text box selected, make the following changes:
   a. Click the Home tab.
   b. Change the font size to 16 points, the font color to Olive Green, Accent 3, Darker 50%, and turn on bold.
   c. Change the line spacing to single.
   d. Click the Center button in the Paragraph group.
   e. Type Miller-Callahan Financial Services can help you plan for retirement and provide you with information to determine your financial direction. (The text will flow to the text box in the bottom arrow.)

8. Save **WordL1_C5_P4.docx**.

Selecting Objects

When a document contains a number of objects you may need to select multiple objects and then perform tasks such as formatting, moving, or aligning the objects. To select multiple objects, click the Select button in the Editing group in the Home tab and then click *Select Objects* at the drop-down list. Using the mouse, draw a border around the objects you want to select. When you click *Select Objects* at the drop-down list, the option in the drop-down list becomes active and the mouse arrow at the left side of the option displays with an orange background. To turn off object selecting, click the Select button and then click *Select Objects*. (This removes the orange background from the mouse arrow at the left side of the option.)

QUICK STEPS

Select Objects
1. Click Select button.
2. Click *Select Objects*.
3. Draw border around objects to select.

Project **4d** **Selecting, Moving, and Aligning Objects**

1. With **WordL1_C5_P4.docx** open, select the beveled shape and text box inside the shape by completing the following steps:
   a. Click the Zoom Out button located at the left side of the Zoom slider bar until *60%* displays at the left side of the button.

   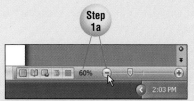

   Step 1a

   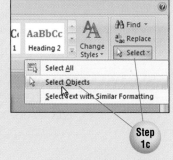

   Step 1c

   b. Click the Home tab.
   c. Click the Select button in the Editing group and then click *Select Objects* at the drop-down list.
   d. Using the mouse, draw a border around the bevel shape. (When you release the mouse button, the shape is selected as well as the text box inside the shape.)

   Retirement Financial Consulting

   Step 1d

e. Position the mouse pointer on the border of the selected shape until the pointer displays as a four-headed arrow and then drag the shape down so the bottom of the shape is positioned at approximately the 8.5-inch mark on the vertical ruler.

f. Click outside the selected objects.

2. Select and move the arrows by completing the following steps:

a. Using the mouse, draw a border around the two arrows. (When you release the mouse button the arrows are selected as well as the text boxes in the arrows.)

b. Drag the arrows down so they are positioned just above the bevel shape.

c. Click outside the selected objects.

3. Select and then align all of the objects by completing the following steps:

a. Using the mouse, draw a border around the two arrows and the bevel shape.

b. Click the Drawing Tools Format tab.

c. Click the Align button in the Arrange group and then click *Align Center* at the drop-down list.

d. Click outside the selected objects.

e. Turn off object selecting by clicking the Select button in the Editing group and then clicking *Select Objects* at the drop-down list.

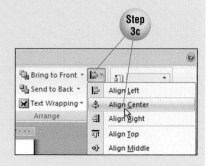

4. Save **WordL1_C5_P4.docx**.

Step 3c

QUICK STEPS

Create WordArt Text
1. Click Insert tab.
2. Click WordArt button.
3. Click desired WordArt style.
4. Type WordArt text.
5. Click OK.

WordArt ▾

Creating and Modifying WordArt Text

Use the WordArt feature to distort or modify text to conform to a variety of shapes. Consider using WordArt to create a company logo, letterhead, flier title, or heading. Insert WordArt in a document by clicking the Insert tab, clicking the WordArt button in the Text group, and then clicking the desired WordArt style at the drop-down list. Type the WordArt text at the Edit WordArt text dialog box and then click OK. You can also change the WordArt font and font size at the Edit WordArt Text dialog box.

You can customize WordArt with options and buttons in the WordArt Tools Format tab as shown in Figure 5.12. This tab displays when WordArt is selected in a document. With options and buttons at the WordArt Tools Format tab you can edit WordArt and change spacing, apply a WordArt style, change the shape fill and outline, apply shadow and 3-D effects, and arrange and size the WordArt.

Figure 5.12 WordArt Tools Format Tab

1. With **WordL1_C5_P4.docx** open, press
   Ctrl + Home to move the insertion point
   to the beginning of the document.
2. Insert WordArt by completing the
   following steps:
   a. Click the Insert tab.
   b. Click the WordArt button in the Text
      group and then click *WordArt style 15* at
      the drop-down list.
   c. Type Miller-Callahan Financial
      Services in the Edit WordArt Text box
      and then click OK.

3. Format the WordArt text by completing the
   following steps:
   a. Click in the *Shape Height* measurement box, type
      1, and then press Enter.
   b. Click in the *Shape Width* measurement box, type
      6.5, and then press Enter.
   c. Click the Position button in the Arrange group
      and then click the middle option in the top row
      of the *With Text Wrapping*
      section (the option named
      *Position Top Center with
      Square Text Wrapping*).

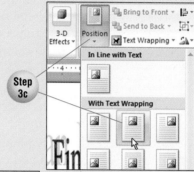

   d. Click the Shadow Effects
      button in the Shadow
      Effects group and then click
      Shadow Style 2 at the drop-
      down gallery (second
      option from the left in the
      top row of the *Drop Shadow*
      section).
   e. Click the Spacing button in the Text
      group and then click *Loose* at the
      drop-down list.
   f. Click the Shape Outline button
      arrow in the WordArt Styles group
      and then click the *Olive Green,
      Accent 3, Darker 50%* option.
   g. Click the Change WordArt Shape
      button in the WordArt Styles group
      and then click *Can Up* (third shape
      from the left in the top row of the *Warp* section).

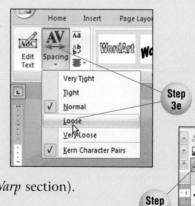

4. Return the display to 100%.
5. Click outside the WordArt to deselect it.
6. Make sure that all of the objects fit on one page.
   Consider deleting blank lines between shapes to
   make sure all of the objects fit on the page.
7. Save, print, and then close **WordL1_C5_P4.docx**.

CHAPTER summary

- Insert a section break in a document to apply formatting to a portion of a document. You can insert a continuous section break or a section break that begins a new page. View a section break in Draft view since section breaks are not visible in Print Layout view.

- Set text in columns to improve readability of documents such as newsletters or reports. Format text in columns using the Columns button in the Page Setup group in the Page Layout tab or with options at the Columns dialog box.

- Remove column formatting with the Columns button in the Page Layout tab or at the Columns dialog box. Balance column text on the last page of a document by inserting a continuous section break at the end of the text.

- Improve the display of text lines by hyphenating long words that fall at the end of the line. You can automatically or manually hyphenate words in a document.

- To enhance the appearance of text, use drop caps to identify the beginning of major sections or parts of a paragraph. Create drop caps with the Drop Cap button in the Text group in the Insert tab.

- Insert symbols with options at the Symbol dialog box with the Symbols tab selected and insert special characters with options at the Symbol dialog box with the Special Characters tab selected.

- Click the Date & Time button in the Text group in the Insert tab to display the Date and Time dialog box. Insert the date or time with options at this dialog box or with keyboard shortcuts. If the date or time is inserted as a field, update the field with the Update Field key, F9.

- Use the click and type feature to center, right-align, and left-align text.

- Vertically align text in a document with the *Vertical alignment* option at the Page Setup dialog box with the Layout tab selected.

- Insert an image such as a picture or clip art with buttons in the Illustrations group in the Insert tab.

- Customize and format an image with options and buttons in the Picture Tools Format tab. Size an image with the *Shape Height* and *Shape Width* measurement boxes in the Picture Tools Format tab or with the sizing handles that display around the selected image.

- Move an image with options from the Position button drop-down gallery located in the Picture Tools Format tab or by choosing a text wrapping style and then moving the image by dragging it with the mouse.

- To insert a picture, click the Insert tab, click the Picture button, navigate to the desired folder at the Insert Picture dialog box, and then double-click the picture.

- To insert a clip art image, click the Insert tab, click the Clip Art button, and then click the desired image in the Clip Art task pane.

- Insert a pull quote in a document with a built-in text box by clicking the Insert tab, clicking the Text Box button, and then clicking the desired built-in text box at the drop-down list.

- Draw shapes in a document by clicking the Shapes button in the Illustrations group in the Insert tab, clicking the desired shape at the drop-down list, and then dragging in the document to draw the shape. Customize a shape with options at the Drawing Tools Format tab. Copy a shape by holding down the Ctrl key while dragging the selected shape.

- Draw a text box by clicking the Text Box button in the Text group in the Insert tab, clicking *Draw Text Box* at the drop-down list, and then clicking in the document or dragging in the document. Customize a text box with buttons at the Text Box Tools Format tab.

- Link drawn text boxes with the Create Link button in the Text group in the Text Box Tools Format tab. Break a link with the Break Link button in the Text group.

- Use WordArt to distort or modify text to conform to a variety of shapes. Customize WordArt with options at the WordArt Tools Format tab.

COMMANDS review

FEATURE	RIBBON TAB, GROUP	BUTTON	OPTION	KEYBOARD SHORTCUT
Continuous section break	Page Layout, Page Setup	Breaks ▾	Continuous	
Columns dialog box	Page Layout, Page Setup	Columns ▾	More Columns	
Columns	Page Layout, Page Setup	Columns ▾		
Hyphenate words automatically	Page Layout, Page Setup	Hyphenation ▾	Automatic	
Manual Hyphenation dialog box	Page Layout, Page Setup	Hyphenation ▾	Manual	
Drop cap	Insert, Text	Drop Cap ▾		
Symbol dialog box	Insert, Symbols	Ω Symbol ▾		
Date and Time dialog box	Insert, Text	Date & Time		
Insert date				Alt + Shift + D
Insert time				Alt + Shift + T
Update field				F9
Page Setup dialog box	Page Layout, Page Setup	🔲		
Insert Picture dialog box	Insert, Illustrations	🖼		
Clip Art task pane	Insert, Illustrations	🔲		
Pull quote (Built-in text box)	Insert, Text	A		
Shapes	Insert, Illustrations	🔲		
Text box	Insert, Text	A	Draw Text Box	
Link text box	Text Box Tools Format, Text	Create Link		
Select objects	Home, Editing	Select ▾	Select Objects	
WordArt	Insert, Text	WordArt ▾		

CONCEPTS check

Test Your Knowledge

Completion: In the space provided at the right, indicate the correct term, symbol, or command.

1. View a section break in this view. _____

2. Format text into columns with the Columns button located in this group in the Page Layout tab. _____

3. Balance column text on the last page of a document by inserting this type of break at the end of the text. _____

4. The first letter of the first word of a paragraph that is set into a paragraph is called this. _____

5. The Symbol button is located in this tab. _____

6. This is the keyboard shortcut to insert the current date. _____

7. Use this feature to position the insertion point at a specific location and alignment in a document. _____

8. Vertically align text with the *Vertical alignment* option at the Page Setup dialog box with this tab selected. _____

9. Insert an image in a document with buttons in this group in the Insert tab. _____

10. Customize and format an image with options and buttons in this tab. _____

11. Size an image with the sizing handles that display around the selected image or with these boxes in the Picture Tools Format tab. _____

12. Click the Picture button in the Insert tab and this dialog box displays. _____

13. Click the Clip Art button in the Insert tab and this displays at the right side of the screen. _____

14. This is the term for a quote that is enlarged and positioned in an attractive location on the page. _____

15. Format text boxes with options and buttons in this tab. _____

16. The Shapes button is located in this tab. _____

17. To copy a selected shape, hold down this key while dragging the shape.   _____

18. Link text boxes using this button in the Text group.   _____

19. To select multiple objects in a document, click the Select button in the Editing group in the Home tab and then click this option.   _____

20. Use this feature to distort or modify text to conform to a variety of shapes.   _____

SKILLS check
Demonstrate Your Proficiency

Assessment

1 ADD VISUAL APPEAL TO A REPORT ON THE FUTURE OF THE INTERNET

1. Open **WordReport02.docx** and then save the document and name it **WordL1_C5_A1**.
2. Remove the first line indent by selecting text from the beginning of the first paragraph of text to the end of the document and then dragging the First Line Indent marker on the horizontal ruler to the 0″ mark.
3. Apply the Heading 1 style to the title of the report and apply the Heading 2 style to the headings in the report.
4. Change the Quick Styles set to *Formal*.
5. Format the text from the first paragraph to the end of the document into two columns with 0.4 inches between columns.
6. Select the title *FUTURE OF THE INTERNET* and then change the font size to 16 points, increase the spacing after the title to 12 points and, if necessary center-align the title.
7. Balance the text on the second page.
8. Insert a clip art image related to *satellite*. (Choose the clip art image that is available with Word and does not require downloading. This clip art image is blue and black and contains a satellite and a person holding a telephone and a briefcase.)
9. Make the following customizations to the clip art image:
   a. Change the height to 1.3″.
   b. Apply tight text wrapping.
   c. Recolor the clip art image to Accent color 6 Dark.
   d. Change the brightness to +10%.
   e. Drag the image so it is positioned at the left margin in the *Satellite Internet Connections* section.
10. Insert the *Alphabet Quote* built-in text box and then make the following customizations:
    a. Type the following text in the text box: "A remedy for the traffic clogging the information highway is Internet2."

b. Select the text and then change the font size to 12 and change the line spacing to 1.15.

c. Apply the Linear Up Gradient - Accent 6 style to the text box (last option in the fifth row of the Text Box Styles drop-down gallery).

d. Apply a shadow effect of your choosing to the text box.

e. Drag the box so it is positioned above the SATELLITE INTERNET CONNECTIONS heading in the first column, below the SECOND INTERNET heading in the second column, and centered between the left and right margins.

11. Press Ctrl + End to move the insertion point to the end of the document. (The insertion point will be positioned below the continuous section break you inserted on the second page to balance the columns of text.)

12. Change back to one column.

13. Press the Enter key twice and then create a shape of your choosing and make the following customizations:

a. Recolor the shape to match the color formatting in the document or the built-in text box.

b. Position the shape centered between the left and right margins.

c. Make any other changes to enhance the visual appeal of the shape.

d. Draw a text box inside the shape.

e. Remove the shape fill and the shape outline.

f. Type the following text inside the text box: ❧Felicité Compagnie❧. Insert the ❧ and ❧ symbols at the Symbol dialog box with the Wingdings font selected. Insert the é symbol at the Symbol dialog box with the *(normal text)* font selected.

g. Insert the current date below ❧*Felicité Compagnie*❧ and insert the current time below the date.

h. Select and then center the text in the text box.

14. Manually hyphenate the document (do not hyphenate headings or proper names).

15. Create a drop cap with the first letter of the word *The* that begins the first paragraph of text.

16. Save, print, and then close **WordL1_C5_A1.docx**.

Assessment

2 CREATE A SALES MEETING ANNOUNCEMENT

1. Create an announcement about an upcoming sales meeting with the following specifications:

a. Insert the company name *Inlet Development Company* as WordArt text.

b. Insert the following text in the document:
   National Sales Meeting
   Northwest Division
   Ocean View Resort
   August 23 through 25, 2010

c. Insert the picture named ***Ocean.jpg*** and size and position the picture behind the text.

d. Make any formatting changes to the WordArt, text, and picture to enhance the visual appeal of the document.

2. Save the announcement document and name it **WordL1_C5_A2**.

3. Print and then close **WordL1_C5_A2.docx**.

CASE study
Apply Your Skills

Part 1

You work for Honoré Financial Services and have been asked by the office manager, Jason Monroe, to prepare an information newsletter. Mr. Monroe has asked you open the document named **WordBudget.docx** and then format it into columns. You determine the number of columns and any additional enhancements to the columns. He also wants you to proofread the document and correct any spelling and grammatical errors. Save the completed newsletter and name it **WordL1_C5_CS_P1** and then print the newsletter. When Mr. Monroe reviews the newsletter, he decides that it needs additional visual appeal. He wants you to insert visual elements in the newsletter such as WordArt, clip art, a built-in text box, and/or a drop cap. Save **WordL1_C5_CS_P1.docx** and then print and close the document.

Part 2

Honoré Financial Services will be offering a free workshop on Planning for Financial Success. Mr. Monroe has asked you to prepare an announcement containing information on the workshop. You determine what to include in the announcement such as the date, time, location, and so forth. Enhance the announcement by inserting a picture or clip art and by applying formatting such as font, paragraph alignment, and borders. Save the completed document and name it **WordL1_C5_CS_P2**. Print and then close the document.

Part 3

Honoré Financial Services has adopted a new slogan and Mr. Monroe has asked you to create a shape with the new slogan inside. Experiment with the shadow and 3-D effects available at the Text Box Tools Format tab and then create a shape and enhance the shape with shadow and/or 3-D effects. Insert the new Honoré Financial Services slogan "Retirement Planning Made Easy" in the shape. Include any additional enhancements to improve the visual appeal of the shape and slogan. Save the completed document and name it **WordL1_C5_CS_P3**. Print and then close the document.

Part 4

Mr. Monroe has asked you to prepare a document containing information on teaching children how to budget. Use the Internet to find Web sites and articles that provide information on how to teach children to budget their money. Write a synopsis of the information you find and include at least four suggestions on how to teach children to manage their money. Format the text in the document into newspaper columns. Add additional enhancements to improve the appearance of the document. Save the completed newsletter and name it **WordL1_C5_CS_P4**. Print and then close the document.

CHAPTER 6

Maintaining Documents

PERFORMANCE OBJECTIVES

Upon successful completion of Chapter 6, you will be able to:

- Create and rename a folder
- Select, delete, copy, move, rename, and print documents
- Save documents in different file formats
- Open, close, arrange, split, maximize, minimize, and restore documents
- Insert a file into an open document
- Print specific pages and sections in a document
- Print multiple copies of a document
- Print envelopes and labels
- Create a document using a Word template

Tutorial 6.1
Managing Folders and Multiple Documents
Tutorial 6.2
Printing Documents

Almost every company that conducts business maintains a filing system. The system may consist of documents, folders, and cabinets; or it may be a computerized filing system where information is stored on the computer's hard drive or other storage medium. Whatever type of filing system a business uses, daily maintenance of files is important to a company's operation. In this chapter, you will learn to maintain files (documents) in Word, including such activities as creating additional folders and copying, moving, and renaming documents. You will also learn how to create and print documents, envelopes, and labels and create a document using a Word template.

Note: Before beginning computer projects, copy to your storage medium the Word2007L1C6 subfolder from the Word2007L1 folder on the CD that accompanies this textbook and then make Word2007L1C6 the active folder.

Project ① Manage Documents

You will perform a variety of file management tasks including creating and renaming a folder; selecting and then deleting, copying, cutting, pasting, and renaming documents; deleting a folder; and opening, printing, and closing a document.

Maintaining Documents

Many file (document) management tasks can be completed at the Open dialog box (and some at the Save As dialog box). These tasks can include copying, moving, printing, and renaming documents; opening multiple documents; and creating a new folder and renaming a folder.

Creating a Folder

In Word, documents are grouped logically and placed in *folders*. The main folder on a storage medium is called the *root folder* and you can create additional folders within the root folder. At the Open or Save As dialog box, documents display in the list box preceded by a document icon 📄 and folders are preceded by a folder icon 📁. Create a new folder by clicking the Create New Folder button located on the dialog box toolbar. At the New Folder dialog box, type a name for the folder, and then press Enter. The new folder becomes the active folder. A folder name can contain a maximum of 255 characters. Numbers, spaces, and symbols can be used in the folder name, except those symbols explained in Chapter 1 in the "Naming a Document" section.

If you want to make the previous folder the active folder, click the Up One Level button on the dialog box toolbar. Clicking this button changes to the folder that is up one level from the current folder. After clicking the Up One Level button, the Back button becomes active. Click this button and the previously active folder becomes active again. You can also use the keyboard shortcut, Alt + 2, to move up one level and make the previous folder active.

Project 1a **Creating a Folder**

1. Create a folder named *Correspondence* on your storage medium by completing the following steps:
   a. Display the Open dialog box and open the Word2007L1C6 folder on your storage medium.
   b. Click the Create New Folder button located on the dialog box toolbar.
   c. At the New Folder dialog box, type Correspondence.
   d. Click OK or press Enter. (The Correspondence folder is now the active folder.)

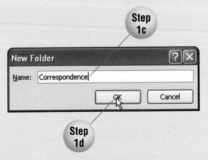

Step 1c

Step 1d

2. Change back to the Word2007L1C6 folder by clicking the Up One Level button on the dialog box toolbar.

Renaming a Folder

As you organize your files and folders, you may decide to rename a folder. Rename a folder using the Tools button in the Open or Save As dialog box or using a shortcut menu. To rename a folder using the Tools button, display the Open or Save As dialog box, click the folder you want to rename, click the Tools button located in the lower left corner of the dialog box, and then click *Rename* at the drop-down list. This selects the folder name and inserts a border around the name. Type the new name for the folder and then press Enter. To rename a folder using a shortcut menu, display the Open dialog box, right-click the folder name in the list box, and then click *Rename* at the shortcut menu. Type a new name for the folder and then press Enter.

QUICK STEPS

Rename a Folder
1. Display Open dialog box.
2. Right-click folder.
3. Click *Rename*.
4. Type new name.
5. Press Enter.

Project 1b Renaming a Folder

1. With the Open dialog box open, right-click the *Correspondence* folder name in the dialog box list box.
2. Click *Rename* at the shortcut menu.
3. Type Documents and then press Enter.

Selecting Documents

You can complete document management tasks on one document or selected documents. To select one document, display the Open dialog box, and then click the desired document. To select several adjacent documents (documents that display next to each other), click the first document, hold down the Shift key, and then click the last document. To select documents that are not adjacent, click the first document, hold down the Ctrl key, click any other desired documents, and then release the Ctrl key.

Deleting Documents

At some point, you may want to delete certain documents from your storage medium or any other drive or folder in which you may be working. To delete a document, display the Open or Save As dialog box, select the document, and then click the Delete button on the dialog box toolbar. At the dialog box asking you to confirm the deletion, click Yes. To delete a document using a shortcut menu, right-click the document name in the list box, click *Delete* at the shortcut menu, and then click Yes at the confirmation dialog box.

QUICK STEPS

Delete Folder/Document
1. Display Open dialog box.
2. Click folder or document name.
3. Click Delete button.
4. Click Yes.

Delete

Deleting to the Recycle Bin

Documents deleted from the hard drive are automatically sent to the Windows Recycle Bin. If you accidentally delete a document to the Recycle Bin, it can be easily restored. To free space on the drive, empty the Recycle Bin on a periodic basis. Restoring a document from or emptying the contents of the Recycle Bin is completed at the Windows desktop (not in Word). To display the Recycle Bin, minimize the Word window, and then double-click the *Recycle Bin* icon located on the Windows desktop. At the Recycle Bin, you can restore file(s) and empty the Recycle Bin.

HINT
Remember to empty the Recycle Bin on a regular basis.

1. Open **WordDocument04.docx** and then save the document and name it **WordL1_C6_P1**.
2. Close **WordL1_C6_P1.docx**.
3. Delete **WordL1_C6_P1.docx** by completing the following steps:
   a. Display the Open dialog box.
   b. Click *WordL1_C6_P1.docx* to select it.
   c. Click the Delete button on the dialog box toolbar.

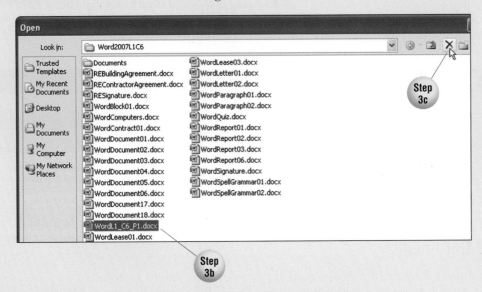

d. At the question asking if you want to delete **WordL1_C6_P1.docx**, click Yes.
4. Delete selected documents by completing the following steps:
   a. At the Open dialog box, click *WordReport01.docx*.
   b. Hold down the Shift key and then click *WordReport03.docx*.
   c. Position the mouse pointer on a selected document and then click the *right* mouse button.
   d. At the shortcut menu that displays, click *Delete*.
   e. At the question asking if you want to delete the items, click Yes.
5. Open **WordDocument01.docx** and then save the document and name it **Keyboards**.
6. Save a copy of the **Keyboards.docx** document in the Documents folder by completing the following steps. (If your system does not contain this folder, check with your instructor to determine if another folder is available for you to use.)
   a. With **Keyboards.docx** open, click the Office button and then click *Save As*.
   b. At the Save As dialog box, double-click the *Documents* folder located at the beginning of the list box (folders are listed before documents).
   c. Click the Save button located in the lower right corner of the dialog box.
7. Close **Keyboards.docx**.
8. Display the Open dialog box and then click the Up One Level button to return to the Word2007L1C6 folder.

Copying and Moving Documents

You can copy a document to another folder without opening the document first. To do this, use the Copy and Paste options from a shortcut menu at the Open or Save As dialog box. You can copy a document or selected documents into the same folder. When you do this, Word names the document(s) "Copy of xxx" (where *xxx* is the current document name). You can copy one document or selected documents into the same folder.

Remove a document from one folder and insert it in another folder using the Cut and Paste options from the shortcut menu at the Open dialog box. To do this, display the Open dialog box, position the arrow pointer on the document to be removed (cut), click the *right* mouse button, and then click *Cut* at the shortcut menu. Change to the desired folder, position the arrow pointer in a white area in the list box, click the *right* mouse button, and then click *Paste* at the shortcut menu.

Copy Documents
1. Display Open dialog box.
2. Right-click document name.
3. Click *Copy*.
4. Navigate to desired folder.
5. Right-click blank area.
6. Click *Paste*.

Project 1d Copying Documents

1. At the Open dialog box with Word2007L1C6 the active folder, copy a document to another folder by completing the following steps:
   a. Position the arrow pointer on **WordDocument02.docx**, click the *right* mouse button, and then click *Copy* at the shortcut menu.
   b. Change to the Documents folder by double-clicking *Documents* at the beginning of the list box.
   c. Position the arrow pointer in any white area (not on a document name) in the list box, click the *right* mouse button, and then click *Paste* at the shortcut menu.
2. Change back to the Word2007L1C6 folder by clicking the Up One Level button located on the dialog box toolbar.
3. Copy several documents to the Documents folder by completing the following steps:
   a. Click once on **WordDocument01.docx**. (This selects the document.)
   b. Hold down the Ctrl key, click **WordDocument04.docx**, click **WordDocument05.docx**, and then release the Ctrl key.
   c. Position the arrow pointer on one of the selected documents, click the *right* mouse button, and then click *Copy* at the shortcut menu.
   d. Double-click the *Documents* folder.
   e. Position the arrow pointer in any white area in the list box, click the *right* mouse button, and then click *Paste* at the shortcut menu.
4. Click the Up One Level button to return to the Word2007L1C6 folder.
5. Move **WordQuiz.docx** to the Documents folder by completing the following steps:
   a. Position the arrow pointer on **WordQuiz.docx**, click the *right* mouse button, and then click *Cut* at the shortcut menu.
   b. Double-click *Documents* to make it the active folder.
   c. Position the arrow pointer in the white area in the list box, click the *right* mouse button, and then click *Paste* at the shortcut menu.
6. Click the Up One Level button to return to the Word2007L1C6 folder.

Renaming Documents

At the Open dialog box, use the *Rename* option from the Tools drop-down list to give a document a different name. The *Rename* option changes the name of the document and keeps it in the same folder. To use Rename, display the Open dialog box, click once on the document to be renamed, click the Tools button, and then click *Rename* at the drop-down list. This causes a black border to surround the document name and the name to be selected. Type the desired name and then press Enter. You can also rename a document by right-clicking the document name at the Open dialog box and then clicking *Rename* at the shortcut menu. Type the desired name for the document and then press the Enter key.

Project 1e   Renaming Documents

1. Rename a document located in the Documents folder by completing the following steps:
   a. At the Open dialog box with the Word2007L1C6 folder open, double-click the *Documents* folder to make it active.
   b. Click once on **WordDocument04.docx** to select it.
   c. Click the Tools button located in the lower left corner of the dialog box.
   d. Click *Rename* at the drop-down list.
   e. Type **Privacy.docx** and then press the Enter key.
2. Click the Up One Level button to return to the Word2007L1C6 folder.

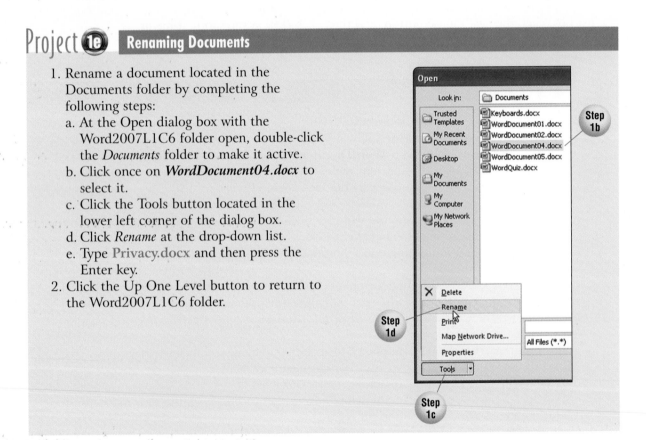

Deleting a Folder

As you learned earlier in this chapter, you can delete a document or selected documents. Delete a folder and all its contents in the same manner as deleting a document.

Project 11 Deleting a Folder

1. At the Open dialog box, click the *Documents* folder to select it.
2. Click the Delete button on the dialog box toolbar.

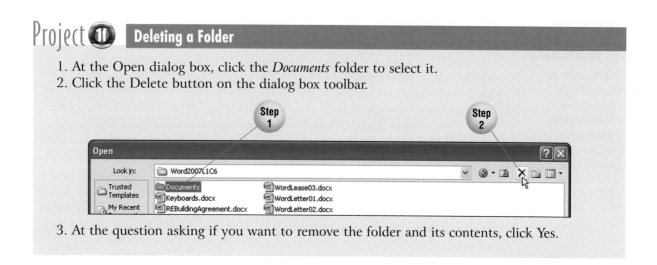

3. At the question asking if you want to remove the folder and its contents, click Yes.

Opening and Printing Multiple Documents

To open more than one document, select the documents in the Open dialog box, and then click the Open button. You can also open multiple documents by positioning the arrow pointer on one of the selected documents, clicking the *right* mouse button, and then clicking *Open* at the shortcut menu. Up to this point, you have opened a document and then printed it. With the *Print* option from the Tools drop-down list or the *Print* option from the shortcut menu at the Open dialog box, you can print a document or several documents without opening them.

HINT
Open a recently opened document by clicking the Office button and then clicking the document in the drop-down list.

Project 1g Opening and Printing Multiple Documents

1. Select **WordDocument01.docx**, **WordDocument02.docx**, **WordDocument03.docx**, and **WordDocument04.docx**.
2. Click the Open button located toward the lower right corner of the dialog box.
3. Close the open documents.
4. Display the Open dialog box and then select **WordDocument03.docx** and **WordDocument04.docx**.
5. Click the Tools button located in the lower left corner of the dialog box.
6. Click *Print* at the drop-down list.

Saving a Document in a Different Format

When you save a document, the document is automatically saved as a Word document. If you need to share a document with someone who is using a different Word processing program or a different version of Word, you can save the document in another format. You can also save a Word document as a Web page, in rich text format, as plain text, or in PDF format. To save a document with a different format, display the Save As dialog box, click the down-pointing arrow at the right side of the *Save as type* option, and then click the desired format at the drop-down list.

HINT
A file's format is indicated by a three- or four-letter extension after the file name.

You can also save a document in a different format with the *Save As* option at the Office button drop-down list. Click the Office button, point to *Save As*, and a side menu displays with options for saving a document in the default format, saving the document as a template, in Office 97 to 2003 format as well as PDF format.

Save Document in Different Format
1. Open document.
2. Click Office button, *Save As*.
3. Click *Save as type* option.
4. Click desired type.
5. Click Save button.

The portable document format (PDF) was developed by Adobe Systems and is a format that captures all of the elements of a file as an electronic image. You can view a PDF file on any application on any computer, making this format the most widely used for transferring files to other users. Before saving a file in PDF format, you must install an add-in download from the Microsoft Web site. If the add-in download is installed, *PDF or XPS* will display in the Office button Save As side menu and if it is not installed, *Find add-ins for other file formats* will display. To download the add-in, click the *Find add-ins for other file formats* option and then follow the steps in the Word Help window.

When you click the *PDF or XPS* option at the Save As side menu, the Save As dialog box displays with *PDF (*.pdf)* specified as the *Save as type* option. At this dialog box, type a name in the *File name* text box and then click the Publish button. By default, the file will open in PDF format in Adobe Reader. The Adobe Reader application is designed to view your file. You will be able to navigate in the file but you will not be able to make any changes to the file. You can open a PDF file in your browser window by clicking the File option on the browser menu bar and then clicking *Open*. At the Open dialog box, browse to the appropriate folder and then double-click the desired file. You may need to change the *Files of type* option to *All Files*.

The Open dialog box generally displays only Word documents, which are documents containing the *.docx* extension. If you want to display all files, display the Open dialog box, click the down-pointing arrow at the right side of the *Files of type* option, and then click *All Files (*.*)* at the drop-down list.

Project 1h   Saving a Document in Different Formats

1. Open **WordDocument18.docx**.
2. Click the Office button, point to *Save As*, and then click *Word 97-2003 Document* at the side menu.
3. At the Save As dialog box, check to make sure that the *Save as type* option displays as *Word 97-2003 Document (*.doc)* and then type WordDocument18in2003format.
4. Click the Save button.
5. Save the document in PDF file format by completing the following steps:
   a. Click the Office button, point to *Save As*, and then click *PDF or XPS* in the side menu. (If this option does not display, the PDF add-in has not been installed.)
   b. At the Save As dialog box with the *Save as type* option set at *PDF (*.pdf)*, click the Publish button.
6. Scroll through the document in Adobe Reader.
7. Close Adobe Reader by clicking the Close button located in the upper right corner of the window.
8. Save the document as plain text by completing the following steps:
   a. Click the Office button and then click *Save As*.
   b. At the Save As dialog box, type WordDocument18PlainText in the *File name* text box.

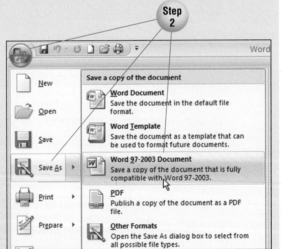

c. Click the down-pointing arrow at the right side of the *Save as type* option, scroll down the drop-down list, and then click *Plain Text (*.txt)*.

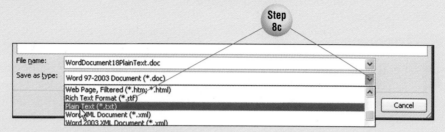

Step
8c

File name:	WordDocument18PlainText.doc	
Save as type:	Word 97-2003 Document (*.doc)	
	Web Page, Filtered (*.htm; *.html)	
	Rich Text Format (*.rtf)	
	Plain Text (*.txt)	Cancel
	Word XML Document (*.xml)	
	Word 2003 XML Document (*.xml)	

d. Click the Save button.
e. At the File Conversion dialog box, click OK.
9. Close the document.
10. Display the Open dialog box and, if necessary, display all files. To do this, click the down-pointing arrow at the right side of the *Files of type* option, and then click *All Files (*.*)* at the drop-down list. (This displays all files containing any extension.)
11. Double-click *WordDocument18PlainText.txt* in the list box. (If a File Conversion dialog box displays, click OK. Notice that the character and margin formatting has been removed from the document.)
12. Close the document.
13. Display the Open dialog box, change the *Files of type* option to *Word Documents (*.docx)*, and then close the dialog box.

Project ② Manage Multiple Documents

You will work with windows by arranging, maximizing, restoring, and minimizing windows; move selected text between split windows; compare formatting of documents side by side; print specific text, pages, and multiple copies; and create and modify document properties.

Working with Windows

You can open multiple documents and move the insertion point between the documents. You can also move and copy information between documents or compare the contents of documents. The maximum number of documents that you can have open at one time depends on the memory of your computer system and the amount of data in each document. When you open a new window, it is placed on top of the original window. Once multiple windows are open, you can resize the windows to see all or a portion of them on the screen.

When a document is open, a button displays on the Taskbar. This button represents the open document and contains a document icon, and the document name. (Depending on the length of the document name and the size of the button, not all of the name may be visible.) Another method for determining what documents are open is to click the View tab and then click the Switch Windows button in the Window group. The document name that displays in the list with

HINT
Press Ctrl + F6 to switch between open documents.

HINT
Press Ctrl + W or Ctrl + F4 to close the active document window.

the check mark in front of it is the *active* document. The active document is the document containing the insertion point. To make one of the other documents active, click the document name. If you are using the keyboard, type the number shown in front of the desired document.

Arranging Windows

Arrange Windows
1. Open documents.
2. Click View tab.
3. Click Arrange All.

If you have more than one document open, you can arrange them so a portion of each document displays. The portions that display are the titles (if present) and opening paragraphs of each document. Seeing this information is helpful if you are preparing a report that needs to incorporate key ideas from several documents.

To arrange a group of open documents, click the View tab and then click the Arrange All button in the Window group. Figure 6.1 shows a document screen with four documents open that have been arranged.

Figure 6.1 Arranged Documents

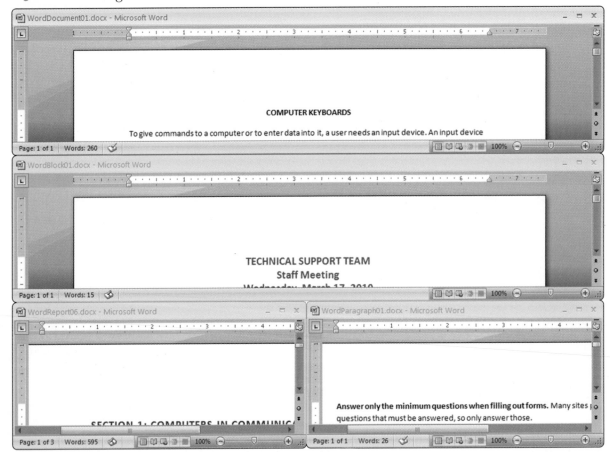

Maximizing, Restoring, and Minimizing Documents

Minimize   Maximize

Use the Maximize and Minimize buttons in the active document window to change the size of the window. The Maximize button is the button in the upper right corner of the active document immediately to the left of the Close button. (The Close button is the button containing the *X*.) The Minimize button is located immediately to the left of the Maximize button.

If you arrange all open documents and then click the Maximize button in the active document, the active document expands to fill the document screen. In addition, the Maximize button changes to the Restore button. To return the active document back to its size before it was maximized, click the Restore button. If you click the Minimize button in the active document, the document is reduced and a button displays on the Taskbar representing the document. To maximize a document that has been minimized, click the button on the Taskbar representing the document.

Restore

Project 2a   Arranging, Maximizing, Restoring, and Minimizing Windows

Note: If you are using Word on a network system that contains a virus checker, you may not be able to open multiple documents at once. Continue by opening each document individually.

1. Open the following documents: **WordBlock01.docx**, **WordDocument01.docx**, **WordParagraph01.docx**, and **WordReport06.docx**.
2. Arrange the windows by clicking the View tab and then clicking the Arrange All button in the Window group.
3. Make **WordDocument01.docx** the active document by positioning the arrow pointer on the title bar for **WordDocument01.docx** and then clicking the left mouse button.
4. Close **WordDocument01.docx**.
5. Make **WordParagraph01.docx** active and then close it.
6. Make **WordReport06.docx** active and minimize it by clicking the Minimize button in the upper right corner of the active window.
7. Maximize **WordBlock01.docx** by clicking the Maximize button at the right side of the Title bar. (The Maximize button is the button at the right side of the Title bar, immediately left of the Close button.)
8. Close **WordBlock01.docx**.
9. Restore **WordReport06.docx** by clicking the button on the Taskbar representing the document.
10. Maximize **WordReport06.docx**.

Step 7

Step 9

Splitting a Window

You can divide a window into two *panes*, which is helpful if you want to view different parts of the same document at one time. You may want to display an outline for a report in one pane, for example, and the portion of the report that you are editing in the other. The original window is split into two panes that extend horizontally across the screen.

Split a window by clicking the View tab and then clicking the Split button in the Window group. This causes a wide gray line to display in the middle of the screen and the mouse pointer to display as a double-headed arrow pointing up and down with a small double line between. Move this double-headed arrow pointer up or down, if desired, by dragging the mouse or by pressing the up- and/or down-pointing arrow keys on the keyboard. When the double-headed arrow is positioned at the desired location in the document, click the left mouse button or press the Enter key.

You can also split the window with the split bar. The split bar is the small gray horizontal bar above the up scroll arrow on the vertical scroll bar. To split the window with the split bar, position the arrow pointer on the split bar until it turns

QUICK STEPS

Split Window
1. Open document.
2. Click View tab.
3. Click Split button.
OR
Drag split bar.

⬛ Split

into a short double line with an up- and down-pointing arrow. Hold down the left mouse button, drag the double-headed arrow into the document screen to the location where you want the window split, and then release the mouse button. With the window split, you may decide you want to move certain objects or sections of text. Do this by selecting the desired object or text and then dragging and dropping it across the split bar.

When a window is split, the insertion point is positioned in the bottom pane. To move the insertion point to the other pane with the mouse, position the I-beam pointer in the other pane, and then click the left mouse button. To remove the split line from the document, click the View tab and then click the Remove Split button in the Window group. You can also double-click the split bar or drag the split bar to the top or bottom of the screen.

Project 2b — Moving Selected Text between Split Windows

1. With **WordReport06.docx** open, save the document with Save As and name it **WordL1_C6_P2**.
2. Click the View tab and then click the Split button in the Window group.
3. With the split line displayed in the middle of the document screen, click the left mouse button.
4. Move the first section below the second section by completing the following steps:
   a. Click the Home tab.
   b. Select the *SECTION 1: COMPUTERS IN COMMUNICATION* section from the title to right above *SECTION 2: COMPUTERS IN ENTERTAINMENT*.
   c. Click the Cut button in the Clipboard group in the Home tab.
   d. Position the arrow pointer at the end of the document in the bottom window pane and then click the left mouse button.
   e. Click the Paste button in the Clipboard group in the Home tab.
   f. Change the number in the two titles to *SECTION 1: COMPUTERS IN ENTERTAINMENT* and *SECTION 2: COMPUTERS IN COMMUNICATION*.
5. Remove the split from the window by clicking the View tab and then clicking the Remove Split button in the Window group.
6. If the Section 2 title displays at the bottom of the first page, move the insertion point to the beginning of the title and then press Ctrl + Enter to insert a page break.
7. Save **WordL1_C6_P2.docx**.

Viewing Documents Side by Side

If you want to compare the contents of two documents, open both documents, click the View tab, and then click the View Side by Side button in the Window group. Both documents are arranged in the screen side by side as shown in Figure 6.2. By default synchronous scrolling is active. With this feature active, scrolling in one document causes the same scrolling to occur in the other document. This feature is useful in situations where you want to compare text, formatting, or other features between documents. If you want to scroll in one document and not the other, click the Synchronous Scrolling button in the Window group in the View tab to turn it off.

Figure 6.2 Viewing Documents Side by Side

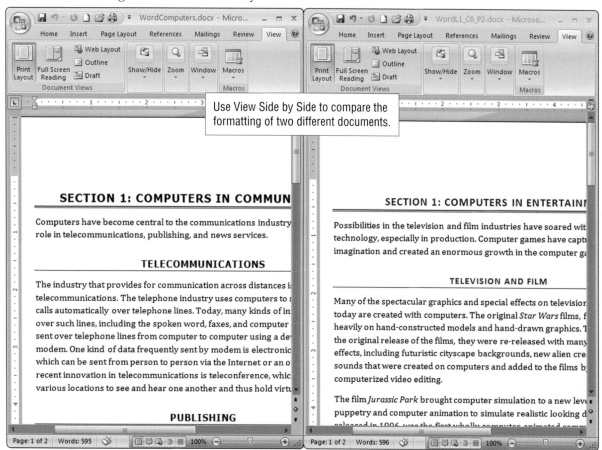

Use View Side by Side to compare the formatting of two different documents.

Project 2c — **Viewing Documents Side by Side**

1. With **WordL1_C6_P2.docx** open, open **WordComputers.docx**.
2. Click the View tab and then click the View Side by Side button in the Window group.

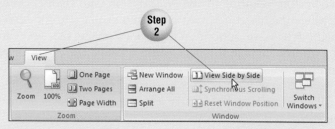

Step 2

3. Scroll through both documents simultaneously. Notice the difference between the two documents. (The title and headings are set in a different font and color.) Select and then format the title and headings in **WordL1_C6_P2.docx** so they match the formatting in **WordComputers.docx**.
4. Save **WordL1_C6_P2.docx**.
5. Make **WordComputers.docx** the active document and then close it.

Inserting a File

Insert a File
1. Open document.
2. Click Insert tab.
3. Click Object button arrow.
4. Click *Text from File*.
5. Navigate to desired folder.
6. Double-click document name.

If you want to insert the contents of one document into another, use the Object button in the Text group in the Insert tab. Click the Object button arrow and then click *Text from File* and the Insert File dialog box displays. This dialog box contains similar features as the Open dialog box. Navigate to the desired folder and then double-click the document you want to insert in the open document.

Project 2d — Inserting a File

1. With **WordL1_C6_P2.docx** open, move the insertion point to the end of the document.
2. Insert a file into the open document by completing the following steps:
   a. Click the Insert tab.
   b. Click the Object button arrow in the Text group.
   c. Click *Text from File* at the drop-down list.
   d. At the Insert File dialog box, navigate to the Word2007L1C6 folder and then double-click ***WordDocument17.docx***.
3. Check the formatting of the inserted text and format it to match the formatting of the original text.
4. Save **WordL1_C6_P2.docx**.

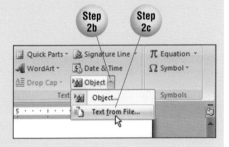

Previewing a Document

Before printing a document, you may want to view the document as it will appear when printed. To do this, display the document in Print Preview by clicking the Office button, pointing to the *Print* option, and then clicking *Print Preview*. The page where the insertion point is located displays in the screen in a manner similar to Figure 6.3. With options in the Print Preview tab, you can send the document to the printer, change the page setup, change the zoom display, and customize the preview window. Viewing a document in Print Preview is especially useful for making sure that a letter is positioned attractively on the page. For example, use Print Preview to help you center letters vertically, which means allowing equal space above and below the beginning and end of the letter.

Figure 6.3 Document in Print Preview

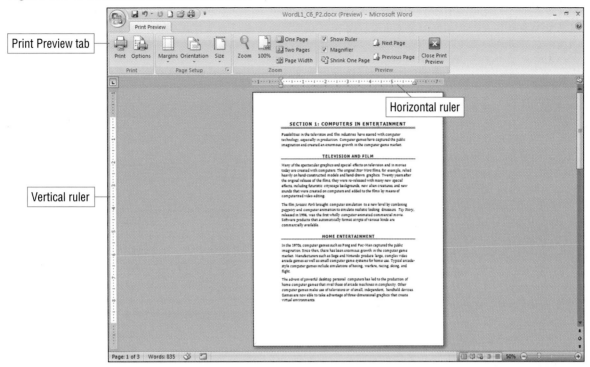

Print Preview tab

Horizontal ruler

Vertical ruler

Project 2e   Previewing the Document

1. With **WordL1_C6_P2.docx** open, press Ctrl + Home to move the insertion point to the beginning of the document.
2. Preview the document by clicking the Office button, pointing to the *Print* option, and then clicking *Print Preview*.
3. Click the Two Pages button in the Zoom group in the Print Preview tab. (This displays the first two pages in the document.)

Step 2

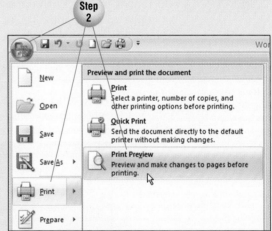

Step 3

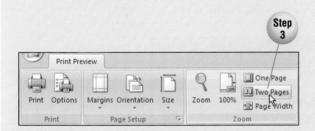

4. Click the Next Page button in the Preview group. (This displays the third page.)
5. Click the Previous Page button in the Preview group. (This redisplays the first two pages.)
6. Click the One Page button in the Zoom group.
7. Change the page orientation by clicking the Orientation button in the Page Setup group and then clicking *Landscape* at the drop-down list.

8. After looking at the page in landscape orientation, you decide to return to portrait orientation. To do this, click the Orientation button in the Page Setup group and then click *Portrait* at the drop-down list.
9. Change margins by completing the following steps:
   a. Click the Margins button in the Page Setup group and then click *Custom Margins* at the drop-down list.
   b. At the Page Setup dialog box with the Margins tab selected, change the top margin to 1.25″.
   c. Click OK to close the dialog box.
10. Change the Zoom by completing the following steps:
    a. Click the Zoom button in the Zoom group.
    b. At the Zoom dialog box, click the *75%* option.
    c. Click OK to close the dialog box.
    d. After viewing the document in 75% view, click the Zoom button.
    e. At the Zoom dialog box, click the *Whole page* option.
    f. Click OK to close the dialog box.
11. Click the Close Print Preview button.
12. Save **WordL1_C6_P2.docx**.

Step 10b

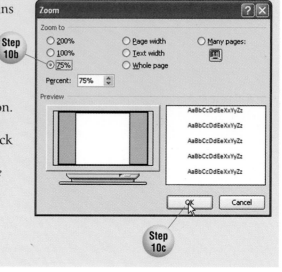

Step 10c

Printing Documents

HINT

Save a document before printing it.

In Chapter 1, you learned to print at the Print dialog box the document displayed in the document screen. By default, one copy of all pages of the currently open document prints. With options at the Print dialog box, you can specify the number of copies to print and also specific pages for printing. To display the Print dialog box shown in Figure 6.4, click the Office button and then click *Print* or press Ctrl + P.

Figure 6.4 Print Dialog Box

Make sure the correct printer displays here.

Click the down-pointing arrow to display a list of installed printers.

Click this button to set options for the selected printer such as paper size, layout, orientation, paper source, and paper quality.

Specify the amount of text to print with options in this section of the dialog box.

Print multiple copies of a document by increasing this number.

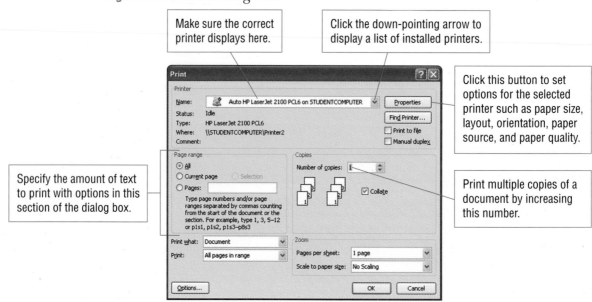

Printing Specific Text or Pages

The *Page range* section of the Print dialog box contains settings you can use to specify the amount of text you want printed. At the default setting of *All*, all pages of the current document are printed. Choose the *Current page* option to print the page where the insertion point is located. If you want to select and then print a portion of the document, choose the *Selection* option at the Print dialog box. This prints only the text that has been selected in the current document. (This option is dimmed unless text is selected in the document.)

With the *Pages* option, you can identify a specific page, multiple pages, and/or a range of pages. If you want specific multiple pages printed, use a comma (,) to indicate *and* and use a hyphen (-) to indicate *through*. For example, to print pages 2 and 5, you would type 2,5 in the *Pages* text box. To print pages 6 through 10, you would type 6-10.

Project 2️⃣ Printing Specific Text and Pages

1. With **WordL1_C6_P2.docx** open, select the heading *Television and Film* and the two paragraphs that follow it.
2. Press Ctrl + P.
3. At the Print dialog box, click the *Selection* option in the *Page range* section.
4. Click OK.
5. Press Ctrl + Home to move the insertion point to the beginning of the document.
6. Click the Office button and then click *Print*.
7. At the Print dialog box, click the *Pages* option in the *Page range* section.
8. Type 1-2 in the *Pages* text box.
9. Click OK.

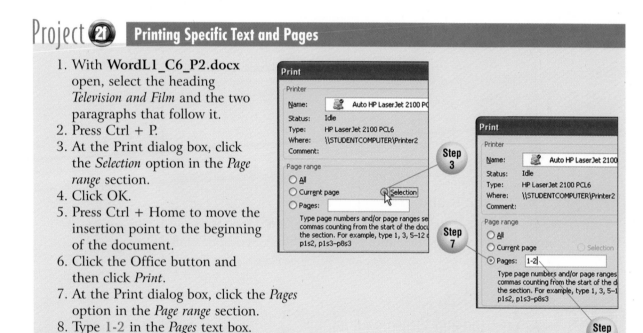

Printing Multiple Copies

If you want to print more than one copy of a document, use the *Number of copies* option from the Print dialog box. If you print several copies of a document containing multiple pages, Word prints the pages in the document collated. For example, if you print two copies of a three-page document, pages 1, 2, and 3 are printed, and then the pages are printed a second time. Printing pages collated is helpful but takes more printing time. To speed up the printing time, you can tell Word *not* to print the pages collated. To do this, remove the check mark from the *Collate* option at the Print dialog box. With the check mark removed, Word will print all copies of the first page, and then all copies of the second page, and so on.

Project 2g   Printing Multiple Copies of a Specific Page

1. With **WordL1_C6_P2.docx** open, press Ctrl + P.
2. Type 2 in the *Number of copies* text box.
3. Click the *Pages* option in the *Page range* section.
4. Type 1,3.
5. Click the *Collate* check box in the *Copies* section to remove the check mark.
6. Click OK.
7. Close **WordL1_C6_P2.docx**.

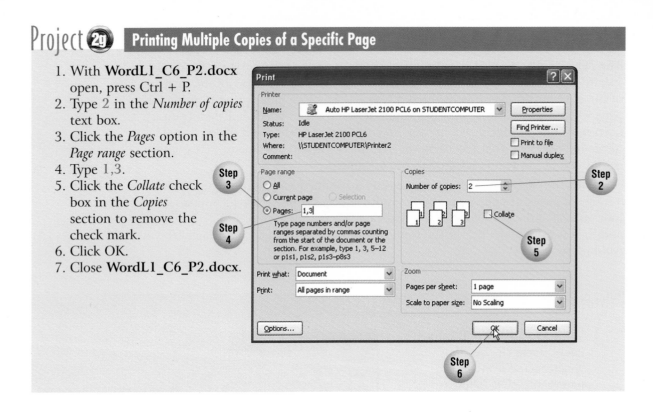

Project 3   Create and Print an Envelope

You will create an envelope document and type the return address and delivery address using envelope addressing guidelines issued by the United States Postal Service.

Create Envelope
1. Click Mailings tab.
2. Click Envelopes button.
3. Type delivery address.
4. Click in *Return address* text box.
5. Type return address.
6. Click Add to Document button or Print button.

Creating and Printing Envelopes

Word automates the creation of envelopes with options at the Envelopes and Labels dialog box with the Envelopes tab selected as shown in Figure 6.5. Display this dialog box by clicking the Mailings tab and then clicking the Envelopes button in the Create group. At the dialog box, type the delivery address in the *Delivery address* text box and the return address in the *Return address* text box. You can send the envelope directly to the printer by clicking the Print button or insert the envelope in the current document by clicking the Add to Document button.

Figure 6.5 Envelopes and Labels Dialog Box with Envelopes Tab Selected

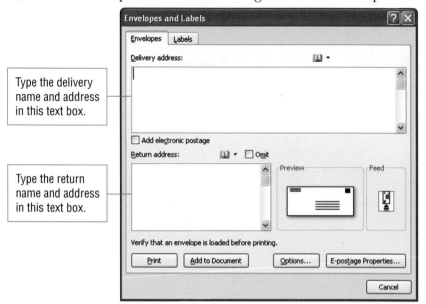

Type the delivery name and address in this text box.

Type the return name and address in this text box.

If you enter a return address before printing the envelope, Word will display the question *Do you want to save the new return address as the default return address?* At this question, click Yes if you want the current return address available for future envelopes. Click No if you do not want the current return address used as the default. If a default return address displays in the *Return address* section of the dialog box, you can tell Word to omit the return address when printing the envelope. To do this, click the *Omit* check box to insert a check mark.

The Envelopes and Labels dialog box contains a *Preview* sample box and a *Feed* sample box. The *Preview* sample box shows how the envelope will appear when printed and the *Feed* sample box shows how the envelope should be inserted into the printer.

When addressing envelopes, consider following general guidelines issued by the United States Postal Service (USPS). The USPS guidelines suggest using all capital letters with no commas or periods for return and delivery addresses. Figure 6.6 shows envelope addresses following the USPS guidelines. Use abbreviations for street suffixes (such as *ST* for *STREET* and *AVE* for *Avenue*). For a complete list of address abbreviations, visit the www.emcp.net/usps site and then search for *Official USPS Abbreviations*.

Project ③ — Printing an Envelope

1. At a blank document, create an envelope that prints the delivery address and return address shown in Figure 6.6. Begin by clicking the Mailings tab.
2. Click the Envelopes button in the Create group.

3. At the Envelopes and Labels dialog box with the Envelopes tab selected, type the delivery address shown in Figure 6.6 (the one containing the name *GREGORY LINCOLN*). (Press the Enter key to end each line in the name and address.)
4. Click in the *Return address* text box. (If any text displays in the *Return address* text box, select and then delete it.)
5. Type the return address shown in Figure 6.6 (the one containing the name *WENDY STEINBERG*). (Press the Enter key to end each line in the name and address.)
6. Click the Add to Document button.
7. At the message *Do you want to save the new return address as the default return address?*, click No.
8. Save the document and name it **WordL1_C6_P3**.
9. Print and then close **WordL1_C6_P3.docx**. *Note: Manual feed of the envelope may be required. Please check with your instructor.*

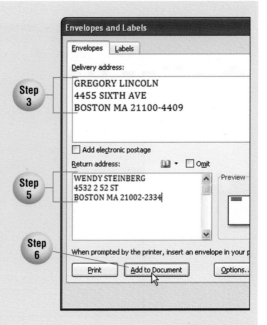

Figure 6.6 **Project 3**

WENDY STEINBERG
4532 S 52 ST
BOSTON MA 21002-2334

GREGORY LINCOLN
4455 SIXTH AVE
BOSTON MA 21100-4409

roject ④ **Create and Print an Envelope and Mailing Labels**

You will open a letter document and then create an envelope using the inside address of the letter and then create mailing labels containing the inside address.

If you open the Envelopes and Labels dialog box in a document containing a name and address (the name and address lines must end with a press of the Enter key and not Shift + Enter), the name and address are automatically inserted in the *Delivery address* section of the dialog box. To do this, open a document containing a name and address and then display the Envelopes and Labels dialog box. The name and address are inserted in the *Delivery address* section as they appear in the letter and may not conform to the USPS guidelines. The USPS guidelines for addressing envelopes are only suggestions, not requirements.

1. Open **WordLetter01.docx**.
2. Click the Mailings tab.
3. Click the Envelopes button in the Create group.
4. At the Envelopes and Labels dialog box (with the Envelopes tab selected), make sure the delivery address displays properly in the *Delivery address* section.
5. If any text displays in the *Return address* section, insert a check mark in the *Omit* check box (located to the right of the *Return address* option). (This tells Word not to print the return address on the envelope.)
6. Click the Print button.

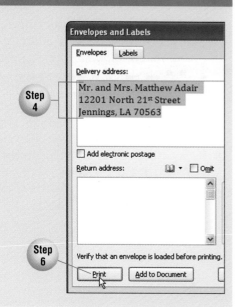

Step 4

Step 6

Creating and Printing Labels

Use Word's labels feature to print text on mailing labels, file labels, disk labels, or other types of labels. Word includes a variety of predefined formats for labels that can be purchased at an office supply store. To create a sheet of mailing labels with the same name and address using the default options, click the Labels button in the Create group in the Mailings tab. At the Envelopes and Labels dialog box with the Labels tab selected as shown in Figure 6.7, type the desired address in the *Address* text box. Click the New Document button to insert the mailing label in a new document or click the Print button to send the mailing label directly to the printer.

QUICK STEPS

Create Labels
1. Click Mailings tab.
2. Click Labels button.
3. Type desired address(es).
4. Click New Document button or Print button.

Labels

Figure 6.7 Envelopes and Labels Dialog Box with Labels Tab Selected

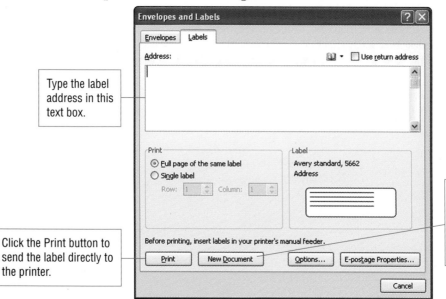

Type the label address in this text box.

Click the Print button to send the label directly to the printer.

Click the New Document button to insert the mailing label in a new document.

Project 4b Creating Mailing Labels

1. With **WordLetter01.docx** open, create mailing labels with the delivery address. Begin by clicking the Mailings tab.
2. Click the Labels button in the Create group.
3. At the Envelopes and Labels dialog box with the Labels tab selected, make sure the delivery address displays properly in the *Address* section.
4. Click the New Document button.
5. Save the mailing label document and name it **WordL1_C6_P4.docx**.
6. Print and then close **WordL1_C6_P4.docx**.
7. Close **WordLetter01.docx**.

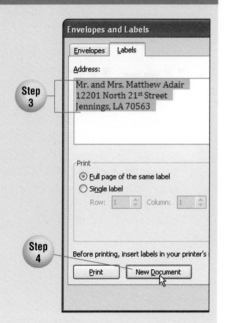

Step 3

Envelopes and Labels

Envelopes   Labels

Address:

Mr. and Mrs. Matthew Adair
12201 North 21ˢᵗ Street
Jennings, LA 70563

Print
◉ Full page of the same label
○ Single label
   Row: 1   Column: 1

Before printing, insert labels in your printer's

Print   New Document

Step 4

Project 5 Create Mailing Labels

You will create mailing labels containing varying names and addresses.

If you open the Envelopes and Labels dialog box with the Labels tab selected in a document containing a name and address, the name and address are automatically inserted in the *Address* section of the dialog box. To enter different names in each of the mailing labels, start at a clear document screen, display the Envelopes and Labels dialog box with the Labels tab selected, and then click the New Document button. The Envelopes and Labels dialog box is removed from the screen and the document screen displays with label forms. The insertion point is positioned in the first label form. Type the name and address in this label and then press the Tab key to move the insertion point to the next label. Pressing Shift + Tab will move the insertion point to the preceding label.

Changing Label Options

Click the Options button at the Envelopes and Labels dialog box with the Labels tab selected and the Label Options dialog box displays as shown in Figure 6.8. At the Label Options dialog box, choose the type of printer, the desired label product, and the product number. This dialog box also displays information about the selected label such as type, height, width, and paper size. When you select a label, Word automatically determines label margins. If, however, you want to customize these default settings, click the Details button at the Label Options dialog box.

Figure 6.8 Label Options Dialog Box

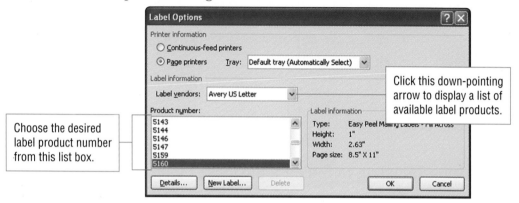

Choose the desired label product number from this list box.

Click this down-pointing arrow to display a list of available label products.

Project ⑤ **Creating Customized Mailing Labels**

1. At a blank document, click the Mailings tab.
2. Click the Labels button in the Create group.
3. At the Envelopes and Labels dialog box with the Labels tab selected, click the Options button.
4. At the Label Options dialog box, click the down-pointing arrow at the right side of the *Label vendors* option and then click *Avery US Letter* at the drop-down list.
5. Scroll down the *Product number* list box and then click *5160*.
6. Click OK or press Enter.
7. At the Envelopes and Labels dialog box, click the New Document button.
8. At the document screen, type the first name and address shown in Figure 6.9 in the first label.
9. Press the Tab key twice to move the insertion point to the next label and then type the second name and address shown in Figure 6.9.

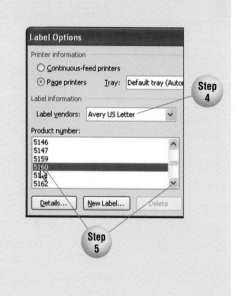

Step 4

Step 5

10. Continue in this manner until all names and addresses in Figure 6.9 have been typed.
11. Save the document and name it **WordL1_C6_P5**.
12. Print and then close **WordL1_C6_P5.docx**.
13. At the blank document, close the document without saving changes.

Figure 6.9 Project 5

DAVID LOWRY	MARCELLA SANTOS	KEVIN DORSEY
12033 S 152 ST	394 APPLE BLOSSOM	26302 PRAIRIE DR
HOUSTON TX 77340	FRIENDSWOOD TX 77533	HOUSTON TX 77316
AL AND DONNA SASAKI	JACKIE RHYNER	MARK AND TINA ELLIS
1392 PIONEER DR	29039 107 AVE E	607 FORD AVE
BAYTOWN TX 77903	HOUSTON TX 77302	HOUSTON TX 77307

Project ⑥ Use a Template to Create a Business Letter

You will use a letter template provided by Word to create a business letter.

Creating a Document Using a Template

Create Document using a Template
1. Click Office button, New.
2. Click *Installed Templates*.
3. Double-click desired template.

Word includes a number of template documents formatted for specific uses. Each Word document is based on a template document with the Normal template the default. With Word templates, you can easily create a variety of documents such as letters, faxes, and awards, with specialized formatting. Templates are available in the *Templates* section of the New Document dialog box. You can choose an installed template or choose from a variety of templates available online.

To create a document based on a template, display the New Document dialog box, click the *Installed Templates* option in the *Templates* section, and then double-click the desired template in the *Installed Templates* list box. This causes a template document to open that contains formatting as well as specific locations where you enter text. Locations for personalized text display in placeholders. Click the placeholder text and then type the personalized text.

If you are connected to the Internet, Microsoft offers a number of predesigned templates you can download. Templates are grouped into categories and the category names display in the *Microsoft Office Online* section of the New Document dialog box. Click the desired template category in the list box and available templates display at the right. Click the desired template and then click the Download button.

Project 6   Creating a Letter Using a Template

1. Click the Office button and then click *New* at the drop-down list.
2. At the New Document dialog box, display available templates by clicking *Installed Templates* in the *Templates* section.
3. Scroll through the list of installed templates and then double-click the **Equity Letter** template.

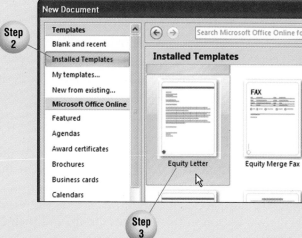

4. At the letter document, click the placeholder text *[Pick the date]*, click the down-pointing arrow at the right side of the placeholder, and then click the Today button located at the bottom of the calendar.
5. Click in the name that displays below the date, select the name, and then type your first and last names.
6. Click the placeholder text *[Type the sender company name]* and then type Sorenson Funds.
7. Click the placeholder text *[Type the sender company address]*, type 4400 Jackson Avenue, press the Enter key, and then type Seattle, WA 98021.
8. Click the placeholder text *[Type the recipient name]* and then type Ms. Jennifer Gonzalez.
9. Click the placeholder text *[Type the recipient address]*, type 12990 California Avenue, press the Enter key, and then type Seattle, WA 98022.
10. Click the placeholder text *[Type the salutation]* and then type Dear Ms. Gonzalez:.
11. Insert a file in the document by completing the following steps:
    a. Click anywhere in the three paragraphs of text in the body of the letter and then click the Delete key.
    b. Click the Insert tab.
    c. Click the Object button arrow in the Text group and then click *Text from File* at the drop-down list.
    d. At the Insert File dialog box, navigate to the Word2007L1C6 folder on your storage medium and then double-click **WordLetter02.docx**.
12. Click the placeholder text *[Type the closing]* and then type Sincerely,.
13. Delete one blank line above Sincerely.
14. Click the placeholder text *[Type the sender title]* and then type Financial Consultant.
15. Save the document and name it **WordL1_C6_P6**.
16. Print and then close **WordL1_C6_P6.docx**.

CHAPTER summary

- Group Word documents logically into folders. Create a new folder at the Open or Save As dialog box.

- You can select one or several documents at the Open dialog box. Copy, move, rename, delete, print, or open a document or selected documents.

- Use the *Cut*, *Copy*, and *Paste* options from the Open dialog box shortcut menu to move or copy a document from one folder to another.

- Delete documents and/or folders with the Delete button on the Open or Save As dialog box toolbar or the *Delete* option from the shortcut menu.

- You can open multiple documents and print multiple documents at the Open dialog box.

- Save a document in a different format with the *Save As* side menu at the Office button drop-down list or with the *Save as type* option at the Save As dialog box.

- Move among the open documents by clicking the button on the Taskbar representing the desired document, or by clicking the View tab, clicking the Switch Windows button in the Window group, and then clicking the desired document name.

- View a portion of all open documents by clicking the View tab and then clicking the Arrange All button in the Window group.

- Use the Minimize, Maximize, and Restore buttons located in the upper right corner of the window to reduce or increase the size of the active window.

- Divide a window into two panes by clicking the View tab and then clicking the Split button in the Window group. This enables you to view different parts of the same document at one time.

- View the contents of two open documents side by side by clicking the View tab, and then clicking the View Side by Side button in the Window group.

- Insert a document into the open document by clicking the Insert tab, clicking the Object button arrow, and then clicking *Text from File* at the drop-down list. At the Insert File dialog box, double-click the desired document.

- Preview a document to display how the document will appear when printed. Use options and buttons in the Print Preview tab to customize the view and to format text in the document.

- Customize a print job with options at the Print dialog box. Use the *Page range* section to specify the amount of text you want printed; use the *Pages* option to identify a specific page, multiple pages, and/or a range of pages for printing; and use the *Number of copies* option to print more than one copy of a document.

- With Word's envelope feature you can create and print an envelope at the Envelopes and Labels dialog box with the Envelopes tab selected.

- If you open the Envelopes and Labels dialog box in a document containing a name and address (with each line ending with a press of the Enter key), that information is automatically inserted in the *Delivery address* text box in the dialog box.

- Use Word's labels feature to print text on mailing labels, file labels, disk labels, or other types of labels.

- Word includes a number of template documents you can use to create a variety of documents. Display the list of template documents by clicking the Office button and then clicking *New* at the drop-down list.

COMMANDS review

FEATURE	RIBBON TAB, GROUP	BUTTON	OPTION	KEYBOARD SHORTCUT
Open dialog box				Ctrl + O
Save As dialog box			Save As	
Print dialog box			Print	Ctrl + P
Arrange all documents	View, Window	Arrange All		
Minimize document				
Maximize document				
Restore				
Split window	View, Window	Split		
View documents side by side	View, Window	View Side by Side		
Insert file	Insert, Text	Object ▾	Text from File	
Preview document			Print, Print Preview	
Envelopes and Labels dialog box with Envelopes tab selected	Mailings, Create			
Envelopes and Labels dialog box with Labels tab selected	Mailings, Create			
New Document dialog box			New	

CONCEPTS check

Test Your Knowledge

Completion: In the space provided at the right, indicate the correct term, command, or number.

1. Create a new folder with this button at the Open or Save As dialog box.

2. Click this button at the Open dialog box to make the previous folder active.

3. Using the mouse, select nonadjacent documents at the Open dialog box by holding down this key while clicking the desired documents.

_____

4. Documents deleted from the hard drive are automatically sent to this bin.

_____

5. Copy a document to another folder without opening the document with the *Copy* option and this option from the Open dialog box shortcut menu.

_____

6. Save a document in a different file format with this option at the Save As dialog box.

_____

7. Click this button in the Window group in the View tab to arrange all open documents so a portion of each document displays.

_____

8. Click this button and the active document fills the editing window.

_____

9. Click this button to reduce the active document to a button on the Taskbar.

_____

10. To display documents side by side, click this button in the Window group in the View tab.

_____

11. Display the Insert File dialog box by clicking the Object button arrow in the Insert tab and then clicking this option.

_____

12. Display a document in this view to determine how a document will appear when printed.

_____

13. Type this in the *Pages* text box in the *Page range* section of the Print dialog box to print pages 3 through 6 of the open document.

_____

14. Type this in the *Pages* text box in the *Page range* section of the Print dialog box to print page 4 and 9 of the open document.

_____

15. The Envelopes button is located in the Create group in this tab.

_____

16. Click the *Installed Templates* option at this dialog box to display a list of templates.

_____

SKILLS check
Demonstrate Your Proficiency

Assessment

1 MANAGE DOCUMENTS

1. Display the Open dialog box with Word2007L1C6 the active folder and then create a new folder named *CheckingTools*.
2. Copy (be sure to copy and not cut) all documents that begin with *WordSpellGrammar* into the CheckingTools folder.
3. With the CheckingTools folder as the active folder, rename **WordSpellGrammar01.docx** to **Technology.docx**.
4. Rename **WordSpellGrammar02.docx** to **Software.docx**.
5. Make Word2007L1C6 the active folder.
6. Delete the CheckingTools folder and all documents contained within it.
7. Open **WordBlock01.docx**, **WordLease03.docx**, and **WordDocument04.docx**.
8. Make **WordLease03.docx** the active document.
9. Make **WordBlock01.docx** the active document.
10. Arrange all of the windows.
11. Make **WordDocument04.docx** the active document and then minimize it.
12. Minimize the remaining documents.
13. Restore **WordBlock01.docx**.
14. Restore **WordLease03.docx**.
15. Restore **WordDocument04.docx**.
16. Maximize and then close **WordBlock01.docx** and then maximize and close **WordDocument04.docx**.
17. Maximize **WordLease03.docx** and then save the document and name it **WordL1_C6_A1**.
18. Open **WordDocument18.docx**.
19. View the **WordL1_C6_A1.docx** document and **WordDocument18.docx** document side by side.
20. Scroll through both documents simultaneously and notice the formatting differences between the title and headings in the two documents. Change the font size and apply shading to the title and headings in **WordL1_C6_A1.docx** to match the font size and shading of the title and headings in **WordDocument18.docx**.
21. Make **WordDocument18.docx** active and then close it.
22. Save **WordL1_C6_A1.docx**.
23. Move the insertion point to the end of the document and then insert the document named **WordSignature.docx**.
24. Save, print, and then close **WordL1_C6_A1.docx**.

Assessment

2 CREATE AN ENVELOPE

1. At a blank document, create an envelope with the text shown in Figure 6.10.
2. Save the envelope document and name it **WordL1_C6_A2**.
3. Print and then close **WordL1_C6_A2.docx**.

Figure 6.10 Assessment 2

DR ROSEANNE HOLT
21330 CEDAR DR
LOGAN UT 84598

GENE MIETZNER
4559 CORRIN AVE
SMITHFIELD UT 84521

Assessment

3 CREATE MAILING LABELS

1. Create mailing labels with the names and addresses shown in Figure 6.11. Use a label option of your choosing. (You may need to check with your instructor before choosing an option.)
2. Save the document and name it **WordL1_C6_A3**.
3. Print and then close **WordL1_C6_A3.docx**.
4. At the clear document screen, close the document screen without saving changes.

Figure 6.11 Assessment 3

SUSAN LUTOVSKY	JIM AND PAT KIEL	IRENE HAGEN
1402 MELLINGER DR	413 JACKSON ST	12930 147TH AVE E
FAIRHOPE OH 43209	AVONDALE OH 43887	CANTON OH 43296
VINCE KILEY	LEONARD KRUEGER	HELGA GUNDSTROM
14005 288TH S	13290 N 120TH	PO BOX 3112
CANTON OH 43287	CANTON OH 43291	AVONDALE OH 43887

Assessment

4 PREPARE A FAX

1. Open the Equity fax template from the New Document dialog box and then insert the following information in the specified fields.
   To: Frank Gallagher
   From: (your first and last names)
   Fax: (206) 555-9010
   Pages: 3
   Phone: (206) 555-9005
   Date: (insert current date)
   Re: Consultation Agreement
   CC: Jolene Yin
   Insert an X in the *For Review* check box
   Comments: Please review the Consultation Agreement and advise me of any legal issues.
2. Save the fax document and name it **WordL1_C6_A4**.
3. Print and then close the document.

Assessment

5 SAVE A DOCUMENT AS A WEB PAGE

1. Experiment with the *Save as type* option at the Save As dialog box and figure out how to save a document as a single file Web page.
2. Open **WordComputers.docx**, display the Save As dialog box, and then change the save as type to a single file Web page. Click the Change Title button that displays in the Save As dialog box. At the Set Page Title dialog box, type Computers in Communication and Entertainment and then close the dialog box. Click the Save button in the Save As dialog box and at the message telling you that some features are not supported by Web browsers, click the Continue button.
3. Close the WordComputers.mht file.
4. Open your Web browser and then open the WordComputers.mht file.
5. Close WordComputers.mht and then close your Web browser.

CASE study
Apply Your Skills

Part 1

You are the office manager for the real estate company, Macadam Realty, and have been asked by the senior sales associate, Lucy Hendricks, to organize contract forms into a specific folder. Create a new folder named *RealEstate* and then copy into the folder documents that begin with the letters "RE." Ms. Hendricks has also asked you to prepare mailing labels for Macadam Realty. Include the name,

Macadam Realty, and the address 100 Third Street, Suite 210, Denver, CO 80803, on the labels. Use a decorative font for the label and make the *M* in *Macadam* and the *R* in *Realty* larger and more pronounced than surrounding text. ***Hint: Format text in the label by selecting text, right-clicking in the selected text, and then choosing the desired option at the shortcut menu.*** Save the completed document and name it **WordL1_C6_CS_P1**. Print and then close the document.

Part 2

One of your responsibilities is to format contract forms. Open the document named **REContractorAgreement.docx** and then save it and name it **WordL1_C6_CS_P2**. The sales associate has asked you to insert signature information at the end of the document and so you decide to insert at the end of the document the file named **RESignature.docx**. With **WordL1_C6_CS_P2.docx** still open, open **REBuildingAgreement.docx**. Format the **WordL1_C6_CS_P2.docx** document so it is formatted in a manner similar to the **REBuildingAreement.docx** document. Consider the following when specifying formatting: margins, fonts, and paragraph shading. Save, print, and then close **WordL1_C6_CS_P2.docx**. Close **REBuildingAgreement.docx**.

Part 3

As part of the organization of contracts, Ms. Hendricks has asked you to insert document properties for the **REBuildingAgreement.docx** and **WordL1_C6_CS_P2.docx** documents. Use the Help feature to learn how to insert document properties. With the information you learn from the Help feature, open each of the two documents separately and then insert document properties in the following fields (you determine the information to type): *Author* (type your first and last names), *Title*, *Subject*, *Keywords*, and *Category*. Print the document properties for each document (change the *Print what* option at the Print dialog box to *Document properties*). Save each document with the original name and close the documents.

Part 4

A client of the real estate company, Anna Hurley, is considering purchasing several rental properties and has asked for information on how to locate real estate rental forms. Using the Internet, locate at least three Web sites that offer real estate rental forms. Write a letter to Anna Hurley at 2300 South 22nd Street, Denver, CO 80205. In the letter, list the Web sites you found and include information on which site you thought offered the most resources. Also include in the letter that Macadam Realty is very interested in helping her locate and purchase rental properties. Save the document and name it **WordL1_C6_CS_P4**. Create an envelope for the letter and add it to the letter document. Save, print, and then close **WordL1_C6_CS_P4.docx**. (You may need to manually feed the envelope in the printer.)

CHAPTER 7

Creating Tables and SmartArt

PERFORMANCE OBJECTIVES

Upon successful completion of Chapter 7, you will be able to:

- Create, edit, and format a table
- Change the table design and layout
- Sort text in a table
- Perform calculations on data in a table
- Create and format a SmartArt diagram
- Create and format a SmartArt organizational chart

word Chapter 7

SNAP

Tutorial 7.1
Using Tables
Tutorial 7.2
Working with Charts

Some Word data can be organized in a table, which is a combination of columns and rows. With the Tables feature, you can insert data in columns and rows. This data can consist of text, values, and formulas. In this chapter you will learn how to create and format a table and insert and format data in the table. Word includes a SmartArt feature that provides a number of predesigned diagrams and organizational charts. Use this feature to create and then customize a diagram or organizational chart.

Note: Before beginning computer projects, copy to your storage medium the Word2007L1C7 subfolder from the Word2007L1 folder on the CD that accompanies this textbook and then make Word2007L1C7 the active folder.

Project ① Create and Format Tables with Company Information

You will create a table containing contact information and another containing information on plans offered by the company. You will then change the design and layout of both tables.

Creating a Table

Use the Tables feature to create boxes of information called *cells*. A cell is the intersection between a row and a column. A cell can contain text, characters, numbers, data, graphics, or formulas. Create a table by clicking the Insert tab,

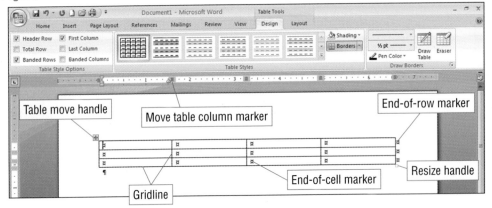
clicking the Table button, dragging down and to the right until the correct number of rows and columns displays, and then clicking the mouse button. You can also create a table with options at the Insert Table dialog box. Display this dialog box by clicking the Table button in the Tables group in the Insert tab and then clicking *Insert Table* at the drop-down list.

Figure 7.1 shows an example of a table with four columns and three rows. Various parts of the table are identified in Figure 7.1 such as the gridlines, move table column marker, end-of-cell marker, end-of-row marker, and the resize handle. In a table, nonprinting characters identify the end of a cell and the end of a row. To view these characters, click the Show/Hide ¶ button in the Paragraph group in the Home tab. The end-of-cell marker displays inside each cell and the end-of-row marker displays at the end of a row of cells. These markers are identified in Figure 7.1.

When you create a table, the insertion point is located in the cell in the upper left corner of the table. Cells in a table contain a cell designation. Columns in a table are lettered from left to right, beginning with *A*. Rows in a table are numbered from top to bottom beginning with *1*. The cell in the upper left corner of the table is cell A1. The cell to the right of A1 is B1, the cell to the right of B1 is C1, and so on.

Figure 7.1 Table

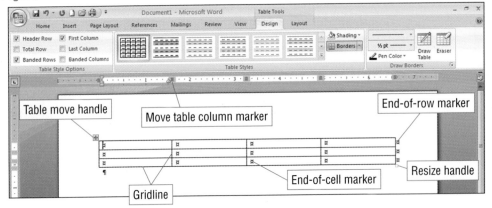

When the insertion point is positioned in a cell in the table, move table column markers display on the horizontal ruler. These markers represent the end of a column and are useful in changing the width of columns. Figure 7.1 identifies a move table column marker.

Entering Text in Cells

With the insertion point positioned in a cell, type or edit text. Move the insertion point to other cells with the mouse by clicking in the desired cell. If you are using the keyboard, press the Tab key to move the insertion point to the next cell or press Shift + Tab to move the insertion point to the previous cell.

If the text you type does not fit on one line, it wraps to the next line within the same cell. Or, if you press Enter within a cell, the insertion point is moved to the next line within the same cell. The cell vertically lengthens to accommodate the text, and all cells in that row also lengthen. Pressing the Tab key in a table causes the insertion point to move to the next cell in the table. If you want to move the insertion point to a tab stop within a cell, press Ctrl + Tab. If the insertion point is located in the last cell of the table and you press the Tab key, Word adds another row to the table. Insert a page break within a table by pressing Ctrl + Enter. The page break is inserted between rows, not within.

Moving the Insertion Point within a Table

To move the insertion point to a different cell within the table using the mouse, click in the desired cell. To move the insertion point to different cells within the table using the keyboard, refer to the information shown in Table 7.1.

Table 7.1 Insertion Point Movement within a Table Using the Keyboard

To move the insertion point	Press these keys
To next cell	Tab
To preceding cell	Shift + Tab
Forward one character	Right Arrow key
Backward one character	Left Arrow key
To previous row	Up Arrow key
To next row	Down Arrow key
To first cell in the row	Alt + Home
To last cell in the row	Alt + End
To top cell in the column	Alt + Page Up
To bottom cell in the column	Alt + Page Down

Project **1a**   **Creating a Table**

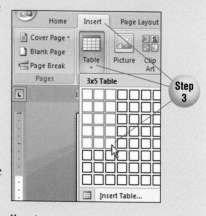

1. At a blank document, turn on bold, and then type the title CONTACT INFORMATION shown in Figure 7.2.
2. Turn off bold and then press the Enter key.
3. Create the table shown in Figure 7.2. To do this, click the Insert tab, click the Table button in the Tables group, drag down and to the right until the number above the grid displays as *3x5*, and then click the mouse button.
4. Type the text in the cells as indicated in Figure 7.2. Press the Tab key to move to the next cell or press Shift + Tab to move to the preceding cell. (If you accidentally press the Enter key within a cell, immediately press the Backspace key. Do not press Tab after typing the text in the last cell. If you do, another row is inserted in the table. If this happens, immediately click the Undo button on the Quick Access toolbar.)
5. Save the table and name it **WordL1_C7_P1**.

Figure 7.2 Project 1a

CONTACT INFORMATION

Maggie Rivera	First Trust Bank	(203) 555-3440
Regina Stahl	United Fidelity	(301) 555-1221
Justin White	Key One Savings	(360) 555-8966
Les Cromwell	Madison Trust	(602) 555-4900
Cecilia Nordyke	American Financial	(509) 555-3995

You can also create a table with options at the Insert Table dialog box shown in Figure 7.3. To display this dialog box, click the Insert tab, click the Table button in the Tables group, and then click *Insert Table.* At the Insert Table dialog box, enter the desired number of columns and rows and then click OK.

Figure 7.3 Insert Table Dialog Box

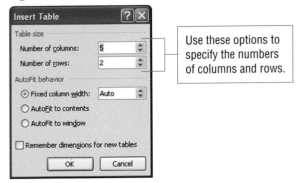

Use these options to specify the numbers of columns and rows.

Project 1b Creating a Table with the Insert Table Dialog Box

1. With **WordL1_C7_P1.docx** open, press Ctrl + End to move the insertion point below the table.
2. Press the Enter key twice.
3. Turn on bold and then type the title OPTIONAL PLAN PREMIUM RATES shown in Figure 7.4.
4. Turn off bold and then press the Enter key.
5. Click the Insert tab, click the Table button in the Tables group, and then click *Insert Table* at the drop-down list.
6. At the Insert Table dialog box, type 3 in the *Number of columns* text box. (The insertion point is automatically positioned in this text box.)
7. Press the Tab key (this moves the insertion point to the *Number of rows* option) and then type 5.
8. Click OK.
9. Type the text in the cells as indicated in Figure 7.4. Press the Tab key to move to the next cell or press Shift + Tab to move to the preceding cell. To indent the text in cells B2 through B5 and cells C2 through C5, press Ctrl + Tab to move the insertion to a tab within cells and then type the text.
10. Save **WordL1_C7_P1.docx**.

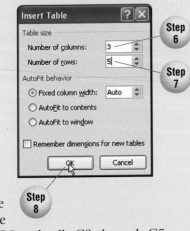

Step 6

Step 7

Step 8

Figure 7.4 Project 1b

OPTIONAL PLAN PREMIUM RATES

Waiting Period	Plan 2010 Employees	Basic Plan Employees
60 days	0.79%	0.67%
90 days	0.59%	0.49%
120 days	0.35%	0.30%
180 days	0.26%	0.23%

Changing the Table Design

When you create a table, the Table Tools Design tab is selected and the tab contains a number of options for enhancing the appearance of the table as shown in Figure 7.5. With options in the Table Styles group, apply a predesigned style that applies color and border lines to a table. Maintain further control over the predesigned style formatting applied to columns and rows with options in the Table Style Options group. For example, if your table contains a total column, you would insert a check mark in the *Total Row* option. Apply additional design formatting to cells in a table with the Shading and Borders buttons in the Table Styles group. Draw a table or draw additional rows and/or columns in a table by clicking the Draw Table button in the Draw Borders group. Click this button and the mouse pointer turns into a pencil. Drag in the table to create the desired columns and rows. Click the Eraser button and the mouse pointer turns into an eraser. Drag through the column and/or row lines you want to erase in the table.

HINT
Draw a freeform table by clicking the Insert tab, clicking the Table button, and then clicking the *Draw Table* option. Drag in the document to create the table.

Draw Table   Eraser

Figure 7.5 Table Tools Design Tab

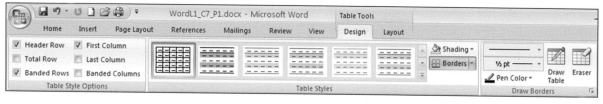

1. With **WordL1_C7_P1.docx** open, click in any cell in the top table.
2. Apply a table style by completing the following steps:

   a. Click the Table Tools Design tab.

   b. Click the More button at the right side of the table styles in the Table Styles group.

   c. Click the *Medium Grid 3 - Accent 5* style (second table style from the *right* in the tenth row in the *Built-in* section).

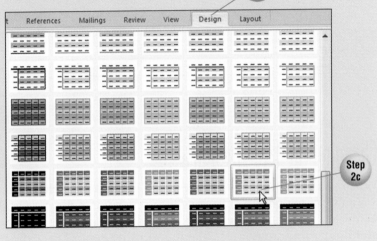

Step 2a

Step 2c

3. After looking at the table, you realize that the first row is not a header row and the first column should not be formatted differently than the other columns. To format the first row and first column in the same manner as the other rows and columns, click the *Header Row* check box and the *First Column* check box in the Table Style Options to remove the check marks.

Step 3

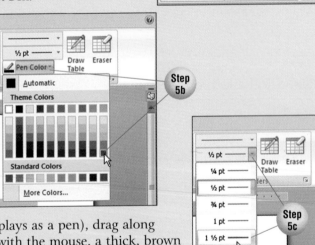

4. Click in any cell in the bottom table, apply the Dark List - Accent 5 table style (second option from the *right* in the eleventh row in the Built-in section), and then remove the check mark from the *First Column* check box.

5. Add color borders to the top table by completing the following steps:

   a. Click in any cell in the top table.

   b. Click the Pen Color button arrow in the Draw Borders group and then click the *Orange, Accent 6, Darker 50%* color.

   c. Click the Line Weight button in the Draw Borders group and then click *1 ½ pt* at the drop-down list. (When you choose a line weight, the Draw Table button is automatically activated.)

   d. Using the mouse (mouse pointer displays as a pen), drag along each side of the table. (As you drag with the mouse, a thick, brown border line is inserted. If you make a mistake or the line does not display as you intended, click the Undo button and then continue drawing along each side of the table.)

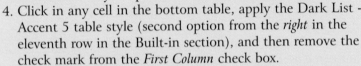
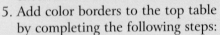

Step 5b

Step 5c

6. Drag along each side of the bottom table.
7. Click the Line Weight button in the Draw Borders group and then click *1 pt* at the drop-down list.
8. Drag along the row boundary separating the first row from the second row in the bottom table.
9. Click the Draw Table button to turn off the feature.
10. Save **WordL1_C7_P1.docx**.

Selecting Cells

You can apply formatting to an entire table or to specific cells, rows, or columns in a table. To identify cells for formatting, select the specific cells using the mouse or the keyboard.

Selecting in a Table with the Mouse

Use the mouse pointer to select a cell, row, column, or an entire table. Table 7.2 describes methods for selecting a table with the mouse. The left edge of each cell, between the left column border and the end-of-cell marker or first character in the cell, is called the *cell selection bar*. When you position the mouse pointer in the cell selection bar, it turns into a small, black arrow pointing up and to the right. Each row in a table contains a *row selection bar*, which is the space just to the left of the left edge of the table. When you position the mouse pointer in the row selection bar, the mouse pointer turns into an arrow pointing up and to the right.

Table 7.2 Selecting in a Table with the Mouse

To select this	Do this
A cell	Position the mouse pointer in the cell selection bar at the left edge of the cell until it turns into a small, black arrow pointing up and to the right and then click the left mouse button.
A row	Position the mouse pointer in the row selection bar at the left edge of the table until it turns into an arrow pointing up and to the right and then click the left mouse button.
A column	Position the mouse pointer on the uppermost horizontal gridline of the table in the appropriate column until it turns into a short, black down-pointing arrow and then click the left mouse button.
Adjacent cells	Position the mouse pointer in the first cell to be selected, hold down the left mouse button, drag the mouse pointer to the last cell to be selected, and then release the mouse button.
All cells in a table	Click the table move handle; or position the mouse pointer in any cell in the table, hold down the Alt key, and then double-click the left mouse button. You can also position the mouse pointer in the row selection bar for the first row at the left edge of the table until it turns into an arrow pointing up and to the right, hold down the left mouse button, drag down to select all rows in the table, and then release the left mouse button.
Text within a cell	Position the mouse pointer at the beginning of the text and then hold down the left mouse button as you drag the mouse across the text. (When a cell is selected, the cell background color changes to blue. When text within cells is selected, only those lines containing text are selected.)

Selecting in a Table with the Keyboard

In addition to the mouse, you can also use the keyboard to select specific cells within a table. Table 7.3 displays the commands for selecting specific amounts of a table.

Table 7.3 Selecting in a Table with the Keyboard

To select	Press
The next cell's contents	Tab
The preceding cell's contents	Shift + Tab
The entire table	Alt + 5 (on numeric keypad with Num Lock off)
Adjacent cells	Hold down Shift key, then press an arrow key repeatedly.
A column	Position insertion point in top cell of column, hold down Shift key, then press down-pointing arrow key until column is selected.

If you want to select only text within cells, rather than the entire cell, press F8 to turn on the Extend mode and then move the insertion point with an arrow key. When a cell is selected, the cell background color changes to blue. When text within a cell is selected, only those lines containing text are selected.

Project 1d Selecting and Formatting Cells in a Table

1. With **WordL1_C7_P1.docx** open, apply shading to a row by completing the following steps:
   a. Position the mouse pointer in the row selection bar at the left edge of the first row in the bottom table until the pointer turns into an arrow pointing up and to the right and then click the left mouse button. (This selects the entire first row of the bottom table.)
   b. Click the Shading button arrow in the Table Styles group and then click the *Red, Accent 2, Darker 50%* color.

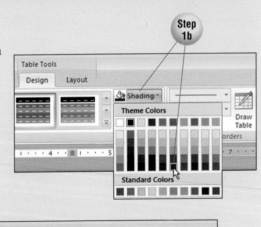

Step 1b

2. Apply a border line to a column by completing the following steps:
   a. Position the mouse pointer on the uppermost horizontal gridline of the first column in the bottom table until the pointer turns into a short, down-pointing arrow and then click the left mouse button.
   b. Click the Borders button arrow and then click *Right Border* at the drop-down list. (This inserts a 1 point dark orange border line at the right side of the column.)

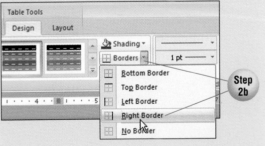

Step 2b

3. Complete steps similar to those in Step 2 to insert a border line at the right side of the second column.
4. Apply italic formatting to a column by completing the following steps:
   a. Position the insertion point in the first cell of the first row in the top table.
   b. Hold down the Shift key and then press the Down Arrow key four times. (This should select all cells in the first column.)
   c. Press Ctrl + I.
5. Save **WordL1_C7_P1.docx**.

Changing Table Layout

To further customize a table, consider changing the table layout by inserting or deleting columns and rows and specifying cell alignments. Change table layout with options at the Table Tools Layout tab shown in Figure 7.6. Use options and buttons in the tab to select specific cells, delete and insert rows and columns, merge and split cells, specify cell height and width, sort data in cells, and insert a formula.

HINT
Some table layout options are available at a shortcut menu that can be viewed by right-clicking a table.

Figure 7.6 Table Tools Layout Tab

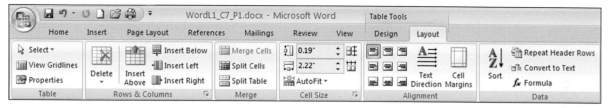

Selecting with the Select Button

Along with selecting cells with the keyboard and mouse, you can also select specific cells with the Select button in the Table group in the Table Tools Layout tab. To select with this button, position the insertion point in the desired cell, column, or row and then click the Select button. At the drop-down list that displays, specify what you want to select—the entire table or a column, row, or cell.

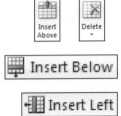

Insert Below

Insert Left

Insert Right

Inserting and Deleting Rows and Columns

With buttons in the Rows & Columns group in the Table Tools Layout tab, you can insert a row or column and delete a row or column. Click the button in the group that inserts the row or column in the desired location such as above, below, to the left, or to the right. Add a row to the bottom of a table by positioning the insertion point in the last cell and then pressing the Tab key. To delete a table, row, or column, click the Delete button and then click the option identifying what you want to delete. If you make a mistake while formatting a table, immediately click the Undo button on the Quick Access toolbar.

Project 1e   Selecting, Inserting, and Deleting Columns and Rows

1. With **WordL1_C7_P1.docx** open, select a column and apply formatting by completing the following steps:
   a. Click in any cell in the first column in the top table.
   b. Click the Table Tools Layout tab.
   c. Click the Select button in the Table group and then click *Select Column* at the drop-down list.

Step 1c   Step 1b

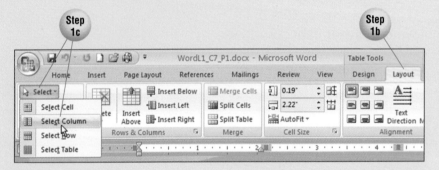

   d. With the first column selected, press Ctrl + I to remove italics and then press Ctrl + B to apply bold formatting.
2. Select a row and apply formatting by completing the following steps:
   a. Click in any cell in the first row in the bottom table.
   b. Click the Select button in the Table group and then click *Select Row* at the drop-down list.
   c. With the first row selected in the bottom table, press Ctrl + I to apply italic formatting.
3. Insert a new row in the bottom table and type text in the new cells by completing the following steps:
   a. Click in the cell containing the text *60 days*.

b. Click the Insert Above button in the Rows & Columns group.

c. Type **30 days** in the first cell of the new row, type **0.85%** in the middle cell of the new row (make sure you press Ctrl + Tab before typing the text), and type **0.81%** in the third cell of the new row (make sure you press Ctrl + Tab before typing the text).

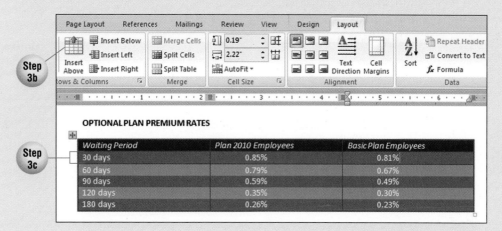

4. Insert three new rows in the top table and type text in the new cells by completing the following steps:

a. Select the three rows of cells that begin with the names *Regina Stahl*, *Justin White*, and *Les Cromwell*.

b. Click the Insert Below button in the Rows & Columns group.

c. Type the following text in the new cells:

Teresa Getty	Meridian Bank	(503) 555-9800
Michael Vazquez	New Horizon Bank	(702) 555-2435
Samantha Roth	Cascade Mutual	(206) 555-6788

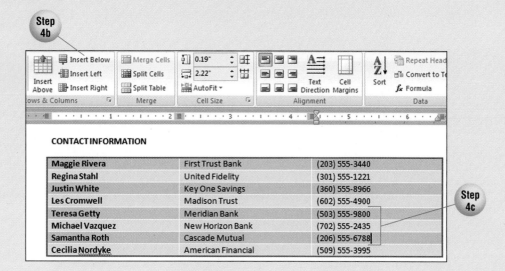

5. Delete a row by completing the following steps:
   a. Click in the cell containing the name *Les Cromwell*.
   b. Click the Delete button in the Rows & Columns group and then click *Delete Rows* at the drop-down list.
6. Insert a new column and type text in the new cells by completing the following steps:
   a. Click in the cell containing the text *First Trust Bank*.
   b. Click the Insert Left button in the Rows & Columns group.
   c. Type the following text in the news cells:
      B1 = Vice President
      B2 = Loan Officer
      B3 = Account Manager
      B4 = Branch Manager
      B5 = President
      B6 = Vice President
      B7 = Regional Manager
7. Save **WordL1_C7_P1.docx**.

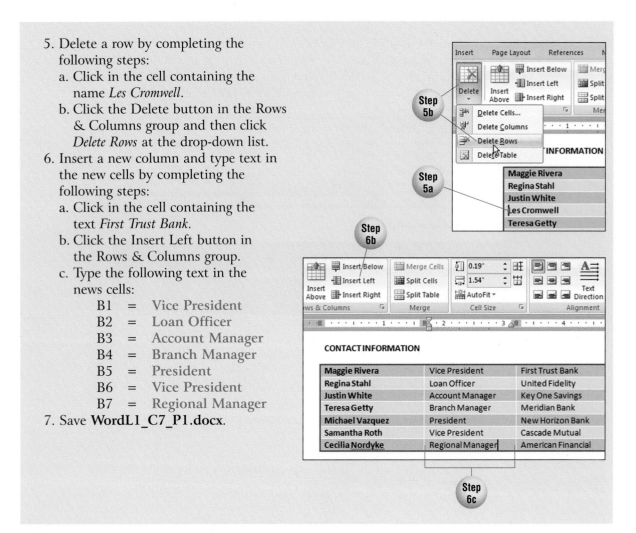

Merging and Splitting Cells and Tables

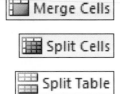

Click the Merge Cells button in the Merge group in the Table Tools Layout tab to merge selected cells and click the Split Cells button to split the currently active cell. When you click the Split Cells button, the Split Cells dialog box displays where you specify the number of columns or rows into which you want to split the active cell. If you want to split one table into two tables, position the insertion point in a cell in the row that you want to be the first row in the new table and then click the Split Table button.

Project 1f Merging and Splitting Cells and Splitting a Table

1. With **WordL1_C7_P1.docx** open, insert a new row and merge cells in the row by completing the following steps:

   a. Click in the cell containing the text *Waiting Period* (located in the bottom table).

   b. Click the Insert Above button in the Rows & Columns group.

   c. With all of the cells in the new row selected, click the Merge Cells button in the Merge group.

   d. Type OPTIONAL PLAN PREMIUM RATES and then press Ctrl + E to center-align the text in the cell. (The text you type will be italicized.)

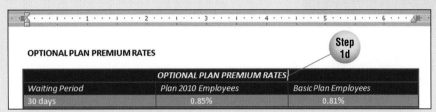

2. Select and then delete the text *OPTIONAL PLAN PREMIUM RATES* that displays above the bottom table.

3. Insert rows and text in the top table and merge cells by completing the following steps:

   a. Click in the cell containing the text *Maggie Rivera*.

   b. Click the Table Tools Layout tab.

   c. Click the Insert Above button twice. (This inserts two rows at the top of the table.)

   d. With the cells in the top row selected, click the Merge Cells button in the Merge group.

   e. Type CONTACT INFORMATION, NORTH and then press Ctrl + E to change the paragraph alignment to center.

   f. Type the following text in the four cells in the new second row.

   Name   Title   Company   Telephone

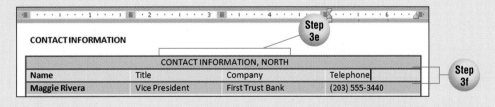

4. Apply heading formatting to the new top row by completing the following steps:

   a. Click the Table Tools Design tab.

   b. Click the *Header Row* check box in the Table Style Options dialog box.

5. Select and then delete the text *CONTACT INFORMATION* that displays above the top table.

6. Split a cell by completing the following steps:

   a. Click in the cell containing the telephone number *(360) 555-8966*.

   b. Click the Table Tools Layout tab.

c. Click the Split Cells button in the Merge group.

d. At the Split Cells dialog box, click OK. (The telephone number will wrap to a new line. You will change this in the next project.)

e. Click in the new cell.

f. Type x453 in the new cell. If AutoCorrect automatically capitalizes the *x*, hover the mouse pointer over the *X* until the AutoCorrect Options button displays. Click the AutoCorrect Options button and then click *Undo Automatic Capitalization* or click *Stop Auto-capitalizing First Letter of Table Cells*.

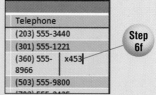

7. Split the cell containing the telephone number *(206) 555-6788* and then type x2310 in the new cell. (If necessary, make the *x* lowercase.)

8. Split the top table into two tables by completing the following steps:

a. Click in the cell containing the name *Teresa Getty*.

b. Click the Split Table button in the Merge group.

c. Click in the cell containing the name *Teresa Getty* (in the first row of the new table).

d. Click the Insert Above button.

e. With the new row selected, click the Merge Cells button.

f. Type CONTACT INFORMATION, SOUTH in the new row and then press Ctrl + E to center-align the text.

9. Draw a dark orange border at the bottom of the top table and the top of the middle table by completing the following steps:

a. Click the Table Tools Design tab.

b. Click the Line Weight button in the Draw Borders group and then click *1 ½ pt* at the drop-down list. (This activates the Draw Table button.)

c. Using the mouse (pointer displays as a pen), drag along the bottom border of the top table.

d. Drag along the top border of the middle table.

e. Click the Draw Table button to turn it off.

10. Save and then print **WordL1_C7_P1.docx**.

11. Delete the middle table by completing the following steps:

a. Click in any cell in the middle table.

b. Click the Table Tools Layout tab.

c. Click the Delete button in the Rows & Columns group and then click *Delete Table* at the drop-down list.

12. Save **WordL1_C7_P1.docx**.

Customizing Cell Size

Distribute Rows

Distribute Columns

When you create a table, column width and row height are equal. You can customize the width of columns or height of rows with buttons in the Cell Size group in the Table Tools Layout tab. Use the *Table Row Height* measurement box to increase or decrease the height of rows and use the *Table Column Width* measurement box to increase or decrease the width of columns. The Distribute Rows button will distribute equally the height of selected rows and the Distribute Columns button will distribute equally the width of selected columns.

You can also change column width using the move table column markers on the horizontal ruler or by using the table gridlines. To change column width using the horizontal ruler, position the mouse pointer on a move table column marker until it turns into a left and right arrow, and then drag the marker to the desired position. Hold down the Shift key while dragging a table column marker and the horizontal ruler remains stationary while the table column marker moves. Hold down the Alt key while dragging a table column marker and measurements display on the horizontal ruler. To change column width using gridlines, position the arrow pointer on the gridline separating columns until the insertion point turns into a left and right arrow with a vertical line between and then drag the gridline to the desired position. If you want to see the column measurements on the horizontal ruler as you drag a gridline, hold down the Alt key.

Adjust row height in a manner similar to adjusting column width. You can drag the adjust table row marker on the vertical ruler or drag the gridline separating rows. Hold down the Alt key while dragging the adjust table row marker or the row gridline and measurements display on the vertical ruler.

Use the AutoFit button in the Cell Size group to make the column widths in a table automatically fit the contents. To do this, position the insertion point in any cell in the table, click the AutoFit button in the Cell Size group, and then click *AutoFit Contents* at the drop-down list.

Project ⑲ Changing Column Width and Row Height

1. With **WordL1_C7_P1.docx** open, change the width of the first column in the top table by completing the following steps:
   a. Click in the cell containing the name *Maggie Rivera*.
   b. Position the mouse pointer on the move table column marker that displays just right of the 1.5-inch marker on the horizontal ruler until the pointer turns into an arrow pointing left and right.
   c. Hold down the Shift key and then the left mouse button.
   d. Drag the marker to the 1.25-inch mark, release the mouse button and then release the Shift key.

2. Complete steps similar to those in Step 1 to drag the move table column marker that displays just right of the 3-inch mark on the horizontal ruler to the 2.5-inch mark. (Make sure the text *Account Manager* in the second column does not wrap to the next line. If it does, slightly increase the width of the column.)

3. Change the width of the third column in the top table by completing the following steps:
   a. Position the mouse pointer on the gridline separating the third and fourth columns until the pointer turns into a left- and right-pointing arrow with a vertical double line between.
   b. Hold down the Alt key and then the left mouse button, drag the gridline to the left until the measurement for the third column on the horizontal ruler displays as *1.4"*, and then release the Alt key and then the mouse button.

4. Position the mouse pointer on the gridline that separates the telephone number *(360) 555-8966* from the extension *x453* and then drag the gridline to the 5.25-inch mark on the horizontal ruler.

5. Drag the right border of the top table to the 5.75-inch marker on the horizontal ruler.

6. Autofit the columns in the bottom table by completing the following steps:
   a. Click in any cell in the bottom table.
   b. Click the AutoFit button in the Cell Size group and then click *AutoFit Contents* at the drop-down list.

7. Increase the height of the first row in the bottom table by completing the following steps:
   a. Make sure the insertion point is located in one of the cells in the bottom table.
   b. Position the mouse pointer on the top adjust table row marker on the vertical ruler.
   c. Hold down the left mouse button and hold down the Alt key.
   d. Drag the adjust table row marker down until the first row measurement on the vertical ruler displays as *0.36"*, release the mouse button and then the Alt key.

8. Increase the height of the first row in the top table by completing the following steps:
   a. Click in any cell in the top table.
   b. Position the arrow pointer on the gridline that displays at the bottom of the top row until the arrow pointer turns into an up- and down-pointing arrow with a vertical double line between.
   c. Hold down the left mouse button and then hold down the Alt key.
   d. Drag the gridline down until the first row measurement on the vertical ruler displays as *0.36"* and release the mouse button and then the Alt key.

9. Save **WordL1_C7_P1.docx**.

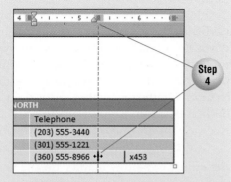

Step 4

Step 6b

Step 7d

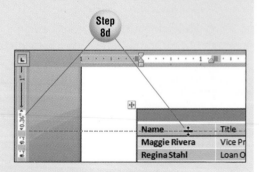

Step 8d

Changing Cell Alignment

The Alignment group in the Table Tools Layout tab contains a number of buttons for specifying the horizontal and vertical alignment of text in cells. The buttons contain a visual representation of the alignment and you can also hover the mouse pointer over a button to determine the alignment.

1. With **WordL1_C7_P1.docx** open, click in the top cell in the top table (the cell containing the title *CONTACT INFORMATION, NORTH*).

Step 2

2. Click the Align Center button in the Alignment group in the Table Tools Layout tab.
3. Format and align text in the second row in the table by completing the following steps:
   a. Select the second row.
   b. Press Ctrl + B (this turns off bold for the entry in the first cell) and then press Ctrl + B again (this turns on bold for all entries in the second row).
   c. Click the Align Top Center button in the Alignment group.
4. Click in the top cell in the bottom table and then click the Align Center button in the Alignment group.
5. Save, print, and then close **WordL1_C7_P1.docx**.

Project 2 Create and Format Tables with Employee Information

You will create and format a table containing information on the names and departments of employees of Tri-State Products and also insert a table containing additional information on employees and then format the table.

Changing Cell Margin Measurements

By default, cells in a table contain specific margin settings. Top and bottom margins in a cell have a default measurement of *0"* and left and right margins have a default setting of *0.08"*. Change these default settings with options at the Table Options dialog box shown in Figure 7.7. Display this dialog box by clicking the Cell Margins button in the Alignment group in the Table Tools Layout tab. Use the options in the *Default cell margins* section to change the top, bottom, left, and/or right cell margin measurements.

Cell Margins

Figure 7.7 Table Options Dialog Box

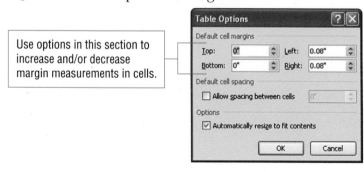

Use options in this section to increase and/or decrease margin measurements in cells.

Changes to cell margins will affect all cells in a table. If you want to change the cell margin measurements for one cell or for selected cells, position the insertion point in the cell or select the desired cells, and then click the Properties button in the Table group in the Table Tools Layout tab. (You can also click the Cell Size group dialog box launcher.) At the Table Properties dialog box that displays, click the Cell tab and then the Options button that displays in the lower right corner of the dialog box. This displays the Cell Options dialog box shown in Figure 7.8.

Figure 7.8 Cell Options Dialog Box

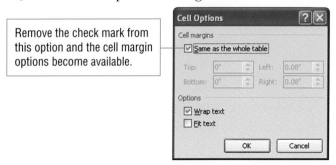

Remove the check mark from this option and the cell margin options become available.

Before setting the new cell margin measurements, remove the check mark from the *Same as the whole table* option. With the check mark removed from this option, the cell margin options become available. Specify the new cell margin measurements and then click OK to close the dialog box.

Project 2a Changing Cell Margin Measurements

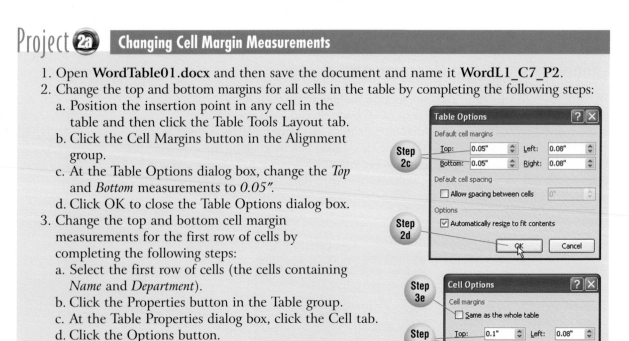

1. Open **WordTable01.docx** and then save the document and name it **WordL1_C7_P2**.
2. Change the top and bottom margins for all cells in the table by completing the following steps:
   a. Position the insertion point in any cell in the table and then click the Table Tools Layout tab.
   b. Click the Cell Margins button in the Alignment group.
   c. At the Table Options dialog box, change the *Top* and *Bottom* measurements to *0.05"*.
   d. Click OK to close the Table Options dialog box.
3. Change the top and bottom cell margin measurements for the first row of cells by completing the following steps:
   a. Select the first row of cells (the cells containing *Name* and *Department*).
   b. Click the Properties button in the Table group.
   c. At the Table Properties dialog box, click the Cell tab.
   d. Click the Options button.
   e. At the Cell Options dialog box, remove the check mark from the *Same as the whole table* option.
   f. Change the *Top* and *Bottom* measurements to *0.1"*.
   g. Click OK to close the Cell Options dialog box.
   h. Click OK to close the Table Properties dialog box.

4. Change the left cell margin measurement for specific cells by completing the following steps:
   a. Select all rows in the table *except* the top row.
   b. Click the Cell Size group dialog box launcher.
   c. At the Table Properties dialog box, click the Cell tab.
   d. Click the Options button.
   e. At the Cell Options dialog box, remove the check mark from the *Same as the whole table* option.
   f. Change the *Left* measurement to *0.3″*.
   g. Click OK to close the Cell Options dialog box.
   h. Click OK to close the Table Properties dialog box.
5. Save **WordL1_C7_P2.docx**.

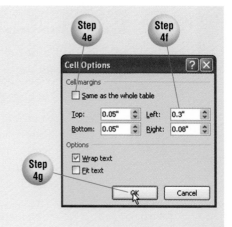

Changing Cell Direction

Change the direction of text in a cell using the Text Direction button in the Alignment group in the Table Tools Layout tab. Each time you click the Text Direction button, the text rotates in the cell 90 degrees.

Text Direction

Changing Table Alignment

By default, a table aligns at the left margin. Change this alignment with options at the Table Properties dialog box with the Table tab selected as shown in Figure 7.9. To change the alignment, click the desired alignment option in the Alignment section of the dialog box.

Figure 7.9 Table Properties Dialog Box with Table Tab Selected

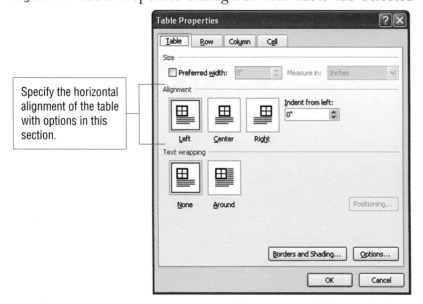

Specify the horizontal alignment of the table with options in this section.

1. With **WordL1_C7_P2.docx** open, insert a new column and change text direction by completing the following steps:
   a. Click in any cell in the first column.
   b. Click the Insert Left button in the Rows & Columns group.
   c. With the cells in the new column selected, click the Merge Cells button in the Merge group.
   d. Type Tri-State Products.
   e. Click the Align Center button in the Alignment group.
   f. Click twice on the Text Direction button in the Alignment group.
   g. With *Tri-State Products* selected, click the Home tab, and then increase the font size to *16*.

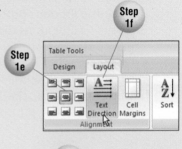

2. Autofit the contents by completing the following steps:
   a. Click in any cell in the table.
   b. Click the Table Tools Layout tab.
   c. Click the AutoFit button in the Cell Size group and then click the *AutoFit Contents* at the drop-down list.

3. Change the table alignment by completing the following steps:
   a. Click the Properties button in the Table group in the Table Tools Layout tab.
   b. At the Table Properties dialog box, click the Table tab.
   c. Click the *Center* option in the *Alignment* section.
   d. Click OK.

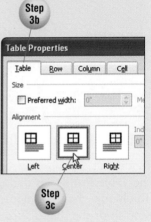

4. Select the two cells containing the text *Name* and *Department* and then click the Align Center button in the Alignment group.

5. Save **WordL1_C7_P2.docx**.

Changing Table Size with the Resize Handle

When you hover the mouse pointer over a table, a resize handle displays in the lower right corner of the table. The resize handle displays as a small, white square. Drag this resize handle to increase and/or decrease the size and proportion of the table.

Moving a Table

Position the mouse pointer in a table and a table move handle displays in the upper left corner. Use this handle to move the table in the document. To move a table, position the mouse pointer on the table move handle until the pointer turns into a four-headed arrow, hold down the left mouse button, drag the table to the desired position, and then release the mouse button.

Project 2C ⟶ Resizing and Moving Tables

1. With **WordL1_C7_P2.docx** open, insert a table into the current document by completing the following steps:
   a. Press Ctrl + End to move the insertion point to the end of the document and then press the Enter key.
   b. Click the Insert tab.
   c. Click the Object button arrow in the Text group and then click *Text from File* at the drop-down list.
   d. At the Insert File dialog box, navigate to the Word2007L1C7 folder and then double-click *WordTable02.docx*.
2. Autofit the bottom table by completing the following steps:
   a. Click in any cell in the bottom table.
   b. Click the Table Tools Layout tab.
   c. Click the AutoFit button in the Cell Size group and then click *AutoFit Contents* at the drop-down list.
3. Format the bottom table by completing the following steps:
   a. Click the Table Tools Design tab.
   b. Click the More button that displays at the right side of the Table Styles group and then click the *Medium Shading 1 - Accent 2* style (third style from the left in the fourth row of the *Built-In* section).

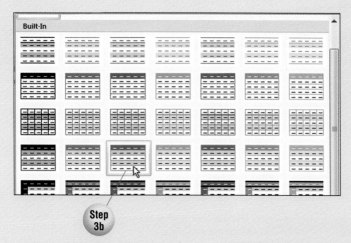

Step 3b

   c. Click the First Column check box to remove the check mark.
   d. Select the first and second rows, click the Table Tools Layout tab, and then click the Align Center button in the Alignment group.
   e. Select the second row and then press Ctrl + B to turn on bold.

4. Resize the bottom table by completing the following steps:
   a. Position the mouse pointer on the resize handle located in the lower right corner of the top table.
   b. Hold down the left mouse button, drag down and to the right until the width and height of the table increases approximately one inch, and then release the mouse button.

Steps 4a–4b

5. Move the bottom table by completing the following steps:
   a. Hover the mouse pointer over the bottom table.
   b. Position the mouse pointer on the table move handle until the pointer displays with a four-headed arrow attached.
   c. Hold down the left mouse button, drag the table so it is positioned equally between the left and right margins, and then release the mouse button.

Step 5c

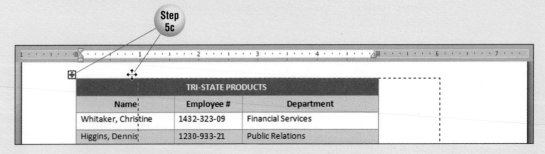

6. Select the cells in the column below the heading *Employee #* and then click the Align Top Center button in the Alignment group.
7. Save **WordL1_C7_P2.docx**.

Converting Text to a Table

You can create a table and then enter data in the cells or you can create the data and then convert it to a table. To convert text to a table, type the text and separate it with a separator character such as a comma or tab. The separator character identifies where you want text divided into columns. To convert text, select the text, click the Insert tab, click the Table button in the Tables group, and then click *Convert Text to Table* at the drop-down list.

Converting a Table to Text

You can convert a table to text by positioning the insertion point in any cell of the table, clicking the Table Tools Layout tab, and then clicking the Convert to Text button in the Data group. At the Convert Table to Text dialog box, specify the desired separator and then click OK.

QUICK STEPS

Convert Text to Table
1. Select text.
2. Click Insert tab.
3. Click Table button.
4. Click *Convert Text to Table*.

Convert Table to Text
1. Position insertion point in any cell of table.
2. Click Table Tools Layout tab.
3. Click *Convert to Text*.
4. Specify desired separator at Convert Table to Text dialog box.
5. Click OK.

Project 2d Converting Text to a Table

1. With **WordL1_C7_P2.docx** open, press Ctrl + End to move the insertion point to the end of the document and then press the Enter key until the insertion point is positioned approximately a double space below the bottom table.
2. Insert the document named **WordList01.docx** into the current document.
3. Convert the text to a table by completing the following steps:
   a. Select the text you just inserted.
   b. Click the Insert tab.
   c. Click the Table button in the Tables group and then click *Convert Text to Table* at the drop-down list.
   d. At the Convert Text to Table dialog box, type 2 in the *Number of columns* text box.
   e. Click the *AutoFit to contents* option in the *AutoFit behavior* section.
   f. Click the *Commas* option in the *Separate text at* section.
   g. Click OK.
4. Select and merge the cells in the top row (the row containing the title *TRI-STATE PRODUCTS* and then change the alignment to Center.
5. Apply the Medium Shading 1 - Accent 2 style (third style from the left in the fourth row of the *Built-In* section) and remove the check mark from the *First Column* check box in the Table Style Options group in the Table Tools Design tab.
6. Drag the table so it is centered and positioned below the table above.
7. Apply the Medium Shading 1 - Accent 2 style to the top table. Increase the width of the columns so the text *TRI-STATE PRODUCTS* is visible and the text in the second and third columns displays on one line.
8. If necessary, drag the table so it is centered and positioned above the middle table. Make sure the three tables fit on one page.
9. Save, print, and then close **WordL1_C7_P2.docx**.

Project ③ Sort and Calculate Sales Data

You will sort data in tables on Tri-State Products sales and then insert formulas to calculate total sales, average sales, and top sales.

QUICK STEPS

Sort Text in Tables
1. Select desired rows in table.
2. Click Sort button in Table Tools Layout tab.
3. Specify the column containing text to sort.
4. Click OK.

Sorting Text in a Table

With the Sort button in the Data group in the Table Tools Layout tab, you can sort text in selected cells in a table in ascending alphabetic or numeric order. To sort text, select the desired rows in the table and then click the Sort button in the Data group. At the Sort dialog box, specify the column containing the text on which you want to sort, and then click OK.

Project ③a Sorting Text in a Table

1. Open **WordTable03.docx** and then save the document and name it **WordL1_C7_P3**.
2. Sort text in the top table by completing the following steps:
   a. Select all of the rows containing names (from *Novak, Diana* through *Sogura, Jeffrey*).
   b. Click Table Tools Layout tab.
   c. Click the Sort button in the Data group.
   d. At the Sort dialog box, click OK. (This sorts the last names in the first column in alphabetical order.)

3. After looking at the table, you decide to sort by 2009 Sales. To do this, complete the following steps:
   a. With the rows still selected, click the Sort button in the Data group.
   b. At the Sort dialog box, click the down-pointing arrow at the right side of the *Sort by* option box and then click *Column 2* at the drop-down list.
   c. Click OK.
   d. Deselect the rows.
4. Save **WordL1_C7_P3.docx**.

Performing Calculations in a Table

You can use the Formula button in the Data group in the Table Tools Layout tab to insert formulas that calculate data in a table. Numbers in cells in a table can be added, subtracted, multiplied, and divided. In addition, you can calculate averages, percentages, and minimum and maximum values. You can calculate data in a Word table, but for complex calculations use an Excel worksheet.

f_x Formula

To perform a calculation on data in a table, position the insertion point in the cell where you want the result of the calculation inserted and then click the Formula button in the Data group in the Table Tools Layout tab. This displays the Formula dialog box shown in Figure 7.10. At this dialog box, accept the default formula that displays in the *Formula* text box or type the desired calculation, and then click OK.

Figure 7.10 Formula Dialog Box

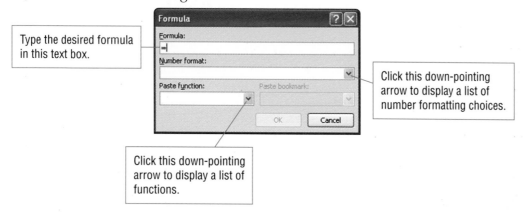

Type the desired formula in this text box.

Click this down-pointing arrow to display a list of number formatting choices.

Click this down-pointing arrow to display a list of functions.

You can use four basic operators when writing a formula including the plus sign (+) for addition, the minus sign (hyphen) for subtraction, the asterisk (*) for multiplication, and the forward slash (/) for division. If a calculation contains two or more operators, Word calculates from left to right. If you want to change the order of calculation, use parentheses around the part of the calculation to be performed first.

In the default formula, the **SUM** part of the formula is called a *function*. Word provides other functions you can use to write a formula. These functions are available with the *Paste function* option in the Formula dialog box. For example, you can use the AVERAGE function to average numbers in cells.

Specify the numbering format with the *Number format* option at the Formula dialog box. For example, if you are calculating money amounts, you can specify that the calculated numbers display with no numbers or two numbers following the decimal point.

1. With **WordL1_C7_P3.docx** open, insert a formula by completing the following steps:
   a. Click in cell B9 (the empty cell located immediately below the cell containing the amount *$623,214*).
   b. Click the Table Tools Layout tab.
   c. Click the Formula button in the Data group.
   d. At the Formula dialog box, make sure *=SUM(ABOVE)* displays in the *Formula* option box.
   e. Click the down-pointing arrow at the right side of the *Number format* option box and then click *#,##0* at the drop-down list (top option in the list).
   f. Click OK to close the Formula dialog box.
   g. At the table, type a dollar sign ($) before the number just inserted in cell B9.

Step 1d   Step 1e

Step 1f

2. Complete steps similar to those in Steps 1c through 1g to insert a formula in cell C9 (the empty cell located immediately below the cell containing the amount *$635,099*).
3. Complete steps similar to those in Steps 1c through 1g to insert in the bottom table formulas that calculate totals. Insert formulas in the cells in the *Total* row and *Total* column. When inserting formulas in cells F3 through F6, you will need to change the formula to *=SUM(LEFT)*.
4. Insert a formula that calculates the average of amounts by completing the following steps:
   a. Click in cell B10 in the top table. (Cell B10 is the empty cell immediately right of the cell containing the word *Average*.)
   b. Click the Formula button in the Data group.
   c. At the Formula dialog box, delete the formula in the *Formula* text box *except* the equals sign.
   d. With the insertion point positioned immediately right of the equals sign, click the down-pointing arrow at the right side of the *Paste function* option box and then click *AVERAGE* at the drop-down list.
   e. With the insertion point positioned between the left and right parentheses, type B2:B8. (When typing cell designations in a formula, you can type either uppercase or lowercase letters.)

Step 4e

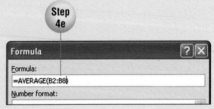

   f. Click the down-pointing arrow at the right side of the *Number format* option box and then click *#,##0* at the drop-down list (top option in the list).
   g. Click OK to close the Formula dialog box.
   h. Type a dollar sign ($) before the number just inserted in cell B10.
5. Complete steps similar to those in Steps 4b through 4h to insert a formula in cell C10 in the top table that calculates the average of cells C2 through C8.

6. Complete steps similar to those in Steps 4b through 4h to insert a formula in cell B7 in the bottom table that calculates the average of cells B2 through B5. Complete similar steps to insert in cell C7 the average of cells C2 through C5; insert in cell D7 the average of cells D2 through D5; insert in cell E7 the average of cells E2 through E5; and insert in cell F7 the average of cells F2 through F5.

7. Insert a formula that calculates the maximum number by completing the following steps:

   a. Click in cell B11 in the top table (the empty cell immediately right of the cell containing the word *Top Sales*).

   b. Click the Formula button in the Data group.

   c. At the Formula dialog box, delete the formula in the *Formula* text box *except* the equals sign.

   d. With the insertion point positioned immediately right of the equals sign, click the down-pointing arrow at the right side of the *Paste function* option box and then click *MAX* at the drop-down list. (You will need to scroll down the list to display the *MAX* option.)

   e. With the insertion point positioned between the left and right parentheses, type B2:B8.

   f. Click the down-pointing arrow at the right side of the *Number format* option box and then click *#,##0* at the drop-down list (top option in the list).

   g. Click OK to close the Formula dialog box.

   h. Type a dollar sign ($) before the number just inserted in cell B11.

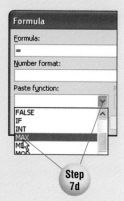

Step 7d

8. Complete steps similar to those in Steps 7b through 7h to insert the maximum number in cell C11.

9. Apply formatting to each table to enhance the visual appeal of the tables.

10. Save, print, and then close **WordL1_C7_P3.docx**.

Project ④ **Prepare and Format a Diagram**

You will prepare a process diagram identifying steps in the production process and then apply formatting to enhance the diagram.

Creating SmartArt

With Word's SmartArt feature you can insert diagrams and organizational charts in a document. SmartArt offers a variety of predesigned diagrams and organizational charts that are available at the Choose a SmartArt Graphic dialog box shown in Figure 7.11. At this dialog box, *All* is selected in the left panel and all available predesigned diagrams display in the middle panel.

HINT
Use SmartArt to communicate your message and ideas in a visual manner.

SmartArt

Figure 7.11 Choose a SmartArt Graphic Dialog Box

Double-click the desired SmartArt graphic in this panel.

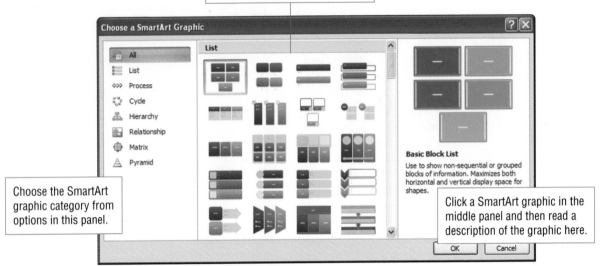

Choose the SmartArt graphic category from options in this panel.

Click a SmartArt graphic in the middle panel and then read a description of the graphic here.

Inserting and Formatting a SmartArt Diagram

QUICK STEPS

Insert a SmartArt Diagram
1. Click Insert tab.
2. Click SmartArt button.
3. Double-click desired diagram.

HINT

Limit the number of shapes and the amount of text to key points.

Predesigned diagrams display in the middle panel of the Choose a SmartArt Graphic dialog box. Use the scroll bar at the right side of the middle panel to scroll down the list of diagram choices. Click a diagram in the middle panel and the name of the diagram displays in the right panel along with a description of the diagram type. SmartArt includes diagrams for presenting a list of data; showing data processes, cycles, and relationships; and presenting data in a matrix or pyramid. Double-click a diagram in the middle panel of the dialog box and the diagram is inserted in the document.

When you double-click a diagram at the dialog box, the diagram is inserted in the document and a text pane displays at the left side of the diagram. You can type text in the diagram in the text pane or directly in the diagram. Apply design formatting to a diagram with options at the SmartArt Tools Design tab shown in Figure 7.12. This tab is active when the diagram is inserted in the document. With options and buttons in this tab you add objects, change the diagram layout, apply a style to the diagram, and reset the diagram back to the original formatting.

Figure 7.12 SmartArt Tools Design Tab

Project 4a Inserting and Formatting a Diagram

1. At a blank document, insert the diagram shown in Figure 7.13 by completing the following steps:
   a. Click the Insert tab.
   b. Click the SmartArt button in the Illustrations group.
   c. At the Choose a SmartArt Graphic dialog box, click *Process* in the left panel and then double-click the *Alternating Flow* diagram (last option in the top row).
   d. If a *Type your text here* text pane does not display at the left side of the diagram, click the Text Pane button in the Create Graphic group to display the pane.
   e. With the insertion point positioned after the top bullet in the *Type your text here* text pane, type Design.
   f. Click *[Text]* that displays below *Design* and then type Mock-up.
   g. Continue clicking occurrences of *[Text]* and typing text so the text pane displays as shown at the right.
   h. Close the text pane by clicking the Close button (contains an X) that displays in the upper right corner of the pane. (You can also click the Text Pane button in the Create Graphic group.)

2. Change the diagram colors by clicking the Change Colors button in the SmartArt Styles group and then clicking the first option in the *Colorful* section (*Colorful – Accent Colors*).

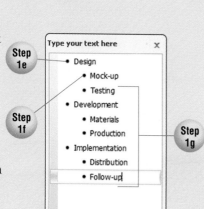

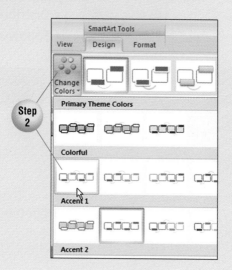

3. Apply a style by clicking the More button that displays at the right side of the SmartArt Styles group and then clicking the second option from the left in the top row of the *3-D* section (*Inset*).

4. Copy the diagram and then change the layout by completing the following steps:
   a. Click inside the diagram border but outside of any shapes.
   b. Click the Home tab and then click the Copy button in the Clipboard group.
   c. Press Ctrl + End, press the Enter key once, and then press Ctrl + Enter to insert a page break.
   d. Click the Paste button in the Clipboard group.
   e. Click the bottom diagram.
   f. Click the SmartArt Tools Design tab.
   g. Click the middle layout (*Continuous Block Process*) in the Layouts group.
   h. Click outside the diagram to deselect it.

5. Save the document and name it **WordL1_C7_P4**.

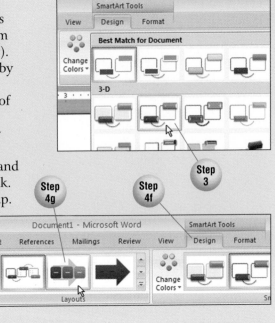

Figure 7.13 Project 4a

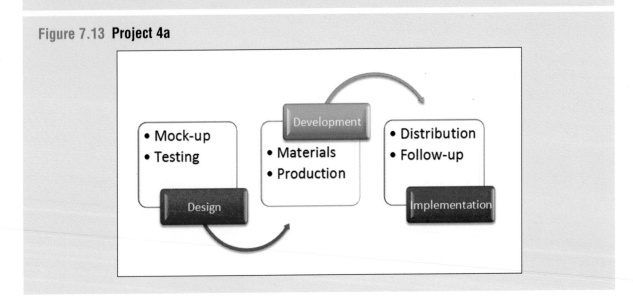

Apply formatting to a diagram with options at the SmartArt Tools Format tab shown in Figure 7.14. With options and buttons in this tab you can change the size and shape of objects in the diagram; apply shape styles and WordArt styles; change the shape fill, outline, and effects; and arrange and size the diagram.

Figure 7.14 SmartArt Tools Format Tab

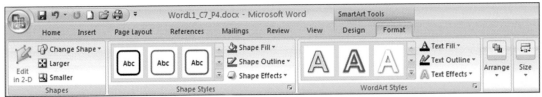

Arranging and Moving a SmartArt Diagram

Before moving a SmartArt diagram, you must select a text wrapping style. Select a text wrapping style with the Arrange button in the SmartArt Tools Format tab. Click the Arrange button, click the Position button, and then click the desired position at the drop-down gallery. You can also choose a text wrapping by clicking the Arrange button, clicking Text Wrapping, and then clicking the desired wrapping style at the drop-down list. Move the diagram by positioning the arrow pointer on the diagram border until the pointer turns into a four-headed arrow, holding down the left mouse button, and then dragging the diagram to the desired location. Nudge selected shape(s) with the up, down, left, or right arrow keys on the keyboard.

Project 4b — Formatting Diagrams

1. With **WordL1_C7_P4.docx** open, format shapes by completing the following steps:
   a. Click the diagram on the first page to select it (light turquoise border surrounds the diagram).
   b. Click the SmartArt Tools Format tab.
   c. In the diagram, click the rectangle shape containing the word *Design*.
   d. Hold down the Shift key and then click the shape containing the word *Development*.
   e. With the Shift key still down, click the shape containing the word *Implementation*. (All three shapes should now be selected.)
   f. Click the Change Shape button in the Shapes group.
   g. Click the seventh shape from the left in the second row of the *Block Arrows* section (the Pentagon shape).
   h. With the shapes still selected, click the Larger button in the Shapes group.
   i. With the shapes still selected, click the Shape Outline button arrow in the Shape Styles group and then click the red color *Red, Accent 2*.

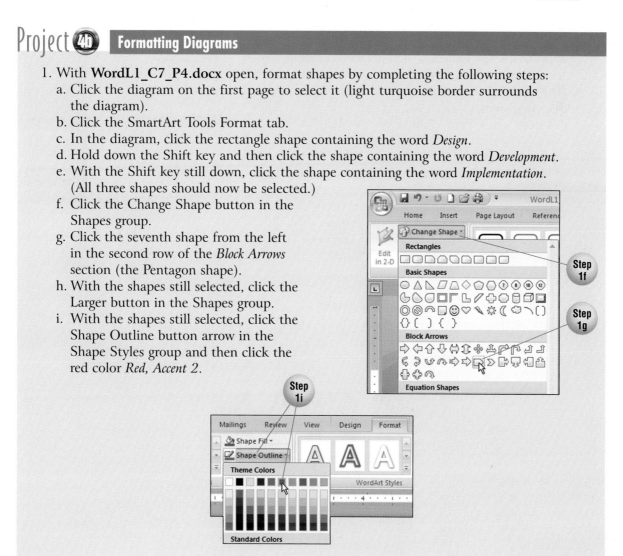

j. Click inside the diagram border but outside any shape. (This deselects the shapes but keeps the diagram selected.)

2. Change the size of the diagram by completing the following steps:

   a. Click the Size button located at the right side of the tab.

   b. Click in the *Height* measurement box, type 4, and then press Enter.

3. Position the diagram by completing the following steps:

   a. Click the Arrange button located toward the right side of the tab.

   b. Click the Position button.

   c. Click the middle option in the second row of the *With Text Wrapping* section (the *Position in Middle Center with Square Text Wrapping* option).

4. Format the bottom diagram by completing the following steps:

   a. Press Ctrl + End to move to the end of the document and then click in the bottom diagram to select it.

   b. Hold down the Shift key and then click each of the three shapes.

   c. Click the More button at the right side of the styles in the WordArt Styles group.

   d. Click the last WordArt style in the lower right corner of the drop-down gallery (*Fill - Accent 1, Metal Bevel, Reflection*).

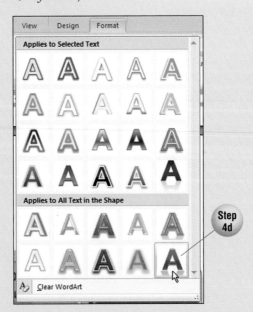

e. Click the Text Outline button arrow in the WordArt Styles group and then click the light blue color in the *Standard Colors* section (the seventh color from the left).

f. Click the Text Effects button in the WordArt Styles group, point to *Glow* at the drop-down list, and then click the last option in the top row.

g. Click inside the diagram border but outside any shape.

5. Arrange the diagram by clicking the Arrange button, clicking the Position button, and then clicking the middle option in the second row of the *With Text Wrapping* section (the *Position in Middle Center with Square Text Wrapping* option).

6. Save, print, and then close **WordL1_C7_P4.docx**.

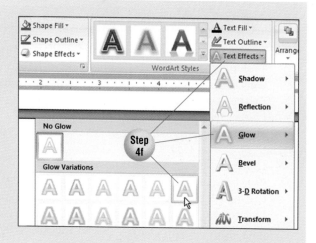

P roject ⑤ Prepare and Format a Company Organizational Chart

You will prepare an organizational chart for a company and then apply formatting to enhance the visual appeal of the organizational chart.

Creating an Organizational Chart with SmartArt

If you need to visually illustrate hierarchical data, consider creating an organizational chart with a SmartArt option. To display organizational chart SmartArt options, click the Insert tab and then click the SmartArt button in the Illustrations group. At the Choose a SmartArt Graphic dialog box, click *Hierarchy* in the left panel. Organizational chart options display in the middle panel of the dialog box. Double-click the desired organizational chart and the chart is inserted in the document. Type text in a diagram by selecting the shape and then typing text in the shape or you can type text in the *Type your text here* window that displays at the left side of the diagram. Format a SmartArt organizational chart with options and buttons in the SmartArt Tools Design tab similar to the one shown in Figure 7.12 and the SmartArt Tools Format tab similar to the one shown in Figure 7.14.

QUICK STEPS

Insert an Organizational Chart
1. Click Insert tab.
2. Click SmartArt button.
3. Click *Hierarchy*.
4. Double-click desired organizational chart.

1. At a blank document, create the organizational chart shown in Figure 7.15. To begin, click the Insert tab.
2. Click the SmartArt button in the Illustrations group.
3. At the Choose a SmartArt Graphic dialog box, click *Hierarchy* in the left panel of the dialog box and then double-click the first option in the middle panel, *Organization Chart*.
4. If a *Type your text here* window displays at the left side of the organizational chart, close the pane by clicking the Text Pane button in the Create Graphic group.
5. Delete one of the boxes in the organizational chart by clicking the border of the box in the lower right corner to select it and then pressing the Delete key. (Make sure that the selection border that surrounds the box is a solid line and not a dashed line. If a dashed line displays, click the box border again. This should change it to a solid line.)
6. With the bottom right box selected, click the Add Shape button arrow and then click the *Add Shape Below* option.
7. Click *[Text]* in the top box, type Blaine Willis, press the Enter key, and then type President. Click in each of the remaining boxes and type the text as shown in Figure 7.15.
8. Click the More button located at the right side of the styles in the SmartArt Styles group and then click the *Inset* style in the *3-D* section (second option from the left in the top row of the *3-D* section).
9. Click the Change Colors button in the SmartArt Styles group and then click the *Colorful Range - Accent Colors 4 to 5* in the *Colorful* section (fourth option from the left in the *Colorful* row).
10. Click the SmartArt Tools Format tab.
11. Click the tab (displays with a right- and left-pointing triangle) that displays at the left side of the diagram border. (This displays the *Type your text here* window.)
12. Using the mouse, select the text that displays in the *Type your text here* window.
13. Click the Change Shape button in the Shapes group and then click the *Round Same Side Corner Rectangle* option (second option from the *right* in the top row).
14. Click the Shape Outline button arrow in the Shape Styles group and then click the dark blue color (second color from the *right* in the *Standard Colors* section).
15. Click the Size button located at the right side of the tab and then change the height to 4″ and the width to 6.5″.
16. Click outside the chart to deselect it.
17. Save the document and name it **WordL1_C7_P5**.
18. Print and then close the document.

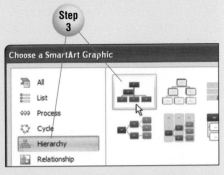

Step
3

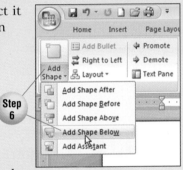

Step
6

Step
9

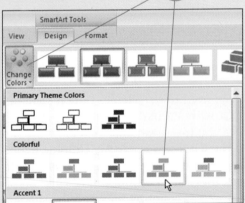

Step
13

Figure 7.15 Project 5

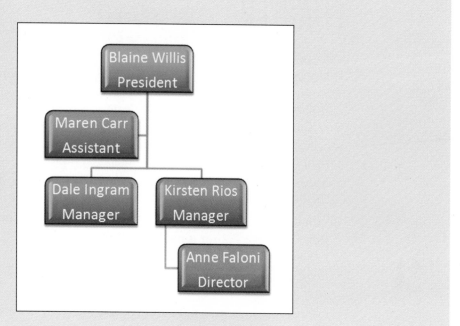

CHAPTER summary

- Use the Tables feature to create columns and rows of information. Create a table with the Table button in the Tables group in the Insert tab or with options at the Insert Table dialog box.

- A cell is the intersection between a row and a column. The lines that form the cells of the table are called gridlines. Columns in a table are lettered from left to right beginning with *A*. Rows are numbered from top to bottom beginning with *1*.

- Move the insertion point to cells in a document using the mouse by clicking in the desired cell or use the keyboard commands shown in Table 7.1.

- Change the table design with options and buttons in the Table Tools Design tab.

- Refer to Table 7.2 for a list of mouse commands for selecting specific cells in a table.

- Refer to Table 7.3 for a list of keyboard commands for selecting specific cells in a table.

- Change the layout of a table with options and buttons in the Table Tools Layout tab.

- You can select a table, column, row, or cell using the Select button in the Table group in the Table Tools Layout tab.

- Insert and delete columns and rows with buttons in the Rows & Columns group in the Table Tools Layout tab.

- Merge selected cells with the Merge Cells button and split cells with the Split Cells button, both located in the Merge group in the Table Tools Layout tab.

- Change column width and row height using the height and width measurement boxes in the Cell Size group in the Table Tools Layout tab; by dragging move table column markers on the horizontal ruler, adjust table row markers on the vertical ruler, gridlines in the table; or with the AutoFit button in the Cell Size group.

- Change alignment of text in cells with buttons in the Alignment group in the Table Tools Layout tab.

- Change cell margins with options in the Table Options dialog box.

- Change text direction in a cell with the Text Direction button in the Alignment group.

- Change the table alignment at the Table Properties dialog box with the Table tab selected.

- You can use the resize handle to change the size of the table and use the table move handle to move the table.

- Convert text to a table with the *Convert Text to Table* option at the Table button drop-down list. Convert a table to text with the Convert to Text button in the Data group in the Table Tools Layout tab.

- Sort selected rows in a table with the Sort button in the Data group.

- Perform calculations on data in a table by clicking the Formula button in the Data group in the Table Tools Layout tab and then specifying the formula and number format at the Formula dialog box.

- Use the SmartArt feature to insert predesigned diagrams and organizational charts in a document. Click the SmartArt button in the Insert tab to display the Choose a SmartArt Graphic dialog box.
- Format a SmartArt diagram or organizational chart with options and buttons in the SmartArt Tools Design tab and the SmartArt Tools Format tab.
- To move a SmartArt diagram, first choose a position or a text wrapping style with the Arrange button in the SmartArt Tools Format tab.

COMMANDS review

FEATURE	RIBBON TAB, GROUP	BUTTON	OPTION
Table	Insert, Tables		
Insert Table dialog box	Insert, Tables		Insert Table
Draw table	Table Tools Design, Draw Borders		
Insert column left	Table Tools Layout, Rows & Columns	Insert Left	
Insert column right	Table Tools Layout, Rows & Columns	Insert Right	
Insert row above	Table Tools Layout, Rows & Columns		
Insert row below	Table Tools Layout, Rows & Columns	Insert Below	
Delete table	Table Tools Layout, Rows & Columns		Delete Table
Delete row	Table Tools Layout, Rows & Columns		Delete Rows
Delete column	Table Tools Layout, Rows & Columns		Delete Columns
Merge cells	Table Tools Layout, Merge	Merge Cells	
Split cells dialog box	Table Tools Layout, Merge	Split Cells	
AutoFit table contents	Table Tools Layout, Cell Size	AutoFit ▾	
Cell alignment	Table Tools Layout, Alignment		
Table Options dialog box	Table Tools Layout, Alignment		
Cell direction	Table Tools Layout, Alignment		
Convert text to table	Insert, Tables		Convert Text to Table
Convert table to text	Table Tools Layout, Data	Convert to Text	

continued

word Level 1

Creating Tables and SmartArt

FEATURE	RIBBON TAB, GROUP	BUTTON	OPTION
Sort text in table	Table Tools Layout, Data	$\begin{smallmatrix}A\\Z\end{smallmatrix}\downarrow$	
Formula dialog box	Table Tools Layout, Data	*f* Formula	
Choose a SmartArt Graphic dialog box	Insert, Illustrations		

CONCEPTS check

Test Your Knowledge

Completion: In the space provided at the right, indicate the correct term, command, or number.

1. The Table button is located in this tab. _____

2. This is another name for the lines that form the cells of the table. _____

3. Use this keyboard shortcut to move the insertion point to the previous cell. _____

4. Use this keyboard shortcut to move the insertion point to a tab within a cell. _____

5. This tab contains table styles you can apply to a table. _____

6. Click this button in the Table Tools Layout tab to insert a column at the left side of the column containing the insertion point. _____

7. Insert and delete columns and rows with buttons in this group in the Table Tools Layout tab. _____

8. One method for changing column width is dragging this on the horizontal ruler. _____

9. Use this button in the Cell Size group to make the column widths in a table automatically fit the contents. _____

10. Change the table alignment at this dialog box with the Table tab selected. _____

11. Hover the mouse pointer over a table and this displays in the lower right corner of the table. _____

12. Position the mouse pointer in a table and this displays in the upper left corner. _____

13. Display the Formula dialog box by clicking the Formula button in this group in the Table Tools Layout tab. _____

14. The SmartArt button is located in this tab. _____

15. Click the SmartArt button and this dialog box displays. _____

16. If you need to visually illustrate hierarchical data, consider creating this with the SmartArt feature. _____

SKILLS check
Demonstrate Your Proficiency

Assessment

1 CREATE AND FORMAT A PROPERTY REPLACEMENT COSTS TABLE

1. At a blank document, create the table shown in Figure 7.16 with the following specifications:
   a. Create a table with two columns and eight rows.
   b. Merge the cells in the top row and then change the alignment to Align Center.
   c. Type the text in the cells as shown in Figure 7.16.
   d. Right-align the cells containing the money amounts as well as the blank line below the last amount (cells B2 through B8).
   e. Autofit the contents of the cells.
   f. Apply the Light List – Accent 4 table style.
   g. Remove the check mark from the *First Column* check box.
   h. Draw a green (Olive Green, Accent 3, Darker 25%) 1½ pt border around the table.
   i. Change the font size to 14 for the text in cell A1.
   j. Use the resize handle located in the lower right corner of the table and increase the width and height of the table by approximately one inch.
2. Click in the *Accounts receivable* cell and insert a row below. Type Equipment in the new cell at the left and type $83,560 in the new cell at the right.
3. Insert a formula in cell B9 that sums the amounts in cell B2 through B8. (Insert a dollar sign before the amount in cell B9.)
4. Save the document and name it **WordL1_C7_A1**.
5. Print and then close **WordL1_C7_A1.docx**.

Figure 7.16 Assessment 1

PROPERTY Replacement Costs	
Business personal property	$1,367,340
Earnings and expenses	$945,235
Domestic and foreign transit	$123,400
Accounts receivable	$95,460
Legal liability	$75,415
Computer coverage	$53,098
Total	

Assessment

2   FORMAT A TABLE CONTAINING TRANSPORTATION SERVICE INFORMATION

1. Open **WordTable04.docx** and then save the document and name it **WordL1_C7_A2**.
2. Format the table so it appears as shown in Figure 7.17.
3. Position the table in the middle of the page.
4. Save, print, and then close **WordL1_C7_A2.docx**.

Figure 7.17 Assessment 2

	Service	Telephone
Metro Area Transportation Services	*Langley City Transit*	
	Subway and bus information	(507) 555-3049
	Service status hotline	(507) 555-4123
	Travel information	(507) 555-4993
	Valley Rail Road	
	Railway information	(202) 555-2300
	Status hotline	(202) 555-2343
	Travel information	(202) 555-2132
	Mainline Bus	
	Bus routes	(507) 555-6530
	Emergency hotline	(507) 555-6798
	Travel information	(507) 555-7542
	Village Travel Card	
	Village office	(507) 555-1232
	Card inquiries	(507) 555-1930

Assessment

3 CREATE AND FORMAT A COMPANY DIAGRAM

1. At a blank document, create the SmartArt diagram shown in Figure 7.18 with the following specifications:
   a. Use the Titled Matrix diagram.
   b. Apply the Colorful - Accent Colors SmartArt style.
   c. Type all of the text shown in Figure 7.18.
   d. Select all of the text and then apply the Gradient Fill - Accent 4, Reflection WordArt style.
2. Save the document and name it **WordL1_C7_A3**.
3. Print and then close **WordL1_C7_A3.docx**.

Figure 7.18 Assessment 3

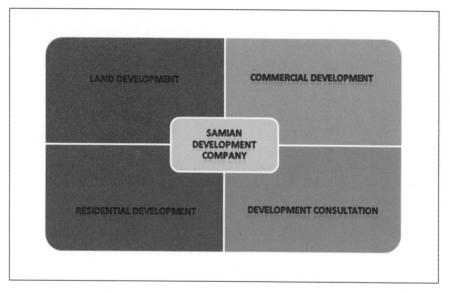

Assessment

4 CREATE AND FORMAT A COMPANY ORGANIZATIONAL CHART

1. At a blank document, create the organizational chart shown in Figure 7.19 with the following specifications:
   a. Use the Hierarchy organizational chart.
   b. Select the top text box and insert a shape above.
   c. Select the top right text box and then add a shape below.
   d. Type the text shown in the organizational chart in Figure 7.19.
   e. Apply the Colorful Range - Accent Colors 2 to 3 option.
   f. Increase the height to 4.5″ and the width to 6.5″.
   g. Position the organizational chart in the middle of the page.
2. Save the document and name it **WordL1_C7_A4**.
3. Print and then close **WordL1_C7_A4.docx**.

Figure 7.19 Assessment 4

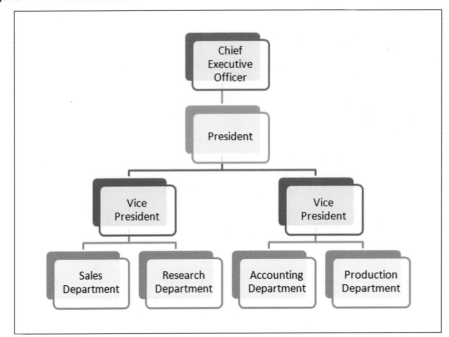

Assessment

5 INSERT FORMULAS IN A TABLE

1. In this chapter, you learned how to insert formulas in a table. Experiment with writing formulas (consider using the Help feature or other reference) and then open **WordTable05.docx**. Save the document and name it **WordL1_C7_A5**.
2. Format the table so it appears as shown in Figure 7.20.
3. Insert a formula in cell B13 that sums the amounts in cells B6 through B12. Complete similar steps to insert a formula in cell C13, D13, and E13.
4. Insert a formula in cell B14 that subtracts the amount in B4 from the amount in B13. *(Hint: The formula should look like this: =(B4-B13).)* Complete similar steps to insert a formula in cells C14, D14, and E14.
5. Save, print, and then close **WordL1_C7_A5.docx**.

Figure 7.20 Assessment 5

TRI-STATE PRODUCTS				
Financial Analysis				
	2007	2008	2009	2010
Revenue	$1,450,348	$1,538,239	$1,634,235	$1,523,455
Expenses				
Facilities	$250,220	$323,780	$312,485	$322,655
Materials	$93,235	$102,390	$87,340	$115,320
Payroll	$354,390	$374,280	$380,120	$365,120
Benefits	$32,340	$35,039	$37,345	$36,545
Marketing	$29,575	$28,350	$30,310	$31,800
Transportation	$4,492	$5,489	$5,129	$6,349
Miscellaneous	$4,075	$3,976	$4,788	$5,120
Total				
Net Revenue				

CASE study
Apply Your Skills

Part 1

You have recently been hired as an accounting clerk for a landscaping business, Landmark Landscaping, which has two small offices in your city. The accounting clerk prior to you kept track of monthly sales using Word, and the manager would prefer that you continue using that application. Open the file named **WordMonthlySales.docx** and then save the document and name it **WordL1_C7_CS_P1**. After reviewing the information, you decide that a table would be a better way of maintaining and displaying the data. Convert the data to a table and modify its appearance so that it is easy to read and understand. Insert a total row at the bottom of the table and then insert formulas to sum the totals in the columns containing amounts. Apply formatting to the table to enhance the visual appeal. Determine a color theme for the table and then continue that same color theme when preparing other documents for Landmark Landscaping. Save, print, and then close the document.

The president of Landmark Landscaping has asked you to prepare an organizational chart for the company that will become part of the company profile. Use a SmartArt organizational chart and create a chart with the following company titles (in the order shown below):

President		
Westside Manager		Eastside Manager
Landscape Architect	Landscape Director	Landscape Architect / Landscape Director
	Assistant	Assistant

Format the organizational chart to enhance the visual appeal and apply colors that match the color scheme you chose for the company in Part 1. Save the document and name it **WordL1_C7_CS_P2**. Print and then close the document.

As part of the company profile, the president of the company would like to include a diagram that represents the services offered by the company and use the diagram as a company marketing tool. Use SmartArt to create a diagram that contains the following services: Maintenance Contracts, Planting Services, Landscape Design, and Landscape Consultation. Format the diagram to enhance the visual appeal and apply colors that match the color scheme you chose for the company in Part 1. Save the document and name it **WordL1_C7_CS_P3**. Print and then close the document.

Help

Since the SmartArt feature is new and others in the company will need training on the feature, the office manager has started a training document with information on using SmartArt. He has asked you to add information on keyboard shortcuts for working with shapes. Use the Help feature to learn about the keyboard shortcuts available for working with shapes and then create a table and insert the information in the table. Format the table to enhance the visual appeal and apply colors that match the color scheme you chose for the company in Part 1. Save the document and name it **WordL1_C7_CS_P4**. Print and then close the document.

Part

5

One of the landscape architects has asked you to prepare a table containing information on trees that need to be ordered next month. She would also like to have you include the Latin name for the trees since this is important when ordering. Create a table that contains the common name of the tree, the Latin name, the number required, and the price per tree as shown in Figure 7.21. Use the Internet (or any other resource available to you) to find the Latin name of each tree listed in Figure 7.21. Create a column in the table that multiplies the number of trees required by the price and include this formula for each tree. Format and enhance the table so it is attractive and easy to read. Save the document and name it **WordL1_C7_CS_P5**. Print and then close the document.

Figure 7.21 Case Study, Part 5

Douglas Fir, 15 required, $1.99 per tree
White Elm, 10 required, $2.49 per tree
Western Hemlock, 10 required, $1.89 per tree
Red Maple, 8 required, $6.99 per tree
Ponderosa Pine, 5 required, $2.69 per tree

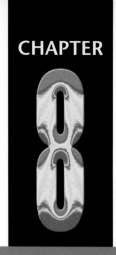

CHAPTER 8

Merging Documents

PERFORMANCE OBJECTIVES

Upon successful completion of Chapter 8, you will be able to:

word Chapter 8

- Create and merge letters, envelopes, labels, and a directory
- Create custom fields for a merge
- Edit main documents and data source files
- Input text during a merge

Tutorial 8.1
Using Mail Merge

Word includes a Mail Merge feature you can use to create customized letters, envelopes, labels, directories, e-mail messages, and faxes. The Mail Merge feature is useful for situations where you need to send the same letter to a number of people and create an envelope for each letter. Use Mail Merge to create a main document that contains a letter, envelope, or other data and then merge the main document with a data source. In this chapter, you will use Mail Merge to create letters, envelopes, labels, and directories.

Note: Before beginning computer projects, copy to your storage medium the Word2007L1C8 subfolder from the Word2007L1 folder in the CD that accompanies this textbook and then make Word2007L1C8 the active folder.

Project ① Merge Letters to Customers

You will create a data source file and a letter main document, and then merge the main document with the records in the data source file.

Completing a Merge

Use buttons and options in the Mailings tab shown in Figure 8.1 to complete a merge. A merge generally takes two files—the ***data source*** file and the ***main document***. The main document contains the standard text along with fields identifying where variable information is inserted during the merge. The data source file contains the variable information that will be inserted in the main document.

Figure 8.1 Mailings Tab

Use the Start Mail Merge button in the Mailings tab to identify the type of main document you want to create and use the Select Recipients button to create a data source file or to specify an existing data source file. You can also use the Mail Merge Wizard to guide you through the merge process. Start the wizard by clicking the Mailings tab, clicking the Start Mail Merge button, and then clicking *Step by Step Mail Merge Wizard*.

Creating a Data Source File

QUICK STEPS

Create Data Source File
1. Click Mailings tab.
2. Click Select Recipients button.
3. Click *Type New List* in drop-down list.
4. Type data in predesigned or custom fields.
5. Click OK.

Before creating a data source file, determine what type of correspondence you will be creating and the type of information you will need to insert in the correspondence. Word provides predetermined field names you can use when creating the data source file. Use these field names if they represent the data you are creating. Variable information in a data source file is saved as a ***record***. A record contains all of the information for one unit (for example, a person, family, customer, client, or business). A series of fields makes one record, and a series of records makes a data source file.

Create a data source file by clicking the Select Recipients button in the Start Mail Merge group in the Mailings tab and then clicking *Type New List* at the drop-down list. At the New Address List dialog box shown in Figure 8.2, use the predesigned fields offered by Word and type the required data or edit the fields by deleting and/or inserting custom fields and then typing the data. Note that fields in the main document correspond to the column headings in the data source file. When all records have been entered, click OK. At the Save Address List dialog box, navigate to the desired folder, type a name for the data source file, and then click OK. Word saves a data source file as an Access database. You do not need Access on your computer to complete a merge with a data source file.

Figure 8.2 New Address List Dialog Box

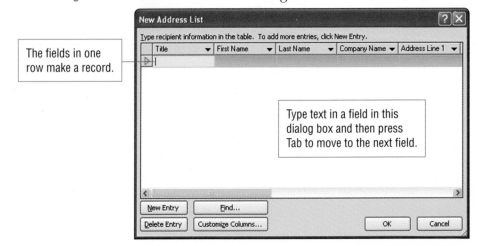

The fields in one row make a record.

Type text in a field in this dialog box and then press Tab to move to the next field.

1. At a blank document, click the Mailings tab.
2. Click the Start Mail Merge button in the Start Mail Merge group and then click *Letters* at the drop-down list.
3. Click the Select Recipients button in the Start Mail Merge group and then click *Type New List* at the drop-down list.

4. At the New Address List dialog box, Word provides you with a number of predesigned fields. Delete the fields you do not need by completing the following steps:
   a. Click the Customize Columns button.
   b. At the Customize Address List dialog box, click *Company Name* to select it and then click the Delete button.

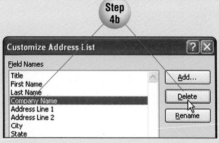

   c. At the message asking if you are sure you want to delete the field, click the Yes button.
   d. Complete steps similar to those in 4b and 4c to delete the following fields:
      Country or Region
      Home Phone
      Work Phone
      E-mail Address
5. Insert a custom field by completing the following steps:
   a. At the Customize Address List box, click the Add button.
   b. At the Add Field dialog box, type **Fund** and then click OK.
   c. Click the OK button to close the Customize Address List dialog box.

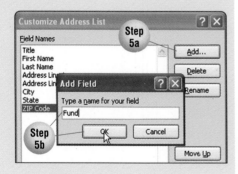

6. At the New Address List dialog box, enter the information for the first client shown in Figure 8.3 by completing the following steps:
   a. Click in the *Title* text box.
   b. Type Mr. and then press the Tab key. (This moves the insertion point to the *First Name* field. You can also press Shift + Tab to move to the previous field.)
   c. Type Kenneth and then press the Tab key.
   d. Type Porter and then press the Tab key.
   e. Type 7645 Tenth Street and then press the Tab key.
   f. Type Apt. 314 and then press the Tab key.
   g. Type New York and then press the Tab key.
   h. Type NY and then press the Tab key.
   i. Type 10192 and then press the Tab key.
   j. Type Mutual Investment Fund and then press the Tab key. (This makes the New Entry button active.)

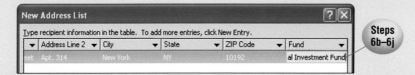

   k. With the insertion point positioned in the *Title* field, complete steps similar to those in 6b through 6j to enter the information for the three other clients shown in Figure 8.3.
7. After entering all of the information for the last client in Figure 8.3 (Mrs. Wanda Houston), click the OK button located in the bottom right corner of the New Address List dialog box.
8. At the Save Address List dialog box, navigate to the Word2007L1C8 folder on your storage medium, type WordL1_C8_P1_DS in the *File name* text box, and then click the Save button.

Figure 8.3 Project 1a

Title	=	Mr.		Title	=	Ms.
First Name	=	Kenneth		First Name	=	Carolyn
Last Name	=	Porter		Last Name	=	Renquist
Address Line 1	=	7645 Tenth Street		Address Line 1	=	13255 Meridian Street
Address Line 2	=	Apt. 314		Address Line 2	=	(leave this blank)
City	=	New York		City	=	New York
State	=	NY		State	=	NY
Zip Code	=	10192		Zip Code	=	10435
Fund	=	Mutual Investment Fund		Fund	=	Quality Care Fund
Title	=	Dr.		Title	=	Mrs.
First Name	=	Amil		First Name	=	Wanda
Last Name	=	Ranna		Last Name	=	Houston
Address Line 1	=	433 South 17th		Address Line 1	=	566 North 22nd Avenue
Address Line 2	=	Apt. 17-D		Address Line 2	=	(leave this blank)
City	=	New York		City	=	New York
State	=	NY		State	=	NY
Zip Code	=	10322		Zip Code	=	10634
Fund	=	Priority One Fund		Fund	=	Quality Care Fund

Creating a Main Document

When you begin a mail merge, you specify the type of main document you are creating. After creating and typing the records in the data source file, type the main document. Insert in the main document fields identifying where you want the variable information inserted when the document is merged with the data source file. Use buttons in the Write & Insert Fields group to insert fields and field blocks in the main document.

Insert all of the fields required for the inside address of a letter with the Address Block button in the Write & Insert Fields group. Click this button and the Insert Address Block dialog box displays with a preview of how the fields will be inserted in the document to create the inside address; the dialog box also contains buttons and options for customizing the fields. Click OK and the «AddressBlock» field is inserted in the document. The «AddressBlock» field is an example of a composite field that groups a number of fields together.

Click the Greeting Line button and the Insert Greeting Line dialog box displays with options for customizing how the fields are inserted in the document to create the greeting line. When you click OK at the dialog box the «GreetingLine» composite field is inserted in the document.

If you want to insert an individual field from the data source file, click the Insert Merge Field button. This displays the Insert Merge Field dialog box with a list of fields from the data source file. Click the Insert Merge Field button arrow and a drop-down list displays containing the fields in the data source file. If you want merged data formatted, you can format the merge fields at the main document.

Address Block

Greeting Line

Insert Merge Field

Project 1b — Creating a Main Document

1. At the blank document, create the letter shown in Figure 8.4. Begin by clicking the No Spacing style in the Styles group in the Home tab.
2. Press the Enter key six times and then type February 23, 2010.
3. Press the Enter key five times and then insert the address fields by completing the following steps:
   a. Click the Mailings tab and then click the Address Block button in the Write & Insert Fields group.
   b. At the Insert Address Block dialog box, click the OK button.
   c. Press the Enter key twice.
4. Insert the greeting line fields by completing the following steps:
   a. Click the Greeting Line button in the Write & Insert Fields group.
   b. At the Insert Greeting Line dialog box, click the down-pointing arrow at the right of the option box containing the comma (the box to the right of the box containing *Mr. Randall*).
   c. At the drop-down list that displays, click the colon.

Step 4b

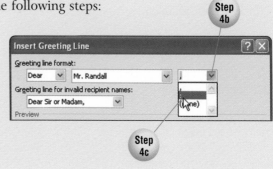

Step 4c

d. Click OK to close the Insert Greeting Line dialog box.

e. Press the Enter key twice.

5. Type the letter to the point where «Fund» displays and then insert the «Fund» field by clicking the Insert Merge Field button arrow and then clicking *Fund* at the drop-down list.

6. Type the letter to the point where the «Title» field displays and then insert the «Title» field by clicking the Insert Merge Field button arrow and then clicking *Title* at the drop-down list.

7. Press the spacebar and then insert the «Last_Name» field by clicking the Insert Merge Field button arrow and then clicking *Last_Name* at the drop-down list.

8. Type the remainder of the letter shown in Figure 8.4. (Insert your initials instead of the *XX* at the end of the letter.)

9. Save the document and name it **WordL1_C8_P1_MD**.

Figure 8.4 Project 1b

February 23, 2010

«AddressBlock»

«GreetingLine»

McCormack Funds is lowering its expense charges beginning May 1, 2010. The reductions in expense charges mean that more of your account investment performance in the «Fund» is returned to you, «Title» «Last_Name». The reductions are worth your attention because most of our competitors' fees have gone up.

Lowering expense charges is noteworthy because before the reduction, McCormack expense deductions were already among the lowest, far below most mutual funds and variable annuity accounts with similar objectives. At the same time, services for you, our client, will continue to expand. If you would like to discuss this change, please call us at (212) 555-2277. Your financial future is our main concern at McCormack.

Sincerely,

Jodie Langstrom
Director, Financial Services

XX:WordL1_C8_P1_MD.docx

Previewing a Merge

To view how the main document will appear when merged with the first record in the data source file, click the Preview Results button in the Mailings tab. You can view the main document merged with other records by using the navigation buttons in the Preview Results group. This group contains the buttons First Record, Previous Record, Go to Record, Next Record, and Last Record. Click the button that will display the main document merged with the desired record. Viewing the merged document before printing is helpful to ensure that the merged data is correct. To use the Go to Record button, click the button, type the number of the desired record, and then press Enter. Turn off the preview feature by clicking the Preview Results button.

First Record   Last Record

Previous Record   Next Record

Merging Documents

To complete the merge, click the Finish & Merge button in the Finish group in the Mailings tab. At the drop-down list that displays, you can choose to merge the records and create a new document, send the merged documents directly to the printer, or send the merged documents by e-mail.

To merge the documents and create a new document with the merged records, click the Finish & Merge button and then click *Edit Individual Documents* at the drop-down list. At the Merge to New Document dialog box, make sure *All* is selected in the *Merge records* section and then click OK. This merges the records in the data source file with the main document and inserts the merged documents in a new document. You can also display the Merge to New Document dialog box by pressing Alt + Shift + N. Press Alt + Shift + M to display the Merge to Printer dialog box.

Project 1c   Merging the Main Document with the Data Source File

1. With **WordL1_C8_P1_MD.docx** open, preview the main document merged with the first record in the data source file by clicking the Preview Results button in the Mailings tab.
2. Click the Next Record button to view the main document merged with the second record in the data source file.
3. Click the Preview Results button to turn it off.
4. Click the Finish & Merge button in the Finish group and then click *Edit Individual Documents* at the drop-down list.

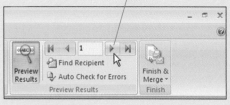

5. At the Merge to New Document dialog box, make sure *All* is selected, and then click OK.
6. Save the merged letters and name the document **WordL1_C8_P1_Ltrs**.
7. Print **WordL1_C8_P1_Ltrs.docx**. (This document will print four letters.)
8. Close **WordL1_C8_P1_Ltrs.docx**.
9. Save and then close **WordL1_C8_P1_MD.docx**.

Project ② Merge Envelopes

You will use Mail Merge to prepare envelopes with customer names and addresses.

Merging Envelopes

If you create a letter as a main document and then merge it with a data source file, more than likely you will need properly addressed envelopes in which to send the letters. To prepare an envelope main document that is merged with a data source file, click the Mailings tab, click the Start Mail Merge button, and then click *Envelopes* at the drop-down list. This displays the Envelope Options dialog box as shown in Figure 8.5. At this dialog box, specify the desired envelope size, make any other changes, and then click OK.

Figure 8.5 Envelope Options Dialog Box

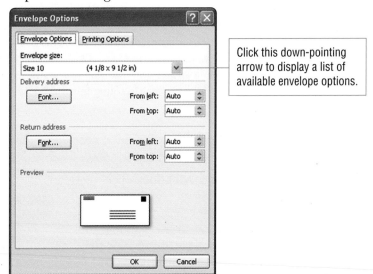

Click this down-pointing arrow to display a list of available envelope options.

The next step in the envelope merge process is to create the data source file or identify an existing data source file. To identify an existing data source file, click the Select Recipients button in the Start Mail Merge group and then click *Use Existing List* at the drop-down list. At the Select Data Source dialog box, navigate to the folder containing the desired data source file and then double-click the file.

With the data source file attached to the envelope main document, the next step is to insert the appropriate fields. Click in the envelope in the approximate location where the recipient's address will appear and a box with a dashed blue border displays. Click the Address Block button in the Write & Insert Fields group and then click OK at the Insert Address Block dialog box.

Project ② Merging Envelopes

1. At a blank document, click the Mailings tab.
2. Click the Start Mail Merge button in the Start Mail Merge group and then click *Envelopes* at the drop-down list.
3. At the Envelope Options dialog box, make sure the envelope size is 10 and then click OK.
4. Click the Select Recipients button in the Start Mail Merge group and then click *Use Existing List* at the drop-down list.
5. At the Select Data Source dialog box, navigate to the Word2007L1C8 folder on your storage medium and then double-click the data source file named *WordL1_C8_P1_DS.mdb*.
6. Click in the approximate location in the envelope document where the recipient's address will appear. (This causes a box with a dashed blue border to display. If you do not see this box, try clicking in a different location on the envelope.)

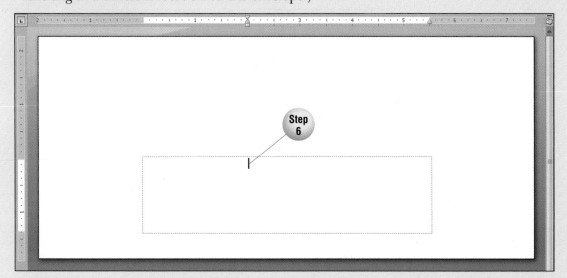

7. Click the Address Block button in the Write & Insert Fields group.
8. At the Insert Address Block dialog box, click the OK button.
9. Click the Preview Results button to see how the envelope appears merged with the first record in the data source file.
10. Click the Preview Results button to turn it off.
11. Click the Finish & Merge button in the Finish group and then click *Edit Individual Documents* at the drop-down list.
12. At the Merge to New Document dialog box, make sure *All* is selected and then click OK.
13. Save the merged envelopes and name the document **WordL1_C8_P2_Envs**.
14. Print **WordL1_C8_P2_Envs.docx**. (This document will print four envelopes.)

15. Close **WordL1_C8_P2_Envs.docx**.
16. Save the envelope main document and name it **WordL1_C8_P2_MD**.
17. Close **WordL1_C8_P2_MD.docx**.

Project 3 Merge Mailing Labels

You will use Mail Merge to prepare mailing labels with customer names and addresses.

Merging Labels

Create mailing labels for records in a data source file in much the same way that you create envelopes. Click the Start Mail Merge button and then click *Labels* at the drop-down list. This displays the Label Options dialog box as shown in Figure 8.6. Make sure the desired label is selected and then click OK to close the dialog box. The next step is to create the data source file or identify an existing data source file. With the data source file attached to the label main document, insert the appropriate fields and then complete the merge.

Figure 8.6 Label Options Dialog Box

Choose the desired label product number from this list box.

Click this down-pointing arrow to display a list of available label vendors.

Project 3 Merging Mailing Labels

1. At a blank document, click the Mailings tab.
2. Click the Start Mail Merge button in the Start Mail Merge group and then click *Labels* at the drop-down list.

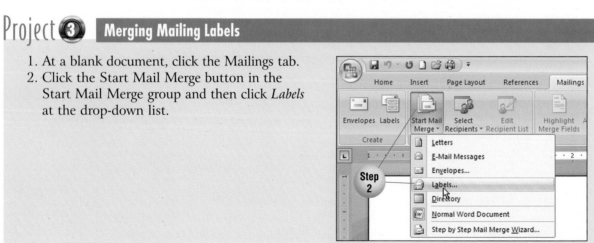

3. At the Label Options dialog box, complete the following steps:
   a. If necessary, click the down-pointing arrow at the right side of the *Label vendors* option and then click *Avery US Letter* at the drop-down list. (If this product vendor is not available, choose a vendor name that offers labels that print on a full page.)
   b. Scroll in the *Product number* list box and then click *5160*. (If this option is not available, choose a label number that prints labels in two or three columns down a full page.)
   c. Click OK to close the dialog box.

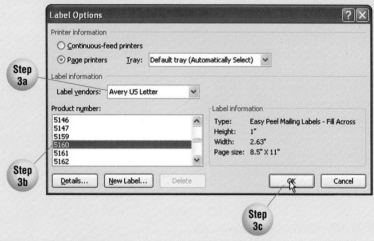

4. Click the Select Recipients button in the Start Mail Merge group and then click *Use Existing List* at the drop-down list.
5. At the Select Data Source dialog box, navigate to the Word2007L1C8 folder on your storage medium and then double-click the data source file named **WordL1_C8_P1_DS.mdb**.
6. At the labels document, click the Address Block button in the Write & Insert Fields group.
7. At the Insert Address Block dialog box, click the OK button. (This inserts «AddressBlock» in the first label. The other labels contain the «Next Record» field.)
8. Click the Update Labels button in the Write & Insert Fields group. (This adds the «AddressBlock» field after each «Next Record» field in the second and subsequent labels.)
9. Click the Preview Results button to see how the labels appear merged with the records in the data source file.
10. Click the Preview Results button to turn it off.
11. Click the Finish & Merge button in the Finish group and then click *Edit Individual Documents* at the drop-down list.
12. At the Merge to New Document dialog box, make sure *All* is selected, and then click OK.
13. Format the labels by completing the following steps:
    a. Click the Table Tools Layout tab.
    b. Click the Select button in the Table group and then click *Select Table*.
    c. Click the Align Center Left button in the Alignment group.
    d. Click the Home tab and then click the Paragraph group dialog box launcher.
    e. At the Paragraph dialog box, click the up-pointing arrow at the right of *Before* and also at the right of *After* to change the measurement to 0″. Click the up-pointing arrow at the right of the *Inside* option to change the measurement to 0.3″ and then click OK.
14. Save the merged labels and name the document **WordL1_C8_P3_Labels**.
15. Print and then close **WordL1_C8_P3_Labels.docx**.
16. Save the label main document and name it **WordL1_C8_P3_MD**.
17. Close **WordL1_C8_P3_MD.docx**.

Project ④ Merge a Directory

You will use Mail Merge to prepare a directory list containing customer names and type of funds.

Merging a Directory

When merging letters, envelopes, or mailing labels, a new form is created for each record. For example, if the data source file merged with the letter contains eight records, eight letters are created. If the data source file merged with a mailing label contains twenty records, twenty labels are created. In some situations, you may want merged information to remain on the same page. This is useful, for example, when creating a list such as a directory or address list.

Begin creating a merged directory by clicking the Start Mail Merge button and then clicking *Directory*. Create or identify an existing data source file and then insert the desired fields in the directory document. You may want to set tabs to insert text in columns.

Project ④ Merging a Directory

1. At a blank document, click the Mailings tab.
2. Click the Start Mail Merge button in the Start Mail Merge group and then click *Directory* at the drop-down list.
3. Click the Select Recipients button in the Start Mail Merge group and then click *Use Existing List* at the drop-down list.
4. At the Select Data Source dialog box, navigate to the Word2007L1C8 folder on your storage medium and then double-click the data source file named ***WordL1_C8_P1_DS.mdb***.

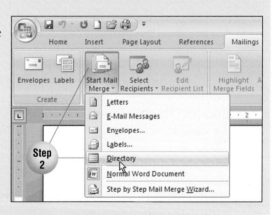

5. At the document screen, set left tabs at the 1-inch mark, the 2.5-inch mark, and the 4-inch mark on the Ruler and then press the Tab key. (This moves the insertion point to the tab set at the 1-inch mark.)
6. Click the Insert Merge Field button arrow and then click *Last_Name* at the drop-down list.
7. Press the Tab key to move the insertion point to the 2.5-inch mark.
8. Click the Insert Merge Field button arrow and then click *First_Name* at the drop-down list.
9. Press the Tab key to move the insertion point to the 4-inch mark.
10. Click the Insert Merge Field button arrow and then click *Fund* at the drop-down list.
11. Press the Enter key once.
12. Click the Finish & Merge button in the Finish group and then click *Edit Individual Documents* at the drop-down list.
13. At the Merge to New Document dialog box, make sure *All* is selected, and then click OK. (This merges the fields in the document.)
14. Press Ctrl + Home, press the Enter key once, and then press the Up Arrow key once.

15. Press the Tab key, turn on bold, and then type Last Name.
16. Press the Tab key and then type First Name.
17. Press the Tab key and then type Fund.

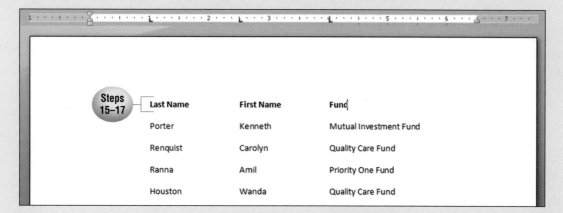

Last Name	First Name	Fund
Porter	Kenneth	Mutual Investment Fund
Renquist	Carolyn	Quality Care Fund
Ranna	Amil	Priority One Fund
Houston	Wanda	Quality Care Fund

Steps
15–17

18. Save the directory document and name it **WordL1_C8_P4_Directory**.
19. Print and then close the document.
20. Close the directory main document without saving it.

Editing a Data Source File

Edit a main document in the normal manner. Open the document, make the required changes, and then save the document. Since a data source is actually an Access database file, you cannot open it in the normal manner. Open a data source file for editing using the Edit Recipient List button in the Start Mail Merge group in the Mailings tab. When you click the Edit Recipient List button, the Mail Merge Recipients dialog box displays as shown in Figure 8.7. Select or edit records at this dialog box.

QUICK STEPS

Edit Data Source File
1. Open main document.
2. Click Mailings tab.
3. Click Edit Recipient List button.
4. Make desired changes at Mail Merge Recipients dialog box.
5. Click OK.

roject **5** **Select Records and Merge Mailing Labels**

You will use Mail Merge to prepare mailing labels with names and addresses of customers living in Baltimore.

Selecting Specific Records

All of the records in the Mail Merge Recipients dialog box contain a check mark before the first field. If you want to select specific records, remove the check mark from those records you do not want included in a merge. In this way you can select and then merge specific records in the data source file with the main document.

Figure 8.7 Mail Merge Recipients Dialog Box

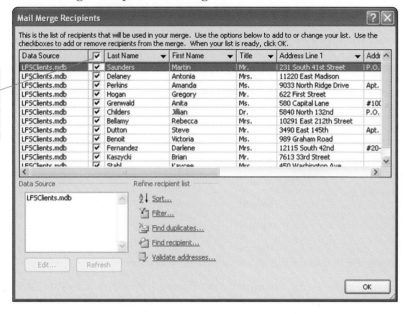

Select specific records by removing the check marks from those records you do not want included in the merge.

Project ⑤ Selecting Records and Merging Mailing Labels

1. At a blank document, create mailing labels for customers living in Baltimore. Begin by clicking the Mailings tab.
2. Click the Start Mail Merge button in the Start Mail Merge group and then click *Labels* at the drop-down list.
3. At the Label Options dialog box, make sure *Avery US Letter* displays in the *Label products* option box, and *5160* displays in the *Product number* list box, and then click OK.
4. Click the Select Recipients button in the Start Mail Merge group and then click *Use Existing List* at the drop-down list.
5. At the Select Data Source dialog box, navigate to the Word2007L1C8 folder on your storage medium and then double-click the data source file named *LFSClients.mdb*.
6. Click the Edit Recipient List button in the Start Mail Merge group.
7. At the Mail Merge Recipients dialog box, complete the following steps:

   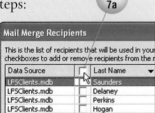

   a. Click the check box located immediately left of the *Last Name* field column heading to remove the check mark. (This removes all of the check marks from the check boxes.)
   b. Click the check box immediately left of each of the following last names: *Saunders, Perkins, Grenwald, Dutton, Fernandez,* and *Stahl*. (These are the customers that live in Baltimore.)
   c. Click OK to close the dialog box.
8. At the labels document, click the Address Block button in the Write & Insert Fields group.
9. At the Insert Address Block dialog box, click the OK button.
10. Click the Update Labels button in Write & Insert Fields group.
11. Click the Preview Results button and then click the Next Record button to display each of the labels and make sure only those customers living in Baltimore display.
12. Click the Preview Results button to turn it off.
13. Click the Finish & Merge button in the Finish group and then click *Edit Individual Documents* at the drop-down list.

14. At the Merge to New Document dialog box, make sure *All* is selected, and then click OK.
15. Format the labels by completing the following steps:
    a. Click the Table Tools Layout tab.
    b. Click the Select button in the Table group and then click *Select Table*.
    c. Click the Align Center Left button in the Alignment group.
    d. Click the Home tab and then click the Paragraph group dialog box launcher.
    e. At the Paragraph dialog box, click the up-pointing arrow at the right of *Before* and also at the right of *After* to change the measurement to 0″. Click the up-pointing arrow at the right of the *Inside* option to change the measurement to 0.3″ and then click OK.
16. Save the merged labels and name the document **WordL1_C8_P5_Labels**.
17. Print and then close **WordL1_C8_P5_Labels.docx**.
18. Close the main labels document without saving it.

Project ⑥ Edit Records in a Data Source File

You will edit records in a data source file and then use Mail Merge to prepare a directory with the edited records that contains customer names, telephone numbers, and cell phone numbers.

Editing Records

A data source file may need editing on a periodic basis to add or delete customer names, update fields, insert new fields, or delete existing fields. To edit a data source file, click the Edit Recipient List button in the Start Mail Merge group. At the Mail Merge Recipients dialog box, click the data source file name in the *Data Source* list box and then click the Edit button that displays below the list box. This displays the Edit Data Source dialog box shown in Figure 8.8. At this dialog box you can add a new entry, delete an entry, find a particular entry, and customize columns.

Figure 8.8 Edit Data Source Dialog Box

Project 6   Editing Records in a Data Source File

1. Make a copy of the **LFSClients.mdb** file by completing the following steps:
   a. Display the Open dialog box and make Word2007L1C8 the active folder.
   b. If necessary, change the *Files of type* option to *All Files (*.*)*.
   c. Right-click on the **LFSClients.mdb** file and then click *Copy* at the shortcut menu.
   d. Position the mouse pointer in a white portion of the Open dialog box list box (outside of any file name), click the right mouse button, and then click *Paste* at the shortcut menu. (This inserts a copy of the file in the dialog box list box and names the file **Copy of LFSClients.mdb**.)
   e. Right-click on the file name *Copy of LFSClients.mdb* and then click *Rename* at the shortcut menu.
   f. Type WordL1_C8_P6_DS.mdb and then press Enter.
   g. Close the Open dialog box.
2. At a blank document, click the Mailings tab.
3. Click the Select Recipients button and then click *Use Existing List* from the drop-down list.
4. At the Select Data Source dialog box, navigate to the Word2007L1C8 folder on your storage medium and then double-click the data source file named *WordL1_C8_P6_DS.mdb*.
5. Click the Edit Recipient List button in the Start Mail Merge group.
6. At the Mail Merge Recipients dialog box, click *WordL1_C8_P6_DS.mdb* that displays in the *Data Source* list box and then click the Edit button.
7. Delete the record for Steve Dutton by completing the following steps:
   a. Click the square that displays at the beginning of the row for *Mr. Steve Dutton*.
   b. Click the Delete Entry button.

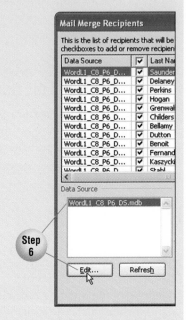

Step 6

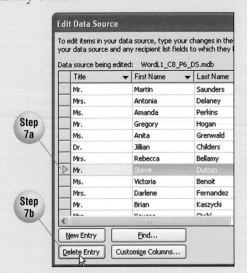

Step 7a

Step 7b

   c. At the message asking if you want to delete the entry, click the Yes button.
8. Insert a new record by completing the following steps:
   a. Click the New Entry button in the dialog box.

b. Type the following text in the new record in the specified fields:

   Title = Ms.
   First Name = Jennae
   Last Name = Davis
   Address Line 1 = 3120 South 21st
   Address Line 2 = (none)
   City = Rosedale
   State = MD
   ZIP Code = 20389
   Home Phone = 410-555-5774

9. Insert a new field and type text in the field by completing the following steps:

   a. At the Edit Data Source dialog box, click the Customize Columns button.
   b. At the message asking if you want to save the changes made to the data source file, click Yes.
   c. At the Customize Address List dialog box, click *ZIP Code* in the *Field Names* list box. (A new field is inserted below the selected field.)
   d. Click the Add button.
   e. At the Add Field dialog box, type **Cell Phone** and then click OK.
   f. You decide that you want the *Cell Phone* field to display after the *Home Phone* field. To move the *Cell Phone* field, make sure it is selected and then click the Move Down button.
   g. Click OK to close the Customize Address List dialog box.

Step 9d

Step 9c

Step 9e

   h. At the Edit Data Source dialog box, scroll to the right to display the *Cell Phone* field (last field in the file) and then type the following cell phone numbers (after typing each cell phone number, except the last number, press the Down Arrow key to make the next cell below active):

      Record 1 = 410-555-1249
      Record 2 = 413-555-3492
      Record 3 = 410-555-0695
      Record 4 = 410-555-9488
      Record 5 = 413-555-1200
      Record 6 = 410-555-7522
      Record 7 = 410-555-8833
      Record 8 = 413-555-9378
      Record 9 = 410-555-4261
      Record 10 = 410-555-9944
      Record 11 = 413-555-2321
      Record 12 = 410-555-9435

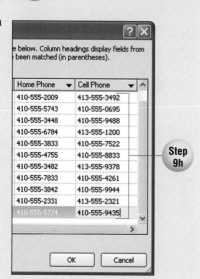

Step 9h

   i. Click OK to close the Edit Data Source dialog box.
   j. At the message asking if you want to update the recipient list and save changes, click Yes.
   k. At the Mail Merge Recipients dialog box, click OK.

10. Create a directory by completing the following steps:

    a. Click the Start Mail Merge button and then click *Directory* at the drop-down list.
    b. At a blank document, set left tabs on the horizontal ruler at the 1-inch mark, the 3-inch mark, and the 4.5-inch mark.
    c. Press the Tab key (this moves the insertion point to the first tab set at the 1-inch mark).

d. Click the Insert Merge Field button arrow and then click *Last_Name* at the drop-down list.

e. Type a comma and then press the spacebar.

f. Click the Insert Merge Field button arrow and then click *First_Name* at the drop-down list.

g. Press the Tab key, click the Insert Merge Field button arrow, and then click *Home_Phone* at the drop-down list.

h. Press the Tab key, click the Insert Merge Field button arrow, and then click *Cell_Phone* at the drop-down list.

i. Press the Enter key once.

j. Click the Finish & Merge button in the Finish group and then click *Edit Individual Documents* at the drop-down list.

k. At the Merge to New Document dialog box, make sure *All* is selected and then click OK. (This merges the fields in the document.)

11. Press Ctrl + Home, press the Enter key once, and then press the Up Arrow key once.

12. Press the Tab key, turn on bold, and then type Name.

13. Press the Tab key and then type Home Phone.

14. Press the Tab key and then type Cell Phone.

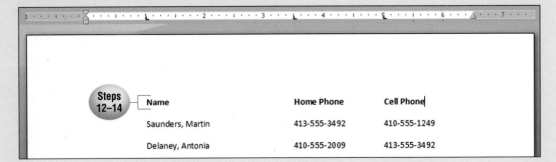

15. Save the directory document and name it **WordL1_C8_P6_Directory**.

16. Print and then close the document.

17. Close the directory main document without saving it.

Project 7 Add Fill-in Fields to a Main Document

You will edit a form letter and insert sales representative contact information during a merge.

Inputting Text during a Merge

Word's Merge feature contains a large number of Word fields you can insert in a main document. In this chapter, you will learn about the *Fill-in* field that is used for information input at the keyboard during a merge. For more information on the other Word fields, please refer to the on-screen help.

Situations may arise in which you do not need to keep all variable information in a data source file. For example, variable information that changes on a regular basis might include a customer's monthly balance, a product price, and so on. Word lets you input variable information into a document during the merge using the keyboard. A Fill-in field is inserted in a main document by clicking the Rules button in the Write & Insert Fields group in the Mailings tab and then clicking *Fill-in* at the drop-down list. This displays the Insert Word Field: Fill-in dialog box shown in Figure 8.9. At this dialog box, type a short message indicating what should be entered at the keyboard and then click OK. At the Microsoft Word dialog box with the message you entered displayed in the upper left corner, type text you want to display in the document and then click OK. When the Fill-in field or fields are added, save the main document in the normal manner. A document can contain any number of Fill-in fields.

QUICK STEPS

Insert Fill-in Field in Main Document
1. Click Mailings tab.
2. Click Rules button.
3. Click *Fill-in* at drop-down list.
4. Type prompt text.
5. Click OK.
6. Type text to be inserted in document.
7. Click OK.

Figure 8.9 Insert Word Field: Fill-in Dialog Box

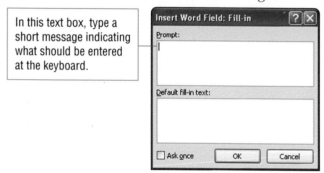

In this text box, type a short message indicating what should be entered at the keyboard.

When you merge the main document with the data source file, the first record is merged with the main document and the Microsoft Word dialog box displays with the message you entered displayed in the upper left corner. Type the required information for the first record in the data source file and then click the OK button. Word displays the dialog box again. Type the required information for the second record in the data source file and then click OK. Continue in this manner until the required information has been entered for each record in the data source file. Word then completes the merge.

Project 7 **Adding Fill-in Fields to a Main Document**

1. Open the document named **WordL1_C8_P1_MD.docx** (at the message asking if you want to continue, click Yes) and then save the document and name it **WordL1_C8_P7_MD**.
2. Change the second paragraph in the body of the letter to the paragraph shown in Figure 8.10. Insert the first Fill-in field (representative's name) by completing the following steps:
   a. Click the Mailings tab.
   b. Click the Rules button in the Write & Insert Fields group and then click *Fill-in* at the drop-down list.

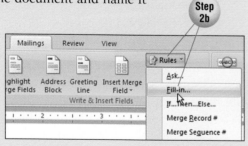

Step 2b

c. At the Insert Word Field: Fill-in dialog box, type Insert rep name in the *Prompt* text box and then click OK.

d. At the Microsoft Office Word dialog box with *Insert rep name* displayed in the upper left corner, type (representative's name) and then click OK.

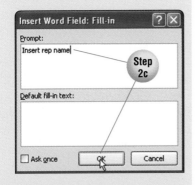

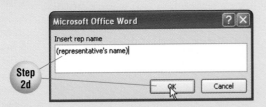

3. Complete steps similar to those in Step 2 to insert the second Fill-in field (phone number), except type Insert phone number in the *Prompt* text box at the Insert Word Field: Fill-in dialog box and type (phone number) at the Microsoft Word dialog box.

4. Save **WordL1_C8_P7_MD.docx**.

5. Merge the main document with the data source file by completing the following steps:

   a. Click the Finish & Merge button and then click *Edit Individual Documents* at the drop-down list.

   b. At the Merge to New Document dialog box, make sure *All* is selected, and then click OK.

   c. When Word merges the main document with the first record, a dialog box displays with the message *Insert rep name* and the text *(representative's name)* selected. At this dialog box, type Marilyn Smythe and then click OK.

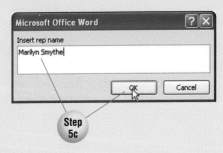

   d. At the dialog box with the message *Insert phone number* and *(phone number)* selected, type (646) 555-8944 and then click OK.

   e. At the dialog box with the message *Insert rep name*, type Anthony Mason (over *Marilyn Smythe*) and then click OK.

   f. At the dialog box with the message *Insert phone number*, type (646) 555-8901 (over the previous number) and then click OK.

   g. At the dialog box with the message *Insert rep name*, type Faith Ostrom (over *Anthony Mason*) and then click OK.

   h. At the dialog box with the message *Insert phone number*, type (646) 555-8967 (over the previous number) and then click OK.

   i. At the dialog box with the message *Insert rep name*, type Thomas Rivers (over *Faith Ostrom*) and then click OK.

   j. At the dialog box with the message *Insert phone number*, type (646) 555-0793 (over the previous number) and then click OK.

6. Save the merged document and name it **WordL1_C8_P7_Ltrs**.

7. Print and then close **WordL1_C8_P7_Ltrs.docx**.

8. Save and then close **WordL1_C8_P7_MD.docx**.

Figure 8.10 Project 7

Lowering expense charges is noteworthy because before the reduction, McCormack expense deductions were already among the lowest, far below most mutual funds and variable annuity accounts with similar objectives. At the same time, services for you, our client, will continue to expand. If you would like to discuss this change, please call our service representative, **(representative's name)**, at **(phone number)**.

CHAPTER summary

- Use the Mail Merge feature to create letters, envelopes, labels, directories, e-mail messages, and faxes, all with personalized information.
- Generally, a merge takes two documents—the data source file containing the variable information and the main document containing standard text along with fields identifying where variable information is inserted during the merge process.
- Variable information in a data source file is saved as a record. A record contains all of the information for one unit. A series of fields makes one record, and a series of records makes a data source file.
- A data source file is saved as an Access database but you do not need Access on your computer to complete a merge with a data source.
- You can use predesigned fields when creating a data source file or you can create your own custom field at the Customize Address List dialog box.
- Use the Address Block button in the Write & Insert Fields group in the Mailings tab to insert all of the fields required for the inside address of a letter. This inserts the «AddressBlock» field, which is considered a composite field because it groups a number of fields together.
- Click the Greeting Line button in the Write & Insert Fields group in the Mailings tab to insert the «GreetingLine» composite field in the document.
- Click the Insert Merge Field button arrow in the Write & Insert Fields group in the Mailings tab to display a drop-down list of fields contained in the data source file.
- Click the Preview Results button in the Mailings tab to view the main document merged with the first record in the data source. Use the navigation buttons in the Preview Results group in the Mailings tab to display the main document merged with the desired record.
- Click the Finish & Merge button in the Mailings tab to complete the merge.
- Select specific records for merging by inserting or removing check marks from the desired records in the Mail Merge Recipients dialog box. Display this dialog box by clicking the Edit Recipient List button in the Mailings tab.
- Edit specific records in a data source file at the Edit Data Source dialog box. Display this dialog box by clicking the Edit Recipient List button in the Mailings tab, clicking the desired data source file name in the *Data Source* list box, and then clicking the Edit button.
- Use the Fill-in field in a main document to insert variable information at the keyboard during a merge.

COMMANDS review

FEATURE	RIBBON TAB, GROUP	BUTTON, OPTION
New Address List dialog box	Mailings, Start Mail Merge	, Type New List
Letter main document	Mailings, Start Mail Merge	, Letters
Envelopes main document	Mailings, Start Mail Merge	, Envelopes
Labels main document	Mailings, Start Mail Merge	, Labels
Directory main document	Mailings, Start Mail Merge	, Directory
Preview merge results	Mailings, Preview Results	
Mail Merge Recipients dialog box	Mailings, Start Mail Merge	
Address Block field	Mailings, Write & Insert Fields	
Greeting Line field	Mailings, Write & Insert Fields	
Insert merge fields	Mailings, Write & Insert Fields	
Fill-in merge field	Mailings, Write & Insert Fields	Rules ▼ , Fill-in

CONCEPTS check

Test Your Knowledge

Completion: In the space provided at the right, indicate the correct term, command, or number.

1. A merge generally takes two files—a data source file and this. _____

2. This term refers to all of the information for one unit in a data source file. _____

3. Create a data source file by clicking this button in the Mailings tab and then clicking *Type New List* at the drop-down list. _____

4. A data source file is saved as this type of file. _____

5. Create your own custom fields in a data source file with options at this dialog box. _____

6. Use this button in the Mailings tab to insert all of the required fields for the inside address in a letter. _____

7. The «GreetingLine» field is considered this type of field because it includes all of the fields required for the greeting line. _____

8. Click this button in the Mailings tab to display the first record merged with the main document. _____

9. To complete a merge, click this button in the Finish group in the Mailings tab. _____

10. Select specific records in a data source file by inserting or removing check marks from the records in this dialog box. _____

11. Use this field to insert variable information at the keyboard during a merge. _____

SKILLS check
Demonstrate Your Proficiency

Assessment

1 PREPARE AND MERGE LETTERS, ENVELOPES, AND LABELS

1. Look at the information shown in Figure 8.11 and Figure 8.12.
2. Use the Mail Merge feature to prepare four letters using the information shown in the figures. Name the data source file **WordL1_C8_A1_DS**, name the main document **WordL1_C8_A1_MD**, and name the merged letters document **WordL1_C8_A1_Ltrs**.
3. Print and then close **WordL1_C8_A1_Ltrs.docx**. Save and then close **WordL1_C8_A1_MD.docx**.
4. Create an envelope main document and merge it with the **WordL1_C8_A1_DS.mdb** data source file. Save the merged envelopes document and name it **WordL1_C8_A1_Envs**. Print and then close document. Close the envelope main document without saving it.
5. Use the Mail Merge feature to prepare mailing labels for the names and addresses in the **WordL1_C8_A1_DS.mdb** data source file.
6. Save the merged labels document and name it **WordL1_C8_A1_Labels**. Print and then close the document.
7. Close the labels main document without saving it.

Figure 8.11 Assessment 1

Mr. Tony Benedetti
1315 Cordova Road
Apt. 402
Santa Fe, NM 87505
Home Phone: 505-555-0489

Ms. Theresa Dusek
12044 Ridgway Drive
(leave this blank)
Santa Fe, NM 87505
Home Phone: 505-555-1120

Mrs. Mary Arguello
2554 Country Drive
#105
Santa Fe, NM 87504
Home Phone: 505-555-7663

Mr. Preston Miller
120 Second Street
(leave this blank)
Santa Fe, NM 87505
Home Phone: 505-555-3551

Figure 8.12 Assessment 1

May 6, 2010

«AddressBlock»

«GreetingLine»

The Cordova Children's Community Center is a nonprofit agency providing educational and recreational activities to children in the Cordova community. We are funded by donations from the community and rely on you and all of our volunteers to provide quality care and services to our children. As a member of our outstanding volunteer team, we are inviting you to attend our summer volunteer open house on Saturday, May 22, at the community center from 1:00 to 4:30 p.m. We want to honor you and our other volunteers for your commitment to children so please plan to attend so we can thank you in person.

The Center's summer volunteer session begins Tuesday, June 1, and continues through August 31. According to our volunteer roster, you have signed up to volunteer during the summer session. Throughout the summer we will be offering a variety of services to our children including tutoring, creative art classes, recreational activities, and a science camp. At the open house, you can sign up for the specific area or areas in which you want to volunteer. We look forward to seeing you at the open house and during the upcoming summer session.

Sincerely,

Andy Amura
Volunteer Coordinator

XX:WordL1_C8_A1_MD.docx

Assessment

2 EDIT AND MERGE LETTERS

1. Open **WordL1_C8_A1_MD.docx** (at the message asking if you want to continue, click Yes) and then save the main document and name it **WordL1_C8_A2_MD**.
2. Edit the **WordL1_C8_A1_DS.mdb** data source file by making the following changes:
   a. Display the record for Ms. Theresa Dusek and then change the address from *12044 Ridgway Drive* to *1390 Fourth Avenue*.
   b. Display the record for Mr. Preston Miller and change the home phone number from *505-555-3551* to *505-555-1289*.
   c. Delete the record for Mrs. Mary Arguello.
   d. Insert a new record with the following information:

   > Mr. Cesar Rivera
   > 3201 East Third Street
   > Santa Fe, NM 87505
   > 505-555-6675

3. At the main document, edit the second sentence of the second paragraph so it reads as follows (insert a *Fill-in* field for the *(number of hours)* shown in the sentence below):

   > According to our volunteer roster, you have signed up to volunteer for *(number of hours)* during the summer session.

4. Merge the main document with the data source file and type the following text for each of the records:

   > Record 1 = four hours a week
   > Record 2 = six hours a week
   > Record 3 = twelve hours a week
   > Record 4 = four hours a week

5. Save the merged document and name it **WordL1_C8_A2_Ltrs**.
6. Print and then close **WordL1_C8_A2_Ltrs.docx**.
7. Save and then close **WordL1_C8_A2_MD.mdb**.

CASE study

Apply Your Skills

Part 1

You are the office manager for Freestyle Extreme, a sporting goods store that specializes in snowboarding and snow skiing equipment and supplies. The store has two branches, one on the east side of town and the other on the west side. One of your job responsibilities is to send letters to customers letting them know about sales, new equipment, and upcoming events. Next month, both stores are having a sale and all snowboard and snow skiing supplies will be 15% off the regular price. Create a data source file that contains the following customer information: first name, last name, address, city, state, ZIP code, and branch. Add six customers to the data source file and indicate that three usually shop at the East branch and the other three usually shop at the West branch. Create a letter as a main document that includes information about the upcoming sale. The letter should contain at least two paragraphs and, in addition to the information on the sale, might include information about the store, snowboarding, and/or snow skiing. Save the data source file with the name **WordL1_C8_CS_DS**, save the main document with the name **WordL1_C8_CS_P1_MD**, and save the merged document with the name **WordL1_C8_CS_P1_Ltrs**. Create envelopes for the six merged letters and name the merged envelope document **WordL_C8_CS_P1_Envs**. Do not save the envelope main document. Print the merged letters document and the merged envelopes document.

Part 2

A well-known extreme snowboarder will be visiting both branches of the store to meet with customers and sign autographs. Use the Help feature to learn how to insert an If . . . Then . . . Else merge field in a document and then create a letter that includes the name of the extreme snowboarder (you determine the name), the time, which is 1:00 p.m. to 4:30 p.m., and any additional information that might interest the customer. Also include in the letter an If . . . Then . . . Else merge field that will insert *Wednesday, September 22* if the customer's Branch is *East* and will insert *Thursday, September 23* if the Branch is *West*. Add visual appeal to the letter by inserting a picture, clip art image, WordArt, or any other feature that will attract the reader's attention. Save the letter main document and name it **WordL1_C8_CS_P2_MD**. Merge the letter main document with the **WordL1_C8_CS_DS.mdb** data source. Save the merged letters document and name it **WordL1_C8_CS_P2_AnnLtrs**. Print the merged letters document.

Part 3

The store owner wants to try selling shorter skis known as "snow blades" or "skiboards." He has asked you to research the shorter skis and identify one type and model to sell only at the West branch of the store. If the model sells well, he will consider selling it at the East branch at a future time. Prepare a main document letter that describes the new snow blade or skiboard that the West branch is selling. Include information about pricing and tell customers that the new item is being offered at a 40% discount if purchased within the next week. Merge the letter main document with the **WordL1_C8_CS_DS.mdb** data source file and include only those customers that shop at the West branch. Save the merged letters document and name it **WordL1_C8_CS_P3_Ltrs**. Print the merged letters document. Save the letter main document and name it **WordL1_C8_CS_P3_MD**. Print and then close the main document

Enhancing and Customizing Documents

ASSESSING proficiency

word Unit 2

In this unit, you have learned to format text into columns; insert, format, and customize objects to enhance the visual appeal of a document; manage files, print envelopes and labels, and create documents using templates; create and edit tables; visually represent data in SmartArt diagrams and organizational charts; and use Mail Merge to create letters, envelopes, labels, and directions.

Note: Before beginning unit assessments, copy to your storage medium the Word2007L1U2 subfolder from the Word2007L1 folder on the CD that accompanies this textbook and then make Word2007L1U2 the active folder.

Assessment 1 Format a Technology Occupations Document

1. Open **WordReport09.docx** and then save the document and name it **WordL1_U2_A1**.
2. Move the insertion point to the beginning of the heading *Telecommuting* and then insert the file named **WordDocument19.docx**.
3. Apply the Heading 1 style to the title and the Heading 2 style to the headings in the document.
4. Change the Quick Styles set to *Formal*.
5. Insert a continuous section break at the beginning of the first paragraph of text (the paragraph that begins *The march of computer technology . . .*).
6. Format the text below the section break into two newspaper columns.
7. Balance the columns on the second page.
8. Insert a pull quote of your choosing on the first page of the document that includes the text *"As the future of wireless unfolds, many new jobs will emerge as well."*
9. Create a drop cap with the first letter of the first word *The* that begins the first paragraph of text and make the drop cap two lines in height.
10. Manually hyphenate words in the document.
11. Insert page numbering that prints at the bottom of each page (you determine the page number formatting).
12. Save, print, and then close **WordL1_U2_A1.docx**.

Assessment 2 Create a Workshop Flyer

1. Create the flyer shown in Figure U2.1 with the following specifications:
   a. Insert the WordArt shape with WordArt style 15 and then customize the WordArt by changing the shadow effect to Shadow Style 1, the shape to Deflate Bottom, and increasing the width of the WordArt to 6.5″ and the height to 1″.

b. Type the text shown in the figure set in 22-point Calibri bold and center the text.

c. Insert the clip art image shown in the figure (use the keyword *buildings* to find the clip art) and then change the wrapping style to *Square*. Position and size the image as shown in the figure.

2. Save the document and name it **WordL1_U2_A2**.
3. Print and then close **WordL1_U2_A2.docx**.

Figure U2.1 Assessment 2

Assessment 3 **Create a Staff Meeting Announcement**

1. Create the announcement shown in Figure U2.2 with the following specifications:

a. Use the *Hexagon* shape in the *Basic Shapes* section of the Shapes drop-down list to create the shape.

b. Apply the Diagonal Gradient - Accent 5 style to the shape.

c. Apply the 3-D Style 2 located in the *Parallel* group in the 3-D Effects drop-down list.

d. Insert a text box in the shape.

e. Display the Home tab and then click the No Spacing style in the Styles group.

f. Insert the text shown in Figure U2.2. Insert the clock as a symbol (in the *Wingdings* font) and insert the ñ as a symbol (in the *(normal text)* font).

g. Increase the size of the shape and text so they display as shown in Figure U2.2.

2. Save the completed document and name it **WordL1_U2_A3**.
3. Print and then close **WordL1_U2_A3.docx**.

Figure U2.2 Assessment 3

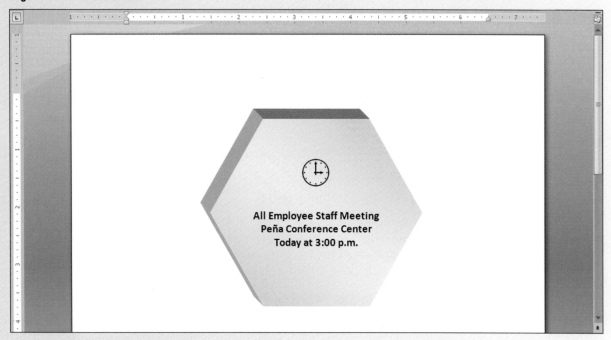

Assessment 4 Create a River Rafting Flyer

1. At a blank document, insert the picture named **River.jpg**. (Insert the picture using the Picture button.)
2. Crop out a portion of the trees at the left and right and a portion of the hill at the top.
3. Change the brightness to *+20%*.
4. Specify that the picture should wrap behind text.
5. Insert the text *River Rafting Adventures* on one line, *Salmon River, Idaho* on the next line, and *1-888-555-3322* on the third line.
6. Increase the size of the picture so it is easier to see and the size of the text so it is easier to read. Center the text and position it on the picture on top of the river so the text is readable.
7. Save the document and name it **WordL1_U2_A4**.
8. Print and then close **WordL1_U2_A4.docx**.

Assessment 5 Create an Envelope

1. At a blank document, create an envelope with the text shown in Figure U2.3.
2. Save the envelope document and name it **WordL1_U2_A5**.
3. Print and then close **WordL1_U2_A5.docx**.

Figure U2.3 Assessment 5

Mrs. Eileen Hebert
15205 East 42nd Street
Lake Charles, LA 71098

Mr. Earl Robicheaux
1436 North Sheldon Street
Jennings, LA 70542

Assessment 6 Create Mailing Labels

1. Create mailing labels with the name and address for Mrs. Eileen Hebert shown in Figure U2.3 using a label vendor and product of your choosing.
2. Save the document and name it **WordL1_U2_A6**.
3. Print and then close **WordL1_U2_A6.docx**.

Assessment 7 Create and Format a Table with Software Training Information

1. At a blank document, create the table shown in Figure U2.4. Format the table and the text in a manner similar to what is shown in Figure U2.4.
2. Insert a formula in B8 that totals the numbers in cells B4 through B7.
3. Insert a formula in C8 that totals the numbers in cells C4 through C7.
4. Save the document and name it **WordL1_U2_A7**.
5. Print and then close **WordL1_U2_A7.docx**.

Figure U2.4 Assessment 7

TRI-STATE PRODUCTS		
Computer Technology Department Microsoft® Office 2007 Training		
Application	# Enrolled	# Completed
Access 2007	20	15
Excel 2007	62	56
PowerPoint 2007	40	33
Word 2007	80	72
Total		

Assessment 8 Create and Format a Table Containing Training Scores

1. Open **WordTable06.docx** and then save the document and name it **WordL1_U2_A8**.
2. Insert formulas that calculate the averages in the appropriate row and column. (When writing the formulas, change the *Number format* option to *0*.)
3. Autofit the contents of the table.
4. Apply a table style of your choosing to the table.
5. Appy any other formatting to improve the visual appeal of the table.
6. Save, print, and then close **WordL1_U2_A8.docx**.

Assessment 9 **Create an Organizational Chart**

1. Use SmartArt to create an organizational chart for the following text (in the order displayed). Apply formatting to enhance the visual appeal of the organizational chart.
2. Save the completed document and name it **WordL1_U2_A9**.
3. Print and then close **WordL1_U2_A9.docx**.

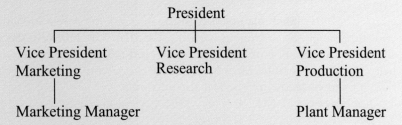

Assessment 10 **Create a SmartArt Diagram**

1. At a blank document, create the WordArt and diagram shown in Figure U2.5 with the following specifications:
   a. Insert the WordArt shape with WordArt style 11 and then customize the WordArt by changing the shape to Can Up and increasing the width to 6.5" and the height to 1".
   b. Create the diagram using the Vertical Picture Accent List diagram. Click the picture icon that displays in the top circle and then insert the picture named **Seagull.jpg** located in the Word2007L1U2 folder. Insert the same picture in the other two circles. Type the text in each rectangle shape as shown in Figure U2.5.
2. Save the document and name it **WordL1_U2_A10**.
3. Print and then close **WordL1_U2_A10.docx**.

Figure U2.5 Assessment 10

Assessment 11 Merge and Print Letters

1. Look at the information shown in Figure U2.6 and Figure U2.7. Use the Mail Merge feature to prepare six letters using the information shown in the figures. When creating the letter main document, insert Fill-in fields in place of the *(coordinator name)* and *(telephone number)* text. Create the data source file with the text shown in Figure U2.6 and name the file **WordL1_U2_DS**.
2. Create the letter main document with the information shown in Figure U2.7 and then merge the document with the **WordL1_U2_DS.mdb** data source file. When merging, enter the first name and telephone number shown below for the first three records and enter the second name and telephone number shown below for the last three records.
   Jeff Greenswald (813) 555-9886
   Grace Ramirez (813) 555-9807
3. Save the merged letters document and name it **WordL1_U2_Letters**. Print and then close the document.
4. Save the main document and name it **WordL1_U2_MD** and then close the document.

Figure U2.6 Assessment 11

Mrs. Antonio Mercado
3241 Court G
Tampa, FL 33623

Ms. Kristina Vukovich
1120 South Monroe
Tampa, FL 33655

Ms. Alexandria Remick
909 Wheeler South
Tampa, FL 33620

Mr. Minh Vu
9302 Lawndale Southwest
Tampa, FL 33623

Mr. Curtis Iverson
10139 93rd Court South
Tampa, FL 33654

Mrs. Holly Bernard
8904 Emerson Road
Tampa, FL 33620

Figure U2.7 Assessment 11

December 12, 2009

«AddressBlock»

«GreetingLine»

Sound Medical is switching hospital care in Tampa to St. Jude's Hospital beginning January 1, 2010. As mentioned in last month's letter, St. Jude's Hospital was selected because it meets our requirements for high-quality, customer-pleasing care that is also affordable and accessible. Our physicians look forward to caring for you in this new environment.

Over the past month, staff members at Sound Medical have been working to make this transition as smooth as possible. Surgeries planned after January 1 are being scheduled at St. Jude's Hospital. Mothers delivering babies any time after January 1 are receiving information about delivery room tours and prenatal classes available at St. Jude's. Your Sound Medical doctor will have privileges at St. Jude's and will continue to care for you if you need to be hospitalized.

You are a very important part of our patient family, «Title» «Last_Name», and we hope this information is helpful. If you have any additional questions or concerns, please call your Sound Medical health coordinator, (coordinator name), at (telephone number), between 8:00 a.m. and 4:30 p.m.

Sincerely,

Jody Tiemann
District Administrator

XX:WordL1_U2_MD.docx

Assessment 12 **Merge and Print Envelopes**

1. Use the Mail Merge feature to prepare envelopes for the letters created in Assessment 11.
2. Specify **WordL1_U2_DS.mdb** as the data source document.
3. Save the merged envelopes document and name the document **WordL1_U2_Envs**.
4. Print and then close **WordL1_U2_Envs.docx**.
5. Do not save the envelope main document.

WRITING activities

The following activities give you the opportunity to practice your writing skills along with demonstrating an understanding of some of the important Word features you have mastered in this unit. Use correct grammar, appropriate word choices, and clear sentence constructions.

Activity 1 Compose a Letter to Volunteers

You are an employee for the City of Greenwater and are responsible for coordinating volunteers for the city's Safe Night program. Compose a letter to the volunteers listed below and include the following information in the letter:

- Safe Night event scheduled for Saturday, June 19, 2010.
- Volunteer orientation scheduled for Thursday, May 20, 2010, at 7:30 p.m. At the orientation, participants will learn about the types of volunteer positions available and the work schedule.

Include any additional information in the letter, including a thank you to the volunteers. Use the Mail Merge feature to create a data source with the names and addresses that is attached to the main document, which is the letter to the volunteers. Save the merged letters as **WordL1_U2_Act01** and then print the letters.

Mrs. Laura Reston
376 Thompson Avenue
Greenwater, OR 99034

Mr. Matthew Klein
7408 Ryan Road
Greenwater, OR 99034

Ms. Cecilia Sykes
1430 Canyon Road
Greenwater, OR 99034

Mr. Brian McDonald
8980 Union Street
Greenwater, OR 99034

Mr. Ralph Emerson
1103 Highlands Avenue
Greenwater, OR 99034

Mrs. Nola Alverez
598 McBride Street
Greenwater, OR 99034

Activity 2 Create a Business Letterhead

You have just opened a new mailing and shipping business and need letterhead stationery. Create a letterhead for your company in a header and/or footer. Use Word's Help feature to learn about creating a header that only displays and prints on the first page. Create the letterhead in a header that displays and prints only on the first page and include *at least* one of the following: a clip art image, a picture, a shape, a text box, and/or WordArt. Include the following information in the header:

Global Mailing
4300 Jackson Avenue
Toronto, ON M4C 3X4
(416) 555-0095
www.emcp.net/globalmailing

Save the completed letterhead and name it **WordL1_U2_Act02**. Print and then close the document.

INTERNET research

Create a Flyer on an Incentive Program

The owner of Evergreen Travel is offering an incentive to motivate travel consultants to increase travel bookings. The incentive is a sales contest with a grand prize of a one-week paid vacation to Cancun, Mexico. The owner has asked you to create a flyer that will be posted on the office bulletin board that includes information about the incentive program and some information about Cancun. Create this flyer using information about Cancun that you find on the Internet. Include a photo you find on a Web site (make sure it is not copyrighted) or include a clip art image representing travel. Include any other information or object to add visual appeal to the flyer. Save the completed flyer and name it **WordL1_U2_InternetResearch**. Print and then close the document.

JOB study

Develop Recycling Program Communications

The Chief Operating Officer of Harrington Engineering has just approved your draft of the company's new recycling policy (see the file named **WordRecyclingPolicy.docx** located in the Word2007L1U2 folder) with a note that you need to add some statistics on national average costs of recycling, which you can locate on the Internet. Edit the draft and prepare a final copy of the policy along with a memorandum to all employees describing the new guidelines. To support the company's energy resources conservation effort, you will send hard copies of the new policy to the Somerset Recycling Program president and to directors of Somerset Chamber of Commerce.

Using the concepts and techniques you learned in this unit, prepare the following documents:

- Format the recycling policy manual, including a cover page, appropriate headers and footers, and page numbers. Add at least one graphic and one diagram where appropriate. Format the document using a Quick Styles set and styles. Save the manual and name it **WordL1_U2_JobStudyManual**. Print the manual.

- Download a memo template from the Microsoft Online Web site and then create a memo from Susan Gerhardt, Chief Operating Officer of Harrington Engineering to all employees introducing the new recycling program. Copy the *Procedure* section of the recycling policy manual into the memo where appropriate. Include a table listing five employees who will act as Recycling Coordinators at Harrington Engineering (make up the names). Add columns for the employees' department names and their telephone extensions. Save the memo and name it **WordL1_U2_JobStudyMemo**. Print the memo.

- Write a letter to the President of the Somerset Recycling Program, William Elizondo, enclosing a copy of the recycling policy manual. Add a notation indicating copies with enclosures were sent to all members of the Somerset Chamber of Commerce. Save the letter and name it **WordL1_U2_JobStudyLetter**. Print the letter.

- Create mailing labels (see Figure U2.8). Save the labels and name the file **WordL1_U2_JobStudyLabels**. Print the file.

Figure U2.8 Mailing Labels

William Elizondo, President
Somerset Recycling Program
700 West Brighton Road
Somerset, NJ 55123

Paul Schwartz
Somerset Chamber of Commerce
45 Wallace Road
Somerset, NJ 55123

Ashley Crighton
Somerset Chamber of Commerce
45 Wallace Road
Somerset, NJ 55123

Carol Davis
Somerset Chamber of Commerce
45 Wallace Road
Somerset, NJ 55123

Robert Knight
Somerset Chamber of Commerce
45 Wallace Road
Somerset, NJ 55123

A

Abbreviations: address, 211
Active documents, 201–202
Addition: table calculations and plus sign (+) operator for, 251
Address Block button: in Write & Insert Fields group, 296
Address Block field, 297
Addresses: United States Postal Service guidelines for, 211
Alignment. *See also* Margins
  of cells, 263
  of cells, changing, 242
  changing, at Paragraph dialog box, 50–52
  of objects, 183–184
  of paragraphs, changing, 48–50
  of tables, changing, 245–246
  of text, 186
  vertical, 168
Alignment button, 63, 82, 83, 96
Alignment group, 242, 262
Alignment option: at Paragraph dialog box, 50
Alphabetical sorting: of paragraphs, 81–82
Arithmetic operations: on numbers in table cells, 251
Arrange All button: in Window group, 202, 219
Arrow bullets, 73
Arrow keys, 17
Arrow shapes: drawing, 178–180
Art list box, 128
Asterisk (*) operator: performing calculations in a table and, 251
Asterisk (*) symbol: in bulleted paragraphs, 73
AutoComplete feature, 10, 29
AutoCorrect dialog box, 96
  with AutoFormat As You Type tab selected, 71, 73
AutoCorrect feature, 9, 29
AutoCorrect Options button, 10, 70, 96
AutoFit button, 262
  in Cell Size group, 241

AutoFit table contents feature, 263
AutoFormat feature, 70, 96
  bulleted paragraphs and, 73
AVERAGE function: for averaging numbers in cells, 251
Averages: calculating, 251

B

Backgrounds: formatting, 126–129
Backspace key, 88
Banners: drawing, 177
Bar tab
  setting at Tabs dialog box, 86–87
  setting on Ruler, 83
Binary numbers, 11
Bits, 11
Blank Page button, 116, 140
Blank pages: inserting, 103, 109, 116, 118–119, 138, 140
Bold button
  in Font group, 38
  keyboard shortcut with, 40
Bold italic type style, 37
Bold text, 35, 63
Bold type style, 37
Borders, 126
  around paragraphs, 75, 76, 96
  customizing, 78–80
Borders and Shading dialog box, 96, 97, 126
  with Borders tab selected, 78
  with Page Border tab selected, 128, 140
  with Shading tab selected, 79
Borders button, 97
  in Paragraph group, 78
  in Table Styles group, 231
Borders gallery, 75
Bottom alignment option, 168
Bottom margins: in cells, 243
Break Link button, 187
  in Text group, 182
Breaks button: in Page Setup group, 154
Brightness: changing in images, 169
Browsing: in document, 17, 18–19

Built-in text boxes: inserting, 176–177
Bulleted lists: with hanging indents, 96
Bulleted paragraphs, 73
  typing, 73–74
Bullets
  inserting before paragraphs, 70
  inserting with Bullets button, 74
Bullets button, 70, 97
  inserting bullets with, 74
  in Paragraph group, 73
Bytes, 11

C

Calculations: performing in tables, 251–252
Calibri typeface: as default typeface in Word, 10, 35, 36
Callouts: drawing, 177
Cambria typeface, 36
Candara typeface, 36
Capitalization: irregular, 24
Case of text: changing, 40
Cell alignment: changing, 242
Cell direction: changing, 245
Cell margins: changing, 243–245, 262
Cell Margins button, 243
Cell Options dialog box, 244
Cells
  alignment of, 263
  alignment of text in, 243
  defined, 227
  direction of, 263
  merging, 263
  merging and splitting, 238
  selecting, 233, 262
  selecting and formatting, in a table, 234–235
  text entered into, 228–229
Cell size: customizing, 240–241
Cell Size group: in Table Tools Layout tab, 240
Center alignment option, 168
Center-align text, 63
Center tabs: setting on Ruler, 83–84
Change Case button, 40
  keyboard shortcut with, 40
Character formatting, 35
  applying to text as you type, 39

Level I

Paradigm
PUBLISHING

Microsoft®
excel
2007

BENCHMARK SERIES

Nita Rutkosky
Pierce College at Puyallup
Puyallup, Washington

Audrey Rutkosky Roggenkamp
Pierce College at Puyallup
Puyallup, Washington

Managing Editor	Sonja Brown
Production Editor	Donna Mears
Cover and Text Designer	Leslie Anderson
Copy Editor	Susan Capecchi
Desktop Production	John Valo, Desktop Solutions
Proofreader	Laura Nelson
Indexer	Nancy Fulton

Acknowledgments: The authors and editors wish to thank Pamela J. Silvers, Chairperson, Business Computer Technologies, Asheville-Buncombe Technical Community College, Asheville, North Carolina, for testing the instruction and exercises for accuracy.

Care has been taken to verify the accuracy of information presented in this book. However, the authors, editors, and publisher cannot accept responsibility for Web, e-mail, newsgroup, or chat room subject matter or content, or for consequences from application of the information in this book, and make no warranty, expressed or implied, with respect to its content.

Photo Credits: Introduction page 1 (clockwise from top), Lexmark International, Inc., courtesy of Dell Inc., all rights Hewlett-Packard Company, Logitech, Micron Technology, Inc.; Excel Level 1 pages 1, 3, 4 © Corbis; photos in Student Resources CD, courtesy of Kelly Rutkosky and Michael Rutkosky.

Trademarks: Microsoft is a trademark or registered trademark of Microsoft Corporation in the United States and/or other countries. Some of the product names and company names included in this book have been used for identification purposes only and may be trademarks or registered trade names of their respective manufacturers and sellers. The authors, editors, and publisher disclaim any affiliation, association, or connection with, or sponsorship or endorsement by, such owners.

We have made every effort to trace the ownership of all copyrighted material and to secure permission from copyright holders. In the event of any question arising as to the use of any material, we will be pleased to make the necessary corrections in future printings. Thanks are due to the aforementioned authors, publishers, and agents for permission to use the materials indicated.

ISBN 978-0-76382-990-2 (Text)
ISBN 978-0-76383-005-2 (Text + CD)

CONTENTS

Unit 2 Enhancing the Display of Workbooks — 155

Benchmark Microsoft Excel 2007 is designed for students who want to learn how to use this powerful spreadsheet program to manipulate numerical data in resolving issues related to finances or other numbers-based information. No prior knowledge of spreadsheets is required. After successfully completing a course using this textbook, students will be able to

- Create and edit spreadsheets of varying complexity
- Format cells, columns, and rows as well as entire workbooks in a uniform, attractive style
- Analyze numerical data and project outcomes to make informed decisions
- Plan, research, create, revise, and publish worksheets and workbooks to meet specific communication needs
- Given a workplace scenario requiring a numbers-based solution, assess the information requirements and then prepare the materials that achieve the goal efficiently and effectively

In addition to mastering Excel skills, students will learn the essential features and functions of computer hardware, the Windows XP operating system, and Internet Explorer 7.0. Upon completing the text, they can expect to be proficient in using Excel to organize, analyze, and present information.

Achieving Proficiency in Excel 2007

Since its inception several Office versions ago, the Benchmark Series has served as a standard of excellence in software instruction. Elements of the book function individually and collectively to create an inviting, comprehensive learning environment that produces successful computer users. On this and following pages, take a visual tour of the structure and features that comprise the highly popular Benchmark model.

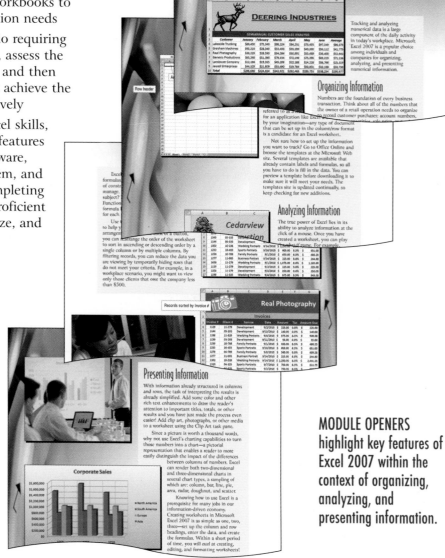

MODULE OPENERS highlight key features of Excel 2007 within the context of organizing, analyzing, and presenting information.

Level 1

Microsoft® excel

Unit 1: Preparing and Formatting a Worksheet

➤ Preparing an Excel Workbook

➤ Inserting Formulas in a Worksheet

➤ Formatting an Excel Worksheet

➤ Enhancing a Worksheet

UNIT OPENERS display the unit's four chapter titles. Each level has two units, which conclude with a comprehensive unit performance assessment.

CHAPTER 2

Inserting Formulas in a Worksheet

CHAPTER OPENERS present the Performance Objectives and highlight the practical relevance of the skills students will learn.

PERFORMANCE OBJECTIVES

Upon successful completion of Chapter 2, you will be able to:

* Write formulas with mathematical operators
* Type a formula in the Formula bar
* Copy a formula
* Use the Insert Function feature to insert a formula in a cell
* Write formulas with the AVERAGE, MAX, MIN, COUNT, PMT, FV, DATE, NOW, and IF functions
* Create an absolute and mixed cell reference

excel Chapter 2

CD icon identifies a folder of data files to be copied to student's storage medium.

S·N·A·P

Tutorial 2.1
Inserting and Editing Formulas
Tutorial 2.2
Working with Cell References

The SNAP icon alerts students to corresponding SNAP tutorial titles.

Excel is a powerful decision-making tool containing data that can be manipulated to answer "what if" situations. Insert a formula in a worksheet and then manipulate the data to make projections, answer specific questions, and use as a planning tool. For example, the owner of a company might prepare a worksheet on production costs and then determine the impact on company revenues if production is increased or decreased.

Insert a formula in a worksheet to perform calculations on values. A formula contains a mathematical operator, value, cell reference, cell range, and a function. Formulas can be written that add, subtract, multiply, and/or divide values. Formulas can also be written that calculate averages, percentages, minimum and maximum values, and much more. As you learned in Chapter 1, Excel includes a Sum button in the Editing group in the Home tab that inserts a formula to calculate the total of a range of cells and also includes some commonly used formulas. Along with the Sum button, Excel includes a Formulas tab that offers a variety of functions to create formulas.

Note: Before beginning computer projects, copy to your storage medium the Excel2007L1C2 subfolder from the Excel2007L1 folder on the CD that accompanies this textbook and make Excel2007L1C2 the active folder.

A prominent note reminds students to copy the appropriate chapter data folder and make it active.

excel Level 1
Inserting Formulas in a Worksheet **37**

New! PROJECT APPROACH: Builds Skill Mastery within Realistic Context

Project 1 Insert Formulas in a Worksheet
You will open a worksheet containing data and then insert formulas to calculate differences, salaries, and percentages of budgets.

Writing Formulas with Mathematical Operators

HINT
After typing a formula in a cell, press the Enter key, the Tab key, Shift + Tab, or click the Enter button on the Formula bar.

As you learned in Chapter 1, the Sum button in the Editing group in the Home tab creates the formula for you. You can also write your own formulas using mathematical operators. Commonly used mathematical operators and their functions are displayed in Table 2.1. When writing your own formula, begin the formula with the equals (=) sign. For example, to create a formula that divides the contents of cell B2 by the contents of cell C2 and inserts the result in cell D2, you would make D2 the active cell and then type =B2/C2.

Table 2.1 Mathematical Operators

Operator	Function
+	Addition
-	Subtraction
*	Multiplication
/	Division
%	Percent
^	Exponentiation

If a formula contains two or more operators, Excel uses the same order of operations used in algebra. From left to right in a formula, this order, called the *order of operations*, is: negations (negative number—a number preceded by -) first, then percents (%), then exponentiations (^), followed by multiplications (*), divisions (/), additions (+), and finally subtractions (-). If you want to change the order of operations, use parentheses around the part of the formula you want calculated first.

Copying a Formula with Relative Cell References

In many worksheets, the same basic formula is used repetitively. In a situation where a formula is copied to other locations in a worksheet, use a *relative cell reference*. Copy a formula containing relative cell references and the cell references change. For example, if you enter the formula =SUM(A2:C2) in cell ___, copy it relatively to cell D3, the formula in cell D3 displays as =SU___. (Additional information on cell references is discussed later in this ch___ "Using an Absolute Cell Reference in a Formula" section.)

38 Chapter Two

Instruction and practice are organized into multipart projects that focus on related program features. A project overview identifies the tasks to accomplish and the key features to use in completing the work.

Typically, a file remains open throughout a project. Students save their work incrementally.

QUICK STEPS provide feature summaries for reference and review.

Following each project part, the text presents instruction on the features and skills necessary to accomplish the next task.

Project 1b Calculating Salary by Inserting and Copying a Formula with the Fill Handle

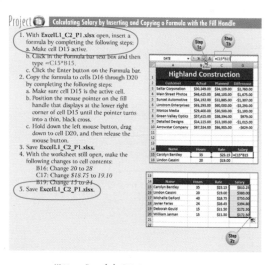

1. With **ExcelL1_C2_P1.xlsx** open, insert a formula by completing the following steps:
   a. Make cell D15 active.
   b. Click in the Formula bar text box and then type =C15*B15.
   c. Click the Enter button on the Formula bar.
2. Copy the formula to cells D16 through D20 by completing the following steps:
   a. Make sure cell D15 is the active cell.
   b. Position the mouse pointer on the fill handle that displays at the lower right corner of cell D15 until the pointer turns into a thin, black cross.
   c. Hold down the left mouse button, drag down to cell D20, and then release the mouse button.
3. Save **ExcelL1_C2_P1.xlsx**.
4. With the worksheet still open, make the following changes to cell contents:
   B16: Change 20 to 28
   C17: Change $18.75 to 19.10
   B19: Change 15 to 24
5. Save **ExcelL1_C2_P1.xlsx**.

Writing a Formula by Pointing

QUICK STEPS

Write Formula by Pointing
1. Click cell that will contain formula.
2. Type equals sign.
3. Click cell you want to reference in formula.
4. Type desired mathematical operator.
5. Click next cell reference.

In Project 1a and Project 1b, you wrote formulas using cell references such as =C3-B3. Another method for writing a formula is to "point" to the specific cells that are to be part of the formula. Creating a formula by pointing is more accurate than typing the cell reference since a mistake can happen when typing the cell reference.

To write a formula by pointing, click the cell that will contain the formula, type the equals sign to begin the formula, and then click the cell you want to reference in the formula. This inserts a moving border around the cell and also changes the mode from Enter to Point. (The word *Point* displays at the left side of the Status bar.) Type the desired mathematical operator and then click the next cell reference. Continue in this manner until all cell references are specified and then press the Enter key. This ends the formula and inserts the result of the calculation of the formula in the active cell. When writing a formula by pointing, you can also select a range of cells you want included in a formula.

40 Chapter Two

Each project exercise guides students step by step to the desired outcome. Screen captures illustrate what the screen should look like at key points.

Text in magenta identifies material to type.

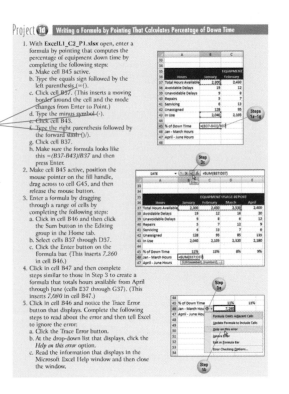

1. With **ExcelL1_C2_P1.xlsx** open, enter a formula by pointing that computes the percentage of equipment down time by completing the following steps:
   a. Make cell B45 active.
   b. Type the equals sign followed by the left parenthesis (=().
   c. Click cell B37. (This inserts a moving border around the cell and the mode changes from Enter to Point.)
   d. Type the minus symbol (-).
   e. Click cell B43.
   f. Type the right parenthesis followed by the forward slash ()/).
   g. Click cell B37.
   h. Make sure the formula looks like this =(B37-B43)/B37 and then press Enter.
2. Make cell B45 active, position the mouse pointer on the fill handle, drag across to cell G45, and then release the mouse button.
3. Enter a formula by dragging through a range of cells by completing the following steps:
   a. Click in cell B46 and then click the Sum button in the Editing group in the Home tab.
   b. Select cells B37 through D37.
   c. Click the Enter button on the Formula bar. (This inserts 7,260 in cell B46.)
4. Click in cell B47 and then complete steps similar to those in Step 3 to create a formula that totals hours available from April through June (cells E37 through G37). (This inserts 7,080 in cell B47.)
5. Click in cell B46 and notice the Trace Error button that displays. Complete the following steps to read about the error and then tell Excel to ignore the error:
   a. Click the Trace Error button.
   b. At the drop-down list that displays, click the *Help on this error* option.
   c. Read the information that displays in the Microsoft Excel Help window and then close the window.

42   Chapter Two

---

d. Click the Trace Error button again and then click *Ignore Error* at the drop-down list.
6. Remove the dark green triangle from cell B47 by completing the following steps:
   a. Click in cell B47.
   b. Click the Trace Error button and then click *Ignore Error* at the drop-down list.
7. Save, print, and then close ExcelL1_C2_P1.xlsx.

Project 2   Insert Formulas with Statistical Functions

You will use the AVERAGE function to determine average test scores, use the MINIMUM and MAXIMUM functions to determine lowest and highest averages, use the COUNT function to count number of students taking a test, and display formulas in a cell rather than the result of the formula.

Inserting Formulas with Functions

In Project 2a in Chapter 1, you used the Sum button to insert the formula =SUM(B2:B5) in a cell. The beginning section of the formula, =SUM, is called a **function**, which is a built-in formula. Using a function takes fewer keystrokes when creating a formula. For example, the =SUM function saved you from having to type each cell to be included in the formula with the plus (+) symbol between cell entries.

Excel provides other functions for writing formulas. A function operates on what is referred to as an **argument**. An argument may consist of a constant, a cell reference, or another function (referred to as a nested function). In the formula =SUM(B2:B5), the cell range (B2:B5) is an example of a cell reference argument. An argument may also contain a **constant**. A constant is a value entered directly into the formula. For example, if you enter the formula =SUM(B3:B9,100), the cell range B3:B9 is a cell reference argument and 100 is a constant. In this formula, 100 is always added to the sum of the cells. If a function is included in an argument within a function, it is called a **nested function**. (You will learn about nested functions later in this chapter.)

When a value calculated by the formula is inserted in a cell, this process is referred to as **returning the result**. The term **returning** refers to the process of calculating the formula and the term **result** refers to inserting the value in the cell.

You can type a function in a cell in a worksheet or you can use the Insert Function button on the Formula bar or in the Formulas tab to help you write the formula. Figure 2.1 displays the Formulas tab. The Formulas tab provides the Insert Function button as well as other buttons for inserting functions in a worksheet. The Function Library group in the Formulas tab contains a number of buttons for inserting functions from a variety of categories such as Financial, Logical, Text, and Date & Time.

Insert Function

excel Level 1
Inserting Formulas in a Worksheet   43

At the end of the project, students save, print, and close the file. Locked, watermarked model answers in PDF format on the Student Resources CD allow students to check their work. This option rewards careful effort and builds software mastery.

CHAPTER REVIEW ACTIVITIES: A Hierarchy of Learning Assessments

CHAPTER summary

- Change column width using the mouse on column boundaries or with options at the Column Width dialog box.
- To automatically adjust a column to accommodate the longest entry in the column, double-click the column header boundary on the right.
- Change row height using the mouse on row boundaries or with options at the Row Height dialog box.
- Insert a row in a worksheet with the Insert button in the Cells group in the Home tab or with options at the Insert dialog box.
- Insert a column in a worksheet with the Insert button in the Cells group or with options at the Insert dialog box.
- Delete a specific cell by clicking the Delete button arrow and then clicking *Delete Cells* at the drop-down list. At the Delete dialog box, specify if you want to delete just the cell or an entire row or column.
- Delete a selected row(s) or column(s) by clicking the Delete button in the Cells group.
- Delete cell contents by pressing the De... the Editing group and then clicking Cl...
- Apply font formatting with buttons in...
- Use the Mini toolbar to apply font for...
- Apply alignment formatting with but... Home tab.
- Preview a worksheet by clicking the O... clicking *Print Preview*.
- Change the size of the worksheet displ... Preview tab or with the Zoom slider ba... Status bar.
- Use the Themes button in the Themes... theme to cells in a worksheet that app... effects. Use the other buttons in the T...
- Format numbers in cells with the Acco... Comma Style, Increase Decimal, and D... group in the home tab. You can also ap... the Format Cells dialog box with the N...
- Apply formatting to cells in a workshe... box. This dialog box includes the follo... Alignment, Font, Border, and Patterns...
- Press F4 or Ctrl + Y to repeat the last...
- Use the Format Painter button in the C... formatting to different locations in a ...
- Hide selected columns or rows in a wo... the Cells group in the Home tab, poin... *Hide Columns* or *Hide Rows*.

CHAPTER SUMMARY captures the purpose and execution of key features.

- To make a hidden column visible, select the column to the left and right, click the Format button in the Cells group, point to *Hide & Unhide*, and then click *Unhide Columns*.
- To make a hidden row visible, select the row above and below, click the Format button in the Cells group, point to *Hide & Unhide*, and then click *Unhide Rows*.

COMMANDS review

FEATURE	RIBBON TAB, GROUP	BUTTON	KEYBOARD SHORTCUT
Format	Home, Cells	Format	
Insert cells, rows, columns	Home, Cells	Insert	
Delete cells, rows, columns	Home, Cells	Delete	
Clear cell or cell contents	Home, Editing		
Font	Home, Font		
Font size	Home, Font		
Increase Font Size	Home, Font		
Decrease Font Size	Home, Font		
Bold	Home, Font		
Italic	Home, Font		
Underline	Home, Font		
Borders	Home, Font		
Fill Color	Home, Font		
Font Color	Home, Font		
Top Align	Home, Alignment		
Middle Align	Home, Alignment		
Bottom Align	Home, Alignment		
Orientation	Home, Alignment		
Align Text Left	Home, Alignment		

COMMANDS REVIEW summarizes visually the major features and alternative methods of access.

FEATURE	RIBBON TAB, GROUP	BUTTON	KEYBOARD SHORTCUT
Center	Home, Alignment		
Align Text Right	Home, Alignment		
Decrease Indent	Home, Alignment		Ctrl + Alt + Shift + Tab
Increase Indent	Home, Alignment		Ctrl + Alt + Tab
Wrap Text	Home, Alignment		
Merge & Center	Home, Alignment		
Print Preview		Print, Print Preview	Ctrl + F2
Themes	Page Layout, Themes		
Number Format	Home, Number	General	
Accounting Number Format	Home, Number	$	
Percent Style	Home, Number	%	Ctrl + Shift + %
Increase Decimal	Home, Number		
Decrease Decimal	Home, Number		
Format Painter	Home, Clipboard		
Repeat			F4 or Ctrl + Y

CONCEPTS check

Test Your Knowledge

Completion: In the space provided at the right, indicate the correct term, symbol, or command.

1. To automatically adjust a column width to accommodate the longest entry in the cell, do this with the mouse on the column boundary.

2. By default, a column is inserted in this direction from the column containing the active cell.

3. To delete a row, select the *row* and then click the Delete button in this group in the Home tab.

CONCEPTS CHECK questions assess knowledge recall.

..., you can clear
... or selected cells.
... a cell.
... enter data within
...ed fashion
... Home tab to
...atus bar, to
... $50.25, Excel
...mber.
... as 25%, Excel
...mber.
...the Alignment
...dialog box with

15. You can repeat the last action performed with the command Ctrl + Y or pressing this function key.

16. The Format Painter button is located in this group in the Home tab.

17. To hide a column, select the column, click this button in the Cells group in the Home tab, point to *Hide & Unhide*, and then click *Hide Columns*.

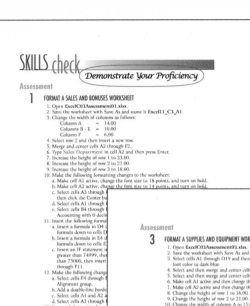

SKILLS check
Demonstrate Your Proficiency

Assessment

1 FORMAT A SALES AND BONUSES WORKSHEET

1. Open **ExcelC03Assessment01.xlsx**.
2. Save the worksheet with Save As and name it **ExcelL1_C3_A1**.
3. Change the width of columns as follows:
   Column A   = 14.00
   Columns B - E   = 10.00
   Column F   =   6.00
4. Select row 2 and then insert a new row.
5. Merge and center cells A2 through F2.
6. Type Sales Department in cell A2 and then press Enter.
7. Increase the height of row 1 to 33.00.
8. Increase the height of row 2 to 21.00.
9. Increase the height of row 3 to 18.00.
10. Make the following formatting changes to the worksheet:
    a. Make cell A1 active, change the font size to 18 points, and turn on bold.
    b. Make cell A2 active, change the font size to 14 points, and turn on bold.
    c. Select cells A3 through [...] then click the Center bu[...]
    d. Select cells A1 through [...]
    e. Select cells B4 through [...] Accounting with 0 deci[...]
11. Insert the following formu[...]
    a. Insert a formula in D4 t[...] formula down to cells D[...]
    b. Insert a formula in E4 t[...] formula down to cells E[...]
    c. Insert an IF statement i[...] greater than 74999, the[...] than 75000, then insert[...] through F11.
12. Make the following change[...]
    a. Select cells F4 through [...] Alignment group.
    b. Add a double-line borde[...]
    c. Select cells A1 and A2 [...]
    d. Select cells A1 through [...]
13. Save and then print the w[...]
14. Apply the Verve theme to [...]
15. Save, print, and then clos[...]

SKILLS CHECK exercises ask students to develop both standard and customized kinds of spreadsheet documents without how-to directions.

Assessment

3 FORMAT A SUPPLIES AND EQUIPMENT WORKSHEET

1. Open **ExcelC03Assessment03.xlsx**.
2. Save the worksheet with Save As and name it **ExcelL1_C3_A3**.
3. Select cells A1 through D19 and then change the font to Garamond and the font color to dark blue.
4. Select and then merge and center cells A1 through D1.
5. Select and then merge and center cells A2 through D2.
6. Make cell A1 active and then change the font size to 22 points and turn on bold.
7. Make cell A2 active and then change the font size to 12 points and turn on bold.
8. Change the height of row 1 to 36.00.
9. Change the height of row 2 to 21.00.
10. Change the width of column A to 15.00.
11. Select cells A3 through A17, turn on bold, and then click the Wrap Text button in the Alignment group.
12. Select cells A1 and A2 and then click the Middle Align button in the Alignment group.
13. Make cell B3 active and then change the number formatting to Currency with no decimal places.
14. Select cells C6 through C19 and then change the number formatting to Percentage with one decimal place.
15. Automatically adjust the width of column C.
16. Make cell D6 active and th[...] reference $B$3 with the pe[...] D7 through D19.
17. With cells D6 through D19 [...] with no decimal places.
18. Make cell D8 active and [...] command, F4, to clear the [...]
19. Add light green fill color to [...] A11–D11, A14–D14, and A[...]
20. Add borders and/or shading[...] the worksheet.
21. Save, print, and then close [...]

Assessment

4 FORMAT A FINANCIAL ANALYSIS [...]

1. Use the Help feature to lea[...] data in a cell (with an opti[...] tab selected).
2. Open **ExcelC03Assessment[...]**.
3. Save the worksheet with Sa[...]
4. Make cell B9 active and th[...] in cells B3 through B8. Co[...]

To complete certain exercises, students must first work with the program's Help feature, learning independently how to use a specific option.

5. Select cells B3 through D9, display the Format Cells dialog box with the Alignment tab selected, change the horizontal alignment to Right (Indent) and the indent to 2, and then close the dialog box.
6. Select cells A1 through D9 and then change the font size to 14.
7. Select cells B2 through D2 and then change the orientation to 45 degrees.
8. With cells B2 through D2 still selected, shrink the font size to show all data in the cells.
9. Save, print, and then close **ExcelL1_C3_A4.xlsx**.

CASE study
Apply Your Skills

Part
1

You are the office manager for HealthWise Fitness Center and you decide to prepare an Excel worksheet that displays the various plans offered by the health club. In this worksheet, you want to include yearly dues for each plan as well as quarterly and monthly payments. Open the **HealthWise.xlsx** workbook and then save it and name it **ExcelL1_C3_CS_P1A**. Make the following changes to the worksheet:

- Select cells B3 through D8 and then change the number formatting to Accounting with two decimal places and a dollar sign.
- Make cell B3 active and then insert 560.00.
- Make cell B4 active and then insert a formula that adds the amount in B3 with the product (multiplication) of B3 multiplied by 10%. (The formula should look like this: **=B3+(B3*10%)**. The Economy plan is the base plan and each additional plan costs 10% more than the previous plan.)
- Copy the formula in cell B4 down to cells B5 through B8.
- Insert a formula in cell C3 that divides the amount in cell B3 by 4 and then copy the formula down to cells C4 through C8.
- Insert a formula in cell D3 that divides the amount in cell B3 by 12 and then copy the formula down to cells D4 through D8.
- Apply formatting to enhance the visual display of the worksheet.

Save and print the completed worksheet.

With **ExcelL1_C3_CS_P1A.xlsx** open, save the workbook with Save As and name it **ExcelL1_C3_CS_P1B**, and then make the following changes:

- You have been informed that the base rate for yearly dues has increased from $500.00 to $600.00. Change this amount in cell B3 of the worksheet.
- If clients are late with their quarterly or monthly dues payments, a late fee is charged. You decide to add the late fee information to the worksheet. Insert a new column to the right of Column C. Type Late Fees in cell D2 and also in cell F2.
- Insert a formula in cell D3 that multiplies the amount in C3 by 5%. Copy this formula down to cells D4 through D8.
- Insert a formula in cell F3 that multiplies the amount in E3 by 7%. Copy this formula down to cells F4 through F8. If necessary, change the number formatting for cells F3 through F8 to Accounting with two decimal places and a dollar sign.
- Apply any additional formatting to enhance the visual display of the worksheet.

Save, print, and then close **ExcelL1_C3_CS_P1B.xlsx**.

The chapter CASE STUDY requires planning and executing multi-part workplace projects.

the fitness center and include the
[...]ss Center
[...]rnal
[...]urs   Weekly Salary   Benefits

[...]that multiplies the hourly wage by
[...] in the *Benefits* column that states that
[...]than 19, then insert "Yes" and if the
[...]ply formatting to enhance the visual
[...] and name it **ExcelL1_C3_CS_P2**.
[...] ` to turn on the display of formulas
[...] Ctrl + ` to turn off the display of

Make the following changes to the worksheet:
- Change the hourly wage for Amanda Turney to $22.00.
- Increase the hours for Emily Dugan to 20.
- Remove the row for Grant Baker.
- Insert a row between Jean Overmeyer and Bonnie Haddon and then type the following information in the cells in the new row: Employee: Tonya McGuire; Hourly Wage: $17.50; Hours: 15.

Save and then print **ExcelL1_C3_CS_P2.xlsx**. Press Ctrl + ` to turn on the display of formulas and then print the worksheet. Press Ctrl + ` to turn off the display of formulas and then save and close **ExcelL1_C3_CS_P2.xlsx**.

Part
3

Your boss is interested in ordering new equipment for the health club. She is interested in ordering three elliptical machines, three recumbent bikes, and three upright bikes. She has asked you to use the Internet to research models and prices for this new equipment. She then wants you to prepare a worksheet with the information. Using the Internet, search for the following equipment:

- Search for elliptical machines for sale. Locate two different models and, if possible, find at least two companies that sell each model. Make a note of the company names, model numbers, and prices.

To complete one or more parts of the Case Study, students search the Web and/or use the Help feature to locate information.

UNIT PERFORMANCE ASSESSMENT: Cross-Disciplinary, Comprehensive Evaluation

Maintaining and Enhancing Workbooks | Unit 2

ASSESSING proficiency

In this unit, you have learned how to work with multiple windows; move, copy, link, and paste data between workbooks and applications; create and customize charts with data in a worksheet; save a workbook as a Web page; insert hyperlinks; and insert and customize pictures, clip art images, shapes, SmartArt diagrams, and WordArt.

Note: Before beginning computer assessments, d...
from your storage medium. Next, copy to your st...
subfolder from the Excel2007L1 folder on the C...
and then make Excel2007L1U2 the active folde...

Assessment 1 Copy and Paste Data and Ins...
Scores Workbook

1. Open ExcelU02Assessment01.xlsx an...
   name it ExcelL1_U2_A1.
2. Delete row 15 (the row for *Kwieciak, Ke...*
3. Insert a formula in cell D4 that averages...
4. Copy the formula in cell D4 down to c...
5. Make cell A22 active, turn on bold, an...
6. Display the Clipboard task pane and m...
7. Select and then copy each of the follow...
   14, 16, and 18.
8. Make cell A23 active and then paste ro...
9. Make cell A24 active and then paste ro...
10. Make cell A25 active and then paste ro...
    Theresa).
11. Make cell A26 active and then paste ro...
12. Make cell A27 active and then paste ro...
13. Click the Clear All button in the Clipb...
    task pane.
14. Insert in cell A1 the text *Roseland* as W...
    to add visual appeal to the worksheet.
15. Save, print, and then close ExcelL1_U2...

ASSESSING PROFICIENCY checks mastery of features.

WRITING activities

The following activities give you the opportunity to practice your writing skills along with demonstrating an understanding of some of the important Excel features you have mastered in this unit. Use correct grammar, appropriate word choices, and clear sentence constructions.

Activity 1 Prepare a Projected Budget

You are the accounting assistant in the financial department of McCormack Funds and you have been asked to prepare a yearly proposed department budget. The total amount for the department is $1,450,000. You are given the percentages for the proposed budget items, which are: Salaries, 45%; Benefits, 12%; Training, 14%; Administrative Costs, 10%; Equipment, 11%; and Supplies, 8%. Create a worksheet with this information that shows the projected yearly budget, the budget items in the department, the percentage of the budget, and the amount for each item. After the worksheet is completed, save the workbook and name it ExcelL1_U2_Act01. Print and then close the workbook.

Optional: Using Word 2007, write a memo to the McCormack Funds Finance Department explaining that the proposed annual department budget is attached for their review. Comments and suggestions are to be sent to you within one week. Save the file and name it ExcelL1_U2_Act01_Memo. Print and then close the file.

Activity 2 Create a Travel Tours Bar Chart

Prepare a worksheet in Excel for Carefree Travels that includes the following information:

Scandinavian Tours

Country	Tours Booked
Norway	52
Sweden	62
Finland	29
Denmark	38

Use the information in the worksh...
separate sheet. Save the workbook...
the sheet containing the chart and...

Activity 3 Prepare a Ski Vacation...

Prepare a worksheet for Carefree Tr...
the following information in the an...
• At the beginning of the work...
  company name *Carefree Trave...*
• Include the heading *Whistler...*
• Include the following below...
  ∘ Round-trip air transporta...
  ∘ Seven nights' hotel accom...
  ∘ Four all-day ski passes: $...

WRITING ACTIVITIES involve applying program skills in a communication context.

∘ Compact rental car with unlimited mileage: $250
∘ Total price of the ski package: (calculate the total price)
• Include the following information somewhere in the worksheet:
  ∘ Book your vacation today at special discount prices.
  ∘ Two-for-one discount at many of the local ski resorts.
Save the workbook and name it ExcelL1_U2_Act03. Print and then close ExcelL1_U2_Act03.xlsx.

INTERNET research

Find Information on Excel Books and Present the Data in a Worksheet

Locate two companies on the Internet that sell new books. At the first new book company site, locate three books on Microsoft Excel. Record the title, author, and price for each book. At the second new book company site, locate the same three books and record the prices. Create an Excel worksheet that includes the following information:

• Name of each new book company
• Title and author of the three books
• Prices for each book from the two book company sites

Create a hyperlink for each book company to the URL on the Internet. Then save the completed workbook and name it ExcelL1_U2_InternetResearch. Print and then close the workbook.

INTERNET RESEARCH project reinforces research and spreadsheet analysis skills.

JOB study

Create a Customized Time Card for a Landscaping Company

You are the manager of a landscaping company and are responsible for employee time cards. Locate the time card template that is available with *Installed Templates* selected in the New Workbook dialog box. Use the template to create a customized time card for your company. With the template open, delete the Company Name that displays in the middle header pane. Insert additional blank rows to increase the spacing above the Employee row. Insert a clip art image related to landscaping or gardening and position and size it attractively in the form. Include a text box with the text Lawn and Landscaping Specialists inside the box. Format, size, and position the text attractively in the form. Fill in the form for the current week with the following employee information:

Employee = Jonathan Holder
Address = 12332 South 152nd Street, Baton Rouge, LA 70804
Manager = (Your name)
Employee phone = (225) 555-3092
Employee e-mail = None

JOB STUDY at the end of Unit 2 presents a capstone assessment requiring critical thinking and problem solving.

Student Courseware

Student Resources CD Each Benchmark Series textbook is packaged with a Student Resources CD containing the data files required for completing the projects and assessments. A CD icon and folder name displayed on the opening page of chapters reminds students to copy a folder of files from the CD to the desired storage medium before beginning the project exercises. Directions for copying folders are printed on the inside back cover. The Student Resources CD also contains the model answers in PDF format for the project exercises within chapters. Files are locked and watermarked, but students can compare their completed documents with the PDF files, either on screen or in hard copy (printed) format.

Internet Resource Center Additional learning tools and reference materials are available at the book-specific Web site at www.emcp.net/BenchmarkExcel07XP. Students can access the same resources that are on the Student Resources CD along with study aids, Web links, and tips for using computers effectively in academic and workplace settings.

SNAP Training and Assessment SNAP is a Web-based program that provides hands-on instruction, practice, and testing for learning Microsoft Office 2007 and Windows. SNAP course work simulates operations of Office 2007. The program is comprised of a Web-based learning management system, multimedia tutorials, performance skill items, a concept test bank, and online grade book and course planning tools. A CD-based set of tutorials teaching the basics of Office and Windows is also available for additional practice not requiring Internet access.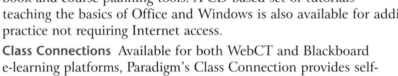

Class Connections Available for both WebCT and Blackboard e-learning platforms, Paradigm's Class Connection provides self-quizzes and study aids and facilitates communication among students and instructors via e-mail and e-discussion.

Instructor Resources

Curriculum Planner and Resources Instructor support for the Benchmark Series has been expanded to include a *Curriculum Planner and Resources* binder with CD. This all-in-one print resource includes planning resources such as Lesson Blueprints and sample course syllabi; presentation resources such as teaching hints and handouts; and assessment resources including an overview of assessment venues, model answers for intrachapter projects, and annotated model answers for end-of-chapter and end-of-unit assessments. Contents of the *Curriculum Planner and Resources* binder are also available on the Instructor's CD and on the password-protected Instructor's section of the Internet Resource Center for this title at www.emcp.com.

Computerized Test Generator Instructors can use ExamView test generating software and the provided bank of multiple-choice items to create customized Web-based or print tests.

System Requirements

This text is designed for the student to complete projects and assessments on a computer running a standard installation of Microsoft Office 2007, Professional Edition, and the Microsoft Windows XP operating system with Service Pack 2 or later. To effectively run this suite and operating system, your computer should be outfitted with the following:

- 500 MHz processor or higher; 256 MB RAM or higher
- DVD drive
- 2 GB of available hard-disk space
- CD-ROM drive
- 800 by 600 minimum monitor resolution; 1024 by 768 recommended
  Note: Screen captures in this book were created using 1024 by 768 resolution; screens with higher resolution may look different.
- Computer mouse or compatible pointing device

About the Authors

Nita Rutkosky began teaching business education courses at Pierce College in Puyallup, Washington, in 1978. Since then she has taught a variety of software applications to students in postsecondary Information Technology certificate and degree programs. In addition to co-authoring texts in the *Benchmark Office 2007 Series*, she has co-authored *Signature Word 2007*, *Marquee Office 2007*, and *Using Computers in the Medical Office: Microsoft Word, Excel, and PowerPoint 2003*. Other textbooks she has written for Paradigm Publishing include books on previous versions of Microsoft Office along with WordPerfect, desktop publishing, keyboarding, and voice recognition.

Audrey Rutkosky Roggenkamp has been teaching courses in the Business Information Technology department at Pierce College in Puyallup including keyboarding, skill building, and Microsoft Office programs. In addition to titles in the *Benchmark Office 2007 Series*, she has co-authored *Using Computers in the Medical Office*, *Marquee Office 2007*, and *Signature Word 2007*.

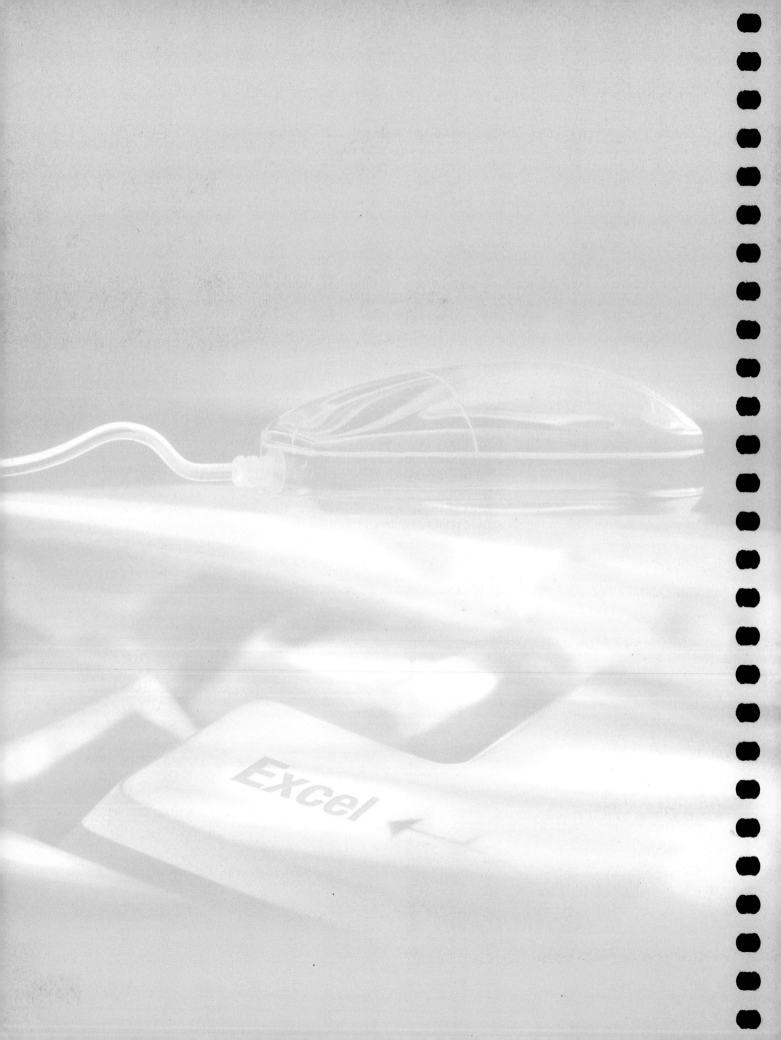

Microsoft® excel

Making Excel Work for You!

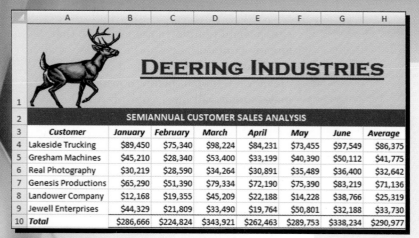

	Customer	January	February	March	April	May	June	Average
	DEERING INDUSTRIES							
	SEMIANNUAL CUSTOMER SALES ANALYSIS							
4	Lakeside Trucking	$89,450	$75,340	$98,224	$84,231	$73,455	$97,549	$86,375
5	Gresham Machines	$45,210	$28,340	$53,400	$33,199	$40,390	$50,112	$41,775
6	Real Photography	$30,219	$28,590	$34,264	$30,891	$35,489	$36,400	$32,642
7	Genesis Productions	$65,290	$51,390	$79,334	$72,190	$75,390	$83,219	$71,136
8	Landower Company	$12,168	$19,355	$45,209	$22,188	$14,228	$38,766	$25,319
9	Jewell Enterprises	$44,329	$21,809	$33,490	$19,764	$50,801	$32,188	$33,730
10	**Total**	$286,666	$224,824	$343,921	$262,463	$289,753	$338,234	$290,977

Tracking and analyzing numerical data is a large component of the daily activity in today's workplace. Microsoft Excel 2007 is a popular choice among individuals and companies for organizing, analyzing, and presenting numerical information.

Organizing Information

Numbers are the foundation of every business transaction. Think about all of the numbers that the owner of a retail operation needs to organize to record customer purchases: account numbers, stock numbers, quantities, sale price, cost price, taxes, total due, amount received—just to name a few. Now consider a different scenario in which the manager of an apple orchard wants to track the volume of apples produced by each of 10 hybrids, along with the associated costs, in order to identify which hybrid apple trees are the most cost-effective. Factors to consider might include the number of apples produced weekly plus the costs of seed, fertilizer, general maintenance, and so on. These are just two examples of the type of information management for which you could use Excel.

Formula bar

Column header

Active cell

Row header

Spreadsheet software organizes data in columns and rows—an electronic version of an accountant's ledger—only with a lot more power and versatility. In Microsoft Excel, information is organized by creating column and row *headers*, also called headings or labels. Numbers, called *values*, are entered below and beside the headers and then formulas are created to perform calculations. The completed document is referred to as a *worksheet*. The potential uses for an application like Excel are only limited by your imagination—any type of document that can be set up in the column/row format is a candidate for an Excel worksheet.

Not sure how to set up the information you want to track? Go to Office Online and browse the templates at the Microsoft Web site. Several templates are available that already contain labels and formulas, so all you have to do is fill in the data. You can preview a template before downloading it to make sure it will meet your needs. The templates site is updated continually, so keep checking for new additions.

Analyzing Information

The true power of Excel lies in its ability to analyze information at the click of a mouse. Once you have created a worksheet, you can play the *what-if* game. For example, suppose you work in the sales department of a construction company and have used Excel to set up a worksheet that tracks sales quotas. You can use Excel's calculating and protecting features to answer questions: What kind of sales increase could we achieve if we added four more salespeople who each sold an average of the total current sales? What if we increase the existing sales quotas by 20 percent? Whenever you change a value in a worksheet, Excel automatically recalculates other values that are dependent on the number you changed. In an instant, you have your answer.

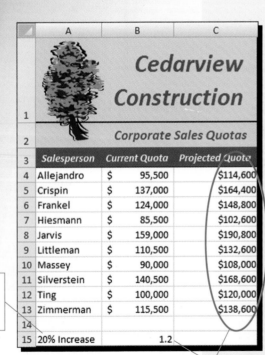

What would be the projected sales quotas with a 20% increase?

Answer appears as soon as you change the percentage.

Excel includes several predefined formulas, called *functions*, that make the task of constructing complex worksheets easier to manage. So math is not your favorite subject? Not a problem with Excel's Insert Function dialog box, which helps you build a formula by prompting you with explanations for each parameter.

Use the sorting and filtering in Excel to help you analyze the data in various arrangements. With the click of a button, you can rearrange the order of the worksheet to sort in ascending or descending order by a single column or by multiple columns. By filtering records, you can reduce the data you are viewing by temporarily hiding rows that do not meet your criteria. For example, in a workplace scenario, you might want to view only those clients that owe the company less than $500.

Original worksheet

Real Photography
Invoices

Invoice #	Client #	Service	Date	Amount	Tax	Amount Due
1199	03-288	Development	9/11/2010	$ 95.00	0.0%	$ 95.00
1326	04-325	Sports Portraits	9/3/2010	$ 750.00	8.5%	$ 813.75
1320	04-325	Sports Portraits	9/7/2010	$ 750.00	8.5%	$ 813.75
1270	04-789	Family Portraits	9/8/2010	$ 560.00	8.8%	$ 609.28
1345	05-335	Development	9/8/2010	$ 400.00	0.0%	$ 400.00
1144	05-335	Development	9/15/2010	$ 140.00	0.0%	$ 140.00
1302	10-226	Wedding Portraits	9/14/2010	$ 2,250.00	8.5%	$ 2,441.25
1233	10-455	Sports Portraits	9/10/2010	$ 600.00	8.5%	$ 651.00
1230	10-788	Family Portraits	9/1/2010	$ 450.00	8.5%	$ 488.25
1277	11-005	Business Portrait	9/14/2010	$ 225.00	8.8%	$ 244.80
1438	11-279	Wedding Portraits	9/1/2010	$ 1,075.00	8.8%	$ 1,169.60
1129	11-279	Development	9/2/2010	$ 225.00	0.0%	$ 225.00
1355	11-279	Development	9/4/2010	$ 350.00	0.0%	$ 350.00
1198	11-325	Wedding Portraits	9/4/2010	$ 875.00	8.5%	$ 949.38

Records sorted by Invoice #

Real Photography
Invoices

Invoice #	Client #	Service	Date	Amount	Tax	Amount Due
1129	11-279	Development	9/2/2010	$ 225.00	0.0%	$ 225.00
1144	05-335	Development	9/15/2010	$ 140.00	0.0%	$ 140.00
1198	11-325	Wedding Portraits	9/4/2010	$ 875.00	8.5%	$ 949.38
1199	03-288	Development	9/11/2010	$ 95.00	0.0%	$ 95.00
1230	10-788	Family Portraits	9/1/2010	$ 450.00	8.5%	$ 488.25
1233	10-455	Sports Portraits	9/10/2010	$ 600.00	8.5%	$ 651.00
1270	04-789	Family Portraits	9/8/2010	$ 560.00	8.8%	$ 609.28
1277	11-005	Business Portrait	9/14/2010	$ 225.00	8.8%	$ 244.80
1302	10-226	Wedding Portraits	9/14/2010	$ 2,250.00	8.5%	$ 2,441.25
1320	04-325	Sports Portraits	9/7/2010	$ 750.00	8.5%	$ 813.75
1326	04-325	Sports Portraits	9/3/2010	$ 750.00	8.5%	$ 813.75
1345	05-335	Development	9/8/2010	$ 400.00	0.0%	$ 400.00
1355	11-279	Development	9/4/2010	$ 350.00	0.0%	$ 350.00
1438	11-279	Wedding Portraits	9/1/2010	$ 1,075.00	8.8%	$ 1,169.60

Real Photog[raphy]

Records filtered to display amounts less than $500.00

Invoices

Invoice	Client #	Service	Date	Amount	Tax	Amount Due
1199	03-288	Development	9/11/2010	$ 95.00	0.0%	$ 95.00
1345	05-335	Development	9/8/2010	$ 400.00	0.0%	$ 400.00
1144	05-335	Development	9/15/2010	$ 140.00	0.0%	$ 140.00
1230	10-788	Family Portraits	9/1/2010	$ 450.00	8.5%	$ 488.25
1277	11-005	Business Portrait	9/14/2010	$ 225.00	8.8%	$ 244.80
1129	11-279	Development	9/2/2010	$ 225.00	0.0%	$ 225.00
1355	11-279	Development	9/4/2010	$ 350.00	0.0%	$ 350.00

Presenting Information

With information already structured in columns and rows, the task of interpreting the results is already simplified. Add some color and other rich text enhancements to draw the reader's attention to important titles, totals, or other results and you have just made the process even easier! Add clip art, photographs, or other media to a worksheet using the Clip Art task pane.

Since a picture is worth a thousand words, why not use Excel's charting capabilities to turn those numbers into a chart—a pictorial representation that enables a reader to more easily distinguish the impact of the differences between columns of numbers. Excel can render both two-dimensional and three-dimensional charts in several chart types, a sampling of which are: column, bar, line, pie, area, radar, doughnut, and scatter.

Knowing how to use Excel is a prerequisite for many jobs in our information-driven economy. Creating worksheets in Microsoft Excel 2007 is as simple as one, two, three—set up the column and row headings, enter the data, and create the formulas. Within a short period of time, you will *excel* at creating, editing, and formatting worksheets!

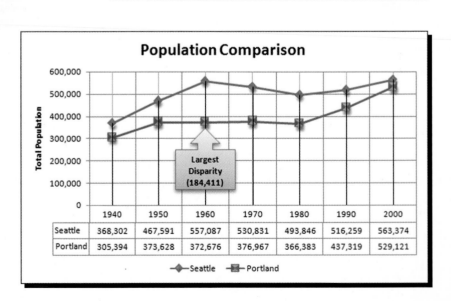

Microsoft®

excel

Unit 1: Preparing and Formatting a Worksheet

➤ Preparing an Excel Workbook

➤ Inserting Formulas in a Worksheet

➤ Formatting an Excel Worksheet

➤ Enhancing a Worksheet

Excel

Benchmark Microsoft® Excel 2007 Level 1

Microsoft Certified Application Specialist Skills—Unit 1

Reference No.	Skill	Pages
1	**Creating and Manipulating Data**	
1.1	Insert data using AutoFill	
1.1.1	Fill a series	16-19
1.1.2	Copy a series	21
1.4	Change worksheet views	
1.4.1	Change views within a single window	79-80, 115-116
2	**Formatting Data and Content**	
2.1	Format worksheets	
2.1.1	Use themes to format worksheets	81-82
2.1.4	Format worksheet backgrounds	118
2.2	Insert and modify rows and columns	
2.2.1	Insert and delete cells, rows, and columns	71-74
2.2.2	Format rows and columns	75-78
2.2.3	Hide and unhide rows and columns	96-98
2.2.4	Modify row height and column width	68-71
2.3	Format cells and cell content	
2.3.1	Apply number formats	51-52, 82-84
2.3.3	Apply and modify cell styles	25-26
2.3.4	Format text in cells	75-78, 85-87
2.3.6	Merge and split cells	76-78
2.3.7	Add and remove cell borders	91-93
3	**Creating and Modifying Formulas**	
3.1	Reference data in formulas	
3.1.1	Create formulas that use absolute and relative cell references	56-59
3.2	Summarize data using a formula	
3.2.1	Use SUM, COUNT, COUNTA, AVERAGE, MIN, and MAX	43-49
3.8	Display and print formulas	49
5	**Collaborating and Securing Data**	
5.5	Set print options for printing data, worksheets, and workbooks	
5.5.1	Define the area of a worksheet to be printed	120-121
5.5.2	Insert and move a page break	114-116
5.5.3	Set margins	110-112
5.5.4	Add and modify headers and footers	121-123
5.5.5	Change the orientation of a worksheet	112-113
5.5.6	Scale worksheet content to fit a printed page	117-118

Note: The Level 1 and Level 2 texts each address approximately half of the Microsoft Certified Application Specialist skills. Complete coverage of the skills is offered in the combined Level 1 and Level 2 text titled *Benchmark Series Microsoft® Excel 2007: Levels 1 and 2*, which has been approved as certified courseware and which displays the Microsoft Certified Application Specialist logo on the cover.

CHAPTER

Preparing an Excel Workbook

Many companies use a spreadsheet for numerical and financial data and to analyze and evaluate information. An Excel spreadsheet can be used for such activities as creating financial statements, preparing budgets, managing inventory, and analyzing cash flow. In addition, numbers and values can be easily manipulated to create "what if" situations. For example, using a spreadsheet, a person in a company can ask questions such as "What if the value in this category is decreased? How would that change affect the department budget?" Questions like these can be easily answered in an Excel spreadsheet. Change the value in a category and Excel will recalculate formulas for the other values. In this way, a spreadsheet can be used not only for creating financial statements or budgets, but also as a planning tool.

Note: Before beginning computer projects, copy to your storage medium the Excel2007L1C1 subfolder from the Excel2007L1 folder on the CD that accompanies this textbook. Steps on how to copy a folder are presented on the inside of the back cover of this textbook. Do this every time you start a chapter's projects.

roject ① **Prepare a Worksheet with Employee Information**

You will create a worksheet containing employee information, edit the contents, and then save and close the workbook.

Creating a Worksheet

start

Open Excel by clicking the Start button at the left side of the Taskbar, pointing to *All Programs*, pointing to *Microsoft Office*, and then clicking *Microsoft Office Excel 2007*. (Depending on your operating system, these steps may vary.) When Excel is open, you are presented with a blank worksheet like the one shown in Figure 1.1. The elements of a blank Excel worksheet are described in Table 1.1.

Figure 1.1 Blank Excel Worksheet

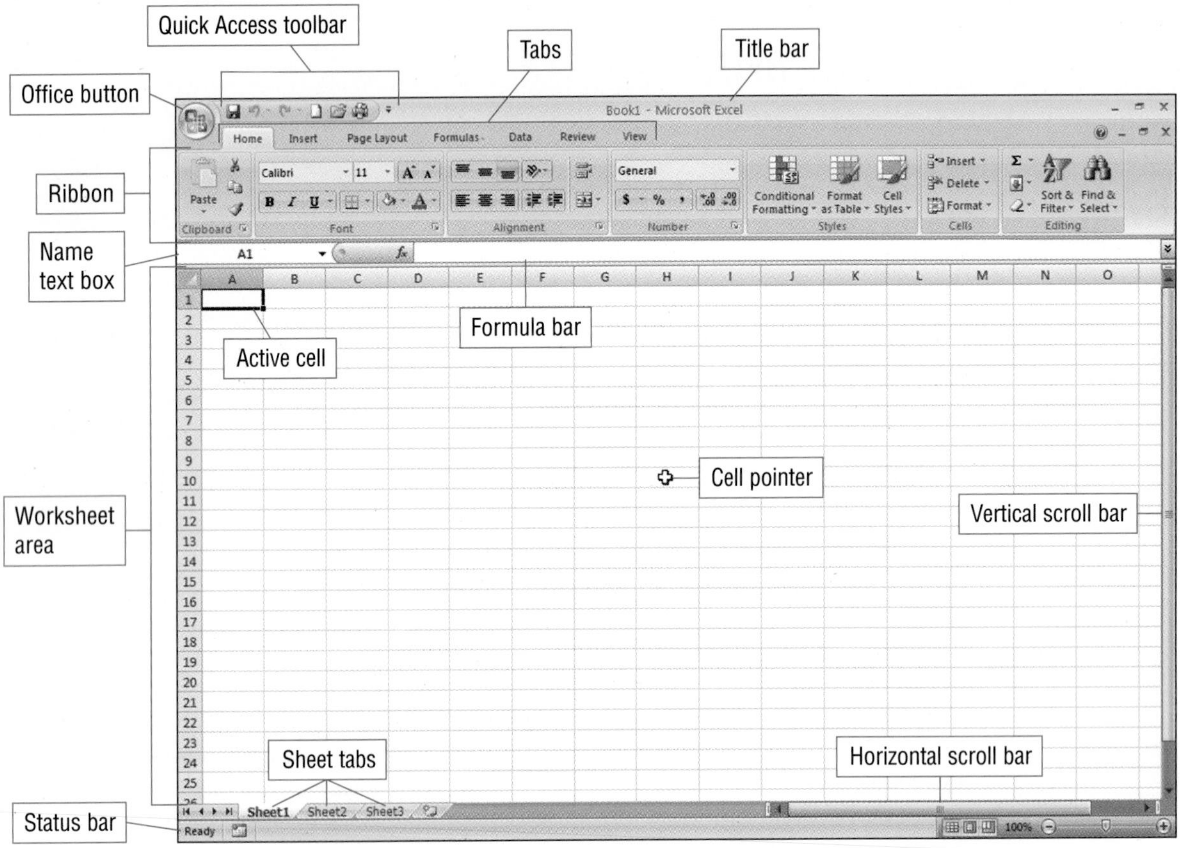

A file created in Excel is referred to as a **workbook**. An Excel workbook consists of individual worksheets (or *sheets*) like the sheets of paper in a notebook. Notice the tabs located toward the bottom of the Excel window that are named *Sheet1*, *Sheet2*, and so on. The area containing the gridlines in the Excel window is called the **worksheet area**. Figure 1.2 identifies the elements of the worksheet area. Create a worksheet in the worksheet area that will be saved as part of a workbook. Columns in a worksheet are labeled with letters of the alphabet and rows are numbered.

Table 1.1 Elements of an Excel Worksheet

Feature	Description
Office button	Displays as a Microsoft Office logo and, when clicked, displays a list of options along with the most recently opened workbooks
Quick Access toolbar	Contains buttons for commonly-used commands
Title bar	Displays workbook name followed by program name
Tab	Contains commands and features organized into groups
Ribbon	Area containing the tabs and commands divided into groups
Name box	Displays cell address (also called the cell reference) and includes the column letter and row number
Formula bar	Provides information about active cell; enter and edit formulas in this bar
Scroll bars	Use vertical and horizontal scroll bars to navigate within a worksheet
Sheet tab	Displays towards bottom of screen and identifies current worksheet
Status bar	Displays information about worksheet and active cell, view buttons, and Zoom slider bar

Figure 1.2 Elements of a Worksheet Area

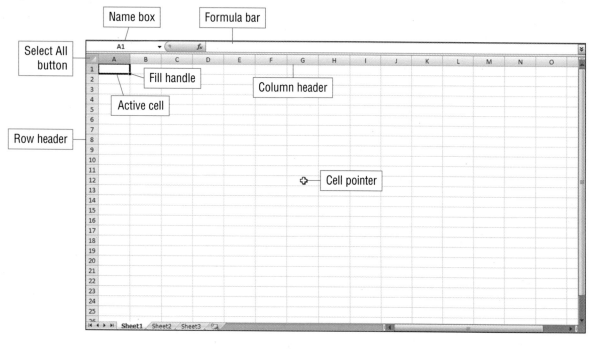

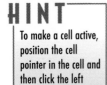

HINT

To make a cell active, position the cell pointer in the cell and then click the left mouse button.

The horizontal and vertical lines that define the cells in the worksheet area are called *gridlines*. When a cell is active (displays with a black border), the *cell address*, also called the *cell reference*, displays in the **Name box**. The cell reference includes the column letter and row number. For example, if the first cell of the worksheet is active, the cell reference *A1* displays in the Name box. A thick black border surrounds the active cell.

Entering Data in a Cell

Enter data such as a heading, number, or value in a cell. To enter data in a cell, make the desired cell active and then type the data. To make the next cell active, press the Tab key. Table 1.2 displays additional commands for making a specific cell active.

Table 1.2 Commands for Making a Specific Cell Active

To make this cell active	Press
Cell below current cell	Enter
Cell above current cell	Shift + Enter
Next cell	Tab
Previous cell	Shift + Tab
Cell at beginning of row	Home
Next cell in the direction of the arrow	Up, Down, Left, or Right Arrow keys
Last cell in worksheet	Ctrl + End
First cell in worksheet	Ctrl + Home
Cell in next window	Page Down
Cell in previous window	Page Up
Cell in window to right	Alt + Page Down
Cell in window to left	Alt + Page Up

HINT

Ctrl + G is the keyboard shortcut to display the Go To dialog box.

Find & Select

Another method for making a specific cell active is to use the Go To feature. To use this feature, click the Find & Select button in the Editing group in the Home tab and then click Go To. At the Go To dialog box, type the cell reference in the *Reference* text box, and then click OK.

When you are ready to type data into the active cell, check the Status bar. The word *Ready* should display at the left side. As you type data, the word *Ready* changes to *Enter*. Data you type in a cell displays in the cell as well as in the Formula bar. If the data you type is longer than the cell can accommodate, the data overlaps the next cell to the right (it does not become a part of the next cell—it simply overlaps it). You will learn how to change column widths to accommodate data later in this chapter.

If the data you enter in a cell consists of text and the text does not fit into the cell, it overlaps the next cell. If, however, you enter a number in a cell, specify it as a number (rather than text) and the number is too long to fit in the cell, Excel changes the display of the number to number symbols *(###)*. This is because Excel does not want you to be misled by a number when you see only a portion of it in the cell.

Along with the keyboard, you can use the mouse to make a specific cell active. To make a specific cell active with the mouse, position the mouse pointer, which displays as a white plus sign (called the *cell pointer*), on the desired cell, and then click the left mouse button. The cell pointer displays as a white plus sign when positioned in a cell in the worksheet and displays as an arrow pointer when positioned on other elements of the Excel window such as options in tabs or scroll bars.

Scroll through a worksheet using the horizontal and/or vertical scroll bars. Scrolling shifts the display of cells in the worksheet area, but does not change the active cell. Scroll through a worksheet until the desired cell is visible and then click the desired cell.

Saving a Workbook

Save an Excel workbook, which may consist of a worksheet or several worksheets, by clicking the Save button on the Quick Access toolbar or by clicking the Office button and then clicking *Save* at the drop-down list. At the Save As dialog box, type a name for the workbook in the *File name* text box and then press Enter or click the Save button. A workbook file name can contain up to 255 characters, including drive letter and any folder names, and can include spaces. Note that you cannot give a workbook the same name in first uppercase and then lowercase letters. Also, some symbols cannot be used in a file name such as:

forward slash (/)	question mark (?)
backslash (\)	quotation mark (")
greater than sign (>)	colon (:)
less than sign (<)	semicolon (;)
asterisk (*)	pipe symbol (|)

To save an Excel workbook in the Excel2007L1C1 folder on your storage medium, display the Save As dialog box and then click the down-pointing arrow at the right side of the *Save in* option box. At the drop-down list that displays, click the drive representing your storage medium and then double-click Excel2007L1C1 in the list box.

Save a Workbook
1. Click Save button.
2. Type workbook name.
3. Press Enter.

HINT
Ctrl + S is the keyboard command to save a document.

Save

Office button

1. Open Excel by clicking the Start button on the Taskbar, pointing to *All Programs*, pointing to *Microsoft Office*, and then clicking *Microsoft Office Excel 2007*. (Depending on your operating system, these steps may vary.)
2. At the Excel worksheet that displays, create the worksheet shown in Figure 1.3 by completing the following steps:
   a. Press the Enter key once to make cell A2 the active cell.
   b. With cell A2 active (displays with a thick black border), type **Employee**.
   c. Press the Tab key. (This makes cell B2 active.)
   d. Type **Location** and then press the Tab key. (This makes cell C2 active.)
   e. Type **Benefits** and then press the Enter key to move the insertion point to cell A3.
   f. With cell A3 active, type the name **Avery**.
   g. Continue typing the data shown in Figure 1.3. (For commands for making specific cells active, refer to Table 1.2.)
3. After typing the data shown in the cells in Figure 1.3, save the workbook by completing the following steps:
   a. Click the Save button on the Quick Access toolbar.
   b. At the Save As dialog box, click the down-pointing arrow to the right of the *Save in* option.
   c. From the drop-down list that displays, click the letter representing your storage medium.
   d. Double-click the Excel2007L1C1 folder that displays in the list box.
   e. Select the text in the *File name* text box and then type **ExcelL1_C1_P1** (for Excel Level 1, Chapter 1, Project 1).
   f. Press the Enter key or click the Save button.

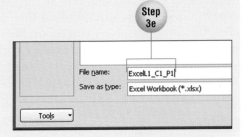

Figure 1.3 Project 1a

	A	B	C	D
1				
2	Employee	Location	Benefits	
3	Avery			
4	Connors			
5	Estrada			
6	Juergens			
7	Mikulich			
8	Talbot			
9				

Editing Data in a Cell

Edit data being typed in a cell by pressing the Backspace key to delete the character to the left of the insertion point or pressing the Delete key to delete the character to the right of the insertion point. To change the data in a cell, click the cell once to make it active and then type the new data. When a cell containing data is active, anything typed will take the place of the existing data.

If you want to edit only a portion of the data in a cell, double-click the cell. This makes the cell active, moves the insertion point inside the cell, and displays the word *Edit* at the left side of the Status bar. Move the insertion point using the arrow keys or the mouse and then make the needed corrections. If you are using the keyboard, you can press the Home key to move the insertion point to the first character in the cell or Formula bar, or press the End key to move the insertion point to the last character.

When you are finished editing the data in the cell, be sure to change out of the Edit mode. To do this, make another cell active. You can do this by pressing Enter, Tab, or Shift + Tab. You can also change out of the Edit mode and return to the Ready mode by clicking another cell or clicking the Enter button on the Formula bar.

If the active cell does not contain data, the Formula bar displays only the cell reference (by column letter and row number). As you type data, the two buttons shown in Figure 1.4 display on the Formula bar to the right of the Name box. Click the Cancel button to delete the current cell entry. You can also delete the cell entry by pressing the Delete key. Click the Enter button to indicate that you are finished typing or editing the cell entry. When you click the Enter button on the Formula bar, the word *Enter* (or *Edit*) located at the left side of the Status bar changes to *Ready*.

Cancel

Enter

Figure 1.4 Buttons on the Formula Bar

Cancel   Enter

A1

Project 1b **Editing Data in a Cell**

1. With **ExcelL1_C1_P1.xlsx** open, double-click cell A7 (contains *Mikulich*).
2. Move the insertion point immediately left of the *k* and then type a **c**. (This changes the spelling to *Mickulich*.)
3. Click once in cell A4 (contains *Connors*), type **Bryant**, and then press the Tab key. (Clicking only once allows you to type over the existing data.)
4. Edit cell C2 by completing the following steps:
   a. Click the Find & Select button in the Editing group in the Home tab and then click *Go To* at the drop-down list.
   b. At the Go To dialog box, type **C2** in the *Reference* text box, and then click OK.
   c. Type **Classification** (over *Benefits*).
5. Click once in any other cell.
6. Click the Save button on the Quick Access toolbar to save the workbook again.

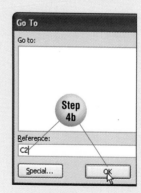

Step 4b

Quick Print

Printing a Workbook

Click the Quick Print button on the Quick Access toolbar to print the active worksheet. If the Quick Print button does not display on the Quick Access toolbar, click the Customize Quick Access Toolbar button that displays at the right side of the toolbar and then click *Quick Print* at the drop-down list. You can also print a worksheet by clicking the Office button, pointing to the *Print* option, and then clicking *Quick Print* at the side menu.

Closing a Workbook

Close Window

To close an Excel workbook, click the Office button and then click *Close* at the drop-down list. You can also close a workbook by clicking the Close Window button located toward the upper right corner of the screen. Position the mouse pointer on the button and a ScreenTip displays with the name *Close Window*.

Exiting Excel

X Exit Excel

Close

To exit Excel, click the Close button that displays in the upper right corner of the screen. The Close button contains an X and if you position the mouse pointer on the button a ScreenTip displays with the name *Close*. You can also exit Excel by clicking the Office button and then clicking the Exit Excel button located at the bottom of the drop-down list.

Using Automatic Entering Features

Excel contains several features that help you enter data into cells quickly and efficiently. These features include *AutoComplete*, which automatically inserts data in a cell that begins the same as a previous entry; *AutoCorrect*, which automatically corrects many common typographical errors; and *AutoFill*, which will automatically insert words, numbers, or formulas in a series.

Using AutoComplete and AutoCorrect

The AutoComplete feature will automatically insert data in a cell that begins the same as a previous entry. If the data inserted by AutoComplete is the data you want in the cell, press Enter. If it is not the desired data, simply continue typing the correct data. This feature can be very useful in a worksheet that contains repetitive data entries. For example, consider a worksheet that repeats the word *Payroll*. The second and subsequent times this word is to be inserted in a cell, simply typing the letter *P* will cause AutoComplete to insert the entire word.

The AutoCorrect feature automatically corrects many common typing errors. To see what symbols and words are in the AutoCorrect feature, click the Office button and then click Excel Options located in the lower right corner of the drop-down list. At the Excel Options dialog box, click *Proofing* in the left panel and then click the AutoCorrect Options button located in the right panel. This displays the AutoCorrect dialog box with the AutoCorrect tab selected as shown in Figure 1.5 with a list box containing the replacement data.

Figure 1.5 AutoCorrect Dialog Box with AutoCorrect Tab Selected

When you type the text displayed in the first column in a worksheet and then press the spacebar, the text is replaced by the text in the second column.

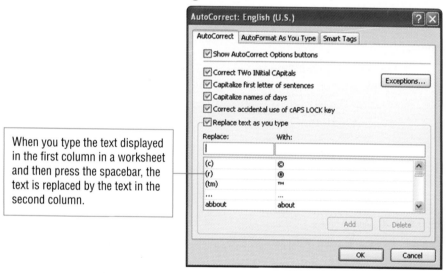

At the AutoCorrect dialog box, type the text shown in the first column in the list box and the text in the second column is inserted in the cell. Along with symbols, the AutoCorrect dialog box contains commonly misspelled words and common typographical errors.

Inserting Data in Cells with AutoComplete

1. With **ExcelL1_C1_P1.xlsx** open make cell A1 active.
2. Type the text in cell A1 as shown in Figure 1.6. Insert the ® symbol by typing (r). (AutoCorrect will change (r) to ®.)
3. Type the remaining text in the cells. When you type the W in *West* in cell B5, the AutoComplete feature will insert *West*. Accept this by pressing the Enter key. (Pressing the Enter key accepts *West* and also makes the cell below active.) Use the AutoComplete feature to enter *West* in B6 and B8 and *North* in cell B7. Use AutoComplete to enter the second and subsequent occurrences of *Salaried* and *Hourly*.
4. Click the Save button on the Quick Access toolbar.
5. Print **ExcelL1_C1_P1.xlsx** by clicking the Quick Print button on the Quick Access toolbar. (The gridlines will not print.) If the Quick Print button does not display on the Quick Access toolbar, click the Customize Quick Access Toolbar button that displays at the right side of the toolbar and then click *Quick Print* at the drop-down list.
6. Close the workbook by clicking the Close Window button (contains an X) that displays in the upper right corner of screen. (Make sure you click the Close Window button and not the Close button.)

Step 5

Step 6

Figure 1.6 **Project 1c**

	A	B	C	D
1	Team Net®			
2	Employee	Location	Classification	
3	Avery	West	Hourly	
4	Bryant	North	Salaried	
5	Estrada	West	Salaried	
6	Juergens	West	Salaried	
7	Mickulich	North	Hourly	
8	Talbot	West	Hourly	
9				

Project ② Open and Format a Workbook and Insert Formulas

You will open an existing workbook, insert formulas to find the sum and averages of numbers and apply predesigned formatting with table and cell styles.

Using AutoFill

When a cell is active, a thick black border surrounds it and a small black square displays in the bottom right corner of the border. This black square is called the AutoFill *fill handle* (see Figure 1.2). With the fill handle, you can quickly fill a range of cells with the same data or with consecutive data. For example, suppose you need to insert the year 2010 in a row or column of cells. To do this quickly, type 2010 in the first cell, position the mouse pointer on the fill handle, hold down the left mouse button, drag across the cells in which you want the year inserted, and then release the mouse button.

You can also use the fill handle to insert a series in a row or column of cells. For example, suppose you are creating a worksheet with data for all of the months in the year. Type January in the first cell, position the mouse pointer on the fill handle, hold down the left mouse button, drag down or across to 11 more cells, and then release the mouse button. Excel automatically inserts the other 11 months in the year in the proper order. When using the fill handle, the cells must be adjacent. Table 1.3 identifies the sequence inserted in cells by Excel when specific data is entered.

Table 1.3 AutoFill Fill Handle Series

Enter this data (Commas represent data in separate cells.)	And the fill handle will insert this sequence in adjacent cells
January	February, March, April, and so on . . .
Jan	Feb, Mar, Apr, and so on . . .
Jan 08, Jan 09	Jan-10, Jan-11, Jan-12, and so on . . .
Monday	Tuesday, Wednesday, Thursday, and so on . . .
Product 1	Product 2, Product 3, Product 4, and so on . . .
Qtr 1	Qtr 2, Qtr 3, Qtr 4
2, 4	6, 8, 10, and so on . . .

Certain sequences, such as *2, 4* and *Jan 08, Jan 09,* require that both cells be selected before using the fill handle. If only the cell containing *2* is active, the fill handle will insert *2*s in the selected cells. The list in Table 1.3 is only a sampling of what the fill handle can do. You may find a variety of other sequences that can be inserted in a worksheet using the fill handle.

An Auto Fill Options button displays when you fill cells with the fill handle. Click this button and a list of options displays for filling the cells. By default, data and formatting are filled in each cell. You can choose to fill only the formatting in the cells or fill only the data without the formatting.

HINT

If you do not want a series to increment, hold down the Ctrl key while dragging the fill handle.

Auto Fill Options

Opening a Workbook

Open an Excel workbook by displaying the Open dialog box and then double-clicking the desired workbook name. Display the Open dialog box by clicking the Open button on the Quick Access toolbar or clicking the Office button and then clicking *Open* at the drop-down list. If the Open button does not display on the Quick Access toolbar, click the Customize Quick Access Toolbar button that displays at the right side of the toolbar and then click *Open* at the drop-down list. You can also use the keyboard shortcut Ctrl + O to display the Open dialog box.

Project 2a — Inserting Data in Cells with the Fill Handle

1. Open **ExcelC01Project02.xlsx**. (This workbook is located in the Excel2007L1C1 folder on your storage medium.)
2. Save the workbook with Save As and name it **ExcelL1_C1_P2**.
3. Add data to cells as shown in Figure 1.7. Begin by making cell B1 active and then typing January.
4. Position the mouse pointer on the fill handle for cell B1, hold down the left mouse button, drag across to cell G1, and then release the mouse button.
5. Type a sequence and then use the fill handle to fill the remaining cells by completing the following steps:
   a. Make cell A2 active and then type Year 1.
   b. Make cell A3 active and then type Year 3.
   c. Select cells A2 and A3 by positioning the mouse pointer in cell A2, holding down the left mouse button, dragging down to cell A3, and then releasing the mouse button.
   d. Drag the fill handle for cell A3 to cell A5. (This inserts *Year 5* in cell A4 and *Year 7* in cell A5.)
6. Use the fill handle to fill adjacent cells with a number but not the formatting by completing the following steps:
   a. Make cell B2 active. (This cell contains *100* with bold formatting.)
   b. Drag the fill handle for cell B2 to cell E2. (This inserts *100* in cells C2, D2, and E2.)
   c. Click the Auto Fill Options button that displays at the bottom right of the selected cells.
   d. Click the *Fill Without Formatting* option at the drop-down list.

	A	B	C	D	E	F	G
1		January	February	March	April	May	June
2		100				125	125
3		150	150	150	150	175	175

Step 4

	A	B	C	D	E	F	G	H
1		January	February	March	April	May	June	
2	Year 1	100	100	100	100	125	125	
3	Year 3	150	150	150	150	175	175	
4	Year 5	200	200	200	150			
5	Year 7	250	250	250	250			
6								
7								
8								
9								

⊙ Copy Cells
○ Fill Series
○ Fill Formatting Only
○ Fill Without Formatting

Step 6c

Step 6d

7. Use the fill handle to apply formatting only by completing the following steps:
   a. Make cell B2 active.
   b. Drag the fill handle to cell B5.
   c. Click the Auto Fill Options button and then click *Fill Formatting Only* at the drop-down list.
8. Make cell A10 active and then type Qtr 1.
9. Drag the fill handle for cell A10 to cell A13.
10. Save **ExcelL1_C1_P2.xlsx**.

Step 7c

Figure 1.7 Project 2a

	A	B	C	D	E	F	G	H
1		January	February	March	April	May	June	
2	Year 1	**100**	100	100	100	125	125	
3	Year 3	**150**	150	150	150	175	175	
4	Year 5	**200**	200	200	150	150	150	
5	Year 7	**250**	250	250	250	250	250	
6								
7								
8								
9								
10	Qtr 1	$5,500	$6,250	$7,000	$8,500	$5,500	$4,500	
11	Qtr 2	$6,000	$7,250	$6,500	$9,000	$4,000	$5,000	
12	Qtr 3	$4,500	$8,000	$6,000	$7,500	$6,000	$5,000	
13	Qtr 4	$6,500	$8,500	$7,000	$8,000	$5,500	$6,000	
14								

Inserting Formulas

Excel is a powerful decision-making tool containing data that can be manipulated to answer "what if" situations. Insert a formula in a worksheet and then manipulate the data to make projections, answer specific questions, and use as a planning tool. For example, the manager of a department might use an Excel worksheet to prepare a department budget and then determine the impact on the budget of hiring a new employee or increasing the volume of production.

Insert a formula in a worksheet to perform calculations on values. A formula contains a mathematical operator, value, cell reference, cell range, and a function. Formulas can be written that add, subtract, multiply, and/or divide values. Formulas can also be written that calculate averages, percentages, minimum and maximum values, and much more. Excel includes a Sum button in the Editing group in the Home tab that inserts a formula to calculate the total of a range of cells.

Using the Sum Button to Add Numbers

You can use the Sum button in the Editing group in the Home tab to insert a formula. The Sum button adds numbers automatically with the SUM function. Make active the cell in which you want to insert the formula (this cell should be empty) and then click the Sum button. Excel looks for a range of cells containing numbers above the active cell. If no cell above contains numbers, then Excel looks to the left of the active cell. Excel suggests the range of cells to be added. If the suggested range is not correct, drag through the desired range with the mouse, and then press Enter. You can also just double-click the Sum button and this will insert the SUM function with the range Excel chooses.

Project 2b · Adding Values with the Sum Button

1. With **ExcelL1_C1_P2.xlsx** open, make cell A6 active and then type Total.
2. Make cell B6 active and then calculate the sum of cells by clicking the Sum button in the Editing group in the Home tab.
3. Excel inserts the formula *=SUM(B2:B5)* in cell B6. This is the correct range of cells, so press Enter.

Step 2

	A	B	C	D	E	F	G	H	I	J	K	L	M	N
1		January	February	March	April	May	June							
2	Year 1	100	100	100	100	125	125							
3	Year 3	150	150	150	150	175	175							
4	Year 5	200	200	200	150	150	150							
5	Year 7	250	250	250	250	250	250							
6	Total	=SUM(B2:B5)												
7		SUM(number1, [number2], ...)												

DATE · f_x =SUM(B2:B5)

Step 3

4. Make cell C6 active and then click the Sum button in the Editing group.
5. Excel inserts the formula *=SUM(C2:C5)* in cell C6. This is the correct range of cells, so press Enter.
6. Make cell D6 active.
7. Double-click the Sum button. (This inserts the formula *=SUM(D2:D5)* in cell D6 and inserts the sum *700.*)
8. Insert the sum in cells E6, F6, and G6.
9. Save **ExcelL1_C1_P2.xlsx**.

QUICK STEPS

Insert Average Formula Using Sum Button
1. Click in desired cell.
2. Click Sum button arrow.
3. Click *Average*.
4. Check range identified and make changes if necessary.
5. Press Enter.

Using the Sum Button to Average Numbers

A common function in a formula is the AVERAGE function. With this function, a range of cells is added together and then divided by the number of cell entries. The AVERAGE function is available on the Sum button. Click the Sum button arrow and a drop-down list displays with a number of common functions.

Using the Fill Handle to Copy a Formula

In a worksheet, you may want to insert the same basic formula in other cells. In a situation where a formula is copied to other locations in a worksheet, use a *relative cell reference*. Copy a formula containing relative cell references and the cell references change. For example, if you enter the formula *=SUM(A2:C2)* in cell D2 and then copy it relatively to cell D3, the formula in cell D3 displays as *=SUM(A3:C3)*. You can use the fill handle to copy a formula relatively in a worksheet. To do this, position the mouse pointer on the fill handle until the mouse pointer turns into a thin black cross. Hold down the left mouse button, drag and select the desired cells, and then release the mouse button.

QUICK STEPS

Copy Formula Using Fill Handle
1. Insert formula in cell.
2. Make active the cell containing formula.
3. Using fill handle, drag through cells you want to contain formula.

Project 2c Inserting the AVERAGE Function and Copying a Formula Relatively

1. With **ExcelL1_C1_P2.xlsx** open, make cell A14 active, and then type Average.
2. Insert the average of cells B10 through B13 by completing the following steps:
   a. Make cell B14 active.
   b. Click the Sum button arrow and then click *Average* at the drop-down list.
   c. Excel inserts the formula *=AVERAGE(B10:B13)* in cell B14. This is the correct range of cells, so press Enter.
3. Copy the formula relatively to cells C14 through G14 by completing the following steps:
   a. Make cell B14 active.
   b. Position the mouse pointer on the fill handle, hold down the left mouse button, drag across to cell G14, and then release the mouse button.

Step 2b

Insert ▾	Σ ▾	
Delete ▾	Σ	Sum
Format ▾		Average
Cells		Count Numbers
		Max
M		Min
		More Functions...

9							
10	Qtr 1	$5,500	$6,250	$7,000	$8,500	$5,500	$4,500
11	Qtr 2	$6,000	$7,250	$6,500	$9,000	$4,000	$5,000
12	Qtr 3	$4,500	$8,000	$6,000	$7,500	$6,000	$5,000
13	Qtr 4	$6,500	$8,500	$7,000	$8,000	$5,500	$6,000
14	Average	$5,625	$7,500	$6,625	$8,250	$5,250	$5,125
15							

4. Save **ExcelL1_C1_P2.xlsx**.

Step 3b

Selecting Cells

You can use a variety of methods for formatting cells in a worksheet. For example, you can change the alignment of data in cells or rows or add character formatting. To identify the cells that are to be affected by the formatting, select the specific cells.

Selecting Cells Using the Mouse

HINT

Select nonadjacent columns or rows by holding down the Ctrl key while selecting cells.

Select specific cells in a worksheet using the mouse or select columns or rows. Methods for selecting cells using the mouse display in Table 1.4.

Selected cells, except the active cell, display with a light blue background (this may vary) rather than a white background. The active cell is the first cell in the selection block and displays in the normal manner (white background with black data). Selected cells remain selected until you click a cell with the mouse or press an arrow key on the keyboard.

Table 1.4 Selecting with the Mouse

To select this	Do this
Column	Position the cell pointer on the column header (a letter) and then click the left mouse button.
Row	Position the cell pointer on the row header (a number) and then click the left mouse button.
Adjacent cells	Drag with mouse to select specific cells.
Nonadjacent cells	Hold down the Ctrl key while clicking column header, row header, or specific cells.
All cells in worksheet	Click Select All button (refer to Figure 1.2).

HINT

The first cell in a range displays with a white background and is the active cell.

Selecting Cells Using the Keyboard

You can use the keyboard to select specific cells within a worksheet. Table 1.5 displays the commands for selecting specific cells.

Table 1.5 Selecting Cells Using the Keyboard

To select	Press
Cells in direction of arrow key	Shift + arrow key
To beginning of row	Shift + Home
To beginning of worksheet	Shift + Ctrl + Home
To last cell in worksheet containing data	Shift + Ctrl + End
An entire column	Ctrl + spacebar
An entire row	Shift + spacebar
An entire worksheet	Ctrl + A or Ctrl + Shift + spacebar

Selecting Data within Cells

The selection commands presented select the entire cell. You can also select specific characters within a cell. To do this with the mouse, position the cell pointer in the desired cell, and then double-click the left mouse button. Drag with the I-beam pointer through the data you want selected. Data selected within a cell displays in white with a black background. If you are using the keyboard to select data in a cell, hold down the Shift key, and then press the arrow key that moves the insertion point in the desired direction. Data the insertion point passes through will be selected. You can also press F8 to turn on the Extend Selection mode, move the insertion point in the desired direction to select the data, and then press F8 to turn off the Extend Selection mode. When the Extend Selection mode is on, the words *Extend Selection* display toward the left side of the Status bar.

Formatting with Predesigned Styles

An Excel worksheet contains default formatting. For example, letters and words are aligned at the left of a cell, numbers are aligned at the right, and data is set in 11-point Calibri. Excel provides predesigned styles you can use to apply formatting to cells in a worksheet. Apply table formatting styles with the Format as Table button or the Cell Styles button, both located in the Styles group in the Home tab.

Formatting with Table Styles

Apply table formatting styles to selected cells in a worksheet using the Format as Table button in the Styles group in the Home tab. When you select cells and then click the Format as Table button, a drop-down list displays as shown in Figure 1.8. Click the desired table style and the Format As Table dialog box displays. Click OK at this dialog box and the formatting is applied to the selected cells. Excel also inserts filtering arrows in each cell in the first row of selected cells. The filtering arrows do not print. You can turn off the display of the filtering arrows by clicking the Data tab and then clicking the Filter button in the Sort & Filter group. You will learn more about these filtering arrows in a later chapter.

Apply Table Formatting
1. Select desired cells.
2. Click Format as Table button.
3. Click desired table style.
4. Click OK at Format As Table dialog box.

Figure 1.8 Format as Table Drop-down List

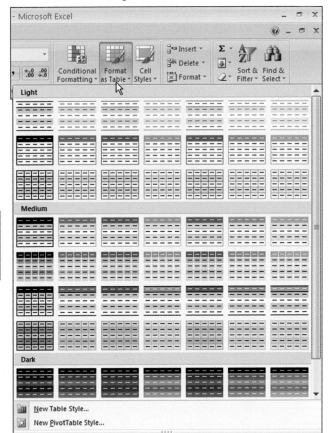

Choose an option at this drop-down list to apply predesigned formatting to selected cells in a worksheet.

Project **2d**   **Formatting Cells with Table Styles**

1. With **ExcelL1_C1_P2.xlsx** open, apply a table style to specific cells by completing the following steps:
   a. Select cells A1 through G6.
   b. Click the Format as Table button in the Styles group in the Home tab.
   c. At the drop-down list, click the *Table Style Light 9* option (second style option from the left in the second row in the *Light* section).

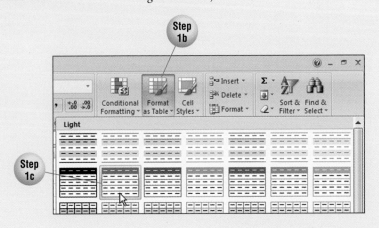

Step 1b

Step 1c

d. At the Format As Table dialog box, click OK. (Excel inserts filtering arrows in the cells in the first row.)

2. Select cells A10 through G14 and then apply the Table Style Light 11 style (fourth style option from the left in the second row in the *Light* section). At the Format As Table dialog box, click OK.

3. Save **ExcelL1_C1_P2.xlsx**. (Excel inserts a row with filtering arrows.)

Step 1d

Formatting with Cell Styles

In some worksheets, you may want to highlight or accentuate certain cells. You can apply formatting to a cell or selected cells with cell styles. Click the Cell Styles button in the Styles group in the Home tab and a drop-down gallery of style options displays as shown in Figure 1.9. Hover your mouse pointer over a style option and the cell or selected cells display with the style formatting applied. You can hover your mouse over different style options to see how the style formatting affects the cell or selected cells. The Cell Styles button drop-down gallery is an example of the *live preview* feature, which allows you to see how the style formatting affects cells in your worksheet without having to return to the worksheet.

QUICK STEPS

Apply Cell Style
1. Select desired cell(s).
2. Click Cell Styles button.
3. Click desired style option.

Cell Styles

Figure 1.9 Cell Styles Drop-down Gallery

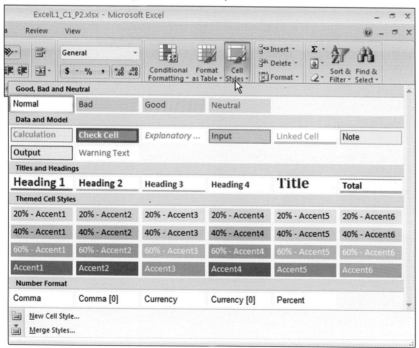

Choose an option at this drop-down gallery to apply a predesigned style to a cell or selected cells in a worksheet.

1. With **ExcelL1_C1_P2.xlsx** open, select cells B2 through G6.
2. Click the Cell Styles button in the Styles group in the Home tab.
3. At the drop-down gallery, hover your mouse over style options to see how the style formatting affects the selected cells.
4. Click the *Currency [0]* option (fourth option from the left in the *Number Format* section).

5. Select cells B6 through G6.
6. Click the Cell Styles button and then click the *Total* option (the last option in the *Titles and Headings* section).

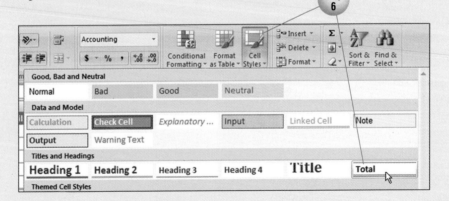

7. Select cells B15 through G15 and then apply the Total cell style.
8. Save, print, and then close **ExcelL1_C1_P2.xlsx**.

Project ③ Use the Help Feature

You will use the Help feature to learn more about entering data in cells and selecting text and saving a workbook. You will also customize Help to search for information offline and for Excel training.

Using Help

Excel's Help feature is an on-screen reference manual containing information about Excel features. Excel's Help feature is similar to the Windows Help and the Help features in Word, PowerPoint, and Access. Get help by clicking the Microsoft Office Excel Help button located in the upper right corner of the screen (a question mark in a circle) or by pressing the keyboard shortcut, F1. This displays the Excel Help window. In this window, type a topic, feature, or question in the *Search* text box and then press Enter. Topics related to the search text display in the Help window. Click a topic that interests you. If the topic window contains a <u>Show All</u> hyperlink in the upper right corner, click this hyperlink and the information expands to show all help information related to the topic. When you click the <u>Show All</u> hyperlink, it becomes the <u>Hide All</u> hyperlink.

Use Help Feature
1. Click Microsoft Office Excel Help button.
2. Type help question.
3. Press Enter.

Help

Project ③a　Using the Help Feature

1. At a blank worksheet, click the Microsoft Office Excel Help button located in the upper right corner of the screen.
2. At the Excel Help window, type enter data in cells in the *Search* text box.
3. Press the Enter key.
4. When the list of topics displays, click the *Enter data manually in worksheet cells* hyperlink.
5. Click the <u>Show All</u> hyperlink that displays in the upper right corner of the window.

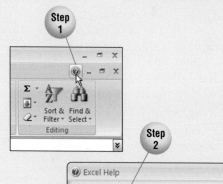

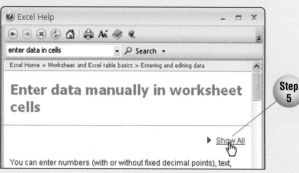

6. Read the information about entering data. (If you want a hard copy of the Help text, click the Print button located toward the top of the Excel Help window, and then click the Print button at the Print dialog box.)
7. Click the Close button to close the Excel Help window.

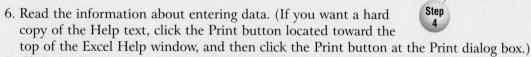

Getting Help in a Dialog Box

Dialog boxes contain a Help button you can click to display help in the Excel Help window that is specific to the dialog box. This button is located in the upper right corner of the dialog box and displays as a question mark inside a circle. Click this button and the Excel Help window displays with topics related to the dialog box.

Getting Help on a Button

When you position the mouse pointer on a button, a ScreenTip displays with information about the button. Some button ScreenTips display with the message "Press F1 for more help." that is preceded by an image of the Help button. With the ScreenTip visible, press the F1 function key and the Excel Help window opens and displays information about the specific button.

Project 3b   **Getting Help in a Dialog Box and Button ScreenTip**

1. At a blank worksheet, click the Office button and then click *Save As* at the drop-down list.
2. At the Save As dialog box, click the Help button located in the upper right corner of the dialog box.
3. At the Excel Help window, click the *Save As* hyperlink.
4. In the Save As list box, click *Microsoft Office Excel*.
5. Read the information that displays about saving in Excel and then click the Close button to close the Excel Help window.
6. Close the Save As dialog box.
7. Position the mouse pointer on the Office button until the ScreenTip displays and then press F1.

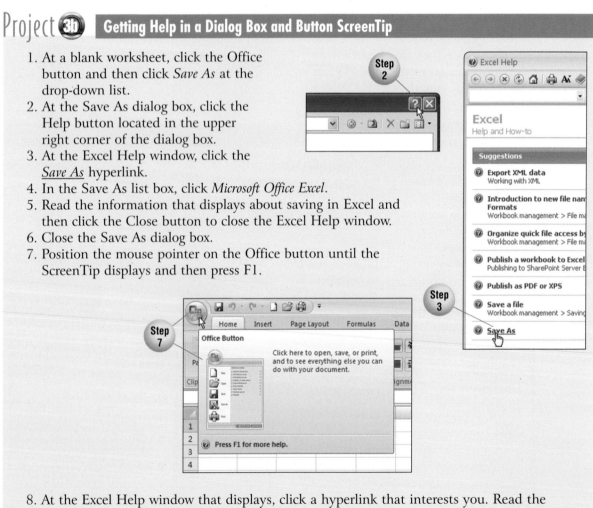

8. At the Excel Help window that displays, click a hyperlink that interests you. Read the information and then close the Excel Help window.

Customizing Help

By default, the Excel Help feature will search for an Internet connection and, if one is found, display help resources from Office Online. If you are connected online to help resources, the message "Connected to Office Online" displays in the lower right corner of the Excel Help window. If you are not connected to the Internet, the message displays as "Offline."

Office Online provides additional help resources such as training and templates. To view the resources, display the Excel Help window and then click the down-pointing arrow at the right side of the Search button. This displays a drop-down list similar to the one shown in Figure 1.10. Generally, the *All Excel* option in the *Content from Office Online* is selected. If you want to search only the Help resources available with your computer (offline), click the *Excel Help* option in the *Content from this computer* section. To access Office Online training, click the *Excel Training* option in the *Content from Office Online* section, type a training topic in the *Search* text box, and then click OK.

Figure 1.10 Excel Help Search Drop-down List

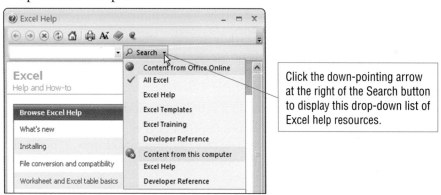

Click the down-pointing arrow at the right of the Search button to display this drop-down list of Excel help resources.

 **Customizing Help**

1. At a blank worksheet, click the Microsoft Office Excel Help button located toward the upper right corner of the screen.
2. Click the down-pointing arrow at the right side of the Search button in the Excel Help window.
3. At the drop-down list that displays, click *Excel Help* in the *Content from this computer* section.
4. Click in the *Search* text box, type formulas in the *Search* text box, and then press Enter.
5. Click a hyperlink that interests you and then read the information that displays.
6. Click the down-pointing arrow at the right side of the Search button and then click *Excel Training* in the *Content from Office Online* section.
7. Click in the *Search* text box (this will select *formulas*) and then press Enter.
8. Click the hyperlink of a training about formulas that interests you.
9. After completing the training, close Internet Explorer and then close the Excel Help window.

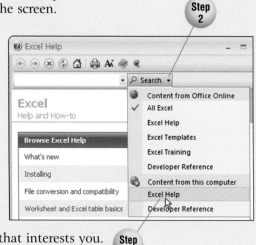

Step 2

Step 3

CHAPTER summary

- Use an Excel spreadsheet to create financial statements, prepare budgets, manage inventory, and analyze cash flow. Numbers and values can be easily manipulated in an Excel spreadsheet to answer "what if" questions.
- A file created in Excel is called a workbook. A workbook consists of individual worksheets. The intersection of columns and rows in a worksheet is referred to as a cell.
- An Excel window contains the following elements: Office button, Quick Access toolbar, Title bar, tabs, ribbon, Name box, Formula bar, scroll bars, sheet tabs, and Status bar.
- The horizontal and vertical lines that define cells in the worksheet area are called gridlines.
- When the insertion point is positioned in a cell, the cell name (also called the cell reference) displays in the Name box located at the left side of the Formula bar. The cell name includes the column letter and row number.
- To enter data in a cell, make the cell active and then type the data. To move the insertion point to the next cell, press the Tab key. To move the insertion point to the previous cell, press Shift + Tab. For other insertion point movement commands, refer to Table 1.2.
- Data being entered in a cell displays in the cell as well as in the Formula bar.
- If data entered in a cell consists of text (letters) and the text does not fit into the cell, it overlaps the cell to the right. However, if the data being entered are numbers and do not fit in the cell, the numbers are changed to number symbols (###).
- Save a workbook by clicking the Save button on the Quick Access toolbar or by clicking the Office button and then clicking *Save* at the drop-down list.
- To replace data in a cell, click the cell once and then type the new data. To edit data within a cell, double-click the cell and then make necessary changes.
- Print a workbook by clicking the Quick Print button on the Quick Access toolbar or by clicking the Office button, pointing to the *Print* option, and then clicking *Quick Print*.
- Close a workbook by clicking the Close Window button located in the upper right corner of the screen or by clicking the Office button and then clicking *Close* at the drop-down list.
- Exit Excel by clicking the Close button located in the upper right corner of the screen or by clicking the Office button and then clicking the Exit Excel button.
- The AutoComplete feature will automatically insert a previous entry if the character or characters being typed in a cell match a previous entry.
- The AutoCorrect feature corrects many common typographical errors.
- Use the AutoFill fill handle to fill a range of cells with the same or consecutive data.
- Open a workbook by clicking the Open button on the Quick Access toolbar or by clicking the Office button and then clicking the *Open* option at the drop-down list. At the Open dialog box, double-click the desired workbook.
- Use the Sum button in the Editing group in the Home tab to find the total or average of data in columns or rows.

- Select all cells in a column by clicking the column header. Select all cells in a row by clicking the row header. Select all cells in a worksheet by clicking the Select All button located immediately to the left of the column headers.
- To select cells with the mouse, refer to Table 1.4; to select cells using the keyboard, refer to Table 1.5.
- Use options from the Format as Table button drop-down gallery to apply predesigned table styles to selected cells.
- Use options from the Cell Styles button drop-down gallery to apply predesigned styles to a cell or selected cells.
- Excel's Help feature is an on-screen reference manual containing information about Excel features.
- Click the Microsoft Office Excel Help button or press F1 to display the Excel Help window. At this window, type a topic and then press Enter.
- Dialog boxes contain a Help button you can click to display the Excel Help window with information specific to the dialog box. The ScreenTip for some buttons displays with a message telling you to press F1. Press F1 and the Excel Help window opens with information about the button.
- Customize Help with options from the Search button drop-down list in the Excel Help window.

COMMANDS review

FEATURE	RIBBON TAB, GROUP	BUTTON	QUICK ACCESS TOOLBAR	OFFICE BUTTON DROP-DOWN LIST	KEYBOARD SHORTCUT
Close workbook		✕		Close	Ctrl + F4
Exit Excel		✕		Exit Excel	
Go To dialog box	Home, Editing	🔍, Go To			Ctrl + G
Excel Help window		⊙			F1
Open workbook			📂	Open	Ctrl + O
Print workbook			🖨	Print, Quick Print	
Save workbook			💾	Save	Ctrl + S
Format as Table drop-down list	Home, Styles	▦			
Cell Styles drop-down gallery	Home, Styles	▦			
Sum button drop-down list	Home, Editing	Σ ▾			

CONCEPTS check

Test Your Knowledge

Completion: In the space provided at the right, indicate the correct term, symbol, or command.

1. Columns in a worksheet are labeled with this. _____

2. Rows in a worksheet are labeled with this. _____

3. The horizontal and vertical lines that define the cells in a worksheet area are referred to as this. _____

4. Press this key on the keyboard to move the insertion point to the next cell. _____

5. Press these keys on the keyboard to move the insertion point to the previous cell. _____

6. If a number entered in a cell is too long to fit inside the cell, the number is changed to this. _____

7. Data being typed in a cell displays in the cell as well as here. _____

8. This is the name of the small black square that displays in the bottom right corner of the active cell. _____

9. To select nonadjacent columns using the mouse, hold down this key on the keyboard while clicking the column headers. _____

10. Use this button in the Editing group in the Home tab to insert a formula in a cell. _____

11. With this function, a range of cells is added together and then divided by the number of cell entries. _____

12. Click this button in the worksheet area to select all of the cells in the table. _____

13. This feature allows you to see how style formatting affects cells in your worksheet without having to return to the worksheet. _____

14. Press this function key to display the Excel Help window. _____

SKILLS check

Demonstrate Your Proficiency

Assessment

1 CREATE AND FORMAT A WORKSHEET WITH A TABLE STYLE

1. Create the worksheet shown in Figure 1.11.
2. Select cells A1 through C5 and then apply the Table Style Medium 3 table style.
3. Save the workbook and name it **ExcelL1_C1_A1**.
4. Print and then close **ExcelL1_C1_A1.xlsx**.

Figure 1.11 Assessment 1

	A	B	C	D
1	Expense	Original	Current	
2	Labor	97000	98500	
3	Material	129000	153000	
4	Permits	1200	1350	
5	Tax	1950	2145	
6				

Assessment

2 CREATE A WORKSHEET USING AUTOCOMPLETE

1. Create the worksheet shown in Figure 1.12. To create the © symbol in cell A1, type (c). Type the misspelled words as shown and let the AutoCorrect feature correct the spelling. Use the AutoComplete feature to insert the second occurrence of *Category*, *Available*, and *Balance*.
2. Apply a table style of your choosing to cells A1 through B7. (Excel inserts a row with filtering arrows.)
3. Save the workbook and name it **ExcelL1_C1_A2**.
4. Print and then close **ExcelL1_C1_A2.xlsx**.

Figure 1.12 Assessment 2

	A	B	C
1	Premiere Plan©		
2	Plan A	Catagory	
3		Availalbe	
4		Balence	
5	Plan B	Category	
6		Available	
7		Balance	
8			

Assessment

3 CREATE A WORKSHEET USING THE FILL HANDLE

1. Create the worksheet shown in Figure 1.13. Type Monday in cell B2 and then use the fill handle to fill in the remaining days of the week. Use the fill handle to enter other repetitive data.
2. Apply a table style of your choosing to cells A1 through F4.
3. Save the workbook and name it **ExcelL1_C1_A3**.
4. Print and then close **ExcelL1_C1_A3.xlsx**.

Figure 1.13 Assessment 3

	A	B	C	D	E	F	G
1	CAPITAL INVESTMENTS						
2		Monday	Tuesday	Wednesday	Thursday	Friday	
3	Budget	350	350	350	350	350	
4	Actual	310	425	290	375	400	
5							

Assessment

4 INSERT FORMULAS IN A WORKSHEET

1. Open **ExcelC01Assessment04.xlsx** and then save the workbook and name it **ExcelL1_C1_A4**.
2. Insert a formula in cell B15 that totals the amounts in cells B4 through B14.
3. Use the fill handle to copy relatively the formula in cell B15 to cell C15.
4. Insert a formula in cell D4 that finds the average of cells B4 and C4.
5. Use the fill handle to copy relatively the formula in cell D4 down to cells D5 through D14.
6. Save, print, and then close **ExcelL1_C1_A4.xlsx**.

Assessment

5 USE HELP FEATURE TO LEARN ABOUT SCROLLING

1. Use the Help feature to learn more about how to scroll within an Excel worksheet.
2. Read and then print the information provided by Help.
3. Create a worksheet containing the information. Set this up as a worksheet with two columns (cells will contain only text—not numbers). Create a title for the worksheet.
4. Select the cells in your worksheet containing data and then apply a table style to the cells.
5. Save the completed workbook and name it **ExcelL1_C1_A5**.
6. Print and then close **ExcelL1_C1_A5.xlsx**.

CASE study

Apply Your Skills

You are the office manager for Deering Industries. One of your responsibilities is creating a monthly calendar containing information on staff meetings, training, and due dates for time cards. Open **DeeringCalendar.xlsx** and then insert the following information:

- Insert the text **September, 2010** in cell A2.
- Insert the days of the week (*Sunday, Monday, Tuesday, Wednesday, Thursday, Friday,* and *Saturday*) in cells A3 through G3.
- Insert the number *1* in cell D4, number *2* in cell E4, number *3* in cell F4, and number *4* in cell G4.
- Insert in the calendar the remaining numbers of the days (numbers 5-11 in cells A6 through G6, numbers 12 through 18 in cells A8 through G8, numbers 19 through 25 in cells A10 through G10, and numbers 26 through 30 in cells A12 through E12).
- Excel training will be held Thursday, September 2, from 9-11 a.m. Insert this information in cell E5. (Insert the text on two lines by typing Excel Training, pressing Alt + Enter to move the insertion point to the next line, and then typing 9-10 a.m.)
- A staff meeting is held the second and fourth Monday of each month from 9-10 a.m. Insert this information in cell B9 and cell B13.
- Time cards are due the first and third Fridays of the month. Insert in cells F5 and F9 information indicating that time cards are due.
- A production team meeting is scheduled for Tuesday, September 21, from 1-3 p.m. Insert this information in cell C11.

Save the workbook and name it **ExcelL1_C1_CS_P1**. Print and then close the workbook.

The manager of the Purchasing Department has asked you to prepare a worksheet containing information on quarterly purchases. Open **DeeringExpenditures.xlsx** and then insert the data as shown in Figure 1.14. After typing the data, insert in the appropriate cells formulas to calculate averages and totals. Save the workbook and name it **ExcelL1_C1_CS_P2**. Print and then close the workbook.

Figure 1.14 **Case Study Part 2**

	A	B	C	D	E	F	G
1	DEERING INDUSTRIES						
2	PURCHASING DEPARTMENT - EXPENDITURES						
3	Category	1st Qtr.	2nd Qtr.	3rd Qtr.	4th Qtr.	Average	
4	Supplies	$ 645.75	$ 756.25	$ 534.78	$ 78,950.00		
5	Equipment	$ 4,520.55	$ 10,789.35	$ 3,825.00	$ 12,890.72		
6	Furniture	$ 458.94	$ 2,490.72	$ 851.75	$ 743.20		
7	Training	$ 1,000.00	$ 250.00	$ 1,200.00	$ 800.00		
8	Software	$ 249.00	$ 1,574.30	$ 155.45	$ 3,458.70		
9	Total						
10							

Part 3

The manager of the Purchasing Department has asked you to prepare a note to the finances coordinator, Jennifer Strauss. In Word, type a note to Jennifer Strauss explaining that you have prepared an Excel worksheet with the Purchasing Department expenditures. You are including the cells from the worksheet containing the expenditure information. In Excel, open **ExcelL1_C1_CS_P2.xlsx**, copy cells A3 through F9, and then paste them in the Word document. Make any corrections to the table so the information is readable. Save the document and name it **WordExcelL1_C1_CS_P3**. Print and then close the document. Close **ExcelL1_C1_CS_P3.xlsx**.

Part 4

You will be ordering copy machines for several departments in the company and decide to research prices. Using the Internet, find three companies that sell copiers and write down information on different copier models. Open **DeeringCopiers.xlsx** and then type the company, model number, and price in the designated cells. Save the completed workbook and name it **ExcelL1_C1_CS_P4**. Print and then close **ExcelL1_C1_CS_P4.xlsx**.

CHAPTER 2

Inserting Formulas in a Worksheet

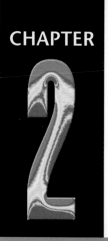

PERFORMANCE OBJECTIVES

Upon successful completion of Chapter 2, you will be able to:

- Write formulas with mathematical operators
- Type a formula in the Formula bar
- Copy a formula
- Use the Insert Function feature to insert a formula in a cell
- Write formulas with the AVERAGE, MAX, MIN, COUNT, PMT, FV, DATE, NOW, and IF functions
- Create an absolute and mixed cell reference

Tutorial 2.1
Inserting and Editing Formulas
Tutorial 2.2
Working with Cell References

Excel is a powerful decision-making tool containing data that can be manipulated to answer "what if" situations. Insert a formula in a worksheet and then manipulate the data to make projections, answer specific questions, and use as a planning tool. For example, the owner of a company might prepare a worksheet on production costs and then determine the impact on company revenues if production is increased or decreased.

Insert a formula in a worksheet to perform calculations on values. A formula contains a mathematical operator, value, cell reference, cell range, and a function. Formulas can be written that add, subtract, multiply, and/or divide values. Formulas can also be written that calculate averages, percentages, minimum and maximum values, and much more. As you learned in Chapter 1, Excel includes a Sum button in the Editing group in the Home tab that inserts a formula to calculate the total of a range of cells and also includes some commonly used formulas. Along with the Sum button, Excel includes a Formulas tab that offers a variety of functions to create formulas.

Note: Before beginning computer projects, copy to your storage medium the Excel2007L1C2 subfolder from the Excel2007L1 folder on the CD that accompanies this textbook and make Excel2007L1C2 the active folder.

Project **①** **Insert Formulas in a Worksheet**

You will open a worksheet containing data and then insert formulas to calculate differences, salaries, and percentages of budgets.

Writing Formulas with Mathematical Operators

HINT

After typing a formula in a cell, press the Enter key, the Tab key, Shift + Tab, or click the Enter button on the Formula bar.

As you learned in Chapter 1, the Sum button in the Editing group in the Home tab creates the formula for you. You can also write your own formulas using mathematical operators. Commonly used mathematical operators and their functions are displayed in Table 2.1. When writing your own formula, begin the formula with the equals (=) sign. For example, to create a formula that divides the contents of cell B2 by the contents of cell C2 and inserts the result in cell D2, you would make D2 the active cell and then type =B2/C2.

Table 2.1 Mathematical Operators

Operator	Function
+	Addition
-	Subtraction
*	Multiplication
/	Division
%	Percent
^	Exponentiation

If a formula contains two or more operators, Excel uses the same order of operations used in algebra. From left to right in a formula, this order, called the *order of operations*, is: negations (negative number—a number preceded by -) first, then percents (%), then exponentiations (^), followed by multiplications (*), divisions (/), additions (+), and finally subtractions (-). If you want to change the order of operations, use parentheses around the part of the formula you want calculated first.

Copying a Formula with Relative Cell References

In many worksheets, the same basic formula is used repetitively. In a situation where a formula is copied to other locations in a worksheet, use a ***relative cell reference***. Copy a formula containing relative cell references and the cell references change. For example, if you enter the formula *=SUM(A2:C2)* in cell D2 and then copy it relatively to cell D3, the formula in cell D3 displays as *=SUM(A3:C3)*. (Additional information on cell references is discussed later in this chapter in the "Using an Absolute Cell Reference in a Formula" section.)

To copy a formula relatively in a worksheet, use the Fill button or the fill handle (you used the fill handle to copy a formula in Chapter 1). To use the Fill button, select the cell containing the formula as well as the cells to which you want the formula copied and then click the Fill button in the Editing group in the Home tab. At the Fill drop-down list, click the desired direction. For example, if you are copying the formula down cells, click the *Down* option.

QUICK STEPS

Copy Relative Formula
1. Insert formula in cell.
2. Select cell containing formula and all cells you want to contain formula.
3. Click Fill button.
4. Click desired direction.

Project **1a** **Finding Differences by Inserting and Copying a Formula**

1. Open **ExcelC02Project01.xlsx**.
2. Save the workbook with Save As and name it **ExcelL1_C2_P1**.
3. Insert a formula by completing the following steps:
   a. Make cell D3 active.
   b. Type the formula =C3-B3.
   c. Press Enter.
4. Copy the formula to cells D4 through D10 by completing the following steps:
   a. Select cells D3 through D10.
   b. Click the Fill button in the Editing group in the Home tab and then click *Down* at the drop-down list.
5. Save **ExcelL1_C2_P1.xlsx**.
6. With the worksheet open, make the following changes to cell contents:
   - B4: Change *$48,290* to *46425*
   - C6: Change *$61,220* to *60000*
   - B8: Change *$55,309* to *57415*
   - B9: Change *$12,398* to *14115*
7. Save **ExcelL1_C2_P1.xlsx**.

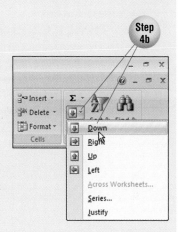

Step 4b

Copying Formulas with the Fill Handle

Use the fill handle to copy a formula up, down, left, or right within a worksheet. To use the fill handle, insert the desired data in the cell (text, value, formula, etc.). With the cell active, position the mouse pointer on the fill handle until the mouse pointer turns into a thin, black cross. Hold down the left mouse button, drag and select the desired cells, and then release the mouse button. If you are dragging a cell containing a formula, a relative version of the formula is copied to the selected cells.

HINT
Use the fill handle to copy a relative version of a formula.

1. With **ExcelL1_C2_P1.xlsx** open, insert a formula by completing the following steps:
   a. Make cell D15 active.
   b. Click in the Formula bar text box and then type **=C15*B15**.
   c. Click the Enter button on the Formula bar.
2. Copy the formula to cells D16 through D20 by completing the following steps:
   a. Make sure cell D15 is the active cell.
   b. Position the mouse pointer on the fill handle that displays at the lower right corner of cell D15 until the pointer turns into a thin, black cross.
   c. Hold down the left mouse button, drag down to cell D20, and then release the mouse button.
3. Save **ExcelL1_C2_P1.xlsx**.
4. With the worksheet still open, make the following changes to cell contents:
   B16: Change *20* to *28*
   C17: Change *$18.75* to *19.10*
   B19: Change *15* to *24*
5. Save **ExcelL1_C2_P1.xlsx**.

Step 1c Step 1b

DATE ▾ × ✓ *fx* =C15*B15

Highland Construction

	A	B	C	D
2	Customer	Actual	Planned	Difference
3	Sellar Corporation	$30,349.00	$34,109.00	$3,760.00
4	Main Street Photos	$46,425.00	$48,100.00	$1,675.00
5	Sunset Automotive	$34,192.00	$32,885.00	-$1,307.00
6	Linstrom Enterprises	$63,293.00	$60,000.00	-$3,293.00
7	Morcos Media	$29,400.00	$30,500.00	$1,100.00
8	Green Valley Optics	$57,415.00	$58,394.00	$979.00
9	Detailed Designs	$14,115.00	$13,100.00	-$1,015.00
10	Arrowstar Company	$87,534.00	$86,905.00	-$629.00
11				
12				
13				
14	Name	Hours	Rate	Salary
15	Carolyn Bentley	35	$23.15	=C15*B15
16	Lindon Cassini	20	$19.00	

13				
14	Name	Hours	Rate	Salary
15	Carolyn Bentley	35	$23.15	$810.25
16	Lindon Cassini	20	$19.00	$380.00
17	Michelle DeFord	40	$18.75	$750.00
18	Javier Farias	24	$16.45	$394.80
19	Deborah Gould	15	$11.50	$172.50
20	William Jarman	15	$11.50	$172.50
21				
22				

Step 2c

Writing a Formula by Pointing

In Project 1a and Project 1b, you wrote formulas using cell references such as *=C3-B3*. Another method for writing a formula is to "point" to the specific cells that are to be part of the formula. Creating a formula by pointing is more accurate than typing the cell reference since a mistake can happen when typing the cell reference.

To write a formula by pointing, click the cell that will contain the formula, type the equals sign to begin the formula, and then click the cell you want to reference in the formula. This inserts a moving border around the cell and also changes the mode from Enter to Point. (The word *Point* displays at the left side of the Status bar.) Type the desired mathematical operator and then click the next cell reference. Continue in this manner until all cell references are specified and then press the Enter key. This ends the formula and inserts the result of the calculation of the formula in the active cell. When writing a formula by pointing, you can also select a range of cells you want included in a formula.

Project 1c   Writing a Formula by Pointing That Calculates Percentage of Actual Budget

1. With **ExcelL1_C2_P1.xlsx** open, enter a formula by pointing that calculates the percentage of actual budget by completing the following steps:
   a. Make cell D25 active.
   b. Type the equals sign.
   c. Click cell C25. (This inserts a moving border around the cell and the mode changes from Enter to Point.)
   d. Type the forward slash symbol (/).
   e. Click cell B25.

	A	B	C	D	E
22					
23					
24	Expense	Actual	Budget	% of Actual	
25	Salaries	$126,000.00	$124,000.00	=C25/B25	
26	Commissions	$58,000.00	$54,500.00		
27	Media space	$8,250.00	$10,100.00		
28	Travel expenses	$6,350.00	$6,000.00		
29	Dealer display	$4,140.00	$4,500.00		
30	Payroll taxes	$2,430.00	$2,200.00		
31	Telephone	$1,450.00	$1,500.00		
32					

Steps
1a–1e

C	D	E
Budget	% of Actual	
$124,000.00	98%	
$54,500.00	94%	
$10,100.00	122%	
$6,000.00	94%	
$4,500.00	109%	
$2,200.00	91%	
$1,500.00	103%	

Step 2

   f. Make sure the formula looks like this =C25/B25 and then press Enter.
2. Make cell D25 active, position the mouse pointer on the fill handle, drag down to cell D31, and then release the mouse button.
3. Save **ExcelL1_C2_P1.xlsx**.

Using the Trace Error Button

As you are working in a worksheet, you may occasionally notice a button pop up near the active cell. The general term for this button is *smart tag*. The display of the smart tag button varies depending on the action performed. In Project 1d, you will insert a formula that will cause a smart tag button, named the Trace Error button, to appear. When the Trace Error button appears, a small dark green triangle also displays in the upper left corner of the cell. Click the Trace Error button and a drop-down list displays with options for updating the formula to include specific cells, getting help on the error, ignoring the error, editing the error in the Formula bar, and completing an error check. In Project 1d, two of the formulas you insert return the desired results. You will click the Trace Error button, read information on what Excel perceives as the error, and then tell Excel to ignore the error.

Trace Error

1. With **ExcelL1_C2_P1.xlsx** open, enter a formula by pointing that computes the percentage of equipment down time by completing the following steps:
   a. Make cell B45 active.
   b. Type the equals sign followed by the left parenthesis (=().
   c. Click cell B37. (This inserts a moving border around the cell and the mode changes from Enter to Point.)
   d. Type the minus symbol (-).
   e. Click cell B43.
   f. Type the right parenthesis followed by the forward slash ()/).
   g. Click cell B37.
   h. Make sure the formula looks like this =(B37-B43)/B37 and then press Enter.
2. Make cell B45 active, position the mouse pointer on the fill handle, drag across to cell G45, and then release the mouse button.
3. Enter a formula by dragging through a range of cells by completing the following steps:
   a. Click in cell B46 and then click the Sum button in the Editing group in the Home tab.
   b. Select cells B37 through D37.
   c. Click the Enter button on the Formula bar. (This inserts *7,260* in cell B46.)
4. Click in cell B47 and then complete steps similar to those in Step 3 to create a formula that totals hours available from April through June (cells E37 through G37). (This inserts *7,080* in cell B47.)
5. Click in cell B46 and notice the Trace Error button that displays. Complete the following steps to read about the error and then tell Excel to ignore the error:
   a. Click the Trace Error button.
   b. At the drop-down list that displays, click the *Help on this error* option.
   c. Read the information that displays in the Excel Help window and then close the window.

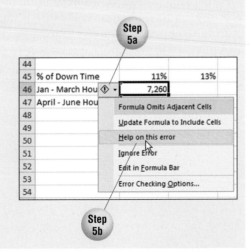

Steps 1a–1g

Step 3c

Step 5a

Step 5b

d. Click the Trace Error button again and then click *Ignore Error* at the drop-down list.

6. Remove the dark green triangle from cell B47 by completing the following steps:
   a. Click in cell B47.
   b. Click the Trace Error button and then click *Ignore Error* at the drop-down list.

7. Save, print, and then close **ExcelL1_C2_P1.xlsx**.

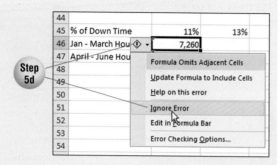

Step 5d

44			
45	% of Down Time	11%	13%
46	Jan - March Hou	7,260	
47	April - June Hou		

Formula Omits Adjacent Cells
Update Formula to Include Cells
Help on this error
Ignore Error
Edit in Formula Bar
Error Checking Options...

Project ② Insert Formulas with Statistical Functions

You will use the AVERAGE function to determine average test scores, use the MINIMUM and MAXIMUM functions to determine lowest and highest averages, use the COUNT function to count number of students taking a test, and display formulas in a cell rather than the result of the formula.

Inserting Formulas with Functions

In Project 2a in Chapter 1, you used the Sum button to insert the formula *=SUM(B2:B5)* in a cell. The beginning section of the formula, *=SUM*, is called a **function**, which is a built-in formula. Using a function takes fewer keystrokes when creating a formula. For example, the *=SUM* function saved you from having to type each cell to be included in the formula with the plus (+) symbol between cell entries.

Excel provides other functions for writing formulas. A function operates on what is referred to as an **argument**. An argument may consist of a constant, a cell reference, or another function (referred to as a nested function). In the formula *=SUM(B2:B5)*, the cell range *(B2:B5)* is an example of a cell reference argument. An argument may also contain a *constant*. A constant is a value entered directly into the formula. For example, if you enter the formula *=SUM(B3:B9,100)*, the cell range *B3:B9* is a cell reference argument and *100* is a constant. In this formula, 100 is always added to the sum of the cells. If a function is included in an argument within a function, it is called a **nested function**. (You will learn about nested functions later in this chapter.)

When a value calculated by the formula is inserted in a cell, this process is referred to as **returning the result**. The term **returning** refers to the process of calculating the formula and the term **result** refers to inserting the value in the cell.

You can type a function in a cell in a worksheet or you can use the Insert Function button on the Formula bar or in the Formulas tab to help you write the formula. Figure 2.1 displays the Formulas tab. The Formulas tab provides the Insert Function button as well as other buttons for inserting functions in a worksheet. The Function Library group in the Formulas tab contains a number of buttons for inserting functions from a variety of categories such as Financial, Logical, Text, and Date & Time.

Insert Function

Figure 2.1 Formulas Tab

HINT

You can also display the Insert Function dialog box by clicking the down-pointing arrow at the right side of the Sum button and then clicking *More Functions.*

Click the Insert Function button on the Formula bar or in the Formulas tab and the Insert Function dialog box displays as shown in Figure 2.2. At the Insert Function dialog box, the most recently used functions display in the *Select a function* list box. You can choose a function category by clicking the down-pointing arrow at the right side of the *Or select a category* list box and then clicking the desired category at the drop-down list. Use the *Search for a function* option to locate a specific function.

Figure 2.2 Insert Function Dialog Box

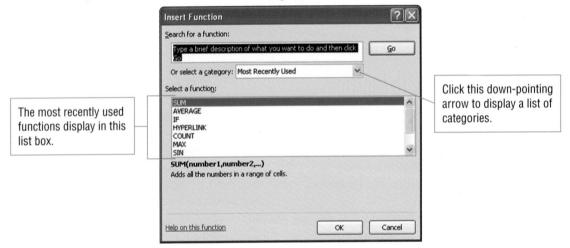

The most recently used functions display in this list box.

Click this down-pointing arrow to display a list of categories.

HINT

Click the down-pointing arrow at the right side of the Sum button in the Formulas tab and common functions display in a drop-down list.

With the desired function category selected, choose a function in the *Select a function* list box and then click OK. This displays a Function Arguments palette like the one shown in Figure 2.3. At this palette, enter in the *Number1* text box the range of cells you want included in the formula, enter any constants that are to be included as part of the formula, or enter another function. After entering a range of cells, a constant, or another function, click the OK button. You can include more than one argument in a function. If the function you are creating contains more than one argument, press the Tab key to move the insertion point to the *Number2* text box, and then enter the second argument. If you need to display a specific cell or cells behind the function palette, move the palette by clicking and dragging it.

Figure 2.3 Example Function Arguments Palette

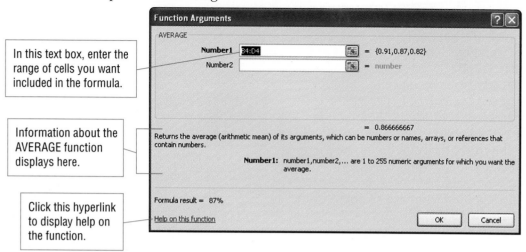

In this text box, enter the range of cells you want included in the formula.

Information about the AVERAGE function displays here.

Click this hyperlink to display help on the function.

Excel includes over 200 functions that are divided into 11 different categories including *Financial, Date & Time, Math & Trig, Statistical, Lookup & Reference, Database, Text, Logical, Information, Engineering,* and *Cube*. Clicking the Sum button in the Function Library group in the Formulas tab or the Editing group in the Home tab automatically adds numbers with the SUM function. The SUM function is included in the *Math & Trig* category. In some projects in this chapter, you will write formulas with functions in other categories including *Statistical, Financial, Date & Time,* and *Logical.*

Excel includes the Formula AutoComplete feature that displays a drop-down list of functions. To use this feature, click in the desired cell or click in the Formula bar text box, type the equals sign (=), and then type the first letter of the desired function. This displays a drop-down list with functions that begin with the letter. Double-click the desired function, enter the cell references, and then press Enter.

Writing Formulas with Statistical Functions

In this section, you will learn to write formulas with the statistical functions AVERAGE, MAX, MIN, and COUNT. The AVERAGE function returns the average (arithmetic mean) of the arguments. The MAX function returns the largest value in a set of values and the MIN function returns the smallest value in a set of values. Use the COUNT function to count the number of cells that contain numbers within the list of arguments.

Finding Averages

A common function in a formula is the AVERAGE function. With this function, a range of cells is added together and then divided by the number of cell entries. In Project 2a you will use the AVERAGE function, which will add all of the test scores for a student and then divide that number by the total number of tests. You will use the Insert Function button to simplify the creation of the formula containing an AVERAGE function.

One of the advantages to using formulas in a worksheet is the ability to easily manipulate data to answer certain questions. In Project 2a you will learn the impact of retaking certain tests on the final average score.

1. Open **ExcelC02Project02.xlsx**.
2. Save the workbook with Save As and name it **ExcelL1_C2_P2**.
3. Use the Insert Function button to find the average of test scores by completing the following steps:
   a. Make cell E4 active.
   b. Click the Insert Function button on the Formula bar.
   c. At the Insert Function dialog box, click the down-pointing arrow at the right side of the *Or select a category* list box and then click *Statistical* at the drop-down list.
   d. Click *AVERAGE* in the *Select a function* list box.
   e. Click OK.
   f. At the Function Arguments palette, make sure *B4:D4* displays in the *Number1* text box. (If not, type **B4:D4** in the *Number1* text box.)
   g. Click OK.
4. Copy the formula by completing the following steps:
   a. Make sure cell E4 is active.
   b. Position the mouse pointer on the fill handle until the pointer turns into a thin black cross.
   c. Hold down the left mouse button, drag down to cell E16, and then release the mouse button.
5. Save and then print **ExcelL1_C2_P2.xlsx**.
6. After viewing the averages of test scores, you notice that a couple of people have a low average. You decide to see what happens to the average score if students make up tests where they scored the lowest. You decide that a student can score a maximum of 70% on a retake of the test. Make the following changes to test scores to see how the changes will affect the test average.

   B9: Change *50* to *70*
   C9: Change *52* to *70*
   D9: Change *60* to *70*
   B10: Change *62* to *70*
   B14: Change *0* to *70*
   D14: Change *0* to *70*
   D16: Change *0* to *70*

7. Save and then print **ExcelL1_C2_P2.xlsx**. (Compare the test averages for Teri Fisher-Edwards, Stephanie Flanery, Claude Markovits, and Douglas Pherson to see what the effect of retaking the tests has on their final test averages.)

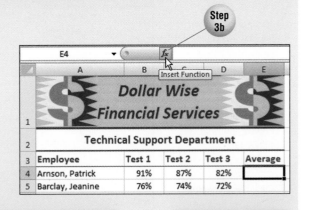

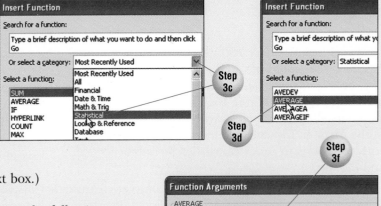

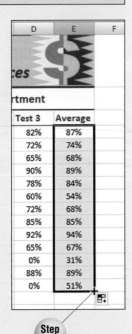

When a formula such as the AVERAGE formula you inserted in a cell in Project 2a calculates cell entries, it ignores certain cell entries. The AVERAGE function will ignore text in cells and blank cells (not zeros). For example, in the worksheet containing test scores, a couple of cells contained a *0%* entry. This entry was included in the averaging of the test scores. If you did not want that particular test to be included in the average, enter text in the cell such as *N/A* (for *not applicable*) or leave the cell blank.

Finding Maximum and Minimum Values

The MAX function in a formula returns the maximum value in a cell range and the MIN function returns the minimum value in a cell range. As an example, you could use the MAX and MIN functions in a worksheet containing employee hours to determine which employee worked the most number of hours and which worked the least. In a worksheet containing sales commissions, you could use the MAX and MIN functions to determine the salesperson who earned the most commission dollars and the one who earned the least.

Insert a MAX and MIN function into a formula in the same manner as an AVERAGE function. In Project 2b, you will use the Formula AutoComplete feature to insert the MAX function in cells to determine the highest test score average and the Insert Function button to insert the MIN function to determine the lowest test score average.

Project 2b Finding Maximum and Minimum Values in a Worksheet

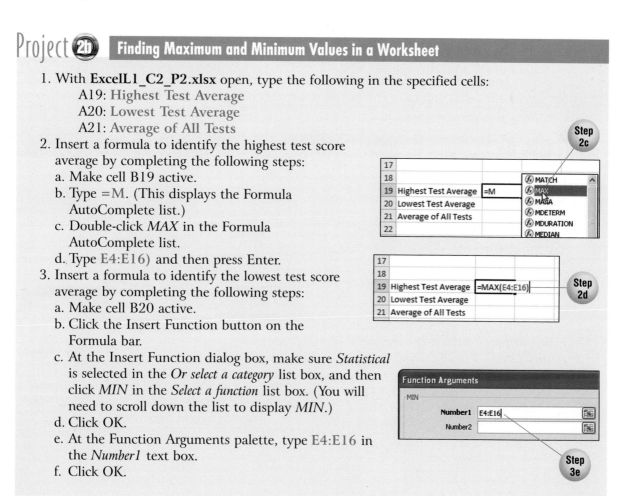

1. With **ExcelL1_C2_P2.xlsx** open, type the following in the specified cells:
   A19: Highest Test Average
   A20: Lowest Test Average
   A21: Average of All Tests
2. Insert a formula to identify the highest test score average by completing the following steps:
   a. Make cell B19 active.
   b. Type =M. (This displays the Formula AutoComplete list.)
   c. Double-click *MAX* in the Formula AutoComplete list.
   d. Type E4:E16) and then press Enter.
3. Insert a formula to identify the lowest test score average by completing the following steps:
   a. Make cell B20 active.
   b. Click the Insert Function button on the Formula bar.
   c. At the Insert Function dialog box, make sure *Statistical* is selected in the *Or select a category* list box, and then click *MIN* in the *Select a function* list box. (You will need to scroll down the list to display *MIN*.)
   d. Click OK.
   e. At the Function Arguments palette, type E4:E16 in the *Number1* text box.
   f. Click OK.

4. Insert a formula to determine the average of all test scores by completing the following steps:
   a. Make cell B21 active.
   b. Click the Formulas tab.
   c. Click the Insert Function button in the Function Library group.
   d. At the Insert Function dialog box, make sure *Statistical* is selected in the *Or select a category* list box and then click *AVERAGE* in the *Select a function* list box.
   e. Click OK.
   f. At the Function Arguments palette, type **E4:E16** in the *Number1* text box, and then click OK.
5. Save and then print **ExcelL1_C2_P2.xlsx**.
6. Change the *70%* values (which were previously *0%*) in cells B14, D14, and D16 to *N/A*. (This will cause the average of test scores for Claude Markovits and Douglas Pherson to increase and will change the minimum number and average of all test scores.)
7. Save and then print **ExcelL1_C2_P2.xlsx**.

Counting Numbers in a Range

Use the COUNT function to count the numeric values in a range. For example, in a range of cells containing cells with text and cells with numbers, you can count how many cells in the range contain numbers. In Project 2c, you will use the COUNT function to specify the number of students taking Test 2 and Test 3. In the worksheet, the cells containing the text N/A are not counted by the COUNT function.

Project 2c · Counting the Number of Students Taking Tests

1. With **ExcelL1_C2_P2.xlsx** open, make cell A22 active.
2. Type Test 2 Completed.
3. Make cell B22 active.
4. Insert a formula counting the number of students who have taken Test 2 by completing the following steps:
   a. With cell B22 active, click in the Formula bar text box.
   b. Type =C.
   c. At the Formula AutoComplete list that displays, scroll down the list until *COUNT* displays and then double-click *COUNT*.
   d. Type C4:C16) and then press Enter.
5. Count the number of students who have taken Test 3 by completing the following steps:
   a. Make cell A23 active.
   b. Type Test 3 Completed.

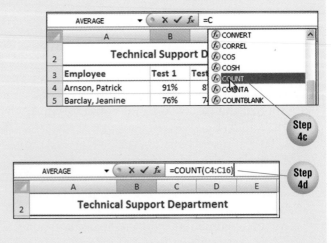

c. Make cell B23 active.

d. Click the Insert Function button on the Formula bar.

e. At the Insert Function dialog box, make sure *Statistical* is selected in the *Or select a category* list box.

f. Scroll down the list of functions in the *Select a function* list box until *COUNT* is visible and then double-click *COUNT*.

g. At the formula palette, type D4:D16 in the *Value1* text box, and then click OK.

6. Save and then print **ExcelL1_C2_P2.xlsx**.

7. Add test scores by completing the following steps:

a. Make cell B14 active and then type 68.

b. Make cell D14 active and then type 70.

c. Make cell D16 active and then type 55.

d. Press Enter.

8. Save and then print **ExcelL1_C2_P2.xlsx**.

Displaying Formulas

In some situations, you may need to display the formulas in a worksheet rather than the results of the formula. You may want to turn on formulas for auditing purposes or check formulas for accuracy. Display all formulas in a worksheet rather than the results by pressing Ctrl + ` (this is the grave accent). Press Ctrl + ` to turn off the display of formulas.

Project **2d**   **Displaying Formulas**

1. With **ExcelL1_C2_P2.xlsx** open, make cell A3 active.

2. Press Ctrl + ` to turn on the display of formulas.

3. Print the worksheet with the formulas.

4. Press Ctrl + ` to turn off the display of formulas.

5. Save and then close **ExcelL1_C2_P2.xlsx**.

Project **3**   **Insert Formulas with Financial and Date and Time Functions**

You will use the PMT financial function to calculate payments and the FV function to find the future value of an investment. You will also use the DATE function to return the serial number for a date and the NOW function to insert the current date and time as a serial number.

Writing Formulas with Financial Functions

In this section, you will learn to write formulas with the financial functions PMT and FV. The PMT function calculates the payment for a loan based on constant payments and a constant interest rate. Use the FV function to return the future value of an investment based on periodic, constant payments and a constant interest rate.

Finding the Periodic Payments for a Loan

The PMT function finds the periodic payment for a loan based on constant payments and a constant interest rate. The PMT function contains the arguments Nper, Pv, Fv, and Type. The Nper argument is the number of payments that will be made to an investment or loan, Pv is the current value of amounts to be received or paid in the future, Fv is the value of a loan or investment at the end of all periods, and Type determines whether calculations will be based on payments made in arrears (at the end of each period) or in advance (at the beginning of each period).

Project 3a Calculating Payments

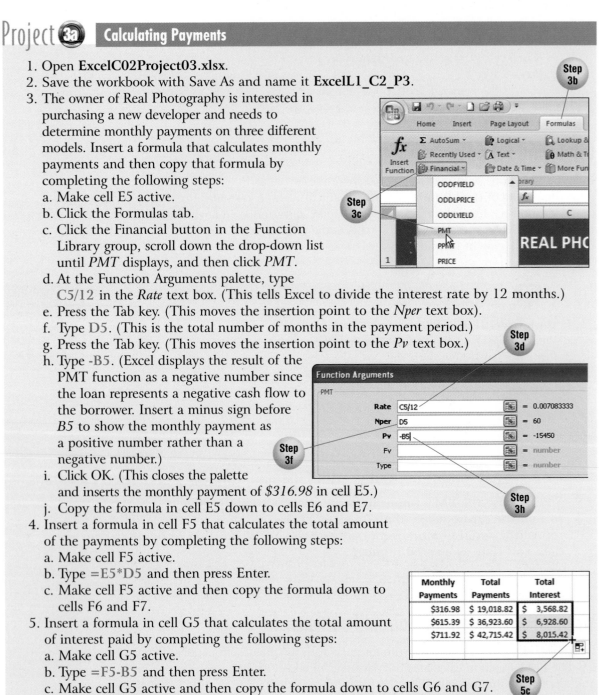

1. Open **ExcelC02Project03.xlsx**.
2. Save the workbook with Save As and name it **ExcelL1_C2_P3**.
3. The owner of Real Photography is interested in purchasing a new developer and needs to determine monthly payments on three different models. Insert a formula that calculates monthly payments and then copy that formula by completing the following steps:
   a. Make cell E5 active.
   b. Click the Formulas tab.
   c. Click the Financial button in the Function Library group, scroll down the drop-down list until *PMT* displays, and then click *PMT*.
   d. At the Function Arguments palette, type C5/12 in the *Rate* text box. (This tells Excel to divide the interest rate by 12 months.)
   e. Press the Tab key. (This moves the insertion point to the *Nper* text box).
   f. Type D5. (This is the total number of months in the payment period.)
   g. Press the Tab key. (This moves the insertion point to the *Pv* text box.)
   h. Type -B5. (Excel displays the result of the PMT function as a negative number since the loan represents a negative cash flow to the borrower. Insert a minus sign before *B5* to show the monthly payment as a positive number rather than a negative number.)
   i. Click OK. (This closes the palette and inserts the monthly payment of *$316.98* in cell E5.)
   j. Copy the formula in cell E5 down to cells E6 and E7.
4. Insert a formula in cell F5 that calculates the total amount of the payments by completing the following steps:
   a. Make cell F5 active.
   b. Type =E5*D5 and then press Enter.
   c. Make cell F5 active and then copy the formula down to cells F6 and F7.
5. Insert a formula in cell G5 that calculates the total amount of interest paid by completing the following steps:
   a. Make cell G5 active.
   b. Type =F5-B5 and then press Enter.
   c. Make cell G5 active and then copy the formula down to cells G6 and G7.
6. Save **ExcelL1_C2_P3.xlsx**.

Finding the Future Value of a Series of Payments

The FV function calculates the future value of a series of equal payments or an annuity. Use this function to determine information such as how much money can be earned in an investment account with a specific interest rate and over a specific period of time.

Project **3h**   **Finding the Future Value of an Investment**

1. Make sure **ExcelL1_C2_P3.xlsx** is open.
2. The owner of Real Photography has decided to save money to purchase a new developer and wants to compute how much money can be earned by investing the money in an investment account that returns 9% annual interest. The owner determines that $1,200 per month can be invested in the account for three years. Complete the following steps to determine the future value of the investment account by completing the following steps:
   a. Make cell B15 active.
   b. Click the Financial button in the Function Library group in the Formulas tab.
   c. At the drop-down list that displays, scroll down the list until *FV* is visible and then click *FV*.
   d. At the Function Arguments palette, type **B12/12** in the *Rate* text box.
   e. Press the Tab key.
   f. Type **B13** in the *Nper* text box.
   g. Press the Tab key.
   h. Type **B14** in the *Pmt* text box.
   i. Click OK. (This closes the palette and also inserts the future value of *$49,383.26* in cell B15.)
3. Save and then print **ExcelL1_C2_P3.xlsx**.
4. The owner decides to determine the future return after two years. To do this, change the amount in cell B13 from *36* to *24* and then press Enter. (This recalculates the future investment amount in cell B15.)
5. Save and then print **ExcelL1_C2_P3.xlsx**.

Step 2d

Step 2f

Step 2h

	Function Arguments		
	FV		
Rate	B12/12		= 0.0075
Nper	B13		= 36
Pmt	B14|		= -1200
Pv			= number
Type			= number

10		
11	**Future Value of Investment**	
12	**Rate**	9%
13	**Number of Months**	24
14	**Monthly Payment**	$ (1,200.00)
15	**Future Value**	$31,426.16
16		

Step 4

Writing Formulas with Date and Time Functions

In this section, you will learn to write formulas with the date and time functions NOW and DATE. The NOW function returns the serial number of the current date and time. The DATE function returns the serial number that represents a particular date. Excel can make calculations using dates because the dates are represented as serial numbers. To calculate a date's serial number, Excel counts the days since the beginning of the twentieth century. The date serial number for January 1, 1900, is 1. The date serial number for January 1, 2000, is 36,526. To access the DATE and NOW functions, click the Date & Time button in the Function Library group in the Formulas tab.

HINT
Ctrl + ; is the keyboard shortcut to insert the current date in the active cell.

Project **3c** **Using the DATE and NOW Functions**

1. Make sure **ExcelL1_C2_P3.xlsx** is open.
2. Certain cells in this worksheet establish overdue dates for Real Photography accounts. Enter a formula in cell D20 that returns the serial number for the date March 17, 2010, by completing the following steps:
   a. Make cell D20 active.
   b. Click the Formulas tab.
   c. Click the Date & Time button in the Function Library group.
   d. At the drop-down list that displays, click *DATE*.
   e. At the Function Arguments palette, type 2010 in the *Year* text box.
   f. Press the Tab key and then type 03 in the *Month* text box.
   g. Press the Tab key and then type 17 in the *Day* text box.
   h. Click OK.
3. Complete steps similar to those in Step 2 to enter the following dates as serial numbers in the specified cells:

   D21 = March 24, 2010
   D22 = March 31, 2010
   D23 = April 7, 2010

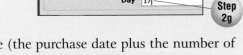

		Step 2e
Year	2010	Step 2f
Month	03	
Day	17	Step 2g

4. Enter a formula in cell F20 that inserts the due date (the purchase date plus the number of days in the *Terms* column) by completing the following steps:
   a. Make cell F20 active.
   b. Type =D20+E20 and then press Enter.
   c. Make cell F20 active and then copy the formula down to cells F21, F22, and F23.
5. Make cell A26 active and then type your name.
6. Insert the current date and time as a serial number by completing the following steps:
   a. Make cell A27 active.
   b. Click the Date & Time button in the Function Library group in the Formulas tab and then click *NOW* at the drop-down list.
   c. At the Function Arguments palette telling you that the function takes no argument, click OK.
7. Save, print, and then close **ExcelL1_C2_P3.xlsx**.

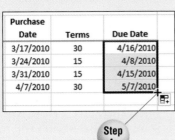

Purchase Date	Terms	Due Date
3/17/2010	30	4/16/2010
3/24/2010	15	4/8/2010
3/31/2010	15	4/15/2010
4/7/2010	30	5/7/2010

Step 4c

Project **4** **Insert Formulas with the IF Logical Function**

You will use the IF logical function to calculate sales bonuses, determine letter grades based on test averages, and identify discounts and discount amounts.

Writing a Formula with the IF Logical Function

The IF function is considered a *conditional function*. With the IF function you can perform conditional tests on values and formulas. A question that can be answered with true or false is considered a *logical test*. The IF function makes a logical test and then performs a particular action if the answer is true and another action if the answer is false.

For example, an IF function can be used to write a formula that calculates a salesperson's bonus as 10% if the quota of $100,000 is met or exceeded, and zero if the quota is less than $100,000. That formula would look like this: *=IF(quota=>100000,quota*0.1,0)*. The formula contains three parts—the condition or logical test *IF(quota=>100000)*, action taken if the condition or logical test is true *(quota*0.1)*, and the action taken if the condition or logical test is false *(0)*. Commas separate the condition and the actions. In the bonus formula, if the quota is equal to or greater than $100,000, then the quota is multiplied by 10%. If the quota is less than $100,000, then the bonus is zero.

In Project 4a, you will write a formula with cell references rather than cell data. The formula in Project 4a is *=IF(C5>B5,C5*0.15,0)*. In this formula the condition or logical test is whether or not the number in cell C5 is greater than the number in cell B5. If the condition is true and the number is greater, then the number in cell C5 is multiplied by 0.15 (providing a 15% bonus). If the condition is false and the number in cell C5 is less than the number in cell B5, then nothing happens (no bonus). Notice how commas are used to separate the logical test from the actions.

Editing a Formula

Edit a formula by making active the cell containing the formula and then editing the formula in the cell or in the Formula bar text box. After editing the formula, press Enter or click the Enter button on the Formula bar and Excel will recalculate the result of the formula.

Enter

Project 4a — Writing a Formula with an IF Function and Editing the Formula

1. Open **ExcelC02Project04.xlsx**.
2. Save the workbook with Save As and name it **ExcelL1_C2_P4**.
3. Write a formula with the IF function by completing the following steps. (The formula will determine if the quota has been met and, if it has, will insert the bonus [15% of the actual sales]. If the quota has not been met, the formula will insert a zero.)
   a. Make cell D5 active.
   b. Type *=IF(C5>B5,C5*0.15,0)* and then press Enter.
   c. Make cell D5 active and then use the fill handle to copy the formula to cells D6 through D10.
4. Print the worksheet.
5. Revise the formula so it will insert a 25% bonus if the quota has been met by completing the following steps:
   a. Make cell D5 active.
   b. Click in the Formula bar, edit the formula so it displays as *=IF(C5>B5,C5*0.25,0)*, and then click the Enter button on the Formula bar.
   c. Copy the formula down to cells D6 through D10.
6. Save and then print **ExcelL1_C2_P4.xlsx**.

	Actual Sales	Bonus
	$ 103,295.00	$ 15,494.25
	$ 129,890.00	$ -
	$ 133,255.00	$ 19,988.25
	$ 94,350.00	$ 14,152.50
	$ 167,410.00	$ 25,111.50
	$ 109,980.00	$ -

Step 3c

Step 5b

NOW ▾ × ✓ ƒx =IF(C5>B5,C5*0.25,0)

IF(logical_test, [value_if_true], [v

	A	B
1		Capstan Marine Prod
2		
3		Sales Department
4	Salesperson	Quota	Actual Sales	Bonus
5	Allejandro	$ 95,500.00	$ 103,295.00	:5>B5,C5*0.25,0
6	Crispin	$ 137,000.00	$ 129,890.00	$ -

Bonus
$ 25,823.75
$ -
$ 33,313.75
$ 23,587.50
$ 41,852.50
$ -

Step 5c

Writing a Nested IF Condition

In Project 4a, the IF function had only two possible actions—the actual sales times 15% or a zero. In a formula where more than two actions are required, use nested IF functions. For example, in Project 4b, you will write a formula with IF conditions that has four possible actions—a letter grade of A, B, C, or D. When writing nested IF conditions, insert symbols such as commas, quotation marks, and parentheses in the proper locations. If you want an IF condition to insert text, insert quotation marks before and after the text. The formula you will be writing in Project 4b is shown below.

=IF(E16>89,"A",IF(E16>79,"B",IF(E16>69,"C",IF(E16>59, "D"))))

This formula begins with the condition =IF(E16>89, "A",. If the number in cell E16 is greater than 89, then the condition is met and the grade of A is returned. The formula continues with a nested condition, IF(E16>79, "B",. If the number in cell E16 does not meet the first condition (greater than 89), then Excel looks to the next condition—is the number in cell E16 greater than 79? If it is, then the grade of B is inserted in cell E16. The formula continues with another nested condition, IF(E16>69, "C",. If the number in cell E16 does not match the first condition, Excel looks to the second condition, and if that condition is not met, then Excel looks to the third condition. If the number in cell E16 is greater than 69, then the grade of C is inserted in cell E16. The final nested condition is IF(E16>59, "D". If the first three conditions are not met but this one is, then the grade of D is inserted in cell E16. The four parentheses at the end of the formula end each condition in the formula.

Project 4b Writing a Formula with Nested IF Conditions

1. With **ExcelL1_C2_P4.xlsx** open, insert a formula to average the scores by completing the following steps:
   a. Make cell E16 active.
   b. Type =AVERAGE(B16:D16) and then press Enter.
   c. Make cell E16 active and then copy the formula down to cells E17 through E20.
2. Insert a formula with nested IF conditions by completing the following steps:
   a. Make cell F16 active.
   b. Type =IF(E16>89,"A",IF(E16>79,"B",IF(E16>69,"C",IF(E16>59,"D")))) and then press Enter.

Step 2b

Step 2c

   c. Make cell F16 active and then use the fill handle to copy the formula down to cells F17 through F20.
3. Save **ExcelL1_C2_P4.xlsx**.

As you typed the formula with nested IF conditions in Step 2b of Project 4b, did you notice that the parentheses were different colors? Each color represents a condition. The four right parentheses at the end of the formula ended each of the conditions and each matched in color a left parenthesis. If an average in column E in **ExcelL1_C2_P4.xlsx** is less than 59, the nested formula inserts *FALSE* in the cell. If you want the formula to insert a letter grade, such as *F*, instead of *FALSE*, include another nested IF condition in the formula. Up to 64 levels of functions can be nested.

You can use the IF function from the Logical button drop-down list in the Function Library in the Formulas tab to write an IF statement. The IF statement you write using the IF function from the Logical button checks whether a condition is met and returns one value if the condition is met and another if the condition is not met. For example, in Project 4c you will insert an IF statement that identifies whether or not a part receives a discount. Parts that sell for more than $499 receive a discount and parts that sell for less do not. If the condition is met (the amount is greater than $499), then the statement will return a *YES* and if the condition is not met, the statement will return a *NO*.

In Project 4c, you will type the second IF statement in the cell rather than using the IF function from the Logical button drop-down list. The IF statement you write will reduce the price by five percent for parts that sell from $500 up to $749, seven percent for parts that sell from $750 up to $999, and ten percent for parts that sell for at least $1,000.

Project 4c   **Writing IF Statements Identifying Discounts and Discount Amounts**

1. With **ExcelL1_C2_P4.xlsx** open, insert an IF statement by completing the following steps:
   a. Make cell C26 active.
   b. Click the Logical button in the Function Library group in the Formulas tab and then click IF at the drop-down list.
   c. At the Function Arguments palette, type **B26>499** in the *Logic_test* text box.
   d. Press the Tab key to move the insertion point to the *Value_if_true* text box and then type **YES**.
   e. Press the Tab key to move the insertion point to the *Value_if_false* text box and then type **NO**.
   f. Click OK to close the Function Arguments palette.
2. Copy the formula in cell C26 down to cells C27 through C38.
3. Make cell D26 active.
4. Insert the following IF statement in the cell:
   =IF(B26>999,B26*0.1,IF(B26>749,B26*0.07,IF(B26>499,B26*0.05,IF(B26>0,"N/A"))))
5. Copy the formula in cell D26 down to cells D27 through D38.
6. Save, print, and then close **ExcelL1_C2_P4.xlsx**.

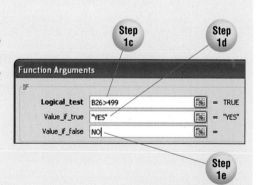

Project ⑤ Insert Formulas Using Absolute and Mixed Cell References

You will insert a formula containing an absolute cell reference that determines the effect on earnings with specific increases, insert a formula with multiple absolute cell references that determine the weighted average of scores, and use mixed cell references to determine simple interest.

Using Absolute and Mixed Cell References in Formulas

A reference identifies a cell or a range of cells in a worksheet and can be relative, absolute, or mixed. Relative cell references refer to cells relative to a position in a formula. Absolute references refer to cells in a specific location. When a formula is copied, a relative cell reference adjusts while an absolute cell reference remains constant. A mixed cell reference does both—either the column remains absolute and the row is relative or the column is relative and the row is absolute. Distinguish between relative, absolute, and mixed cell references using the dollar sign ($). Type a dollar sign before the column and/or row cell reference in a formula to specify that the column or row is an absolute cell reference.

Using an Absolute Cell Reference in a Formula

In this chapter you have learned to copy a relative formula. For example, if the formula =SUM(A2:C2) in cell D2 is copied relatively to cell D3, the formula changes to =SUM(A3:C3). In some situations, you may want a formula to contain an absolute cell reference, which always refers to a cell in a specific location. In Project 5a, you will add a column for projected job earnings and then perform "what if" situations using a formula with an absolute cell reference. To identify an absolute cell reference, insert a $ symbol before the row and the column. For example, the absolute cell reference C12 would be typed as $C$12 in a formula.

Project ⑤a Inserting and Copying a Formula with an Absolute Cell Reference

1. Open **ExcelC02Project05.xlsx**.
2. Save the workbook with Save As and name it **ExcelL1_C2_P5**.
3. Determine the effect on actual job earnings with a 20% increase by completing the following steps:
   a. Make cell C3 active, type the formula =B3*$B$12, and then press Enter.
   b. Make cell C3 active and then use the fill handle to copy the formula to cells C4 through C10.
4. Save and then print **ExcelL1_C2_P5.xlsx**.

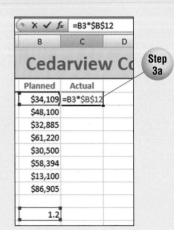

5. With the worksheet still open, determine the effect on actual job earnings with a 10% decrease by completing the following steps:
   a. Make cell B12 active.
   b. Type 0.9 and then press Enter.
6. Save and then print the **ExcelL1_C2_P5.xlsx**.
7. Determine the effects on actual job earnings with a 10% increase. (To do this, type 1.1 in cell B12.)
8. Save and then print **ExcelL1_C2_P5.xlsx**.

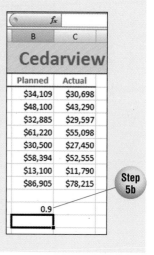

Step 5b

In Project 5a, you created a formula with one absolute cell reference. You can also create a formula with multiple absolute cell references. For example, in Project 5b you will create a formula that contains both relative and absolute cell references to determine the average of training scores based on specific weight percentages.

Project 5b Inserting and Copying a Formula with Multiple Absolute Cell References

1. With **ExcelL1_C2_P5.xlsx** open, insert the following formulas:
   a. Insert a formula in cell B23 that averages the percentages in cells B17 through B22.
   b. Copy the formula in cell B23 to the right to cells C23 and D23.
2. Insert a formula that determines the weighted average of training scores by completing the following steps:
   a. Make cell E17 active.
   b. Type the following formula:
      =$B$24*B17+$C$24*C17+$D$24*D17
   c. Press the Enter key.
   d. Copy the formula in cell E17 down to cells E18 through E22.
3. Save and then print the **ExcelL1_C2_P5.xlsx**.
4. With the worksheet still open, determine the effect on weighted training scores if the weighted values change by completing the following steps:
   a. Make cell B24 active, type 30, and then press Enter.
   b. Make cell D24 active, type 40, and then press Enter.
5. Save and then print **ExcelL1_C2_P5.xlsx**.

15		Employee Training			
16	Name	Plumbing	Electrical	Carpentry	Weighted Average
17	Allesandro	76%	80%	84%	89%
18	Ellington	66%	72%	64%	73%
19	Goodman	90%	88%	94%	100%
20	Huntington	76%	82%	88%	91%
21	Kaplan-Downing	90%	84%	92%	98%
22	Larimore	58%	62%	60%	66%
23	Training Averages	76%	78%	80%	
24	Training Weights	30%	30%	50%	
25					

Step 4a

Using a Mixed Cell Reference in a Formula

The formula you created in Step 3a in Project 5a contained a relative cell reference (B3) and an absolute cell reference ($B$12). A formula can also contain a mixed cell reference. In a mixed cell reference either the column remains absolute and the row is relative or the column is relative and the row is absolute. In Project 5c you will insert a number of formulas, two of which will contain mixed cell references. You will insert the formula *=E29*E$26* to calculate withholding tax and *=E29*H$36* to calculate Social Security tax. The dollar sign before the rows indicates that the row is an absolute cell reference.

Project **5c** | **Determining Payroll Using Formulas with Absolute and Mixed Cell References**

1. With **ExcelL1_C2_P5.xlsx** open, make cell E29 active and then insert the following formula containing mixed cell references:
   =(B29*C29+(B29*$B$36*D29))
2. Copy the formula in cell E29 down to cells E30 through E34.
3. Make cell F29 active and then insert the following formula that calculates the amount of withholding tax:
   =E29*E$36
4. Copy the formula in cell F29 down to cells F30 through F34.
5. Make cell G29 active and then insert the following formula that calculates the amount of Social Security tax:
   =E29*H$36
6. Copy the formula in cell G29 down to cells G30 through G34.
7. Make cell H29 active and then insert the following formula that calculates net pay:
   =E29-(F29+G29)
8. Copy the formula in cell H29 down to cells H30 through H34.
9. Save **ExcelL1_C2_P5.xlsx**.

As you learned in Project 5c, a formula can contain a mixed cell reference. In a mixed cell reference either the column remains absolute and the row is relative or the column is relative and the row is absolute. In Project 5d, you will create the formula *=$A41*B$40*. In the first cell reference in the formula, *$A41*, the column is absolute and the row is relative. In the second cell reference, *B$40*, the column is relative and the row is absolute. The formula containing the mixed cell references allows you to fill in the column and row data using only one formula.

Identify an absolute or mixed cell reference by typing a dollar sign before the column and/or row reference or press the F4 function key to cycle through the various cell references. For example, type *=A41* in a cell, press F4, and the cell reference changes to *=$A$41*. Press F4 again and the cell reference changes to *=A$41*. The next time you press F4, the cell reference changes to *=$A41* and press it again to change the cell reference back to *=A41*.

Project 5b   **Determining Simple Interest Using a Formula with Mixed Cell References**

1. With **ExcelL1_C2_P5.xlsx** open, make cell B41 the active cell and then insert a formula containing mixed cell references by completing the following steps:
   a. Type =A41 and then press the F4 function key three times. (This changes the cell reference to $A41.)
   b. Type *B40 and then press the F4 function key twice. (This changes the cell reference to B$40.)
   c. Make sure the formula displays as =$A41*B$40 and then press Enter.

39		SIMPLE INTEREST LOAN TABLE					
40		$ 1,000	$ 2,000	$ 3,000	$ 4,000	$ 5,000	
41	5%	=$A41*B$40					
42	6%						
43	7%						

Step 1c

2. Copy the formula to the right by completing the following steps:
   a. Make cell B41 active and then use the fill handle to copy the formula right to cell F41.

39		SIMPLE INTEREST LOAN TABLE					
40		$ 1,000	$ 2,000	$ 3,000	$ 4,000	$ 5,000	
41	5%	$ 50	$ 100	$ 150	$ 200	$ 250	
42	6%						
43	7%						

Step 2a

   b. With cells B41 through F41 selected, use the fill handle to copy the formula down to cell F51.

39		SIMPLE INTEREST LOAN TABLE					
40		$ 1,000	$ 2,000	$ 3,000	$ 4,000	$ 5,000	
41	5%	$ 50	$ 100	$ 150	$ 200	$ 250	
42	6%	$ 60	$ 120	$ 180	$ 240	$ 300	
43	7%	$ 70	$ 140	$ 210	$ 280	$ 350	
44	8%	$ 80	$ 160	$ 240	$ 320	$ 400	
45	9%	$ 90	$ 180	$ 270	$ 360	$ 450	
46	10%	$ 100	$ 200	$ 300	$ 400	$ 500	
47	11%	$ 110	$ 220	$ 330	$ 440	$ 550	
48	12%	$ 120	$ 240	$ 360	$ 480	$ 600	
49	13%	$ 130	$ 260	$ 390	$ 520	$ 650	
50	14%	$ 140	$ 280	$ 420	$ 560	$ 700	
51	15%	$ 150	$ 300	$ 450	$ 600	$ 750	
52							

Step 2b

3. Save, print, and then close **ExcelL1_C2_P5.xlsx**. (This worksheet will print on two pages.)

CHAPTER summary

- Type a formula in a cell and the formula displays in the cell as well as in the Formula bar. If cell entries are changed, a formula will automatically recalculate the values and insert the result in the cell.

- Create your own formula with commonly used operators such as addition (+), subtraction (-), multiplication (*), division (/), percent (%), and exponentiation (^). When writing a formula, begin with the equals (=) sign.

- Copy a formula to other cells in a row or column with the Fill button in the Editing group in the Home tab or with the fill handle that displays in the bottom right corner of the active cell.

- Another method for writing a formula is to point to specific cells that are part of the formula.

- If Excel detects an error in a formula, a Trace Error button appears and a dark green triangle displays in the upper left corner of the cell containing the formula.

- Excel includes over 200 functions that are divided into eleven categories. Use the Insert Function feature to create formulas using built-in functions.

- A function operates on an argument, which may consist of a cell reference, a constant, or another function. When a value calculated by a formula is inserted in a cell, this is referred to as returning the result.

- The AVERAGE function returns the average (arithmetic mean) of the arguments. The MAX function returns the largest value in a set of values, and the MIN function returns the smallest value in a set of values. The COUNT function counts the number of cells containing numbers within the list of arguments.

- Use the keyboard shortcut, Ctrl + ` (grave accent) to turn on the display of formulas in a worksheet.

- The PMT function calculates the payment for a loan based on constant payments and a constant interest rate. The FV function returns the future value of an investment based on periodic, constant payments and a constant interest rate.

- The NOW function returns the serial number of the current date and time and the DATE function returns the serial number that represents a particular date.

- Use the IF function, considered a conditional function, to perform conditional tests on values and formulas.

- Use nested IF functions in a formula where more than two actions are required.

- A reference identifies a cell or a range of cells in a worksheet and can be relative, absolute, or mixed. Identify an absolute cell reference by inserting a $ symbol before the column and row. Cycle through the various cell reference options by typing the cell reference and then pressing F4.

COMMANDS review

FEATURE	RIBBON TAB, GROUP	BUTTON	KEYBOARD SHORTCUT
SUM function	Home, Editing OR Formulas, Function Library	Σ AutoSum ▾	Alt + =
Insert Function dialog box	Formulas, Function Library	*fx*	Shift + F3
Display formulas			Ctrl + `

CONCEPTS check

Test Your Knowledge

Completion: In the space provided at the right, indicate the correct term, symbol, or command.

1. When typing a formula, begin the formula with this sign.

2. This is the operator for division that is used when writing a formula.

3. This is the operator for multiplication that is used when writing a formula.

4. This is the name of the small black box located at the bottom right corner of a cell that can be used to copy a formula to adjacent cells.

5. A function operates on this, which may consist of a constant, a cell reference, or other function.

6. This function returns the largest value in a set of values.

7. This is the keyboard shortcut to display formulas in a worksheet.

8. This function finds the periodic payment for a loan based on constant payments and a constant interest rate.

9. This function returns the serial number of the current date and time.

10. This function is considered a conditional function.

11. To identify an absolute cell reference, type this symbol before the column and row. _____

12. Suppose that cell B2 contains the budgeted amount and cell C2 contains the actual amount. Write the formula (including the IF conditions) that would insert the word *under* if the actual amount was less than the budgeted amount and insert the word *over* if the actual amount was greater than the budgeted amount. _____

SKILLS check
Demonstrate Your Proficiency

Assessment

1 INSERT AVERAGE, MAX, AND MIN FUNCTIONS

1. Open **ExcelC02Assessment01.xlsx**.
2. Save the workbook with Save As and name it **ExcelL1_C2_A1**.
3. Use the AVERAGE function to determine the monthly sales (cells H4 through H9).
4. Total each monthly column including the Average column (cells B10 through H10).
5. Use the MAX function to determine the highest monthly total (for cells B4 through G9) and insert the amount in cell B11.
6. Use the MIN function to determine the lowest monthly total (for cells B4 through G9) and insert the amount in cell B12.
7. Save, print, and then close **ExcelL1_C2_A1.xlsx**.

Assessment

2 INSERT PMT FUNCTION

1. Open **ExcelC02Assessment02.xlsx**.
2. Save the workbook with Save As and name it **ExcelL1_C2_A2**.
3. The manager of Clearline Manufacturing is interested in refinancing a loan for either $125,000 or $300,000 and wants to determine the monthly payments, total payments, and total interest paid. Insert a formula with the following specifications:
   a. Make cell E5 active.
   b. Use the Insert Function button on the Formula bar to insert a formula using the PMT function. At the formula palette, enter the following:
      Rate = C5/12
      Nper = D5
      Pv = -B5
   c. Copy the formula in cell E5 down to cells E6 through E8.
4. Insert a formula in cell F5 that multiplies the amount in E5 by the amount in D5.

5. Copy the formula in cell F5 down to cells F6 through F8.
6. Insert a formula in cell G5 that subtracts the amount in B5 from the amount in F5. (The formula is *=F5-B5*.)
7. Copy the formula in cell G5 down to cells G6 through G8.
8. Save, print, and then close **ExcelL1_C2_A2.xlsx**.

Assessment

3 INSERT FV FUNCTION

1. Open **ExcelC02Assessment03.xlsx**.
2. Save the workbook with Save As and name it **ExcelL1_C2_A3**.
3. Make the following changes to the worksheet:
   a. Change the percentage in cell B3 from *9%* to *10%*.
   b. Change the number in cell B4 from *36* to *60*.
   c. Change the amount in cell B5 from *($1,200) to -500*.
   d. Use the FV function to insert a formula that calculates the future value of the investment. **Hint: For help with the formula, refer to Project 3b.**
4. Save, print, and then close **ExcelL1_C2_A3.xlsx**.

Assessment

4 WRITE IF STATEMENT FORMULAS

1. Open **ExcelC02Assessment04.xlsx**.
2. Save the workbook with Save As and name it **ExcelL1_C2_A4**.
3. Insert a formula in cell C4 that contains an IF statement with the following details:

   If the contents of cell B4 are greater than 150000, then insert the word Platinum.
   If the contents of cell B4 are greater than 100000, then insert the word Gold.
   If the contents of cell B4 are greater than 75000, then insert the word Silver.
   If the contents of cell B4 are greater than 0 (zero), then insert the word Bronze.

   When writing the IF statement, make sure you insert quotes around the words *Platinum*, *Gold*, *Silver*, and *Bronze*. Copy the formula in cell C4 down to cell C14.
4. Insert a formula in cell D4 that contains in IF statement with the following details:

   If the content of cell C4 is Bronze, then insert the word None.
   If the content of cell C4 is Silver, then insert $3,000.
   If the content of cell C4 is Gold, then insert $5,000.
   If the content of cell C4 is Platinum, then insert $10,000.

   When writing the IF statement, you will need to insert quotes around the words *Platinum*, *Gold*, *Silver*, *Bronze*, and *None* as well as the amounts *$3,000*, *$5,000*, and *$10,000*. Copy the formula in cell D4 down to cell D14.
5. Save and then print **ExcelL1_C2_A4.xlsx**.

6. Display the formulas in the worksheet.
7. Print **ExcelL1_C2_A4.xlsx**.
8. Turn off the display of the formulas.
9. Save and then close **ExcelL1_C2_A4.xlsx**.

Assessment

5 WRITE FORMULAS WITH ABSOLUTE CELL REFERENCES

1. Open **ExcelC02Assessment05.xlsx**.
2. Save the workbook with Save As and name it **ExcelL1_C2_A5**.
3. Make the following changes to the worksheet:
   a. Insert a formula using an absolute reference to determine the projected quotas at 10% of the current quotas.
   b. Save and then print **ExcelL1_C2_A5.xlsx**.
   c. Determine the projected quotas at 15% of the current quota by changing cell A15 to *15% Increase* and cell B15 to *1.15*.
   d. Save and then print **ExcelL1_C2_A5.xlsx**.
   e. Determine the projected quotas at 20% of the current quota.
4. Save, print, and then close **ExcelL1_C2_A5.xlsx**.

Assessment

6 USE HELP TO LEARN ABOUT EXCEL OPTIONS

1. Learn about specific options in the Excel Options dialog box by completing the following steps:
   a. Display the Excel Options dialog box by clicking the Office button and then clicking the Excel Options button that displays in the lower right corner of the drop-down list.
   b. At the Excel Options dialog box, click the *Advanced* option located in the left panel.
   c. Click the Help button that displays in the upper right corner of the dialog box, read the information that displays about advanced features, and then close the Excel Help window.
   d. Write down the check box options available in the *Display options for this workbook* section and the *Display options for this worksheet* section of the dialog box and identify whether or not the check box contains a check mark. (Record only check box options and ignore buttons and options preceded by circles.)
2. With the information you wrote down about the options, create an Excel spreadsheet with the following information:
   a. In column C, type each option you wrote down. (Include an appropriate heading.)
   b. In column B, insert an X in the cell that precedes any option that contains a check mark in the check box. (Include an appropriate heading.)
   c. In column A, write a formula with the IF function that inserts the word ON in the cell if the cell in column B contains an X and inserts the word OFF if it does not (the cell is blank). (Include an appropriate heading.)
   d. Apply formatting to improve the visual appeal of the worksheet.

3. Save the workbook and name it **ExcelL1_C2_A6**.
4. Turn on the display of formulas.
5. Print the worksheet.
6. Turn off the display of formulas.
7. Save, print, and then close **ExcelL1_C2_A6.xlsx**.

CASE study
Apply Your Skills

Part 1

You are a loan officer for Dollar Wise Financial Services and work in the department that specializes in home loans. You have decided to prepare a sample home mortgage worksheet to show prospective clients. This sample home mortgage worksheet will show the monthly payments on variously priced homes with varying interest rates. Open the **DollarWise.xlsx** worksheet and then complete the home mortgage worksheet by inserting the following formulas:

- Since many homes in your area sell for at least $400,000, you decide to add that amount to the worksheet with a 5%, 10%, 15%, and 20% down payment.
- In column C, insert a formula that determines the down payment amount.
- In column D, insert a formula that determines the loan amount.
- In column G, insert a formula using the PMT function (the monthly payment will display as a negative number).

Save the worksheet and name it **ExcelL1_C2_CS_P1**.

Part 2

If home buyers put down less than twenty percent of the home's purchase price, mortgage insurance is required. With **ExcelL1_C2_C1.xlsx** open, insert an IF statement in the cells in column H that inserts the word "No" if the percentage in column B is equal to or greater than 20% or inserts the word "Yes" if the percentage in column B is less than 20%. Save and then print **ExcelL1_C2_CS_P1.xlsx**.

Part 3

Interest rates fluctuate on a regular basis. Using the resources available to you, determine a current interest rate in your area. Delete the interest rate of 7% in the Dollar Wise worksheet and insert the interest rate for your area. Save and then print **ExcelL1_C2_CS_P1.xlsx**.

Part

4

When a client is required to purchase mortgage insurance, you would like to provide information to the client concerning this insurance. Use the Help feature to learn about creating hyperlinks in Excel. Locate a helpful Web site that specializes in private mortgage insurance. Create a hyperlink in the worksheet that will display the Web site. Save, print, and then close **ExcelL1_C2_CS_P1.xlsx**.

Part

5

Once a loan has been approved and finalized, a letter is sent to the client explaining the details of the loan. Use a letter template in Word to create a letter that is sent to the client. Copy and link the information in the **ExcelL1_C2_CS_P1.xlsx** worksheet to the client letter. Save the letter document and name it **WordDollarWiseLetter**. Print and then close **WordDollarWiseLetter.docx**.

Formatting an Excel Worksheet

PERFORMANCE OBJECTIVES

Upon successful completion of Chapter 3, you will be able to:

- Change column widths
- Change row heights
- Insert rows and columns in a worksheet
- Delete cells, rows, and columns in a worksheet
- Clear data in cells
- Apply formatting to data in cells
- Apply formatting to selected data using the Mini toolbar
- Preview a worksheet
- Apply a theme and customize the theme font and color
- Format numbers
- Repeat the last action
- Automate formatting with Format Painter
- Hide and unhide rows and columns

Tutorial 3.1
Working with Excel
Tutorial 3.2
Enhancing the Appearance of a
Worksheet

The appearance of a worksheet on the screen and how it looks when printed is called the *format*. In Chapter 1, you learned how to apply formatting to a table with the Format as Table button in the Styles group in the Home tab and apply formatting to a cell or selected cells with the Cell Styles button. Other types of formatting you may want to apply to a worksheet include changing column width and row height; applying character formatting such as bold, italics, and underlining; specifying number formatting; inserting and deleting rows and columns; and applying borders, shading, and patterns to cells. You can also apply formatting to a worksheet with a theme. A theme is a set of formatting choices that include colors and fonts.

Note: Before beginning computer projects, copy to your storage medium the Excel2007L1C3 subfolder from the Excel2007L1 folder on the CD that accompanies this textbook and then make Excel2007L1C3 the active folder.

Project ① Format a Product Pricing Worksheet

You will open a workbook containing a worksheet with product pricing data, and then format the worksheet by changing column widths and row heights, inserting and deleting rows and columns, deleting rows and columns, and clearing data in cells. You will also apply font and alignment formatting to data in cells and then preview the worksheet.

Changing Column Width

Columns in a worksheet are the same width by default. In some worksheets you may want to change column widths to accommodate more or less data. You can change column width using the mouse on column boundaries or at a dialog box.

Changing Column Width Using Column Boundaries

You can use the mouse to change the width of a column or selected columns. For example, to change the width of column B, you would position the mouse pointer on the blue boundary line between columns B and C in the column header until the mouse pointer turns into a double-headed arrow pointing left and right and then drag the boundary to the right to increase the size or to the left to decrease the size.

You can change the width of selected adjacent columns at the same time. To do this, select the columns and then drag one of the column boundaries within the selected columns. As you drag the boundary the column width changes for all selected columns. To select adjacent columns, position the cell pointer on the first desired column header (the mouse pointer turns into a black, down-pointing arrow), hold down the left mouse button, drag the cell pointer to the last desired column header, and then release the mouse button.

As a column boundary is being dragged, the column width displays in a box above the mouse pointer. The column width number that displays represents the average number of characters in the standard font that can fit in a cell.

A column width in an existing worksheet can be adjusted to fit the longest entry in the column. To automatically adjust a column width to the longest entry, position the cell pointer on the column boundary at the right side of the column and then double-click the left mouse button.

> **HINT**
>
> To change the width of all columns in a worksheet, click the Select All button and then drag a column boundary to the desired position.

Project ⓐ Changing Column Width Using a Column Boundary

1. Open **ExcelC03Project01.xlsx**.
2. Save the workbook with Save As and name it **ExcelL1_C3_P1**.
3. Insert a formula in cell D2 that multiplies the price in cell B2 with the number in cell C2. Copy the formula in cell D2 down to cells D3 through D14.

4. Change the width of column D by completing the following steps:
   a. Position the mouse pointer on the column boundary in the column header between columns D and E until it turns into a double-headed arrow pointing left and right.
   b. Hold down the left mouse button, drag the column boundary to the right until *Width: 11.00 (82 pixels)* displays in the box, and then release the mouse button.

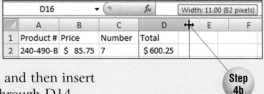

5. Make cell D15 active and then insert the sum of cells D2 through D14.

Step 4b

6. Change the width of columns A and B by completing the following steps:
   a. Select columns A and B. To do this, position the cell pointer on the column A header, hold down the left mouse button, drag the cell pointer to the column B header, and then release the mouse button.
   b. Position the cell pointer on the column boundary between columns A and B until it turns into a double-headed arrow pointing left and right.
   c. Hold down the left mouse button, drag the column boundary to the right until *Width: 10.14 (76 pixels)* displays in the box, and then release the mouse button.

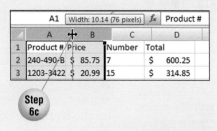

Step 6c

7. Adjust the width of column C to accommodate the longest entry in the column by completing the following steps:
   a. Position the cell pointer on the column boundary between columns C and D until it turns into a double-headed arrow pointing left and right.
   b. Double-click the left mouse button.
8. Save **ExcelL1_C3_P1.xlsx**.

Changing Column Width at the Column Width Dialog Box

At the Column Width dialog box shown in Figure 3.1, you can specify a column width number. Increase the column width number to make the column wider or decrease the column width number to make the column narrower.

To display the Column Width dialog box, click the Format button in the Cells group in the Home tab and then click *Column Width* at the drop-down list. At the Column Width dialog box, type the number representing the average number of characters in the standard font that you want to fit in the column, and then press Enter or click OK.

Figure 3.1 Column Width Dialog Box

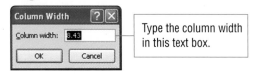

Type the column width in this text box.

Format

Project 1b | Changing Column Width at the Column Width Dialog Box

1. With **ExcelL1_C3_P1.xlsx** open, change the width of column A by completing the following steps:
   a. Make any cell in column A active.
   b. Click the Format button in the Cells group in the Home tab and then click *Column Width* at the drop-down list.
   c. At the Column Width dialog box, type *12.75* in the *Column width* text box.
   d. Click OK to close the dialog box.
2. Make any cell in column B active and then change the width of column B to *12.75* by completing steps similar to those in Step 1.
3. Make any cell in column C active and then change the width of column C to *8* by completing steps similar to those in Step 1.
4. Save **ExcelL1_C3_P1.xlsx**.

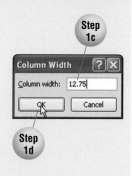

Step 1c

Step 1d

QUICK STEPS

Change Row Height
Drag row boundary line.
OR
1. Click Format button.
2. Click *Row Height* at drop-down list.
3. Type desired height.
4. Click OK.

Changing Row Height

Row height can be changed in much the same manner as column width. For example, you can change the row height using the mouse on a row boundary, or at the Row Height dialog box. Change row height using a row boundary in the same manner as you learned to change column width. To do this, position the cell pointer on the boundary between rows in the row header until it turns into a double-headed arrow pointing up and down, hold down the left mouse button, drag up or down until the row is the desired height, and then release the mouse button.

The height of selected rows that are adjacent can be changed at the same time. (The height of nonadjacent rows will not all change at the same time.) To do this, select the rows and then drag one of the row boundaries within the selected rows. As the boundary is being dragged the row height changes for all selected rows.

As a row boundary is being dragged, the row height displays in a box above the mouse pointer. The row height number that displays represents a point measurement. A vertical inch contains approximately 72 points. Increase the point size to increase the row height; decrease the point size to decrease the row height.

At the Row Height dialog box shown in Figure 3.2, you can specify a row height number. To display the Row Height dialog box, click the Format button in the Cells group in the Home tab and then click *Row Height* at the drop-down list.

HINT

To change the height of all rows in a worksheet, click the Select All button and then drag a row boundary to the desired position.

Figure 3.2 Row Height Dialog Box

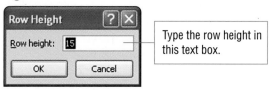

Type the row height in this text box.

Project 1c — Changing Row Height

1. With **ExcelL1_C3_P1.xlsx** open, change the height of row 1 by completing the following steps:
   a. Position the cell pointer in the row header on the row boundary between rows 1 and 2 until it turns into a double-headed arrow pointing up and down.
   b. Hold down the left mouse button, drag the row boundary down until *Height: 19.50 (26 pixels)* displays in the box, and then release the mouse button.
2. Change the height of rows 2 through 14 by completing the following steps:
   a. Select rows 2 through 14. To do this, position the cell pointer on the number 2 in the row header, hold down the left mouse button, drag the cell pointer to the number 14 in the row header, and then release the mouse button.
   b. Position the cell pointer on the row boundary between rows 2 and 3 until it turns into a double-headed arrow pointing up and down.
   c. Hold down the left mouse button, drag the row boundary down until *Height: 16.50 (22 pixels)* displays in the box, and then release the mouse button.
3. Change the height of row 15 by completing the following steps:
   a. Make cell A15 active.
   b. Click the Format button in the Cells group in the Home tab and then click *Row Height* at the drop-down list.
   c. At the Row Height dialog box, type 20 in the *Row height* text box, and then click OK.
4. Save **ExcelL1_C3_P1.xlsx**.

Step 1b

	B	C
Height: 19.50 (26 pixels)		
Product #	Price	Numb
240-490-B	$ 85.75	7
1203-3422	$ 20.99	15
443-22-0	$ 148.50	8

Step 2c

A2		
	A	B
Height: 16.50 (22 pixels)		
240-490-B	$	85.75
1203-3422	$	20.99
443-22-0	$	148.50
A-4302-5	$	1,540.00
43-GB-39	$	45.00
341-453	$	19.99
CT-342	$	304.75
83-492	$	9.75
L-756-M	$	95.40
340-19	$	15.99
T-3491-S	$	450.50
900-599	$	35.95
43-49CE	$	120.00
Total		

Row Height

Row height: 20

OK   Cancel

Step 3c

Inserting/Deleting Cells, Rows, and Columns

New data may need to be included in an existing worksheet. For example, a row or several rows of new data may need to be inserted into a worksheet, or data may need to be removed from a worksheet.

Inserting Rows

After you create a worksheet, you can add (insert) rows to the worksheet. Insert a row with the Insert button in the Cells group in the Home tab or with options at the Insert dialog box. By default, a row is inserted above the row containing the active cell. To insert a row in a worksheet, select the row below where the row is to be inserted, and then click the Insert button. If you want to insert more than one row, select the number of rows in the worksheet that you want inserted and then click the Insert button.

HINT
When you insert rows in a worksheet, all references affected by the insertion are automatically adjusted.

Insert

You can also insert a row by making a cell active in the row below where the row is to be inserted, clicking the Insert button arrow, and then clicking *Insert Sheet Rows*. Another method for inserting a row is to click the Insert button arrow and then click *Insert Cells*. This displays the Insert dialog box as shown in Figure 3.3. At the Insert dialog box, click *Entire row*. This inserts a row above the active cell.

Figure 3.3 Insert Dialog Box

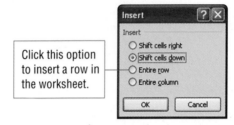

Click this option to insert a row in the worksheet.

Project 1d Inserting Rows

1. With **ExcelL1_C3_P1.xlsx** open, insert two rows at the beginning of the worksheet by completing the following steps:
   a. Make cell A1 active.
   b. Click the Insert button arrow in the Cells group in the Home tab.
   c. At the drop-down list that displays, click *Insert Sheet Rows*.
   d. With cell A1 active, click the Insert button arrow and then click *Insert Sheet Rows* at the drop-down list.

   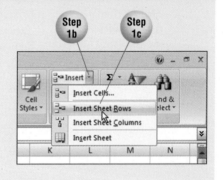

   Step 1b   Step 1c

2. Type the text **Capstan Marine Products** in cell A1.
3. Make cell A2 active and then type **Purchasing Department**.
4. Change the height of row 1 to *42.00 (56 pixels)*.
5. Change the height of row 2 to *21.00 (28 pixels)*.
6. Insert two rows by completing the following steps:
   a. Select rows 7 and 8 in the worksheet.
   b. Click the Insert button in the Cells group in the Home tab.

   Step 6b

7. Type the following data in the specified cells (you do not need to type the dollar sign in cells containing money amounts):

A7	=	855-495
B7	=	42.75
C7	=	5
A8	=	ST039
B8	=	12.99
C8	=	25

8. Make D6 the active cell and then use the fill handle to copy the formula down to cells D7 and D8.
9. Save **ExcelL1_C3_P1.xlsx**.

Inserting Columns

Insert columns in a worksheet in much the same way as rows. Insert a column with options from the Insert button drop-down list or with options at the Insert dialog box. By default, a column is inserted immediately to the left of the column containing the active cell. To insert a column in a worksheet, make a cell active in the column immediately to the right of where the new column is to be inserted, click the Insert button arrow and then click *Insert Sheet Columns* at the drop-down list. If you want to insert more than one column, select the number of columns in the worksheet that you want inserted, click the Insert button arrow and then click *Insert Sheet Columns*.

You can also insert a column by making a cell active in the column immediately to the right of where the new column is to be inserted, clicking the Insert button arrow, and then clicking *Insert Cells* at the drop-down list. This causes the Insert dialog box to display. At the Insert dialog box, click *Entire column*. This inserts an entire column immediately to the left of the active cell.

Excel includes an especially helpful and time-saving feature related to inserting columns. When you insert columns in a worksheet, all references affected by the insertion are automatically adjusted.

QUICK STEPS

Insert Column
Click Insert button.
OR
1. Click Insert button arrow.
2. Click *Insert Sheet Columns* at drop-down list.
OR
1. Click Insert button arrow.
2. Click *Insert Cells*.
3. Click *Entire column*.
4. Click OK.

Project 1e   Inserting a Column

1. With **ExcelL1_C3_P1.xlsx** open, insert a column by completing the following steps:
   a. Click in any cell in column A.
   b. Click the Insert button arrow in the Cells group in the Home tab and then click *Insert Sheet Columns* at the drop-down list.
2. Type the following data in the specified cell:

A3	=	Company
A4	=	RD Manufacturing
A8	=	Smithco, Inc.
A11	=	Sunrise Corporation
A15	=	Geneva Systems

3. Make cell A1 active and then adjust the width of column A to accommodate the longest entry.
4. Insert another column by completing the following steps:
   a. Make cell B1 active.
   b. Click the Insert button arrow and then click *Insert Cells* at the drop-down list.
   c. At the Insert dialog box, click *Entire column*.
   d. Click OK.
5. Type Date in cell B3 and then press Enter.
6. Save **ExcelL1_C3_P1.xlsx**.

Deleting Cells, Rows, or Columns

You can delete specific cells in a worksheet or rows or columns in a worksheet. To delete a row, select the row and then click the Delete button in the Cells group in the Home tab. To delete a column, select the column and then click the Delete button. Delete a specific cell by making the cell active, clicking the Delete button arrow, and then clicking *Delete Cells* at the drop-down list. This displays the Delete dialog box shown in Figure 3.4. At the Delete dialog box, specify what you want deleted, and then click OK. You can also delete adjacent cells by selecting the cells and then displaying the Delete Cells dialog box.

Figure 3.4 Delete Dialog Box

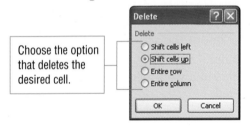

Choose the option that deletes the desired cell.

Clearing Data in Cells

If you want to delete cell contents but not the cell, make the cell active or select desired cells and then press the Delete key. A quick method for clearing the contents of a cell is to right-click the cell and then click *Clear Contents* at the shortcut menu. Another method for deleting cell contents is to make the cell active or select desired cells, click the Clear button in the Editing group in the Home tab, and then click *Clear Contents* at the drop-down list.

With the options at the Clear button drop-down list you can clear the contents of the cell or selected cells as well as formatting and comments. Click the *Clear Formats* option to remove formatting from cells or selected cells while leaving the data. You can also click the *Clear All* option to clear the contents of the cell or selected cells as well as the formatting.

Project 1j   Deleting and Clearing Rows in a Worksheet

1. With **ExcelL1_C3_P1.xlsx** open, delete column B in the worksheet by completing the following steps:
   a. Click in any cell in column B.
   b. Click the Delete button arrow in the Cells group in the Home tab and then click *Delete Sheet Columns* at the drop-down list.
2. Delete row 5 by completing the following steps:
   a. Select row 5.
   b. Click the Delete button in the Cells group.

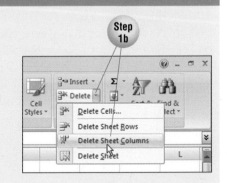

Step 1b

3. Clear row contents by completing the following steps:
   a. Select rows 7 and 8.
   b. Click the Clear button in the Editing group in the Home tab and then click *Clear Contents* at the drop-down list.
4. Type the following data in the specified cell:

A7	=	Ray Enterprises
B7	=	S894-T
C7	=	4.99
D7	=	30
B8	=	B-3448
C8	=	25.50
D8	=	12

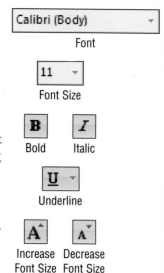

Step 3b

Step 4

6		855-495	$	42.75	5	$	213.75
7	Ray Enterprises	S894-T	$	4.99	30		
8		B-3448	$	25.50	12		
9		43-GB-39	$	45.00	20	$	900.00

5. Make cell E6 active and then copy the formula down to cells E7 and E8.
6. Save **ExcelL1_C3_P1.xlsx**.

Applying Formatting

With many of the groups in the Home tab you can apply formatting to text in the active cells or selected cells. Use buttons in the Font group to apply font formatting to text and use buttons in the Alignment group to apply alignment formatting to text.

Applying Font Formatting

You can apply a variety of formatting to cells in a worksheet with buttons in the Font group in the Home tab. With buttons in the Font group shown in Figure 3.5, you can change the font, font size, and font color; bold, italicize, and underline data in cells; change the text color; and apply a border or add fill to cells.

Figure 3.5 Font Group

Use buttons in the font group to apply formatting to cells or data in cells.

Calibri (Body) — Font

11 — Font Size

B Bold   *I* Italic

U Underline

A▲ Increase Font Size   A▼ Decrease Font Size

Use the Font button in the Font group to change the font of text in a cell and use the Font Size button to specify size for the text. Apply bold formatting to text in a cell with the Bold button, italic formatting with the Italic button, and underlining with the Underline button.

Click the Increase Font Size button and the text in the active cell or selected cells increases from 11 points to 12 points. Click the Increase Font Size button again and the font size increases to 14. Each additional time you click the button, the font size increases by two points. Click the Decrease Font Size button and text in the active cell or selected cells decreases in point size.

Border

Fill Color

Font Color

With the Borders button in the Font group, you can insert a border on any or all sides of the active cell or any or all sides of selected cells. The name of the button changes depending on the most recent border applied to a cell or selected cells. Use the Fill Color button to insert color in the active cell or in selected cells. With the Font Color button, you can change the color of text within a cell.

Formatting with the Mini Toolbar

Double-click in a cell and then select data within the cell and the Mini toolbar displays in a dimmed fashion above the selected data. Hover the mouse pointer over the Mini toolbar and it becomes active. The Mini toolbar contains buttons for applying font formatting such as font, font size, and font color as well as bold and italic formatting. Click a button on the Mini toolbar to apply formatting to selected text.

Applying Alignment Formatting

Merge & Center

Orientation

Wrap Text

The alignment of data in cells depends on the type of data entered. Enter words or text combined with numbers in a cell and the text is aligned at the left edge of the cell. Enter numbers in a cell and the numbers are aligned at the right side of the cell. Use options in the Alignment group to align text at the left, center, or right side of the cell; align text at the top, center, or bottom of the cell; increase and/or decrease the indent of text; and change the orientation of text in a cell. Click the Merge & Center button to merge selected cells and center data within the merged cells. If you have merged cells and want to split them again, select the cells and then click the Merge & Center button.

Click the Orientation button to rotate data in a cell. Click the Orientation button and a drop-down list displays with options for rotating text in a cell. If data typed in a cell is longer than the cell, it overlaps the next cell to the right. If you want data to remain in a cell and wrap to the next line within the same cell, click the Wrap Text button in the Alignment group.

Project ⑩   **Applying Font and Alignment Formatting**

1. With **ExcelL1_C3_P1.xlsx** open, make cell B1 active and then click the Wrap Text button in the Alignment group in the Home tab. (This wraps the company name within the cell.)
2. Make cell B2 active and then click the Wrap Text button.
3. Instead of wrapping text within cells, you decide to spread out the text over several cells and vertically align text in cells by completing the following steps:
   a. Select cells A1 through E1.
   b. Click the Merge & Center button in the Alignment group in the Home tab.
   c. Click the Middle Align button in the Alignment group.
   d. Select cells A2 through E2, click the Merge & Center button, and then click the Middle Align button.

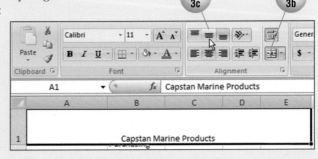

4. Rotate text in the third row by completing the following steps:
   a. Select cells A3 through E3.
   b. Click the Orientation button in the Alignment group and then click *Angle Counterclockwise* at the drop-down list.
   c. After looking at the rotated text, you decide to return the orientation back to the horizontal by clicking the Undo button on the Quick Access toolbar.

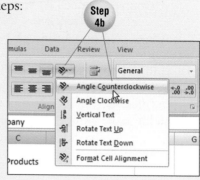

Step 4b

5. Change the font, font size, and font color for text in specific cells by completing the following steps:
   a. Make cell A1 active.
   b. Click the Font button arrow in the Font group in the Home tab, scroll down the drop-down gallery, and then click *Bookman Old Style*.

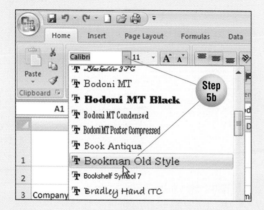

Step 5b

   c. Click the Font Size button arrow in the Font group and then click *22* at the drop-down gallery.
   d. Click the Font Color button arrow and then click *Dark Blue* in the *Standard* section of the drop-down color palette.

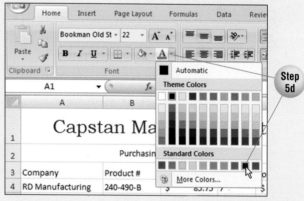

Step 5d

6. Make cell A2 active and then complete steps similar to those in Step 5 to change the font to Bookman Old Style, the font size to 16, and the font color to Dark Blue.
7. Select cells A3 through E3 and then click the Center button in the Alignment group.
8. With cells A3 through E3 still selected, click the Bold button in the Font group and then click the Italic button.
9. Select cells A3 through E18 and then change the font to Bookman Old Style.
10. Apply formatting to selected data using the Mini toolbar by completing the following steps:
    a. Double-click cell A4.
    b. Select the letters *RD*. (This displays the dimmed Mini toolbar above the selected word.)
    c. Click the Increase Font Size button on the Mini toolbar.

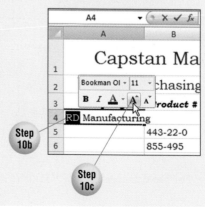

Step 10b

Step 10c

d. Double-click cell A14.

e. Select the word *Geneva* and then click the Italic button on the Mini toolbar.

11. Adjust columns A through E to accommodate the longest entry in each column.

12. Select cells D4 through D17 and then click the Center button in the Alignment group.

13. Add a double-line bottom border to cell A2 by completing the following steps:

a. Make cell A2 active.

b. Click the Borders button arrow in the Font group in the Home tab.

c. Click the *Bottom Double Border* option at the drop-down list.

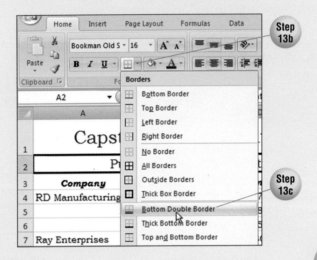

14. Add a single-line bottom border to cells A3 through E3 by completing the following steps:

a. Select cells A3 through E3.

b. Click the Borders button arrow and then click the *Bottom Border* option.

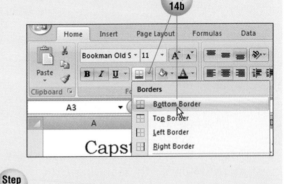

15. Apply fill color to specific cells by completing the following steps:

a. Select cells A1 through E3.

b. Click the Fill Color button arrow in the Font group.

c. Click the *Aqua, Accent 5, Lighter 80%* color option.

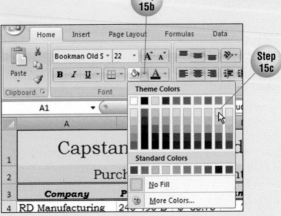

16. Save **ExcelL1_C3_P1.xlsx**.

Previewing a Worksheet

Before printing a worksheet, consider previewing it to see how it will appear when printed. To preview a worksheet, click the Office button, point to the *Print* option, and then click the *Print Preview* option. You can also display a worksheet in Print Preview by clicking the Preview button that displays in the lower left corner of the Print dialog box. A document displays in Print Preview as it will appear when printed. Figure 3.6 displays the **ExcelL1_C3_P1.xlsx** worksheet in Print Preview. Notice that the gridlines in the worksheet do not print.

Figure 3.6 Worksheet in Print Preview

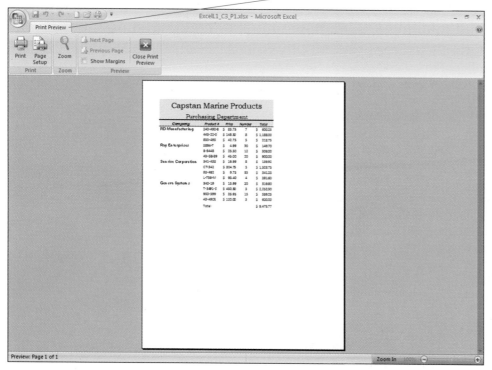

To zoom in on the worksheet, position the mouse pointer (displays as a magnifying glass) in the worksheet text and then click the left mouse button. You can also click the Zoom In option located at the left slide of the Zoom slider bar located at the right side of the Status bar (lower right corner of the Excel window). Click the Print button in the Print Preview tab to send the worksheet to the printer. Click the Page Setup button in the Print Preview tab and the Page Setup dialog box displays with options for changing the paper size and orientation of the page. Insert a check mark in the *Show Margins* check box and margin boundary lines display around the worksheet. Insert a check mark in the *Show Margins* check box and you can change worksheet margins by dragging margin borders. Close Print Preview by clicking the Close Print Preview button.

Preview a Worksheet
1. Click Office button.
2. Point to *Print.*
3. Click *Print Preview.*

Changing the Zoom Setting

Zoom Out Zoom In

In Print Preview, you can zoom in on the worksheet and make the display bigger. You can also change the size of worksheet display in Normal view using the Zoom slider bar that displays at the right side of the Status bar. To change the percentage of display, drag the button on the Zoom slider bar to increase or decrease the percentage of display. You can also click the Zoom Out button located at the left side of the slider bar to decrease the percentage of display or click the Zoom In button located at the right side of the slider bar to increase the percentage of display.

Project **1h** **Previewing a Worksheet**

1. With **ExcelL1_C3_P1.xlsx** open, click the Office button, point to the *Print* option, and then click the *Print Preview* option.
2. At the print preview screen, click in the worksheet. (This increases the display of the worksheet cells.)
3. After viewing the worksheet, click the Close Print Preview button.
4. At the worksheet, drag the button on the Zoom slider bar to the right until the zoom displays as 190%. (The percentage amount displays at the left side of the slider.)

Step 4

5. After viewing the worksheet at 190% display, click the Zoom Out button located at the left side of the slider until the display percentage is 100%.

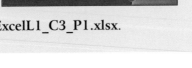

Step 5

6. Save, print, and then close **ExcelL1_C3_P1.xlsx**.

Project **2** **Apply a Theme to a Payroll Worksheet**

You will open a workbook containing a worksheet with payroll information and then insert text, apply formatting to cells and cell contents, apply a theme, and then change the theme font and colors.

Applying a Theme

Excel provides a number of themes you can use to format text and cells in a worksheet. A theme is a set of formatting choices that include a color theme (a set of colors), a font theme (a set of heading and body text fonts), and an effects theme (a set of lines and fill effects). To apply a theme, click the Page Layout tab and then click the Themes button in the Themes group. At the drop-down gallery that displays, click the desired theme. Position the mouse pointer over a theme and the *live preview* feature will display the worksheet with the theme formatting applied. With the live preview feature you can see how the theme formatting affects your worksheet before you make your final choice.

H I N T

Apply a theme to give your worksheet a professional look.

Project ② Applying a Theme

1. Open **ExcelC03Project02.xlsx** and then save it and name it **ExcelL1_C3_P2**.
2. Make G4 the active cell and then insert a formula that calculates the amount of Social Security tax (multiply the gross pay amount in E4 with the Social Security rate in cell H11 [you will need to use the mixed cell reference H$11 when writing the formula]).
3. Copy the formula in cell G4 down to cells G5 through G9.
4. Make H4 the active cell and then insert a formula that calculates the net pay (gross pay minus withholding and Social Security tax).
5. Automatically adjust the width of column H.
6. Copy the formula in H4 down to cells H5 through H9.
7. Increase the height of row 1 to 36.00.
8. Make A1 the active cell, click the Middle Align button in the Alignment group, click the Font Size button arrow and click *18* at the drop-down list, and then click the Bold button.
9. Type Stanton & Barnett Associates in cell A1.
10. Select cells A2 through H3 and then click the Bold button in the Font group.
11. Apply a theme and customize the font and colors by completing the following steps:
    a. Click the Page Layout tab.
    b. Click the Themes button in the Themes group and then click *Aspect* at the drop-down gallery. (You might want to point the mouse to various themes to see how the theme formatting affects the worksheet).

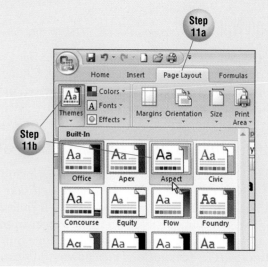

c. Click the Colors button in the Themes group and then click *Flow* at the drop-down gallery.

d. Click the Fonts button in the Themes group, scroll down the drop-down gallery, and then click *Opulent*.

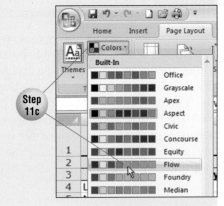

Step 11c

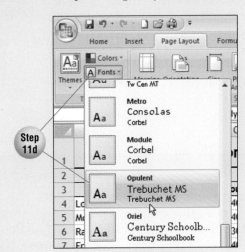

Step 11d

12. Select columns A through H and then adjust the width of the columns to accommodate the longest entries.

13. Save, print, and then close **ExcelL1_C3_P2.xlsx**.

Project ③ Format an Invoices Worksheet

You will open a workbook containing an invoice worksheet and apply number formatting to numbers in cells.

Formatting Numbers

Numbers in a cell, by default, are aligned at the right and decimals and commas do not display unless they are typed in the cell. Change the format of numbers with buttons in the Number group in the Home tab or with options at the Format Cells dialog box with the Number tab selected.

Formatting Numbers Using Number Group Buttons

Format symbols you can use to format numbers include a percent sign (%), a comma (,), and a dollar sign ($). For example, if you type the number *$45.50* in a cell, Excel automatically applies Currency formatting to the number. If you type *45%*, Excel automatically applies the Percent formatting to the number. The Number group in the Home tab contains five buttons you can use to format numbers in cells. The five buttons are shown and described in Table 3.1.

Table 3.1 Number Formatting Buttons on Formatting Toolbar

	Click this button	To do this
$ ▾	Accounting Number Format	Add a dollar sign, any necessary commas, and a decimal point followed by two decimal digits, if none are typed; right-align number in cell
%	Percent Style	Multiply cell value by 100 and display result with a percent symbol; right-align number in cell
,	Comma Style	Add any necessary commas and a decimal point followed by two decimal digits, if none are typed; right-align number in cell
←.0 .00	Increase Decimal	Increase number of decimal places displayed after decimal point in selected cells
.00 →.0	Decrease Decimal	Decrease number of decimal places displayed after decimal point in selected cells

Specify the formatting for numbers in cells in a worksheet before typing the numbers, or format existing numbers in a worksheet. The Increase Decimal and Decrease Decimal buttons in the Number group in the Home tab will change decimal places for existing numbers only.

Increase   Decrease
Decimal   Decimal

The Number group in the Home tab also contains the Number Format button. Click the Number Format button arrow and a drop-down list displays of common number formats. Click the desired format at the drop-down list to apply the number formatting to the cell or selected cells.

General ▾

Number Format

Project 3a   Formatting Numbers with Buttons in the Number Group

1. Open **ExcelC03Project03.xlsx**.
2. Save the workbook with Save As and name it **ExcelL1_C3_P3**.
3. Make the following changes to column widths:
   a. Change the width of column C to 17.00.
   b. Change the width of column D to 10.00.
   c. Change the width of column E to 7.00.
   d. Change the width of column F to 12.00.
4. Select row 1 and then click the Insert button in the Cells group.
5. Change the height of row 1 to 42.00.
6. Select cells A1 through F1 and then make the following changes:
   a. Click the Merge & Center button in the Alignment group.
   b. With cell A1 active, change the font size to 24 points.
   c. Click the Fill Color button arrow in the Font group and then click *Olive Green, Accent 3, Lighter 80%*.

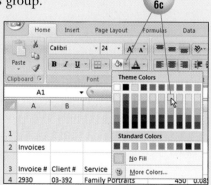

Step 6c

d. Click the Borders button arrow in the Font group and then click the *Top and Thick Bottom Border* option.

e. With cell A1 active, type REAL PHOTOGRAPHY and then press Enter.

7. Change the height of row 2 to 24.00.

8. Select cells A2 through F2 and then make the following changes:

a. Click the Merge & Center button in the Alignment group.

b. With cell A2 active, change the font size to 18.

c. Click the Fill Color button in the Font group. (This will fill the cell with light green color.)

d. Click the Borders button arrow in the Font group and then click the *Bottom Border* option.

9. Make the following changes to row 3:

a. Change the height of row 3 to 18.00.

b. Select cells A3 through F3, click the Bold button in the Font group, and then click the Center button in the Alignment group.

c. With the cells still selected, click the Borders button arrow and then click the *Bottom Border* option.

10. Make the following number formatting changes:

a. Select cells E4 through E16 and then click the *Percent Style* button in the Number group.

b. With the cells still selected, click once on the Increase Decimal button in the Number group. (The percent numbers should contain one decimal place.)

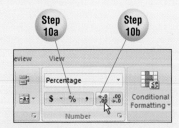

c. Select cells A4 through B16.

d. Click the Number Format button arrow, scroll down the drop-down list, and then click *Text*.

e. With A4 through B16 still selected, click the Center button in the Alignment group.

11. Save **ExcelL1_C3_P3.xlsx**.

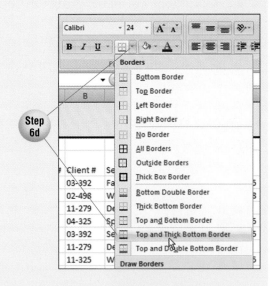

Step 6d

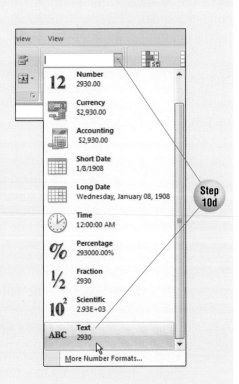

Step 10d

Formatting Numbers Using the Format Cells Dialog Box

Along with buttons in the Number group, you can format numbers with options at the Format Cells dialog box with the Number tab selected as shown in Figure 3.7. Display this dialog box by clicking the Number group dialog box launcher or by clicking the Number Format button arrow and then clicking *More Number Formats* at the drop-down list. The left side of the dialog box displays number categories with a default category of *General*. At this setting no specific formatting is applied to numbers except right-aligning numbers in cells. The other number categories are described in Table 3.2.

Figure 3.7 Format Cells Dialog Box with Number Tab Selected

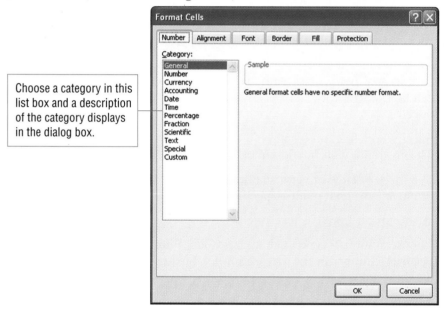

Choose a category in this list box and a description of the category displays in the dialog box.

Table 3.2 Number Categories at the Format Cells Dialog Box

Click this category	*To apply this number formatting*
Number	Specify number of decimal places and whether or not a thousand separator should be used; choose the display of negative numbers; right-align numbers in cell.
Currency	Apply general monetary values; dollar sign is added as well as commas and decimal points, if needed; right-align numbers in cell.
Accounting	Line up the currency symbol and decimal points in a column; add dollar sign and two digits after a decimal point; right-align numbers in cell.
Date	Display date as date value; specify the type of formatting desired by clicking an option in the *Type* list box; right-align date in cell.
Time	Display time as time value; specify the type of formatting desired by clicking an option in the *Type* list box; right-align time in cell.
Percentage	Multiply cell value by 100 and display result with a percent symbol; add decimal point followed by two digits by default; number of digits can be changed with the *Decimal places* option; right-align number in cell.
Fraction	Specify how fraction displays in cell by clicking an option in the *Type* list box; right-align fraction in cell.
Scientific	Use for very large or very small numbers. Use the letter *E* to tell Excel to move a decimal point a specified number of positions.
Text	Treat number in cell as text; number is displayed in cell exactly as typed.
Special	Choose a number type, such as Zip Code, Phone Number, or Social Security Number in the *Type* option list box; useful for tracking list and database values.
Custom	Specify a numbering type by choosing an option in the *Type* list box.

Project 3h   **Formatting Numbers at the Format Cells Dialog Box**

1. With **ExcelL1_C3_P3.xlsx** open, make cell F4 active and then insert the following formula: =(D4*E4)+D4.
2. Make cell F4 active and then copy the formula down to cells F5 through F16.
3. Change number formatting by completing the following steps:
   a. Select cells D4 through D16.
   b. Click the Number group dialog box launcher.

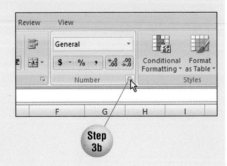

Step 3b

c. At the Format Cells dialog box with the Number tab selected, click *Accounting* in the *Category* section.

d. Make sure a *2* displays in the *Decimal places* option box and a dollar sign *$* displays in the *Symbol* option box.

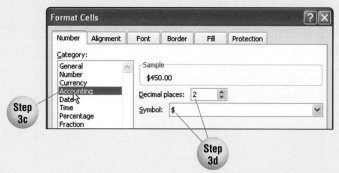

e. Click OK.

4. Apply Accounting formatting to cells F4 through F16 by completing steps similar to those in Step 3.

5. Save, print, and then close **ExcelL1_C3_P3.xlsx**.

P roject ④ Format a Company Budget Worksheet

You will open a workbook containing a company budget worksheet and then apply formatting to cells with options at the Format Cells dialog box, use the Format Painter to apply formatting, and hide and unhide rows and columns in the worksheet.

Formatting Cells Using the Format Cells Dialog Box

In the previous section, you learned how to format numbers with options at the Format Cells dialog box with the Number tab selected. This dialog box contains a number of other tabs you can select to format cells.

Aligning and Indenting Data

You can align and indent data in cells using buttons in the Alignment group in the Home tab or with options at the Format Cells dialog box with the Alignment tab selected as shown in Figure 3.8. Display this dialog box by clicking the Alignment group dialog box launcher.

Figure 3.8 Format Cells Dialog Box with Alignment Tab Selected

Specify horizontal and vertical alignment with options in this section.

Use options in this section to control how text fits in a cell.

Rotate text in a cell by clicking a point on the arc or by entering a number in the *Degrees* text box.

In the *Orientation* section, you can choose to rotate data. A portion of the *Orientation* section shows points on an arc. Click a point on the arc to rotate the text along that point. You can also type a rotation degree in the *Degrees* text box. Type a positive number to rotate selected text from the lower left to the upper right of the cell. Type a negative number to rotate selected text from the upper left to the lower right of the cell.

If data typed in a cell is longer than the cell, it overlaps the next cell to the right. If you want data to remain in a cell and wrap to the next line within the same cell, click the *Wrap text* option in the *Text control* section of the dialog box. Click the *Shrink to fit* option to reduce the size of the text font so all selected data fits within the column. Use the *Merge cells* option to combine two or more selected cells into a single cell.

If you want to enter data on more than one line within a cell, enter the data on the first line and then press Alt + Enter. Pressing Alt + Enter moves the insertion point to the next line within the same cell.

Project 4a Aligning and Rotating Data in Cells

1. Open **ExcelC03Project04.xlsx**.
2. Save the workbook with Save As and name it **ExcelL1_C3_P4**.
3. Make the following changes to the worksheet:
   a. Insert a new row at the beginning of the worksheet.
   b. Change the height of row 1 to 66.00.
   c. Merge and center cells A1 through E1.
   d. Type **Harris & Briggs** in cell A1 and then press Alt + Enter. (This moves the insertion point down to the next line in the same cell.)
   e. Type **Construction** and then press Enter.
   f. With cell A2 active, type **Preferred**, press Alt + Enter, type **Customer**, and then press Enter.

g. Change the width of column A to 20.00.

h. Change the width of column B to 7.00.

i. Change the width of columns C, D, and E to 10.00.

4. Change number formatting for specific cells by completing the following steps:

a. Select cells C3 through E11.

b. Click the Number group dialog box launcher.

c. At the Format Cells dialog box with the Number tab selected, click *Accounting* in the *Category* section.

d. Click the down-pointing arrow at the right side of the *Decimal places* option until *0* displays.

e. Make sure a dollar sign *$* displays in the *Symbol* option box.

f. Click OK.

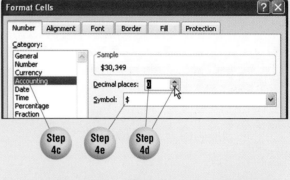

Step 4c   Step 4e   Step 4d

5. Make cell E3 active and then insert a formula that subtracts the *Planned* amount from the *Actual* amount. Copy this formula down to cells E4 through E11.

6. Change the orientation of data in cells by completing the following steps:

a. Select cells B2 through E2.

b. Click the Alignment group dialog box launcher.

c. At the Format Cells dialog box with the Alignment tab selected, select *0* in the *Degrees* text box and then type 45.

d. Click OK.

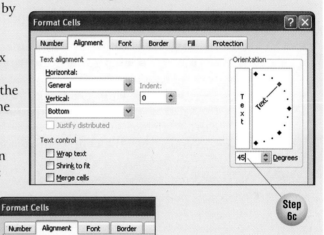

Step 6c

7. Change the vertical alignment of text in cells by completing the following steps:

a. Select cells A1 through E2.

b. Click the Alignment group dialog box launcher.

c. At the Format Cells dialog box with the Alignment tab selected, click the down-pointing arrow at the right side of the *Vertical* alignment option.

d. Click *Center* at the drop-down list.

e. Click OK.

Step 7c

Step 7d

8. Change the horizontal alignment of text in cells by completing the following steps:

a. Select cells A2 through E2.

b. Click the Alignment group dialog box launcher.

c. At the Format Cells dialog box with the Alignment tab selected, click the down-pointing arrow at the right side of the *Horizontal* alignment option.

d. Click *Center* at the drop-down list.

e. Click OK.

Step 8c

Step 8d

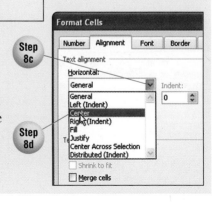

9. Change the horizontal alignment and indent of text in cells by completing the following steps:
   a. Select cells B3 through B11.
   b. Click the Alignment group dialog box launcher.
   c. At the Format Cells dialog box with the Alignment tab selected, click the down-pointing arrow at the right side of the *Horizontal* alignment option and then click *Right (Indent)* at the drop-down list.
   d. Click once on the up-pointing arrow at the right side of the *Indent* option box (this displays *1* in the box).
   e. Click OK.
10. Save **ExcelL1_C3_P4.xlsx**.

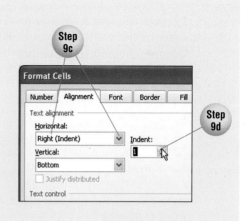

Changing the Font at the Format Cells Dialog Box

As you learned earlier in this chapter, the Font group in the Home tab contains buttons for applying font formatting to data in cells. You can also change the font for data in cells with options at the Format Cells dialog box with the Font tab selected as shown in Figure 3.9. At the Format Cells dialog box with the Font tab selected, you can change the font, font style, font size, and font color. You can also change the underlining method and add effects such as superscript and subscript. Click the Font group dialog box launcher to display this dialog box.

Figure 3.9 Format Cells Dialog Box with Font Tab Selected

1. With **ExcelL1_C3_P4.xlsx** open, change the font and font color by completing the following steps:
   a. Select cells A1 through E11.
   b. Click the Font group dialog box launcher.
   c. At the Format Cells dialog box with the Font tab selected, click *Garamond* in the *Font* list box (you will need to scroll down the list to make this font visible).
   d. Click *12* in the *Size* list box.
   e. Click the down-pointing arrow at the right of the *Color* option box.
   f. At the palette of color choices that displays, click the *Dark Red* color (first color option from the left in the *Standard Colors* section).
   g. Click OK to close the dialog box.
2. Make cell A1 active and then change the font to 24-point Garamond bold.
3. Select cells A2 through E2 and then apply bold formatting.
4. Save and then print **ExcelL1_C3_P4.xlsx**.

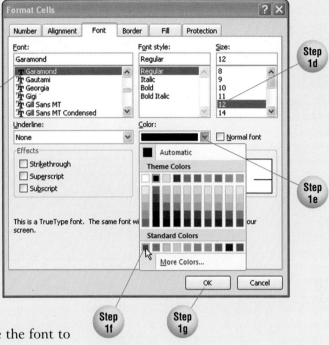

Adding Borders to Cells

The gridlines that display in a worksheet do not print. As you learned earlier in this chapter, you can use the Borders button in the Font group to add borders to cells that will print. You can also add borders to cells with options at the Format Cells dialog box with the Border tab selected as shown in Figure 3.10. Display this dialog box by clicking the Borders button arrow in the Font group and then clicking *More Borders* at the drop-down list.

With options in the *Presets* section, you can remove borders with the *None* option, add only outside borders with the *Outline* option, or click the *Inside* option to add borders to the inside of selected cells. In the *Border* section of the dialog box, specify the side of the cell or selected cells to which you want to apply a border. Choose the style of line desired for the border with the options that display in the *Style* list box. Add color to border lines with choices from the color palette that displays when you click the down-pointing arrow located at the right side of the *Color* option box.

QUICK STEPS

Add Borders to Cells
1. Select cells.
2. Click Borders button arrow.
3. Click desired border.
OR
1. Select cells.
2. Click Borders button arrow.
3. Click *More Borders*.
4. Use options in dialog box to apply desired border.
5. Click OK.

Figure 3.10 Format Cells Dialog Box with Border Tab Selected

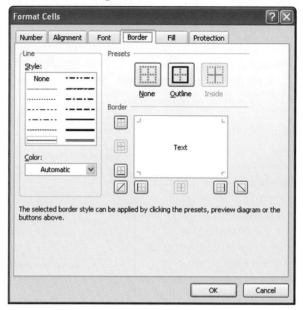

![Project icon] Project ④C **Adding Borders to Cells**

1. With **ExcelL1_C3_P4.xlsx** open, remove the 45 degrees orientation you applied in Project 4a by completing the following steps:
   a. Select cells B2 through E2.
   b. Click the Alignment group dialog box launcher.
   c. At the Format Cells dialog box with the Alignment tab selected, select *45* in the *Degrees* text box and then type 0.
   d. Click OK.

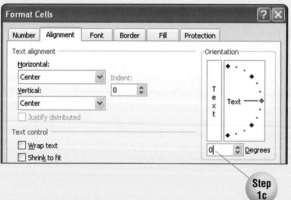

Step 1c

2. Change the height of row 2 to 33.00.
3. Add a thick, dark red border line to cells by completing the following steps:
   a. Select cells A1 through E11 (cells containing data).
   b. Click the Border button arrow in the Font group and then click the *More Borders* option at the drop-down list.

c. At the Format Cells dialog box with the Border tab selected, click the down-pointing arrow at the right side of the *Color* option and then click *Dark Red* at the color palette (first color option from the left in the *Standard Colors* section).

d. Click the thick single line option located in the second column (sixth option from the top) in the *Style* option box in the *Line* section.

e. Click the *Outline* option in the *Presets* section.

f. Click OK.

4. Add a border above and below cells by completing the following steps:

a. Select cells A2 through E2.

b. Click the Border button arrow in the Font group and then click *More Borders* at the drop-down list.

c. At the Format Cells dialog box with the Border tab selected, make sure the color is Dark Red.

d. Make sure the thick single line option (sixth option from the top in the second column) is selected in the *Style* option box in the *Line* section.

e. Click the top border of the sample cell in the *Border* section of the dialog box.

f. Click the double-line option (bottom option in the second column) in the *Style* option box.

g. Click the bottom border of the sample cell in the *Border* section of the dialog box.

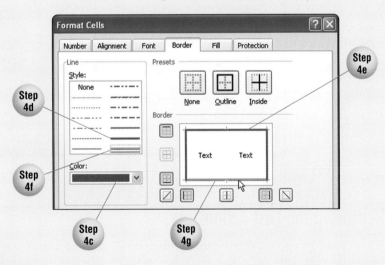

h. Click OK.

5. Save **ExcelL1_C3_P4.xlsx**.

Adding Fill and Shading to Cells

Add Shading to Cells
1. Select cells.
2. Click Fill Color button arrow.
3. Click desired color.
OR
1. Select cells.
2. Click Format button.
3. Click *Format Cells* at drop-down list.
4. Click Fill tab.
5. Use options in dialog box to apply desired shading.
6. Click OK.

To enhance the visual display of cells and data within cells, consider adding fill and/or shading to cells. As you learned earlier in this chapter, you can add fill color to cells with the Fill Color button in the Font group. You can also add fill color and/or shading to cells in a worksheet with options at the Format Cells dialog box with the Fill tab selected as shown in Figure 3.11. Display the Format Cells dialog box by clicking the Format button in the Cells group and then clicking *Format Cells* at the drop-down list. You can also display the dialog box by clicking the Font group, Alignment group, or Number group dialog box launcher. At the Format Cells dialog box, click the Fill tab.

Choose a fill color for a cell or selected cells by clicking a color choice in the *Color* palette. To add shading to a cell or selected cells, click the Fill Effects button, and then click the desired shading style at the Fill Effects dialog box.

Figure 3.11 Format Cells Dialog Box with Fill Tab Selected

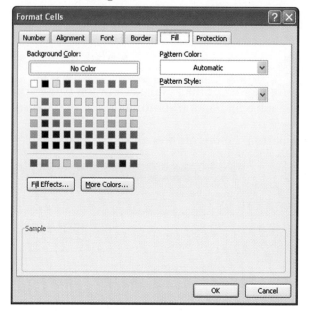

Repeating the Last Action

If you want to apply other types of formatting, such as number, border, or shading formatting to other cells in a worksheet, use the Repeat command by pressing F4 or Ctrl + Y. The Repeat command repeats the last action performed.

1. With **ExcelL1_C3_P4.xlsx** open, add fill color to cell A1 and repeat the formatting by completing the following steps:
   a. Make cell A1 active.
   b. Click the Format button in the Cells group and then click *Format Cells* at the drop-down list.
   c. At the Format Cells dialog box, click the Fill tab.
   d. Click a light purple color in the *Color* section (click the eighth color from the left in the second row).

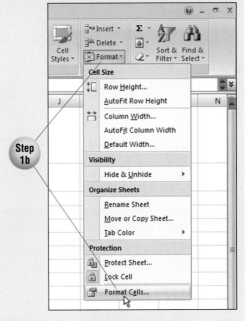

Step 1c

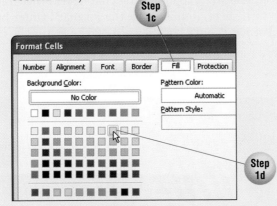

Step 1d

Step 1b

   e. Click OK.
   f. Select cells A2 through E2 and then press the F4 function key. (This repeats the light purple fill.)
2. Select row 2, insert a new row, and then change the height of the new row to 12.00.
3. Add shading to cells by completing the following steps:
   a. Select cells A2 through E2.
   b. Click the Format button in the Cells group and then click *Format Cells* at the drop-down list.
   c. At the Format Cells dialog box, if necessary, click the Fill tab.
   d. Click the Fill Effects button.
   e. At the Fill Effects dialog box, click the down-pointing arrow at the right side of the *Color 2* option box and then click *Purple, Accent 4* (eighth color from the left in the top row).
   f. Click *Horizontal* in the *Shading styles* section of the dialog box.
   g. Click OK to close the Fill Effects dialog box.
   h. Click OK to close the Format Cells dialog box.
4. Save **ExcelL1_C3_P4.xlsx**.

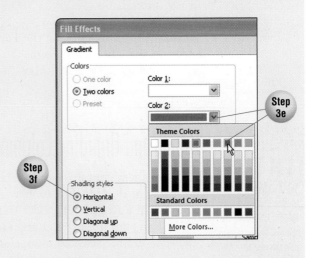

Step 3e

Step 3f

Formatting with Format Painter

Format with Format Painter
1. Select cells with desired formatting.
2. Double-click Format Painter button.
3. Select cells.
4. Click Format Painter button.

Format Painter

The Clipboard group in the Home tab contains a button you can use to copy formatting to different locations in the worksheet. This button is the Format Painter button and displays in the Clipboard group as a paintbrush. To use the Format Painter button, make a cell or selected cells active that contain the desired formatting, click the Format Painter button, and then click the cell or selected cells to which you want the formatting applied.

When you click the Format Painter button, the mouse pointer displays with a paintbrush attached. If you want to apply formatting a single time, click the Format Painter button once. If, however, you want to apply the character formatting in more than one location in the worksheet, double-click the Format Painter button. If you have double-clicked the Format Painter button, turn off the feature by clicking the Format Painter button once.

Project 4e   Formatting with Format Painter

1. With **ExcelL1_C3_P4.xlsx** open, select cells A5 through E5.
2. Click the Font group dialog box launcher.
3. At the Format Cells dialog box, click the Fill tab.
4. Click the light green color (seventh color from the left in the second row).
5. Click OK to close the dialog box.
6. Use Format Painter to "paint" formatting to rows by completing the following steps:
   a. With A5 through E5 selected, double-click the Format Painter button in the Clipboard group.
   b. Select cells A7 through E7.
   c. Select cells A9 through E9.
   d. Select cells A11 through E11.
   e. Turn off Format Painter by clicking the Format Painter button in the Clipboard group.
7. Save and then print **ExcelL1_C3_P4.xlsx**.

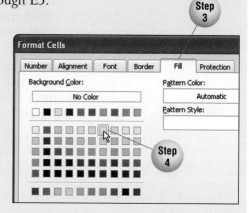

Hiding and Unhiding Columns/Rows

If a worksheet contains columns and/or rows of sensitive data or data that you are not using or do not want to view, consider hiding the columns and/or rows. To hide columns in a worksheet, select the columns to be hidden, click the Format button in the Cells group in the Home tab, point to *Hide & Unhide*, and then click *Hide Columns*. To hide selected rows, click the Format button in the Cells group, point to *Hide & Unhide*, and then click *Hide Rows*. To make a hidden column visible, select the column to the left and the column to the right of the hidden column, click the Format button in the Cells group, point to *Hide & Unhide*, and then click *Unhide Columns*. To make a hidden row visible, select the row above and the row below the hidden row, click the Format button in the Cells group, point to *Hide & Unhide*, and then click *Unhide Rows*.

If the first row or column is hidden, use the Go To feature to make the row or column visible. To do this, click the Find & Select button in the Editing group in the Home tab and then click *Go To* at the drop-down list. At the Go To dialog box, type **A1** in the *Reference* text box, and then click OK. At the worksheet, click the Format button in the Cells group, point to *Hide & Unhide*, and then click *Unhide Columns* or click *Unhide Rows*.

You can also unhide columns or rows using the mouse. If a column or row is hidden, the light blue boundary line in the column or row header displays as a slightly thicker blue line. To unhide a column, position the mouse pointer on the slightly thicker blue line that displays in the column header until the mouse pointer changes to left- and right-pointing arrows with a double line between. (Make sure the mouse pointer displays with two lines between the arrows. If a single line displays, you will simply change the size of the visible column.) Hold down the left mouse button, drag to the right until the column displays at the desired width, and then release the mouse button. Unhide a row in a similar manner. Position the mouse pointer on the slightly thicker blue line in the row header until the mouse pointer changes to up- and down-pointing arrows with a double line between. Drag down to display the row and then release the mouse button. If two or more adjacent columns or rows are hidden, you will need to unhide each column or row separately.

QUICK STEPS

Hide Columns
1. Select columns.
2. Click Format button.
3. Point to *Hide & Unhide*.
4. Click *Hide Columns*.

Hide Rows
1. Select rows.
2. Click Format button.
3. Point to *Hide & Unhide*.
4. Click *Hide Rows*

Project ④ Hiding/Unhiding Columns and Rows

1. With **ExcelL1_C3_P4.xlsx** open, hide the row for Linstrom Enterprises and the row for Summit Services by completing the following steps:
   a. Click the row 7 header to select the entire row.
   b. Hold down the Ctrl key and then click the row 11 header to select the entire row.
   c. Click the Format button in the Cells group in the Home tab, point to *Hide & Unhide*, and then click *Hide Rows*.
2. Hide the column containing the planned amounts by completing the following steps:
   a. Click cell D3 to make it the active cell.
   b. Click the Format button in the Cells group, point to *Hide & Unhide*, and then click *Hide Columns*.
3. Save and then print **ExcelL1_C3_P4.xlsx**.

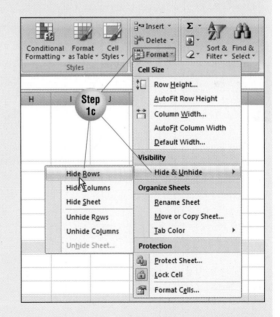

4. Unhide the rows by completing the following steps:
   a. Select rows 6 through 12.
   b. Click the Format button in the Cells group, point to *Hide & Unhide*, and then click
      Unhide Rows.
   c. Click in cell A4.

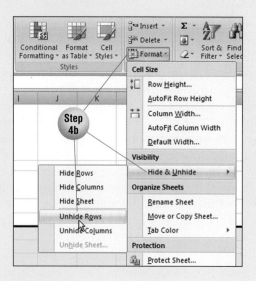

5. Unhide column D by completing the following steps:
   a. Position the mouse pointer on the thicker blue line that displays between columns C
      and E in the column header until the pointer turns into arrows pointing left and right
      with a double line between.
   b. Hold down the left mouse button, drag to the right until *Width: 12.57 (93 pixels)*
      displays in a box above the mouse pointer, and then release the mouse button.

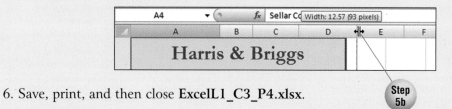

6. Save, print, and then close **ExcelL1_C3_P4.xlsx**.

CHAPTER summary

- Change column width using the mouse on column boundaries or with options at the Column Width dialog box.
- To automatically adjust a column to accommodate the longest entry in the column, double-click the column header boundary on the right.
- Change row height using the mouse on row boundaries or with options at the Row Height dialog box.
- Insert a row in a worksheet with the Insert button in the Cells group in the Home tab or with options at the Insert dialog box.
- Insert a column in a worksheet with the Insert button in the Cells group or with options at the Insert dialog box.
- Delete a specific cell by clicking the Delete button arrow and then clicking *Delete Cells* at the drop-down list. At the Delete dialog box, specify if you want to delete just the cell or an entire row or column.
- Delete a selected row(s) or column(s) by clicking the Delete button in the Cells group.
- Delete cell contents by pressing the Delete key or clicking the Clear button in the Editing group and then clicking *Clear Contents* at the drop-down list.
- Apply font formatting with buttons in the Font group in the Home tab.
- Use the Mini toolbar to apply font formatting to selected data in a cell.
- Apply alignment formatting with buttons in the Alignment group in the Home tab.
- Preview a worksheet by clicking the Office button, pointing to *Print*, and then clicking *Print Preview*.
- Change the size of the worksheet display with the Zoom button in the Print Preview tab or with the Zoom slider bar that displays at the right side of the Status bar.
- Use the Themes button in the Themes group in the Page Layout tab to apply a theme to cells in a worksheet that applies formatting such as color, font, and effects. Use the other buttons in the Themes group to customize the theme.
- Format numbers in cells with the Accounting Number Format, Percent Style, Comma Style, Increase Decimal, and Decrease Decimal buttons in the Number group in the home tab. You can also apply number formatting with options at the Format Cells dialog box with the Number tab selected.
- Apply formatting to cells in a worksheet with options at the Format Cells dialog box. This dialog box includes the following tabs for formatting cells: Number, Alignment, Font, Border, and Fill.
- Press F4 or Ctrl + Y to repeat the last action performed.
- Use the Format Painter button in the Clipboard group in the Home tab to apply formatting to different locations in a worksheet.
- Hide selected columns or rows in a worksheet by clicking the Format button in the Cells group in the Home tab, pointing to *Hide & Unhide*, and then clicking *Hide Columns* or *Hide Rows*.

- To make a hidden column visible, select the column to the left and right, click the Format button in the Cells group, point to *Hide & Unhide*, and then click *Unhide Columns*.
- To make a hidden row visible, select the row above and below, click the Format button in the Cells group, point to *Hide & Unhide*, and then click *Unhide Rows*.

COMMANDS review

FEATURE	RIBBON TAB, GROUP	BUTTON	KEYBOARD SHORTCUT
Format	Home, Cells	Format	
Insert cells, rows, columns	Home, Cells	Insert	
Delete cells, rows, columns	Home, Cells	Delete	
Clear cell or cell contents	Home, Editing		
Font	Home, Font	Calibri	
Font size	Home, Font	11	
Increase Font Size	Home, Font	A	
Decrease Font Size	Home, Font	A	
Bold	Home, Font	B	Ctrl + B
Italic	Home, Font	I	Ctrl + I
Underline	Home, Font	U	Ctrl + U
Borders	Home, Font		
Fill Color	Home, Font		
Font Color	Home, Font	A	
Top Align	Home, Alignment		
Middle Align	Home, Alignment		
Bottom Align	Home, Alignment		
Orientation	Home, Alignment		
Align Text Left	Home, Alignment		

continued

FEATURE	RIBBON TAB, GROUP	BUTTON	KEYBOARD SHORTCUT
Center	Home, Alignment		
Align Text Right	Home, Alignment		
Decrease Indent	Home, Alignment		Ctrl + Alt + Shift + Tab
Increase Indent	Home, Alignment		Ctrl + Alt + Tab
Wrap Text	Home, Alignment		
Merge & Center	Home, Alignment		
Print Preview		, Print, Print Preview	Ctrl + F2
Themes	Page Layout, Themes		
Number Format	Home, Number	General	
Accounting Number Format	Home, Number	$	
Percent Style	Home, Number	%	Ctrl + Shift + %
Increase Decimal	Home, Number		
Decrease Decimal	Home, Number		
Format Painter	Home, Clipboard		
Repeat			F4 or Ctrl + Y

CONCEPTS check

Test Your Knowledge

Completion: In the space provided at the right, indicate the correct term, symbol, or command.

1. To automatically adjust a column width to accommodate the longest entry in the cell, do this with the mouse on the column boundary.

2. By default, a column is inserted in this direction from the column containing the active cell.

3. To delete a row, select the row and then click the Delete button in this group in the Home tab.

4. With the options at this button drop-down list, you can clear the contents of the cell or selected cells.

_____

5. Use this button to insert color in the active cell or selected cells.

_____

6. By default, numbers are aligned at this side of a cell.

_____

7. Click this button to merge selected cells and center data within the merged cells.

_____

8. Select data in a cell and this displays in a dimmed fashion above the selected text.

_____

9. Click this button in the Alignment group in the Home tab to rotate data in a cell.

_____

10. Use this bar, located at the right side of the Status bar, to zoom the display of the worksheet.

_____

11. The Themes button is located in this tab.

_____

12. If you type a number with a dollar sign, such as $50.25, Excel automatically applies this formatting to the number.

_____

13. If you type a number with a percent sign, such as 25%, Excel automatically applies this formatting to the number.

_____

14. Align and indent data in cells using buttons in the Alignment group in the Home tab or with options at this dialog box with the Alignment tab selected.

_____

15. You can repeat the last action performed with the command Ctrl + Y or pressing this function key.

_____

16. The Format Painter button is located in this group in the Home tab.

_____

17. To hide a column, select the column, click this button in the Cells group in the Home tab, point to *Hide & Unhide*, and then click *Hide Columns*.

_____

SKILLS check

Demonstrate Your Proficiency

Assessment

1 FORMAT A SALES AND BONUSES WORKSHEET

1. Open **ExcelC03Assessment01.xlsx**.
2. Save the workbook with Save As and name it **ExcelL1_C3_A1**.
3. Change the width of columns as follows:

Column A	=	14.00
Columns B - E	=	10.00
Column F	=	6.00

4. Select row 2 and then insert a new row.
5. Merge and center cells A2 through F2.
6. Type Sales Department in cell A2 and then press Enter.
7. Increase the height of row 1 to 33.00.
8. Increase the height of row 2 to 21.00.
9. Increase the height of row 3 to 18.00.
10. Make the following formatting changes to the worksheet:
    a. Make cell A1 active, change the font size to 18 points, and turn on bold.
    b. Make cell A2 active, change the font size to 14 points, and turn on bold.
    c. Select cells A3 through F3, click the Bold button in the Font group, and then click the Center button in the Alignment group.
    d. Select cells A1 through F3, change the vertical alignment to Middle Align.
    e. Select cells B4 through E11 and then change the number formatting to Accounting with 0 decimal places and a dollar sign.
11. Insert the following formulas in the worksheet:
    a. Insert a formula in D4 that adds the amounts in B4 and C4. Copy the formula down to cells D5 through D11.
    b. Insert a formula in E4 that averages the amounts in B4 and C4. Copy the formula down to cells E5 through E11.
    c. Insert an IF statement in cell F4 that says that if the amount in cell E4 is greater than 74999, then insert the word "Yes" and if the amount is less than 75000, then insert the word "No." Copy this formula down to cells F5 through F11.
12. Make the following changes to the worksheet:
    a. Select cells F4 through F11 and then click the Center button in the Alignment group.
    b. Add a double-line border around cells A1 through F11.
    c. Select cells A1 and A2 and then apply a light orange fill color.
    d. Select cells A3 through F3 and then apply an orange fill color.
13. Save and then print the worksheet.
14. Apply the Verve theme to the worksheet.
15. Save, print, and then close **ExcelL1_C3_A1.xlsx**.

Assessment

2 FORMAT AN OVERDUE ACCOUNTS WORKSHEET

1. Open **ExcelC03Assessment02.xlsx**.
2. Save the workbook with Save As and name it **ExcelL1_C3_A2**.
3. Change the width of columns as follows:

    Column A = 21.00
    Column B = 10.00
    Column C = 10.00
    Column D = 12.00
    Column E = 7.00
    Column F = 12.00

4. Make cell A1 active and then insert a new row.
5. Merge and center cells A1 through F1.
6. Type Compass Corporation in cell A1 and then press Enter.
7. Increase the height of row 1 to 42.00.
8. Increase the height of row 2 to 24.00.
9. Make the following formatting changes to the worksheet:
    a. Select cells A1 through F11 and then change the font to 10-point Bookman Old Style.
    b. Make cell A1 active, change the font size to 24 points, and turn on bold.
    c. Make cell A2 active, change the font size to 18 points, and turn on bold.
    d. Select cells A3 through F3, click the Bold button in the Font group and then click the Center button in the Alignment group.
    e. Select cells A1 through F3, click the Middle Align button in the Alignment group.
    f. Select cells B4 through C11 and then click the Center button in the Alignment group.
    g. Select cells E4 through E11 and then click the Center button in the Alignment group.
10. Use the DATE function in the following cells to enter a formula that returns the serial number for the following dates:

    D4 = September 1, 2010
    D5 = September 3, 2010
    D6 = September 8, 2010
    D7 = September 22, 2010
    D8 = September 15, 2010
    D9 = September 30, 2010
    D10 = October 6, 2010
    D11 = October 13, 2010

11. Enter a formula in cell F4 that inserts the due date (the purchase date plus the number of days in the Terms column). Copy the formula down to cells F5 through F11.
12. Apply the following borders and fill color:
    a. Add a thick line border around cells A1 through F11.
    b. Make cell A2 active and then add a double-line border at the top and bottom of the cell.
    c. Select cells A3 through F3 and then add a single line border to the bottom of the cells.
    d. Select cells A1 and A2 and then apply a light blue fill color.
13. Save, print, and then close **ExcelL1_C3_A2.xlsx**.

3 FORMAT A SUPPLIES AND EQUIPMENT WORKSHEET

1. Open **ExcelC03Assessment03.xlsx**.
2. Save the workbook with Save As and name it **ExcelL1_C3_A3**.
3. Select cells A1 through D19 and then change the font to Garamond and the font color to dark blue.
4. Select and then merge and center cells A1 through D1.
5. Select and then merge and center cells A2 through D2.
6. Make cell A1 active and then change the font size to 22 points and turn on bold.
7. Make cell A2 active and then change the font size to 12 points and turn on bold.
8. Change the height of row 1 to 36.00.
9. Change the height of row 2 to 21.00.
10. Change the width of column A to 15.00.
11. Select cells A3 through A17, turn on bold, and then click the Wrap Text button in the Alignment group.
12. Select cells A1 and A2 and then click the Middle Align button in the Alignment group.
13. Make cell B3 active and then change the number formatting to Currency with no decimal places.
14. Select cells C6 through C19 and then change the number formatting to Percentage with one decimal place.
15. Automatically adjust the width of column B.
16. Make cell D6 active and then type a formula that multiplies the absolute cell reference $B$3 with the percentage in cell C6. Copy the formula down to cells D7 through D19.
17. With cells D6 through D19 selected, change the number formatting to Currency with no decimal places.
18. Make cell D8 active and then clear the cell contents. Use the Repeat command, F4, to clear the contents from cells D11, D14, and D17.
19. Add light green fill color to the following cells: A1, A2, A5–D5, A8–D8, A11–D11, A14–D14, and A17–D17.
20. Add borders and/or shading of your choosing to enhance the visual appeal of the worksheet.
21. Save, print, and then close **ExcelL1_C3_A3.xlsx**.

4 FORMAT A FINANCIAL ANALYSIS WORKSHEET

1. Use the Help feature to learn how to use the shrink to fit option to show all data in a cell (with an option at the Format Cells dialog box with the Alignment tab selected).
2. Open **ExcelC03Assessment04.xlsx**.
3. Save the workbook with Save As and name it **ExcelL1_C3_A4**.
4. Make cell B9 active and then insert a formula that averages the percentages in cells B3 through B8. Copy the formula to the right to cells C9 and D9.

5. Select cells B3 through D9, display the Format Cells dialog box with the Alignment tab selected, change the horizontal alignment to Right (Indent) and the indent to *2*, and then close the dialog box.
6. Select cells A1 through D9 and then change the font size to 14.
7. Select cells B2 through D2 and then change the orientation to 45 degrees.
8. With cells B2 through D2 still selected, shrink the font size to show all data in the cells.
9. Save, print, and then close **ExcelL1_C3_A4.xlsx**.

CASE study

Apply Your Skills

Part 1

You are the office manager for HealthWise Fitness Center and you decide to prepare an Excel worksheet that displays the various plans offered by the health club. In this worksheet, you want to include yearly dues for each plan as well as quarterly and monthly payments. Open the **HealthWise.xlsx** workbook and then save it and name it **ExcelL1_C3_CS_P1A**. Make the following changes to the worksheet:

- Select cells B3 through D8 and then change the number formatting to Accounting with two decimal places and a dollar sign.
- Make cell B3 active and then insert *500.00*.
- Make cell B4 active and then insert a formula that adds the amount in B3 with the product (multiplication) of B3 multiplied by 10%. (The formula should look like this: =B3+(B3*10%). The Economy plan is the base plan and each additional plan costs 10% more than the previous plan.)
- Copy the formula in cell B4 down to cells B5 through B8.
- Insert a formula in cell C3 that divides the amount in cell B3 by 4 and then copy the formula down to cells C4 through C8.
- Insert a formula in cell D3 that divides the amount in cell B3 by 12 and then copy the formula down to cells D4 through D8.
- Apply formatting to enhance the visual display of the worksheet.

Save and print the completed worksheet.

With **ExcelL1_C3_CS_P1A.xlsx** open, save the workbook with Save As and name it **ExcelL1_C3_CS_P1B**, and then make the following changes:

- You have been informed that the base rate for yearly dues has increased from $500.00 to $600.00. Change this amount in cell B3 of the worksheet.
- If clients are late with their quarterly or monthly dues payments, a late fee is charged. You decide to add the late fee information to the worksheet. Insert a new column to the right of Column C. Type Late Fees in cell D2 and also in cell F2.
- Insert a formula in cell D3 that multiplies the amount in C3 by 5%. Copy this formula down to cells D4 through D8.
- Insert a formula in cell F3 that multiplies the amount in E3 by 7%. Copy this formula down to cells F4 through F8. If necessary, change the number formatting for cells F3 through F8 to Accounting with two decimal places and a dollar sign.
- Apply any additional formatting to enhance the visual display of the worksheet.

Save, print, and then close **ExcelL1_C3_CS_P1B.xlsx**.

106   Chapter Three

Part 2

Prepare a payroll sheet for the employees of the fitness center and include the following information:

| HealthWise Fitness Center | | | | |
| Weekly Payroll | | | | |
Employee	Hourly Wage	Hours	Weekly Salary	Benefits
Heaton, Kelly	$26.50	40		
Severson, Joel	$25.00	40		
Turney, Amanda	$20.00	15		
Walters, Leslie	$19.65	30		
Overmeyer, Jean	$18.00	20		
Haddon, Bonnie	$16.00	20		
Baker, Grant	$15.00	40		
Calveri, Shannon	$12.00	15		
Dugan, Emily	$10.50	10		
Joyner, Daniel	$10.50	10		
Lee, Alexander	$10.50	10		

Insert a formula in the *Weekly Salary* column that multiplies the hourly wage by the number of hours. Insert an IF statement in the *Benefits* column that states that if the number in the *Hours* column is greater than 19, then insert "Yes" and if the number is less than 20, then insert "No." Apply formatting to enhance the visual display of the worksheet. Save the workbook and name it **ExcelL1_C3_CS_P2**. Print **ExcelL1_C3_CS_P2.xlsx**. Press Ctrl + ` to turn on the display of formulas, print the worksheet, and then press Ctrl + ` to turn off the display of formulas.

Make the following changes to the worksheet:

- Change the hourly wage for Amanda Turney to $22.00.
- Increase the hours for Emily Dugan to 20.
- Remove the row for Grant Baker.
- Insert a row between Jean Overmeyer and Bonnie Haddon and then type the following information in the cells in the new row: Employee: Tonya McGuire; Hourly Wage: $17.50; Hours: 15.

Save and then print **ExcelL1_C3_CS_P2.xlsx**. Press Ctrl + ` to turn on the display of formulas and then print the worksheet. Press Ctrl + ` to turn off the display of formulas and then save and close **ExcelL1_C3_CS_P2.xlsx**.

Part 3

Your boss is interested in ordering new equipment for the health club. She is interested in ordering three elliptical machines, three recumbent bikes, and three upright bikes. She has asked you to use the Internet to research models and prices for this new equipment. She then wants you to prepare a worksheet with the information. Using the Internet, search for the following equipment:

- Search for elliptical machines for sale. Locate two different models and, if possible, find at least two companies that sell each model. Make a note of the company names, model numbers, and prices.

- Search for recumbent bikes for sale. Locate two different models and, if possible, find at least two companies that sell each model. Make a note of the company names, model numbers, and prices.
- Search for upright bikes for sale. Locate two different models and, if possible, find at least two companies that sell each model. Make a note of the company names, model numbers, and prices.

Using the information you found on the Internet, prepare an Excel worksheet with the following information:

- Equipment name
- Equipment model
- Price
- A column that multiplies the price by the number required (which is 3).

Include the fitness center name, HealthWise Fitness Center, and any other information you determine is necessary to the worksheet. Apply formatting to enhance the visual display of the worksheet. Save the workbook and name it **ExcelL1_C3_CS_P3**. Print and then close **ExcelL1_C3_CS_P3.xlsx**.

Part 4

When a prospective client contacts HealthWise about joining, you send a letter containing information about the fitness center, the plans offered, and the dues amounts. Use a letter template in Word to create a letter to send to a prospective client (you determine the client's name and address). Copy the cells in **ExcelL1_C3_CS_P1B.xlsx** containing data and paste them into the body of the letter. Make any formatting changes to make the data readable. Save, print, and then close the letter.

Enhancing a Worksheet

PERFORMANCE OBJECTIVES

Upon successful completion of Chapter 4, you will be able to:

- Change worksheet margins
- Center a worksheet horizontally and vertically on the page
- Insert a page break in a worksheet
- Print gridlines and row and column headings
- Set and clear a print area
- Insert headers and footers
- Customize print jobs
- Complete a spelling check on a worksheet
- Find and replace data and cell formatting in a worksheet
- Sort data in cells in ascending and descending order
- Filter a list using AutoFilter
- Plan and create a worksheet

excel Chapter 4

Tutorial 4.1
Printing Worksheets
Tutorial 4.2
Finding, Sorting, and Filtering
Data

Excel contains features you can use to enhance and control the formatting of a worksheet. In this chapter, you will learn how to change worksheet margins, orientation, size, and scale; print column and row titles; print gridlines; and center a worksheet horizontally and vertically on the page. You will also learn how to complete a spell check on text in a worksheet, find and replace specific data and formatting in a worksheet, sort and filter data, and plan and create a worksheet.

Note: Before beginning computer projects, copy to your storage medium the Excel2007L1C4 subfolder from the Excel2007L1 folder on the CD that accompanies this textbook and make Excel2007L1C4 the active folder.

Project ① Format a Yearly Budget Worksheet

You will format a yearly budget worksheet by inserting formulas; changing margins, page orientation, and page size; inserting a page break; printing column headings on multiple pages; scaling data to print on one page; inserting a background picture; inserting headers and footers; and identifying a print area and customizing print jobs.

QUICK STEPS

Change Worksheet Margins
1. Click Page Layout tab.
2. Click Margins button.
3. Click desired predesigned margin.

OR
1. Click Page Layout tab.
2. Click Margins button.
3. Click *Custom Margins* at drop-down list.
4. Change the top, left, right, and/or bottom measurements.
5. Click OK.

Formatting a Worksheet Page

An Excel worksheet contains default page formatting. For example, a worksheet contains left and right margins of 0.7 inch and top and bottom margins of 0.75 inch, a worksheet prints in portrait orientation, and the worksheet page size is 8.5 inches by 11 inches. These default settings as well as additional options can be changed and/or controlled with options in the Page Layout tab.

Changing Margins

The Page Setup group in the Page Layout tab contains buttons for changing margins, the page orientation and size, as well as buttons for establishing a print area, inserting a page break, applying a picture background, and printing titles.

Change the worksheet margins by clicking the Margins button in the Page Setup group in the Page Layout tab. This displays a drop-down list of predesigned margin choices. If one of the predesigned choices is what you want to apply to the worksheet, click the option. If you want to customize margins, click the *Custom Margins* option at the bottom of the Margins drop-down list. This displays the Page Setup dialog box with the Margins tab selected as shown in Figure 4.1.

Figure 4.1 Page Setup Dialog Box with Margins Tab Selected

Changes made to margin measurements are reflected in the sample worksheet page.

A worksheet page showing the cells and margins displays in the dialog box. As you increase or decrease the top, bottom, left, or right margin measurements, the sample worksheet page reflects the change. You can also increase or decrease the measurement from the top of the page to the header with the *Header* option or the measurement from the footer to the bottom of the page with the *Footer* option. (You will learn about headers and footers later in this chapter.)

QUICK STEPS

Center Worksheet Horizontally/ Vertically
1. Click Page Layout tab.
2. Click *Custom Margins* at drop-down list.
3. Click *Horizontally* option and/or click *Vertically* option.
4. Click OK.

Centering a Worksheet Horizontally and/or Vertically

By default, worksheets print in the upper left corner of the page. You can center a worksheet on the page by changing the margins; however, an easier method for centering a worksheet is to use the *Horizontally* and/or *Vertically* options that display at the bottom of the Page Setup dialog box with the Margins tab selected. If you choose one or both of these options, the worksheet page in the preview section displays how the worksheet will print on the page.

Project 1a   **Changing Margins and Horizontally and Vertically Centering a Worksheet**

1. Open **ExcelC04Project01.xlsx**.
2. Save the workbook with Save As and name it **ExcelL1_C4_P1**.
3. Insert the following formulas in the worksheet:
   a. Insert formulas in column N, rows 5 through 10 that sum the totals for each income item.
   b. Insert formulas in row 11, columns B through N that sum the income as well as the total for all income items.
   c. Insert formulas in column N, rows 14 through 19 that sum the totals for each expense item.
   d. Insert formulas in row 20, columns B through N that sum the expenses as well as the total of expenses.
   e. Insert formulas in row 21, columns B through N that subtract the total expenses from the income. (To begin the formula, make cell B21 active and then type the formula *=B11-B20*. Copy this formula to columns C through N.)
4. Click the Page Layout tab.
5. Click the Margins button in the Page Setup group and then click *Custom Margins* at the drop-down list.

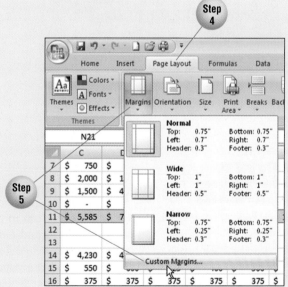

6. At the Page Setup dialog box with the Margins tab selected, click the up-pointing arrow at the right side of the *Top* text box until *3.5* displays.
7. Click the up-pointing arrow at the right side of the *Bottom* text box until *1.5* displays.
8. Preview the worksheet by clicking the Print Preview button located toward the bottom of the Page Setup dialog box. The worksheet appears to be a little low on the page so you decide to horizontally and vertically center it by completing the following steps:
   a. Click the Close Print Preview button.
   b. Click the Margins button in the Page Setup group and then click *Custom Margins* at the drop-down list.
   c. At the Page Setup dialog box with the Margins tab selected, change the *Top* and *Bottom* measurements to *1*.
   d. Click the *Horizontally* option. (This inserts a check mark.)
   e. Click the *Vertically* option. (This inserts a check mark.)
   f. Click OK to close the dialog box.
9. Save **ExcelL1_C4_P1.xlsx**.

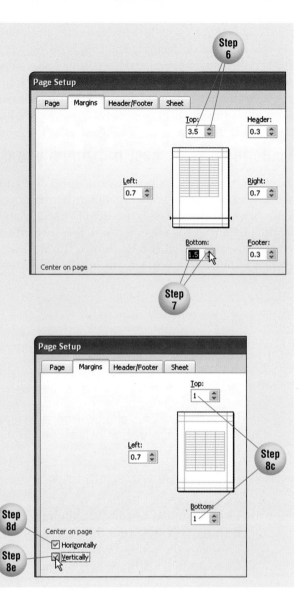

Changing Page Orientation

Change Page Orientation
1. Click Page Layout tab.
2. Click Orientation button.
3. Click desired orientation at drop-down list.

Click the Orientation button in the Page Setup group and a drop-down list displays with two choices, *Portrait* and *Landscape*. The two choices are represented by sample pages. A sample page that is taller than it is wide shows how the default orientation (*Portrait*) prints data on the page. The other choice, *Landscape*, will rotate the data and print it on a page that is wider than it is tall.

Changing the Page Size

An Excel worksheet page size, by default, is set at 8.5 × 11 inches. You can change this default page size by clicking the Size button in the Page Setup group. At the drop-down list that displays, notice that the default setting is *Letter* and the measurement *8.5" × 11"* displays below *Letter*. This drop-down list also contains a number of page sizes such as *Executive*, *Legal*, and a number of envelope sizes.

Project **1b** — **Changing Page Orientation and Size**

1. With **ExcelL1_C4_P1.xlsx** open, click the Orientation button in the Page Setup group in the Page Layout tab and then click *Landscape* at the drop-down list.

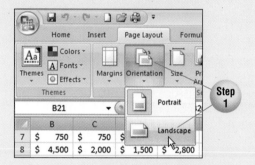

2. Click the Size button in the Page Setup group and then click *Legal* at the drop-down list.

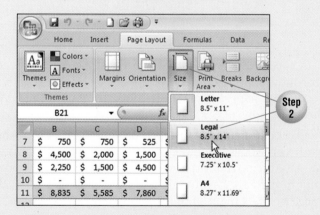

3. Preview the worksheet by clicking the Office button, pointing to *Print*, and then clicking *Print Preview*. After viewing the worksheet in Print Preview, click the Close Print Preview button.
4. Save **ExcelL1_C4_P1.xlsx**.

Inserting and Removing Page Breaks

The default left and right margins of 0.7 inch allow approximately 7 inches of cells across the page (8.5 inches minus 1.4 inches equals 7.1 inches). If a worksheet contains more than 7 inches of cells across the page, a page break is inserted in the worksheet and the remaining columns are moved to the next page. A page break displays as a broken line along cell borders. Figure 4.2 shows the page break in **ExcelL1_C4_P1.xlsx**.

Figure 4.2 Page Break

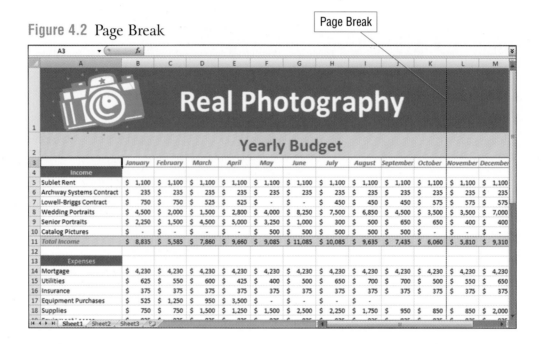

Page Break

QUICK STEPS

Insert Page Break
1. Select column or row.
2. Click Page Layout tab.
3. Click Breaks button.
4. Click *Insert Page Break* at drop-down list.

A page break also displays horizontally in a worksheet. By default, a worksheet can contain approximately 9.5 inches of cells vertically down the page. This is because the paper size is set by default at 11 inches. With the default top and bottom margins of 0.75 inch, this allows 9.5 inches of cells to print on one page.

Excel automatically inserts a page break in a worksheet. You can insert your own if you would like more control over what cells print on a page. To insert your own page break, select the column or row, click the Breaks button in the Page Setup group in the Page Layout tab, and then click *Insert Page Break* at the drop-down list. A page break is inserted immediately left of the selected column or immediately above the selected row.

If you want to insert both a horizontal and vertical page break at the same time, make a cell active, click the Breaks button in the Page Setup group and then click *Insert Page Break*. This causes a horizontal page break to be inserted immediately above the active cell, and a vertical page break to be inserted at the left side of the active cell. To remove a page break, select the column or row or make the desired cell active, click the Breaks button in the Page Setup group, and then click *Remove Page Break* at the drop-down list.

The page break automatically inserted by Excel may not be visible initially in a worksheet. One way to display the page break is to preview the worksheet. When you close Print Preview, the page break will display in the worksheet.

Displaying a Worksheet in Page Break Preview

Excel provides a page break view that displays worksheet pages and page breaks. To display this view, click the Page Break Preview button located in the view area at the right side of the Status bar or click the View tab and then click the Page Break Preview button in the Workbook Views group. This causes the worksheet to display similar to the worksheet shown in Figure 4.3. The word *Page* along with the page number is displayed in gray behind the cells in the worksheet. A solid blue line indicates a page break inserted by Excel and a dashed blue line indicates a page break inserted manually.

You can move the page break by positioning the arrow pointer on the blue line, holding down the left mouse button, dragging the line to the desired location, and then releasing the mouse button. To return to the Normal view, click the Normal button in the view area on the Status bar or click the View tab and then click the Normal button in the Workbook Views group.

HINT
You can edit a worksheet in Page Break Preview.

Page Break Preview

Normal

Figure 4.3 Worksheet in Page Break Preview

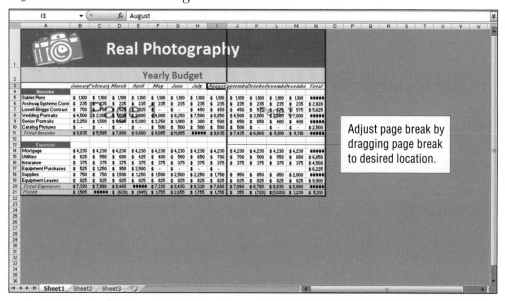

Adjust page break by dragging page break to desired location.

Project ⑩ **Inserting a Page Break in a Worksheet**

1. With **ExcelL1_C4_P1.xlsx** open, click the Size button in the Page Setup group in the Page Layout tab and then click *Letter* at the drop-down list.
2. Click the Margins button and then click *Custom Margins* at the drop-down list.
3. At the Page Setup dialog box with the Margins tab selected, click *Horizontally* to remove the check mark, click *Vertically* to remove the check mark, and then click OK to close the dialog box.
4. Insert a page break between columns I and J by completing the following steps:
   a. Select column J.
   b. Click the Breaks button in the Page Setup group and then click *Insert Page Break* at the drop-down list. Click in any cell in column I.

Step 4b

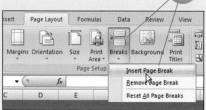

5. View the worksheet in Page Break Preview by completing the following steps:
   a. Click the Page Break Preview button located in the view area on the Status bar. (If a welcome message displays, click OK.)
   b. View the pages and page breaks in the worksheet.
   c. You decide to include the first six months of the year on one page. To do this, position the arrow pointer on the vertical blue line, hold down the left mouse button, drag the line to the left so it is positioned between columns G and H, and then release the mouse button.
   d. Click the Normal button located in the view area on the Status bar.
6. Save **ExcelL1_C4_P1.xlsx**.

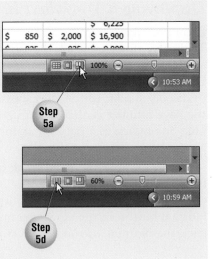

Step 5a

Step 5d

Printing Column and Row Titles on Multiple Pages

Print Titles

Columns and rows in a worksheet are usually titled. For example, in **ExcelL1_C4_P1.xlsx**, column titles include *Income*, *Expenses*, *January*, *February*, *March*, and so on. Row titles include the income and expenses categories. If a worksheet prints on more than one page, having column and/or row titles printing on each page can be useful. To do this, click the Print Titles button in the Page Setup group in the Page Layout tab. This displays the Page Setup dialog box with the Sheet tab selected as shown in Figure 4.4.

Figure 4.4 Page Setup Dialog Box with Sheet Tab Selected

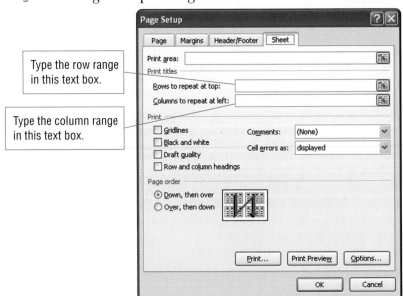

Type the row range in this text box.

Type the column range in this text box.

At the Page Setup dialog box with the Sheet tab selected, specify the range of row cells you want to print on every page in the *Rows to repeat at top* text box. Type a cell range using a colon. For example, if you want cells A1 through J1 to print on every page, you would type A1:J1 in the *Rows to repeat at top* text box. Type the range of column cells you want to print on every page in the *Columns to repeat at left* text box. To make rows and columns easier to identify on the printed page, specify that row and/or column headings print on each page.

QUICK STEPS

Print Column and Row Titles
1. Click Page Layout tab.
2. Click Print Titles button.
3. Type row range in *Rows to repeat at top* option.
4. Type column range in *Columns to repeat at left* option.
5. Click OK.

Project 1d   Printing Column Titles on Each Page of a Worksheet

1. With **ExcelL1_C4_P1.xlsx** open, click the Page Layout tab and then click the Print Titles button in the Page Setup group.
2. At the Page Setup dialog box with the Sheet tab selected, click in the *Columns to repeat at left* text box.
3. Type A1:A21.

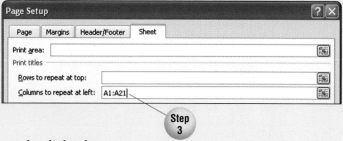

Step 3

4. Click OK to close the dialog box.
5. Save, preview, and then print **ExcelL1_C4_P1.xlsx**.

Scaling Data

With buttons in the Scale to Fit group in the Page Layout tab, you can adjust the printed output by a percentage to fit the number of pages specified. For example, if a worksheet contains too many columns to print on one page, click the down-pointing arrow at the right side of the *Width* box in the Scale to Fit group in the Page Layout tab and then click *1 page*. This causes the data to shrink so all columns display and print on one page.

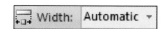

Project **1e**   **Scaling Data to Fit on One Page**

1. With **ExcelL1_C4_P1.xlsx** open, click the down-pointing arrow at the right side of the *Width* box in the Scale to Fit group in the Page Layout tab.
2. At the drop-down list that displays, click the *1 page* option.

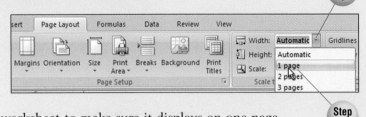

Step 1

Step 2

3. Preview the worksheet to make sure it displays on one page.
4. Save and then print **ExcelL1_C4_P1.xlsx**.

Inserting a Background Picture

With the Background button in the Page Setup group in the Page Layout tab you can insert a picture as a background to the worksheet. The picture displays only on the screen and does not print. To insert a picture, click the Background button in the Page Setup group. At the Sheet Background dialog box navigate to the folder containing the desired picture and then double-click the picture. To remove the picture from the worksheet, click the Delete Background button.

Project **1f**   **Inserting a Background Picture**

1. With **ExcelL1_C4_P1.xlsx** open, change the scaling back to the default by completing the following steps:
   a. Click the down-pointing arrow at the right side of the *Width* box in the Scale to Fit group and then click *Automatic* at the drop-down list.
   b. Click the up-pointing arrow at the right side of the *Scale* measurement box until *100%* displays in the box.
2. Remove titles from printing on second and subsequent pages by completing the following steps:
   a. Click the Print Titles button in the Page Setup group.
   b. At the Page Setup dialog box with the Sheet tab selected, select the text that displays in the *Columns to repeat at left* text box and then press the Delete key.
   c. Click OK to close the dialog box.
3. Insert a background picture by completing the following steps:
   a. Click the Background button in the Page Setup group.
   b. At the Sheet Background dialog box, navigate to the Excel2007L1C4 folder, and then double-click *Mountain.jpg*.
4. Preview the worksheet. (Notice that the picture does not display in Print Preview.)
5. Remove the picture by clicking the Delete Background button in the Page Setup group.
6. Save **ExcelL1_C4_P1.xlsx**.

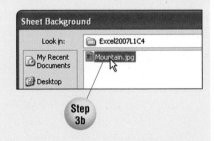

Step 3b

Printing Gridlines and Row and Column Headings

By default, the gridlines that create the cells in a worksheet and the row numbers and column letters do not print. The Sheet Options group in the Page Layout tab contain check boxes for gridlines and headings. The *View* check boxes for Gridlines and Headings contain check marks. At these settings, gridlines and row and column headings display on the screen but do not print. If you want them to print, insert check marks in the *Print* check boxes. Complex worksheets may be easier to read with the gridlines printed.

You can also control the display and printing of gridlines and headings with options at the Page Setup dialog box with the Sheet tab selected. Display this dialog box by clicking the Sheet Options dialog box launcher. To print gridlines and headings, insert check marks in the check boxes located in the *Print* section of the dialog box. The *Print* section contains two additional options—*Black and white* and *Draft quality*. If you are printing with a color printer, you can print the worksheet in black and white by inserting a check mark in the *Black and white* check box. Insert a check mark in the *Draft* option if you want to print a draft of the worksheet. With this option checked, some formatting such as shading and fill are not printed.

QUICK STEPS

Print Gridlines
1. Click Page Layout tab.
2. Click *Print* check box in Gridlines section in Sheet Options group.
OR
1. Click Page Layout tab.
2. Click Sheet Options dialog box launcher.
3. Click *Gridlines* option.
4. Click OK.

Print Row and Column Headings
1. Click Page Layout tab.
2. Click *Print* check box in Headings section in Sheet Options group.
OR
1. Click Page Layout tab.
2. Click Sheet Options dialog box launcher.
3. Click *Row and column headings* option.
4. Click OK.

Project 🅑 Printing Gridlines and Row and Column Headings

1. With **ExcelL1_C4_P1.xlsx** open, click in the *Print* check box below Gridlines in the Sheet Options group to insert a check mark.
2. Click in the *Print* check box below Headings in the Sheet Options group to insert a check mark.

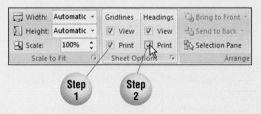

Step 1   Step 2

3. Click the Margins button in the Page Setup group and then click *Custom Margins* at the drop-down list.
4. At the Page Setup dialog box with the Margins tab selected, click in the *Horizontally* check box to insert a check mark.
5. Click in the *Vertically* check box to insert a check mark.
6. Click OK to close the dialog box.
7. Save, preview, and then print **ExcelL1_C4_P1.xlsx**.
8. Click in the *Print* check box below Headings in the Sheet Options group to remove the check mark.
9. Click in the *Print* check box below Gridlines in the Sheet Options group to remove the check mark.
10. Save **ExcelL1_C4_P1.xlsx**.

Printing a Specific Area of a Worksheet

With the Print Area button in the Page Setup group in the Page Layout tab you can select and print specific areas in a worksheet. To do this, select the cells you want to print, click the Print Area button in the Page Setup group in the Page Layout tab, and then click *Set Print Area* at the drop-down list. This inserts a border around the selected cells. Click the Quick Print button on the Quick Access toolbar and the cells within the border are printed.

You can specify more than one print area in a worksheet. To do this, select the first group of cells, click the Print Area button in the Page Setup group, and then click *Set Print Area*. Select the next group of cells, click the Print Area button, and then click *Add to Print Area*. Clear a print area by clicking the Print Area button in the Page Setup group and then clicking *Clear Print Area* at the drop-down list.

Each area specified as a print area will print on a separate page. If you want nonadjacent print areas to print on the same page, consider hiding columns and/or rows in the worksheet to bring the areas together.

Project 1h   Printing Specific Areas

1. With **ExcelL1_C4_P1.xlsx** open, print the first half expenses by completing the following steps:
   a. Select cells A3 through G21.
   b. Click the Print Area button in the Page Setup group in the Page Layout tab and then click *Set Print Area* at the drop-down list.

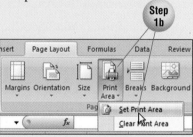

   c. With the border surrounding the cells A3 through G21, click the Quick Print button on the Quick Access toolbar.
   d. Clear the print area by clicking the Print Area button in the Page Setup group and then clicking *Clear Print Area* at the drop-down list.
2. Suppose you want to print the income and expenses information as well as the totals for the month of April. To do this, hide columns and select a print area by completing the following steps:
   a. Select columns B through D.
   b. Click the Home tab.
   c. Click the Format button in the Cells group, point to *Hide & Unhide*, and then click *Hide Columns*.
   d. Click the Page Layout tab.
   e. Select cells A3 through E21. (Columns A and E are now adjacent.)
   f. Click the Print Area button in the Page Setup group and then click *Set Print Area* at the drop-down list.

3. Click the Quick Print button on the Quick Access toolbar.
4. Clear the print area by making sure cells A3 through E21 are selected, clicking the Print Area button in the Page Setup group, and then clicking *Clear Print Area* at the drop-down list.
5. Unhide the columns by completing the following steps:
    a. Click the Home tab.
    b. Select columns A and E (these columns are adjacent).
    c. Click the Format button in the Cells group, point to *Hide & Unhide*, and then click *Unhide Columns*.
    d. Deselect the text by clicking in any cell containing data in the worksheet.
6. Save **ExcelL1_C4_P1.xlsx**.

Inserting Headers/Footers

Text that prints at the top of each worksheet page is called a **header** and text that prints at the bottom of each worksheet page is called a **footer**. You can create a header and/or footer with the Header & Footer button in the Text group in the Insert tab, in Page Layout View, or with options at the Page Setup dialog box with the Header/Footer tab selected.

To create a header with the Header & Footer button, click the Insert tab and then click the Header & Footer button in the Text group. This displays the worksheet in Page Layout view and displays the Header & Footer Tools Design tab. Use buttons in this tab, shown in Figure 4.5, to insert predesigned headers and/or footers or insert header and footer elements such as the page number, date, time, path name, and file name. You can also create a different header or footer on the first page of the worksheet or create a header or footer for even pages and another for odd pages.

QUICK
STEPS

Insert a Header or Footer
1. Click Insert tab.
2. Click Header & Footer button.
3. Click Header button and then click predesigned header or click Footer button and then click predesigned footer.
OR
1. Click Insert tab.
2. Click Header & Footer button.
3. Click desired header or footer elements.

HINT
Close the header or footer pane by clicking in the worksheet or pressing Esc.

Figure 4.5 Header & Footer Tools Design Tab

Project ⓤ Inserting a Header in a Worksheet

1. With **ExcelL1_C4_P1.xlsx** open, create a header by completing the following steps:
   a. Click the Insert tab.
   b. Click the Header & Footer button in the Text group.

c. Click the Header button located at the left side of the Header & Footer Tools Design tab and then click *Page 1, ExcelL1_C4_P1.xlsx* at the drop-down list. (This inserts the page number in the middle header box and the workbook name in the right header box.)
2. Click in any cell in the worksheet containing data.
3. Click the Normal view button located in the view area on the Status bar.
4. Save **ExcelL1_C4_P1.xlsx**.

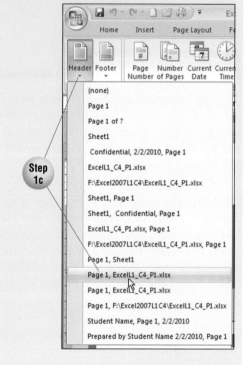

You also can insert a header and/or footer by switching to Page Layout view. In Page Layout view, the top of the worksheet page displays with the text *Click to add header*. Click this text and the insertion point is positioned in the middle header box. Type the desired header in this box or click in the left box or the right box and then type the header. Create a footer in a similar manner. Scroll down the worksheet until the bottom of the page displays and then click the text *Click to add footer*. Type the footer in the center footer box or click the left or right box and then type the footer.

Project ⑩ Inserting a Footer and Modifying a Header in a Worksheet

1. With **ExcelL1_C4_P1.xlsx** open, click the Page Layout button located in the view area on the Status bar.
2. Scroll down the worksheet until the text *Click to add footer* displays and then click the text.

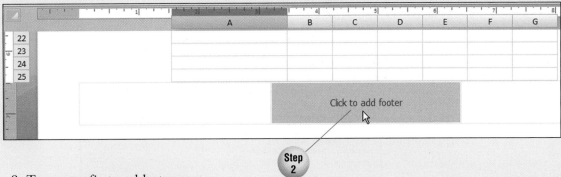

Step 2

3. Type your first and last names.
4. Click in the left footer box and then click the Current Date button in the Header & Footer Elements group in the Header & Footer Tools Design tab.
5. Click in the right footer box and then click the Current Time button in the Header & Footer Elements group.
6. Click in a cell in the worksheet.
7. Save and then print **ExcelL1_C4_P1.xlsx**.
8. Modify the header by completing the following steps:
    a. Scroll to the beginning of the worksheet and display the header text.
    b. Click the page number in the middle header box. (This displays the Header & Footer Tools Design tab, changes the header to a field, and selects the field.)
    c. Press the Delete key to delete the header.
    d. Click the header text that displays in the right header box and then press the Delete key.
    e. Insert the page number by clicking the Page Number button in the Header & Footer Elements group.
    f. Click in the left header box and then click the File Name button in the Header & Footer Elements group.

Step 8f

9. Click in any cell in the worksheet containing data.
10. Click the Normal button in the view area on the Status bar.
11. Preview the worksheet to determine how the header and footer print on each page.
12. Save and then print **ExcelL1_C4_P1.xlsx**.

Customizing Print Jobs

The Print dialog box provides options for customizing a print job. Display the Print dialog box shown in Figure 4.6 by clicking the Office button and then clicking *Print* at the drop-down list or by pressing the keyboard shortcut Ctrl + P. Use options at the Print dialog box to print a specific range of cells, selected cells, or multiple copies of a workbook.

Figure 4.6 Print Dialog Box

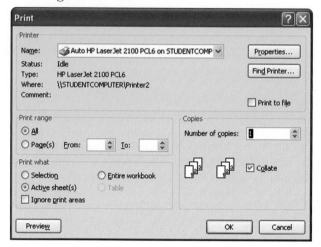

At the Print dialog box, the currently selected printer name displays in the *Name* option box. If other printers are installed, click the down-pointing arrow at the right side of the *Name* option box to display a list of printers.

The *Active sheet(s)* option in the *Print what* section is selected by default. At this setting, the currently active worksheet will print. If you want to print an entire workbook that contains several worksheets, click *Entire workbook* in the *Print what* section. Click the *Selection* option in the *Print what* section to print the currently selected cells.

If you want more than one copy of a worksheet or workbook printed, change the desired number of copies with the *Number of copies* option in the *Copies* section. If you want the copies collated, make sure the *Collate* check box in the *Copies* section contains a check mark.

A worksheet within a workbook can contain more than one page. If you want to print specific pages of a worksheet within a workbook, click *Page(s)* in the *Print range* section, and then specify the desired page numbers in the *From* and *To* text boxes.

If you want to preview the worksheet before printing, click the Preview button that displays at the bottom left corner of the dialog box. This displays the worksheet as it will appear on the printed page. After viewing the worksheet, click the Close Print Preview button that displays at the right side of the Print Preview tab.

Project 1k Printing Specific Cells in a Worksheet

1. With **ExcelL1_C4_P1.xlsx** open, print selected cells by completing the following steps:
   a. Select cells A3 through G11.
   b. Click the Office button and then click *Print* at the drop-down list.
   c. At the Print dialog box, click *Selection* in the *Print what* section.
   d. Click OK.
2. Close **ExcelL1_C4_P1.xlsx**.

Project 2 Format a May Sales and Commissions Worksheet

You will format a sales commission worksheet by inserting a formula, completing a spelling check, and finding and replacing data and cell formatting.

Completing a Spelling Check

Excel includes a spelling checker you can use to check the spelling of text in a worksheet. Before checking the spelling in a worksheet, make the first cell active. The spell checker checks the worksheet from the active cell to the last cell in the worksheet that contains data.

To use the spelling checker, click the Review tab and then click the Spelling button. Figure 4.7 displays the Spelling dialog box. At this dialog box, you can click a button to tell Excel to ignore a word or you can replace a misspelled word with a word from the *Suggestions* list box.

QUICK STEPS

Complete a Spelling Check
1. Click Review tab.
2. Click Spelling button.
3. Replace or ignore selected words.

HINT

Customize spell checking options at the Excel Options dialog box with Proofing selected.

Figure 4.7 Excel Spelling Dialog Box

The word in the worksheet not found in the spell check dictionary displays here.

Suggested spellings display in the *Suggestions* list box.

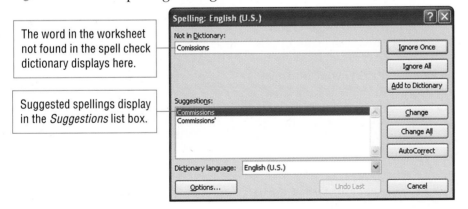

Using Undo and Redo

HINT

Ctrl + Z is the keyboard shortcut to undo a command.

Undo

Redo

Excel includes an Undo button on the Quick Access toolbar that will reverse certain commands or delete the last data typed in a cell. For example, if you apply an autoformat to selected cells in a worksheet and then decide you want the autoformatting removed, click the Undo button on the Quick Access toolbar. If you decide you want the autoformatting back again, click the Redo button on the Quick Access toolbar.

Excel maintains actions in temporary memory. If you want to undo an action performed earlier, click the down-pointing arrow at the right side of the Undo button and a drop-down list displays containing the actions performed on the worksheet. Click the desired action at the drop-down list. Any actions preceding a chosen action are also undone. You can do the same with the Redo drop-down list. Multiple actions must be undone or redone in sequence.

Project 2a   Spell Checking and Formatting a Worksheet

1. Open **ExcelC04Project02.xlsx**.
2. Save the workbook with Save As and name it **ExcelL1_C4_P2**.
3. Complete a spelling check on the worksheet by completing the following steps:
   a. Make sure cell A1 is the active cell.
   b. Click the Review tab.
   c. Click the Spelling button.
   d. Click the Change button as needed to correct misspelled words in the worksheet. (When the spell checker stops at proper names *Pirozzi*, *Valona*, and *Yonemoto*, click the Ignore All button.)
   e. At the message telling you the spelling check is completed, click OK.

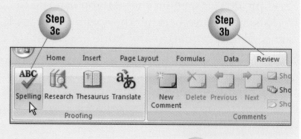

Step 3c

Step 3b

4. Make cell G4 active and then insert a formula that multiplies the sale price by the commission percentage. Copy the formula down to cells G5 through G26.
5. Make cell G27 active and then insert the sum of cells G4 through G26.
6. Apply a theme by clicking the Page Layout button, clicking the Themes button, and then clicking *Civic* at the drop-down gallery.
7. After looking at the worksheet with the Civic theme applied, you decide you want to return to the original formatting. To do this, click the Undo button on the Quick Access toolbar.
8. You realize that copying the formula in cell G4 down to cells G5 through G26 caused the yellow fill to be removed from certain cells and you decide to insert the shading. To do this, complete the following steps:
   a. Make cell G5 active.
   b. Click the Home tab.

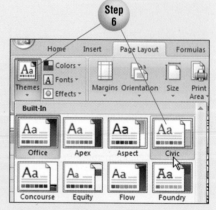

Step 6

Step 7

c. Click the Fill Color button arrow and then click *More Colors* at the drop-down gallery.

d. At the Colors dialog box with the Standard tab selected, click the yellow color as shown at the right.

e. Click OK to close the dialog box.

f. Make cell G7 active and then press F4 (the Repeat command).

g. Use F4 to apply yellow shading to cells G9, G11, G13, G15, G17, G19, G21, G23, and G25.

9. Save **ExcelL1_C4_P2.xlsx**.

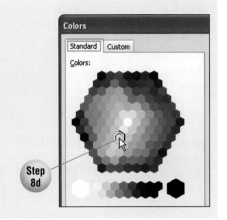

Step 8d

Finding and Replacing Data in a Worksheet

Excel provides a Find feature you can use to look for specific data and either replace it with nothing or replace it with other data. This feature is particularly helpful in a large worksheet with data you want to find quickly. Excel also includes a find and replace feature. Use this to look for specific data in a worksheet and replace it with other data.

To find specific data in a worksheet, click the Find & Select button located in the Editing group in the Home tab and then click *Find* at the drop-down list. This displays the Find and Replace dialog box with the Find tab selected as shown in Figure 4.8. Type the data you want to find in the *Find what* text box and then click the Find Next button. Continue clicking the Find Next button to move to the next occurrence of the data. If the Find and Replace dialog box obstructs your view of the worksheet, use the mouse pointer on the title bar to drag the box to a different location.

Figure 4.8 Find and Replace Dialog Box with Find Tab Selected

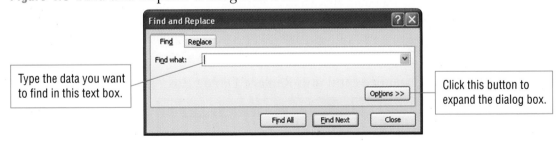

Type the data you want to find in this text box.

Click this button to expand the dialog box.

To find specific data in a worksheet and replace it with other data, click the Find & Select button in the Editing group in the Home tab and then click *Replace* at the drop-down list. This displays the Find and Replace dialog box with the Replace tab selected as shown in Figure 4.9. Enter the data for which you are looking in the *Find what* text box. Press the Tab key or click in the *Replace with* text box and then enter the data that is to replace the data in the *Find what* text box.

Figure 4.9 Find and Replace Dialog Box with Replace Tab Selected

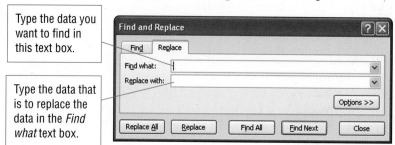

Type the data you want to find in this text box.

Type the data that is to replace the data in the *Find what* text box.

Click the Find Next button to tell Excel to find the next occurrence of the data. Click the Replace button to replace the data and find the next occurrence. If you know that you want all occurrences of the data in the *Find what* text box replaced with the data in the *Replace with* text box, click the Replace All button. Click the Close button to close the Replace dialog box.

Display additional find and replace options by clicking the Options button. This expands the dialog box as shown in Figure 4.10. By default, Excel will look for any data that contains the same characters as the data in the *Find what* text box, without concern for the characters before or after the entered data. For example, in Project 2b, you will be looking for sale prices of $450,000 and replacing with $475,000. If you do not specify to Excel that you want to find cells that contain only *450000,* Excel will stop at any cell containing *450000.* In this example, Excel would stop at a cell containing *$1,450,000* or a cell containing *$2,450,000.* To specify that the only data that should be contained in the cell is what is entered in the *Find what* text box, click the Options button to expand the dialog box, and then insert a check mark in the *Match entire cell contents* check box.

Figure 4.10 Expanded Find and Replace Dialog Box

Search the active worksheet or the entire workbook with the *Within* option.

With this option you can search by rows or by columns.

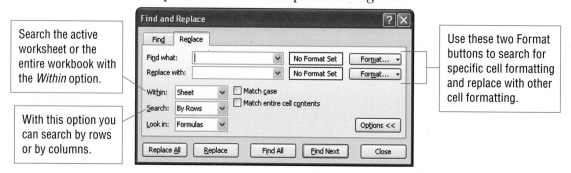

Use these two Format buttons to search for specific cell formatting and replace with other cell formatting.

If the *Match case* option is active (contains a check mark), Excel will look for only that data that exactly matches the case of the data entered in the *Find what* text box. Remove the check mark from this check box if you do not want Excel to find exact case matches. Excel will search in the current worksheet. If you want Excel to search an entire workbook, change the *Within* option to *Workbook*. Excel, by default, searches by rows in a worksheet. You can change this to *By Columns* with the *Search* option.

Project **2b**   **Finding and Replacing Data**

1. With **ExcelL1_C4_P2.xlsx** open, find all occurrences of *Land* in the worksheet and replace with *Acreage* by completing the following steps:

   a. Click the Find & Select button in the Editing group in the Home tab and then click *Replace* at the drop-down list.

   b. At the Find and Replace dialog box with the Replace tab selected, type Land in the *Find what* text box.

   c. Press the Tab key (this moves the insertion point to the *Replace with* text box).

   d. Type Acreage.

   e. Click the Replace All button.

   f. At the message telling you that four replacements were made, click OK.

   g. Click the Close button to close the Find and Replace dialog box.

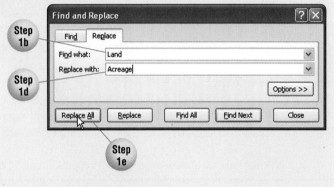

2. Find all occurrences of *$450,000* and replace with *$475,000* by completing the following steps:

   a. Click the Find & Select button in the Editing group and then click *Replace* at the drop-down list.

   b. At the Find and Replace dialog box with the Replace tab selected, type 450000 in the *Find what* text box.

   c. Press the Tab key.

   d. Type 475000.

   e. Click the Options button to display additional options. (If additional options already display, skip this step.)

   f. Click the *Match entire cell contents* option to insert a check mark in the check box.

   g. Click Replace All.

   h. At the message telling you that two replacements were made, click OK.

   i. At the Find and Replace dialog box, click the *Match entire cell contents* option to remove the check mark.

   j. Click the Close button to close the Find and Replace dialog box.

3. Save **ExcelL1_C4_P2.xlsx**.

Finding and Replacing Cell Formatting

Use the Format buttons at the expanded Find and Replace dialog box (see Figure 4.10) to search for specific cell formatting and replace with other formatting. Click the down-pointing arrow at the right side of the Format button and a drop-down list displays. Click the *Format* option and the Find Format dialog box displays with the Number, Alignment, Font, Border, Fill, and Protection tabs. Specify formatting at this dialog box. Click the *Choose Format From Cell* option and the mouse pointer displays with a pointer tool attached. Click in the cell containing the desired formatting and the formatting displays in the *Preview* box to the left of the Format button. Click the *Clear Find Format* option and any formatting in the *Preview* box is removed.

Project 2c Finding and Replacing Cell Formatting

1. With **ExcelL1_C4_P2.xlsx** open, search for light turquoise fill color and replace with a purple fill color by completing the following steps:
   a. Click the Find & Select button in the Editing group and then click *Replace* at the drop-down list.
   b. At the Find and Replace dialog box with the Replace tab selected, make sure the dialog box is expanded. (If not, click the Options button.)
   c. Select and then delete any text that displays in the *Find what* text box.
   d. Select and then delete any text that displays in the *Replace with* text box.
   e. Make sure the boxes immediately preceding the two Format buttons display with the text *No Format Set*. (If not, click the down-pointing arrow at the right of the Format button, and then click the *Clear Find Format* option at the drop-down list. Do this for each Format button.)
   f. Click the top Format button.
   g. At the Find Format dialog box, click the Fill tab.
   h. Click the More Colors button.
   i. At the Colors dialog box with the Standard tab selected, click the light turquoise color shown at the right.
   j. Click OK to close the Colors dialog box.
   k. Click OK to close the Find Format dialog box.
   l. Click the bottom Format button.
   m. At the Replace Format dialog box with the Fill tab selected, click the purple color shown at the right.
   n. Click OK to close the dialog box.
   o. At the Find and Replace dialog box, click the Replace All button.
   p. At the message telling you that ten replacements were made, click OK.

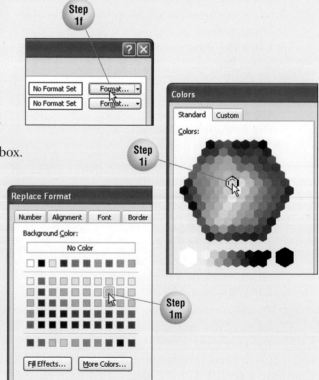

2. Search for yellow fill color and replace with a green fill color by completing the following steps:
   a. At the Find and Replace dialog box, click the top Format button.
   b. At the Find Format dialog box, click the Fill tab.
   c. Click the More Colors button.
   d. At the Colors dialog box with the Standard tab selected, click the yellow color as shown at the right.
   e. Click OK to close the Colors dialog box.
   f. Click OK to close the Find Format dialog box.
   g. Click the bottom Format button.
   h. At the Replace Format dialog box with the Fill tab selected, click the green color shown at the right.
   i. Click OK to close the dialog box.
   j. At the Find and Replace dialog box, click the Replace All button.
   k. At the message telling you that 78 replacements were made, click OK.

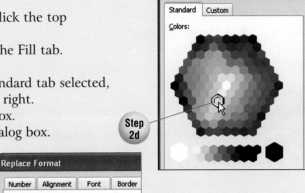

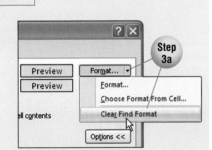

3. Search for 11-point Calibri formatting and replace with 10-point Arial formatting by completing the following steps:
   a. With the Find and Replace dialog box open, clear formatting from the top Format button by clicking the down-pointing arrow and then clicking the *Clear Find Format* option at the drop-down list.
   b. Clear formatting from the bottom Format button by clicking the down-pointing arrow and then clicking *Clear Replace Format*.
   c. Click the top Format button.
   d. At the Find Format dialog box, click the Font tab.
   e. Click *Calibri* in the *Font* list box (you may need to scroll down the list to display this typeface).
   f. Click *11* in the *Size* text box.
   g. Click OK to close the dialog box.
   h. Click the bottom Format button.
   i. At the Replace Format dialog box with the Font tab selected, click *Arial* in the *Font* list box (you may need to scroll down the list to display this typeface).
   j. Click *10* in the *Size* list box.
   k. Click OK to close the dialog box.
   l. At the Find and Replace dialog box, click the Replace All button.
   m. At the message telling you that 174 replacements were made, click OK.
   n. At the Find and Replace dialog box, remove formatting from both Format buttons.
   o. Click the Close button to close the Find and Replace dialog box.
4. Save, print, and then close **ExcelL1_C4_P2.xlsx**.

roject ③ **Format a Billing Worksheet**

You will insert a formula in a weekly billing worksheet and then sort and filter specific data in the worksheet.

QUICK STEPS

Sort Data
1. Select cells.
2. Click Sort & Filter button.
3. Click desired sort option at drop-down list.

HINT

If you are not satisfied with the results of the sort, immediately click the Undo button.

Sorting Data

Excel is primarily a spreadsheet program, but it also includes some basic database functions. With a database program, you can alphabetize information or arrange numbers numerically. Data can be sorted by columns in a worksheet. Sort data in a worksheet with the Sort & Filter button in the Editing group in the Home tab.

To sort data in a worksheet, select the cells containing data you want to sort, click the Sort & Filter button in the Editing group and then click the option representing the desired sort. The sort option names vary depending on the data in selected cells. For example, if the first column of selected cells contains text, the sort options in the drop-down list display as *Sort A to Z* and *Sort Z to A*. If the selected cells contain dates, the sort options in the drop-down list display as *Sort Oldest to Newest* and *Sort Newest to Oldest* and if the cells contain numbers or values, the sort options display as *Sort Smallest to Largest* and *Sort Largest to Smallest*. If you select more than one column in a worksheet, Excel will sort the data in the first selected column.

Project ③a　Sorting Data

1. Open **ExcelC04Project03.xlsx** and save it and name it **ExcelL1_C4_P3**.
2. Insert a formula in cell F4 that multiplies the rate by the hours. Copy the formula down to cells F5 through F29.
3. Sort the data in the first column in descending order by completing the following steps:
   a. Make cell A4 active.
   b. Click the Sort & Filter button in the Editing group.
   c. Click the *Sort Largest to Smallest* option at the drop-down list.
4. Sort in ascending order by clicking the Sort & Filter button and then clicking *Sort Smallest to Largest* at the drop-down list.
5. Save and then print **ExcelL1_C4_P3.xlsx**.

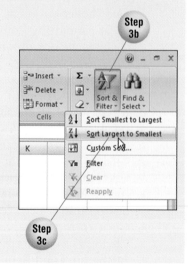

Step 3b

Step 3c

Completing a Custom Sort

If you want to sort data in a column other than the first column, use the Sort dialog box. If you select just one column in a worksheet, click the Sort & Filter button, and then click the desired sort option, only the data in that column is sorted. If this data is related to data to the left or right of the data in the sorted column, that relationship is broken. For example, if you sort cells C4 through C29 in **ExcelL1_C4_P3.xlsx**, the client number, treatment, hours, and total would no longer match the date.

Use the Sort dialog box to sort data and maintain the relationship of all cells. To sort using the Sort dialog box, select the cells you want sorted, click the Sort & Filter button, and then click *Custom Sort*. This displays the Sort dialog box shown in Figure 4.11.

The data displayed in the *Sort by* option box will vary depending on what you have selected. Generally, the data that displays is the title of the first column of selected cells. If the selected cells do not have a title, the data may display as *Column A*. Use this option to specify what column you want sorted. Using the Sort dialog box to sort data in a column maintains the relationship of the data.

QUICK STEPS

Complete Custom Sort
1. Select cells.
2. Click Sort & Filter button.
3. Click *Custom Sort* at drop-down list.
4. Specify options at Sort dialog box.
5. Click OK.

Figure 4.11 Sort Dialog Box

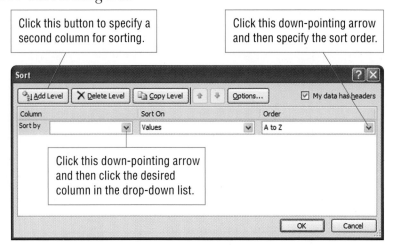

Click this button to specify a second column for sorting.

Click this down-pointing arrow and then specify the sort order.

Click this down-pointing arrow and then click the desired column in the drop-down list.

Project 3b Sorting Data Using the Sort Dialog Box

1. With **ExcelL1_C4_P3.xlsx** open, sort the rates in cells E4 through E29 in ascending order and maintain the relationship to the other data by completing the following steps:
   a. Select cells A3 through F29.
   b. Click the Sort & Filter button and then click *Custom Sort*.
   c. At the Sort dialog box, click the down-pointing arrow at the right of the *Sort by* option box, and then click *Rate* at the drop-down list.
   d. Click the down-pointing arrow at the right of the *Order* option box and then click *Largest to Smallest* at the drop-down list.
   e. Click OK to close the Sort dialog box.
   f. Deselect the cells.

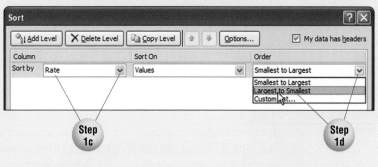

Step 1c

Step 1d

2. Save and then print **ExcelL1_C4_P3.xlsx**.
3. Sort the dates in ascending order (oldest to newest) by completing steps similar to those in Step 1.
4. Save and then print **ExcelL1_C4_P3.xlsx**.

Sorting More Than One Column

When sorting data in cells, you can sort in more than one column. For example, in Project 3c you will be sorting the date from oldest to newest and then sorting client numbers from lowest to highest. In this sort, the dates are sorted first and then client numbers are sorted in ascending order within the same date.

To sort in more than one column, select all columns in the worksheet that need to remain relative and then display the Sort dialog box. At the Sort dialog box, specify the first column you want sorted in the *Sort by* option box, click the *Add Level* button, and then specify the second column in the first *Then by* option box. In Excel, you can sort on multiple columns. Add additional *Then by* option boxes by clicking the *Add Level* button.

Project 3c Sorting Data in Two Columns

1. With **ExcelL1_C4_P3.xlsx** open, select cells A3 through F29.
2. Click the Sort & Filter button and then click *Custom Sort*.
3. At the Sort dialog box, click the down-pointing arrow at the right side of the *Sort by* option box, and then click *Date* in the drop-down list.
4. Make sure *Oldest to Newest* displays in the *Order* option box.
5. Click the *Add Level* button.
6. Click the down-pointing arrow at the right of the first *Then by* option box and then click *Client #* in the drop-down list.
7. Click OK to close the dialog box.
8. Deselect the cells.
9. Save and then print **ExcelL1_C4_P3.xlsx**.

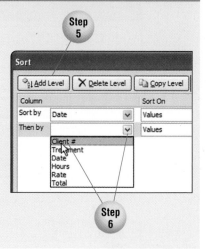

Step 5

Step 6

QUICK STEPS

Filter a List
1. Select cells.
2. Click Filter & Sort button.
3. Click *Filter* at drop-down list.
4. Click down-pointing arrow of heading to filter.
5. Click desired option at drop-down list.

Filtering Data

You can place a restriction, called a *filter*, on data in a worksheet to isolate temporarily specific data. To turn on filtering, make a cell containing data active, click the Filter & Sort button in the Editing group in the Home tab, and then click *Filter* at the drop-down list. This turns on filtering and causes a filter arrow to appear in each column label in the worksheet as shown in Figure 4.12. You do not need to select before turning on filtering because Excel automatically searches for column labels in a worksheet.

To filter data in a worksheet, click the filter arrow in the heading you want to filter. This causes a drop-down list to display with options to filter all records, create a custom filter, or select an entry that appears in one or more of the cells in the column. When you filter data, the filter arrow changes to a funnel icon. The funnel icon indicates that rows in the worksheet have been filtered. To turn off filtering, click the Sort & Filter button and then click *Filter*.

If a column contains numbers, click the filter arrow, point to *Number Filters*, and a side menu displays with options for filtering numbers. For example, you can filter numbers that are equal to, greater than, or less than a number you specify; filter the top ten numbers; and filter numbers that are above or below a specified number.

Figure 4.12 Filtering Data

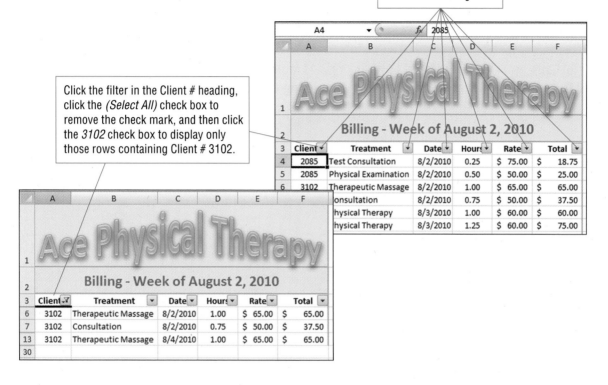

Turn on the filter feature and filter arrows display in column headings.

Click the filter in the *Client #* heading, click the *(Select All)* check box to remove the check mark, and then click the *3102* check box to display only those rows containing Client # 3102.

Project **3d**   **Filtering Data**

1. With **ExcelL1_C4_P3.xlsx** open, click in cell A4.
2. Turn on filtering by clicking the Sort & Filter button in the Editing group in the Home tab and then clicking *Filter* at the drop-down list.
3. Filter and then print rows for client number 3102 by completing the following steps:
   a. Click the filter arrow in the *Client #* heading.
   b. Click the *(Select All)* check box to remove the check mark.
   c. Scroll down the list box and then click *3102* to insert a check mark in the check box.
   d. Click OK.
   e. Print the worksheet by clicking the Quick Print button on the Quick Access toolbar.
4. Redisplay all rows containing data by completing the following steps:
   a. Click the funnel icon in the *Client #* heading.
   b. Click the *(Select All)* check box to insert a check mark (this also inserts a check mark for all items in the list).
   c. Click OK.

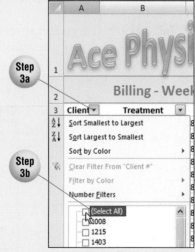

Step 3a

Step 3b

5. Filter and then print a list of clients receiving physical therapy by completing the following steps:
   a. Click the filter arrow in the *Treatment* heading.
   b. Click the *(Select All)* check box.
   c. Click the *Physical Therapy* check box.
   d. Click OK.
   e. Click the Quick Print button on the Quick Access toolbar.
6. Redisplay all rows containing data by completing the following steps:
   a. Click the funnel icon in the *Treatment* heading.
   b. Click the *(Select All)* check box to insert a check mark (this also inserts a check mark for all items in the list).
   c. Click OK.
7. Display the top two highest rates by completing the following steps:
   a. Click the filter arrow in the *Rate* heading.
   b. Point to *Number Filters* and then click *Top 10* at the side menu.
   c. At the Top 10 AutoFilter dialog box, select the *10* that displays in the middle text box and then type *2*.
   d. Click OK to close the dialog box.
   e. Click the Quick Print button on the Quick Access toolbar.
8. Redisplay all rows containing data by completing the following steps:
   a. Click the funnel icon in the *Rate* heading.
   b. Click the *(Select All)* check box to insert a check mark (this also inserts a check mark for all items in the list).
   c. Click OK.

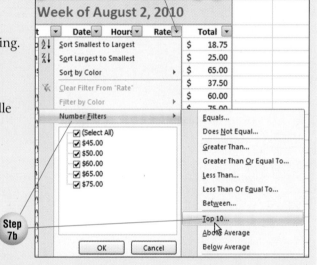

9. Display totals greater than $60 by completing the following steps:
   a. Click the filter arrow in the *Total* heading.
   b. Point to *Number Filters* and then click *Greater Than*.
   c. At the Custom AutoFilter dialog box, type *60* and then click OK.

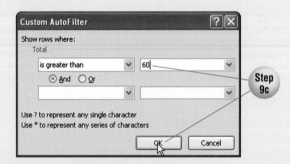

   d. Click the Quick Print button on the Quick Access toolbar.
10. Turn off the filtering feature by clicking the Sort & Filter button and then clicking *Filter* at the drop-down list.
11. Save and then close **ExcelL1_C4_P3.xlsx**.

Project 4 Plan and Create a Worksheet

You will use steps presented to plan a worksheet and then create, save, print, and then close the worksheet.

Planning a Worksheet

The worksheets you have worked with so far basically have already been planned. If you need to plan a worksheet yourself, some steps you can follow are listed below. These are basic steps—you may think of additional steps or additional information to help you plan a worksheet.

- **Step 1: Identify the purpose of the worksheet.** The more definite you are about your purpose, the easier organizing your data into an effective worksheet will be. Consider things such as the purpose of the worksheet, the intended audience, the desired output or results, and the data required.

- **Step 2: Design the worksheet.** To do this, you need to determine how the data is to be organized, the titles of columns and rows, and how to emphasize important information. Designing the worksheet also includes determining any calculations that need to be performed.

- **Step 3: Create a sketch of the worksheet.** A diagram or sketch can help create a logical and well-ordered worksheet. With a sketch, you can experiment with alternative column and row configurations and titles and headings. When creating a sketch, start with the heading or title of the worksheet, which should provide a quick overview of what the data represents in the worksheet. Determine appropriate column and row titles that clearly identify the data.

- **Step 4: Enter the data in the worksheet.** Type the data in the worksheet, including the worksheet title, column titles, row titles, and data within cells. Enter any required formulas into the worksheet and then format the worksheet to make it appealing and easy to read.

- **Step 5: Test the worksheet data.** After preparing the worksheet and inserting any necessary formulas, check the data to be sure that the calculations are performed correctly. Consider verifying the formula results by completing the formula on a calculator.

Project 4 Planning and Creating a Worksheet

1. Look at the data shown in Figure 4.13. (The first paragraph is simply a description of the data—do not include this in the worksheet.) After reviewing the data, complete the following steps:
   a. Create a sketch of how you think the worksheet should be organized.
   b. Create a worksheet from the sketch. (Be sure to include the necessary formula to calculate the total costs.)
   c. Apply formatting to enhance the appearance of the worksheet.
2. Save the workbook and name it **ExcelL1_C4_P4**.
3. Print and then close **ExcelL1_C4_P4.xlsx**.

Figure 4.13 **Project 4**

The following data itemizes budgeted direct labor hours and dollars by department for planning purposes. This data is prepared quarterly and sent to the plant manager and production manager.

DIRECT LABOR BUDGET

	Labor Rate	Total Hours	Total Costs
April			
Assembly	12.75	723	
Electronics	16.32	580	
Machining	27.34	442	
May			
Assembly	12.75	702	
Electronics	16.32	615	
Machining	27.34	428	
June			
Assembly	12.75	694	
Electronics	16.32	643	
Machining	27.34	389	

CHAPTER summary

- The Page Setup group in the Page Layout tab contains buttons for changing margins, page orientation and size, and buttons for establishing a print area, inserting page break, applying a picture background, and printing titles.

- The default left and right margins are 0.7 inch and the default top and bottom margins are 0.75 inch. Change these default margins with the Margins button in the Page Setup group in the Page Layout tab.

- Display the Page Setup dialog box with the Margins tab selected by clicking the Margins button and then clicking *Custom Margins* at the drop-down list.

- Center a worksheet on the page with the *Horizontally* and *Vertically* options at the Page Setup dialog box with the Margins tab selected.

- Click the Orientation button in the Page Setup group in the Page Layout tab to display the two orientation choices—*Portrait* and *Landscape*.

- Insert a page break by selecting the column or row, clicking the Breaks button in the Page Setup group in the Page Layout tab, and then clicking *Insert Page Break* at the drop-down list.

- To insert both a horizontal and vertical page break at the same time, make a cell active, click the Breaks button, and then click *Insert Page Break* at the drop-down list.

- Display a worksheet in page break preview by clicking the Page Break Preview button in the view area on the Status bar or clicking the View tab and then clicking the Page Break Preview button.

- Use options at the Page Setup dialog box with the Sheet tab selected to specify that you want column or row titles to print on each page. Display this dialog box by clicking the Print Titles button in the Page Setup group in the Page Layout tab.

- Use options in the Scale to Fit group in the Page Layout tab to scale data to fit on a specific number of pages.

- Use the Background button in the Page Setup group in the Page Layout tab to insert a worksheet background picture. A background picture displays on the screen but does not print.

- Use options in the Sheet Options group in the Page Layout tab to specify if you want gridlines and headings to view and/or print.

- Specify a print area by selecting the desired cells, clicking the Print Area button in the Page Setup group in the Page Layout tab and then clicking *Set Print Area* at the drop-down list. Add another print area by selecting the desired cells, clicking the Print Area button, and then clicking *Add to Print Area* at the drop-down list.

- Create a header and/or footer with the Header & Footer button in the Text group in the Insert tab, in Page Layout view, or with options at the Page Setup dialog box with the Header/Footer tab selected.

- Customize print jobs with options at the Print dialog box.

- To check spelling in a worksheet, click the Review tab and then click the Spelling button.

- Click the Undo button on the Quick Access toolbar to reverse the most recent action and click the Redo button to redo a previously reversed action.
- Use options at the Find and Replace dialog box with the Find tab selected to find specific data and/or formatting in a worksheet.
- Use options at the Find and Replace dialog box with the Replace tab selected to find specific data and/or formatting and replace with other data and/or formatting.
- Sort data in a worksheet with options from the Sort & Filter button in the Editing group in the Home tab.
- Create a custom sort with options at the Sort dialog box. Display this dialog box by clicking the Sort & Filter button and then clicking *Custom Sort* at the drop-down list.
- Use the filter feature to temporarily isolate specific data. Turn on the filter feature by clicking the Sort & Filter button in the Editing group in the Home tab and then clicking *Filter* at the drop-down list. This inserts filter arrows in each column label. Click a filter arrow and then use options at the drop-down list that displays to specify the filter data.
- Plan a worksheet by completing these basic steps: identify the purpose of the worksheet, design the worksheet, create a sketch of the worksheet, enter the data in the worksheet, and test the worksheet data.

COMMANDS review

FEATURE	RIBBON TAB, GROUP	BUTTON, OPTION	KEYBOARD SHORTCUT
Margins	Page Layout, Page Setup		
Page Setup dialog box with Margins tab selected	Page Layout, Page Setup	, Custom Margins	
Orientation	Page Layout, Page Setup		
Size	Page Layout, Page Setup		
Insert page break	Page Layout, Page Setup	, Insert Page Break	
Remove page break	Page Layout, Page Setup	, Remove Page Break	
Page Break Preview	View, Workbook Views		
Page Setup dialog box with Sheet tab selected	Page Layout, Page Setup		
Scale width	Page Layout, Scale to Fit	Width: Automatic	
Scale height	Page Layout, Scale to Fit	Height: Automatic	
Scale	Page Layout, Scale to Fit	Scale: 100%	
Background picture	Page Layout, Page Setup		
Print Area	Page Layout, Page Setup		
Header and footer	Insert, Text		
Page Layout view	View, Workbook Views		
Spelling	Review, Proofing	ABC	F7
Find and Replace dialog box with Find tab selected	Home, Editing	, Find	Ctrl + F
Find and Replace dialog box with Replace tab selected	Home, Editing	, Replace	Ctrl + H
Sort data	Home, Editing		
Filter data	Home, Editing		

CONCEPTS check

Test Your Knowledge

Completion: In the space provided at the right, indicate the correct term, symbol, or command.

1. This is the default left and right margin measurement. _____

2. This is the default top and bottom margin measurement. _____

3. The Margins button is located in this tab. _____

4. By default, a worksheet prints in this orientation on a page. _____

5. Click the Print Titles button in the Page Setup group in the Page Layout tab and the Page Setup dialog box displays with this tab selected. _____

6. Use options in this group in the Page Layout tab to adjust the printed output by a percentage to fit the number of pages specified. _____

7. Use this button in the Page Setup group in the Page Layout tab to select and print specific areas in a worksheet. _____

8. Click the Header & Footer button in the Text group in the Insert tab and the worksheet displays in this view. _____

9. This tab contains options for formatting and customizing a header and/or footer. _____

10. Click this tab to display the Spelling button. _____

11. The Undo and Redo buttons are located on this toolbar. _____

12. Click this button in the Find and Replace dialog box to expand the dialog box. _____

13. Use these two buttons at the expanded Find and Replace dialog box to search for specific cell formatting and replace with other formatting. _____

14. Use this button in the Home tab to sort data in a worksheet. _____

15. Use this feature to isolate temporarily a specific data in a worksheet. _____

SKILLS check

Demonstrate Your Proficiency

1 FORMAT A DATA ANALYSIS WORKSHEET

1. Open **ExcelC04Assessment01.xlsx**.
2. Save the workbook with Save As and name it **ExcelL1_C4_A1**.
3. Make the following changes to the worksheet:
   a. Insert a formula in cell H4 that averages the amounts in cells B4 through G4.
   b. Copy the formula in cell H4 down to cells H5 through H9.
   c. Insert a formula in cell B10 that adds the amounts in cells B4 through B9.
   d. Copy the formula in cell B10 over to cells C10 through H10. (Click the AutoFill Options button and then click *Fill With Formatting* at the drop-down list.)
   e. Change the orientation of the worksheet to landscape.
   f. Change the top margin to 3 inches and the left margin to 1.5 inches.
4. Save and then print **ExcelL1_C4_A1.xlsx**.
5. Make the following changes to the worksheet:
   a. Change the top margin to 1 inch and the left margin to 0.7 inch.
   b. Change the orientation back to portrait.
   c. Horizontally and vertically center the worksheet on the page.
   d. Scale the worksheet so it fits on one page.
6. Save, print, and then close **ExcelL1_C4_A1.xlsx**.

2 FORMAT A TEST RESULTS WORKSHEET

1. Open **ExcelC04Assessment02.xlsx**.
2. Save the workbook with Save As and name it **ExcelL1_C4_A2**.
3. Make the following changes to the worksheet.
   a. Insert a formula in cell N4 that averages the test scores in cells B4 through M4.
   b. Copy the formula in cell N4 down to cells N5 through N21.
   c. Type Average in cell A22.
   d. Insert a formula in cell B22 that averages the test scores in cells B4 through B21.
   e. Copy the formula in cell B22 across to cells C22 through N22.
   f. Insert a page break between columns G and H.
4. View the worksheet in Page Break Preview.
5. Change back to the Normal view.
6. Specify that the column row titles (A3 through A22) are to print on each page.
7. Create a header that prints the page number at the right side of the page.
8. Create a footer that prints your name at the left side of the page and the workbook file name at the right side of the page.
9. Save and then print the worksheet.
10. Set a print area for cells N4 through N22 and then print the cells.
11. Clear the print area.
12. Save and then close **ExcelL1_C4_A2.xlsx**.

Assessment

3 FORMAT AN EQUIPMENT RENTAL WORKSHEET

1. Open **ExcelC04Assessment03.xlsx**.
2. Save the workbook with Save As and name it **ExcelL1_C4_A3**.
3. Insert a formula in cell H3 that multiplies the rate in cell G3 by the hours in cell F3. Copy the formula in cell H3 down to cells H4 through H16.
4. Insert a formula in cell H17 that sums the amounts in cells H3 through H16.
5. Complete the following find and replaces:
   a. Find all occurrences of cells containing *75* and replace with *90*.
   b. Find all occurrences of cells containing *55* and replace with *60*.
   c. Find all occurrences of *Barrier Concrete* and replace with *Lee Sand and Gravel*.
   d. Find all occurrences of 11-point Calibri and replace with 10-point Cambria.
6. Insert a header that prints the date at the left side of the page and the time at the right side of the page.
7. Insert a footer that prints your name at the left side of the page and the workbook name at the right side of the page.
8. Print the worksheet horizontally and vertically centered on the page.
9. Save and then close **ExcelL1_C4_A3.xlsx**.

Assessment

4 FORMAT AN INVOICES WORKSHEET

1. Open **ExcelC04Assessment04.xlsx**.
2. Save the workbook with Save As and name it **ExcelL1_C4_A4**.
3. Search for the light green fill (the lightest fill in the worksheet that fills cells in every other row beginning with row 5) and replace it with no fill. (Do this at the Find and Replace dialog box with the Replace tab selected.)
4. Insert a formula in G4 that multiplies the amount in E4 with the percentage in F4 and then adds the product to cell E4. (If you write the formula correctly, the result in G4 will display as *$488.25*.)
5. Copy the formula in cell G4 down to cells G5 through G17.
6. Complete a spelling check on the worksheet.
7. Find all occurrences of *Picture* and replace with *Portrait*. (Do not type a space after *Picture* or *Portrait* because you want to find occurrences that end with an "s.")
8. Sort the records by invoice number in ascending order (smallest to largest).
9. Sort the records by client number in ascending order (A to Z) and then by date in ascending order (oldest to newest).
10. Insert a footer in the worksheet that prints your name at the left side of the page and the current date at the right side of the page.
11. Center the worksheet horizontally and vertically on the page.
12. Save and then print **ExcelL1_C4_A4.xlsx**.
13. Select cells A3 through G3 and then turn on the filter feature and complete the following filters:
    a. Filter and then print a list of rows containing client number 11-279.

b. Filter and then print a list of rows containing the top three highest amounts due.

c. Filter and then print a list of rows containing amounts due that are less than $500.

14. Save and then close **ExcelL1_C4_A4.xlsx**.

5   CREATE A WORKSHEET CONTAINING SORT ORDER INFORMATION

1. Use Excel's Help feature and learn about the default sort order. After reading and printing the information presented, create a worksheet containing a summary of the information. Create the worksheet with the following features:

a. Create a title for the worksheet.

b. Set the data in cells in a serif typeface and change the data color.

c. Add borders to the cells (you determine the border style).

d. Add a color shading to cells (you determine the color—make it complementary to the data color).

e. Create a footer that prints your name at the left margin and the file name at the right margin.

2. Save the workbook and name it **ExcelL1_C4_A5**.

3. Print and then close **ExcelL1_C4_A5.xlsx**.

CASE study

Part

1

Apply Your Skills

You are the sales manager for Macadam Realty. You decide that you want to display sample mortgage worksheets in the reception area display rack. Open the **MacadamMortgages.xlsx** workbook, save it with Save As and name it **ExcelL1_C4_CS_P1A**, and then add the following information and make the following changes:

- In column C, insert a formula that determines the down payment amount.
- In column D, insert a formula that determines the loan amount.
- In column G, insert a formula using the PMT function (enter the *Pv* as a negative).
- Insert the date and time as a header and your name and the workbook name (**ExcelL1_C4_CS_P1A.xlsx**) as a footer.
- Find 11-point Calibri formatting and replace with 11-point Candara formatting.
- Scale the worksheet so it prints on one page.

Save and then print **ExcelL1_C4_CS_P1A.xlsx**. After looking at the printed worksheet, you decide that you need to make the following changes:

- Sort the *Price of Home* column from smallest to largest.
- Change the percentage amount in column E from 6% to 7%.
- Shade the cells in row 4 in the light yellow color that matches the fill in cell A2. Copy this shading to every other row of cells in the worksheet (stopping at row 46).

Save the edited worksheet with Save As and name it **ExcelL1_C4_CS_P1B**. Edit the footer to reflect the workbook name change (from *ExcelL1_C4_CS_P1A.xlsx* to *ExcelL1_C4_CS_P1B.xlsx*). Save, print and then close **ExcelL1_C4_CS_P1B.xlsx**. (Make sure the worksheet prints on one page.)

Part 2

You are preparing for a quarterly sales meeting during which you will discuss retirement issues with the sales officers. You want to encourage them to consider opening an Individual Retirement Account (IRA) to supplement the retirement contributions made by Macadam Realty. You have begun an IRA worksheet but need to complete it. Open **MacadamIRA.xlsx** and then save it with Save As and name it **ExcelL1_C4_CS_P2A**. Make the following changes to the worksheet:

- Insert in cell C6 a formula that calculates the future value of an investment. Use the FV function to write the formula. You must use absolute and mixed cell references for the formula. When entering the *Rate* (percentage), the column letter is variable but the row number is fixed; when entering the *Nper* (years), the column letter is fixed but the row number is variable; and when entering the *Pmt* (the contribution amount), both the column letter and row number are absolute.
- Copy the formula in cell C6 down to cells C7 through C19. Copy the formula in cell C6 across to cells D6 through K6. Continue in this manner until the amounts are entered in all the appropriate cells.
- Select and then merge and center cells A6 through A19. Type the text *Number of Years* and then rotate the text up. Make sure the text is centered in the merged cell. Apply 12-point Calibri bold formatting to the text.
- Adjust the column widths so all text is visible in the cells.
- Change the page orientation to landscape.
- Vertically and horizontally center the worksheet.
- Include a header that prints the page number and insert a footer that prints your name.

Save the worksheet and then print it so that the row titles print on both pages. After looking at the worksheet, you decide to make the following changes:

- Remove the header containing the page number.
- Edit the footer so the date prints at the left margin and your name prints at the right margin.
- Scale the worksheet so it prints on one page.

Save the workbook and name it **ExcelL1_C4_CS_P2B** and then print the worksheet. Change the amount in cell D3 to *$2,500* and then print the worksheet again. Change the amount in cell D3 to *$3,000* and then print the worksheet again. Save and then close **ExcelL1_C4_CS_P2B.xlsx**.

Part 3

You have clients living in Canada that are interested in purchasing real estate in the United States. For those clients, you like to keep a conversion worksheet available. Using the Internet, search for the MS MoneyCentral Investor Currency Rates site. Determine the current currency exchange rate for Canada and then create a worksheet with the following specifications:

- Apply formatting that is similar to the formatting in the worksheets you worked with in the first two parts of the case study.
- Create the following columns:
  - Column for home price in American dollars.
  - Column for home price in Canadian dollars.
  - Column for amount of down payment.
  - Column for loan total.
  - Column for monthly payment.
- In the column for home prices, insert home amounts beginning with $100,000, incrementing every $50,000, and ending with $1,000,000.
- Insert a formula in the home price in the Canadian dollars column that displays the home price in Canadian dollars.
- Insert a formula in the down payment column that multiplies the Canadian home price by 20%.
- Insert a formula in the loan total column that subtracts the down payment from the Canadian home price.
- Insert a formula in the monthly payment column that determines the monthly payment using the PMT function. Use 6% as the rate (be sure to divide by 12 months), 360 as the number of payments, and the loan amount as a negative as the present value.
- Apply any other formatting you feel necessary to improve the worksheet.

Save the completed workbook and name it **ExcelL1_C4_CS_P3**. Display formulas and then print the worksheet. Redisplay the formulas and then save and close the workbook.

Part 4

After working with the commissions worksheet, you decide to maintain the information in an Access table. Before importing the information to an Access table, open **MacadamCommissions.xlsx** and then save the workbook with Save As and name it **ExcelL1_C4_CS_P4**. Insert a formula in G4 that multiplies the sale price by the commission percentage. Copy the formula down to cells G5 through G24. Insert a formula in cell G25 that totals the commissions and then adjust the column width so the entire total is visible. Select cells A3 through G25 and then save the selected cells in a separate workbook named **ExcelMacadamComm**. Create a database in Access named **Macadam** and then import the **ExcelMacadamComm.xlsx** Excel workbook as an Access table. Save the database and print the newly imported table.

Preparing and Formatting a Worksheet

ASSESSING proficiency

In this unit, you have learned to create, save, print, edit, and format Excel worksheets; create and insert formulas; and enhance worksheets with features such as headers and footers, page numbering, sorting, and filtering.

Excel Unit 1

Note: Before beginning computer assessments, copy to your storage medium the Excel2007L1U1 subfolder from the Excel2007L1 folder on the CD that accompanies this textbook and then make Excel2007L1U1 the active folder.

Assessment 1 Create Sales Bonuses Workbook

1. Create the Excel worksheet shown in Figure U1.1. Format the cells as you see them in the figure. Format the money amounts in Accounting format with no decimal places.
2. Insert an IF statement in cell C4 that inserts *7%* if B4 is greater than 99999 and inserts *5%* if B4 is less than 100000.
3. Format the number in cell C4 so it displays as a percentage with no decimal places. Copy the formula in cell C4 down to cells C5 through C11.
4. Insert a formula in cell D4 that multiplies the amount in B4 with the percentage in cell C4. Copy the formula in D4 down to cells D5 through D11.
5. Insert a footer that contains your first and last names and the current date.
6. Print the worksheet horizontally and vertically centered on the page.
7. Save the workbook and name it **ExcelL1_U1_A1**.
8. Close **ExcelL1_U1_A1.xlsx**.

Figure U1.1 Assessment 1

	A	B	C	D	E
1	**Capstan Marine Products**				
2		Sales Department			
3	**Salesperson**	**Sales**	**Bonus**	**Bonus Amount**	
4	Allejandro, Eduardo	$ 105,345			
5	Crispin, Juliette	$ 96,345			
6	Frankel, Hayden	$ 89,234			
7	Hiesmann, Denae	$ 120,455			
8	Jarvis, Robert	$ 131,095			
9	Littleman, Marcus	$ 99,850			
10	Weisen, George	$ 103,125			
11	Schoenfeld, Allie	$ 78,495			
12					

Assessment 2 Format Equipment Purchase Plan Workbook

1. Open **ExcelU01Assessment02.xlsx** and then save the workbook and name it **ExcelL1_U1_A2**.
2. The owner of Hilltop Equipment Rental is interested in purchasing a new tractor and needs to determine monthly payments on three different models. Insert a formula in cell E4 that uses the PMT function to calculate monthly payments. Copy the formula down to cells E5 and E6.
3. Insert a formula in cell F4 that multiplies the amount in E4 by the amount in D4.
4. Copy the formula in cell F4 down to cells F5 and F6.
5. Insert a formula in cell G4 that subtracts the amount in B4 from the amount in F4.
6. Copy the formula in cell G4 down to cells G5 and G6.
7. Change the vertical alignment of cell A2 to Middle Align.
8. Change the vertical alignment of cells A3 through G3 to Bottom Align.
9. Save, print, and then close **ExcelL1_U1_A2.xlsx**.

Assessment 3 Format Accounts Due Workbook

1. Open **ExcelU01Assessment03.xlsx** and then save the workbook and name it **ExcelL1_U1_A3**.
2. Using the DATE function, enter a formula in each of the specified cells that returns the serial number for the specified date:

    C4   =   October 26, 2010
    C5   =   October 27, 2010
    C6   =   October 27, 2010
    C7   =   October 29, 2010
    C8   =   November 3, 2010
    C9   =   November 5, 2010
    C10 =   November 5, 2010
    C11 =   November 12, 2010
    C12 =   November 12, 2010

3. Enter a formula in cell E4 that inserts the due date (date of service plus the number of days in the *Terms* column).
4. Copy the formula in cell E4 down to cells E5 through E12.
5. Make cell A14 active and then type your name.
6. Make cell A15 active and then use the NOW function to insert the current date as a serial number.
7. Save, print, and then close **ExcelL1_U1_A3.xlsx**.

Assessment 4 Format First Quarter Sales Workbook

1. Open **ExcelU01Assessment04.xlsx** and then save the workbook and name it **ExcelL1_U1_A4**.
2. Insert a formula in cell E4 that totals the amounts in B4, C4, and D4. Copy the formula in cell E4 down to cells E5 through E18.
3. Insert an IF statement in cell F4 that inserts *10%* if E4 is greater than 99999 and inserts *7%* if E4 is greater than 49999 and inserts *5%* if E4 is greater than 24999 and inserts *0%* if E4 is greater than 0.
4. Make sure the result of the IF formula displays in cell F4 as a percentage with no decimal points and then copy the formula down to cells F5 through F18.

5. Select cells A5 through F5 and then insert the same yellow fill as cell A2. Apply the same yellow fill to cells A7 through F7, A9 through F9, A11 through F11, A13 through F13, A15 through F15, and cells A17 through F17.
6. Insert a footer that prints your name at the left, the current date at the middle, and the current time at the right.
7. Print the worksheet horizontally and vertically centered on the page.
8. Save, print, and then close **ExcelL1_U1_A4.xlsx**.

Assessment 5 Format Weekly Payroll Workbook

1. Open **ExcelU01Assessment05.xlsx** and then save the workbook and name it **ExcelL1_U1_A5**.
2. Insert a formula in cell E4 that multiplies the hourly wage by the hours and then adds that to the multiplication of the hourly wage by the overtime pay rate (1.5) and then overtime hours. (Use parentheses in the formula and use an absolute cell reference for the overtime pay rate (1.5). Refer to Chapter 2, Project 5c.) Copy the formula down to cells E5 through E17.
3. Insert a formula in cell F4 that multiplies the gross pay by the withholding tax rate (W/H Rate). (Use a mixed cell reference for the cell containing the withholding rate. Refer to Chapter 2, Project 5c.) Copy the formula down to cells F5 through F17.
4. Insert a formula in cell G4 that multiplies the gross pay by the Social Security rate (SS Rate). (Use a mixed cell reference for the cell containing the Social Security rate. Refer to Chapter 2, Project 5c.) Copy the formula down to cells G5 through G17.
5. Insert a formula in cell H4 that adds together the Social Security tax and the withholding tax and subtracts that from the gross pay. Copy the formula down to cells H5 through H17.
6. Sort the employee last names alphabetically in ascending order (A to Z).
7. Center the worksheet horizontally and vertically on the page.
8. Insert a footer that prints your name at the left side of the page and the worksheet name at the right side of the page.
9. Save, print, and then close **ExcelL1_U1_A5.xlsx**.

Assessment 6 Format Customer Sales Analysis Workbook

1. Open **ExcelU01Assessment06.xlsx** and then save the workbook and name it **ExcelL1_U1_A6**.
2. Insert formulas and drag down formulas to complete the worksheet.
3. Change the orientation to landscape.
4. Insert a header that prints the page number at the right side of the page.
5. Insert a footer that prints your name at the right side of the page.
6. Horizontally and vertically center the worksheet on the page.
7. Specify that the column headings in cells A3 through A9 print on both pages.
8. Save, print, and then close **ExcelL1_U1_A6.xlsx**.

Assessment 7 Format Invoices Workbook

1. Open **ExcelU01Assessment07.xlsx** and then save the workbook and name it **ExcelL1_U1_A7**.
2. Insert a formula in cell G4 that multiplies the amount in E4 by the percentage in F4 and then adds that total to the amount in E4. (Use parentheses in this formula.)
3. Copy the formula in cell G4 down to cells G5 through G18.

4. Find all occurrences of cells containing *11-279* and replace with *10-005*.
5. Find all occurrences of cells containing *8.5* and replace with *9.0*.
6. Search for the Calibri font and replace with the Candara font (do not specify a type size so that Excel replaces all sizes of Calibri with Candara).
7. Print **ExcelL1_U1_A7.xlsx**.
8. Filter and then print a list of rows containing only the client number *04-325*. (After printing, return the list to *(All)*.)
9. Filter and then print a list of rows containing only the service *Development*. (After printing, return the list to *(All)*.)
10. Filter and then print a list of rows containing the top three highest totals in the *Amount Due* column. (After printing, turn off the filter feature.)
11. Save and then close **ExcelL1_U1_A7.xlsx**.

WRITING activities

The following activities give you the opportunity to practice your writing skills along with demonstrating an understanding of some of the important Excel features you have mastered in this unit. Use correct grammar, appropriate word choices, and clear sentence construction.

Activity 1 Plan and Prepare Orders Summary Workbook

Plan and prepare a worksheet with the information shown in Figure U1.2. Apply formatting of your choosing to the worksheet either with a cell or table style or with formatting at the Format Cells dialog box. Save the completed worksheet and name it **ExcelL1_U1_Act01**. Print and then close **ExcelL1_U1_Act01.xlsx**.

Figure U1.2 Activity 1

Prepare a weekly summary of orders taken that itemizes the products coming into the company and the average order size.

The products and average order size include:

Black and gold wall clock—$2,450 worth of orders, average order size of $125
Traveling alarm clock—$1,358 worth of orders, average order size of $195
Water-proof watch—$890 worth of orders, average order size of $90
Dashboard clock—$2,135 worth of orders, average order size of $230
Pyramid clock—$3,050 worth of orders, average order size of $375
Gold chain watch—$755 worth of orders, average order size of $80

In the worksheet, total the amount ordered and also calculate the average weekly order size. Sort the data in the worksheet by the order amount in descending order.

Activity 2 Prepare Depreciation Workbook

Assets within a company, such as equipment, can be depreciated over time. Several methods are available for determining the amount of depreciation such as the straight-line depreciation method, fixed-declining balance method, and the double-declining method. Use Excel's Help feature to learn about two depreciation methods—straight-line and double-declining depreciation. After reading about the two methods, create an Excel worksheet with the following information:

- An appropriate title
- A heading for straight-line depreciation
- The straight-line depreciation function
- The name and a description for each straight-line depreciation function argument category
- A heading for double-declining depreciation
- The double-declining depreciation function
- The name and a description for each double-declining depreciation function argument category

Apply formatting of your choosing to the worksheet. Save the completed workbook and name it **ExcelL1_U1_Act02**. Print the worksheet horizontally and vertically centered on the page. Close **ExcelL1_U1_Act02.xlsx**.

Activity 3 Insert Straight-Line Depreciation Formula

Open **ExcelU01Activity03.xlsx** and then save the workbook and name it **ExcelL1_U1_Act03**. Insert the function to determine straight-line depreciation in cell E3. Copy the formula down to cells E4 through E10. Apply formatting of your choosing to the worksheet. Print the worksheet horizontally and vertically centered on the page. Save and then close **ExcelL1_U1_Act03.xlsx**.

Optional: Briefly research the topic of straight-line and double-declining depreciation to find out why businesses depreciate their assets. What purpose does it serve? Locate information about the topic on the Internet or in your school library. Then use Word 2007 to write a half-page, single-spaced report explaining the financial reasons for using depreciation methods. Save the document and name it **ExcelL1_U1_Act03Report**. Print and then close the document.

Create a Travel Planning Worksheet

Make sure you are connected to the Internet. Use a search engine of your choosing to look for information on traveling to a specific country that interests you. Find sites that provide cost information for airlines, hotels, meals, entertainment, and car rentals. Create a travel planning worksheet for the country that includes the following:

- appropriate title
- appropriate headings
- airline costs

- hotel costs (off-season and in-season rates if available)
- estimated meal costs
- entertainment costs
- car rental costs

Save the completed workbook and name it **ExcelL1_U1_Act04**. Print and then close the workbook.

Level 1

Microsoft excel

Unit 2: Enhancing the Display of Workbooks

➤ Moving Data within and between Workbooks

➤ Maintaining Workbooks

➤ Creating a Chart in Excel

➤ Adding Visual Interest to Workbooks

Benchmark Microsoft® Excel 2007 Level 1

Microsoft Certified Application Specialist Skills—Unit 2

Reference No.	Skill	Pages
1	**Creating and Manipulating Data**	
1.3	Modify cell contents and formats	
1.3.1	Cut, copy, and paste data and cell contents	158-164, 181-182
1.4	Change worksheet views	
1.4.1	Change views within a single window	171-174
1.4.2	Split windows	171-174
1.4.3	Open and arrange new windows	177-180
1.5	Manage worksheets	
1.5.1	Copy worksheets	167-168, 207-208
1.5.2	Reposition worksheets within workbooks	167-168
1.5.3	Rename worksheets	167-168
1.5.4	Hide and unhide worksheets	169-170
1.5.5	Insert and delete worksheets	164-166
2	**Formatting Data and Content**	
2.1	Format worksheets	
2.1.3	Add color to worksheet tabs	167-168
2.1.4	Format worksheet backgrounds	291-292
2.3	Format cells and cell content	
2.3.8	Insert, modify, and remove hyperlinks	275-277
4	**Presenting Data Visually**	
4.1	Create and format charts	
4.1.1	Select appropriate data sources for charts	239-243
4.1.2	Select appropriate chart types to represent data sources	243-245
4.1.3	Format charts using Quick Styles	246-248, 257-259
4.2	Modify charts	
4.2.1	Add and remove chart elements	249-253
4.2.2	Move and size charts	241-243, 260-261
4.2.3	Change chart types	243-245
4.4	Insert and modify illustrations	
4.4.1	Insert and modify pictures from files (not clip art files)	255-256, 288-289
4.4.2	Insert and modify SmartArt graphics	292-297
4.4.3	Insert and modify shapes	284-287
5	**Collaborating and Securing Data**	
5.1	Manage changes to workbooks	
5.1.2	Insert, display, modify, and delete comments	222-226
5.4	Save workbooks	
5.4.1	Save workbooks for use in a previous version of Excel	211-212
5.4.2	Using the correct format, save a workbook as a template, a Web page, a macro-enabled document, or another appropriate format	213-214, 272-274

Note: The Level 1 and Level 2 texts each address approximately half of the Microsoft Certified Application Specialist skills. Complete coverage of the skills is offered in the combined Level 1 and Level 2 text titled *Benchmark Series Microsoft® Excel 2007: Levels 1 and 2,* which has been approved as certified courseware and which displays the Microsoft Certified Application Specialist logo on the cover.

CHAPTER 5

Moving Data within and between Workbooks

PERFORMANCE OBJECTIVES

Upon successful completion of Chapter 5, you will be able to:

- Create a workbook with multiple worksheets
- Move, copy, and paste cells within a worksheet
- Split a worksheet into windows and freeze panes
- Name a range of cells and use a range in a formula
- Open multiple workbooks
- Arrange, size, and move workbooks
- Copy and paste data between workbooks
- Link data between worksheets
- Link worksheets with a 3-D reference
- Copy and paste a worksheet between programs

excel Chapter 5

SNAP

Tutorial 5.1
Managing Worksheets and
Workbooks
Tutorial 5.2
Working with Multiple
Worksheets

Up to this point, the workbooks in which you have been working have consisted of only one worksheet. In this chapter, you will learn to create a workbook with several worksheets and complete tasks such as copying and pasting data within and between worksheets. Moving and pasting or copying and pasting selected cells in and between worksheets is useful for rearranging data or for saving time. You will also work with multiple workbooks and complete tasks such as arranging, sizing, and moving workbooks, and opening and closing multiple workbooks.

Note: Before beginning computer projects, copy to your storage medium the Excel2007L1C5 subfolder from the Excel2007L1 folder on the CD that accompanies this textbook and then make Excel2007L1C5 the active folder.

Project ① Manage Data in a Multiple-Worksheet Account Workbook

You will open an account workbook containing three worksheets and then move, copy, and paste data between the worksheets. You will also hide and unhide worksheets, and format and print multiple worksheets in the workbook.

Creating a Workbook with Multiple Worksheets

An Excel workbook can contain multiple worksheets. You can create a variety of worksheets within a workbook for related data. For example, a workbook may contain a worksheet for the expenses for each salesperson in a company and another worksheet for the monthly payroll for each department within the company. Another example is recording sales statistics for each quarter in individual worksheets within a workbook.

By default, a workbook contains three worksheets named *Sheet1*, *Sheet2*, and *Sheet3*. (Later in this chapter, you will learn how to change these default names.) Display various worksheets in the workbook by clicking the desired tab.

Project 1a Displaying Worksheets in a Workbook

1. Open **ExcelC05Project01.xlsx** and then save the workbook and name it **ExcelL1_C5_P1**.
2. This workbook contains three worksheets. Display the various worksheets by completing the following steps:
   a. Display the second worksheet by clicking the Sheet2 tab that displays immediately above the Status bar.
   b. Display the third worksheet by clicking the Sheet3 tab that displays immediately above the Status bar.
   c. Return to the first worksheet by clicking the Sheet1 tab.

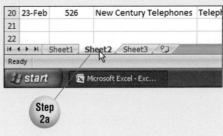

Step 2a

3. Make the following changes to worksheets in the workbook:
   a. Click the Sheet2 tab and then change the column width for columns E, F, and G to 11.00.
   b. Click the Sheet3 tab and then change the column width for columns E, F, and G to 11.00.
   c. Click the Sheet1 tab to display the first worksheet.
4. Save **ExcelL1_C5_P1.xlsx**.

Cutting, Copying, and Pasting Selected Cells

Situations may arise where you need to move cells to a different location within a worksheet, or you may need to copy repetitive data in a worksheet. You can perform these actions by selecting cells and then using the Cut, Copy, and/or Paste buttons in the Clipboard group in the Home tab. You can also perform these actions with the mouse.

Moving Selected Cells

Cut

Paste

You can move selected cells and cell contents in a worksheet and between worksheets. Move selected cells with the Cut and Paste buttons in the Clipboard group in the Home tab or by dragging with the mouse.

To move selected cells with buttons in the Home tab, select the cells and then click the Cut button in the Clipboard group. This causes a moving dashed line border (called a marquee) to display around the selected cells. Click the cell where you want the first selected cell inserted and then click the Paste button in the Clipboard group. If you change your mind and do not want to move the selected cells, press the Esc key to remove the moving dashed line border or double-click in any cell.

To move selected cells with the mouse, select the cells and then position the mouse pointer on any border of the selected cells until the pointer turns into an arrow pointer with a four-headed arrow attached. Hold down the left mouse button, drag the outline of the selected cells to the desired location, and then release the mouse button.

QUICK STEPS

Move and Paste Cells
1. Select cells.
2. Click Cut button.
3. Click desired cell.
4. Click Paste button.

HINT
Ctrl + X is the keyboard shortcut to cut selected data. Ctrl + V is the keyboard shortcut to paste data.

Project 1b Moving Selected Cells

1. With **ExcelL1_C5_P1.xlsx** open, you realize that the sublet rent deposit was recorded on the wrong day. The correct day is January 11. To move the cells containing information on the deposit, complete the following steps:
   a. Make cell A13 active and then insert a row. (The new row should display above the row containing information on *Rainer Suppliers*.)
   b. Select cells A7 through F7.
   c. Click the Cut button in the Clipboard group in the Home tab.

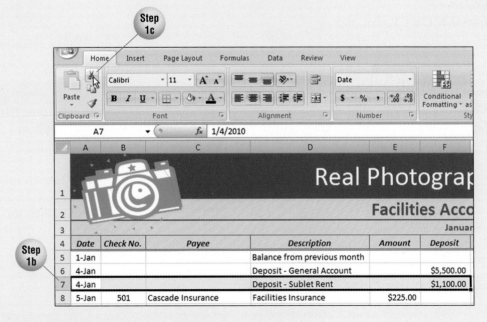

   d. Click cell A13 to make it active.
   e. Click the Paste button in the Clipboard group.

f. Change the date of the deposit from January 4 to January 11.

g. Select row 7 and then delete it.

2. Click the Sheet2 tab and then complete steps similar to those in Step 1 to move the sublet deposit row so it is positioned above the *Rainier Suppliers* row and below the *Clear Source* row. Change the date of the deposit to February 11 and make sure you delete row 7.

3. Move cells using the mouse by completing the following steps:

a. Click the Sheet3 tab.

b. Make cell A13 active and then insert a new row.

c. Using the mouse, select cells A7 through F7.

d. Position the mouse pointer on any boundary of the selected cells until it turns into an arrow pointer with a four-headed arrow attached.

e. Hold down the left mouse button, drag the outline of the selected cells to row 13, and then release the mouse button.

4	Date	Check No.	Payee	Description	Amount	Deposit
5	1-Mar			Balance from previous month		
6	1-Mar			Deposit - General Account		$5,500.00
7	1-Mar			Deposit - Sublet Rent		$1,100.00
8	2-Mar	527				
9	3-Mar	528				
10	3-Mar	529				
11	8-Mar	530	Stationery Plus	Paper Supplies	$113.76	
12	9-Mar	531	Clear Source	Developer Supplies	$251.90	
13						
14	10-Mar	532	Rainier S A13:F13	Camera Supplies	$119.62	
15	11-Mar	533	A1 Wedding Supplies	Photo Albums	$323.58	

Step 3c

Step 3e

f. Change the date of the deposit to March 10.

g. Delete row 7.

4. Save **ExcelL1_C5_P1.xlsx**.

Copy

Paste Options

Copying Selected Cells

Copying selected cells can be useful in worksheets that contain repetitive data. To copy cells, select the cells, and then click the Copy button in the Clipboard group in the Home tab. Click the cell where you want the first selected cell copied and then click the Paste button in the Clipboard group.

You can also copy selected cells using the mouse and the Ctrl key. To do this, select the cells you want to copy and then position the mouse pointer on any border around the selected cells until it turns into an arrow pointer. Hold down the Ctrl key and the left mouse button, drag the outline of the selected cells to the desired location, release the left mouse button, and then release the Ctrl key.

Using the Paste Options Button

The Paste Options button displays in the lower right corner of the pasted cell(s) when you paste a cell or cells. Hover the mouse over this button until it displays with a down-pointing arrow and then click the left mouse button. This causes a drop-down list to display as shown in Figure 5.1. With the options from this list you can specify what you want pasted. You can specify that you want to keep source formatting or use destination themes or destination formatting. You can also keep the column widths of the source worksheet.

Figure 5.1 Paste Options Button Drop-down List

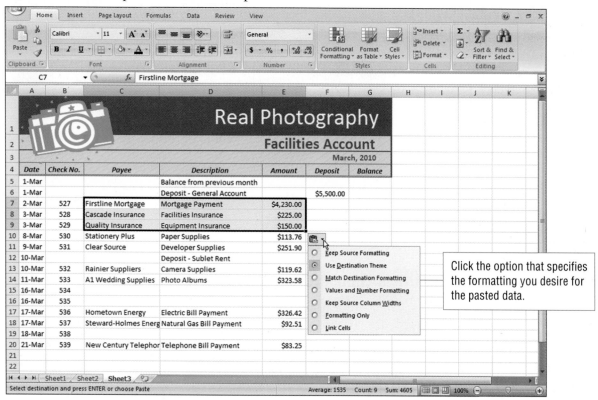

Click the option that specifies the formatting you desire for the pasted data.

Project 1C   Copying Selected Cells in a Worksheet

1. With **ExcelL1_C5_P1.xlsx** open, make Sheet2 active.
2. Select cells C7 through E9.
3. Click the Copy button in the Clipboard group in the Home tab.

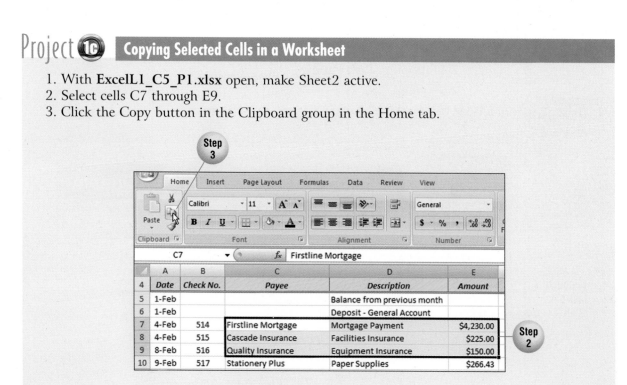

4. Make Sheet3 active.
5. Make cell C7 active.
6. Click the Paste button in the Clipboard group.
7. Click the Paste Options button that displays in the lower right corner of the pasted cells and then click *Keep Source Column Widths* at the drop-down list.
8. Make Sheet2 active and then press the Esc key to remove the moving marquee.
9. Save **ExcelL1_C5_P1.xlsx**.

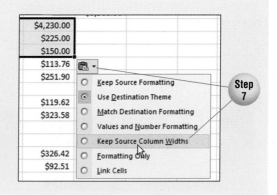

Step 7

QUICK STEPS

Copy and Paste Multiple Items
1. Click Clipboard group dialog box launcher.
2. Select desired cells.
3. Click Copy button.
4. Continue selecting desired cells and then clicking the Copy button.
5. Make active the desired cell.
6. Click item in Clipboard task pane that you want inserted in the worksheet.
7. Continue pasting desired items from the Clipboard task pane.

Using the Office Clipboard

Use the Office Clipboard feature to collect and paste multiple items. To use the Office Clipboard, display the Clipboard task pane by clicking the Clipboard group dialog box launcher. This button is located in the lower right corner of the Clipboard group in the Home tab. The Clipboard task pane displays at the left side of the screen in a manner similar to what you see in Figure 5.2.

Figure 5.2 Clipboard Task Pane

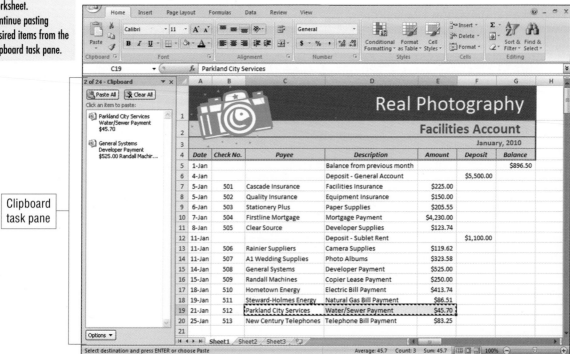

Clipboard task pane

Select data or an object you want to copy and then click the Copy button in the Clipboard group. Continue selecting text or items and clicking the Copy button. To insert an item, position the insertion point in the desired location and then click the item in the Clipboard task pane. If the copied item is text, the first 50 characters display. When all desired items are inserted, click the Clear All button to remove any remaining items. Sometimes, you may have a situation in which you want to copy all of the selected items to a single location. If so, position the insertion point in the desired location and then click the Paste All button in the Clipboard task pane.

Project ⑩   Copying and Pasting Cells Using the Office Clipboard

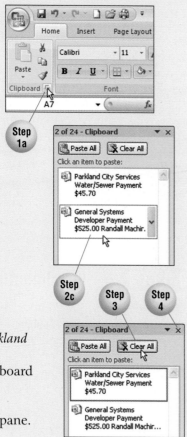

1. With **ExcelL1_C5_P1.xlsx** open, select cells for copying by completing the following steps:
   a. Display the Clipboard task pane by clicking the Clipboard group dialog box launcher. (If the Clipboard contains any copied data, click the Clear All button.)
   b. Click the Sheet1 tab.
   c. Select cells C15 through E16.
   d. Click the Copy button in the Clipboard group.
   e. Select cells C19 through E19.
   f. Click the Copy button in the Clipboard group.
2. Paste the copied cells by completing the following steps:
   a. Click the Sheet2 tab.
   b. Make cell C15 active.
   c. Click the item in the Clipboard task pane representing *General Systems Developer*.
   d. Click the Sheet3 tab.
   e. Make C15 active.
   f. Click the item in the Clipboard task pane representing *General Systems Developer*.
   g. Make cell C19 active.
   h. Click the item in the Clipboard task pane representing *Parkland City Services*.
3. Click the Clear All button located toward the top of the Clipboard task pane.
4. Close the Clipboard task pane by clicking the Close button (contains an X) located in the upper right corner of the task pane.
5. Save **ExcelL1_C5_P1.xlsx**.

Pasting Values Only

When you copy and then paste a cell containing a value as well as a formula, the Paste Options button contains the options shown in Figure 5.1 as well as the additional option *Values Only*. Click this option if you want to copy only the value and not the formula.

Project 1e — Copying and Pasting Values

1. With **ExcelL1_C5_P1.xlsx** open, make Sheet1 active.
2. Make cell G6 active, insert the formula =(F6-E6)+G5, and then press Enter.
3. Copy the formula in cell G6 down to cells G7 through G20.
4. Copy the final balance amount from Sheet1 to Sheet2 by completing the following steps:
   a. Make cell G20 active.
   b. Click the Copy button in the Clipboard group.
   c. Click the Sheet2 tab.
   d. Make cell G5 active and then click the Paste button in the Clipboard group.
   e. Hover the mouse over the Paste Options button until the button displays with a down-pointing arrow and then click the left mouse button.
   f. At the drop-down list, click the *Values Only* option. (This inserts the value and not the formula.)

February, 2010		
Deposit	**Balance**	
◈	#VALUE!	
$5,500.00		📋 ▾

Step 4e

- ○ Keep Source Formatting
- ◉ Use Destination Theme
- ○ Match Destination Formatting
- ○ Values Only
- ○ Values and Number Formatting
- ○ Values and Source Formatting
- ○ Keep Source Column Widths
- ○ Formatting Only
- ○ Link Cells

$1,100.00   Step 4f

5. Make cell G6 active, insert a formula that determines the balance, and then copy the formula down to cells G7 through G20.
6. Copy the amount in cell G20 and then paste the value only into cell G5 in Sheet3.
7. With Sheet3 active, make cell G6 active, insert a formula that determines the balance, and then copy the formula down to cells G7 through G20.
8. Save **ExcelL1_C5_P1.xlsx**.

Inserting a Worksheet

Insert Worksheet
Click Insert Worksheet tab.
OR
Press Shift + F11.

A workbook, by default, contains three worksheets. You can insert additional worksheets in a workbook. To do this, click the Insert Worksheet tab located to the right of the Sheet3 tab. This inserts a new worksheet labeled *Sheet4* at the right of the Sheet3 tab. You can also press Shift + F11 to insert a new worksheet. Or, you can insert a worksheet by clicking the Insert button arrow in the Cells group in the Home tab and then clicking *Insert Sheet*.

Project 1f — Inserting a Worksheet

1. With **ExcelL1_C5_P1.xlsx** open, make the following changes:
   a. Make Sheet1 active.
   b. Make cell D21 active, turn on bold, and then type Total.
   c. Make cell E21 active and then click once on the Sum button located in the Editing group in the Home tab. (This inserts the formula =SUM(E13:E20).)
   d. Change the formula to =SUM(E7:E20) and then press Enter.

Water/Sewer Payment	$45.70	
Telephone Bill Payment	$83.25	
Total	=SUM(E7:E20)	
	SUM(number1, [number2], ...)	

Step 1d

e. Make cell F21 active and then click once on the Sum button in the Editing group. (This inserts the formula =SUM(F12:F20).)

f. Change the formula to =SUM(F6:F20) and then press Enter.

2. Make Sheet2 active and then complete the steps in Step 1 to insert the totals of the *Amount* and *Deposit* columns.

3. Make Sheet3 active and then complete the steps in Step 1 to insert the totals of the *Amount* and *Deposit* columns.

4. Insert a new worksheet by clicking the Insert Worksheet tab located to the right of the Sheet3 tab.

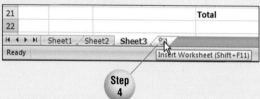

Step 4

5. Make Sheet1 active, copy cells A1 through G3, make Sheet4 active (with cell A1 active), and then paste the cells. (When copying the cells, position the cell pointer to the right of the image, make sure the pointer displays as a white plus symbol, and then drag to select the cells.)

6. Make the following changes to the worksheet:

a. Make cell A3 active and then type First Quarter Summary, 2010.

b. Change the width of column A to 20.00.

c. Change the width of columns B, C, and D to 12.00.

d. Select cells B4 through D4, click the Bold button in the Font group in the Home tab, and then click the Center button in the Alignment group.

e. Select cells B5 through D7 and then change the number formatting to Currency with two decimal places and include the dollar sign symbol.

f. Type the following text in the specified cells:

B4	=	January
C4	=	February
D4	=	March
A5	=	Checks Amount
A6	=	Deposit Amount
A7	=	End-of-month Balance

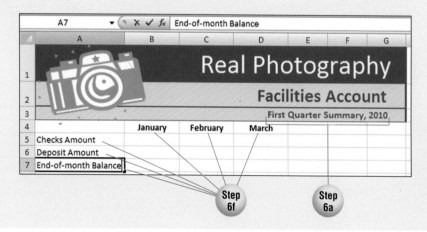

Step 6f   Step 6a

7. Copy a value by completing the following steps:
   a. Make Sheet1 active.
   b. Make cell E21 active and then click the Copy button in the Clipboard group in the Home tab.
   c. Make Sheet4 active.
   d. Make cell B5 active and then click the Paste button in the Clipboard group.
   e. Click the Paste Options button and then click *Values Only* at the drop-down list.

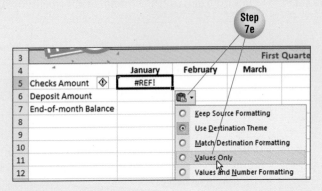

   f. Make Sheet1 active.
   g. Press the Esc key to remove the moving marquee.
   h. Make cell F21 active and then click the Copy button.
   i. Make Sheet4 active.
   j. Make cell B6 active and then click the Paste button.
   k. Click the Paste Options button and then click *Values Only* at the drop-down list.
   l. Make Sheet1 active.
   m. Press the Esc key to remove the moving marquee.
   n. Make cell G20 active and then click the Copy button.
   o. Make Sheet4 active.
   p. Make cell B7 active and then click the Paste button.
   q. Click the Paste Options button and then click *Values Only* at the drop-down list.
8. Complete steps similar to those in Step 7 to insert amounts and balances for February and March.
9. Save **ExcelL1_C5_P1.xlsx**.

Managing Worksheets

Right-click a sheet tab and a shortcut menu displays as shown in Figure 5.3 with the options for managing worksheets. For example, remove a worksheet by clicking the *Delete* option. Move or copy a worksheet by clicking the *Move or Copy* option. Clicking this option causes a Move or Copy dialog box to display where you specify before what sheet you want to move or copy the selected sheet. By default, Excel names worksheets in a workbook *Sheet1, Sheet2, Sheet3,* and so on. To rename a worksheet, click the *Rename* option (this selects the default sheet name) and then type the desired name.

Figure 5.3 Sheet Tab Shortcut Menu

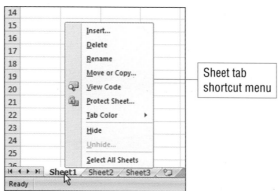

Sheet tab shortcut menu

In addition to the shortcut menu options, you can use the mouse to move or copy worksheets. To move a worksheet, position the mouse pointer on the worksheet tab, hold down the left mouse button (a page icon displays next to the mouse pointer), drag the page icon to the desired position, and then release the mouse button. For example, to move Sheet2 tab after Sheet3 tab you would position the mouse pointer on the Sheet2 tab, hold down the left mouse button, drag the page icon so it is positioned after the Sheet3 tab, and then release the mouse button. To copy a worksheet, hold down the Ctrl key while dragging the sheet tab.

Use the *Tab Color* option at the shortcut menu to apply a color to a worksheet tab. Right-click a worksheet tab, point to *Tab Color* at the shortcut menu, and then click the desired color at the color palette.

QUICK STEPS

Move or Copy a Worksheet
1. Right-click sheet tab.
2. Click *Move or Copy.*
3. At Move or Copy dialog box, click desired worksheet name in *Before sheet* list box.
4. Click OK.
OR
Drag worksheet tab to the desired position (to copy, hold down Ctrl key while dragging).

HINT

Use the tab scroll buttons, located to the left of the sheet tabs, to bring into view any worksheet tabs not currently visible.

QUICK STEPS

Recolor Sheet Tab
1. Right-click sheet tab.
2. Point to *Tab Color.*
3. Click desired color at color palette.

1. With **ExcelL1_C5_P1.xlsx** open, move Sheet4 by completing the following steps:
   a. Right-click Sheet4 and then click *Move or Copy* at the shortcut menu.

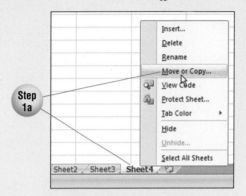

Step 1a

   b. At the Move or Copy dialog box, make sure *Sheet1* is selected in the *Before sheet* section, and then click OK.

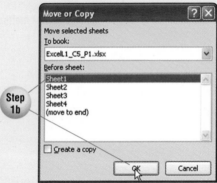

Step 1b

2. Rename Sheet4 by completing the following steps:
   a. Right-click the Sheet4 tab and then click *Rename*.
   b. Type **Summary** and then press Enter.

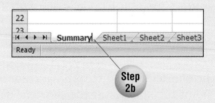

Step 2b

3. Complete steps similar to those in Step 2 to rename Sheet1 to *January*, Sheet2 to *February*, and Sheet3 to *March*.
4. Change the color of the Summary sheet tab by completing the following steps:
   a. Right-click the Summary sheet tab.
   b. Point to *Tab Color* at the shortcut menu.
   c. Click a red color of your choosing at the color palette.
5. Follow steps similar to those in Step 4 to change the January sheet tab to a blue color, the February sheet tab to a purple color, and the March sheet tab to a green color.
6. Save **ExcelL1_C5_P1.xlsx**.

Hiding a Worksheet in a Workbook

In a workbook containing multiple worksheets, you can hide a worksheet that may contain sensitive data or data you do not want to display or print with the workbook. To hide a worksheet in a workbook, click the Format button in the Cells group in the Home tab, point to *Hide & Unhide*, and then click *Hide Sheet*. You can also hide a worksheet by right-clicking a worksheet tab and then clicking the *Hide* option at the shortcut menu. To make a hidden worksheet visible, click the Format button in the Cells group, point to *Hide & Unhide*, and then click *Unhide Sheet*, or right-click a worksheet tab and then click *Unhide* at the shortcut menu. At the Unhide dialog box shown in Figure 5.4, double-click the name of the hidden worksheet you want to display.

Figure 5.4 Unhide Dialog Box

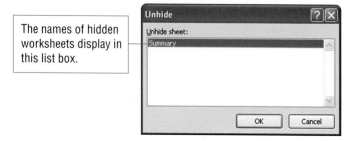

The names of hidden worksheets display in this list box.

Formatting Multiple Worksheets

When you apply formatting to a worksheet, such as changing margins, orientation, or inserting a header or footer, and so on, the formatting is applied only to the active worksheet. If you want formatting to apply to multiple worksheets in a workbook, select the tabs of the desired worksheets and then apply the formatting. For example, if a workbook contains three worksheets and you want to apply formatting to the first and second worksheets only, select the tabs for the first and second worksheets and then apply the formatting.

To select adjacent worksheet tabs, click the first tab, hold down the Shift key, and then click the last tab. To select nonadjacent worksheet tabs, click the first tab, hold down the Ctrl key, and then click any other tabs you want selected.

QUICK STEPS

Hide a Worksheet
1. Click Format button.
2. Point to *Hide & Unhide*.
3. Click *Hide Sheet*.
OR
1. Right-click worksheet tab.
2. Click *Hide* at shortcut menu.

Unhide a Worksheet
1. Click Format button.
2. Point to *Hide & Unhide*.
3. Click *Unhide Sheet*.
4. Double-click desired hidden worksheet in Unhide dialog box.
OR
1. Right-click worksheet tab.
2. Click *Unhide* at shortcut menu.
3. Double-click desired hidden worksheet in Unhide dialog box.

HINT
If the *Hide* option is unavailable, the workbook is protected from change.

1. With **ExcelL1_C5_P1.xlsx** open, hide the Summary worksheet by completing the following steps:
   a. Click the Summary tab.
   b. Click the Format button in the Cells group in the Home tab, point to *Hide & Unhide*, and then click *Hide Sheet*.

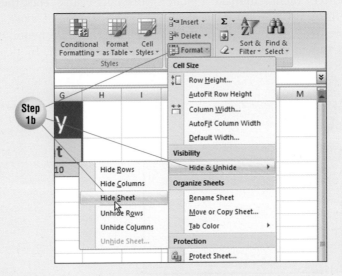

2. Unhide the worksheet by completing the following steps:
   a. Click the Format button in the Cells group, point to *Hide & Unhide*, and then click *Unhide Sheet*.
   b. At the Unhide dialog box, make sure *Summary* is selected and then click OK.
3. Insert a header for each worksheet by completing the following steps:
   a. Click the Summary tab.
   b. Hold down the Shift key and then click the March tab. (This selects all four tabs.)

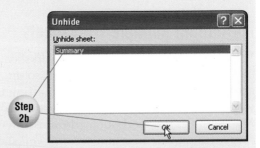

   c. Click the Insert tab.
   d. Click the Header & Footer button in the Text group.
   e. Click the Header button in the Header & Footer group in the Header & Footer Tools Design tab and then click the option at the drop-down list that prints your name at the left side of the page, the page number in the middle, and the date at the right side of the page.
4. With all the sheet tabs selected, horizontally and vertically center each worksheet on the page. ***Hint: Do this at the Page Setup dialog box with the Margins tab selected.***
5. With all of the sheet tabs still selected, change the page orientation to landscape. ***Hint: Do this with the Orientation button in the Page Layout tab.***
6. Save **ExcelL1_C5_P1.xlsx**.

Printing a Workbook Containing Multiple Worksheets

By default, Excel prints the currently displayed worksheet. If you want to print all worksheets in a workbook, display the Print dialog box by clicking the Office button and then clicking *Print*. At the Print dialog box, click *Entire workbook* in the *Print what* section, and then click OK. You can also print specific worksheets in a workbook by selecting the tabs of the worksheets you want to print.

QUICK STEPS

Print all Worksheets in a Workbook
1. Click Office button, *Print*.
2. Click *Entire workbook*.
3. Click OK.

Project 1i — **Printing All Worksheets in a Workbook**

1. With **ExcelL1_C5_P1.xlsx** open, click the Office button and then click *Print*.
2. At the Print dialog box, click the *Entire workbook* option in the *Print what* section.
3. Click OK.
4. Close **ExcelL1_C5_P1.xlsx**.

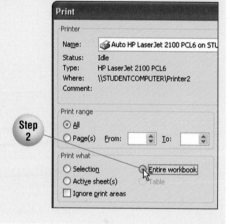

Step 2

Project 2 — **Write Formulas Using Ranges in an Equipment Usage Workbook**

You will open an equipment usage workbook and then split the window and edit cells. You will also name ranges and then use the range names to write formulas in the workbook.

Splitting a Worksheet into Windows and Freezing and Unfreezing Panes

In some worksheets, not all cells display at one time in the worksheet area (such as ExcelC05Project02.xlsx). When working in worksheets with more cells than can display at one time, you may find splitting the worksheet window into panes helpful. Split the worksheet window into panes with the Split button in the Window group in the View tab or with the split bars that display at the top of the vertical scroll bar and at the right side of the horizontal scroll bar. Figure 5.5 identifies these split bars.

QUICK STEPS

Split a Worksheet
1. Click View tab.
2. Click Split button.
OR
Drag horizontal and/or vertical split bars.

Split

Figure 5.5 Split Bars

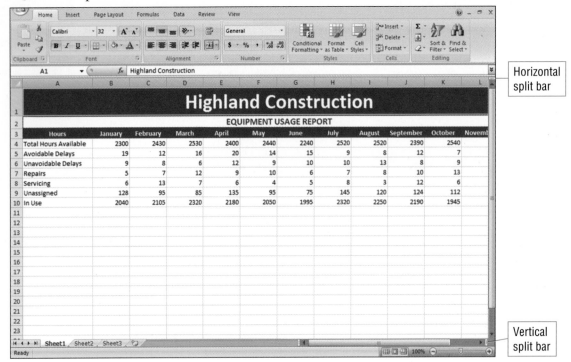

Horizontal split bar

Vertical split bar

HINT

Restore a split window by double-clicking anywhere on the split bar that divides the panes.

To split a window with the split bar located at the top of the vertical scroll bar, position the mouse pointer on the split bar until it turns into a double-headed arrow with a short double line in the middle. Hold down the left mouse button, drag down the thick gray line that displays until the pane is the desired size, and then release the mouse button. Split the window vertically with the split bar at the right side of the horizontal scroll bar.

To split a worksheet window with the Split button, click the View tab, and then click the Split button. This causes the worksheet to split into four window panes as shown in Figure 5.6. The windows are split by thick, light blue lines (with a three-dimensional look). To remove a split from a worksheet click the Split button to deactivate it or drag the split bars to the upper left corner of the worksheet.

Figure 5.6 Split Window

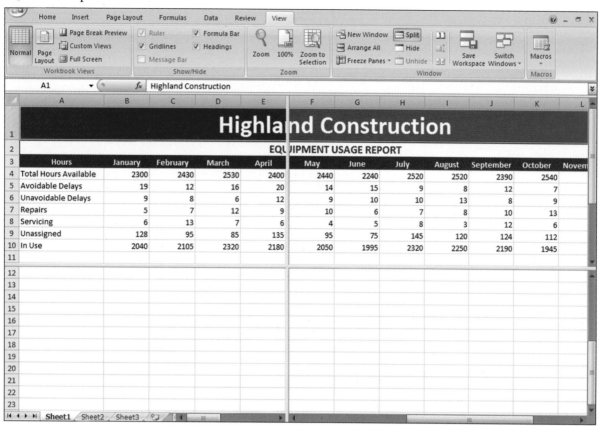

A window pane will display the active cell. As the insertion point is moved through the pane, another active cell with a blue background may display. This additional active cell displays when the insertion point passes over one of the light blue lines that creates the pane. As you move through a worksheet, you may see both active cells—one with a normal background and one with a blue background. If you make a change to the active cell, the change is made in both. If you want only one active cell to display, freeze the window panes by clicking the Freeze Panes button in the Window group in the View tab and then clicking *Freeze Panes* at the drop-down list. You can maintain the display of column headings while editing or typing text in cells by clicking the Freeze Panes button and then clicking *Freeze Top Row*. Maintain the display of row headings by clicking the Freeze Panes button and then clicking *Freeze First Column*. Unfreeze window panes by clicking the Freeze Panes button and then clicking *Unfreeze Panes* at the drop-down list.

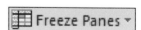

Using the mouse, you can move the thick, light blue lines that divide the window into panes. To do this, position the mouse pointer on the line until the pointer turns into a double-headed arrow with a double line in the middle. Hold down the left mouse button, drag the outline of the light blue line to the desired location, and then release the mouse button. If you want to move both the horizontal and vertical lines at the same time, position the mouse pointer on the intersection of the thick, light blue lines until it turns into a four-headed arrow. Hold down the left mouse button, drag the thick, light blue lines in the desired direction, and then release the mouse button.

Project 2a — Splitting Windows and Editing Cells

1. Open **ExcelC05Project02.xlsx** and then save the workbook and name it **ExcelL1_C5_P2**.
2. Make sure cell A1 is active and then split the window by clicking the View tab and then clicking the Split button in the Window group. (This splits the window into four panes.)
3. Drag the vertical light blue line by completing the following steps:
   a. Position the mouse pointer on the vertical split line until the pointer turns into a double-headed arrow pointing left and right with a double-line between.
   b. Hold down the left mouse button, drag to the left until the vertical light blue line is immediately to the right of the first column, and then release the mouse button.
4. Freeze the window panes by clicking the Freeze Panes button in the Window group in the View tab and then clicking *Freeze Panes* at the drop-down list.
5. Make cell L4 active and then type the following data in the specified cells:

L4	=	2310	M4	=	2210
L5	=	12	M5	=	5
L6	=	5	M6	=	7
L7	=	9	M7	=	8
L8	=	11	M8	=	12
L9	=	95	M9	=	120
L10	=	2005	M10	=	1830

6. Unfreeze the window panes by clicking the Freeze Panes button and then clicking *Unfreeze Panes* at the drop-down list.
7. Remove the panes by clicking the Split button in the Window group to deactivate it.
8. Save **ExcelL1_C5_P2.xlsx**.

Working with Ranges

Name a Range
1. Select cells.
2. Click in Name box.
3. Type range name.
4. Press Enter.

A selected group of cells is referred to as a ***range***. A range of cells can be formatted, moved, copied, or deleted. You can also name a range of cells and then move the insertion point to the range or use a named range as part of a formula.

To name a range, select the cells, and then click in the Name box located at the left of the Formula bar. Type a name for the range (do not use a space) and then press Enter. To move the insertion point to a specific range and select the range, click the down-pointing arrow at the right side of the Name box and then click the range name.

You can also name a range using the Define Name button in the Formulas tab. To do this, click the Formulas tab and then click the Define Name button in the Defined Names group. At the New Name dialog box, type a name for the range and then click OK.

You can use a range name in a formula. For example, if a range is named *Profit* and you want to insert the average of all cells in the *Profit* range, you would make the desired cell active and then type =AVERAGE(Profit). You can use a named range in the current worksheet or in another worksheet within the workbook.

HINT
Another method for moving to a range is to click the Find & Select button in the Editing group in the Home tab and then click *Go To*. At the Go To dialog box, double-click the range name.

🗐 Define Name ▾

Project 2b Naming a Range and Using a Range in a Formula

1. With **ExcelL1_C5_P2.xlsx** open, click the Sheet2 tab and then type the following text in the specified cells:

   A1 = EQUIPMENT USAGE REPORT
   A2 = Yearly Hours
   A3 = Avoidable Delays
   A4 = Unavoidable Delays
   A5 = Total Delay Hours
   A6 = (leave blank)
   A7 = Repairs
   A8 = Servicing
   A9 = Total Repair/Servicing Hours

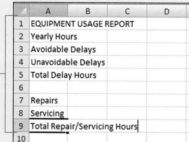

Step 1

	A	B	C	D
1	EQUIPMENT USAGE REPORT			
2	Yearly Hours			
3	Avoidable Delays			
4	Unavoidable Delays			
5	Total Delay Hours			
6				
7	Repairs			
8	Servicing			
9	Total Repair/Servicing Hours			
10				

2. Make the following formatting changes to the worksheet:
   a. Automatically adjust the width of column A.
   b. Center and bold the text in cells A1 and A2.
3. Select a range of cells in worksheet 1, name the range, and use it in a formula in worksheet 2 by completing the following steps:
   a. Click the Sheet1 tab.
   b. Select cells B5 through M5.
   c. Click in the Name box located to the left of the Formula bar.
   d. Type **adhours** (for Avoidable Delays Hours) and then press Enter.
   e. Click the Sheet2 tab.
   f. Make cell B3 active.
   g. Type the equation =SUM(adhours) and then press Enter.
4. Click the Sheet1 tab and then complete the following steps:
   a. Select cells B6 through M6.
   b. Click the Formulas tab.
   c. Click the Define Name button in the Defined Names group.

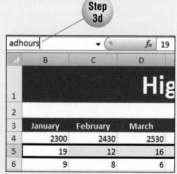

Step 3d

adhours		fx	19
	B	C	D
1			Hig
2			
3	January	February	March
4	2300	2430	2530
5	19	12	16
6	9	8	6

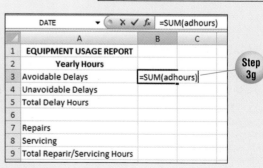

Step 3g

DATE		X ✓ fx	=SUM(adhours)
	A	B	C
1	EQUIPMENT USAGE REPORT		
2	Yearly Hours		
3	Avoidable Delays	=SUM(adhours)	
4	Unavoidable Delays		
5	Total Delay Hours		
6			
7	Repairs		
8	Servicing		
9	Total Reparir/Servicing Hours		

d. At the New Name dialog box, type **udhours** and then click OK.

e. Make worksheet 2 active, make cell B4 active, and then insert the equation =*SUM(udhours)*.

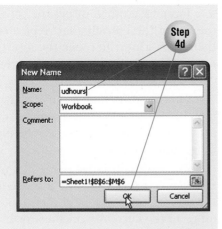

Step 4d

5. Make worksheet 1 active and then complete the following steps:

a. Select cells B7 through M7 and then name the range *rhours*.

b. Make worksheet 2 active, make cell B7 active, and then insert the equation =*SUM(rhours)*.

c. Make worksheet 1 active.

d. Select cells B8 through M8 and then name the range *shours*.

e. Make worksheet 2 active, make cell B8 active, and then insert the equation =*SUM(shours)*.

6. With worksheet 2 still active, make the following changes:

a. Make cell B5 active.

b. Double-click the Sum button in the Editing group in the Home tab.

c. Make cell B9 active.

d. Double-click the Sum button in the Editing group in the Home tab.

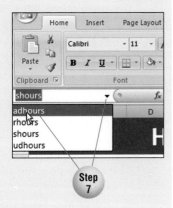

7. Make worksheet 1 active and then move to the range *adhours* by clicking the down-pointing arrow at the right side of the Name box and then clicking *adhours* at the drop-down list.

8. Select both sheet tabs, change the orientation to landscape, scale the contents to fit on one page (in Page Layout tab, change width to *1 page*), and insert a custom footer with your name, page number, and date.

9. Print both worksheets in the workbook.

10. Save and then close **ExcelL1_C5_P2.xlsx**.

Step 7

Project ③ Arrange, Size, and Copy Data between Workbooks

You will open, arrange, hide, unhide, size, and move multiple workbooks. You will also copy cells from one workbook and paste in another workbook.

Working with Windows

You can open multiple workbooks in Excel and arrange the open workbooks in the Excel window. With multiple workbooks open, you can cut and paste or copy and paste cell entries from one workbook to another using the same techniques discussed earlier in this chapter with the exception that you activate the destination workbook before executing the Paste command.

Opening Multiple Workbooks

With multiple workbooks open, you can move or copy information between workbooks or compare the contents of several workbooks. When you open a new workbook, it is placed on top of the original workbook. Once multiple workbooks are opened, you can resize the workbooks to see all or a portion of them on the screen.

Open multiple workbooks at one time at the Open dialog box. If workbooks are adjacent, display the Open dialog box, click the first workbook name to be opened, hold down the Shift key, and then click the last workbook name to be opened. If the workbooks are nonadjacent, click the first workbook name to be opened and then hold down the Ctrl key while clicking the remaining desired workbook names. Release the Shift key or the Ctrl key and then click the Open button.

To see what workbooks are currently open, click the View tab and then click the Switch Windows button in the Window group. The names of the open workbooks display in a drop-down list and the workbook name preceded by a check mark is the active workbook. To make one of the other workbooks active, click the desired workbook name at the drop-down list.

Switch Windows ▾

Arranging Workbooks

If you have more than one workbook open, you can arrange the workbooks at the Arrange Windows dialog box shown in Figure 5.7. To display this dialog box, open several workbooks, and then click the Arrange All button in the Window group in the View tab. At the Arrange Windows dialog box, click *Tiled* to display a portion of each open workbook. Figure 5.8 displays four tiled workbooks.

Arrange Workbooks
1. Click View tab.
2. Click Arrange All button.
3. At Arrange Windows dialog box, click desired arrangement.
4. Click OK.

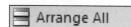

Figure 5.7 Arrange Windows Dialog Box

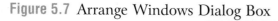

Use options at this dialog box to choose an arrange method.

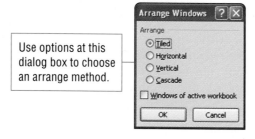

Figure 5.8 Tiled Workbooks

Choose the *Horizontal* option at the Arrange Windows dialog box and the open workbooks display across the screen. The *Vertical* option displays the open workbooks up and down the screen. The last option, *Cascade*, displays the Title bar of each open workbook. Figure 5.9 shows four cascaded workbooks.

The option you select for displaying multiple workbooks depends on which part of the workbooks is most important to view simultaneously. For example, the tiled workbooks in Figure 5.8 allow you to view the company logos and the first few rows and columns of each workbook.

Figure 5.9 Cascaded Workbooks

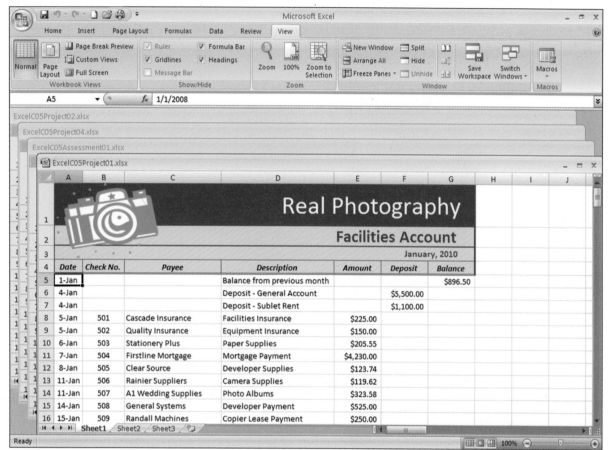

Hiding/Unhiding Workbooks

With the Hide button in the Window group in the View tab, you can hide the active workbook. If a workbook has been hidden, redisplay the workbook by clicking the Unhide button in the Window group in the View tab. At the Unhide dialog box, make sure the desired workbook is selected in the list box, and then click OK.

Project **3a**   **Opening, Arranging, and Hiding/Unhiding Workbooks**

1. Open several workbooks at the same time by completing the following steps:
   a. Display the Open dialog box.
   b. Click the workbook named *ExcelC05Project01.xlsx*.
   c. Hold down the Ctrl key, click *ExcelC05Project02.xlsx*, click *ExcelC05Project04.xlsx*, and click *ExcelC05Assessment01.xlsx*.
   d. Release the Ctrl key and then click the Open button in the dialog box.

2. Make **ExcelC05Assessment01.xlsx** the active workbook by clicking the View tab, clicking the Switch Windows button in the Window group, and then clicking *4* at the drop-down list.

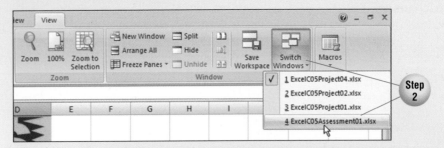

3. Make **ExcelC05Project01.xlsx** the active workbook by clicking the Switch Windows button and then clicking *ExcelC05Project01.xlsx* at the drop-down list.
4. Tile the workbooks by completing the following steps:
   a. Click the Arrange All button in the Window group in the View tab.
   b. At the Arrange Windows dialog box, make sure *Tiled* is selected and then click OK.

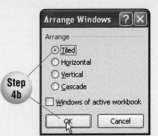

5. Tile the workbooks horizontally by completing the following steps:
   a. Click the Arrange All button.
   b. At the Arrange Windows dialog box, click *Horizontal*.
   c. Click OK.
6. Cascade the workbooks by completing the following steps:
   a. Click the Arrange All button.
   b. At the Arrange Windows dialog box, click *Cascade*.
   c. Click OK.
7. Hide and unhide workbooks by completing the following steps:
   a. Make sure **ExcelC05Project01.xlsx** is the active workbook (displays on top of the other workbooks).
   b. Click the Hide button in the Window group in the View tab.
   c. Make sure **ExcelC05Assessment01.xlsx** is the active workbook (displays on top of the other workbooks).
   d. Click the Hide button.
   e. Click the Unhide button.
   f. At the Unhide dialog box, click *ExcelC05Project01.xlsx* in the list box, and then click OK.

   g. Click the Unhide button.
   h. At the Unhide dialog box, make sure **ExcelC05Assessment01.xlsx** is selected in the list box and then click OK.
8. Close all of the open workbooks without saving changes.

Sizing and Moving Workbooks

You can use the Maximize and Minimize buttons located in the upper right corner of the active workbook to change the size of the window. The Maximize button is the button in the upper right corner of the active workbook immediately to the left of the Close button. (The Close button is the button containing the *X*.) The Minimize button is located immediately to the left of the Maximize button.

Maximize   Minimize

Close   Restore

If you arrange all open workbooks and then click the Maximize button in the active workbook, the active workbook expands to fill the screen. In addition, the Maximize button changes to the Restore button. To return the active workbook back to its size before it was maximized, click the Restore button.

Clicking the Minimize button causes the active workbook to be reduced and positioned as a button on the Taskbar. In addition, the Minimize button changes to the Restore button. To maximize a workbook that has been reduced, click the button on the Taskbar representing the workbook.

Project 3b   Minimizing, Maximizing, and Restoring Workbooks

1. Open **ExcelC05Project01.xlsx**.
2. Maximize **ExcelC05Project01.xlsx** by clicking the Maximize button at the right side of the workbook Title bar. (The Maximize button is the button at the right side of the Title bar, immediately to the left of the Close button.)
3. Open **ExcelC05Project02.xlsx** and **ExcelC05Project03.xlsx**.
4. Make the following changes to the open workbooks:
   a. Tile the workbooks.
   b. Make **ExcelC05Project01.xlsx** the active workbook (Title bar displays with a light blue background [the background color may vary depending on how Windows is customized]).
   c. Minimize **ExcelC05Project01.xlsx** by clicking the Minimize button that displays at the right side of the Title bar.
   d. Make **ExcelC05Project02.xlsx** the active workbook and then minimize it.
   e. Minimize **ExcelC05Project03.xlsx**.
5. Close all workbooks.

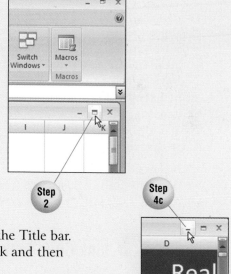

Step 2

Step 4c

Moving, Copying, and Pasting Data

With more than one workbook open, you can move, copy, and/or paste data from one workbook to another. To move, copy, and/or paste data between workbooks, use the cutting and pasting options you learned earlier in this chapter, together with the information about windows in this chapter.

1. Open **ExcelC05Project03.xlsx**.
2. If you just completed Project 3b, click the Maximize button so the worksheet fills the entire worksheet window.
3. Save the workbook and name it **ExcelL1_C5_P3**.
4. With **ExcelL1_C5_P3.xlsx** open, open **ExcelC05Deering.xlsx**.
5. Select and then copy text from **ExcelC05Deering.xlsx** to **ExcelL1_C5_P3.xlsx** by completing the following steps:
   a. With **ExcelC05Deering.xlsx** the active workbook, select cells A3 through D10.
   b. Click the Copy button in the Clipboard group in the Home tab.
   c. Click the button on the Taskbar representing **ExcelL1_C5_P3.xlsx**.

Step 5c

Step 5d

   d. Make cell A8 the active cell and then click the Paste button in the Clipboard group in the Home tab.
   e. Make cell E7 active and then drag the fill handle down to cell E15.
6. Print **ExcelL1_C5_P3.xlsx** horizontally and vertically centered on the page.
7. Save and then close **ExcelL1_C5_P3.xlsx**.
8. Close **ExcelC05Deering.xlsx**.

Project 4 Link Cells between Quarterly Expenses Worksheets

You will open a workbook containing worksheets with quarterly expenses data and then link cells between the worksheets.

Linking Data between Worksheets

You may want to create a link between worksheets or workbooks with data in cells in related workbooks or workbooks containing multiple worksheets. When data is linked, a change made in a linked cell is automatically made to the other cells in the link. You can make links with individual cells or with a range of cells.

Linking cells between worksheets creates what is called a *dynamic link*. Dynamic links are useful in worksheets or workbooks that need to maintain consistency and control over critical data. The worksheet that contains the original data is called the *source* worksheet and the worksheet relying on the source worksheet for the data in the link is called the *dependent* worksheet.

To create a link, make active the cell containing the data to be linked (or select the cells), and then click the Copy button in the Clipboard group in the Home tab. Make active the worksheet where you want to paste the cell or cells, click the Paste button arrow, and then click *Paste Link* at the drop-down list. When a change is made to the cell or cells in the source worksheet, the change is automatically made to the linked cell or cells in the dependent worksheet. You can also create a link by clicking the Paste button, clicking the Paste Options button, and then clicking the *Link Cells* option.

You can also link cells with options at the Paste Special dialog box. Display this dialog box by clicking the Paste button arrow and then clicking *Paste Special* at the drop-down list. At the Paste Special dialog box, specify what in the cell you want to copy and what operators you want to include and then click the Paste Link button.

Project ④ Linking Cells between Worksheets

1. Open **ExcelC05Project04.xlsx** and then save the workbook and name it **ExcelL1_C5_P4**.
2. Link cells in the first quarter worksheet to the other three worksheets by completing the following steps:
   a. Select cells C4 through C10.
   b. Click the Copy button in the Clipboard group in the Home tab.
   c. Click the 2nd Qtr. tab.
   d. Make cell C4 active.
   e. Click the Paste button arrow and then click *Paste Link* at the drop-down list.
   f. Click the 3rd Qtr. tab.
   g. Make cell C4 active.
   h. Click the Paste button.
   i. Click the Paste Options button that displays in the lower right corner of the pasted cell and then click *Link Cells* at the drop-down list.
   j. Click the 4th Qtr. tab.
   k. Make cell C4 active.
   l. Click the Paste button arrow and then click *Paste Link*.
   m. Click the 1st Qtr. tab and then press the Esc key to remove the moving marquee.

3. Insert a formula in all worksheets that subtracts the Budget amount from the Variance amount by completing the following steps:
   a. Make sure the first quarter worksheet displays.
   b. Hold down the Shift key and then click the 4th Qtr. tab. (This selects all four tabs.)
   c. Make cell D4 active and then insert the formula =C4-B4.
   d. Copy the formula in cell D4 down to cells D5 through D10.
   e. Click the 2nd Qtr. tab and notice that the formula was inserted and copied in this worksheet.
   f. Click the other worksheet tabs and notice the formula.
   g. Click the 1st Qtr. tab.

	C	D
	Wise Services	
uarter		
	Budget	Variance
	$126,000.00	$4,000.00
	$54,500.00	-$3,500.00
	$10,100.00	$1,850.00
	$6,000.00	-$350.00
	$4,500.00	$360.00
	$2,200.00	-$230.00
	$1,500.00	$50.00

Step 3d

4. With the first quarter worksheet active, make the following changes to some of the linked cells:
   C4: Change $126,000 to 128,000
   C5: Change $54,500 to 56,000
   C9: Change $2,200 to 2,400
5. Click the 2nd Qtr. tab and notice that the values in cells C4, C5, and C9 automatically changed (because they are linked to the first quarter worksheet).
6. Click the 3rd Qtr. tab and notice that the values in cells C4, C5, and C9 automatically changed.
7. Click the 4th Qtr. tab and notice that the values in cells C4, C5, and C9 automatically changed.
8. Save **ExcelL1_C5_P4.xlsx** and then print all the worksheets in the workbook.
9. Close **ExcelL1_C5_P4.xlsx**.

Project  Link Worksheets with 3-D References

You will open a workbook containing worksheets with quarterly sales data and then link the sales data in the worksheets with a 3-D reference.

Linking Worksheets with a 3-D Reference

In multiple worksheet workbooks, you can use a 3-D reference to analyze data in the same cell or range of cells. A 3-D reference includes the cell or range of cells, preceded by a range of worksheet names. For example, you can add all of the values contained in cells in B2 through B5 in worksheets 1 and 2 in a workbook using a 3-D reference. To do this, you would complete these basic steps:

1. Make active the cell where you want to enter the function.
2. Type =SUM(and then click the Sheet1 tab.
3. Hold down the Shift key and then click the Sheet2 tab.
4. Select cells B2 through B5 in the worksheet.
5. Type) (this is the closing parenthesis that ends the formula) and then press Enter.

Project ⑤   Linking Worksheets with a 3-D Reference

1. Open **ExcelC05Project05.xlsx** and then save the workbook and name it **ExcelL1_C5_P5**.
2. Make sure Sales 2007 is the active worksheet.
3. Make the following changes to the Sales 2007 worksheet:
   a. Make cell B12 active.
   b. Click the Center button in the Alignment group and then click the Bold button in the Font group.
   c. Type *January Sales* and then press Alt + Enter.
   d. Type *2007-2009* and then press Enter.
4. Link the Sales 2007, Sales 2008, and Sales 2009 worksheets with a 3-D reference by completing the following steps:
   a. With cell B13 active, type =SUM(.
   b. Hold down the Shift key, click the Sales 2009 sheet tab, and then release the Shift key. (This selects all three sheet tabs.)
   c. Select cells B5 through B10.
   d. Type) and then press Enter.

	FIRST-QUARTER SALES - 2007					
4	*Customer*		*January*		*February*	*March*
5	Lakeside Trucking	$	84,231	$	73,455	$ 97,549
6	Gresham Machines	$	33,199	$	40,390	$ 50,112
7	Real Photography	$	30,891	$	35,489	$ 36,400
8	Genesis Productions	$	72,190	$	75,390	$ 83,219
9	Landower Company	$	22,188	$	14,228	$ 38,766
10	Jewell Enterprises	$	19,764	$	50,801	$ 32,188
11						
12			January Sales 2007-2009			
13			=SUM('Sales 2007:Sales 2009'!B5:B10)			
14						

Steps 4a–4d

5. Complete steps similar to those in Step 3 to add *February Sales 2007-2009* (on two lines) in cell C12 and complete steps similar to those in Step 4 to insert the formula with the 3-D reference in cell C13. (Select cells C5 through C10.)
6. Complete steps similar to those in Step 3 to add *March Sales 2007-2009* (on two lines) in cell D12 and complete steps similar to those in Step 4 to insert the formula with the 3-D reference in cell D13. (Select cells D5 through D10.)
7. Save the workbook.
8. Print only the Sales 2007 worksheet.
9. Close **ExcelL1_C5_P5.xlsx**.

Project ⑥   Copy and Paste a Worksheet in a Word Document

You will copy cells in a worksheet and paste the cells in a Word letter document. You will then edit some of the data in cells in the Word document.

Copying and Pasting a Worksheet between Programs

Microsoft Office is a suite that allows integration, which is the combining of data from two or more programs into one file. Integration can occur by copying and pasting data between programs. The program containing the data to be copied is called the *source* program and the program where the data is pasted is called the *destination* program. For example, you can create a worksheet in Excel and then copy it to a Word document. The steps to copy and paste between programs are basically the same as copying and pasting within the same program.

When copying data between worksheets or from one program to another, you can copy and paste, copy and link, or copy and embed the data. Consider the following when choosing a method for copying data:

- Copy data in the source program and paste it in the destination program when the data will not need to be edited.

- Copy data in the source program and then link it in the destination program when the data is updated regularly in the source program and you want the update reflected in the destination program.

- Copy data in the source program and then embed it in the destination program when the data will be edited in the destination program (with the tools of the source program).

Earlier in this chapter, you copied and pasted cells within and between worksheets and you also copied and linked cells between worksheets. You can also copy and link data between programs. Copy and embed data using options at the Paste Special dialog box. In Project 6, you will copy cells in a worksheet and then embed the cells in a Word document. With the worksheet embedded in a Word document, double-click the worksheet and Excel tools display in the document for editing the worksheet.

Project **6** **Copying and Pasting a Worksheet into a Word Document**

1. Open the Word program and then open **WordC05_Letter01.docx**.
2. Save the document and name it **WordExcelL1_C5_P6**.
3. With **WordExcelL1_C5_P6.docx** open, make Excel the active program.
4. Open **ExcelC05Project06.xlsx** and then save the workbook and name it **ExcelL1_C5_P6**.
5. Copy the worksheet to the letter by completing the following steps:
   a. Select cells A1 through D8.
   b. Click the Copy button in the Clipboard group in the Home tab.
   c. Click the button on the Taskbar representing the Word document **WordExcelL1_C5_P6.docx**.
   d. Position the insertion point on the blank line below the first paragraph of text in the body of the letter.
   e. Click the Paste button arrow in the Clipboard group in the Home tab and then click *Paste Special* at the drop-down list.
   f. At the Paste Special dialog box, click *Microsoft Office Excel Worksheet Object* in the *As* list box, and then click OK.

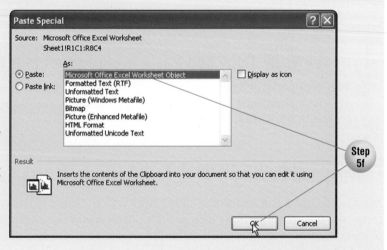

Step 5f

6. Edit a few of the cells in the worksheet by completing the following steps:
   a. Double-click anywhere in the worksheet. (This displays the Excel ribbon for editing.)
   b. Click in each of the following cells and make the change indicated:
       B6: Change *196%* to *110%*.
       C6: Change *190%* to *104%*.
       D6: Change *187%* to *101%*.

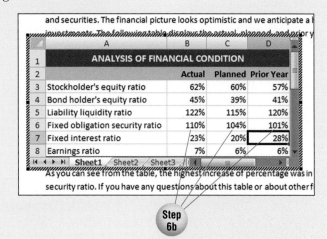

Step
6b

   c. Click outside the worksheet to remove the Excel tools (and deselect the worksheet).
7. Save, print, and then close **WordExcelL1_C5_P6.docx**.
8. Exit Word.
9. With Excel the active program, close **ExcelL1_C5_P6.xlsx**.

CHAPTER summary

- An Excel workbook, by default, contains three worksheets. Click a worksheet tab to display the worksheet.

- Move selected cells and cell contents in and between worksheets using the Cut, Copy, and Paste buttons in the Clipboard group in the Home tab or by dragging with the mouse.

- Move selected cells with the mouse by dragging the outline of the selected cells to the desired position.

- Copy selected cells with the mouse by holding down the Ctrl key and the left mouse button, dragging the outline of the selected cells to the desired location, releasing the left mouse button, and then releasing the Ctrl key.

- When pasting data, use the Paste Options button to specify what you want pasted. Click the Paste Options button and a drop-down list displays with options to specify that you want to keep source formatting, use destination themes, use destination formatting, or keep the column widths of the source worksheet. If you are pasting a cell containing a value as well as a formula, the Paste Options button drop-down list also includes the *Values Only* option.

- Use the Clipboard task pane to collect and paste data within and between worksheets and workbooks. Display the Clipboard task pane by clicking the Clipboard group dialog box launcher.

- Insert a worksheet in a workbook by clicking the Insert Worksheet tab located to the right of the Sheet3 tab or pressing Shift + F11.

- Perform maintenance activities, such as deleting and renaming, on worksheets within a workbook by clicking the *right* mouse button on a sheet tab and then clicking the desired option at the shortcut menu.

- You can use the mouse to move or copy worksheets. To move a worksheet, drag the worksheet tab with the mouse. To copy a worksheet, hold down the Ctrl key and then drag the worksheet tab with the mouse.

- Use the *Tab Color* option at the sheet tab shortcut menu to apply a color to a worksheet tab.

- Hide and unhide a worksheet by clicking the Format button in the Cells group and then clicking the desired option at the drop-down list, or by right-clicking the worksheet tab and then clicking the desired option at the shortcut menu.

- Manage more than one worksheet at a time by first selecting the worksheets. Use the mouse together with the Shift key to select adjacent worksheet tabs and use the mouse together with the Ctrl key to select nonadjacent worksheet tabs.

- If you want formatting to apply to multiple worksheets in a workbook, select the tabs of the desired worksheets and then apply the formatting.

- To print all worksheets in a workbook, click *Entire workbook* in the *Print what* section of the Print dialog box. You can also print specific worksheets by selecting the tabs of the worksheets you want to print.

- Split the worksheet window into panes with the Split button in the Window group in the View tab or with the split bars on the horizontal and vertical scroll bars.

- To remove a split from a worksheet, click the Split button to deactivate it or drag the split bars to the upper left corner of the worksheet.
- Freeze window panes by clicking the Freeze Panes button in the Window group in the View tab and then clicking *Freeze Panes* at the drop-down list. Unfreeze window panes by clicking the Freeze Panes button and then clicking *Unfreeze Panes* at the drop-down list.
- A selected group of cells is referred to as a range. A range can be named and used in a formula. Name a range by typing the name in the Name box located to the left of the Formula bar or at the New Name dialog box.
- To open multiple workbooks that are adjacent, display the Open dialog box, click the first workbook, hold down the Shift key, click the last workbook, and then click the Open button. If workbooks are nonadjacent, click the first workbook, hold down the Ctrl key, click the desired workbooks, and then click the Open button.
- To see a list of open workbooks, click the View tab and then click the Switch Windows button in the Window group.
- Arrange multiple workbooks in a window with options at the Arrange Windows dialog box.
- Hide the active workbook by clicking the Hide button and unhide a workbook by clicking the Unhide button in the Window group in the View tab.
- Click the Maximize button located in the upper right corner of the active workbook to make the workbook fill the entire window area. Click the Minimize button to shrink the active workbook to a button on the Taskbar. Click the Restore button to return the workbook to its previous size.
- You can move, copy, and/or paste data between workbooks.
- Copy and then link data if you make changes in the source worksheet and you want the changes reflected in the destination worksheet. The worksheet containing the original data is called the source worksheet and the worksheet relying on the source worksheet for data in the link is called the dependent worksheet.
- Copy and link data using the Paste Special dialog box or the *Link Cells* option at the Paste Options button drop-down list.
- You can copy data from a file in one program (called the source program) and paste the data into a file in another program (called the destination program).
- Use a 3-D reference to analyze data in the same cell or range of cells.
- You can copy and then paste, link, or embed data between programs in the Office suite. Integrating is the combining of data from two or more programs in the Office suite.

COMMANDS review

FEATURE	RIBBON TAB, GROUP	BUTTON, OPTION	KEYBOARD SHORTCUT
Cut selected cells	Home, Clipboard	✂	Ctrl + X
Copy selected cells	Home, Clipboard	📋	Ctrl + C
Paste selected cells	Home, Clipboard	📋	Ctrl + V
Clipboard task pane	Home, Clipboard	⬜	
Insert worksheet		📊	Shift + F11
Hide worksheet	Home, Cells	Format ▾, Hide & Unhide, Hide Sheet	
Unhide worksheet	Home, Cells	Format ▾, Hide & Unhide, Unhide Sheet	
Split window into pane	View, Window	Split	
Freeze window panes	View, Window	Freeze Panes ▾, Freeze Panes	
Unfreeze window panes	View, Window	Freeze Panes ▾, Unfreeze Panes	
New Name dialog box	Formulas, Defined Names	Define Name ▾	
Arrange Windows dialog box	View, Window	Arrange All	
Maximize window		⬜	
Restore		⬜	
Minimize window		—	
Paste Special dialog box	Home, Clipboard	📋, Paste Special	

CONCEPTS check

Test Your Knowledge

Completion: In the space provided at the right, indicate the correct term, symbol, or command.

1. By default, a workbook contains this number of worksheets. _____

2. To copy selected cells with the mouse, hold down this key while dragging the outline of the selected cells to the desired location. _____

3. The Cut, Copy, and Paste buttons are located in this group in the Home tab. _____

4. This button displays in the lower right corner of pasted cells. _____

5. Use this task pane to collect and paste multiple items. _____

6. Click this tab to insert a new worksheet. _____

7. Click this option at the sheet tab shortcut menu to apply a color to a worksheet tab. _____

8. To select adjacent worksheet tabs, click the first tab, hold down this key, and then click the last tab. _____

9. To select nonadjacent worksheet tabs, click the first tab, hold down this key, and then click any other tabs you want selected. _____

10. Click this option in the *Print what* section of the Print dialog box to print all worksheets in a workbook. _____

11. The Split button is located in this tab. _____

12. Display the Arrange Windows dialog box by clicking this button in the Window group in the View tab. _____

13. Click this button to make the active workbook expand to fill the screen. _____

14. Click this button to reduce the active workbook to a button on the Taskbar. _____

15. When copying and pasting data between programs, the program containing the original data is called this. _____

SKILLS check
Demonstrate Your Proficiency

Assessment

1 COPY AND PASTE DATA BETWEEN WORKSHEETS IN A SALES WORKBOOK

1. Open **ExcelC05Assessment01.xlsx** and then save the workbook and name it **ExcelL1_C5_A1**.
2. Turn on the display of the Clipboard task pane, click the Clear All button to clear any content, and then complete the following steps:
   a. Select and copy cells A7 through C7.
   b. Select and copy cells A10 through C10.
   c. Select and copy cells A13 through C13.
   d. Display the second worksheet, make cell A7 active, and then paste the *Avalon Clinic* cells.
   e. Make cell A10 active and then paste the *Stealth Media* cells.
   f. Make A13 active and then paste the *Danmark Contracting* cells.
   g. Make the third worksheet active and then complete similar steps to paste the cells in the same location as the second worksheet.
   h. Clear the contents of the Clipboard task pane and then close the task pane.
3. Change the name of the Sheet1 tab to *2007 Sales*, the name of the Sheet2 tab to *2008 Sales*, and the name of the Sheet3 tab to *2009 Sales*.
4. Change the color of the 2007 Sales tab to blue, the color of the 2008 Sales tab to green, and the color of the 2009 Sales tab to yellow.
5. Display the 2007 Sales worksheet, select all three tabs, and then insert a formula in cell D4 that sums the amounts in cells B4 and C4. Copy the formula in cell D4 down to cells D5 through D14.
6. Make cell D15 active and then insert a formula that sums the amounts in cells D4 through D14.
7. Insert a footer on all three worksheets that prints your name at the left side and the current date at the right.
8. Save, print, and then close **ExcelL1_C5_A1.xlsx**.

Assessment

2 COPY, PASTE, AND FORMAT WORKSHEETS IN AN INCOME STATEMENT WORKBOOK

1. Open **ExcelC05Assessment02.xlsx** and then save the workbook and name it **ExcelL1_C5_A2**.
2. Copy cells A1 through B17 in Sheet1 and paste them into Sheet2. (Click the Paste Options button and then click *Keep Source Column Widths* at the drop-down list.)
3. Make the following changes to the Sheet2 worksheet:
   a. Adjust the row heights so they match the heights in the Sheet1 worksheet.
   b. Change the month from *January* to *February*.
   c. Change the amount in B4 to *97,655*.
   d. Change the amount in B5 to *39,558*.
   e. Change the amount in B11 to *1,105*.

4. Select both sheet tabs and then insert the following formulas:
   a. Insert a formula in B6 that subtracts the Cost of Sales from the Sales Revenue (*=B4-B5*).
   b. Insert a formula in B16 that sums the amounts in B8 through B15.
   c. Insert a formula in B17 that subtracts the Total Expenses from the Gross Profit (*=B6-B16*).
5. Change the name of the Sheet1 tab to *January* and the name of the Sheet2 tab to *February*.
6. Change the color of the January tab to blue and the color of the February tab to red.
7. Insert a custom footer on both worksheets that prints your name at the left side, the date in the middle, and the file name at the right side.
8. Save, print, and then close **ExcelL1_C5_A2.xlsx**.

Assessment

3 FREEZE AND UNFREEZE WINDOW PANES IN A TEST SCORES WORKBOOK

1. Open **ExcelC05Assessment03.xlsx** and then save the workbook and name it **ExcelL1_C5_A3**.
2. Make cell A1 active and then split the window by clicking the View tab and then clicking the Split button in the Window group. (This causes the window to split into four panes.)
3. Drag both the horizontal and vertical gray lines up and to the left until the horizontal gray line is immediately below the second row and the vertical gray line is immediately to the right of the first column.
4. Freeze the window panes.
5. Add two rows immediately above row 18 and then type the following text in the specified cells:

A18	=	Nauer, Sheryl	A19	=	Nunez, James
B18	=	75	B19	=	98
C18	=	83	C19	=	96
D18	=	85	D19	=	100
E18	=	78	E19	=	90
F18	=	82	F19	=	95
G18	=	80	G19	=	93
H18	=	79	H19	=	88
I18	=	82	I19	=	91
J18	=	92	J19	=	89
K18	=	90	K19	=	100
L18	=	86	L19	=	96
M18	=	84	M19	=	98

6. Insert a formula in cell N3 that averages the percentages in cells B3 through M3 and then copy the formula down to cells N4 through N22.
7. Unfreeze the window panes.
8. Remove the split.
9. Save the worksheet and then print it in landscape orientation.
10. Close **ExcelL1_C5_A3.xlsx**.

Assessment

4 CREATE, COPY, PASTE, AND FORMAT CELLS IN AN EQUIPMENT USAGE WORKBOOK

1. Create the worksheet shown in Figure 5.10 (change the width of column A to 21.00).
2. Save the workbook and name it **ExcelL1_C5_A4**.
3. With **ExcelL1_C5_A4.xlsx** open, open **ExcelC05Project02.xlsx**.
4. Select and copy the following cells from **ExcelC05Project02.xlsx** to **ExcelL1_C5_A4.xlsx**:
   a. Copy cells A4 through G4 in **ExcelC05Project02.xlsx** and paste them into **ExcelL1_C5_A4.xlsx** beginning with cell A12.
   b. Copy cells A10 through G10 in **ExcelC05Project02.xlsx** and paste them into **ExcelL1_C5_A4.xlsx** beginning with cell A13.
5. With **ExcelL1_C5_A4.xlsx** the active workbook, make cell A1 active and then apply the following formatting:
   a. Change the height of row 1 to 25.50.
   b. Change the font size of the text in cell A1 to 14 points.
   c. Insert Olive Green, Accent 3, Lighter 60% fill color to cell A1.
6. Select cells A2 through G2 and then insert Olive Green, Accent 3, Darker 50% fill color.
7. Select cells B2 through G2 and then change to right alignment, change the text color to white, and turn on italics.
8. Select cells A3 through G3 and then insert Olive Green, Accent 3, Lighter 80% fill color.
9. Select cells A7 through G7 and then insert Olive Green, Accent 3, Lighter 80% fill color.
10. Select cells A11 through G11 and then insert Olive Green, Accent 3, Lighter 80% fill color.
11. Change the orientation to landscape.
12. Print the worksheet centered horizontally and vertically on the page.
13. Save and then close **ExcelL1_C5_A4.xlsx**.
14. Close **ExcelC05Project02.xlsx** without saving the changes.

Figure 5.10 Assessment 4

	A	B	C	D	E	F	G	H
1	EQUIPMENT USAGE REPORT							
2		January	February	March	April	May	June	
3	Machine #12							
4	Total Hours Available	2300	2430	2530	2400	2440	2240	
5	In Use	2040	2105	2320	2180	2050	1995	
6								
7	Machine #25							
8	Total Hours Available	2100	2240	2450	2105	2390	1950	
9	In Use	1800	1935	2110	1750	2215	1645	
10								
11	Machine #30							
12								

Assessment

5 LINK WORKSHEETS IN A SALES WORKBOOK WITH 3-D REFERENCES

1. Open **ExcelC05Assessment05.xlsx** and then save the workbook and name it **ExcelL1_C5_A5**.
2. Change the color of the Sales 2007 tab to purple, the color of the Sales 2008 tab to blue, and the color of the Sales 2009 tab to green.
3. Make the following changes to the workbook:
   a. Make Sales 2007 the active worksheet.
   b. Select columns B, C, and D and then change the width to 16.00.
   c. Insert the heading *Average January Sales 2007-2009* (on multiple lines) in cell B11, centered and bolded.
   d. Insert a formula in cell B12 with a 3-D reference that averages the total in cells B4 through B9 in the Sales 2007, Sales 2008, and Sales 2009 worksheets.
   e. Insert the heading *Average February Sales 2007-2009* (on multiple lines) in cell C11, centered and bolded.
   f. Insert a formula in cell C12 with a 3-D reference that averages the total in cells C4 through C9 in the Sales 2007, Sales 2008, and Sales 2009 worksheets.
   g. Insert the heading *Average March Sales 2007-2009* (on multiple lines) in cell D11, centered and bolded.
   h. Insert a formula in cell D12 with a 3-D reference that averages the total in cells D4 through D9 in the Sales 2007, Sales 2008, and Sales 2009 worksheets.
4. Save the workbook and then print only the Sales 2007 worksheet.
5. Close **ExcelL1_C5_A5.xlsx**.

Assessment

6 LINK DATA BETWEEN A WORD LETTER AND AN EXCEL WORKSHEET

1. Use Excel's Help feature to learn about linking data between programs.
2. After locating and reading the information on linking, open the Word program and then open **WordC05_Letter02.docx**.
3. Save the document and name it **WordExcelL1_C5_A6**.
4. Make Excel the active program and then open **ExcelC05Assessment06.xlsx**.
5. Save the workbook with Save As and name it **ExcelL1_C5_A6**.
6. In column G, insert a formula using the PMT function.
7. Save and then print the worksheet.
8. Select cells A2 through G10 and then copy and link the cells to **WordExcelL1_C5_A6.docx** (between the two paragraphs in the body of the letter).
9. Save, print, and then close **WordExcelL1_C5_A6.docx**.
10. Click the button on the Taskbar representing the Excel workbook **ExcelL1_C5_A6.xlsx** and then change the percentages in cells E3 through E6 to 7.5% and the percentages in cells E7 through E10 to 8.5%.
11. Save, print, and then close **ExcelL1_C5_A6.xlsx**.
12. Make Word the active program and then open **WordExcelL1_C5_A6.docx**.
13. At the message that displays, click Yes.
14. Save, print, and then close **WordExcelL1_C5_A6.docx**.
15. Exit Word.

CASE study
Apply Your Skills

Part 1

You are an administrator for Gateway Global, an electronics manufacturing corporation. You are gathering information on money spent on supplies and equipment purchases. You have gathered information for the first quarter of the year and decide to create a workbook containing worksheets for monthly information. To do this, create a worksheet that contains the following information:

- Company name is Gateway Global.
- Create the title *January Expenditures*.
- Create the following columns:

Department	Supplies	Equipment	Total
Production	$25,425	$135,500	
Research and Development	$50,000	$125,000	
Technical Support	$14,500	$65,000	
Finance	$5,790	$22,000	
Sales and Marketing	$35,425	$8,525	
Facilities	$6,000	$1,200	
Total			

- Insert a formula in the *Total* column that sums the amounts in the *Supplies* and *Equipment* columns and insert a formula in the *Total* row that sums the Supplies amounts, Equipment amounts, and Total amounts.
- Apply formatting such as fill color, borders, font color, and shading to enhance the visual appeal of the worksheet.

After creating and formatting the worksheet, complete the following:

- Copy the worksheet data to Sheet2 and then to Sheet3.
- Make the following changes to data in Sheet2:
  - Change *January Expenditures* to *February Expenditures*.
  - Change the Production Department Supplies amount to *$38,550* and the Equipment amount to *$88,500*.
  - Change the Technical Support Department Equipment amount to *$44,250*.
  - Change the Finance Department Supplies amount to *$7,500*.
- Make the following changes to data in Sheet3:
  - Change *January Expenditures* to *March Expenditures*.
  - Change the Research and Development Department Supplies amount to *$65,000* and the Equipment amount to *$150,000*.
  - Change the Technical Support Department Supplies amount to *$21,750* and the Equipment amount to *$43,525*.
  - Change the Facilities Department Equipment amount to *$18,450*.

Create a new worksheet that summarizes the Supplies and Equipment totals for January, February, and March. Apply the same formatting to the worksheet as applied to the other three. Change the tab name for Sheet1 to *Jan. Expenditures*, the tab name for Sheet2 to *Feb. Expenditures*, the tab name for Sheet3 to *Mar. Expenditures*, and the tab name for Sheet4 to *Qtr. Summary*. Change the color of each tab (you determine the colors).

Insert a footer that prints your name at the left side of each worksheet and the current date at the right side of each worksheet. Save the workbook and name it **ExcelL1_C5_CS_P1**. Print all the worksheets in the workbook and then close the workbook.

Part 2

Employees of Gateway Global have formed two intramural co-ed softball teams and you have volunteered to keep statistics for the players. Open **ExcelGGStats.xlsx** and then make the following changes to both worksheets in the workbook:

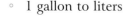

- Insert a formula that calculates a player's batting average (Hits divided by At Bats).
- Insert a formula that calculates a player's on-base percentage (Walks + Hits divided by At Bats plus Walks). Make sure you insert parentheses in the formula.
- Insert the company name.
- Apply formatting to enhance the visual appeal of the worksheets.
- Horizontally and vertically center the worksheets.
- Insert a footer that prints on both worksheets and prints your name at the left side of the worksheet and the date at the right of the worksheet.

Using Help, learn how to apply conditional formatting to data in a worksheet. Select both worksheets and then apply conditional formatting that inserts red fill and changes text color to dark red for cells in the *Batting Average* column with an average over .400. Save the workbook and name it **ExcelL1_C5_CS_P2**. Print and then close **ExcelL1_C5_CS_P2.xlsx**.

Part 3

Many of the suppliers for Gateway Global are international and use different length, weight, and volume measurements. The purchasing manager has asked you to prepare a conversion chart in Excel that displays conversion tables for length, weight, volume, and temperature. Use the Internet to locate conversion tables for length, weight, and volume. When preparing the workbook, create a worksheet with the following information:

- Include the following length conversions:
  - 1 inch to centimeters
  - 1 foot to centimeters
  - 1 yard to meters
  - 1 mile to kilometers
- Include the following weight conversions:
  - 1 ounce to grams
  - 1 pound to kilograms
  - 1 ton to metric tons
- Include the following volume conversions:
  - 1 fluid ounce to milliliters
  - 1 pint to liters
  - 1 quart to liters
  - 1 gallon to liters

Locate a site on the Internet that provides the formula for converting Fahrenheit temperatures to Celsius temperatures and then create another worksheet in the workbook with the following information:

- Insert Fahrenheit temperatures beginning with zero, continuing to 100, and incrementing by 5 (for example, 0, 5, 10, 15, and so on).
- Insert a formula that converts the Fahrenheit temperature to a Celsius temperature.

Include the company name, Gateway Global, in both worksheets. Apply additional formatting to improve the visual appeal of both worksheets. Rename both sheet names and apply a color to each tab (you determine the names and colors). Save the workbook and name it **ExcelL1_C5_CS_P3**. Print both worksheets centered horizontally and vertically on the page and then close **ExcelL1_C5_CS_P3.xlsx**.

Part
4

Open Microsoft Word and then create a letterhead document that contains the company name *Gateway Global*, the address (you decide the address including street address, city, state, and ZIP code or street address, city, province, and postal code), and the telephone number (you determine the telephone number). Apply formatting to improve the visual display of the letterhead. Save the document and name it **WordGGLtrhd**. Save the document again with Save As and name it **WordL1_C5_CS_P4A**. In Excel, open **ExcelL1_C5_CS_P3.xlsx**. In the first worksheet, copy the cells containing data and then paste them in **WordL1_C5_CS_P4A.docx** using Paste Special. Save, print, and then close **WordL1_C5_CS_P4A.docx**. In Word, open **WordGGLtrd.docx**. Save the document with Save As and name it **WordL1_C5_CS_P4B**. In Excel, make the worksheet active that contains the Fahrenheit conversion information, copy the cells containing data, and then paste them in the Word document using Paste Special. Save, print, and then close **WordL1_C5_CS_P4B.docx**. Close Microsoft Word and then, in Excel, close **ExcelL1_C5_CS_P3.xlsx**.

CHAPTER

6

Maintaining Workbooks

PERFORMANCE OBJECTIVES

Upon successful completion of Chapter 6, you will be able to:

- Create and rename a folder
- Delete workbooks and folders
- Copy and move workbooks within and between folders
- Copy, move, and rename worksheets within a workbook
- Save a workbook in a variety of formats
- Maintain consistent formatting with styles
- Use comments for review and response
- Create financial forms using templates

Tutorial 6.1
Managing Folders and
Workbooks
Tutorial 6.2
Advanced Formatting Techniques

Once you have been working with Excel for a period of time you will have accumulated several workbook files. Workbooks should be organized into folders to facilitate fast retrieval of information. Occasionally you should perform file maintenance activities such as copying, moving, renaming, and deleting workbooks to ensure the workbook list in your various folders is manageable. You will learn these file management tasks in this chapter along with creating and applying styles, inserting and printing comments, and using Excel templates to create a workbook.

Note: Before beginning computer projects, copy to your storage medium the Excel2007L1C6 subfolder from the Excel2007L1 folder on the CD that accompanies this textbook and then make Excel2007L1C6 the active folder.

Project ① Manage Workbooks

You will perform a variety of file management tasks including creating and renaming a folder; selecting and then deleting, copying, cutting, pasting, and renaming workbooks; deleting a folder; and opening, printing, and closing a workbook.

Maintaining Workbooks

You can complete many workbook management tasks at the Open and Save As dialog boxes. These tasks can include copying, moving, printing, and renaming workbooks; opening multiple workbooks; and creating and renaming a new folder. Some file maintenance tasks such as creating a folder and deleting files are performed by using buttons on the Open dialog box or Save As dialog box toolbar. Figure 6.1 displays the Open dialog box toolbar buttons.

Figure 6.1 Open Dialog Box Toolbar Buttons

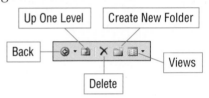

QUICK STEPS

Create a Folder
1. Click Office button, *Open*.
2. Click Create New Folder button.
3. Type folder name.
4. Press Enter.

Creating a Folder

In Excel, you should logically group and store workbooks in folders. For example, you could store all of the workbooks related to one department in one folder with the department name being the folder name. You can create a folder within a folder (called a ***subfolder***). If you create workbooks for a department by individuals, each individual name could have a subfolder within the department folder. The main folder on a disk or drive is called the root folder. You create additional folders as branches of this root folder.

At the Open or Save As dialog boxes, workbook file names display in the list box preceded by a workbook icon and a folder name displays preceded by a folder icon. Create a new folder by clicking the Create New Folder button located on the dialog box toolbar at the Open dialog box or Save As dialog box. At the New Folder dialog box shown in Figure 6.2, type a name for the folder in the *Name* text box, and then click OK or press Enter. The new folder becomes the active folder.

If you want to make the previous folder the active folder, click the Up One Level button on the dialog box toolbar. After clicking the Up One Level button, the Back button becomes active. Click this button and the previously active folder becomes active again.

A folder name can contain a maximum of 255 characters. Numbers, spaces, and symbols can be used in the folder name, except those symbols explained in Chapter 1 in the "Saving a Workbook" section.

HINT
Change the default folder with the *Default file location* option at the Excel Options dialog box with Save selected.

Create New Folder

Up One Level

Figure 6.2 New Folder Dialog Box

Type the new folder name in the *Name* text box.

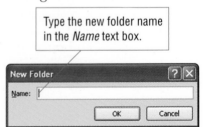

Project 1a Creating a Folder

1. Create a folder named *Payroll* on your storage medium. To begin, display the Open dialog box.
2. Double-click the *Excel2007L1C6* folder name to make it the active folder.
3. Click the Create New Folder button (located on the dialog box toolbar).
4. At the New Folder dialog box, type Payroll.
5. Click OK. (The Payroll folder is now the active folder.)

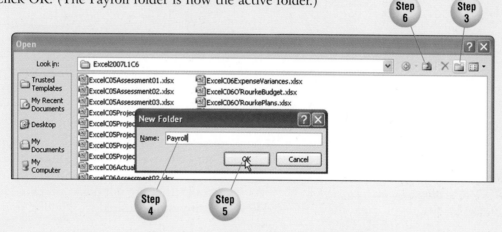

Step 6

Step 3

Step 4

Step 5

6. Click the Up One Level button on the dialog box toolbar to change back to the Excel2007L1C6 folder.

Renaming a Folder

As you organize your files and folders, you may decide to rename a folder. Rename a folder using the Tools button in the Open dialog box or using a shortcut menu. To rename a folder using the Tools button, display the Open dialog box, click in the list box the folder you want to rename, click the Tools button located in the lower left corner of the dialog box, and then click *Rename* at the drop-down list. This selects the folder name and inserts a border around the name. Type the new name for the folder and then press Enter. To rename a folder using a shortcut menu, display the Open dialog box, right-click the folder name in the list box, and then click *Rename* at the shortcut menu. Type a new name for the folder and then press Enter.

A tip to remember when you are organizing files and folders is to be sure that your system is set up to display all of the files in a particular folder and not just the Excel files, for example. You can display all files in a folder by changing the *Files of type* option at the Open dialog box to *All Files (*.*)*.

QUICK STEPS

Rename a Folder
1. Click Office button, *Open*.
2. Click desired folder.
3. Click Tools button, *Rename*.
4. Type new name.
5. Press Enter.
OR
1. Click Office button, *Open*.
2. Right-click folder name.
3. Click *Rename*.
4. Type new name.
5. Press Enter.

[Tools ▾]

Project **1b** **Renaming a Folder**

1. At the Open dialog box, right-click the *Payroll* folder name in the Open dialog box list box.
2. Click *Rename* at the shortcut menu.
3. Type Finances and then press Enter.

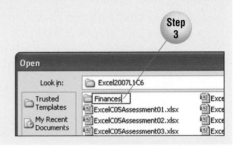

Step 3

Selecting Workbooks

You can complete workbook management tasks on one workbook or selected workbooks. To select one workbook, display the Open dialog box, and then click the desired workbook. To select several adjacent workbooks (workbooks that display next to each other), click the first workbook, hold down the Shift key, and then click the last workbook. To select workbooks that are not adjacent, click the first workbook, hold down the Ctrl key, click any other desired workbooks, and then release the Ctrl key.

Deleting Workbooks and Folders

Delete Workbook/ Folder
1. Click Office button, *Open.*
2. Click workbook or folder name.
3. Click Delete button.
4. Click Yes.

At some point, you may want to delete certain workbooks from your storage medium or any other drive or folder in which you may be working. To delete a workbook, display the Open or Save As dialog box, select the workbook, and then click the Delete button on the dialog box toolbar. At the dialog box asking you to confirm the deletion, click Yes. To delete a workbook using a shortcut menu, display the Open dialog box, right-click the workbook name in the list box, and then click *Delete* at the shortcut menu. Click Yes at the confirmation dialog box.

Delete

Deleting to the Recycle Bin

Workbooks deleted from the hard drive are automatically sent to the Windows Recycle Bin. You can easily restore a deleted workbook from the Recycle Bin. To free space on the drive, empty the Recycle Bin on a periodic basis. Restoring a workbook from or emptying the contents of the Recycle Bin is completed at the Windows desktop (not in Excel). To display the Recycle Bin, minimize the Excel window, and then double-click the *Recycle Bin* icon located on the Windows desktop. At the Recycle Bin, you can restore file(s) and empty the Recycle Bin.

Project **1c** **Selecting and Deleting Workbooks**

1. At the Open dialog box, open **ExcelC05Project01.xlsx** (located in the Excel2007L1C6 folder).
2. Save the workbook with Save As and name it **ExcelL1_C6_P1**.
3. Close **ExcelL1_C6_P1.xlsx**.

4. Delete **ExcelL1_C6_P1.xlsx** by completing the following steps:
   a. Display the Open dialog box with Excel2007L1C6 the active folder.
   b. Click *ExcelL1_C6_P1.xlsx* to select it.
   c. Click the Delete button on the dialog box toolbar.

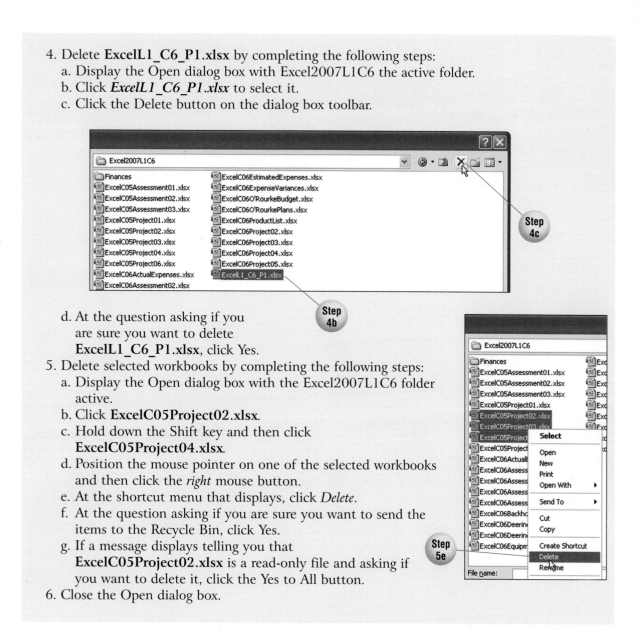

   d. At the question asking if you are sure you want to delete **ExcelL1_C6_P1.xlsx**, click Yes.
5. Delete selected workbooks by completing the following steps:
   a. Display the Open dialog box with the Excel2007L1C6 folder active.
   b. Click **ExcelC05Project02.xlsx**.
   c. Hold down the Shift key and then click **ExcelC05Project04.xlsx**.
   d. Position the mouse pointer on one of the selected workbooks and then click the *right* mouse button.
   e. At the shortcut menu that displays, click *Delete*.
   f. At the question asking if you are sure you want to send the items to the Recycle Bin, click Yes.
   g. If a message displays telling you that **ExcelC05Project02.xlsx** is a read-only file and asking if you want to delete it, click the Yes to All button.
6. Close the Open dialog box.

Copying Workbooks

In previous chapters, you have been opening a workbook from your storage medium and saving it with a new name in the same location. This process makes an exact copy of the workbook, leaving the original on your storage medium. You have been copying workbooks and saving the new workbook in the same folder as the original workbook. You can also copy a workbook into another folder.

Project 1d   Saving a Copy of an Open Workbook

1. Open **ExcelC05Assessment01.xlsx**.
2. Save the workbook with Save As and name it **TotalSales**. (Make sure Excel2007L1C6 is the active folder.)
3. Save a copy of the **TotalSales.xlsx** workbook in the Finances folder you created in Project 1a by completing the following steps:
   a. With **TotalSales.xlsx** open, display the Save As dialog box.
   b. At the Save As dialog box, change to the Finances folder. To do this, double-click *Finances* at the beginning of the list box (folders are listed before workbooks).
   c. Click the Save button located in the lower right corner of the dialog box.
4. Close **TotalSales.xlsx**.
5. Change back to the Excel2007L1C6 folder by completing the following steps:
   a. Display the Open dialog box.
   b. Click the Up One Level button located on the dialog box toolbar.
   c. Close the Open dialog box.

Step 5b

You can copy a workbook to another folder without opening the workbook first. To do this, use the *Copy* and *Paste* options from a shortcut menu at the Open (or Save As) dialog box. You can also copy a workbook or selected workbooks into the same folder. When you do this, Excel names the workbook(s) "Copy of xxx" (where *xxx* is the current workbook name). You can copy one workbook or selected workbooks into the same folder.

Project 1e   Copying a Workbook at the Open Dialog Box

1. Copy **ExcelC05Assessment02.xlsx** to the Finance folder. To begin, display the Open dialog box with the Excel2007L1C6 folder active.
2. Position the arrow pointer on **ExcelC05Assessment02.xlsx**, click the right mouse button, and then click *Copy* at the shortcut menu.
3. Change to the Finance folder by double-clicking *Finances* at the beginning of the list box.
4. Position the arrow pointer in any white area (not on a workbook name) in the list box, click the right mouse button, and then click *Paste* at the shortcut menu.
5. Change back to the Excel2007L1C6 folder by clicking the Up One Level button located on the dialog box toolbar.
6. Close the Open dialog box.

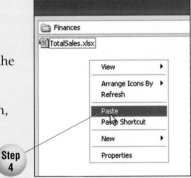

Step 4

Sending Workbooks to a Different Drive or Folder

Copy workbooks to another folder or drive with the *Copy* and *Paste* options from the shortcut menu at the Open or Save As dialog box. With the *Send To* option, you can send a copy of a workbook to another drive or folder. To use this option, position the arrow pointer on the workbook you want copied, click the *right* mouse button, point to *Send To* (this causes a side menu to display), and then click the desired drive or folder.

Cutting and Pasting a Workbook

You can remove a workbook from one folder and insert it in another folder using the *Cut* and *Paste* options from the shortcut menu at the Open dialog box. To do this, display the Open dialog box, position the arrow pointer on the workbook to be removed (cut), click the *right* mouse button, and then click *Cut* at the shortcut menu. Change to the desired folder or drive, position the arrow pointer in a white area in the list box, click the *right* mouse button, and then click *Paste* at the shortcut menu.

QUICK STEPS

Move a Workbook
1. Click Office button, *Open.*
2. Right-click workbook name.
3. Click *Cut.*
4. Navigate to desired folder.
5. Right-click white area in list box.
6. Click *Paste.*

Project — Cutting and Pasting a Workbook

1. Move a workbook to a different folder. To begin, display the Open dialog box with the Excel2007L1C6 folder active.
2. Position the arrow pointer on **ExcelC05Project06.xlsx**, click the right mouse button, and then click *Cut* at the shortcut menu.
3. Double-click *Finances* to make it the active folder.
4. Position the arrow pointer in the white area in the list box, click the right mouse button, and then click *Paste* at the shortcut menu.
5. If a Confirm File Move dialog box displays asking if you are sure you want to move the file, click Yes. (This dialog box usually does not appear when you cut and paste. Since the files you copied from your student CD-ROM are read-only files, this warning message appears.)
6. Click the Up One Level button to make the Excel2007L1C6 folder the active folder.

Renaming Workbooks

At the Open dialog box, use the *Rename* option from the Tools button drop-down list or the shortcut menu to give a workbook a different name. The *Rename* option changes the name of the workbook and keeps it in the same folder. To use *Rename*, display the Open dialog box, click once on the workbook to be renamed, click the Tools button located in the lower left corner of the dialog box, and then click *Rename*. This causes a thin black border to surround the workbook name and the name to be selected. Type the new name and then press Enter.

You can also rename a workbook by right-clicking the workbook name at the Open dialog box and then clicking *Rename* at the shortcut menu. Type the new name for the workbook and then press the Enter key.

QUICK STEPS

Rename Workbook
1. Click Office button, *Open.*
2. Click desired workbook.
3. Click Tools button, *Rename.*
4. Type new name.
5. Press Enter.
OR
1. Click Office button, *Open.*
2. Right-click workbook name.
3. Click *Rename.*
4. Type new name.
5. Press Enter.

Project 1g — Renaming a Workbook

1. Rename a workbook located in the Finances folder. To begin, make sure the Open dialog box displays with Excel2007L1C6 the active folder.
2. Double-click *Finances* to make it the active folder.
3. Click once on **ExcelC05Project06.xlsx** to select it.
4. Click the Tools button that displays in the lower left corner of the dialog box.
5. Click *Rename* at the drop-down list.
6. Type Analysis.xlsx and then press the Enter key.
7. If a message displays asking if you are sure you want to change the name of the read-only file, click Yes.
8. Complete steps similar to those in Steps 3 through 6 to rename **ExcelC05Assessment02.xlsx** to *SoftwareTests.xlsx*.
9. Click the Up One Level button.

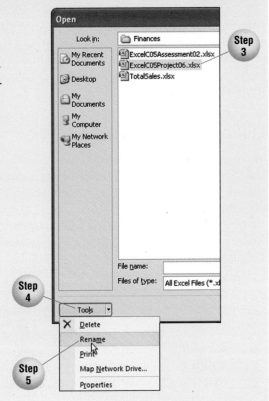

Deleting a Folder and Its Contents

As you learned earlier in this chapter, you can delete a workbook or selected workbooks. In addition to workbooks, you can delete a folder and all of its contents. Delete a folder in the same manner as you delete a workbook.

Project 1h — Deleting a Folder and Its Contents

1. Delete the Finances folder and its contents. To begin, make sure the Open dialog box displays with the Excel2007L1C6 folder active.
2. Right-click on the *Finances* folder.
3. Click *Delete* at the shortcut menu.
4. At the Confirm Folder Delete dialog box, click Yes.
5. If the Confirm File Delete dialog box displays, click the Yes to All button.

Printing Workbooks

Up to this point, you have opened a workbook and then printed it. With the *Print* option from the Tools button drop-down list or the *Print* option from the shortcut menu at the Open dialog box, you can print a workbook or several workbooks without opening them.

1. At the Open dialog box with the Excel2007L1C6 folder active, select
   ExcelC05Assessment01.xlsx and *ExcelC05Assessment02.xlsx*.
2. Click the Tools button located in the lower left corner of the dialog box.
3. Click *Print* at the drop-down list.

roject ② **Copy and Move Worksheets into an Equipment Rental Workbook**

You will open an equipment rental workbook, open two other workbooks containing equipment rental information, and then copy and move worksheets between the workbooks.

Managing Worksheets

You can move or copy individual worksheets within the same workbook or to another existing workbook. Exercise caution when moving sheets since calculations or charts based on data on a worksheet might become inaccurate if you move the worksheet. To make a duplicate of a worksheet in the same workbook, hold down the Ctrl key and then drag the worksheet tab to the desired position.

Copying a Worksheet to Another Workbook

To copy a worksheet to another existing workbook, open both the source and the destination workbooks. Right-click the sheet tab and then click *Move or Copy* at the shortcut menu. At the Move or Copy dialog box shown in Figure 6.3, select the destination workbook name from the *To book* drop-down list, select the worksheet that you want the copied worksheet placed before in the *Before sheet* list box, click the *Create a copy* check box, and then click OK.

Figure 6.3 Move or Copy Dialog Box

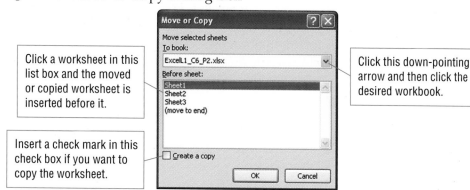

excel Level 1
Maintaining Workbooks **207**

1. Open **ExcelC06Project02.xlsx** and then save the workbook and name it **ExcelL1_C6_P2**.
2. With **ExcelL1_C6_P2.xlsx** open, open **ExcelC06Equipment.xlsx**.
3. Copy the Front Loader worksheet by completing the following steps:
   a. With **ExcelC06Equipment.xlsx** the active workbook, right-click the Front Loader tab and then click *Move or Copy* at the shortcut menu.
   b. Click the down-pointing arrow next to the *To book* option box and then click **ExcelL1_C6_P2.xlsx** at the drop-down list.
   c. Click *Sheet2* in the *Before sheet* list box.
   d. Click the *Create a copy* check box to insert a check mark.
   e. Click OK. (Excel switches to the **ExcelL1_C6_P2.xlsx** workbook and inserts the copied Front Loader worksheet between Sheet1 and Sheet2.)
4. Complete steps similar to those in Step 3 to copy the Tractor worksheet to the **ExcelL1_C6_P2.xlsx** workbook. (Insert the Tractor worksheet between Front Loader and Sheet2.)
5. Complete steps similar to those in Step 3 to copy the Forklift worksheet to the **ExcelL1_C6_P2.xlsx** workbook. (Insert the Forklift worksheet between Tractor and Sheet2.)
6. Save **ExcelL1_C6_P2.xlsx**.
7. Make **ExcelC06Equipment.xlsx** the active workbook and then close it.

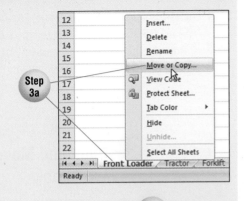

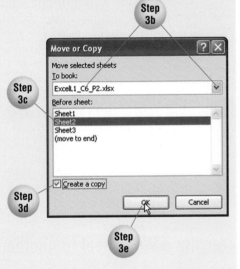

Moving a Worksheet to Another Workbook

To move a worksheet to another existing workbook, open both the source and the destination workbooks. Make active the sheet you want to move in the source workbook, right-click the sheet tab and then click *Move or Copy* at the shortcut menu. At the Move or Copy dialog box shown in Figure 6.3, select the destination workbook name from the *To book* drop-down list, select the worksheet that you want the worksheet placed before in the *Before sheet* list box, and then click OK. If you need to reposition a worksheet tab, drag the tab to the desired position.

Be careful when moving a worksheet to another workbook file. If formulas exist in the workbook that depend on the contents of the cells in the worksheet that is moved, they will no longer calculate properly.

1. With **ExcelL1_C6_P2.xlsx** open, open **ExcelC06Backhoe.xlsx**.
2. Move Sheet1 from **ExcelC06Backhoe.xlsx** to **ExcelL1_C6_P2.xlsx** by completing the following steps:
   a. With **ExcelC06Backhoe.xlsx** the active workbook, right-click the Sheet1 tab and then click *Move or Copy* at the shortcut menu.
   b. Click the down-pointing arrow next to the *To book* option box and then click **ExcelL1_C6_P2.xlsx** at the drop-down list.
   c. Click *Sheet2* in the *Before sheet* list box.
   d. Click OK.
3. Make **ExcelC06Backhoe.xlsx** the active workbook and then close it without saving the changes.
4. With **ExcelL1_C6_P2.xlsx** open, make the following changes:
   a. Delete Sheet2 and Sheet3 tabs. (These worksheets are blank.)
   b. Rename Sheet1 to Equipment Hours.
   c. Rename Sheet1 (2) to Backhoe.
5. Create a range for the Forklift total hours available by completing the following steps:
   a. Click the Front Loader tab.
   b. Select cells B4 through E4.
   c. Click in the Name box.
   d. Type FrontLoaderHours.

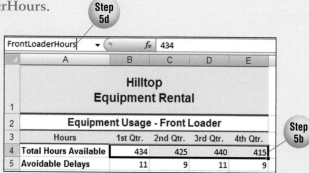

   e. Press Enter.
6. Complete steps similar to those in Step 5 to create the following ranges:
   a. In the Front Loader worksheet, create a range with cells B10 through E10 and name it *FrontLoaderHoursInUse*.
   b. Click the Tractor tab and then create a range with cells B4 through E4 and name it *TractorHours* and create a range with cells B10 through E10 and name it *TractorHoursInUse*.
   c. Click the Forklift tab and then create a range with cells B4 through E4 and name it *ForkliftHours* and create a range with cells B10 through E10 and name it *ForkliftHoursInUse*.
   d. Click the Backhoe tab and then create a range with cells B4 through E4 and name it *BackhoeHours* and create a range with cells B10 through E10 and name it *BackhoeHoursInUse*.

7. Click the EquipmentHours tab to make it the active worksheet and then insert a formula that inserts the total hours for the Front Loader by completing the following steps:
   a. Make cell C4 active.
   b. Type =SUM(Fr.
   c. When you type *Fr* a drop-down list displays with the Front Loader ranges. Double-click *FrontLoaderHours*.
   d. Type) (the closing parenthesis).
   e. Press Enter.

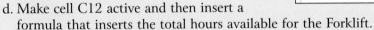

8. Complete steps similar to those in Step 7 to insert ranges in the following cells:
   a. Make cell C5 active and then insert a formula that inserts the total in-use hours for the Front Loader.
   b. Make cell C8 active and then insert a formula that inserts the total hours available for the Tractor.
   c. Make cell C9 active and then insert a formula that inserts the total in-use hours for the Tractor.
   d. Make cell C12 active and then insert a formula that inserts the total hours available for the Forklift.
   e. Make cell C13 active and then insert a formula that inserts the total in-use hours for the Forklift.
   f. Make cell C16 active and then insert a formula that inserts the total hours available for the Backhoe.
   g. Make cell C17 active and then insert a formula that inserts the total in-use hours for the Backhoe.
9. Make the following changes to specific worksheets:
   a. Click the Front Loader tab and then change the number in cell E4 from *415* to *426* and change the number in cell C6 from *6* to *14*.
   b. Click the Forklift tab and then change the number in cells E4 from *415* to *426* and change the number in cell D8 from *4* to *12*.
10. Select all of the worksheet tabs and then create a footer that prints your name at the left side of each worksheet, the page number in the middle, and the current date at the right side of each worksheet.
11. Save, print, and then close **ExcelL1_C6_P2.xlsx**.

 roject **3** **Save Workbooks in Various Formats**

You will open a workbook and then save it in a previous version of Excel, in text format, and in PDF format.

Saving a Workbook in a Different Format

When you save a workbook, the workbook is automatically saved as an Excel workbook with the *.xlsx* file extension. If you need to share a workbook with someone who is using a different version of Excel, or someone who will open it in an application other than Excel, save the workbook in another format. You can also save an Excel workbook as a Web page and in text format. Save a workbook in a different format with options from the Office button Save As side menu or with the *Save as type* option at the Save As dialog box.

Saving a Workbook in a Previous Version of Excel

If you create workbooks that others will open in a previous version of Excel, consider saving the workbook in the Excel 97-2003 format. If you save a workbook in a previous version, the workbook name displays in the title bar followed by the words *[Compatibility Mode]*. In this mode, some Excel 2007 features may not be available.

You can save a workbook in a previous version with the Office button Save As side menu or with the *Save as type* option at the Save As dialog box. To save using the side menu, click the Office button, point to the *Save As* option, and then click *Excel 97-2003 Workbook* at the side menu as shown in Figure 6.4. At the Save As dialog box, type the name for the workbook, and then click the Save button. Note also that some file formats save the active worksheet and others save the entire workbook. If you want to save a specific worksheet, hide the other worksheets and then save.

QUICK STEPS

Save Workbook in Different Format
1. Click Office button.
2. Point to *Save As*.
3. Click desired format type.
4. Type name for workbook.
5. Click Save button.
OR
1. Click Office button, *Save As*.
2. Type name for workbook.
3. Click down-pointing arrow at right of *Save as type* option box.
4. Click desired type in drop-down list.
5. Click Save button.

Figure 6.4 Save As Side Menu

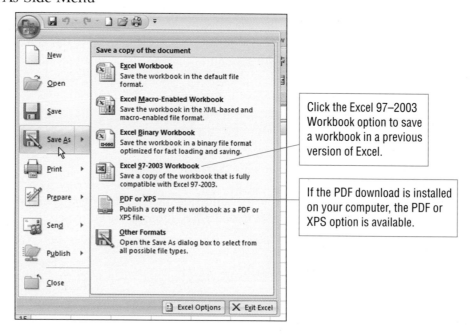

Click the Excel 97–2003 Workbook option to save a workbook in a previous version of Excel.

If the PDF download is installed on your computer, the PDF or XPS option is available.

Project **3a** | **Saving a Workbook in a Previous Version of Excel**

1. Open **ExcelC06Project03.xlsx**.
2. Click the Office button, point to the *Save As* option, and then click the *Excel 97-2003 Workbook* option that displays in the side menu.
3. At the Save As dialog box with the *Save as type* option changed to *Excel 97-2003 Workbook (*.xls)*, type ExcelL1_C6_P3_xlsformat in the *File name* text box and then press Enter.

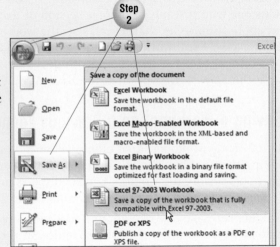

Step 2

Step 3

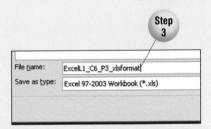

4. At the Compatibility Checker dialog box, click Continue.
5. Close **ExcelL1_C6_P3_xlsformat.xls**.
6. Open **ExcelL1_C6_P3_xlsformat.xls** and then notice that *[Compatibility Mode]* displays after the workbook title at the top of the screen.
7. Close **ExcelL1_C6_P3_xlsformat.xls**.

Saving a Workbook in Text Format

Along with the Save As side menu, you can also save workbooks in different formats with options at the *Save as type* drop-down list at the Save As dialog box. In Project 3b, you will save an Excel worksheet as a text file with tab delimiters.

Project **3b** | **Saving a Workbook in Text Format**

1. Open **ExcelC06Project03.xlsx**.
2. Click the Office button and then click *Save As*.
3. At the Save As dialog box, type ExcelL1_C6_P3tab in the *File name* text box.
4. Click the down-pointing arrow at the right side of the *Save as type* list box and then click *Text (Tab delimited) (*.txt)* at the drop-down list. (You will need to scroll down the list box to display this option.)

Step 3

Step 4

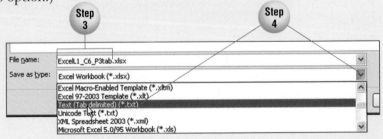

5. Click the Save button.
6. At the message telling you that the selected file type does not support workbooks that contain multiple worksheets, click OK.
7. At the message telling you that the file may contain features that are not compatible with Text (Tab delimited) and asking if you want to keep the workbook in the format, click Yes.
8. Close the workbook. (At the message asking if you want to save the changes, click Yes. At the message asking if you want to keep the workbook in the format, click Yes.)
9. Open Microsoft Word.
10. Display the Open dialog box, change the *Files of type* to *All Files (*.*)* and then open **ExcelL1_C6_P3tab.txt**.
11. Close **ExcelL1_C6_P3tab.txt** and then exit Word.

Saving in PDF Format

The portable document format (PDF) was developed by Adobe Systems and is a format that captures all of the elements of a file as an electronic image. You can view a PDF file on any application on any computer making this format the most widely used for transferring files to other users. A workbook saved in PDF format is printer friendly and most, if not all, of the workbook's original appearance is maintained.

Before saving an Excel workbook in PDF format, you must install an add-in download from the Microsoft Web site. To determine whether or not the download is installed, click the Office button and then point to the *Save As* option. If the add-in is installed, you will see the option *PDF or XPS* in the side menu with the following text below the option: *Publish a copy of the document as a PDF or XPS file*. If the add-in is not downloaded, you will see the option *Find add-ins for other file formats* in the side menu with the following text below the option: *Learn about add-ins to save to other formats such as PDF or XPS*.

If the add-in is not downloaded and you want to download it, click the *Find add-ins for other file formats* option at the side menu. This displays the Excel Help window with information on how to download the add-in. The steps in Project 3c assume that the PDF add-in is downloaded and installed and available on your computer. Before completing Project 3c, check with your instructor.

When you click the *PDF or XPS* option at the Save As side menu, the Save As dialog box displays with *PDF (*.pdf)* specified as the *Save as type* option. At this dialog box, type a name in the *File name* text box and then click the Publish button. By default, the workbook will open in PDF format in Adobe Reader. The Adobe Reader application is designed to view your workbook. You will be able to navigate in the workbook but you will not be able to make any changes to the workbook. After viewing the workbook in Adobe Reader, click the Close button located in the upper right corner of the Adobe Reader window. This closes the workbook and also closed Adobe Reader.

You can open your PDF file in Adobe Reader or in your browser window. To open a PDF workbook in your browser window, click File on the browser Menu bar and then click *Open*. (If the Menu bar is not visible, click the Tools button located in the upper right corner of the window and then click *Menu Bar* at the drop-down list.) At the Open dialog box, browse to the folder containing your PDF workbook and then double-click the workbook. You may need to change the *Files of type* option to *All Files (*.*)*.

1. Open **ExcelC06Project03.xlsx**.
2. Save the workbook in PDF file format by completing the following steps:
   a. Click the Office button and then point to the *Save As* option.
   b. Click *PDF or XPS* in the side menu. (If this option does not display, the PDF add-in download has not been installed.)

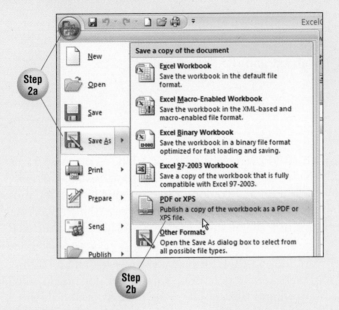

Step 2a

Step 2b

   c. At the Save As dialog box with the *Save as type* option set at *PDF (*.pdf)*, click the Publish button.

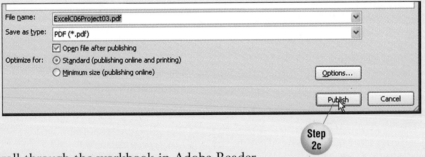

Step 2c

3. Scroll through the workbook in Adobe Reader.
4. Click the Close button located in the upper right corner of the window to close Adobe Reader.
5. Close **ExcelC06Project03.xlsx**.

Project 4   Create and Apply Styles to a Payroll Workbook

You will open a payroll workbook, define styles and apply styles and then modify the styles. You will also copy the styles to another workbook and then apply the styles in the new workbook.

Formatting with Cell Styles

In Chapter 1 you learned how to apply formatting to cells with the Cell Styles button in the Styles group in the Home tab. A style is a predefined set of formatting attributes such as font, font size, alignment, borders, shading, and so forth. You can apply the styles from the Cell Styles drop-down gallery or create your own style. Using a style to apply formatting has several advantages. A style helps to ensure consistent formatting from one worksheet to another. Once you define all attributes for a particular style, you do not have to redefine them again. If you need to change the formatting, change the style and all cells formatted with that style automatically reflect the change.

Defining a Cell Style

Two basic methods are available for defining your own cell style. You can define a style with formats already applied to a cell or you can display the Style dialog box, click the Format button, and then choose formatting options at the Format Cells dialog box. Styles you create are only available in the workbook in which they are created. To define a style with existing formatting, select the cell or cells containing the desired formatting, click the Cell Styles button in the Styles group in the Home tab, and then click the *New Cell Style* option located toward the bottom of the drop-down gallery. At the Style dialog box, shown in Figure 6.5, type a name for the new style in the *Style name* text box, and then click OK to close the dialog box.

Figure 6.5 Style Dialog Box

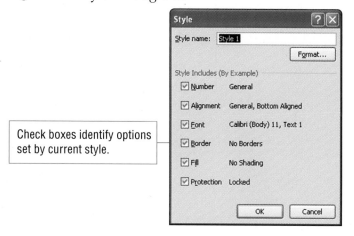

Check boxes identify options set by current style.

> ## QUICK STEPS
>
> **Define a Cell Style with Existing Formatting**
> 1. Select cell containing formatting.
> 2. Click Cell Styles button.
> 3. Click *New Cell Style*.
> 4. Type name for new style.
> 5. Click OK.
>
> **Define a Style**
> 1. Click in a blank cell.
> 2. Click Cell Styles button.
> 3. Click *New Cell Style*.
> 4. Type name for new style.
> 5. Click Format button.
> 6. Choose formatting options.
> 7. Click OK to close Format Cells dialog box.
> 8. Click OK to close Style dialog box.

> ## HINT
> Cell styles are based on the workbook theme.

Cell Styles ▾

Project 4a   Defining a Style

1. Open **ExcelC06Project04.xlsx** and then save the workbook and name it **ExcelL1_C6_P4**.
2. Make Sheet1 the active worksheet and then insert the necessary formulas to calculate gross pay, withholding tax amount, Social Security tax amount, and net pay. *Hint: Refer to Project 5c in Chapter 2 for assistance.*
3. Make Sheet2 the active worksheet and then insert a formula that calculates the amount due.

4. Make Sheet3 the active worksheet and then insert a formula in the *Due Date* column that inserts the purchase date plus the number of days in the *Terms* column. **Hint: Refer to Project 3c in Chapter 2 for assistance.**

5. Define a style named *C06Title* with the formatting in cell A1 by completing the following steps:

   a. Make *Sheet1* active and then make cell A1 active.

   b. Click the Cell Styles button in the Styles group in the Home tab and then click the *New Cell Style* option located toward the bottom of the drop-down gallery.

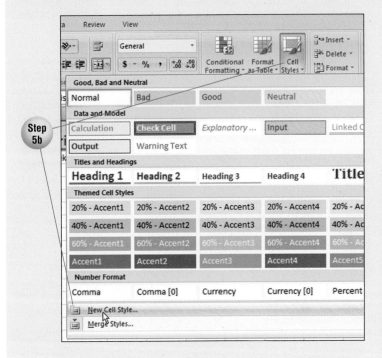

   c. At the Style dialog box, type C06Title in the *Style name* text box.

   d. Click OK.

6. Save **ExcelL1_C6_P4.xlsx**.

QUICK STEPS

Apply a Style
1. Select cells.
2. Click Cell Styles button.
3. Click desired style at drop-down gallery.

Applying a Style

To apply a style, select the cells you want to format, click the Cell Styles button in the Styles group, and then click the desired style at the drop-down gallery. The styles you create display at the top of the drop-down gallery.

Project 4b   Applying a Style

1. With **ExcelL1_C6_P4.xlsx** open, apply the C06Title style to cell A1 by completing the following steps:
   a. Make sure cell A1 is the active cell. (Even though cell A1 is already formatted, the style has not been applied to it. Later, you will modify the style and the style must be applied to the cell for the change to affect it.)
   b. Click the Cell Styles button in the Styles group in the Home tab.
   c. Click the *C06Title* style in the *Custom* section located toward the top of the drop-down gallery.

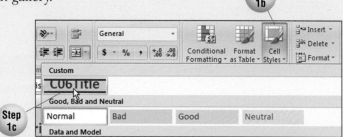

2. Apply the C06Title style to other cells by completing the following steps:
   a. Click the Sheet2 tab.
   b. Make cell A1 active.
   c. Click the Cell Styles button in the Styles group and then click the *C06Title* style at the drop-down gallery. (Notice that the style did not apply the row height formatting. The style applies only cell formatting.)
   d. Click the Sheet3 tab.
   e. Make cell A1 active.
   f. Click the Cell Styles button and then click the *C06Title* style at the drop-down gallery.
   g. Click the Sheet1 tab.
3. Save **ExcelL1_C6_P4.xlsx**.

In addition to defining a style based on cell formatting, you can also define a new style without first applying the formatting. To do this, you would display the Style dialog box, type a name for the new style, and then click the Format button. At the Format Cells dialog box, apply any desired formatting and then click OK to close the dialog box. At the Style dialog box, remove the check mark from any formatting that you do not want included in the style and then click OK to close the Style dialog box.

Project 4c   Defining a Style without First Applying Formatting

1. With **ExcelL1_C6_P4.xlsx** open, define a new style named *C06Subtitle* without first applying the formatting by completing the following steps:
   a. With Sheet1 active, click in any empty cell.
   b. Click the Cell Styles button in the Styles group and then click *New Cell Style* at the drop-down gallery.

c. At the Style dialog box, type **C06Subtitle** in the *Style name* text box.

d. Click the Format button in the Style dialog box.

e. At the Format Cells dialog box, click the Font tab.

f. At the Format Cells dialog box with the Font tab selected, change the font to Candara, the font style to bold, the size to 12, and the color to white.

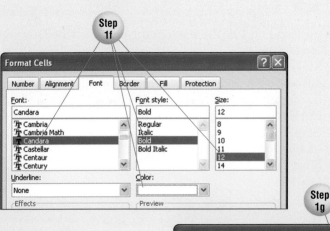

Step 1f

g. Click the Fill tab.

h. Click the bottom color in the green column as shown at the right.

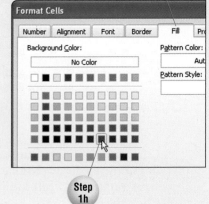

Step 1g

Step 1h

i. Click the Alignment tab.

j. Change the Horizontal alignment to Center.

k. Click OK to close the Format Cells dialog box.

l. Click OK to close the Style dialog box.

2. Apply the C06Subtitle style by completing the following steps:

a. Make cell A2 active.

b. Click the Cell Styles button and then click the *C06Subtitle* style located toward the top of the drop-down gallery in the *Custom* section.

c. Click the Sheet2 tab.

d. Make cell A2 active.

e. Click the Cell Styles button and then click the *C06Subtitle* style.

f. Click the Sheet3 tab.

g. Make cell A2 active.

h. Click the Cell Styles button and then click the *C06Subtitle* style.

i. Click the Sheet1 tab.

3. Apply the following predesigned cell styles:

a. Select cells A3 through G3.

b. Click the Cell Styles button and then click the *Heading 3* style at the drop-down gallery.

c. Select cells A5 through G5.

d. Click the Cell Styles button and then click the *20% - Accent3* style.

e. Apply the 20% - Accent3 style to cells A7 through G7 and cells A9 through G9.

f. Click the Sheet2 tab.

g. Select cells A3 through F3 and then apply the Heading 3 style.

h. Select cells A5 through F5 and then apply the 20% - Accent3 style.

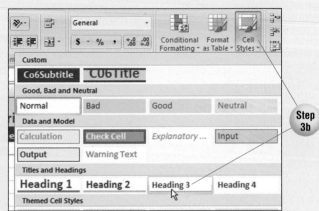

Step 3b

i. Apply the 20% - Accent3 style to every other row of cells (A7 through F7, A9 through F9, and so on, finishing with A17 through F17).

j. Click the Sheet3 tab.

k. Select cells A3 through F3 and then apply the Heading 3 style.

l. Apply the 20% - Accent3 style to A5 through F5, A7 through F7, and A9 through F9.

4. Make Sheet2 active and then change the height of row 1 to 36.00 (48 pixels).

5. Make Sheet3 active and then change the height of row 1 to 36.00 (48 pixels).

6. Make Sheet1 active.

7. Save **ExcelL1_C6_P4.xlsx** and then print only the first worksheet.

Modifying a Style

One of the advantages to formatting with a style is that you can modify the formatting of the style and all cells formatted with that style automatically reflect the change. You can modify a style you create or one of the predesigned styles provided by Word. When you modify a predesigned style, only the style in the current workbook is affected. If you open a blank workbook, the cell styles available are the default styles.

To modify a style, click the Cell Styles button in the Styles group in the Home tab and then right-click the desired style at the drop-down gallery. At the shortcut menu that displays, click *Modify*. At the Style dialog box, click the Format button. Make the desired formatting changes at the Format Cells dialog box and then click OK. Click OK to close the Style dialog box and any cells formatted with the specific style are automatically updated.

QUICK STEPS

Modify a Style
1. Click Cell Styles button.
2. Right-click desired style at drop-down gallery.
3. Click *Modify*.
4. Click Format button.
5. Make desired formatting changes.
6. Click OK to close Format Cells dialog box.
7. Click OK to close Style dialog box.

Project 4d Modifying Styles

1. With **ExcelL1_C6_P4.xlsx** open, modify the C06Title style by completing the following steps:
   a. Click in any empty cell.
   b. Click the Cell Styles button in the Styles group.
   c. At the drop-down gallery, right-click on the *C06Title* style located toward the top of the gallery in the *Custom* section, and then click Modify.
   d. At the Style dialog box, click the Format button.
   e. At the Format Cells dialog box, click the Font tab, and then change the font to Candara.

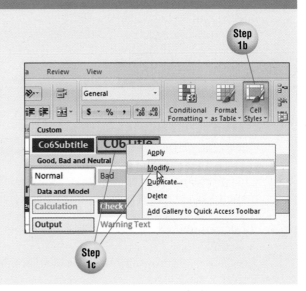

f. Click the Alignment tab.

g. Click the down-pointing arrow to the right of the *Vertical* option box, and then click *Center* at the drop-down list.

h. Click the Fill tab.

i. Click the light turquoise fill color as shown at the right.

j. Click OK to close the Format Cells dialog box.

k. Click OK to close the Style dialog box.

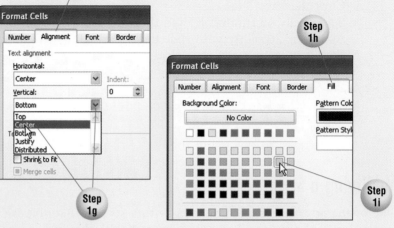

2. Modify the C06Subtitle style by completing the following steps:

   a. Click in any empty cell.

   b. Click the Cell Styles button in the Styles group.

   c. At the drop-down gallery, right-click on the *C06Subtitle* style located toward the top of the gallery in the *Custom* section, and then click *Modify*.

   d. At the Style dialog box, click the Format button.

   e. At the Format Cells dialog box, click the Font tab, and then change the font to Calibri.

   f. Click the Fill tab.

   g. Click the dark turquoise fill color as shown at the right.

   h. Click OK to close the Format Cells dialog box.

   i. Click OK to close the Style dialog box.

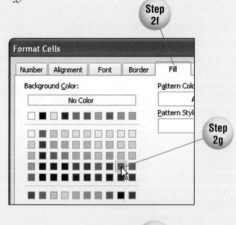

3. Modify the predefined 20% - Accent3 style by completing the following steps:

   a. Click the Cell Styles button in the Styles group.

   b. At the drop-down gallery, right-click on the *20% - Accent3* style and then click *Modify*.

   c. At the Style dialog box, click the Format button.

   d. At the Format Cells dialog box, click the Fill tab.

   e. Click the light turquoise fill color as shown at the right.

   f. Click OK to close the Format Cells dialog box.

   g. Click OK to close the Style dialog box.

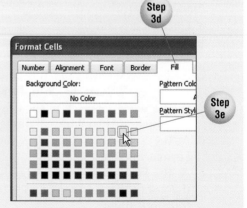

4. Click each sheet tab and notice the formatting changes made by the modified styles.

5. Change the name of Sheet1 to *Weekly Payroll*, the name of Sheet2 to *Invoices*, and the name of Sheet3 to *Overdue Accounts*.

6. Apply a different color to each of the three worksheet tabs.

7. Save and then print all the worksheets in **ExcelL1_C6_P4.xlsx**.

Copying Styles to Another Workbook

Styles you define are saved with the workbook in which they are created. You can, however, copy styles from one workbook to another. To do this, open the workbook containing the styles you want to copy and open the workbook into which you want to copy the styles. Click the Cell Styles button in the Styles group in the Home tab, and then click the *Merge Styles* option located at the bottom of the drop-down gallery. At the Merge Styles dialog box shown in Figure 6.6, double-click the name of the workbook that contains the styles you want to copy, and then click OK.

Figure 6.6 Merge Styles Dialog Box

Removing a Style

If you apply a style to text and then decide you do not want the formatting applied, return the formatting to Normal, which is the default formatting. To do this, select the cells formatted with the style you want to remove, click the Cell Styles button, and then click *Normal* at the drop-down gallery.

Deleting a Style

To delete a style, click the Cell Styles button in the Styles group in the Home tab. At the drop-down gallery that displays, right-click the style you want to delete, and then click *Delete* at the shortcut menu. Formatting applied by the deleted style is removed from cells in the workbook.

QUICK STEPS

Copy Styles to Another Workbook
1. Open workbook containing desired styles.
2. Click Cell Styles button.
3. Click *Merge Styles* option.
4. Double-click name of workbook that contains styles you want to copy.

Remove a Style
1. Select cells formatted with style you want removed.
2. Click Cell Styles button.
3. Click *Normal* at drop-down gallery.

Delete a Style
1. Click Cell Styles button.
2. Right-click desired style to delete.
3. Click *Delete* at shortcut menu.

HINT
The Undo command will not reverse the effects of the Merge Styles dialog box.

HINT
You cannot delete the Normal style.

Project 4e — **Copying and Removing Styles**

1. With **ExcelL1_C6_P4.xlsx** open, open **ExcelC06O'RourkePlans.xlsx**.
2. Save the workbook with Save As and name it **ExcelL1_C6_P4b**.

3. Copy the styles in **ExcelL1_C6_P4.xlsx** into **ExcelL1_C6_P4b.xlsx** by completing the following steps:

   a. Click the Cell Styles button in the Styles group in the Home tab.

   b. Click the *Merge Styles* option located toward the bottom of the drop-down gallery.

   c. At the Merge Styles dialog box, double-click **ExcelL1_C6_P4.xlsx** in the *Merge styles from* list box.

   d. At the message that displays asking if you want to merge styles that have the same names, click Yes.

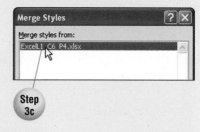

Step 3c

4. Apply the C06Title style to cell A1 and the C06Subtitle style to cell A2.

5. Increase the height of row 1 to 36.00 (48 pixels).

6. Insert the required formulas in the workbook. ***Hint: Refer to Project 3a of Chapter 2 for assistance.***

7. If neccessary, adjust column widths so all text is visible in cells.

8. Save, print, and then close **ExcelL1_C6_P4b.xlsx**.

9. Close **ExcelL1_C6_P4.xlsx**.

Project ⑤ Insert, Modify, and Print Comments in an Equipment Rental Workbook

You will open an equipment rental workbook and then insert, edit, delete and print comments.

Insert a Comment
1. Click in desired cell.
2. Click Review tab.
3. Click New Comment button.
4. Type comment.
OR
1. Right-click desired cell.
2. Click *Insert Comment*.
3. Type comment.

Inserting Comments

If you want to make comments in a worksheet, or if a reviewer wants to make comments in a worksheet prepared by someone else, insert a comment. A comment is useful for providing specific instructions, identifying critical information, or for multiple individuals reviewing the same worksheet to insert comments. Some employees in a company may be part of a ***workgroup***, which is a networked collection of computers sharing files, printers, and other resources. In a workgroup, you may collaborate with coworkers on a specific workbook. Comments provide a method for reviewing the workbook and responding to others in the workgroup.

Inserting a Comment

HINT

You can resize and/or move overlapping comments.

New Comment

Insert a comment by clicking the Review tab and then clicking the New Comment button in the Comments group. This displays a color shaded box with the user's name inside. Type the desired information or comment in this comment box and then click outside the comment box. A small, red triangle appears in the upper right corner of a cell containing a comment. You can also insert a comment by right-clicking a cell and then clicking *Insert Comment* at the shortcut menu.

Displaying a Comment

Hover the mouse over a cell containing a comment and the comment box displays. You can also display comments by right-clicking the cell containing a comment and then clicking *Show/Hide Comments* at the shortcut menu. Turn on the display of all comments by clicking the Show All Comments button in the Comments group in the Review tab. Turn on the display of an individual comment by making the cell active and then clicking the Show/Hide Comment button in the Comments group in the Review tab. Hide the display of an individual comment by clicking the same button. Move to comments in a worksheet by clicking the Next or Previous buttons in the Comments group in the Review tab.

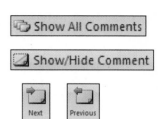

Project 5a **Inserting and Displaying Comments**

1. Open **ExcelC06Project05.xlsx**.
2. Save the workbook with Save As and name it **ExcelL1_C6_P5**.
3. Insert a formula in cell H3 that multiplies the rate by the hours and then copy the formula down to cells H4 through H16. (When you copy the formula, click the Auto Fill Options button and then click *Fill Without Formatting* at the drop-down list.)
4. Make cell H17 active and then insert a formula that sums the amounts in cells H3 through H16.
5. Insert a comment by completing the following steps:
   a. Click cell F3 to make it active.
   b. Click the Review tab.
   c. Click the New Comment button in the Comments group.
   d. In the comment box, type Bill Lakeside Trucking for only 7 hours for the backhoe and front loader on May 1.
   e. Click outside the comment box.
6. Insert another comment by completing the following steps:
   a. Click cell C6 to make it active.
   b. Click the New Comment button in the Comments group.
   c. In the comment box, type I think Country Electrical has changed their name to Northwest Electrical.
   d. Click outside the comment box.

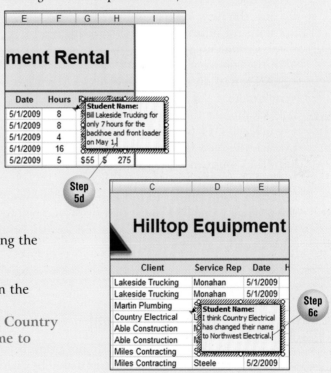

7. Assume that more than one person is reviewing and commenting on this worksheet. Change the user name and then insert additional comments by completing the following steps:

a. Click the Office button and then click the Excel Options button located toward the bottom of the drop-down list.

b. At the Excel Options dialog box make sure *Popular* is selected in the left panel.

c. Select the current name in the *User name* text box (remember the name you are selecting) and then type Jean Coen.

d. Click OK to close the dialog box.

e. Click cell D11 to make it active.

f. Click the New Comment button in the Comments group.

g. In the comment box, type This rental should be credited to Monahan instead of Leuke.

h. Click outside the comment box.

i. Click cell G11 to make it active.

j. Click the New Comment button in the Comments group.

k. In the comment box, type The hourly rental for the pressure sprayer is $25.

l. Click outside the comment box.

8. Complete steps similar to those in Steps 7a through 7d to return the user name back to the original name (the name that displayed before you changed it to *Jean Coen*).

9. Click the Show All Comments button to turn on the display of all comments.

10. Save **ExcelL1_C6_P5.xlsx**.

HINT

Display the document in Print Preview to view how comments will print.

Printing a Comment

By default, comments do not print. If you want comments to print, use the *Comments* option at the Page Setup dialog box with the Sheet tab selected. Display this dialog box by clicking the Page Layout tab, clicking the Page Setup group dialog box launcher, and then clicking the Sheet tab. Click the down-pointing arrow at the right side of the *Comments* option box. At the drop-down list that displays, choose *At end of sheet* to print comments on the page after cell contents, or choose the *As displayed on sheet* option to print the comments in the comment box in the worksheet.

Project 5b   Printing Comments

1. With **ExcelL1_C6_P5.xlsx** open, click the Page Layout tab.
2. Click the Orientation button in the Page Setup group and then click *Landscape* at the drop-down list.
3. Click the Page Setup group dialog box launcher.
4. At the Page Setup dialog box, click the Sheet tab.
5. Click the down-pointing arrow at the right side of the *Comments* option box and then click *As displayed on sheet*.
6. Click the Print button that displays toward the bottom of the dialog box and then click OK at the Print dialog box.
7. Turn off the display of comments by clicking the Review tab and then clicking the Show All Comments button.
8. Save **ExcelL1_C6_P5.xlsx**.

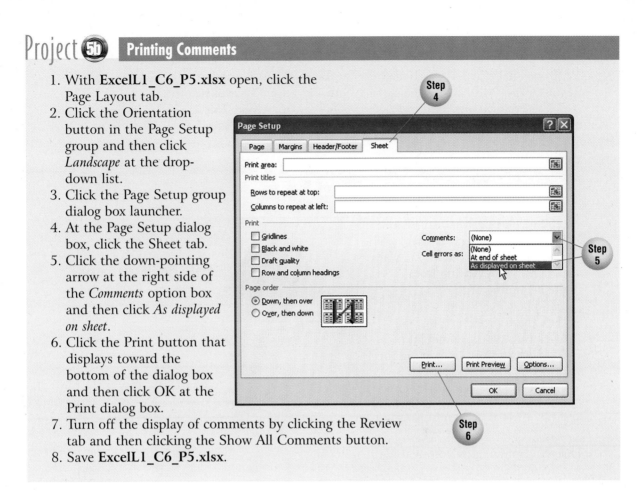

Editing a Comment

To edit a comment, click the cell containing the comment and then click the Edit Comment button in the Comments group in the Review tab. (The New Comment button changes to the Edit Comment button when the active cell contains a comment.) You can also edit a comment by right-clicking the cell containing the comment and then clicking *Edit Comment* at the shortcut menu.

Deleting a Comment

Cell comments exist in addition to data in a cell. Deleting data in a cell does not delete the comment. To delete a comment, click the cell containing the comment and then click the Delete button in the Comments group in the Review tab. You can also delete a comment by right-clicking the cell containing the comment and then clicking *Delete Comment* at the shortcut menu.

Project 5c Editing, Deleting, and Responding to Comments

1. With **ExcelL1_C6_P5.xlsx** open, display comments by completing the following steps:
   a. Click cell A3 to make it the active cell.
   b. Click the Review tab.
   c. Click the Next button in the Comments group.
   d. Read the comment and then click the Next button.
   e. Continue clicking the Next button until a message displays telling you that Microsoft Excel has reached the end of the workbook and asking if you want to continue reviewing from the beginning of the workbook. At this message, click the Cancel button.
   f. Click outside the comment box.

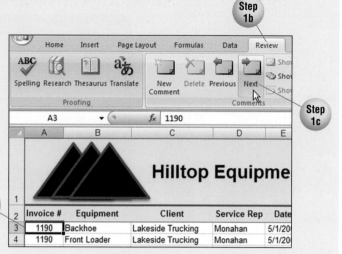

Step 1b

Step 1c

Step 1a

2. Edit a comment by completing the following steps:
   a. Click cell D11 to make it active.
   b. Click the Edit Comment button.
   c. Edit the comment so it displays as *This rental should be credited to Steele instead of Leuke.*

3. Delete a comment by completing the following steps:
   a. Click cell C6 to make it active.
   b. Click the Delete button in the Comments group.

4. Respond to the comments by making the following changes:
   a. Change the contents of F3 from *8* to *7*.
   b. Change the contents of F4 from *8* to *7*.
   c. Change the contents of D11 from *Leuke* to *Steele*.
   d. Change the contents of G11 from *$20* to *$25*.

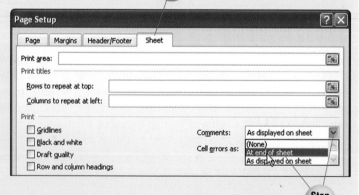

Step 2c

5. Print the worksheet and the comments by completing the following steps:
   a. Click the Page Layout tab.
   b. Click the Page Setup group dialog box launcher.
   c. At the Page Setup dialog box, click the Sheet tab.
   d. Click the down-pointing arrow at the right side of the *Comments* option and then click *At end of sheet*.
   e. Click the Print button that displays toward the bottom of the dialog box.
   f. At the Print dialog box, click OK. (The worksheet will print on one page and the comments will print on a second page.)

Step 5c

Step 5d

6. Save and then close **ExcelL1_C6_P5.xlsx**.

Project 6 Create a Billing Statement Workbook Using a Template

You will open a Billing Statement template provided by Excel, add data, save it as an Excel workbook, and then print the workbook.

Using Excel Templates

Excel has included a number of *template* worksheet forms formatted for specific uses. For example, Excel has provided template forms for a balance sheet, billing statement, loan amortization, sales invoice, and timecard. To view the templates available, click the Office button and then click *New* at the drop-down list. At the New Workbook dialog box shown in Figure 6.7, click the *Installed Templates* option in the *Templates* section. This displays the installed templates in the middle panel of the dialog box. Note that the first time you download a template, Microsoft checks to determine if you are using a genuine Office product.

QUICK STEPS

Use an Excel Template
1. Click Office button, *New*.
2. Click *Installed Templates* option.
3. Double-click desired template.

Figure 6.7 New Workbook Dialog Box

Click the *Installed Templates* option to display available templates.

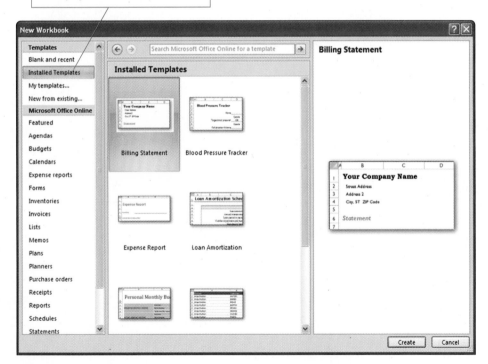

Entering Data in a Template

Templates contain unique areas where information is entered at the keyboard. For example, in the Billing Statement template shown in Figure 6.8, you enter information such as the customer name, address, and telephone number, and also the date, time, description, amount, payment, and balance of items. To enter information in the appropriate location, position the mouse pointer (white plus sign) in the location where you want to type data and then click the left mouse button. After typing the data, click the next location. You can also move the insertion point to another cell using the commands learned in Chapter 1. For example, press the Tab key to make the next cell active, press Shift + Tab to make the previous cell active.

Figure 6.8 Billing Statement Template

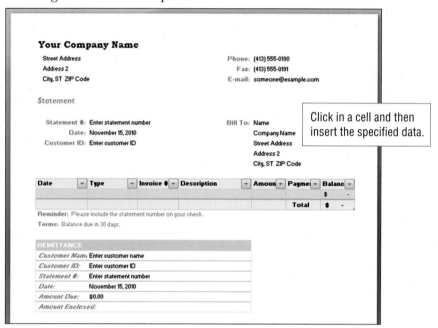

Click in a cell and then insert the specified data.

Project ⑥ Preparing a Billing Statement Using a Template

1. Click the Office button and then click *New* at the drop-down list.
2. At the New Workbook dialog box, click the *Installed Templates* option in the *Templates* section.
3. Double-click the *Billing Statement* template in the *Installed Templates* section of the dialog box.

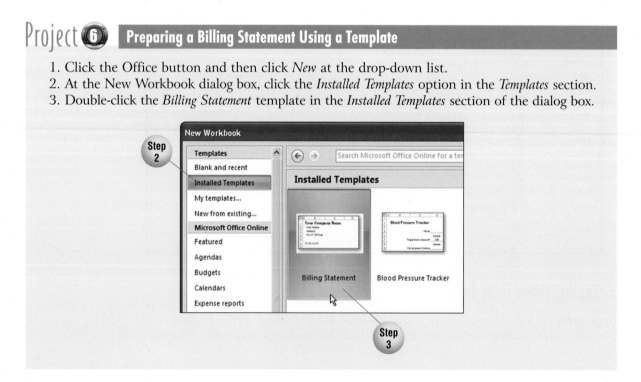

4. With cell B1 active, type **IN-FLOW SYSTEMS**.
5. Click the text *Street Address* (cell B2) and then type 320 Milander Way.
6. Click in the specified location (cell) and then type the text indicated:
    Address 2 (cell B3) = P.O. Box 2300
    City, ST ZIP Code (cell B4) = Boston, MA 02188
    Phone (cell F2) = (617) 555-3900
    Fax (cell F3) = (617) 555-3945
    Statement # (cell C8) = 5432
    Customer ID (cell C10) = 25-345
    Name (cell F8) = Aidan Mackenzie
    Company Name (cell F9) = Stanfield Enterprises
    Street Address (cell F10) = 9921 South 42nd Avenue
    Address 2 (cell F11) = P.O. Box 5540
    City, ST ZIP Code (cell F12) = Boston, MA 02193
    Date (cell B15) = (insert current date in numbers as ##/##/####)
    Type (cell C15) = System Unit
    Invoice # (cell D15) = 7452
    Description (cell E15) = Calibration Unit
    Amount (cell F15) = 950
    Payment (cell G15) = 200
    Customer Name (cell C21) = Stanfield Enterprises
    Amount Enclosed (C26) = 750

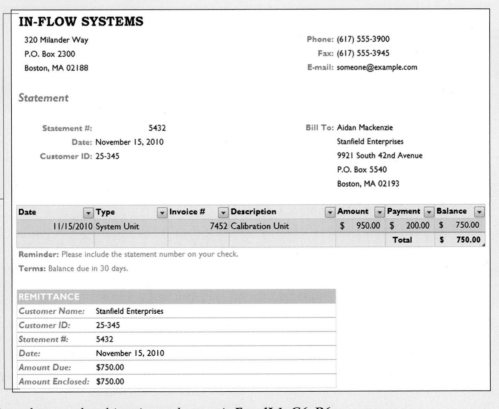

Steps
4-6

7. Save the completed invoice and name it **ExcelL1_C6_P6**.
8. Print and then close **ExcelL1_C6_P6.xlsx**.

CHAPTER summary

- Perform file management tasks such as copying, moving, printing, and renaming workbooks and creating a new folder and renaming a folder at the Open or Save As dialog boxes.
- Create a new folder by clicking the Create New Folder button located on the dialog box toolbar at the Open dialog box or Save As dialog box.
- Rename a folder with the *Rename* option from the Tools button drop-down list or with a shortcut menu.
- To select adjacent workbooks in the Open dialog box, click the first workbook, hold down the Shift key, and then click the last workbook. To select nonadjacent workbooks, click the first workbook, hold down the Ctrl key, and then click any desired workbooks.
- To delete a workbook, use the Delete button on the Open or Save As dialog box toolbar, the *Delete* option at the Tools button drop-down list, or with a shortcut menu option.
- Workbooks deleted from the hard drive are automatically sent to the Windows Recycle Bin where they can be restored or permanently deleted.
- Create a copy of an existing workbook by opening the workbook and then using the *Save As* command to assign the workbook a different file name.
- Use the *Copy* and *Paste* options from the shortcut menu at the Open (or Save As) dialog box to copy a workbook from one folder to another folder or drive.
- When you copy a workbook into the same folder from which it originates, Excel names the duplicated workbook(s) "Copy of xxx" (where *xxx* is the original workbook name).
- Use the *Send To* option from the shortcut menu to send a copy of a workbook to another drive or folder.
- Remove a workbook from a folder or drive and insert it in another folder or drive using the *Cut* and *Paste* options from the shortcut menu.
- Use the *Rename* option from the Tools button drop-down list or the shortcut menu to give a workbook a different name.
- Print multiple workbooks by selecting the desired workbooks at the Print dialog box, clicking the Tools button, and then clicking *Print* at the drop-down list.
- To move or copy a worksheet to another existing workbook, open both the source and the destination workbook and then open the Move or Copy dialog box.
- Save a workbook in a different format with options from the Office button Save As side menu or with the *Save as type* option at the Save As dialog box. Click the down-pointing arrow at the right side of the *Save as type* option and a drop-down list displays with the available formats.
- Automate the formatting of cells in a workbook by defining and then applying styles. A style is a predefined set of formatting attributes.
- A style helps to ensure consistent formatting from one worksheet to another. All formatting attributes for a particular style are defined only once. Define a style with formats already applied to a cell or display the Style dialog box, click the Format button, and then choose formatting options at the Format Cells dialog box.

- To apply a style, select the desired cells, click the Cell Styles button in the Styles group in the Home tab, and then click the desired style at the drop-down gallery.
- Modify a style and all cells to which the style is applied automatically reflect the change. To modify a style, click the Cell Styles button in the Styles group in the Home tab, right-click the desired style, and then click *Modify* at the shortcut menu.
- Styles are saved in the workbook in which they are created. Styles can be copied, however, to another workbook. Do this with options at the Merge Styles dialog box.
- Insert comments in a worksheet to provide specific instructions, identify critical information, review a workbook, and respond to others in a workgroup about the workbook.
- Insert, display, edit, and delete comments using buttons in the Comments group in the Review tab.
- By default, comments do not print. To print comments, display the Page Setup dialog box with the Sheet tab selected, and then choose the printing location with the *Comments* option.
- Excel provides preformatted templates for creating forms such as a balance sheet, billing statement, loan amortization, sales invoice, and timecard. Display the available templates by clicking the *Installed Templates* option in the *Templates* section of the New Workbook dialog box.
- Templates contain unique areas where information is entered at the keyboard. These areas vary depending on the template.

COMMANDS review

FEATURE	RIBBON TAB, GROUP	BUTTON, OPTION	OFFICE BUTTON DROP-DOWN LIST	KEYBOARD SHORTCUT
Open dialog box			Open	Ctrl + O
Save As dialog box			Save As	Ctrl + S
Print dialog box			Print	Ctrl + P
Save in PDF format			Save As, PDF or XPS	
Style dialog box	Home, Styles	, New Cell Style		
Merge Styles dialog box	Home, Styles	, Merge Styles		
Insert comment	Review, Comments			Shift + F2
Display all comments	Review, Comments	Show All Comments		
Delete comment	Review, Comments			
Display next comment	Review, Comments			
Display previous comment	Review, Comments			
New Workbook dialog box			New	

CONCEPTS check

Test Your Knowledge

Completion: In the space provided at the right, indicate the correct term, symbol, or command.

1. Perform file management tasks such as copying, moving, or deleting workbooks with options at the Open dialog box or this dialog box. _____

2. Click this button on the Open dialog box toolbar to display the folder that is up a level from the current folder. _____

3. At the Open dialog box, hold down this key while selecting nonadjacent workbooks.

   _____

4. Workbooks deleted from the hard drive are automatically sent to this location.

   _____

5. Click the down-pointing arrow at the right side of this option at the Save As dialog box to display a drop-down list of available workbook formats.

   _____

6. If the PDF format is installed, this option for saving a workbook in PDF file format displays at the Office button Save As side menu.

   _____

7. The Cell Styles button is located in this group in the Home tab.

   _____

8. Click the *New Cell Style* option at the Cell Styles button drop-down gallery and this dialog box displays.

   _____

9. A style you create displays in this section of the Cell Styles button drop-down gallery.

   _____

10. Copy styles from one workbook to another with options at this dialog box.

   _____

11. This displays in the upper right corner of a cell containing a comment.

   _____

12. The New Comment button is located in the Comments group in this tab.

   _____

13. Print comments by choosing the desired printing location with the *Comments* option at the Page Setup dialog box with this tab selected.

   _____

14. Click this button in the Comments group to display all comments in the worksheet.

   _____

15. Click this option at the New Workbook dialog box to display available templates.

   _____

SKILLS check

Demonstrate Your Proficiency

Assessment

1 **MANAGE WORKBOOKS**

1. Display the Open dialog box with Excel2007L1C6 the active folder.
2. Create a new folder named *O'Rourke* in the Excel2007L1C6 folder.
3. Copy **ExcelC06O'RourkeBudget.xlsx**, **ExcelC06O'RourkePlans.xlsx**, and **ExcelC06Project04.xlsx** to the O'Rourke folder.
4. Display the contents of the O'Rourke folder and then rename **ExcelC06O'RourkeBudget.xlsx** to **EquipmentBudget.xlsx**.
5. Rename **ExcelC06O'RourkePlans.xlsx** to **PurchasePlans.xlsx** in the O'Rourke folder.
6. Change the active folder back to Excel2007L1C6.
7. Delete all of the workbooks in the Excel2007L1C6 folder that begin with *ExcelC05*.
8. Close the Open dialog box.

Assessment

2 **MOVE AND COPY WORKSHEETS BETWEEN SALES ANALYSIS WORKBOOKS**

1. Open **ExcelC06Assessment02.xlsx**.
2. Save the workbook with Save As and name it **ExcelL1_C6_A2**.
3. Rename Sheet1 to *1st Qtr.*
4. Rename Sheet2 to *Yearly Summary*.
5. Move the Yearly Summary sheet before the 1st Qtr. sheet.
6. Open **ExcelC06DeeringQtrs.xlsx**.
7. Rename Sheet1 to *2nd Qtr.* and then copy it to **ExcelL1_C6_A2.xlsx** (following the 1st Qtr. worksheet).
8. Make **ExcelC06DeeringQtrs.xlsx** active, rename Sheet2 to *3rd Qtr.* and then copy it to **ExcelL1_C6_A2.xlsx** (following the 2nd Qtr. worksheet).
9. Make **ExcelC06DeeringQtrs.xlsx** active and then close it without saving the changes.
10. Open **ExcelC06DeeringFourthQtr.xlsx**.
11. Rename Sheet1 to *4th Qtr.* and then move it to **ExcelL1_C6_A2.xlsx** (following the 3rd Qtr. worksheet).
12. Make **ExcelC06DeeringFourthQtr.xlsx** active and then close it without saving the changes.
13. With **ExcelL1_C6_A2.xlsx** active, make the following changes:
    a. Make 1st Qtr. the active worksheet and then insert a formula to calculate the averages and another to calculate the totals. (Use the Auto Fill Options button to fill without formatting.)
    b. Make 2nd Qtr. the active worksheet and then insert a formula to calculate the averages and another to calculate the totals. (Use the Auto Fill Options button to fill without formatting.)

c. Make 3rd Qtr. the active worksheet and then insert a formula to calculate the averages and another to calculate the totals. (Use the Auto Fill Options button to fill without formatting.)

d. Make 4th Qtr. the active worksheet and then insert a formula to calculate the averages and another to calculate the totals. (Use the Auto Fill Options button to fill without formatting.)

e. Make Yearly Summary the active worksheet and then insert a formula that inserts in cell B4 the average of the amounts in cell E4 for the 1st Qtr., 2nd Qtr., 3rd Qtr., and 4th Qtr. worksheets.

f. Copy the formula in cell B4 down to cells B5 through B9.

g. Make cell B10 active and then insert a formula that calculates the total of cells B4 through B9.

14. Delete the Sheet3 tab.

15. Insert a footer on all worksheets that prints your name at the left, the page number in the middle, and the current date at the right.

16. Horizontally and vertically center the worksheets.

17. Save and then print all of the worksheets in **ExcelL1_C6_A2.xlsx**.

18. Close **ExcelL1_C6_A2.xlsx**.

Assessment

3 DEFINE AND APPLY STYLES TO A PROJECTED EARNINGS WORKBOOK

1. At a blank worksheet, define a style named *C06Heading* that contains the following formatting:
   a. 14-point Cambria bold in dark blue color
   b. Horizontal alignment of Center
   c. Top and bottom border in a dark red color
   d. Light purple fill

2. Define a style named *C06Subheading* that contains the following formatting:
   a. 12-point Cambria bold in dark blue color
   b. Horizontal alignment of Center
   c. Top and bottom border in dark red color
   d. Light purple fill

3. Define a style named *C06Column* that contains the following formatting:
   a. 12-point Cambria in dark blue color
   b. Light purple fill

4. Save the workbook and name it **ExcelL1_C6_A3_Styles**.

5. With **ExcelL1_C6_A3_Styles.xlsx** open, open **ExcelC06Assessment03.xlsx**.

6. Save the workbook with Save As and name it **ExcelL1_C6_A3**.

7. Make cell C6 active and then insert a formula that multiplies the content of cell B6 with the amount in cell B3. (When writing the formula, identify cell B3 as an absolute reference.) Copy the formula down to cells C7 through C17.

8. Copy the styles from **ExcelL1_C6_A3_Styles.xlsx** into **ExcelL1_C6_A3.xlsx**. *Hint: Do this at the Merge Styles dialog box.*

9. Apply the following styles:
   a. Select cells A1 and A2 and then apply the C06Heading style.
   b. Select cells A5 through C5 and then apply the C06Subheading style.
   c. Select cells A6 through A17 and then apply the C06Column style.

10. Save the workbook again and then print **ExcelL1_C6_A3.xlsx**.

11. With **ExcelL1_C6_A3.xlsx** open, modify the following styles:
   a. Modify the C06Heading style so it changes the font color to dark purple (instead of dark blue), changes the vertical alignment to Center, and inserts a top and bottom border in dark purple (instead of dark red).
   b. Modify the C06Subheading style so it changes the font color to dark purple (instead of dark blue) and inserts a top and bottom border in dark purple (instead of dark red).
   c. Modify the C06Column style so it changes the font color to dark purple (instead of dark blue). Leave all of the other formatting attributes.
12. Save the workbook and then print **ExcelL1_C6_A3.xlsx**.
13. Close **ExcelL1_C6_A3.xlsx** and then close **ExcelL1_C6_A3_Styles.xlsx** without saving the changes.

Assessment

4 INSERT, DELETE AND PRINT COMMENTS IN A TRAVEL WORKBOOK

1. Open **ExcelC06Asessment04.xlsx**.
2. Save the workbook with Save As and name it **ExcelL1_C6_A4.xlsx**.
3. Insert the following comments in the specified cells:

B7	=	Should we include Sun Valley, Idaho, as a destination?
B12	=	Please include the current exchange rate.
G8	=	What other airlines fly into Aspen, Colorado?

4. Save **ExcelL1_C6_A4.xlsx**.
5. Turn on the display of all comments.
6. Print the worksheet in landscape orientation with the comments as displayed on the worksheet.
7. Turn off the display of all comments.
8. Delete the comment in cell B12.
9. Print the worksheet again with the comments printed at the end of the worksheet. (The comments will print on a separate page from the worksheet.)
10. Save and then close **ExcelL1_C6_A4.xlsx**.

Assessment

5 APPLY CONDITIONAL FORMATTING TO A SALES WORKBOOK

1. Use Excel Help files to learn more about conditional formatting.
2. Open **ExcelC06Assessment05.xlsx** and then save the workbook and name it **ExcelL1_C6_A5**.
3. Select cells D5 through D19 and then use conditional formatting to display the amounts as data bars.
4. Insert a footer that prints your name, a page number, and the current date.
5. Save, print, and then close **ExcelL1_C6_A5.xlsx**.

CASE study

Apply Your Skills

Part 1

You are the office manager for Leeward Marine and you decide to consolidate into one workbook worksheets containing information on expenses. Copy **ExcelC06EstimatedExpenses.xlsx**, **ExcelC06ActualExpenses.xlsx**, and **ExcelC06ExpenseVariances.xlsx** into one workbook. Apply appropriate formatting to numbers and insert necessary formulas. Include the company name, Leeward Marine, in each worksheet. Create styles and apply the styles to cells in each worksheet to maintain consistent formatting. Rename and recolor the three worksheet tabs (you determine the names and colors). Save the workbook and name it **ExcelC06LeewardExpenses**.

Part 2

As you look at the information in each worksheet in the **ExcelC06LeewardExpenses.xlsx** workbook, you decide that the information should be summarized for easy viewing. Include a new worksheet in the workbook that summarizes each category in Employee Costs, Facilities Costs, and Marketing Costs by estimated costs, actual costs, and expense variances. Insert formulas in the summary worksheet that insert the appropriate totals from each of the three other worksheets. Insert an appropriate header or footer in the workbook. Scale the worksheets so each print on one page. Save, print (all of the worksheets in the workbook), and then close **ExcelC06LeewardExpenses.xlsx**.

Part 3

You are not happy with the current product list form so you decide to look at template forms available at the Microsoft online site. Display the New Workbook dialog box and then download the Product price list template located in the *Lists* category. Open **ExcelC06ProductList.xlsx** and then copy the product information into the Produce price list template. Insert the following company information as required by the template:

> Leeward Marine
> 4500 Shoreline Drive,
> Ketchikan, AK 99901
> (907) 555-2200
> (907) 555-2595 (fax)
> www.emcp.com/leewardmarine

Format the product list form with formatting similar to the formatting you applied to the **ExcelC06LeewardExpenses.xlsx** workbook. Save the completed products list form and name it **ExcelC06ProductsList**. Print and then close the workbook.

You need to print a number of copies of the product list and you want the company letterhead to print at the top of the page. You decide to use the letterhead you created in Word and copy the product list information from Excel into the Word letterhead document. To do this, open Word and then open the document named **LeewardMarineLtrhd.docx**. Open **ExcelC06ProductList.xlsx** and then copy the cells containing data and paste them into the Word letterhead document using *Paste Special*. When the product list information is pasted into the Word document, apply blue font color to the data in the cells. Apply any other formatting you think will enhance the cells in the document. Save the Word document with *Save As* and name it **WordC06ProductList**. Print and then close **WordC06ProductList.docx** and then close **ExcelC06ProductList.xlsx**.

Creating a Chart in Excel

PERFORMANCE OBJECTIVES

Upon successful completion of Chapter 7, you will be able to:

- Create a chart with data in an Excel worksheet
- Size, move, and delete charts
- Print a selected chart and print a worksheet containing a chart
- Preview a chart
- Choose a chart style, layout, and formatting
- Change chart location
- Insert, move, size, and delete chart labels, shapes, and pictures

excel Chapter 7

SNAP

Tutorial 7.1
Creating and Formatting Charts

In the previous Excel chapters, you learned to create data in worksheets. While a worksheet does an adequate job of representing data, you can present some data more visually by charting the data. A chart is sometimes referred to as a *graph* and is a picture of numeric data. In this chapter, you will learn to create and customize charts in Excel.

Note: Before beginning computer projects, copy to your storage medium the Excel2007L1C7 subfolder from the Excel2007L1 folder on the CD that accompanies this textbook and then make Excel2007L1C7 the active folder.

Project ① Create a Quarterly Sales Column Chart

You will open a workbook containing quarterly sales data and then use the data to create a column chart. You will decrease the size of the chart, move it to a different location in the worksheet and then make changes to sales numbers.

Creating a Chart

In Excel, create a chart with buttons in the Charts group in the Insert tab as shown in Figure 7.1. With buttons in the Charts group you can create a variety of charts such as a column chart, line chart, pie chart, and much more. Excel provides 11

QUICK STEPS

Create a Chart
1. Select cells.
2. Click Insert tab.
3. Click desired chart button.
4. Click desired chart style at drop-down list.

Create Chart as Default Chart Type
1. Select cells.
2. Press Alt + F1.

basic chart types as described in Table 7.1. To create a chart, select cells in a worksheet that you want to chart, click the Insert tab, and then click the desired chart button in the Charts group. At the drop-down gallery that displays, click the desired chart style. You can also create a chart by selecting the desired cells and then pressing Alt + F1. This keyboard shortcut, by default, inserts the data in a 2-D column chart (unless the default chart type has been changed).

Figure 7.1 Chart Group Buttons

These buttons display in the Insert tab and you can use them to create a variety of charts.

Table 7.1 Types of Charts

Chart	Description
Area	An Area chart emphasizes the magnitude of change, rather than time and the rate of change. It also shows the relationship of parts to a whole by displaying the sum of the plotted values.
Bar	A Bar chart shows individual figures at a specific time, or shows variations between components but not in relationship to the whole.
Bubble	A Bubble chart compares sets of three values in a manner similar to a scatter chart, with the third value displayed as the size of the bubble marker.
Column	A Column chart compares separate (noncontinuous) items as they vary over time.
Doughnut	A Doughnut chart shows the relationship of parts of the whole.
Line	A Line chart shows trends and change over time at even intervals. It emphasizes the rate of change over time rather than the magnitude of change.
Pie	A Pie chart shows proportions and relationships of parts to the whole.
Radar	A Radar chart emphasizes differences and amounts of change over time and variations and trends. Each category has its own value axis radiating from the center point. Lines connect all values in the same series.
Stock	A Stock chart shows four values for a stock—open, high, low, and close.
Surface	A Surface chart shows trends in values across two dimensions in a continuous curve.
XY (Scatter)	A Scatter chart either shows the relationships among numeric values in several data series or plots the interception points between x and y values. It shows uneven intervals of data and is commonly used in scientific data.

Sizing, Moving, and Deleting a Chart

When you create a chart, the chart is inserted in the same worksheet as the selected cells. Figure 7.2 displays the worksheet and chart you will create in Project 1a. The chart is inserted in a box which you can size and/or move in the worksheet.

To size the worksheet, position the mouse pointer on the four dots located in the middle of the border you want to size until the pointer turns into a two-headed arrow, hold down the left mouse button, and then drag to increase or decrease the size of the chart. To increase or decrease the height and width of the chart at the same time, position the mouse pointer on the three dots that display in a chart border corner until the pointer displays as a two-headed arrow, hold down the left mouse button, and then drag to the desired size. To increase or decrease the size of the chart and maintain the proportions of the chart, hold down the Shift key while dragging a chart corner border.

To move the chart, make sure the chart is selected (light turquoise box displays around the chart), position the mouse pointer on a border until it turns into a four-headed arrow, hold down the left mouse button, and then drag to the desired position.

HINT

Hide rows or columns that you do not want to chart.

Figure 7.2 Project 1a Chart

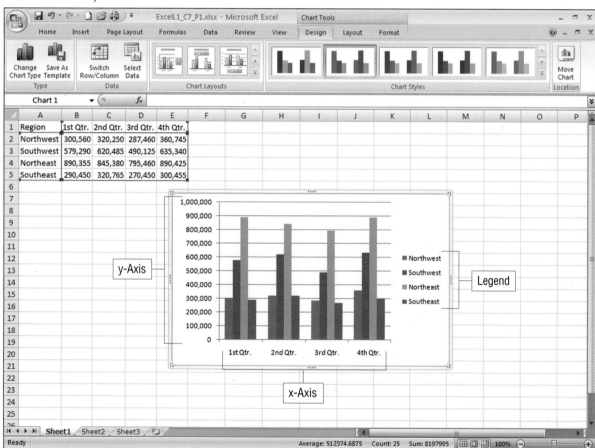

Editing Data

The cells you select to create the chart are linked to the chart. If you need to change data for a chart, edit the data in the desired cell and the corresponding section of the chart is automatically updated.

Project 1a Creating a Chart

1. Open **ExcelC07Project01.xlsx** and then save the workbook and name it **ExcelL1_C7_P1**.
2. Select cells A1 through E5.
3. Press Alt + F1.
4. Slightly increase the size of the chart and maintain the proportions of the chart by completing the following steps:
   a. Position the mouse pointer on the bottom right corner of the chart border until the pointer turns into a two-headed arrow pointing diagonally.
   b. Hold down the Shift key and then hold down the left mouse button.
   c. Drag out approximately one-half inch and then release the mouse button and then the Shift key.

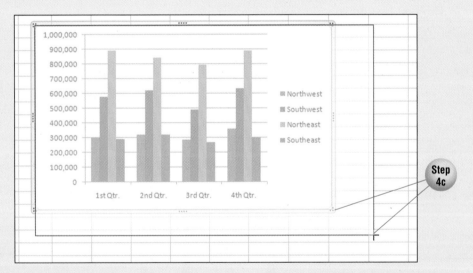

Step 4c

5. Move the chart below the cells containing data by completing the following steps:
   a. Make sure the chart is selected (light turquoise border surrounds the chart).

Step 5c

b. Position the mouse pointer on the chart border until the pointer turns into a four-headed arrow.
   c. Hold down the left mouse button, drag the chart so it is positioned below the cells containing data, and then release the mouse button.
6. Make the following changes to the specified cells:
   a. Make cell B2 active and then change *300,560* to *421,720*.
   b. Make cell C2 active and then change *320,250* to *433,050*.
   c. Make cell D2 active and then change *287,460* to *397,460*.
   d. Make cell E2 active and then change *360,745* to *451,390*.
7. Save **ExcelL1_C7_P1.xlsx**.

Printing Only the Chart

In a worksheet containing data in cells as well as a chart, you can print only the chart. To do this, click the chart to select it and then display the Print dialog box. At the Print dialog box, *Selected Chart* will automatically be selected in the *Print what* section. Click OK to print only the selected chart.

Previewing a Chart

Preview a chart by clicking the Office button, pointing to the *Print* option, and then clicking *Print Preview*. After previewing the chart, click the Close Preview button, or print the worksheet by clicking the Print button in the Print Preview tab.

Project **1b**   **Previewing and Printing the Chart**

1. With **ExcelL1_C7_P1.xlsx** open, make sure the chart displays.
2. Preview the chart by completing the following steps:
   a. Click the Office button.
   b. Point to the *Print* option.
   c. Click *Print Preview*.
   d. After viewing the chart in Print Preview, click the Close Print Preview button.
3. Print the worksheet by clicking the Quick Print button in the Quick Access toolbar.
4. Save and then close **ExcelL1_C7_P1.xlsx**.

Project **2**   **Create a Technology Purchases Bar Chart and Column Chart**

You will open a workbook containing technology purchases data by department and then create a bar chart with the data. You will then change the chart type, layout, and style and move the chart to a new sheet.

Changing the Chart Design

When you insert a chart in a worksheet, the Chart Tools Design tab displays as shown in Figure 7.3. With options in this tab, you can change the chart type, specify a different layout or style for the chart, and change the location of the chart so it displays in a separate worksheet.

Figure 7.3 Chart Tools Design Tab

QUICK STEPS

Change Chart Type and Style
1. Make the chart active.
2. Click Chart Tools Design tab.
3. Click Change Chart Type button.
4. Click desired chart type.
5. Click desired chart style.
6. Click OK.

Choosing a Custom Chart Style

The chart feature offers a variety of preformatted custom charts and offers varying styles for each chart type. You can choose a chart style with buttons in the Charts group by clicking a chart button and then choosing from the styles offered at the drop-down list. You can also choose a chart style with the Change Chart Type button in the Chart Tools Design tab. Click this button and the Change Chart Type dialog box displays as shown in Figure 7.4. Click the desired chart type in the panel at the left side of the dialog box and then click the desired chart style at the right. If you create a particular chart type on a regular basis, you may want to set that chart type as the default. To do this, click the Set as Default Chart button in the Change Chart Type dialog box.

Figure 7.4 Change Chart Type Dialog Box

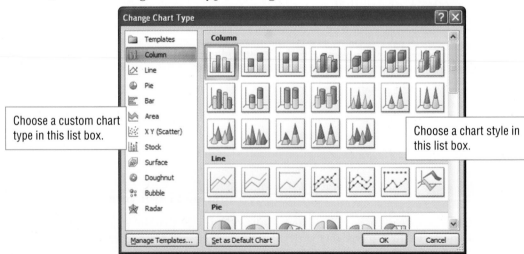

Choose a custom chart type in this list box.

Choose a chart style in this list box.

Changing the Data Series

A data series is information represented on the chart by bars, lines, columns, pie slices, and so on. When Excel creates a chart, the data in the first column (except the first cell) is used to create the x-axis (the information along the bottom of the chart) and the data in the first row (except the first cell) is used to create the legend. You can switch the data in the axes by clicking the Switch Row/Column button in the Data group in the Chart Tools Design tab. This moves the data on the x-axis to the y-axis and the y-axis data to the x-axis.

QUICK STEPS

Change Chart Data Series
1. Make the chart active.
2. Click Chart Tools Design tab.
3. Click Switch Row/Column button.

Switch Row/Column

Project 2a — Creating a Chart and Changing the Design

1. Open **ExcelC07Project02.xlsx** and then save the workbook and name it **ExcelL1_C7_P2**.
2. Create a bar chart by completing the following steps:
   a. Select cells A3 through B9.
   b. Click the Insert tab.
   c. Click the Bar button in the Charts group.
   d. Click the first option from the left in the *Cylinder* section (*Clustered Horizontal Cylinder*).
3. With the chart selected and the Chart Tools Design tab displayed, change the data series by clicking the Switch Row/Column button located in the Data group.

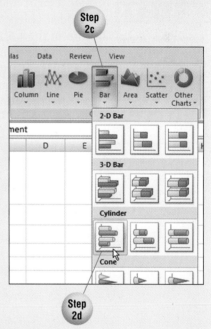

Step 2c

Step 2d

Step 3

4. Change the chart type and style by completing the following steps:
   a. Click the Change Chart Type button located in the Type group.
   b. At the Change Chart Type dialog box, click the *Column* option in the left panel.
   c. Click the *3-D Cylinder* option in the *Column* section (fourth chart style from the left in the second row of the *Column* section).
   d. Click OK to close the Change Chart Type dialog box.
5. Save **ExcelL1_C7_P2.xlsx**.

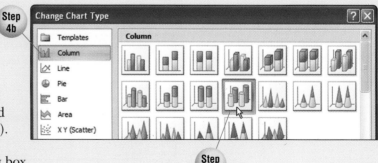

Step 4b

Step 4c

Changing Chart Layout and Style

HINT

Click the Save As Template button in the Type group in the Chart Tools Design tab to save the formatting and layout of the current chart as a template you can use to create future charts.

The Chart Tools Design tab contains options for changing the chart layout and style. The Chart Layouts group in the tab contains preformatted chart layout options. Click the More button (contains an underline and a down-pointing arrow) to display a drop-down list of layout options. Hover the mouse pointer over an option and a ScreenTip displays with the option name. You can also scroll through layout options by clicking the up-pointing arrow or the down-pointing arrow located at the right side of the Chart Layouts group.

Use options in the Chart Styles group to apply a particular style of formatting to a chart. Click the More button located at the right side of the Chart Styles group to display a drop-down list with all the style options or click the up-pointing or down-pointing arrow at the right of the group to scroll through the options.

Changing Chart Location

QUICK STEPS

Change Chart Location
1. Make the chart active.
2. Click Chart Tools Design tab.
3. Click Move Chart button.
4. Click *New Sheet* option.
5. Click OK.

[Move Chart icon]

Move Chart

Create a chart and the chart is inserted in the currently open worksheet as an embedded object. You can change the location of a chart with the Move Chart button in the Location group. Click this button and the Move Chart dialog box displays as shown in Figure 7.5. Click the *New sheet* option to move the chart to a new sheet within the workbook. Excel automatically names the sheet *Chart1*. Click the down-pointing arrow at the right side of the *Object in* option box and then click the desired location. The drop-down list will generally display the names of the worksheets within the open workbook. You can use the keyboard shortcut, F11, to create a default chart type (usually a column chart) and Excel automatically inserts the chart in a separate sheet.

If you have moved a chart to a separate sheet, you can move it back to the original sheet or move it to a different sheet within the workbook. To move a chart to a sheet, click the Move Chart button in the Location group in the Chart Tools Design tab. At the Move Chart dialog box, click the down-pointing arrow at the right side of the *Object in* option and then click the desired sheet at the drop-down list. Click OK and the chart is inserted in the specified sheet as an object that you can move, size, and format.

Figure 7.5 Move Chart Dialog Box

Click the *New sheet* option to insert the chart in a separate sheet.

To move the chart to a different sheet, click this down-pointing arrow and then click the desired sheet.

Deleting a Chart

Delete a chart created in Excel by clicking once in the chart to select it and then pressing the Delete key. If you move a chart to a different worksheet in the workbook and then delete the chart, the chart is deleted but not the worksheet. To delete the chart as well as the worksheet, position the mouse pointer on the Chart1 tab, click the *right* mouse button, and then click *Delete* at the shortcut menu. At the message box telling you that selected sheets will be permanently deleted, click Delete.

QUICK STEPS

Delete a Chart
1. Click once in chart.
2. Press Delete key.
OR
1. Right-click chart tab.
2. Click Cut.

Project 2b Changing Chart Layout, Style, and Location

1. With **ExcelL1_C7_P2.xlsx** open, make sure the Chart Tools Design tab displays. (If it does not, make sure the chart is selected and then click the Chart Tools Design tab.)
2. Change the chart type by completing the following steps:
   a. Click the Change Chart Type button in the Type tab.
   b. Click *3-D Clustered Column* (fourth column style from the left in the top row).
   c. Click OK to close the dialog box.
3. Change the chart layout by clicking the *Layout 1* option in the Chart Layouts group (first option from the left). This layout inserts the words *Chart Title* at the top of the chart.
4. Change the chart style by clicking the More button located at the right side of the Chart Styles group and the clicking *Style 34* (second option from the left in the fifth row).

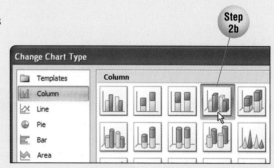

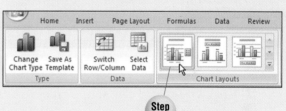

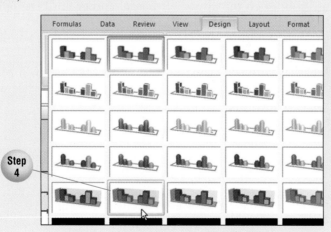

5. Move the chart to a new location by completing the following steps:
   a. Click the Move Chart button in the Location group.
   b. At the Move Chart dialog box, click the *New sheet* option and then click OK. (The chart is inserted in a worksheet named *Chart1*.)
6. Save **ExcelL1_C7_P2.xlsx**.
7. Print the Chart1 worksheet containing the chart.
8. Move the chart from Chart1 to Sheet2 by completing the following steps:
   a. Make sure Chart1 is the active sheet and that the chart is selected (not an element in the chart).
   b. Make sure the Chart Tools Design tab is active.
   c. Click the Move Chart button in the Location group.
   d. At the Move Chart dialog box, click the down-pointing arrow at the right side of the *Object in* option and then click *Sheet2* at the drop-down list.

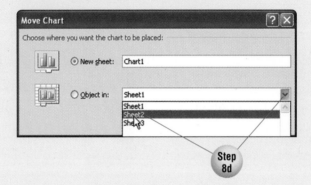

Step 5b

Step 8d

   e. Click OK.
9. Increase the size of the chart and maintain the proportions by completing the following steps:
   a. Click inside the chart but outside any chart elements. (This displays a light turquoise border around the chart.)
   b. Hold down the Shift key.
   c. Position the mouse pointer on the upper left border corner until the pointer turns into a double-headed arrow pointing diagonally.
   d. Hold down the left mouse button, drag left approximately one inch and then release the mouse button and then the Shift key.
   e. Display the worksheet in Print Preview to determine if the chart will print on one page. If the chart does not fit on the page, close Print Preview and then decrease the size of the chart until it fits on one page.
10. Change amounts in Sheet1 by completing the following steps:
    a. Click Sheet1.
    b. Make cell B4 active and then change the number from *$33,500* to *$12,750*.
    c. Make cell B9 active and then change the number from *$19,200* to *$5,600*.
    d. Make cell A2 active.
    e. Click the Sheet2 tab and notice that the chart displays the updated amounts.
11. Print the active worksheet (Sheet2).
12. Save and then close **ExcelL1_C7_P2.xlsx**.

 roject ❸ **Create a Population Comparison Bar Chart**

You will open a workbook containing population comparison data for Seattle and Portland and then create a bar chart with the data. You will also add chart labels and shapes and move, size, and delete labels/shapes.

Changing the Chart Layout

Customize the layout of labels in a chart with options in the Chart Tools Layout tab as shown in Figure 7.6. With buttons in this tab, you can change the layout and/or insert additional chart labels. Certain chart labels are automatically inserted in a chart including a chart legend and labels for the x-axis and y-axis. Add chart labels to an existing chart with options in the Labels group in the Chart Tools Layout tab. In addition to chart labels, you can also insert shapes, pictures, and/or clip art and change the layout of 3-D chart labels.

Figure 7.6 Chart Tools Layout Tab

Inserting, Moving, and Deleting Chart Labels

Certain chart labels are automatically inserted in a chart, including a chart legend and labels for the x-axis and y-axis. The legend identifies which data series is represented by which data marker. Insert additional chart labels with options in the Labels group in the Chart Tools Layout tab. For example, click the Chart Title button in the Labels group and a drop-down list displays with options for inserting a chart title in a specific location in the chart.

You can move and/or size a chart label. To move a chart label, click the label to select it and then move the mouse pointer over the border line until the pointer turns into a four-headed arrow. Hold down the left mouse button, drag the label to the desired location, and then release the mouse button. To size a chart label, use the sizing handles that display around the selected label to increase or decrease the size. To delete a chart label, click the label to select it and then press the Delete key. You can also delete a label by right-clicking the label and then clicking *Delete* at the shortcut menu.

Add Chart Labels
1. Make the chart active.
2. Click Chart Tools Layout tab.
3. Click desired chart labels button.
4. Choose desired option at drop-down list.

1. Open **ExcelC07Project03.xlsx** and then save the workbook and name it **ExcelL1_C7_P3**.
2. Create a Bar chart by completing the following steps:
   a. Select cells A2 through H4.
   b. Click the Insert tab.
   c. Click the Bar button in the Charts group and then click the *Clustered Horizontal Cylinder* option in the *Cylinder* section.
3. Change to a Line chart by completing the following steps:
   a. Click the Change Chart Type button in the Type group.
   b. At the Change Chart Type dialog box, click *Line* located at the left side of the dialog box.
   c. Click the *Line with Markers* option in the *Line* section (fourth option from the left).

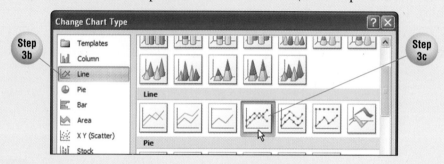

   d. Click OK to close the Change Chart Type dialog box.
4. Click the More button in the Chart Styles group in the Chart Tools Design tab and then click *Style 18* at the drop-down gallery (second option from left in the third row).

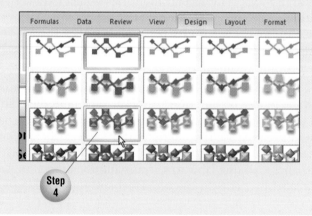

5. Change the layout of the chart by completing the following steps:
   a. Click the Chart Tools Layout tab.
   b. Click the Legend button in the Labels group.
   c. At the drop-down list, click the *Show Legend at Bottom* option.

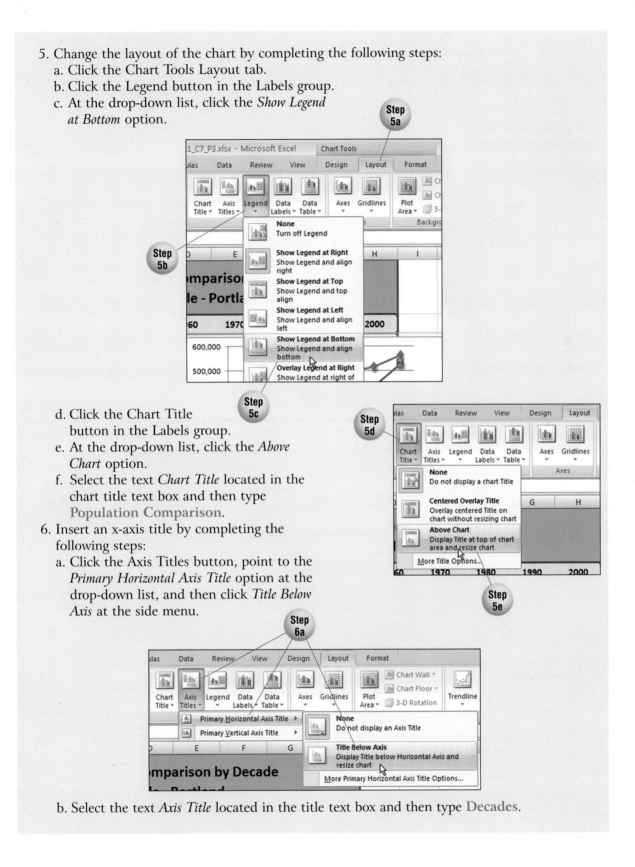

   d. Click the Chart Title button in the Labels group.
   e. At the drop-down list, click the *Above Chart* option.
   f. Select the text *Chart Title* located in the chart title text box and then type Population Comparison.
6. Insert an x-axis title by completing the following steps:
   a. Click the Axis Titles button, point to the *Primary Horizontal Axis Title* option at the drop-down list, and then click *Title Below Axis* at the side menu.

   b. Select the text *Axis Title* located in the title text box and then type Decades.

7. Insert a y-axis title by completing the following steps:
   a. Click the Axis Titles button, point to the *Primary Vertical Axis Title* option at the drop-down list, and then click *Rotated Title* at the side menu. (This inserts a rotated title at the left side of the chart containing the text *Axis Title*).

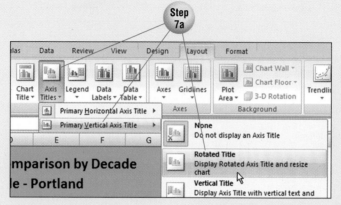

   b. Select the text *Axis Title* located in the axis title text box and then type Total Population.
8. Click the Gridlines button in the Axes group, point to *Primary Vertical Gridlines*, and then click the *Major & Minor Gridlines* option at the side menu.

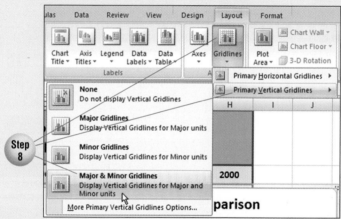

9. Click the Data Table button in the Labels group and then click the *Show Data Table* option. (This inserts cells toward the bottom of the chart containing cell data.)
10. Click the Lines button in the Analysis group and then click *Drop Lines* at the drop-down list.

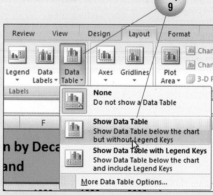

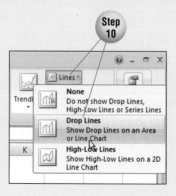

11. Drag the bottom right corner of the chart border to increase the size by approximately one inch.
12. Drag the chart so it is positioned below the data in cells but not overlapping the data.
13. Click the x-axis title (*Decades*) to select the title text box and then drag the box so it is positioned as shown below.

	1940	1950	1960	1970	1980	1990	2000
0							
Seattle	368,302	467,591	557,087	530,831	493,846	516,259	563,374
Portland	305,394	373,628	372,676	376,967	366,383	437,319	529,121

Decades

——— Seattle ——— Portland

Step
13

14. Print only the selected chart.
15. Delete the horizontal axis title by clicking the axis title *Decades* and then pressing the Delete key.
16. Save **ExcelL1_C7_P3.xlsx**.

Inserting Shapes

The Insert group in the Chart Tools Layout tab contains three buttons with options for inserting shapes or images in a chart. Click the Shapes button in the Insert group and a drop-down list displays with a variety of shape options as shown in Figure 7.7. Click the desired shape at the drop-down list and the mouse pointer turns into a thin, black plus symbol. Drag with this pointer symbol to create the shape in the chart. The shape is inserted in the chart with default formatting. You can change this formatting with options in the Drawing Tools Format tab. This tab contains many of the same options as the Chart Tools Format tab. For example, you can insert a shape, apply a shape or WordArt style, and arrange and size the shape.

Moving, Sizing, and Deleting Shapes

Move, size, and delete shapes in the same manner as moving, sizing, and deleting chart elements. To move a shape, select the shape, position the mouse pointer over the border line until the pointer turns into a four-headed arrow. Hold down the left mouse button, drag the shape to the desired location, and then release the mouse button. To size a shape, select the shape and then use the sizing handles that display around the shape to increase or decrease the size. Delete a selected shape by clicking the Delete key or right-clicking the shape and then clicking *Cut* at the shortcut menu.

QUICK STEPS

Insert Shape
1. Make the chart active.
2. Click Chart Tools Layout tab.
3. Click Shapes button.
4. Click desired shape at drop-down list.
5. Drag pointer symbol to create shape in chart.

Shapes

HINT
Chart elements can be repositioned for easier viewing.

Figure 7.7 Shapes Button Drop-down List

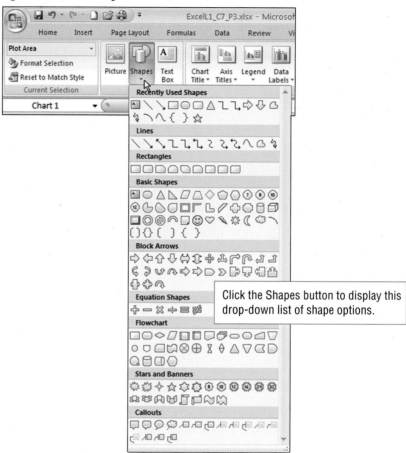

Click the Shapes button to display this drop-down list of shape options.

Project 3b   Inserting and Customizing a Shape

1. With **ExcelL1_C7_P3.xlsx** open, make sure the Chart Tools Layout tab displays.
2. Create a shape similar to the shape shown in Figure 7.8. Begin by clicking the Shapes button in the Insert group.
3. Click the *Up Arrow Callout* shape in the *Block Arrows* section (last shape in the second row).
4. Drag in the chart to create the shape.

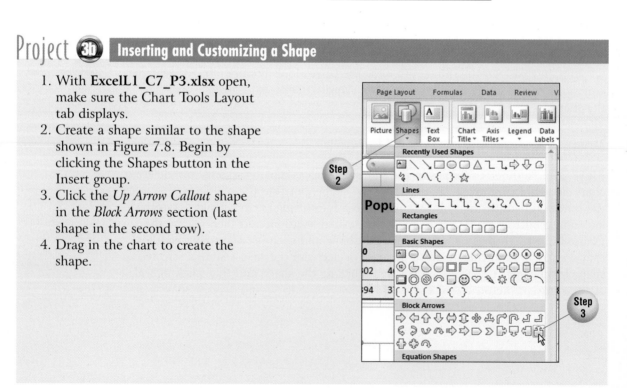

5. Click the More button in the Shapes Styles group (located at the right side of the three shapes) and then click *Subtle Effect - Accent 1* at the drop-down gallery.

6. With the shape selected, use the sizing handles around the shape to increase and/or decrease the size so it displays as shown in Figure 7.8.

7. Type **Largest Disparity** in the shape box, press Enter, and then type (184,411).

8. Select the text you just typed and then complete the following steps:
   a. Click the Home tab.
   b. Click the Center button in the Alignment group.
   c. Click the Bold button in the Font group.
   d. Click the Font Size button arrow and then click *10*.

9. With the shape selected, drag the shape so it is positioned as shown in Figure 7.8.

10. Save **ExcelL1_C7_P3.xlsx**.

Figure 7.8 Project 3b Chart

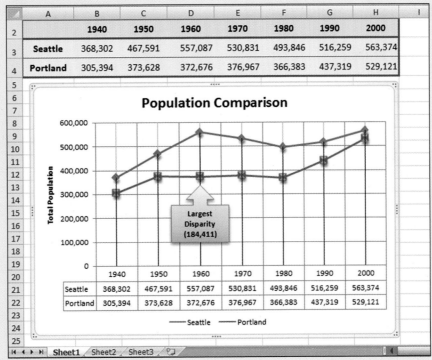

QUICK STEPS

Insert Image
1. Make the chart active.
2. Click Chart Tools Layout tab.
3. Click Picture button.
4. Double-click desired file name.

Inserting Images

Click the Picture button in the Insert group in the Chart Tools Layout tab and the Insert Picture dialog box displays. If you have a picture or image file saved in a folder, navigate to the desired folder and then double-click the file name. This inserts the picture or image in the chart. Drag the picture or image to the desired position in the chart and use the sizing handles to change the size.

Project 3c Inserting a Picture in a Chart

1. With **ExcelL1_C7_P3.xlsx** open, make sure the chart is selected and then click the Chart Tools Layout tab.
2. Insert the company logo by completing the following steps:
   a. Click the Picture button in the Insert group.
   b. At the Insert Picture dialog box, navigate to the Excel2007L1C7 folder on your storage medium and then double-click *WELogo.jpg* in the list box.
3. With the logo image inserted in the chart, use the sizing handles to decrease the size of the image and then move the image so it displays in the upper left corner of the chart area as shown in Figure 7.9.
4. Print only the selected chart.
5. Save and then close **ExcelL1_C7_P3.xlsx**.

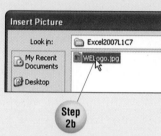

Step 2b

Figure 7.9 **Project 3c Chart**

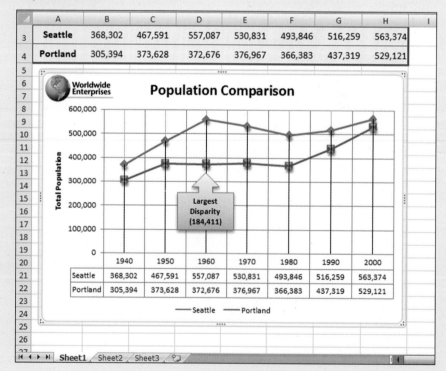

 roject **4** **Create a Costs Percentage Pie Chart**

You will open a workbook containing percentage of costs for company departments and then create a pie chart with the data. You will apply formatting to the chart and then move the chart to a new worksheet.

Changing the Chart Formatting

Customize the format of the chart and chart elements with options in the Chart Tools Format tab as shown in Figure 7.10. With buttons in the Current Selection group you can identify a specific element in the chart and then apply formatting to that element. You can also click the Reset to Match Style button in the Current Selection group to return the formatting of the chart back to the original layout.

Figure 7.10 Chart Tools Format Tab

With options in the Shape Styles group, you can apply formatting styles to specific elements in a chart. Identify the desired element either by clicking the element to select it or by clicking the down-pointing arrow at the right side of the Chart Elements button in the Current Selection group and then clicking the desired element name at the drop-down list. With the chart element specified, apply formatting by clicking a style button in the Shape Styles group. You can also apply a style from a drop-down gallery. Display this gallery by clicking the More button located at the right side of the shape styles. Click the up-pointing or the down-pointing arrow at the right of the shape styles to cycle through the available style options.

H I N T

Apply a WordArt style to make numbers stand out.

Chart Elements

1. Open **ExcelC07Project04.xlsx** and then save the workbook and name it **ExcelL1_C7_P4**.
2. Create the pie chart as shown in Figure 7.11 by completing the following steps:
   a. Select cells A3 through B10.
   b. Click the Insert tab.
   c. Click the Pie button in the Charts group and then click the first pie option in the *2-D Pie* section.
3. Click the More button located at the right side of the Chart Styles group.
4. At the drop-down gallery, click the *Style 32* option (last option in the fourth row).

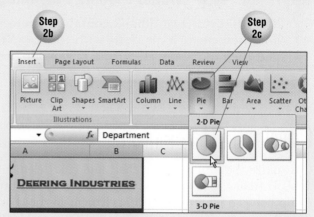

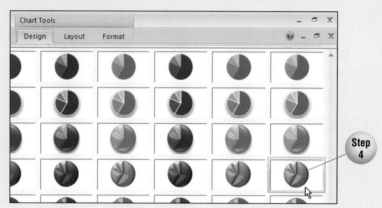

5. Click the Chart Tools Layout tab.
6. Insert data labels by clicking the Data Labels button in the Labels group and then clicking *Outside End* at the drop-down list.
7. Format chart elements by completing the following steps:
   a. Click the Chart Tools Format tab.
   b. Click the down-pointing arrow at the right side of the Chart Elements button in the Current Selection group and then click *Legend* at the drop-down list.
   c. Click the More button in the Shape Styles group and then click the last option in the fourth row (*Subtle Effect - Accent 6*).
   d. Click the down-pointing arrow at the right side of the Chart Elements button in the Current Selection group and then click *Chart Title*.

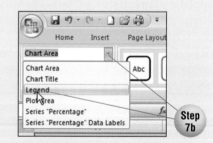

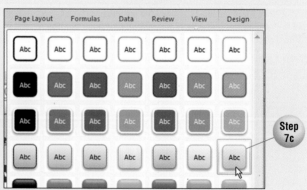

e. Click the More button at the right side of the WordArt styles in the WordArt Styles group and then click the *Gradient Fill - Accent 6, Inner Shadow* (second option from the left in the fourth row).

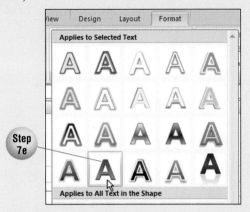

8. Insert the chart in a new sheet by completing the following steps:
   a. With the chart selected, click the Chart Tools Design tab.
   b. Click the Move Chart button in the Location group.
   c. At the Move Chart dialog box, click the *New sheet* option.
   d. Click OK.
9. Print only the worksheet containing the chart.
10. Save and then close **ExcelL1_C7_P4.xlsx**.

Figure 7.11 Project 4

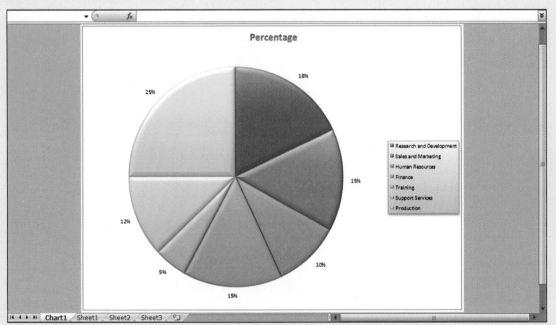

P roject ⑤ Create a Regional Sales Column Chart

You will create a column chart using regional sales data, change the layout of the chart, apply formatting, and change the height and width of the chart.

QUICK STEPS

Change Chart Height and/or Width
1. Make the chart active.
2. Click Chart Tools Format tab.
3. Insert desired height and/or width with *Shape Height* and/or *Shape Width* text boxes.

Changing the Chart Height and Width

You can size a chart by selecting the chart and then dragging a sizing handle. You can also size a chart to specific measurements with the *Shape Height* and *Shape Width* measurement boxes in the Size group in the Chart Tools Format tab. Change the height or width by clicking the up- or down-pointing arrows that display at the right side of the button or select the current measurement in the measurement box and then type a specific measurement.

Project ⑤ | Changing the Height and Width of a Chart

1. Open **ExcelC07Project05.xlsx**.
2. Save the workbook with Save As and name it **ExcelL1_C7_P5**.
3. Create a Column chart by completing the following steps:
   a. Select cells A3 through B8.
   b. Click the Insert tab.
   c. Click the Column button in the Charts group.
   d. Click the *3-D Clustered Column* option (first option in the *3-D Column* section).
   e. Click the Switch Row/Column button located in the Data group to change the data series.
   f. Click the *Layout 1* option in the Chart Layouts group (first option from the left in the group).
   g. Select the text *Chart Title* and then type Northeast Regional Sales.
   h. Click the More button located at the right side of the Chart Styles group and then click *Style 32* at the drop-down gallery (last option in fourth row).

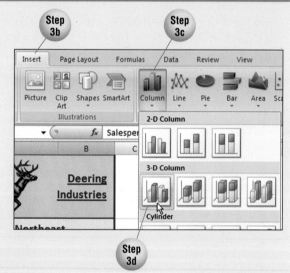

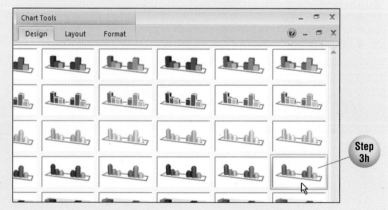

4. Change a series color by completing the following steps:
   a. Click the Chart Tools Format tab.
   b. Click the down-pointing arrow at the right side of the Chart Elements button and then click *Series "Newman, Jared"* at the drop-down list.

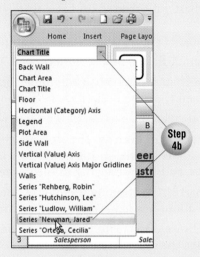

Step
4b

c. Click the Shape Fill button arrow in the Shape Styles group and then click the dark red color *Red, Accent 2, Darker 25%*.

Step
4c

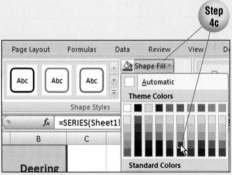

5. Change a series color by completing the following steps:
   a. With the Chart Tools Format tab active, click the down-pointing arrow at the right side of the Chart Elements button and then click *Series "Hutchinson, Lee"* at the drop-down list.
   b. Click the Shape Fill button arrow in the Shape Styles group and then click the dark green color *Olive Green, Accent 3, Darker 25%*.
6. Drag the chart down below the cells containing data.
7. Click the Chart Tools Format tab.
8. Click in the *Shape Height* measurement box in the Size group and then type 3.8.
9. Click the up-pointing arrow at the right side of the *Shape Width* measurement box in the Size group until 5.5 displays in the text box.
10. Print only the chart.
11. Save and then close **ExcelL1_C7_P5.xlsx**.

Step
8

Step
9

CHAPTER summary

- Create a chart with data in an Excel worksheet. A chart is a visual presentation of data.

- Excel provides 11 basic chart types: Area, Bar, Bubble, Column, Doughnut, Line, Pyramid, Radar, Stock, Surface, and XY (Scatter).

- To create a chart, select cells containing data you want to chart, click the Insert tab, and then click the desired chart button in the Charts group.

- A chart you create is inserted in the same worksheet as the selected cells.

- You can increase or decrease the size of a chart by positioning the mouse pointer on the four dots located in the middle of each border line or the three dots at each corner, and then dragging to the desired size.

- Move a chart by positioning the mouse pointer on the chart border until it turns into a four-headed arrow and then dragging with the mouse.

- Data in cells used to create the chart are linked to the chart. If you change the data in cells, the chart reflects the changes.

- Print by selecting the chart and then displaying the Print dialog box. At the Print dialog box, make sure *Selected Chart* is selected and then click OK.

- Preview a chart by clicking the Office button, pointing to *Print*, and then clicking *Print Preview* at the side menu.

- When you insert a chart in a worksheet, the Chart Tools Design tab is active. Use options in this tab to change the chart type, specify a different layout or style, and change the location of the chart.

- Choose a chart style with buttons in the Charts group in the Insert tab or at the Change Chart Type dialog box. Display this dialog box by clicking the Change Chart Type button in the Type group in the Chart Tools Design tab.

- The Chart Layouts group in the Chart Tools Design tab contains preformatted chart layout options. Use options in the Chart Styles group to apply a particular style of formatting to a chart.

- By default, a chart is inserted in the active worksheet. You can move the chart to a new sheet within the workbook with the *New sheet* option at the Move Chart dialog box. Display this dialog box by clicking the Move Chart button in the Location group in the Chart Tools Design tab.

- To delete a chart in a worksheet, click the chart to select it, and then press the Delete key. To delete a chart created in a separate sheet, position the mouse pointer on the chart tab, click the *right* mouse button, and then click Delete.

- Use options in the Chart Tools Layout tab to change the layout and/or insert additional chart labels, shapes, pictures, or clip art images.

- Insert additional chart labels with options in the Labels group in the Chart Tools Layout tab.

- Use buttons in the Insert group in the Chart Tools Layout tab to insert shapes, pictures, or text boxes.

- To move a chart label, click the label to select it and then drag the label with the mouse. To delete a label, click the label and then press the Delete key.

- Use options in the Chart Tools Format tab to customize the format of the chart and chart elements.
- Change the chart size by dragging the chart sizing handles or by entering a measurement in the *Shape Height* and *Shape Width* measurement boxes in the Size group in the Chart Tools Format tab.

COMMANDS review

FEATURE	RIBBON TAB, GROUP	BUTTON, OPTION	KEYBOARD SHORTCUT
Default chart in worksheet			Alt + F1
Default chart in separate sheet			F11
Change Chart Type dialog box	Chart Tools Design, Type		
Move Chart dialog box	Chart Tools Design, Location		
Shapes button drop-down list	Chart Tools Layout, Insert		
Insert Picture dialog box	Chart Tools Layout, Insert		

CONCEPTS check

Test Your Knowledge

Completion: In the space provided at the right, indicate the correct term, symbol, or command.

1. This is the keyboard shortcut to create a chart with the default chart type.

2. This type of chart shows proportions and relationships of parts to the whole.

3. The Charts group contains buttons for creating charts and is located in this tab.

4. When you create a chart, the chart is inserted in this location by default.

5. Select a chart in a worksheet, display the Print dialog box, and this option is automatically selected in the *Print what* section.

6. When Excel creates a chart, the data in the first row (except the first cell) is used to create this.

7. Click the Picture button in the Chart Tools Layout tab and this dialog box displays.

8. Click this option at the Move Chart dialog box to move the chart to a separate sheet.

9. Use buttons in the Insert group in this tab to insert shapes, pictures, or text boxes.

10. Change the chart size by entering measurements in these text boxes in the Size group in the Chart Tools Format tab.

SKILLS check
Demonstrate Your Proficiency

Assessment

1 CREATE A COMPANY SALES COLUMN CHART

1. Open **ExcelC07Assessment01.xlsx** and then save the workbook and name it **ExcelL1_C7_A1**.
2. Select cells A3 through C15 and then create a Column chart with the following specifications:
   a. Choose the *3-D Clustered Column* chart at the Chart button drop-down list.
   b. At the Chart Tools Design tab, click the *Layout 3* option in the Chart Layouts group.
   c. Change the chart style to *Style 26*.
   d. Select the text *Chart Title* and then type Company Sales.
   e. Move the location of the chart to a new sheet.
3. Print only the worksheet containing the chart.
4. Save and then close **ExcelL1_C7_A1.xlsx**.

Assessment

2 CREATE QUARTERLY DOMESTIC AND FOREIGN SALES BAR CHART

1. Open **ExcelC07Assessment02.xlsx** and then save the workbook and name it **ExcelL1_C7_A2**.
2. Select cells A3 through E5 and then create a Bar chart with the following specifications:
   a. Click the *Clustered Bar in 3-D* option at the Bar button drop-down list.
   b. At the Chart Tools Design tab choose the *Layout 2* option in the Chart Layouts group.
   c. Choose the *Style 23* option in the Chart Styles group.
   d. Select the text *Chart Title*, type Quarterly Sales, and then click in the chart but outside any chart elements.
   e. Display the Chart Tools Layout tab and then insert primary vertical minor gridlines. (Do this with the Gridlines button.)
   f. Display the Chart Tools Format tab and then apply to the chart the *Subtle Effect - Accent 3* option in the Shape Styles group.
   g. Select the *Domestic* series (using the Chart Elements button) and then apply a purple fill (Purple, Accent 4, Darker 25%) using the Shape Fill button in the Shape Styles group.
   h. Select the Foreign series and then apply a dark aqua fill (Aqua, Accent 5, Darker 25%) using the Shape Fill button in the Shape Styles group.
   i. Select the chart title and then apply the *Gradient Fill - Accent 6, Inner Shadow* option with the WordArt Styles button.
   j. Increase the height of the chart to 4 inches and the width to 6 inches.
   k. Move the chart below the cells containing data and make sure the chart fits on the page with the data. (**Hint: Display the worksheet in Print Preview.**)
3. Print only the worksheet.
4. Save and then close **ExcelL1_C7_A2.xlsx**.

Assessment

3 CREATE AND FORMAT A CORPORATE SALES COLUMN CHART

1. Open **ExcelC07Assessment03.xlsx** and then save the workbook and name it **ExcelL1_C7_A3**.
2. Create a column chart and format the chart so it displays as shown in Figure 7.12.
3. Print only the worksheet containing the chart.
4. Save and then close **ExcelL1_C7_A3.xlsx**.

Figure 7.12 Assessment 3

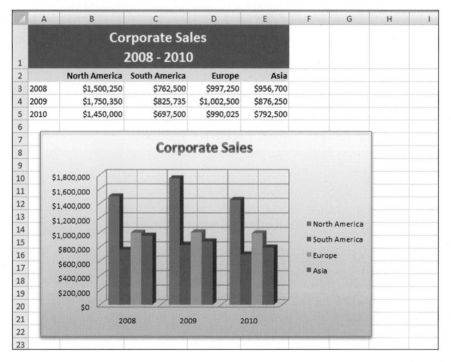

Assessment

4 CREATE A FUNDS ALLOCATIONS PIE CHART

1. At a blank worksheet, create a worksheet with the following data:

   Fund Allocations

Fund	Percentage
Annuities	23%
Stocks	42%
Bonds	15%
Money Market	20%

2. Using the data above, create a pie chart as a separate worksheet with the following specifications:
   a. Create a title for the pie chart.
   b. Add data labels to the chart.
   c. Add any other enhancements that will improve the visual presentation of the data.

3. Save the workbook and name it **ExcelL1_C7_A4**.
4. Print only the sheet containing the chart.
5. Close **ExcelL1_C7_A4.xlsx**.

Assessment

5 CREATE AN ACTUAL AND PROJECTED SALES CHART

1. Open **ExcelC07Assessment05.xlsx** and then save the workbook and name it **ExcelL1_C7_A5**.
2. Look at the data in the worksheet and then create a chart to represent the data. Add a title to the chart and add any other enhancements to improve the visual display of the chart.
3. Save the workbook and then print the chart.
4. Close **ExcelL1_C7_A5.xlsx**.

Assessment

6 CREATE AN ATTENDANCE SCATTER CHART

1. Use Excel's Help feature to learn more about chart types and then create a worksheet with the data shown in Figure 7.13. Create a scatter chart from the data in a separate sheet and create an appropriate title for the chart. Use the DATE function to enter the dates in the first column and enter the current year for the date.
2. Save the completed workbook and name it **ExcelL1_C7_A6**.
3. Print both sheets of the workbook (the sheet containing the data in cells and the sheet containing the chart).
4. Close **ExcelL1_C7_A6.xlsx**.

Figure 7.13 Assessment 6

HIGHLAND PARK ATTENDANCE

Week	Projected	Actual
July 1	35,000	42,678
July 8	33,000	41,065
July 15	30,000	34,742
July 22	28,000	29,781
July 29	28,000	26,208

CASE study
Apply Your Skills

You are an administrator for Dollar Wise Financial Services and you need to prepare charts indicating home loan and commercial loan amounts for the past year. Use the information below to prepare two charts in Excel. You determine the type and style of chart and the layout and formatting of the chart. Insert a shape in the Commercial Loans chart that contains the text *All-time High* and points to the second quarter amount (*$6,785,250*).

> Home Loans
>> 1st Qtr. = $2,675,025
>> 2nd Qtr. = $3,125,750
>> 3rd Qtr. = $1,975,425
>> 4th Qtr. = $875,650
>
> Commercial Loans
>> 1st Qtr. = $5,750,980
>> 2nd Qtr. = $6,785,250
>> 3rd Qtr. = $4,890,625
>> 4th Qtr. = $2,975,900

Save the workbook containing the two charts and name it **ExcelL1_C7_CS_P1**. Print only the two charts and then close **ExcelL1_C7_CS_P1.xlsx**.

Part 2

You need to present information on the budget for the company. You have the dollar amounts and need to convert the amounts to a percentage of the entire budget. Use the information below to calculate the percentage of the budget for each item and then create a pie chart with the information. You determine the chart style, layout, and formatting.

Total Budget: $6,000,000

Building Costs	=	$720,000
Salaries	=	$2,340,000
Benefits	=	$480,000
Advertising	=	$840,000
Marketing	=	$600,000
Client Expenses	=	$480,000
Equipment	=	$420,000
Supplies	=	$120,000

Save the workbook containing the pie chart and name it **ExcelL1_C7_CS_P2**. Print only the chart and then close **ExcelL1_C7_CS_P2.xlsx**.

Part 3

One of your clients owns a number of stocks and you like to prepare a daily chart of the stocks' high, low, and close price. Use the Help feature to learn about stock charts and then create a stock chart with the following information (the company stock symbols are fictitious):

	IDE	POE	QRR
High	$23.75	$18.55	$34.30
Low	$18.45	$15.00	$31.70
Close	$19.65	$17.30	$33.50

Save the workbook containing the stock chart and name it **ExcelL1_C7_CS_P3**. Print only the chart and then close **ExcelL1_C7_CS_P3.xlsx**.

Part 4

You need to prepare information on mortgage rates for a community presentation. You decide to include the information on mortgage rates in a chart for easy viewing. Use the Internet to search for historical data on the national average for mortgage rates. Determine the average mortgage rate for a 30-year FRM (fixed-rate mortgage) for each January and July beginning with the year 2005 and continuing to the current year. Also include the current average rate. Use this information to create the chart. Save the workbook and name it **ExcelL1_C7_CS_P4**. Print only the chart and then close **ExcelL1_C7_CS_P4.xlsx**.

Part 5

You will be presenting information at an upcoming meeting on the information in the previous challenges for which you created a chart. You decide to include the charts in a PowerPoint presentation so you can display the charts on a screen while presenting. Open PowerPoint and then open the presentation named **ExcelC07Presentation.pptx**. Copy the chart you created in Part 1 to the second slide, copy the chart for Part 2 into the third slide, and then copy the chart for Part 4 into the fourth slide. Increase the size of the charts to better fill the slides. Save the presentation and name it **PPL1_C7_CS_P5**. Print the three slides containing charts. Close **PPL1_C7_CS_P5.pptx**.

CHAPTER 8

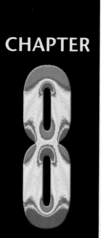

Adding Visual Interest to Workbooks

PERFORMANCE OBJECTIVES

Upon successful completion of Chapter 8, you will be able to:

- Save a workbook as a Web page
- Create and modify a hyperlink
- Insert symbols and special characters
- Insert, size, move, and format a clip art image
- Draw, format, and copy shapes
- Insert, size, move, and format a picture image
- Insert, format, and type text in a text box
- Insert a picture image as a watermark
- Insert and format SmartArt diagrams
- Insert and format WordArt

excel Chapter 8

Tutorial 8.1
Using Web-Based Features
Tutorial 8.2
Adding Graphic Elements

You can save an Excel workbook as a Web page and then view it in a Web browser. You can also insert hyperlinks in a workbook that connect to a Web site or to another workbook. Microsoft Excel includes a variety of features that you can use to enhance the visual appeal of a workbook. Some methods for adding visual appeal that you will learn in this chapter include inserting and modifying clip art images, shapes, pictures, text boxes, SmartArt, and WordArt.

Note: Before beginning computer projects, copy to your storage medium the Excel2007L1C8 subfolder from the Excel2007L1 folder on the CD that accompanies this textbook and make Excel2007L1C8 the active folder.

Project ① Save a Travel Workbook as a Web Page

You will open a travel destinations workbook and then save the workbook as a single page Web page. You will also create hyperlinks in the Web page that link you to sites on the Internet.

QUICK
STEPS

**Save Workbook as
Single File Web Page**
1. Click Office button,
   Save As.
2. Change *Save as type*
   option to *Single File
   Web Page (*.mht;
   .mhtml).
3. Type name in *File name*
   text box.
4. Click Save button.

HINT
Web pages are files
containing special
formatting codes
written in HTML
(Hypertext Markup
Language).

Creating a Web Page

You can save an Excel workbook as a Web page and then view it in the default Web browser software. You can also insert hyperlinks in the Web page to jump to other workbooks or sites on the Internet with additional information pertaining to the workbook content.

Saving a Workbook as a Web Page

You can save the entire workbook, a worksheet, or a single item in a worksheet. Save a workbook as a Web page by changing the *Save as type* option at the Save As dialog box. You can save the data in the workbook as a single Web page or as a conventional Web page. If you choose the *Single File Web Page (*.mht; *.mhtml)* option, all data in the workbook such as graphics and other supplemental data is saved in a single Web file. If you choose the *Web Page (*.htm; *.html)* option, Excel creates additional files for supplemental data and saves the files in a subfolder.

When you choose a Web page option at the *Save as type* drop-down list, the Save As dialog box changes as shown in Figure 8.1. At this dialog box, specify which part of the workbook you want published and if you want to add a title to the Web page. Click the Publish button and the Publish as Web Page dialog box appears as shown in Figure 8.2. This dialog box contains advanced options for publishing a Web page.

Figure 8.1 Save As Dialog Box

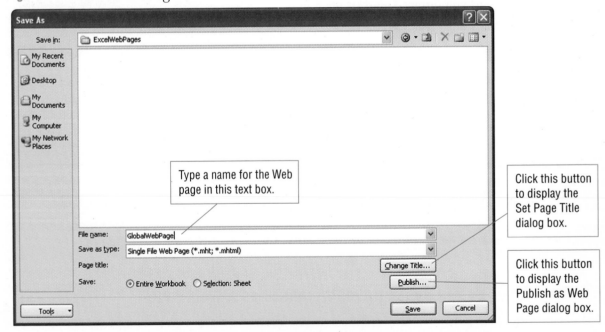

Figure 8.2 Publish as Web Page Dialog Box

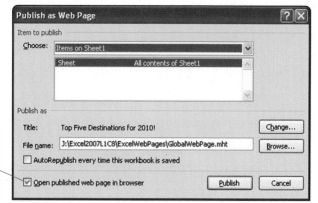

Insert a check mark in this check box if you want the worksheet to automatically display in the default Web browser.

Project 1a Saving a Workbook as a Web Page

1. Create a folder named *ExcelWebPages* within the Excel2007L1C8 folder on your storage medium.
2. Open **ExcelC08Project01.xlsx** and then save the workbook with Save As and name it **ExcelL1_C8_P1**.
3. Click the Office button and then click *Save As*.
4. At the Save As dialog box, double-click *ExcelWebPages* in the list box.
5. Click the down-pointing arrow at the right side of the *Save as type* list box and then click *Single File Web Page (*.mht; *.mhtml)* at the drop-down list.
6. Select the text in the *File name* text box and then type GlobalWebPage.
7. Click the Change Title button.

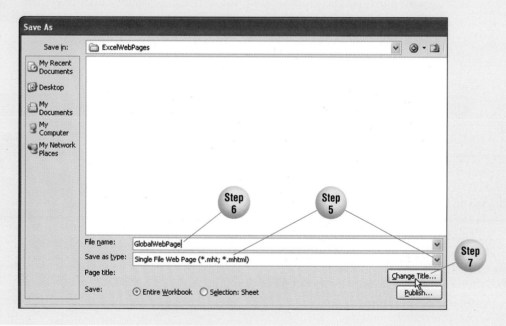

8. At the Set Page Title dialog box, type **Top Five Destinations for 2010!** in the *Page title* text box and then click OK.
9. At the Save As dialog box, click the Publish button.
10. At the Publish as Web Page dialog box, click the *Open published web page in browser* option to insert a check mark.
11. Click the Publish button. (This automatically displays the worksheet in your default Web browser.)

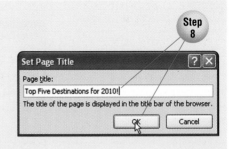

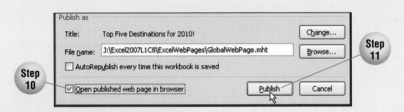

12. After viewing your Web page, close the Web page browser.
13. Save and then close **ExcelL1_C8_P1.xlsx**.

Opening a Workbook in Internet Explorer

Another method for opening a workbook saved as a Web page is to open Internet Explorer, click the File option on the Menu bar, and then click *Open* at the drop-down list. At the Open dialog box, click the Browse button. At the Microsoft Internet Explorer dialog box, navigate to the folder containing the saved Web page and then double-click the Web page file.

Project **1b** **Opening the Web Page in Internet Explorer**

1. Open Internet Explorer.
2. Click File in the Menu bar and then click *Open* at the drop-down list. (If the Menu bar is not visible, click the Tools button and then click *Menu Bar*.)
3. At the Open dialog box, click the Browse button.
4. At the Microsoft Internet Explorer dialog box, navigate to the ExcelWebPages folder and then double-click **GlobalWebPage.mht**.
5. Click OK at the Open dialog box.
6. After viewing the Web page in Internet Explorer, close **GlobalWebPage.mht**.
7. Close Internet Explorer.

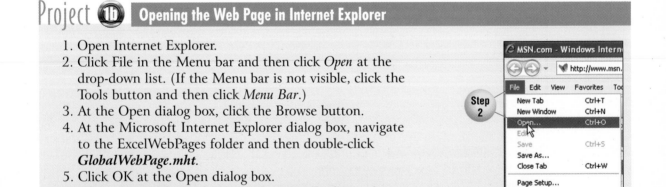

Creating Hyperlinks

A hyperlink is text or an object that you click to go to a different file, an HTML page on the Internet, or an HTML page on an intranet. Create a hyperlink in an Excel worksheet by typing the address of an existing Web page such as *www.emcp.com*. By default, the automatic formatting of hyperlinks is turned on and the Web address is formatted as a hyperlink (text is underlined and the color changes to blue). (You can turn off the automatic formatting of hyperlinks at the AutoCorrect dialog box. Display this dialog box by clicking the Office button, clicking the Excel Options button, and then clicking *Proofing* in the left panel of the Excel Options dialog box. Click the AutoCorrect Options button to display the AutoCorrect dialog box. At this dialog box, click the AutoFormat As You Type tab and then remove the check mark from the *Internet and network paths with hyperlinks* check box.)

You can also create a customized hyperlink by clicking the desired cell in a workbook, clicking the Insert tab, and then clicking the Hyperlink button in the Links group. At the Insert Hyperlink dialog box shown in Figure 8.3, type the file name or Web site address in the *Address* text box and then click OK. You can also use the *Look in* option to browse to the desired folder and file and then double-click the file name. To link to the specified file or Web page, position the mouse pointer (white plus symbol) on the hyperlink until the mouse pointer displays as a hand and then click the left mouse button.

QUICK STEPS

Create Hyperlink
1. Click desired cell.
2. Click Insert tab.
3. Click Hyperlink button.
4. Type Web address or file name.
5. Click OK.

HINT

Ctrl + K is the keyboard shortcut to display the Insert Hyperlink dialog box.

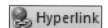

Figure 8.3 Insert Hyperlink Dialog Box

Project 1c Creating Hyperlinks

1. Display the Open dialog box and then double-click *GlobalWebPage.mht*.
2. Create a hyperlink so that clicking *American Airlines* displays the American Airlines Web page by completing the following steps:
   a. Click cell G10 (this is the cell containing *American Airlines*).
   b. Click the Insert tab.
   c. Click the Hyperlink button in the Links group.

d. At the Insert Hyperlink dialog box, type www.aa.com in the *Address* text box. (The *http://* is automatically inserted in the address.)

e. Click OK. (This changes the color of the *American Airlines* text and also adds underlining to the text.)

f. Repeat Steps 2c through 2e in cell G13.

3. Complete steps similar to those in Step 2 to create a hyperlink from *Northwest Airlines* to the URL *www.nwa.com* in cells G11 and G12.

4. Complete steps similar to those in Step 2 to create a hyperlink from *Air Canada* to the URL *www.aircanada.ca* in cell G14.

5. Click the Save button on the Quick Access toolbar. At the compatibility dialog box, click Yes.

6. Jump to the hyperlinked sites by completing the following steps:

a. Make sure you are connected to the Internet.

b. Position the mouse pointer on one of the <u>American Airlines</u> hyperlinks until the mouse pointer turns into a hand and then click the left mouse button.

c. When the American Airlines Web page displays, scroll through the page, and then click a hyperlink that interests you.

d. After looking at this next page, click File and then *Exit*.

e. At the **GlobalWebPage.mht** workbook, click the <u>Air Canada</u> hyperlink.

f. At the Air Canada Web page, click the hyperlink to see their site displayed in English.

g. After viewing the Air Canada page, click File and then *Exit*.

h. At the **GlobalWebPage.mht** workbook, click one of the <u>Northwest</u> hyperlinks.

i. At the Northwest Airlines Web page, click a link that interests you.

j. After viewing the Northwest Airlines page, click File and then *Exit*.

7. Change the orientation to landscape.

8. Save **GlobalWebPage.mht** and click Yes at the compatibility dialog box.

9. Print and then close **GlobalWebPage.mht**.

Project ② Insert a Hyperlink in a Company Sales Workbook

You will open a company sales workbook and then create a hyperlink that links you to another Excel workbook.

Edit Hyperlink
1. Right-click hyperlink.
2. Click *Edit Hyperlink.*
3. Make desired changes.
4. Click OK.

Creating a Hyperlink to an Excel Worksheet

In Project 1c, you created hyperlinks from an Excel workbook to sites on the Web. You can also insert hyperlinks in a workbook that link to other Excel workbooks or files in other programs in the Office suite. In Project 2, you will create a hyperlink that displays another Excel workbook.

You can modify or change hyperlink text or the hyperlink destination. To do this, right-click the hyperlink, and then click *Edit Hyperlink*. At the Edit Hyperlink dialog box, make any desired changes and then close the dialog box. The Edit Hyperlink dialog box contains the same options as the Insert Hyperlink dialog box.

HINT

Deactivate a hyperlink by right-clicking the hyperlink and then clicking *Remove Hyperlink* at the shortcut menu.

Project ② Creating and Modifying a Hyperlink to an Excel Worksheet

1. Open **ExcelC08Project02.xlsx**.
2. Save the workbook with Save As and name it **ExcelL1_C8_P2**.
3. Create a hyperlink that will display **ExcelC08Sales.xlsx** by completing the following steps:
   a. Make cell A12 active.
   b. Type **Semiannual Sales** and then press Enter.
   c. Click cell A12 to make it the active cell.
   d. Click the Insert tab.
   e. Click the Hyperlink button in the Links group.
   f. At the Insert Hyperlink dialog box, click the down-pointing arrow at the right side of the *Look in* option and then navigate to the Excel2007L1C8 folder on your storage medium.
   g. Double-click **ExcelC08Sales.xlsx**. (This closes the Insert Hyperlink dialog box and displays the *Semiannual Sales* text as a hyperlink in the workbook.)
4. Display **ExcelC08Sales.xlsx** by clicking the Semiannual Sales hyperlink.
5. Close **ExcelC08Sales.xlsx**.
6. Print **ExcelL1_C8_P2.xlsx**.
7. Modify the hyperlink text in **ExcelL1_C8_P2.xlsx** by completing the following steps:
   a. Position the mouse pointer on the Semiannual Sales hyperlink, click the *right* mouse button, and then click *Edit Hyperlink*.
   b. At the Edit Hyperlink dialog box, select the text *Semiannual Sales* in the *Text to display* text box and then type **Customer Sales Analysis**.
   c. Click OK.
8. Click the Customer Sales Analysis hyperlink.
9. Close **ExcelC08Sales.xlsx**.
10. Save, print, and then close **ExcelL1_C8_P2.xlsx**.

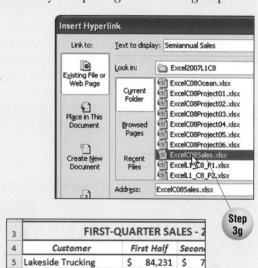

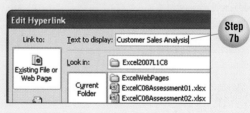

Project ③ Insert a Clip Art Image and Shapes in a Financial Analysis Workbook

You will open a financial analysis workbook and then insert, move, size, and format a clip art image in the workbook. You will also insert an arrow shape, type and format text in the shape, and then copy the shape.

QUICK STEPS

Insert Symbol
1. Click in desired cell.
2. Click the Insert tab.
3. Click Symbol button.
4. Double-click desired symbol.
5. Click Close.

Insert Special Character
1. Click in desired cell.
2. Click Insert tab.
3. Click Symbol button.
4. Click Special Characters tab.
5. Double-click desired special character.
6. Click Close.

HINT
You can increase and/or decrease the size of the Symbol dialog box by positioning the mouse pointer on the lower right corner until the pointer displays as a two-headed arrow and then dragging with the mouse.

Inserting Symbols and Special Characters

You can use the Symbol button in the Insert tab to insert special symbols in a worksheet. Click the Symbol button in the Text group in the Insert tab and the Symbol dialog box displays as shown in Figure 8.4. At the Symbol dialog box, double-click the desired symbol, and then click Close; or click the desired symbol, click the Insert button, and then click Close. At the Symbol dialog box with the Symbols tab selected, you can change the font with the *Font* option. When you change the font, different symbols display in the dialog box. Click the Special Characters tab at the Symbol dialog box and a list of special characters displays along with keyboard shortcuts to create the special character.

Figure 8.4 Symbol Dialog Box with Symbols Tab Selected

Use the *Font* option to select the desired set of characters.

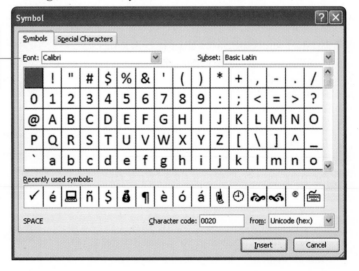

1. Open **ExcelC08Project03.xlsx** and then save the workbook and name it **ExcelL1_C8_P3**.
2. Insert a symbol by completing the following steps:
   a. Double-click cell A2.
   b. Delete the *e* that displays at the end of *Qualite*.
   c. With the insertion point positioned immediately right of the *t* in *Qualit*, click the Insert tab.
   d. Click the Symbol button in the Text group.
   e. At the Symbol dialog box, scroll down the list box and then click the *é* symbol (ninth symbol from the left in the eleventh row).
   f. Click the Insert button and then click the Close button.

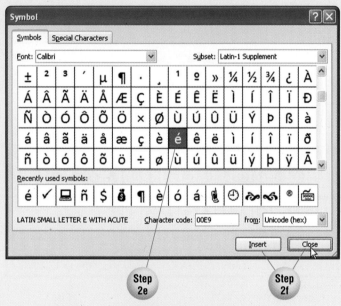

Step 2e

Step 2f

3. Insert a special character by completing the following steps:
   a. With cell A2 selected and in Edit mode, move the insertion point so it is positioned immediately right of *Group*.
   b. Click the Symbol button in the Text group.
   c. At the Symbol dialog box, click the Special Characters tab.
   d. Double-click the ® symbol (tenth option from the top).
   e. Click the Close button.

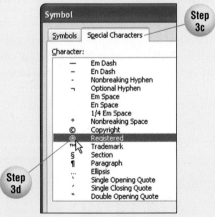

Step 3c

Step 3d

4. Insert a symbol by completing the following steps:
   a. With cell A2 selected and in Edit mode, move the insertion point so it is positioned immediately left of the *Q* in *Qualité*.
   b. Click the Symbol button in the Text group.
   c. At the Symbol dialog box, click the down-pointing arrow at the right side of the *Font* option box and then click *Wingdings* at the drop-down list. (You will need to scroll down the list to display this option.)
   d. Click the ❖ symbol (seventh option from the left in the sixth row).
   e. Click the Insert button and then click the Close button.

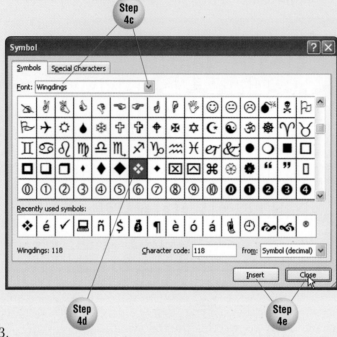

Step 4c

Step 4d

Step 4e

5. Click in cell A3.
6. Save **ExcelL1_C8_P3.xlsx**.

Inserting an Image

You can insert an image such as a picture or clip art in an Excel workbook with buttons in the Illustrations group in the Insert tab. Click the Picture button to display the Insert Picture dialog box where you can specify the desired picture file, or click the Clip Art button and then choose from a variety of images available at the Clip Art task pane. When you insert a picture or a clip art image in a worksheet, the Picture Tools Format Tab displays as shown in Figure 8.5.

Figure 8.5 Picture Tools Format Tab

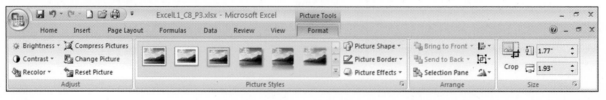

Customizing and Formatting an Image

With options in the Adjust group in the Picture Tools Format tab you can recolor the picture or clip art image and change the brightness and contrast of the image. You can also reset the picture or clip art back to its original color or change to a different image. Use the Compress Pictures button to compress the size of the image file. Apply predesigned styles with options in the Picture Styles group. Use options in the Arrange group to position the image on the page, specify text wrapping in relation to the image, align the image with other objects in the worksheet, and rotate the image. Use the Crop button in the Size group to remove any unnecessary parts of the image and specify the image size with the *Shape Height* and *Shape Width* measurement boxes.

Sizing and Moving an Image

You can change the size of an image with the *Shape Height* and *Shape Width* measurement boxes in the Size group in the Picture Tools Format tab or with the sizing handles that display around the selected image. To change size with a sizing handle, position the mouse pointer on a sizing handle until the pointer turns into a double-headed arrow and then hold down the left mouse button. Drag the sizing handle in or out to decrease or increase the size of the image and then release the mouse button. Use the middle sizing handles at the left or right side of the image to make the image wider or thinner. Use the middle sizing handles at the top or bottom of the image to make the image taller or shorter. Use the sizing handles at the corners of the image to change both the width and height at the same time. Hold down the Shift key while dragging a sizing handle to maintain the proportions of the image.

Move an image by positioning the mouse pointer on the image border until the pointer displays with a four-headed arrow attached. Hold down the left mouse button, drag the image to the desired position, and then release the mouse button. Rotate the image by positioning the mouse pointer on the green, round rotation handle until the pointer displays as a circular arrow. Hold down the left mouse button, drag in the desired direction, and then release the mouse button.

Inserting a Clip Art Image

Microsoft Office includes a gallery of media images you can insert in a worksheet such as clip art, photographs, and movie images, as well as sound clips. To insert an image in a worksheet, click the Insert tab and then click the Clip Art button in the Illustrations group. This displays the Clip Art task pane at the right side of the screen as shown in Figure 8.6.

HINT

You can use arrow keys on the keyboard to move a selected object. To move the image in small increments, hold down the Ctrl key while pressing one of the arrow keys.

QUICK STEPS

Insert Clip Art Image
1. Click Insert tab.
2. Click Clip Art button.
3. Type desired word or topic in *Search for* text box.
4. Click Go button or press Enter.
5. Click desired image.

Figure 8.6 Clip Art Task Pane

Type in this text box the word or topic for which you are searching.

Use these options to specify where to search and the media types.

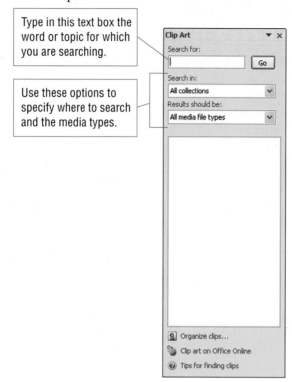

Clip Art

Search for:

[   ] [Go]

Search in:

All collections

Results should be:

All media file types

Organize clips...

Clip art on Office Online

Tips for finding clips

HINT

You can insert a clip art image by dragging the image from the Clip Art task pane into the worksheet.

HINT

Insert multiple clip art images by holding down the Ctrl key, clicking each desired clip art in the Clip Art task pane, and then dragging the images into the worksheet.

To view all picture, sound, and motion files, make sure the *Search for* text box in the Clip Art task pane does not contain any text and then click the Go button. When the desired image is visible, click the image to insert it in the worksheet. Use buttons in the Picture Tools Format tab shown in Figure 8.5 to format and customize the clip art image.

By default (unless it has been customized), the Clip Art task pane looks for all media images and sound clips found in all locations. You can narrow the search to specific locations and to specific images. The *Search in* option at the Clip Art task pane has a default setting of *All collections*. This can be changed to *My Collections*, *Office Collections*, and *Web Collections*. The *Results should be* option has a default setting of *Selected media file types*. Click the down-pointing arrow at the right side of this option to display media types. To search for a specific media type, remove the check mark before all options at the drop-down list but the desired type. For example, if you are searching only for photograph images, remove the check mark before Clip Art, Movies, and Sound.

If you are searching for specific images, click in the *Search for* text box, type the desired topic, and then click the Go button. For example, if you want to find images related to business, click in the *Search for* text box, type business, and then click the Go button. Clip art images related to *business* display in the viewing area of the task pane. If you are connected to the Internet, Word will search for images at the Office Online Web site matching the topic.

Project 3b — Inserting an Image

1. With **ExcelL1_C8_P3.xlsx** open, insert a clip art image by completing the following steps:
   a. Click the Insert tab.
   b. Click the Clip Art button in the Illustrations group.
   c. At the Clip Art task pane, click the down-pointing arrow at the right side of the *Results should be* option box and then click the *Photographs*, *Movies*, and *Sounds* check boxes at the drop-down list to remove the check marks. Click in the task pane to remove the drop-down list.

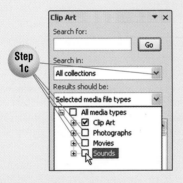

   d. Select any text that displays in the *Search for* text box, type stock market, and then press Enter.
   e. Click the image in the list box as shown at the right. (If you are not connected to the Internet and this image is not available, click a similar image.)
   f. Click the down-pointing at the right side of the *Results should be* option box and then click the *Photographs*, *Movies*, and *Sounds* check boxes at the drop-down list to insert check marks.
   g. Close the Clip Art task pane by clicking the Close button (contains an X) located in the upper right corner of the task pane.
2. Size and move the clip art image by completing the following steps:
   a. Click in the *Shape Width* measurement box, type 2.52, and then press Enter.

b. Position the mouse pointer on a border of the clip art image until the mouse pointer displays with a four-headed arrow attached. Hold down the left mouse button, drag the upper left corner of the clip art image so it is positioned in the upper left corner of cell A1, and then release the mouse button.

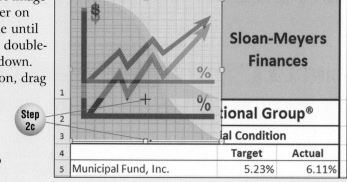

c. Change the height of the clip art image by positioning the mouse pointer on the bottom middle sizing handle until the mouse pointer displays as a double-headed arrow pointing up and down. Hold down the left mouse button, drag up until the bottom of the clip art image is aligned with the bottom of cell A1, and then release the mouse button.

3. Click outside the clip art image to deselect it.

4. Save **ExcelL1_C8_P3.xlsx**.

QUICK STEPS

Insert Shape
1. Click Insert tab.
2. Click Shapes button.
3. Click desired shape at drop-down list.
4. Drag in worksheet to create shape.

Inserting a Shape

In Chapter 7, you learned how to insert shapes in a chart. With the Shapes button in the Illustrations group in the Insert tab, you can also insert shapes in a worksheet. Use the Shapes button in the Insert tab to draw shapes in a worksheet including lines, basic shapes, block arrows, flow chart shapes, callouts, stars, and banners. Click a shape and the mouse pointer displays as crosshairs (plus sign). Position the crosshairs where you want the shape to begin, hold down the left mouse button, drag to create the shape, and then release the mouse button. This inserts the shape in the worksheet and also displays the Drawing Tools Format tab shown in Figure 8.7. Use buttons in this tab to change the shape, apply a style to the shape, arrange the shape, and change the size of the shape.

If you choose a shape in the *Lines* section of the drop-down list, the shape you draw is considered a *line drawing*. If you choose an option in the other sections of the drop-down list, the shape you draw is considered an *enclosed object*. When drawing an enclosed object, you can maintain the proportions of the shape by holding down the Shift key while dragging with the mouse to create the shape. You can type text in an enclosed object and then use buttons in the WordArt Styles group to format the text.

Figure 8.7 Drawing Tools Format Tab

Copying Shapes

If you have drawn or inserted a shape, you may want to copy it to other locations in the worksheet. To copy a shape, select the shape and then click the Copy button in the Clipboard group in the Home tab. Position the insertion point at the location where you want the copied image and then click the Paste button. You can also copy a selected shape by holding down the Ctrl key while dragging the shape to the desired location.

Copy Shape
1. Click in shape to select it.
2. Click Copy button.
3. Position insertion point in desired location.
4. Click Paste button.
OR
1. Click in shape to select.
2. Hold down Ctrl key.
3. Drag shape to desired location.

Project 3C Drawing Arrow Shapes

1. With **ExcelL1_C8_P3.xlsx** open, create the tallest arrow shown in Figure 8.8 by completing the following steps:
   a. Click the Insert tab.
   b. Click the Shapes button and then click the *Up Arrow* shape (third option from the left in the top row of the *Block Arrows* section).
   c. Position the mouse pointer (displays as a thin, black cross) near the upper left corner of cell D1, hold down the left mouse button, drag down and to the right to create the shape as shown below, and then release the mouse button.

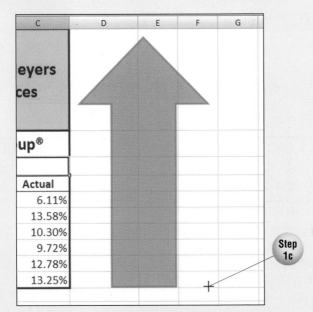

   d. Click in the *Shape Height* measurement box and then type 3.9.
   e. Click in the *Shape Width* measurement box, type 2.2, and then press Enter.

f. If necessary, drag the arrow so it is positioned as shown in Figure 8.8. (To drag the arrow, position the mouse pointer on the border of the selected arrow until the pointer turns into a four-headed arrow, hold down the left mouse button, drag the arrow to the desired position, and then release the mouse button.)

g. Click the More button at the right side of the shapes in the Shape Styles group and then click the *Intense Effect - Accent 1* option (second option from the left in the bottom row).

h. Click the Shape Effects button in the Shape Styles group, point to *Glow*, and then click the last option in the bottom row (*Accent color 6, 18 pt glow*).

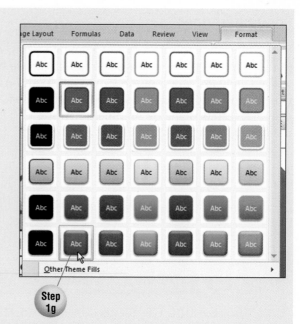

Step 1g

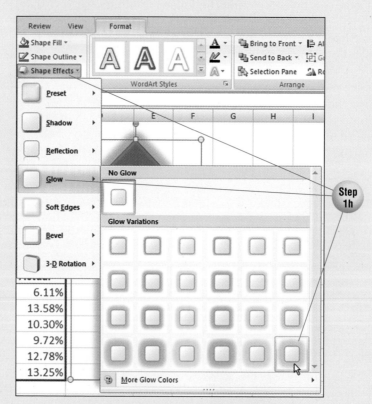

Step 1h

2. Insert text in the arrow shape by completing the following steps:
   a. With the arrow shape selected, type **McGuire Mutual Shares 5.33%**.
   b. Select the text you just typed (*McGuire Mutual Shares 5.33%*).

c. Click the More button at the right side of the styles in the WordArt Styles group and then click the second option from the left in the second row (*Fill - None, Outline - Accent 6, Glow - Accent 6*).

d. Click the Home tab.

e. Click the Top Align button in the Alignment group.

3. With the arrow selected, copy the arrow by completing the following steps:

a. Hold down the Ctrl key.

b. Position the mouse pointer on the arrow border until the pointer displays with a square box and plus symbol attached.

c. Hold down the left mouse button and drag to the right so the outline of the arrow is positioned at the right side of the existing arrow.

d. Release the mouse button and then release the Ctrl key.

4. Format the second arrow by completing the following steps:

a. With the second arrow selected, click the Drawing Tools Format tab.

b. Click in the *Shape Height* measurement box and then type 2.

c. Click in the *Shape Width* measurement box, type 1.7, and then press Enter

d. Select the text *McGuire Mutual Shares 5.33%* and then type SR Linus Fund 0.22%.

e. Drag the arrow so it is positioned as shown in Figure 8.8.

5. Change the orientation to landscape. (Make sure the cells containing data and the arrows will print on the same page.)

6. Save, print, and then close **ExcelL1_C8_P3.xlsx**.

Figure 8.8 Project 3c

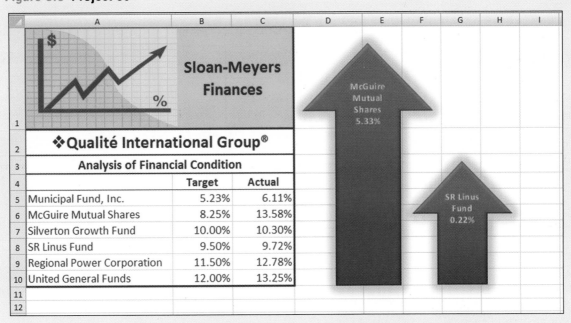

Project ④ Insert a Picture and Text Box in a Division Sales Workbook

You will open a division sales workbook and then insert, move, and size a picture. You will also insert a text box and then format the text.

QUICK STEPS

Insert Picture
1. Click Insert tab.
2. Click Picture button.
3. Navigate to desired folder.
4. Double-click desired picture.

Inserting a Picture

To insert a picture in a worksheet, click the Insert tab and then click the Picture button in the Illustrations group. At the Insert Picture dialog box, navigate to the folder containing the desired picture and then double-click the picture. Use buttons in the Picture Tools Format tab to format and customize the picture.

Project ④a Inserting and Customizing a Picture

1. Open **ExcelC08Project04.xlsx** and then save the workbook and name it **ExcelL1_C8_P4**.
2. Make the following changes to the bird clip art image:
   a. Click the bird clip art image to select it.
   b. Click the Picture Tools Format tab.
   c. Click the Rotate button in the Arrange group and then click *Flip Horizontal* at the drop-down list.

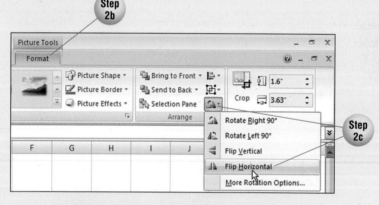

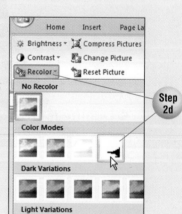

   d. Click the Recolor button in the Adjust group and then click the *Black and White* option in the *Color Modes* section.

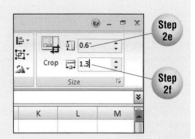

e. Click in the *Shape Height* measurement box and then type 0.6.

f. Click in the *Shape Width* measurement box, type 1.3, and then press Enter.

3. Insert and format a picture by completing the following steps:

   a. Click in cell A1 outside of the bird image.

   b. Click the Insert tab.

   c. Click the Picture button in the Illustrations group.

   d. At the Insert Picture dialog box, navigate to the Excel2007L1C8 folder on your storage medium and then double-click *Ocean.jpg*.

   e. With the picture selected, click the Send to Back button in the Arrange group in the Picture Tools Format tab.

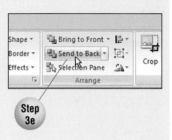

   f. Use the sizing handles that display around the picture image to move and size it so it fills cell A1 as shown in Figure 8.9.

   g. Click the bird clip art image and then drag the image so it is positioned as shown in Figure 8.9.

4. Save **ExcelL1_C8_P4.xlsx**.

Drawing and Formatting a Text Box

Use the Text Box button in the Insert tab to draw a text box in a worksheet. To draw a text box, click the Insert tab and then click the Text Box button in the Text group. This causes the mouse pointer to display as a thin, down-pointing arrow. Position the arrow in the worksheet and then drag to create the text box. When a text box is selected, the Drawing Tools Format tab displays with options for customizing the text box.

Click a text box to select it and a dashed border and sizing handles display around the text box. If you want to delete the text box, click the text box border again to change the dashed border lines to solid border lines and then press the Delete key.

QUICK STEPS

Draw Text Box
1. Click Insert tab.
2. Click Text Box button.
3. Drag in worksheet to create text box.

Project 4b **Inserting and Formatting a Text Box**

1. With **ExcelL1_C8_P4.xlsx** open, draw a text box by completing the following steps:

   a. Click the Insert tab.

   b. Click the Text Box button in the Text group.

   c. Drag in cell A1 to draw a text box the approximate size and shape shown at the right.

2. Format the text box by completing the
   following steps:
   a. Make sure the Drawing Tools Format tab
      is active.
   b. Click the Shape Fill button arrow in the
      Shape Styles group and then click *No Fill*
      at the drop-down gallery.
   c. Click the Shape Outline button arrow in
      the Shape Styles group and then click *No
      Outline* at the drop-down gallery.
3. Insert text in the text box by completing the
   following steps:
   a. With the text box selected, click the
      Home tab.
   b. Click the Font button arrow and then click *Lucida Calligraphy* at the drop-down gallery.
      (You will need to scroll down the gallery to display this font.)
   c. Click the Font Size button arrow and then click *32* at the drop-down gallery.
   d. Click the Font Color button arrow and then click *White, Background 1* (first option in the
      first row in the *Theme Colors* section).
   e. Type Seabird Productions.
4. Move the text box so the text is positioned in cell A1 as shown in Figure 8.9. If necessary,
   move the bird clip art image. (To move the bird image, you may need to move the text box
   so you can select the image. Move the text box back to the desired location after moving
   the bird image.)
5. Save, print, and then close **ExcelL1_C8_P4.xlsx**.

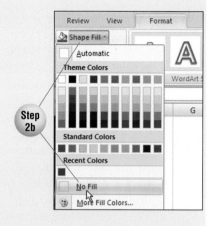

Figure 8.9 **Projects 4a and 4b**

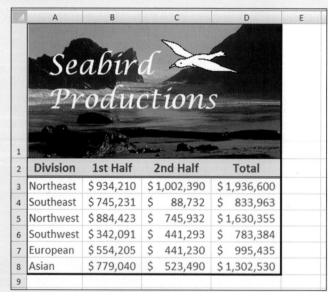

Project 5 Insert a Watermark in an Equipment Usage Workbook

You will open an equipment usage report workbook and then insert a picture watermark that prints on both pages of the worksheet.

Inserting a Picture as a Watermark

A watermark is a lightened image that displays behind data in a file. You can create a watermark in a Word document but the watermark functionality is not available in Excel. You can, however, insert a picture in a header or footer and then resize and format the picture to display behind each page of the worksheet.

To create a picture watermark in a worksheet, click the Insert tab and then click the Header & Footer button in the Text group. With the worksheet in Print Layout view, click the Picture button in the Header & Footer Elements group in the Header & Footer Tools Design tab. At the Insert Picture dialog box, navigate to the desired folder and then double-click the desired picture. This inserts &[Picture] in the header. Resize and format the picture by clicking the Format Picture button in the Header & Footer Elements group. Use options at the Format Picture dialog box with the Size tab selected to specify the size of the picture and use options in the dialog box with the Picture tab selected to specify brightness and contrast.

QUICK STEPS

Insert Picture as Watermark
1. Click Insert tab.
2. Click Header & Footer button.
3. Click Picture button.
4. Navigate to desired folder.
5. Double-click desired picture.

 Picture
 Format Picture

Project 5 Inserting a Picture as a Watermark

1. Open **ExcelC08Project05.xlsx** and then save the workbook and name it **ExcelL1_C8_P5**.
2. Insert a picture as a watermark by completing the following steps:
   a. Click the Insert tab.
   b. Click the Header & Footer button in the Text group.
   c. Click the Picture button in the Header & Footer Elements group in the Header & Footer Tools Design tab.
   d. At the Insert Picture dialog box, navigate to the Excel2007L1C8 folder on your storage medium and then double-click *Olympics.jpg*.
   e. Click the Format Picture button in the Header & Footer Elements group.
   f. At the Format Picture dialog box with the Size tab selected, click the *Lock aspect ratio* in the *Scale* section to remove the check mark.
   g. Select the current measurement in the *Height* measurement box in the *Size and rotate* section and then type 10.
   h. Select the current measurement in the *Width* measurement box in the *Size and rotate* section and then type 7.5.

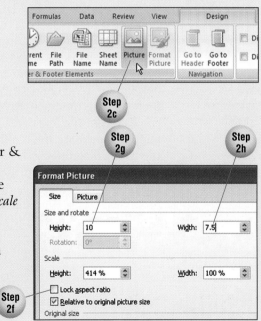

i. Click the Picture tab.
j. At the Format Picture dialog box with the Picture tab selected, select the current percentage number in the *Brightness* option box in the *Image control* section and then type 75.
k. Select the current percentage number in the *Contrast* option box and then type 25.
l. Click OK to close the Format Picture dialog box.

3. Click in the worksheet.
4. Display the worksheet in Print Preview to view how the image will print on page 1 and page 2 and then close Print Preview.
5. Save, print, and then close **ExcelL1_C8_P5.xlsx**. (If you are printing on a laser printer, the text may not print in the worksheet. Check with your instructor before printing this worksheet.)

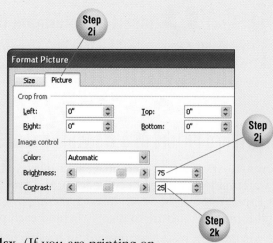

Step 2i

Step 2j

Step 2k

Project ⑥ Insert and Format Diagrams in a Company Sales Workbook

You will open a workbook that contains two company sales worksheets. You will insert and format a cycle diagram in one worksheet and insert and format a relationship diagram in the other. You will also create and format WordArt text.

Inserting a SmartArt Diagram

QUICK STEPS

Insert SmartArt Diagram
1. Click Insert tab.
2. Click SmartArt button.
3. Double-click desired diagram.

HINT

Generally, you would use a SmartArt diagram to represent text and a chart to represent numbers.

SmartArt

Excel includes the SmartArt feature you can use to insert diagrams and organizational charts in a worksheet. SmartArt offers a variety of predesigned diagrams and organizational charts that are available at the Choose a SmartArt Graphic dialog box shown in Figure 8.10. Display this dialog box by clicking the Insert tab and then clicking the SmartArt button in the Illustrations group. At the dialog box, *All* is selected in the left panel and all available predesigned diagrams display in the middle panel. Use the scroll bar at the right side of the middle panel to scroll down the list of diagram choices. Click a diagram in the middle panel and the name of the diagram displays in the right panel along with a description of the diagram type. SmartArt includes diagrams for presenting a list of data; showing data processes, cycles, and relationships; and presenting data in a matrix or pyramid. Double-click a diagram in the middle panel of the dialog box and the diagram is inserted in the worksheet.

Figure 8.10 Choose a SmartArt Graphic Dialog Box

Double-click the desired
SmartArt graphic in this panel.

Choose the SmartArt
graphic category from
options in this panel.

Click a SmartArt graphic in the
middle panel and then read a
description of the graphic here.

Entering Data in a Diagram

Some diagrams are designed to include text. You can type text in a diagram by
selecting the shape and then typing text in the shape or you can display a text
pane and then type text in the pane. Display the text pane by clicking the Text
Pane button in the Create Graphic group in the SmartArt Tools Design tab. Turn
off the display of the pane by clicking the Text Pane button or by clicking the Close
button that displays in the upper right corner of the text pane.

Sizing, Moving, and Deleting a Diagram

Increase or decrease the size of a diagram by dragging the diagram border. Increase
or decrease the width of the diagram by positioning the mouse pointer on the set of
four dots that displays in the middle of the left and right borders until the pointer
turns into a left- and right-pointing arrow, hold down the left mouse button and
then drag the border to the desired size. Increase or decrease the height of the
diagram in a similar manner using the set of four dots that displays in the middle
of the top and bottom borders. To increase or decrease both the height and the
width of the diagram, drag one of the sets of three dots that displays in each corner
of the border.

To move a diagram, select the diagram and then position the mouse pointer
on the diagram border until the pointer turns into a four-headed arrow. Hold down
the left mouse button, drag the diagram to the desired position, and then release
the mouse button. Delete a diagram by selecting the diagram and then pressing
the Delete key.

1. Open **ExcelC08Project06.xlsx** and then save the workbook and name it **ExcelL1_C8_P6**.
2. Create the diagram shown in Figure 8.11. To begin, click the Insert tab.
3. Click the SmartArt button in the Illustrations group.
4. At the Choose a SmartArt Graphic dialog box, click *Cycle* in the left panel.
5. Double-click *Radial Cycle* as shown at the right.
6. If the text pane is not open, click the Text Pane button in the Create Graphic group. (The text pane will display at the left side of the diagram.)
7. With the insertion point positioned after the top bullet in the text pane, type Evergreen Products.
8. Click the *[Text]* box below *Evergreen Products* and then type Seattle.
9. Click the next *[Text]* box and then type Olympia.
10. Click the next *[Text]* box and then type Portland.
11. Click the next *[Text]* box and then type Spokane.
12. Click the Text Pane button to turn off the display of the text pane.
13. Drag the diagram so it is positioned as shown in Figure 8.11. To drag the diagram, position the mouse pointer on the diagram border until the pointer turns into a four-headed arrow. Hold down the left mouse button, drag the diagram to the desired position, and then release the mouse button.
14. Increase or decrease the size of the diagram so it displays as shown in Figure 8.11. Use the sets of dots on the diagram border to drag the border to the desired size.
15. Save **ExcelL1_C8_P6.xlsx**.

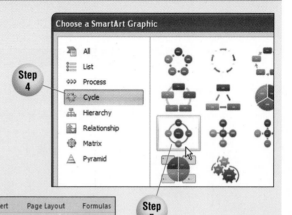

HINT
To restore the SmartArt default layout and color, click the Reset Graphic button in the Reset group in the SmartArt Tools Design tab.

Changing the Diagram Design

When you double-click a diagram at the dialog box, the diagram is inserted in the worksheet and the SmartArt Tools Design tab is active. With options and buttons in this tab, you can add objects, change the diagram layout, apply a style to the diagram, and reset the diagram back to the original formatting.

Project 6b Changing the Diagram Design

1. With **ExcelL1_C8_P6.xlsx** open, make sure the SmartArt Tools Design tab is active and the *Spokane* circle shape is selected.
2. Click the Right to Left button in the Create Graphic group. (This switches *Olympia* and *Spokane*.)
3. Click the More button located at the right side of the SmartArt Styles group and then click the *Polished* option at the drop-down list (first option from the left in the top row of the *3-D* section).

Step 2

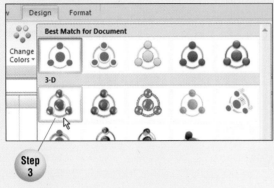

Step 3

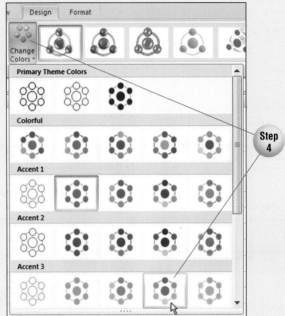

Step 4

4. Click the Change Colors button in the SmartArt Styles group and then click the fourth option from the left in the *Accent 3* section (*Gradient Loop - Accent 3*).
5. Click outside the diagram to deselect it.
6. Change the orientation to landscape. (Make sure the diagram fits on the first page.)
7. Save **ExcelC1_C8_P6.xlsx** and then print the Total Sales worksheet.

Figure 8.11 Projects 6a and 6b

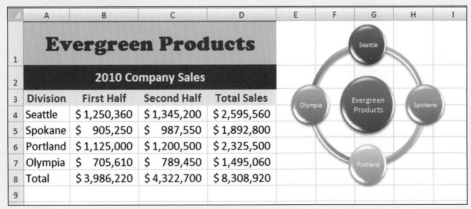

Changing the Diagram Formatting

Click the SmartArt Tools Format tab and options display for formatting a diagram. Use buttons in this tab to insert and customize shapes; apply a shape quick style; customize shapes; insert WordArt quick styles; and specify the position, alignment, rotation, wrapping style, height, and width of the diagram.

Project **6C** **Changing the Diagram Formatting**

1. With **ExcelL1_C8_P6.xlsx** open, click the Seattle Sales worksheet tab.
2. Create the diagram shown in Figure 8.12. To begin, click the Insert tab and then click the SmartArt button in the Illustrations group.
3. At the Choose a SmartArt Graphic dialog box, click *Relationship* in the left panel and then double-click *Gear* in the middle panel.

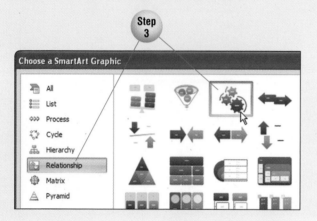

Step 3

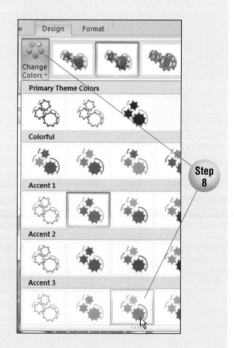

Step 8

4. Click *[Text]* that appears in the bottom gear and then type Quality Products.
5. Click *[Text]* that appears in the left gear and then type Customized Plans.
6. Click *[Text]* that appears in the top gear and then type Exemplary Service.
7. Click the More button that displays at the right side of the SmartArt Styles group and then click the *Inset* option (second option from the left in the top row of the *3-D* section).
8. Click the Change Colors button in the SmartArt Styles group and then click the third option from the left in the *Accent 3* section (*Gradient Range - Accent 3*).
9. Click the SmartArt Tools Format tab.

10. Click the Size button located at the right side of the tab.
11. Click in the *Height* text box and then type 3.75.
12. Click in the *Width* text box, type 5.25, and then press Enter.

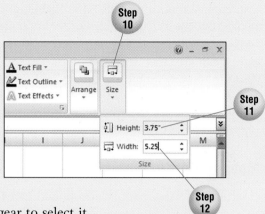

Step 10

Step 11

Step 12

13. Click the bottom gear to select it.
14. Click the Shape Fill button arrow in the Shape Styles group and then click the bottom dark green color (*Olive Green, Accent 3, Darker 50%*) that displays in the *Theme Colors* section.
15. Click the top gear to select it.
16. Click the Shape Fill button arrow and then click the dark green color (*Olive Green, Accent 3, Darker 25%*) that displays in the *Theme Colors* section.
17. Change the orientation to landscape.
18. Move the diagram so it fits on the first page and displays as shown in Figure 8.12.
19. Save **ExcelL1_C8_P6.xlsx** and then print the Seattle Sales worksheet.

Step 14

Figure 8.12 Project 6c

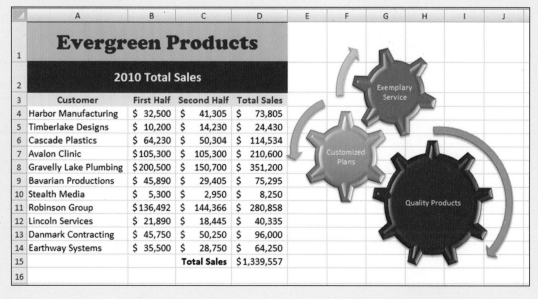

Creating WordArt

With the WordArt application, you can distort or modify text to conform to a variety of shapes. This is useful for creating company logos and headings. With WordArt, you can change the font, style, and alignment of text. You can also use different fill patterns and colors, customize border lines, and add shadow and three-dimensional effects.

To insert WordArt in an Excel worksheet, click the Insert tab, click the WordArt button in the Text group, and then click the desired option at the drop-down list. This displays *Your Text Here* inserted in the worksheet in the WordArt option you selected at the gallery. Type the desired text and then use the buttons on the Drawing Tools Format tab to format the WordArt.

Create WordArt
1. Click Insert tab.
2. Click WordArt button.
3. Click desired WordArt style at drop-down list.
4. Type desired text.

HINT

To remove WordArt style from text and retain the text, click the More button in the WordArt Styles group in the Drawing Tools Format tab and then click *Clear WordArt*.

Sizing and Moving WordArt

WordArt text inserted in a worksheet is surrounded by white sizing handles. Use the white sizing handles to change the height and width of the WordArt text. To move WordArt text, position the arrow pointer on the border of the WordArt until the pointer displays with a four-headed arrow attached. Hold down the left mouse button, drag the outline of the WordArt text box to the desired position, and then release the mouse button. When you change the shape of the WordArt text, the WordArt border displays with a purple diamond shape. Use this shape to change the slant of the WordArt text.

Project 6d   **Inserting and Formatting WordArt**

1. With **ExcelL1_C8_P6.xlsx** open, click the Total Sales worksheet tab.
2. Make cell A1 active and then press the Delete key. (This removes the text from the cell.)
3. Increase the height of row 1 to 136.50.
4. Click the Insert tab.
5. Click the WordArt button in the Text group and then click the last option in the top row (*Fill - Accent 3, Outline - Text 2*).

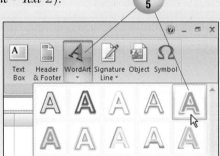

6. Type Evergreen, press the Enter key, and then type Products.
7. Position the mouse pointer on the WordArt border until the pointer displays with a four-headed arrow attached and then drag the WordArt inside cell A1.

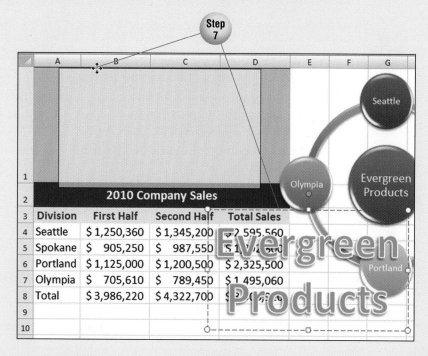

8. Click the Text Fill button arrow in the WordArt Styles group and then click the dark green color (*Olive Green, Accent 3, Darker 25%*).
9. Click the Text Outline button arrow in the WordArt Styles group and then click the dark green color (*Olive Green, Accent 3, Darker 50%*).
10. Resize the chart and position it so it prints on one page with the data.
11. Click the Seattle Sales worksheet tab and then complete steps similar to those in Steps 2 through 10 to insert *Evergreen Products* as WordArt.
12. Save **ExcelL1_C8_P6.xlsx** and then print both worksheets.
13. Close **ExcelL1_C8_P6.xlsx**.

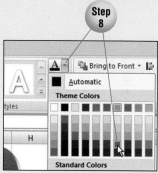

CHAPTER summary

- Save a workbook as a Web page by changing the *Save as type* option at the Save As dialog box to *Single File Web Page (*.mht; *.mhtml)* or *Web Page (*.htm; *.html).*

- To open a Web page in Internet Explorer, open the browser, click File on the Menu bar, and then click *Open* at the drop-down list.

- To create a hyperlink in a workbook, select the text, click the Insert tab, and then click the Hyperlink button in the Links group. At the Insert Hyperlink dialog box, type the file name or Web site URL in the *Address* text box.

- To modify or edit a hyperlink, right-click the hyperlink and then click *Edit Hyperlink* at the shortcut menu.

- Insert symbols with options at the Symbol dialog box with the Symbols tab or the Special Characters tab selected. Click the Insert tab and then click the Symbol button to display the dialog box.

- With buttons in the Illustrations group in the Insert tab, you can insert a picture, clip art image, shapes, or a SmartArt diagram.

- When you insert a picture or clip art image in a worksheet, the Picture Tools Format tab is active and includes options for adjusting the image, applying preformatted styles, and arranging and sizing the image.

- Change the size of an image with the *Shape Height* and *Shape Width* measurement boxes in the Size group in the Picture Tools Format tab or with the sizing handles that display around the selected image.

- Move an image by positioning the mouse pointer on the image border until the pointer displays with a four-headed arrow attached and then drag the image to the desired location.

- Delete a selected image by pressing the Delete key.

- Rotate an image by positioning the mouse pointer on the green rotation handle until the pointer displays as a circular arrow and then dragging in the desired direction.

- Insert an image in a workbook with options at the Clip Art task pane. Display this task pane by clicking the Insert tab and then clicking the Clip Art button in the Illustrations group.

- With options at the Clip Art task pane, you can narrow the search for images to specific locations and to specific images.

- To draw shapes in a workbook, click the Insert tab, click the Shapes button in the Illustrations group, and then click the desired shape at the drop-down list. Drag in the worksheet to draw the shape. To maintain the proportions of the shape, hold down the Shift key while dragging in the worksheet.

- Copy a shape with the Copy and Paste buttons in the Clipboard group in the Home tab or by holding down the Ctrl key while dragging the shape.

- You can type text in an enclosed drawn object.

- To insert a picture in a worksheet, click the Insert tab and then click the Picture button in the Illustrations group. At the Insert Picture dialog box, navigate to the desired folder and then double-click the file name.

- Draw a text box in a worksheet by clicking the Insert tab, clicking the Text Box button in the Text group and then dragging in the worksheet. Use options at the Drawing Tools Format tab to format and customize the text box.
- A watermark is a lightened image that displays behind data in a file. You can create a picture watermark in a worksheet by inserting a picture in a header or footer and then changing the size and formatting of the picture.
- Insert a SmartArt diagram in a worksheet by clicking the Insert tab, clicking the SmartArt button in the Illustrations group, and then double-clicking the desired diagram at the Choose a SmartArt Graphic dialog box. Customize a diagram with options in the SmartArt Tools Design tab or the SmartArt Tools Format tab.
- Use WordArt to create, distort, modify, and/or conform text to a variety of shapes. Insert WordArt in a worksheet by clicking the Insert tab, clicking the WordArt button in the Text group, and then clicking the desired option at the drop-down list.
- Customize WordArt text with options in the Drawing Tools Format tab.
- Size WordArt using the sizing handles that display around selected WordArt text and move selected WordArt by dragging it to the desired location using the mouse.

COMMANDS review

FEATURE	RIBBON TAB, GROUP	BUTTON	KEYBOARD SHORTCUT
Insert Hyperlink dialog box	Insert, Links		Ctrl + K
Symbol dialog box	Insert, Text		
Clip Art task pane	Insert, Illustrations		
Shapes drop-down list	Insert, Illustrations		
Insert Picture dialog box	Insert, Illustrations		
Text box	Insert, Text		
Choose a SmartArt Graphic dialog box	Insert, Illustrations		
WordArt drop-down list	Insert, Text		

CONCEPTS check

Test Your Knowledge

Completion: In the space provided at the right, indicate the correct term, symbol, or command.

1. Change the *Save as type* option at the Save As dialog box to this to save the open workbook as a single Web page. _____

2. Click the Insert tab and then click the Hyperlink button and this dialog box displays. _____

3. The Symbol button is located in this tab. _____

4. The *Font* option is available at the Symbol dialog box with this tab selected. _____

5. Insert a picture, clip art image, shape, or SmartArt diagram with buttons in this group in the Insert tab. _____

6. When you insert a picture or clip art image in a worksheet, this tab is active. _____

7. Maintain the proportions of the image by holding down this key while dragging a sizing handle. _____

8. To move an image, position the mouse pointer on the image border until the mouse pointer displays with this attached and then drag the image to the desired location. _____

9. To copy a shape, hold down this key while dragging the shape. _____

10. When you draw a text box in a worksheet and then release the mouse button, this tab is active. _____

11. This term refers to a lightened image that displays behind data in a file. _____

12. Click the SmartArt button in the Illustrations group in the Insert tab and this dialog box displays. _____

SKILLS check
Demonstrate Your Proficiency

Assessment

1 INSERT A TEXT BOX IN AND SAVE A BOOK CLUB WORKBOOK AS A WEB PAGE

1. Display the Open dialog box with Excel2007L1C8 the active folder.
2. Open **ExcelC08Assessment01.xlsx** and then save the workbook and name it **ExcelL1_C8_A1**.
3. Draw a text box at the right side of the Books Galore clip art image with the following specifications:
   a. Change the height to 1.7" and the width to 2.7".
   b. Remove the text box outline.
   c. Click the Middle Align button and the Center button in the Alignment group in the Home tab.
   d. Change the font to 32-point Forte and change the font color to blue.
   e. Type Book of the Month Club News, 2010 in the text box.
4. Change the orientation to landscape.
5. Save and then print **ExcelL1_C8_A1.xlsx**.
6. Save **ExcelL1_C8_A1.xlsx** as a single Web page in the ExcelWebPages folder (you created this folder in Project 8a) on your storage medium and name it **BooksGaloreWebPage**.
7. Open Internet Explorer and then open **BooksGaloreWebPage.mht**.
8. Close Internet Explorer.
9. Print **BooksGaloreWebPage.mht** in landscape orientation.
10. Select E12 and hyperlink it to *www.microsoft.com*.
11. Select E13 and hyperlink it to *www.symantec.com*.
12. Select E14 and hyperlink it to *www.nasa.gov*.
13. Select E15 and hyperlink it to *www.cnn.com*.
14. Make sure you are connected to the Internet and then click the hyperlink to NASA.
15. Jump to a link from the NASA Web page that interests you.
16. Print the page you viewed from NASA and then close the browser application window.
17. Jump to each of the remaining links in the Web page. At each Web page, jump to a link that interests you, print the page, and then close the browser application window.
18. Save (click Yes at the compatibility dialog box) and then close **BooksGaloreWebPage.mht**.

Assessment 2

INSERT A CLIP ART IMAGE AND WORDART IN AN EQUIPMENT PURCHASE WORKBOOK

1. Open **ExcelC08Assessment02.xlsx** and then save the workbook and name it **ExcelL1_C8_A2**.
2. Insert a formula in cell E4 using the PMT function that calculates monthly payments. ***Hint: Refer to Chapter 2, Project 3a.***
3. Copy the formula in cell E4 down to cells E5 and E6.
4. Insert a formula in cell F4 that calculates the total amount of the payments. ***Hint: Refer to Chapter 2, Project 3a.***
5. Copy the formula in cell F4 down to cells F5 and F6.
6. Insert a formula in cell G4 that calculates to the total amount of interest paid. ***Hint: Refer to Chapter 2, Project 3a.***
7. Copy the formula in cell G4 down to cells G5 and G6.
8. Increase the height of row 1 to 75.00.
9. Delete *BAYSIDE TRAVEL* in cell A1.
10. Insert the clip art image shown in Figure 8.13 (search for this clip art by searching only for clip art images [remove check marks from *Photographs*, *Movies*, and *Sound*] and typing travel in the *Search for* text box). If this clip art image is not available, choose another image related to travel. (Before closing the Clip Art task pane, reinsert check marks in the *Photographs*, *Movies*, and *Sound* check boxes at the *Results should be* option drop-down list.)
11. Size and move the clip art image so it is positioned as shown in Figure 8.13.
12. Insert the company name as WordArt as shown in Figure 8.13 with the following specifications:
    a. Create the WordArt with the second option from the left in the bottom row of the WordArt drop-down list (*Fill - Accent 6, Warm Matte Bevel*).
    b. Select the WordArt text, click the Text Fill button arrow in the WordArt Styles group, and then click the light blue color (in the *Standard Colors* section) at the drop-down gallery.
13. Change the worksheet orientation to landscape
14. Save, print, and then close **ExcelL1_C8_A2.xlsx**.

Figure 8.13 Assessment 2

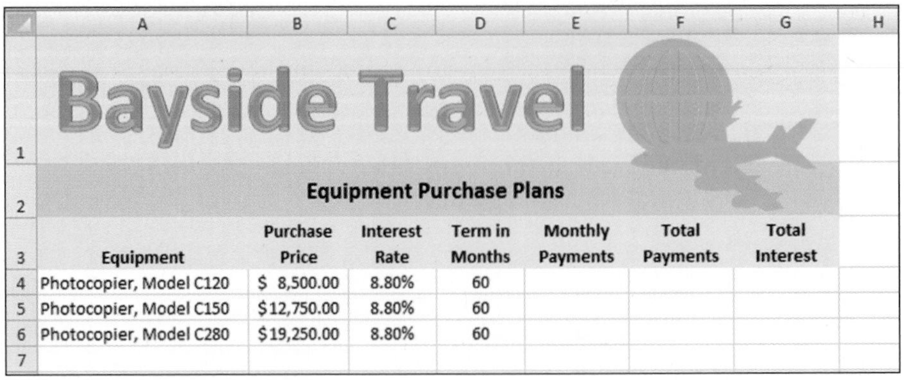

	A	B	C	D	E	F	G	H
1	Bayside Travel							
2	Equipment Purchase Plans							
3	Equipment	Purchase Price	Interest Rate	Term in Months	Monthly Payments	Total Payments	Total Interest	
4	Photocopier, Model C120	$ 8,500.00	8.80%	60				
5	Photocopier, Model C150	$12,750.00	8.80%	60				
6	Photocopier, Model C280	$19,250.00	8.80%	60				
7								

Assessment 3

INSERT AND FORMAT SHAPES IN A COMPANY SALES WORKBOOK

1. Open **ExcelC08Assessment03.xlsx** and then save the workbook and name it **ExcelL1_C8_A3**.
2. In cell A1, type Mountain, press Alt + Enter, and then type Systems.
3. Select *Mountain Systems* and then change the font to 24-point Calibri bold.
4. Change the horizontal alignment of cell A1to left and the vertical alignment to center.
5. Display the Format Cells dialog box with the Alignment tab selected and then change the *Indent* measurement to *1*. ***Hint: Display the Format Cells dialog box by clicking the Alignment group dialog box launcher in the Home tab.***
6. Click outside cell A1.
7. Use the *Isosceles Triangle* shape located in the *Basic Shapes* section of the Shapes drop-down palette to draw a triangle as shown in Figure 8.14.
8. Copy the triangle three times. Add green fill, dark green outline color, and a shadow effect of your choosing to the triangles so they appear in a similar manner to the triangles in Figure 8.14. Position the triangles as shown in the figure.
9. Save, print, and then close **ExcelL1_C8_A3.xlsx**.

Figure 8.14 Assessment 3

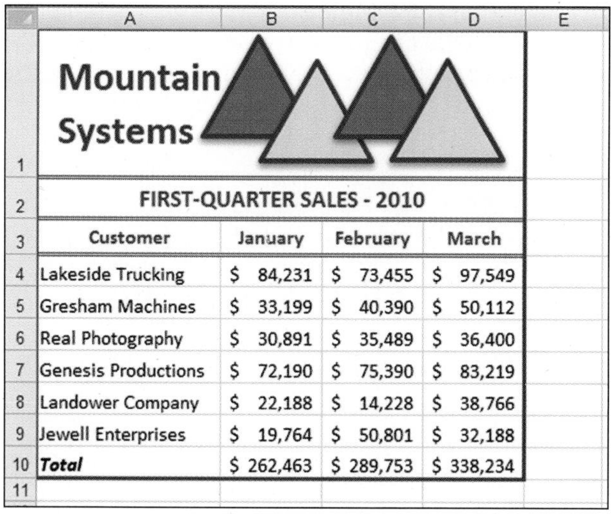

	A	B	C	D	E
1	Mountain Systems				
2	FIRST-QUARTER SALES - 2010				
3	Customer	January	February	March	
4	Lakeside Trucking	$ 84,231	$ 73,455	$ 97,549	
5	Gresham Machines	$ 33,199	$ 40,390	$ 50,112	
6	Real Photography	$ 30,891	$ 35,489	$ 36,400	
7	Genesis Productions	$ 72,190	$ 75,390	$ 83,219	
8	Landower Company	$ 22,188	$ 14,228	$ 38,766	
9	Jewell Enterprises	$ 19,764	$ 50,801	$ 32,188	
10	***Total***	$ 262,463	$ 289,753	$ 338,234	
11					

Assessment 4

INSERT AND FORMAT A SMARTART DIAGRAM IN A SALES WORKBOOK

1. Open **ExcelC08Assessment04.xlsx** and then save the workbook and name it **ExcelL1_C8_A4**.
2. Change the orientation to landscape.
3. Insert a pyramid shape at the right side of the worksheet data using the *Basic Pyramid* SmartArt diagram and insert the following information in the pyramid:
   a. In the bottom shape, type Red Level, press Enter, and then type $25,000 - $49,999.

b. In the middle shape, type Blue Level, press Enter, and then type $50,000 - $99,999.

c. In the top shape, type Gold Level, press Enter, and then type $100,000+.

d. Change the font size and/or move the text so the text displays in each shape.

e. Change the color of the shapes to match the color level.

f. If necessary, change the color of the text inside the shapes so it is easy to read.

g. Size and/or move the diagram so it displays attractively at the right side of the worksheet data. (Make sure the entire diagram will print on the same page as the worksheet data.)

4. Save, print, and then close **ExcelL1_C8_A4.xlsx**.

Assessment

5 APPLY CONDITIONAL FORMATTING TO CELLS IN A SALES WORKBOOK

1. Using the Help feature, learn about applying conditional formatting to numbers in cells that match a specific range.

2. Open **ExcelL1_C8_A4.xlsx** and then save the workbook and name it **ExcelL1_C8_A5**.

3. Using the conditional formatting feature, apply the following formatting to amounts in the *Total* column:

a. Apply red color formatting to numbers between $25,000 and $49,999.

b. Apply blue color formatting to numbers between $50,000 and $99,999.

c. Apply gold color formatting to numbers between $100,000 and $500,000.

4. Save, print, and then close **ExcelL1_C8_A5.xlsx**.

CASE study
Apply Your Skills

Part 1

You are the office manager for Ocean Truck Sales and are responsible for maintaining a spreadsheet of the truck and SUV inventory. Open **ExcelC08Ocean.xlsx** and then save the workbook and name it **ExcelL1_C8_CS_P1**. Apply formatting to improve the appearance of the worksheet and insert at least one clip art image (related to "truck" or "ocean"). Save **ExcelL1_C8_CS_P1.xlsx** and then print the worksheet.

Part 2

You have been asked to save the inventory worksheet as a Web page for viewing online and also to insert hyperlinks to various sites. With **ExcelL1_C8_CS_P1.xlsx** open, locate at least one financial institution in your area that will finance an automobile and then insert in the worksheet a hyperlink to that site. Locate another site that provides information on book value of a used automobile and then insert in the worksheet a hyperlink to that site. Save the workbook as a single Web page with the name **ExcelC08OceanWebPage**. Open your Internet browser and then open the Web page. Click each hyperlink to make sure it takes you to the proper Web site. Close your Internet browser and then close **ExcelC08OceanWebPage.mht**.

Open **ExcelL1_C8_CS_P1.xlsx** and then save it with Save As and name it **ExcelL1_C8_CS_P3**. You make the inventory workbook available to each salesperson at the beginning of the week. For easier viewing, you decide to divide the workbook into two worksheets with one worksheet containing all Ford vehicles and the other worksheet containing all Chevrolet vehicles. Rename the worksheet tabs to reflect the contents. Sort each worksheet by price from the most expensive to the least expensive. The owner offers incentives each week to help motivate the sales force. Insert in the first worksheet a SmartArt diagram of your choosing that contains the following information:

> Small-sized truck = $100
> 2WD Regular Cab = $75
> SUV 4x4 = $50

Copy the diagram in the first worksheet and then paste it into the second worksheet. Change the orientation to landscape and then save, print, and close **ExcelL1_C8_CS_P3.xlsx**.

As part of your weekly duties, you need to post the incentive diagram in various locations throughout the company. You decide to insert the diagram in PowerPoint for easy printing. Open **ExcelL1_C8_CS_P3.xlsx** and then open PowerPoint. Change the slide layout in PowerPoint to Blank. Copy the diagram in the first worksheet and paste it into the PowerPoint blank slide. Increase and/or move the diagram so it better fills the slide. Print the slide and then close PowerPoint without saving the presentation. Close **ExcelL1_C8_CS_P3.xlsx**.

Maintaining and Enhancing Workbooks

ASSESSING proficiency

In this unit, you have learned how to work with multiple windows; move, copy, link, and paste data between workbooks and applications; create and customize charts with data in a worksheet; save a workbook as a Web page; insert hyperlinks; and insert and customize pictures, clip art images, shapes, SmartArt diagrams, and WordArt.

Note: Before beginning computer assessments, copy to your storage medium the Excel2007L1U2 subfolder from the Excel2007L1 folder on the CD that accompanies this textbook and then make Excel2007L1U2 the active folder.

Assessment 1 Copy and Paste Data and Insert WordArt in a Training Scores Workbook

1. Open **ExcelU02Assessment01.xlsx** and then save the workbook and name it **ExcelL1_U2_A1**.
2. Delete row 15 (the row for *Kwieciak, Kathleen*).
3. Insert a formula in cell D4 that averages the percentages in cells B4 and C4.
4. Copy the formula in cell D4 down to cells D5 through D20.
5. Make cell A22 active, turn on bold, and then type Highest Averages.
6. Display the Clipboard task pane and make sure it is empty.
7. Select and then copy each of the following rows (individually): row 7, 10, 14, 16, and 18.
8. Make cell A23 active and then paste row 14 (the row for *Jewett, Troy*).
9. Make cell A24 active and then paste row 7 (the row for *Cumpston, Kurt*).
10. Make cell A25 active and then paste row 10 (the row for *Fisher-Edwards, Theresa*).
11. Make cell A26 active and then paste row 16 (the row for *Mathias, Caleb*).
12. Make cell A27 active and then paste row 18 (the row for *Nyegaard, Curtis*).
13. Click the Clear All button in the Clipboard task pane and then close the task pane.
14. Insert in cell A1 the text *Roseland* as WordArt. Format the WordArt text to add visual appeal to the worksheet.
15. Save, print, and then close **ExcelL1_U2_A1.xlsx**.

Assessment 2 Manage Multiple Worksheets in a Projected Earnings Workbook

1. Open **ExcelU02Assessment02.xlsx** and then save the workbook and name it **ExcelL1_U2_A2**.
2. Delete *Roseland* in cell A1. Open **ExcelL1_U2_A1.xlsx** and then copy the *Roseland* WordArt text and paste it into cell A1 in **ExcelL1_U2_A2.xlsx**. If necessary, increase the height of row 1 to accommodate the WordArt text.
3. Notice the fill color in cells in **ExcelL1_U2_A1.xlsx** and then apply the same fill color to cells of data in **ExcelL1_U2_A2.xlsx**. Close **ExcelL1_U2_A1.xlsx**.
4. Select cells A1 through C11 and then copy and paste the cells to Sheet2 keeping the source column widths.
5. With Sheet2 displayed, make the following changes:
   a. Increase the height of row 1 to accommodate the WordArt text.
   b. Delete the contents of cell B2.
   c. Change the contents of the following cells:
      - A6: Change *January* to *July*
      - A7: Change *February* to *August*
      - A8: Change *March* to *September*
      - A9: Change *April* to *October*
      - A10: Change *May* to *November*
      - A11: Change *June* to *December*
      - B6: Change *8.30%* to *8.10%*
      - B8: Change *9.30%* to *8.70%*
6. Make Sheet1 active and then copy cell B2 and paste link it to cell B2 in Sheet2.
7. Rename Sheet1 to *First Half* and rename Sheet2 to *Second Half*.
8. Make the First Half worksheet active and then determine the effect on projected monthly earnings if the projected yearly income is increased by 10% by changing the number in cell B2 to *$1,480,380*.
9. Save the workbook (two worksheets) again and then print both worksheets of the workbook so they are horizontally and vertically centered on each page.
10. Determine the effect on projected monthly earnings if the projected yearly income is increased by 20% by changing the number in cell B2 to *$1,614,960*.
11. Save the workbook again and then print both worksheets of the workbook so they are horizontally and vertically centered on each page.
12. Close **ExcelL1_U2_A2.xlsx**.

Assessment 3 Create Charts in Worksheets in a Sales Totals Workbook

1. Open **ExcelU02Assessment03** and then save the workbook and name it **ExcelL1_U2_A3**.
2. Insert the heading **Average Sales 2008-2010** (on multiple lines) in cell A13.
3. Insert a formula in cell B13 with a 3-D reference that averages the total in cells B4 through B11 in Sheet1, Sheet2, and Sheet3.
4. Insert a formula in cell C13 with a 3-D reference that averages the total in cells C4 through C11 in Sheet1, Sheet2, and Sheet3.
5. Rename Sheet1 to *2008 Sales*, rename Sheet2 to *2009 Sales*, and rename Sheet3 to *2010 Sales*.
6. Make the 2008 Sales worksheet active, select cells A3 through C11 and create a column chart. Click the Switch Row/Column button at the Chart Tools Design tab. Apply formatting to increase the visual appeal of the chart. Drag the chart below the worksheet data. (Make sure the chart fits on the page.)

7. Make the 2009 Sales worksheet active and then create the same type of chart you created in Step 6.
8. Make the 2010 Sales worksheet active and then create the same type of chart you created in Step 6.
9. Save the workbook and then print the entire workbook.
10. Close **ExcelL1_U2_A3.xlsx**.

Assessment 4 **Create and Format a Line Chart**

1. Type the following information in a worksheet:

Country	Total Sales
Denmark	$85,345
Finland	$71,450
Norway	$135,230
Sweden	$118,895

2. Using the data just entered in the worksheet, create a line chart with the following specifications:
   a. Apply a chart style of your choosing.
   b. Insert major and minor primary vertical gridlines.
   c. Insert drop lines. (Do this with the Lines button in the Analysis group in the Chart Tools Layout tab.)
   d. Apply any other formatting to improve the visual appeal of the chart.
   e. Move the chart to a new sheet.
3. Save the workbook and name it **ExcelL1_U2_A4**.
4. Print only the sheet containing the chart.
5. Change the line chart to a bar chart of your choosing.
6. Save the workbook and then print only the sheet containing the chart.
7. Close **ExcelL1_U2_A4.xlsx**.

Assessment 5 **Create and Format a Pie Chart**

1. Open **ExcelU02Assessment05.xlsx** and then save the workbook and name it **ExcelL1_U2_A5**.
2. Create a pie chart as a separate sheet with the data in cells A3 through B10. You determine the type of pie. Include an appropriate title for the chart and include percentage labels.
3. Print only the sheet containing the chart.
4. Save and then close **ExcelL1_U2_A5.xlsx**.

Assessment 6 **Insert a Text Box in and Save a Travel Workbook as a Web Page**

1. Open **ExcelU02Assessment06.xlsx** and then save the workbook and name it **ExcelL1_U2_A6**.
2. Insert a text box in the workbook with the following specifications:
   a. Draw the text box at the right side of the clip art image.
   b. Remove the fill in the text box and the outline around the text box.
   c. Type **Call 1-888-555-1288 for last-minute vacation specials!**
   d. Select the text and then change the font to 20-point Bradley Hand ITC in blue color and turn on bold.
   e. Size and position the text box so it appears visually balanced with the travel clip art image.
3. Make sure you are connected to the Internet and then search for sites that might be of interest to tourists for each of the cities in the worksheet. Write down the URL for the best Web page you find for each city.

4. Create a hyperlink for each city to jump to the URL you wrote down in Step 3. (Select the hyperlink text in each cell and change the font size to 18 points.)
5. Save **ExcelL1_U2_A6.xlsx** and then print the worksheet.
6. Create a new folder named TravelWebPages in the Excel2007L1U2 folder.
7. Save **ExcelL1_U2_A6.xlsx** as a single file Web page in the TravelWebPages folder with the following specifications:
   a. Name the Web page **TravelAdvantageWebPage**.
   b. Change the title to *Winter Getaway Destinations!*
8. Open Internet Explorer and then open **TravelAdvantageWebPage.mht**.
9. Test the hyperlinks to make sure you entered the URLs correctly by clicking each hyperlink and then closing the Web browser.
10. Close **TravelAdvantageWebPage.mht** and then close Internet Explorer.
11. Save and then close **ExcelL1_U2_A6.xlsx**.

Assessment 7 Insert Clip Art Image and Smart Diagram in a Projected Quotas Workbook

1. Open **ExcelU02Assessment07.xlsx** and then save the workbook and name it **ExcelL1_U2_A7**.
2. Insert a formula in cell C3 using an absolute reference to determine the projected quotas at 10% of the current quotas.
3. Copy the formula in cell C3 down to cells C4 through C12.
4. Insert a clip art image in row 1 related to money. You determine the size and position of the clip art image. If necessary, increase the height of the row.
5. Apply the following conditional formatting to the values in cells C3 through C12:
   Apply green color to values from $50,000 to $99,999.
   Apply blue color to values from $100,000 to $149,999.
   Apply red color to values from $150,000 to $200,000.
6. Insert a SmartArt diagram at the right side of the chart that contains three shapes. Insert the quota ranges in the shapes as identified in Step 5 and apply color fill to match the conditional formatting. (For example, type $50,000 to $99,999 in a shape and then apply green fill color to the shape.)
7. Change the orientation to landscape and make sure the diagram fits on the page.
8. Save, print, and then close **ExcelL1_U2_A7.xlsx**.

Assessment 8 Insert Symbol, Clip Art, and Comments in a Sales Workbook

1. Open **ExcelU02Assessment08.xlsx** and then save the workbook and name it **ExcelL1_U2_A8**.
2. Delete the text *Landower Company* and then type Económico in the cell. (Use the Symbol dialog box to insert ó.)
3. Insert a new row at the beginning of the worksheet.
4. Select and then merge cells A1 through D1.
5. Increase the height of row 1 to approximately 100.50.
6. Insert the text *Custom Interiors* as WordArt in cell A1. You determine the formatting of the WordArt. Move and size the WordArt so it fits in cell A1.
7. Insert the following comments in the specified cells:
   D4 = Increase amount to $100,000.
   A5 = Change the name to Gresham Technology.
   A9 = Decrease amounts for this company by 5%.

8. Turn on the display of all comments.
9. Print the worksheet with the comments as displayed on the worksheet.
10. Turn off the display of all comments.
11. Delete the comment in A5.
12. Print the worksheet again with the comments printed at the end of the worksheet. (The comments will print on a separate page from the worksheet.)
13. Save and then close **ExcelL1_U2_A8.xlsx**.

Assessment 9 Insert and Format a Shape in a Budget Workbook

1. Open **ExcelU02Assessment09.xlsx** and then save the workbook and name it **ExcelL1_U2_A9**.
2. Make the following changes to the worksheet so it displays as shown in Figure U2.1:
   a. Select and then merge cells A1 through D1.
   b. Add fill to the cells as shown in Figure U2.1.
   c. Increase the height of row 1 to the approximate size shown in Figure U2.1.
   d. Insert the text **SOLAR ENTERPRISES** in cell A1 set in 20-point Calibri bold, center and middle aligned, and set in aqua (Aqua, Accent 5, Darker 25%).
   e. Insert the sun shape (located in the *Basic Shapes* section of the Shapes button drop-down list). Apply orange shape fill and change the shape outline to aqua (Aqua, Accent 5, Darker 25%)
3. Save, print, and then close **ExcelL1_U2_A9.xlsx**.

Figure U2.1 Assessment 9

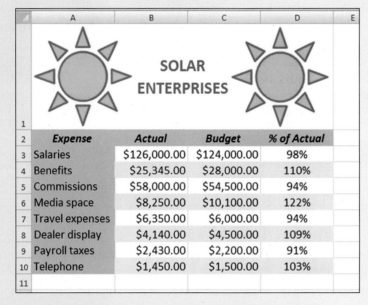

WRITING activities

The following activities give you the opportunity to practice your writing skills along with demonstrating an understanding of some of the important Excel features you have mastered in this unit. Use correct grammar, appropriate word choices, and clear sentence constructions.

Activity 1 Prepare a Projected Budget

You are the accounting assistant in the financial department of McCormack Funds and you have been asked to prepare a yearly proposed department budget. The total amount for the department is $1,450,000. You are given the percentages for the proposed budget items, which are: Salaries, 45%; Benefits, 12%; Training, 14%; Administrative Costs, 10%; Equipment, 11%; and Supplies, 8%. Create a worksheet with this information that shows the projected yearly budget, the budget items in the department, the percentage of the budget, and the amount for each item. After the worksheet is completed, save the workbook and name it **ExcelL1_U2_Act01**. Print and then close the workbook.

Optional: Using Word 2007, write a memo to the McCormack Funds Finance Department explaining that the proposed annual department budget is attached for their review. Comments and suggestions are to be sent to you within one week. Save the file and name it **ExcelL1_U2_Act01_Memo**. Print and then close the file.

Activity 2 Create a Travel Tours Bar Chart

Prepare a worksheet in Excel for Carefree Travels that includes the following information:

Scandinavian Tours

Country	Tours Booked
Norway	52
Sweden	62
Finland	29
Denmark	38

Use the information in the worksheet to create and format a bar chart as a separate sheet. Save the workbook and name it **ExcelL1_U2_Act02**. Print only the sheet containing the chart and then close **ExcelL1_U2_Act02.xlsx**.

Activity 3 Prepare a Ski Vacation Worksheet

Prepare a worksheet for Carefree Travels that advertises a snow skiing trip. Include the following information in the announcement:

- At the beginning of the worksheet, create a company logo that includes the company name *Carefree Travels* and a clip art image related to travel.
- Include the heading *Whistler Ski Vacation Package* in the worksheet.
- Include the following below the heading:
  - Round-trip air transportation: $395
  - Seven nights' hotel accommodations: $1,550
  - Four all-day ski passes: $425

- Compact rental car with unlimited mileage: $250
- Total price of the ski package: (calculate the total price)
- Include the following information somewhere in the worksheet:
  - Book your vacation today at special discount prices.
  - Two-for-one discount at many of the local ski resorts.

Save the workbook and name it **ExcelL1_U2_Act03**. Print and then close **ExcelL1_U2_Act03.xlsx**.

Find Information on Excel Books and Present the Data in a Worksheet

Locate two companies on the Internet that sell new books. At the first new book company site, locate three books on Microsoft Excel. Record the title, author, and price for each book. At the second new book company site, locate the same three books and record the prices. Create an Excel worksheet that includes the following information:

- Name of each new book company
- Title and author of the three books
- Prices for each book from the two book company sites

Create a hyperlink for each book company to the URL on the Internet. Then save the completed workbook and name it **ExcelL1_U2_InternetResearch**. Print and then close the workbook.

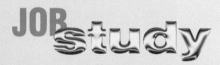

Create a Customized Time Card for a Landscaping Company

You are the manager of a landscaping company and are responsible for employee time cards. Locate the time card template that is available with *Installed Templates* selected in the New Workbook dialog box. Use the template to create a customized time card for your company. With the template open, delete the Company Name that displays in the middle header pane. Insert additional blank rows to increase the spacing above the Employee row. Insert a clip art image related to landscaping or gardening and position and size it attractively in the form. Include a text box with the text Lawn and Landscaping Specialists inside the box. Format, size, and position the text attractively in the form. Fill in the form for the current week with the following employee information:

Employee = Jonathan Holder
Address = 12332 South 152nd Street, Baton Rouge, LA 70804
Manager = (Your name)
Employee phone = (225) 555-3092
Employee e-mail = None

Regular hours = 8 hours for Monday, Tuesday, Wednesday, and Thursday
Overtime = 2 hours on Wednesday
Sick hours = None
Vacation = 8 hours on Friday
Rate per hour = $20.00
Overtime pay = $30.00

Save the completed form and name it **ExcelL1_U2_JobStudy**. Print and then close **ExcelL1_U2_JobStudy.xlsx**.

Edit mode: changing out of, 13
Effects theme, 81, 99
Embedding: data in worksheets, 186, 189
Enclosed objects: drawing, 284, 300
Engineering function category: in Excel, 43, 45
Enter button, 13, 53
Envelope sizes, 113
Equals (=) sign: formulas beginning with, 38, 60
Esc key, 13
Even pages: headers or footers for, 121
Excel
   answering "what if" questions with, 37
   charts created in, 239–263
   exiting, 14, 30, 31
   functions within categories in, 45, 60
   opening, 8
   workbooks saved in previous version of, 211–212
Excel 97-2003 format: saving workbooks in, 211
Excel Help Search drop-down list, 29
Excel Help window
   displaying, 27, 31
   downloading PDF add-ins information at, 213
Excel Options button, 275
Excel Options dialog box, 15, 275
Excel spreadsheets, 30
   uses for, 7
Excel templates, 199
   using, 227–229, 230
Excel window: elements within, 30
Excel workbooks. *See also* Workbooks, 8
   saving, 11–12
   saving, as a Web page and in text format, 211
Excel worksheets. *See also* Worksheets
   blank, 8
   default formatting in, 23
   default page size for, 113
   elements of, 9
   formatting, 67–101
Executive page size, 113
Exponentiation operator (^): formulas written with, 38, 60
Extend Selection mode, 23

F

Files
   displaying all in a folder, 201
   maintenance activities for, 199

Files of type option: at Open dialog box, 201
File transfer: in PDF format, 213
Fill: adding to cells, 94
Fill button, 39, 60
Fill color: adding to cells, 94, 95
Fill Color button, 76, 94, 100
Fill handle, 39
   copying formulas with, 21, 39, 40, 60
   in Excel worksheets, 9
   inserting data in cells with, 16–17, 18
   using, 16–17
Fill patterns: WordArt and, 298
Fill tab: in Find Format dialog box, 130
Filtering
   data, 134–136, 139, 141
   turning on, 134
Filtering arrows: turning off display of, 23, 139
Filters, 134
Filter & Sort button, 134
Financial function category: in Excel, 43, 45
Financial functions: writing formulas with, 49–51
Financial statements, 30
   creating, 7
Find and Replace dialog box
   expanded, 128
   expanded, finding and replacing cell formatting at, 130–131
   with Find tab selected, 127, 139, 141
   with Replace tab selected, 128, 139, 141
Find and replace feature, 127
Find feature, 127
Find Format dialog box, 130
Finding and replacing: cell formatting, 130–131
Find Next button, 127, 128
Find & Select button, 10, 97, 127, 128
Find what text box: in Find and Replace dialog box, 128, 129
Flow chart shapes: drawing, 284
Folder icon, 200
Folders
   copying workbooks into, 203
   creating, 200–201, 230
   deleting, 202
   deleting contents of, 206
   different, sending workbooks to, 205
   renaming, 201–202, 230
   root, 200
   workbooks organized into, 199, 200, 230

Font button, 75, 100
Font color: changing, 90
Font Color button, 76, 100
Font Color button arrow, 290
Font formatting
   applying, 75–78, 99
   applying at Format Cells dialog box, 91
Font group, 75, 76, 90, 91, 94, 99
Fonts
   changing at Format Cells dialog box, 90
   changing at Symbol dialog box, 278
Font size
   changing, 90
   specifying, 75
Font Size button, 75
Font Size button arrow, 290
Font style: changing, 90
Font tab
   in Find Format dialog box, 130
   in Format Cells dialog box, 99
Font theme, 81, 99
Footer option: in Page Setup dialog box, 111
Footers
   defined, 121
   inserting in worksheets, 121–122, 139
   pictures inserted in, 291, 301
Format: defined, 67
Format as Table button, 23, 67
Format As Table dialog box, 23
Format as Table drop-down gallery, 31
Format as Table drop-down list, 24
Format button, 69, 70, 94, 96, 100, 169, 188, 217, 219, 230
Format buttons: at expanded Find and Replace dialog box, 130
Format Cells dialog box, 82, 215, 217, 219, 230
   with Alignment tab selected, 88
   with Border tab selected, 91, 92
   changing font at, 90
   with Fill tab selected, 94
   with Font tab selected, 90
   formatting numbers with, 85, 86–87, 99
   number categories at, 86
   with Number tab selected, 85, 87, 99
Format Painter: formatting with, 96, 99
Format Painter button, 96, 99, 101
Format Picture button, 291
Format Picture dialog box, 291
Formatting. *See also* Customizing
   applying, 75–78

excel Level 1

CONTENTS

Project ④ Insert Headers and Footers in a Computer Report

You will open a report on computers in communication and entertainment, then create and position headers and footers. You will also create headers and footers for different pages in a document, divide a document into sections, and then create footers for specific sections.

Inserting Headers and Footers

Text that appears at the top of every page is called a ***header*** and text that appears at the bottom of every page is referred to as a ***footer***. Headers and footers are commonly used in manuscripts, textbooks, reports, and other publications to display the page number and section or chapter title. For example, see the footer at the bottom of this page. You can insert a predesigned header by clicking the Insert tab and then clicking the Header button. This displays a drop-down list of header choices. Click the predesigned header and the formatted header is inserted in the document. Complete similar steps to insert a predesigned footer. Note that headers and footers only appear in Print Layout view, Print Preview, and in the printed document.

If the predesigned headers and footers do not meet your needs, you can create your own. For example, to create a header you would click the Insert tab, click the Header button in the Header & Footer group, and then click *Edit Header* at the drop-down list. This displays a Header pane in the document and also displays the Header & Footer Tools Design tab as shown in Figure 1.7. With options in this tab you can insert elements such as page numbers, pictures, and clip art; navigate to other headers or footers in the document; and position headers and footers on different pages in a document.

Inserting Elements in Headers and Footers

Use buttons in the Insert group in the Header & Footer Tools Design tab to insert elements into the header or footer such as the date and time, quick parts, pictures, and clip art images. Click the Date & Time button and the Date and Time dialog box displays with options for inserting the current date as well as the current time. Click the Picture button and the Insert Picture dialog box displays. At this dialog box, navigate to the desired folder and double-click the picture file. Click the Clip Art button and the Clip Art task pane displays where you can search for and then insert an image into the header or footer.

HINT

If predesigned headers and footers do not display, building block add-ins may not be available.

HINT

One method for formatting a header or footer is to select the header or footer text and then use options on the Mini toolbar.

Header   Footer

QUICK STEPS

Insert Element in Header
1. Click Insert tab.
2. Click Header button.
3. Click *Edit Header* at drop-down gallery.
4. Click desired elements.

Insert Element in Footer
1. Click Insert tab.
2. Click Footer button.
3. Click *Edit Footer* at drop-down gallery.
4. Click desired elements.

Date & Time

Picture   Clip Art

Figure 1.7 Header & Footer Tools Design tab

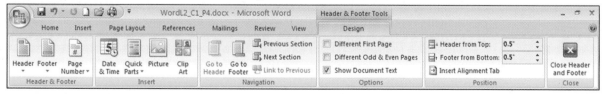

1. Open **WordReport06.docx** and then save the document and name it **WordL2_C1_P4**.
2. Change the top margin by completing the following steps:
   a. Click the Page Layout tab.
   b. Click the Margins button in the Page Setup group.
   c. Click *Custom Margins* at the drop-down list.
   d. At the Page Setup dialog box with the Margins tab selected, click the up-pointing arrow at the right side of the *Top* measurement box until *1.5"* displays.
   e. Click the up-pointing arrow at the right side of the *Bottom* measurement box until *1.5"* displays.
   f. Click OK to close the dialog box.

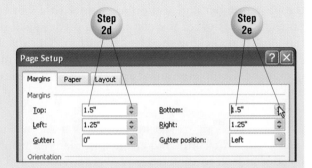

Step 2d

Step 2e

3. Click the Theme Colors button in the Themes group in the Page Layout tab and then click *Oriel* at the drop-down list.
4. Insert spacing above paragraphs by completing the following steps:
   a. Move the insertion point to the paragraph of text in the *TELEVISION AND FILM* section that begins *The film* Jurassic Park . . . .
   b. Make sure the Page Layout tab is selected.
   c. Click once on the up-pointing arrow at the right side of the *Before* measurement box below *Spacing*. (This inserts *6 pt* in the measurement box.)

Step 3

Step 4c

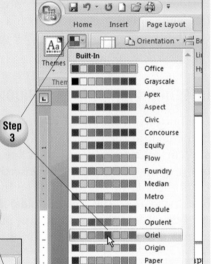

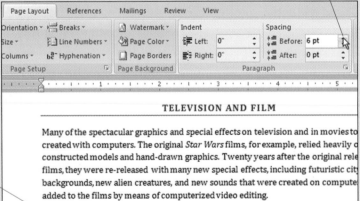

Step 4a

   d. Move the insertion point to the paragraph of text in the *HOME ENTERTAINMENT* section that begins *The advent of powerful* . . . and then press F4. (This is the Repeat command that repeats the spacing above formatting.)

5. Insert a header by completing the following steps:
   a. Click the Insert tab.
   b. Click the Header button in the Header & Footer group.
   c. Click *Edit Header* at the drop-down list.
   d. With the insertion point positioned in the Header pane, click the Picture button in the Insert group in the Header & Footer Tools Design tab.

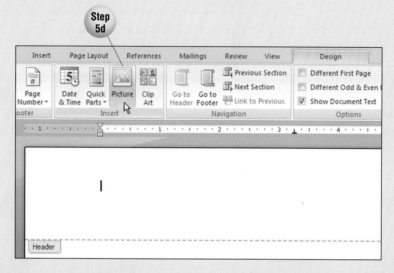

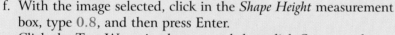

   e. At the Insert Picture dialog box, navigate to the Word2007L2C1 folder on your storage medium and then double-click *Worldwide.jpg*.
   f. With the image selected, click in the *Shape Height* measurement box, type 0.8, and then press Enter.
   g. Click the Text Wrapping button and then click *Square* at the drop-down list.

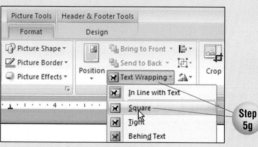

   h. Drag the image up approximately one-third of an inch.
   i. Click to the right of the picture to deselect it.
   j. Press the Tab key. (This moves the insertion point to approximately the middle of the page.)
   k. Click the Date & Time button in the Insert group in the Header & Footer Tools Design tab.
   l. At the Date and Time dialog box, click the twelfth option from the top (the option that displays the date in numbers and the time) and then click OK to close the dialog box.
   m. Select the date and time text and then click the Home tab. Click the Bold button, click the Font Size button arrow, and then click *10* at the drop-down gallery.
   n. Double-click in the document to make the document active and dim the header.
6. Save **WordL2_C1_P4.docx**.

Positioning a Header or Footer

Word inserts a header 0.5 inch from the top of the page and a footer 0.5 inch from the bottom of the page. You can change these default positions with buttons in the Position group in the Header & Footer Tools Design tab. Use the *Header from Top* and *Footer from Bottom* measurement boxes to adjust the position of the header or footer on the page.

By default a header and footer contain two tab settings. A center tab is set at 3.25 inches and a right tab is set at 6.5 inches. If the document contains default left and right margin settings of 1 inch, the center tab set at 3.25 inches is the center of the document and the right tab set at 6.5 inches is at the right margin. If you make changes to the default margins, you may need to move the default tabs before inserting header or footer text at the center or right tabs. You can also set and position tabs with the Insert Alignment Tab button in the Position group. Click this button and the Alignment Tab dialog box displays. Use options at this dialog box to change tab alignment and set tabs with leaders.

Project 4b Positioning Headers and Footers

1. With **WordL2_C1_P4.docx** open, create a footer by completing the following steps:
   a. Click the Insert tab.
   b. Click the Footer button in the Header & Footer group and then click *Edit Footer* at the drop-down list.
   c. With the insertion point positioned in the Footer pane, type your first and last names at the left margin.
   d. Press the Tab key. (This moves the insertion point to the center tab position.)
   e. Click the Page Number button in the Header & Footer group, point to *Current Position*, and then click *Accent Bar 2* at the drop-down list.

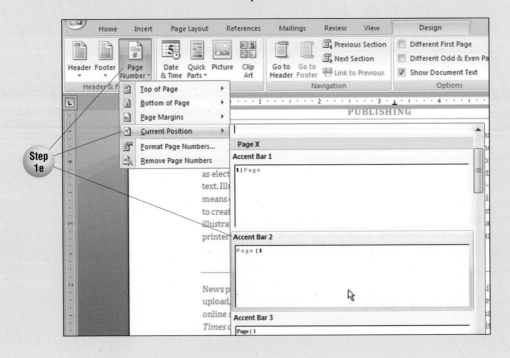

f. Press the Tab key and then type WordL2_C1_P4.
g. You notice that the center tab and the right tab are off slightly since the left and right margins in the document are set at 1.25″ instead of 1″. To correctly align the text, drag the center tab marker to the 3-inch mark on the Ruler and drag the right tab marker to the 6-inch mark on the Ruler.

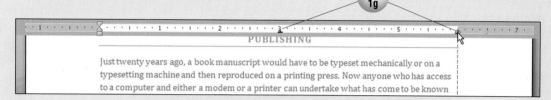

h. Select all of the footer text and then change the font to 10-point Cambria bold.
2. Edit the header by completing the following steps:
   a. Click the Header & Footer Tools Design tab.
   b. Click the Go to Header button in the Navigation group.
   c. Move the insertion point to the beginning of the date and then press the Tab key.
   d. Drag the right tab marker to the 6-inch mark on the ruler.
3. Change the position of the header and footer by completing the following steps:
   a. With the Header & Footer Tools Design tab active, click the up-pointing arrow at the right side of the *Header from Top* measurement box until *0.8″* displays.

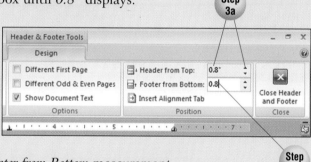

   b. Click in the *Footer from Bottom* measurement box, type 0.8, and then press Enter.
   c. Click the Close Header and Footer button.
4. Save and then print **WordL2_C1_P4.docx**.

QUICK STEPS

Create Different First Page Header or Footer
1. Click Insert tab.
2. Click Header or Footer button.
3. Click *Edit Header* or *Edit Footer* at drop-down gallery.
4. Click *Different First Page* check box.
5. Insert desired elements and/or text.
6. Click Next Section button.
7. Insert desired elements and/or text.

Creating a Different First Page Header or Footer

By default, Word will insert a header or footer on every page in the document. You can create different headers or footers within one document. For example, you can create a unique header or footer on the first page and then insert a different header or footer on subsequent pages. To create a different first page header, click the Insert tab, click the Header button, and then click *Edit Header* at the drop-down list. Click the *Different First Page* check box to insert a check mark and the First Page Header pane displays with the insertion point inside. Insert elements or type text to create the first page header and then click the Next Section button in the Navigation group. This displays the Header pane with the insertion point positioned inside. Insert elements and/or type text to create the header. Complete similar steps to create a different first page footer.

In some situations you may want the first page header or footer to be blank. This is particularly useful if a document contains a title page and you do not want the header or footer to print at the top or bottom of the first page.

Project 4C   Creating a Header That Prints on all Pages Except the First Page

1. With **WordL2_C1_P4.docx** open, press Ctrl + A to select the entire document and then press Ctrl + 2 to change the line spacing to 2.
2. Move the insertion point to the beginning of the title *SECTION 2: COMPUTERS IN ENTERTAINMENT* and then press Ctrl + Enter. (This inserts a page break at the location of the insertion point.)
3. Remove the header and footer by completing the following steps:
   a. Click the Insert tab.
   b. Click the Header button in the Header & Footer group and then click *Remove Header* at the drop-down list.
   c. Click the Footer button in the Header & Footer group and then click *Remove Footer* at the drop-down list.
4. Press Ctrl + Home and then create a header that prints on all pages except the first page by completing the following steps:
   a. With the Insert tab active, click the Header button in the Header & Footer group.
   b. Click *Edit Header* at the drop-down list.
   c. Click the *Different First Page* check box located in the Options group.

Step 4c

   d. With the insertion point positioned in the First Page Header pane, click the Next Section button in the Navigation group. (This tells Word that you want the first page header to be blank.)
   e. With the insertion point positioned in the Header pane, click the Page Number button, point to *Top of Page*, and then click *Accent Bar 2* at the drop-down gallery.
   f. Click the Close Header and Footer button.
5. Scroll through the document and notice that the header appears on the second through fourth pages.
6. Save and then print **WordL2_C1_P4.docx**.

Creating Odd and Even Page Headers or Footers

If your document will be read in book form with facing pages, consider inserting odd and even page headers or footers. When presenting pages in a document in book form with facing pages, the outside margin is the left side of the left page and the right side of the right page. Also, when a document has facing pages, the page at the right side is generally numbered with odd page numbers and the page at the left side is generally numbered with even page numbers. You can create even and odd headers or footers to insert this type of page numbering. Use the *Different Odd & Even Pages* check box in the Options group in the Header & Footer Tools Design tab to create odd and even headers and/or footers.

QUICK STEPS

Create Odd and Even Page Headers or Footers
1. Click Insert tab.
2. Click Header or Footer button.
3. Click *Edit Header* or *Edit Footer* at drop-down gallery.
4. Click *Different Odd & Even Pages* check box.
5. Insert desired elements and/or text.

Project 4d Creating an Even Page and Odd Page Footer

1. With **WordL2_C1_P4.docx** open, remove the headers from the document by completing the following steps:
   a. Click the Insert tab.
   b. Click the Header button in the Header & Footer group and then click *Edit Header* at the drop-down list.
   c. Click the *Different First Page* check box in the Options group to remove the check mark.
   d. Click the Header button in the Header & Footer group in the Header & Footer Tools Design tab and then click *Remove Header* at the drop-down list. (This displays the insertion point in an empty Header pane.)

2. Create a footer that prints on odd pages and another that prints on even pages by completing the following steps:
   a. Click the Go to Footer button in the Navigation group in the Header & Footer Tools Design tab.
   b. Click the *Different Odd & Even Pages* check box in the Options group. (This displays the Odd Page Footer pane with the insertion point inside.)
   c. Click the Footer button in the Header & Footer group.
   d. Scroll down the list of predesigned footers and then click the *Mod (Odd Page)* option.
   e. Click the Next Section button in the Navigation group. (This displays the Even Page Footer pane with the insertion point inside.)
   f. Click the Footer button in the Header & Footer group.
   g. Scroll down the list of predesigned footers and then click the *Mod (Even Page)* option.
   h. Click the Close Header and Footer button.

3. Scroll through the document and notice the odd page and even page footers. After looking at the footers, you decide that you want the color of the circles in the footers to match the color of the titles and headings in the document. To do that, change the theme color by completing the following steps:

a. Click the Page Layout tab.

b. Click the Theme Colors button in the Themes group.

c. Click the *Foundry* option at the drop-down gallery.

4. Save and then print **WordL2_C1_P4.docx**.

Create Header/Footer for Different Sections

1. Insert section break in desired location.
2. Click Insert tab.
3. Click Header or Footer button.
4. Click *Edit Header* or *Edit Footer* at drop-down gallery.
5. Click Link to Previous button to deactivate.
6. Insert desired elements and/or text.
7. Click Next Section button.
8. Insert desired elements and/or text.

Link to Previous

Creating a Header/Footer for Different Sections

You can divide a document into sections and then apply different formatting in each section. You can insert a section break that begins a new page or insert a continuous section break. If you want different headers and/or footers for pages in a document, divide the document into sections.

For example, if a document contains several chapters, you can create a section for each chapter, and then create a different header or footer for each section. When dividing a document into sections by chapter, insert a section break that also begins a new page.

When a header or footer is created for a specific section in a document, the header or footer can be created for all previous and next sections or just for next sections. If you want a header or footer to print on only those pages in a section and not the previous or next sections, you must deactivate the Link to Previous button. This tells Word not to print the header or footer on previous sections. Word will, however, print the header or footer on following sections. If you do not want the header or footer to print on following sections, create a blank header or footer at the next section. When creating a header or footer for a specific section in a document, preview the document to determine if the header or footer appears on the correct pages.

Project 4e   Creating Footers for Different Sections

1. With **WordL2_C1_P4.docx** open, remove the odd and even page footers by completing the following steps:

a. Click the Insert tab.

b. Click the Footer button and then click *Edit Footer* at drop-down list.

c. Click the *Different Odd & Even Pages* check box to remove the check mark.

d. Click the Footer button and then click *Remove Footer* at the drop-down list.

e. Click the Close Header and Footer button.

2. Insert a section break that begins a new page by completing the following steps:

a. Move the insertion point to the beginning of the title *SECTION 2: COMPUTERS IN ENTERTAINMENT*.

b. Click the Page Layout tab.

c. Click the Breaks button in the Page Setup dialog box and then click *Next Page* in the *Section Breaks* section of the drop-down list. (The section break takes the place of the hard page break.)

3. Create section and page numbering footers for the two sections by completing the following steps:

a. Position the insertion point at the beginning of the document.

b. Click the Insert tab.

c. Click the Footer button in the Header & Footer group and then click *Edit Footer* at the drop-down list.

d. At the Footer -Section 1- pane, make sure bold is on, type Section 1, and then press the Tab key twice. (This moves the insertion point to the right margin.)

e. Type Page and then press the spacebar.

f. Click the Header & Footer Tools Design tab.

g. Click the Page Number button in the Header & Footer group, point to *Current Position*, and then click *Plain Number* at the side menu.

h. Click the Next Section button in the Navigation group.

i. Click the Link to Previous button to deactivate it. (This removes the message *Same as Previous* from the top right side of the footer pane.)

j. Edit the text *Section 1* to *Section 2* in the footer.

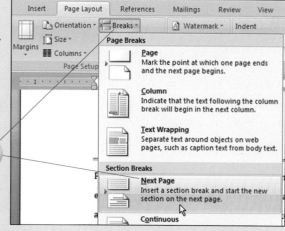

Step 2c

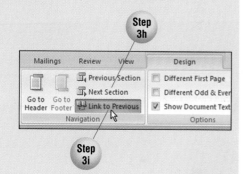

Step 3h

Step 3i

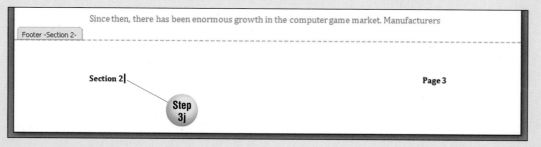

Step 3j

k. Click the Close Header and Footer button.

4. Save and then print **WordL2_C1_P4.docx**.

Printing Sections

You can print specific pages in a document by inserting page numbers in the *Pages* option at the Print dialog box. When entering page numbers in this option, you use a hyphen to indicate a range of consecutive pages for printing or a comma to specify nonconsecutive pages. If a document contains sections, use the *Pages* option at the Print dialog box to specify the section and pages within the section that you want printed. For example, if a document is divided into three sections and you want to print only section two, you would type s2 in the *Pages* option. If a document contains six sections and you want to print sections three through five, you would type s3-s5 in the *Pages* option.

You can also identify specific pages within or between sections for printing. For example, to print pages two through five of section four, you would type p2s4-p5s4; to print from page three of section one through page five of section four, you would type p3s1-p5s4; to print page one of section three, page four of section five, and page six of section eight, you would type p1s3,p4s5,p6s8.

Project ④ **Printing Sections**

1. With **WordL2_C1_P4.docx** open, click the Office button and then click *Print* at the drop-down list.
2. Specify that you want to print only section 2 by clicking the *Pages* option and then typing s2 in the *Pages* text box.
3. Click OK.
4. Save and then close **WordL2_C1_P4.docx**.

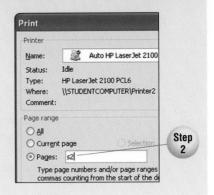

Automating and Customizing Formatting

PERFORMANCE OBJECTIVES

Upon successful completion of Chapter 3, you will be able to:

- Add words to and delete words from the AutoCorrect dialog box
- Use the AutoCorrect Options button
- Sort and insert building blocks
- Create, edit, modify, and delete building blocks
- Insert and update fields from Quick Parts
- Customize the Quick Access toolbar

word Chapter 3

Tutorial 3.1
Customizing Word's Writing Tools
and Using Building Blocks
Tutorial 3.2
Using Fields and the Quick
Access Toolbar

Microsoft Word offers a number of features to help you customize documents and to streamline the formatting of documents. In this chapter you will also learn how to customize the AutoCorrect feature and use the AutoCorrect Options button. You will also learn how to build a document using building blocks and create, save, and edit your own building blocks.

Note: Before beginning computer projects, copy to your storage medium the Word2007L2C3 subfolder from the Word2007L2 folder on the CD that accompanies this textbook and then make Word2007L2C3 the active folder.

Project ① Create a Travel Document Using AutoCorrect

You will create several AutoCorrect entries, open a letterhead document, and then use the AutoCorrect entries to type text in the document.

Customizing AutoCorrect

Word's AutoCorrect feature automatically corrects certain words as you type them. You can add words to AutoCorrect during spell checking or you can add, delete, or change words at the AutoCorrect dialog box. To display the AutoCorrect dialog box with the AutoCorrect tab selected as shown in Figure 3.1, click the Office button and then click the Word Options button. At the Word Options dialog box, click *Proofing* in the left panel and then click the AutoCorrect Options button.

Figure 3.1 AutoCorrect Dialog Box with AutoCorrect Tab Selected

Remove the check mark from those corrections you do not want AutoCorrect to make.

If you type the text shown in the first column of this list box and then press the spacebar, it is replaced by the text shown in the second column.

Adding Words to AutoCorrect

Insert Word(s) to AutoCorrect
1. Click Office button, Word Options.
2. Click *Proofing*.
3. Click AutoCorrect Options button.
4. Click AutoCorrect tab.
5. Type misspelled or abbreviated word.
6. Press Tab.
7. Type correctly spelled word or complete word(s).
8. Click Add button.
9. Click OK.

You can add commonly misspelled words or typographical errors to AutoCorrect. For example, if you consistently type *relavent* instead of *relevant*, you can add *relavent* to AutoCorrect and tell it to correct it as *relevant*. The AutoCorrect dialog box contains a few symbols you can insert in a document. For example, type (c) and AutoCorrect changes the text to ©. Type (r) and AutoCorrect changes the text to ®. The symbols display at the beginning of the AutoCorrect dialog box list box.

You can also add an abbreviation to AutoCorrect that, when typed, will insert the entire word (or words). For example, in Project 1a, you will add *fav* to AutoCorrect that will insert *Family Adventure Vacations* when you type *fav* and then press the spacebar. You can also control the capitalization of the word (or words) inserted by controlling the capitalization of the abbreviation. For example, in Project 1a, you will add *Na* to AutoCorrect that will insert *Namibia* when you type *Na*. If you want to insert NAMIBIA in the document, you would type NA and then press the spacebar.

Note that the AutoCorrect feature does not automatically correct text in hyperlinks. Also, AutoCorrect is only available in Word, Outlook, and Visio.

Project 1a Adding Text to AutoCorrect

1. At a blank document, click the Office button and then click the Word Options button at the bottom of the drop-down list.
2. At the Word Options dialog box, click *Proofing* in the left panel.
3. Click the AutoCorrect Options button in the *AutoCorrect options* section.
4. At the AutoCorrect dialog box with the AutoCorrect tab selected, make sure the insertion point is positioned in the *Replace* text box. If not, click in the *Replace* text box.
5. Type fav.
6. Press the Tab key (this moves the insertion point to the *With* text box) and then type Family Adventure Vacations.
7. Click the Add button. (This adds *fav* and *Family Adventure Vacations* to the AutoCorrect and also selects *fav* in the *Replace* text box.)
8. Type Na in the *Replace text* box. (The text *fav* is automatically deleted when you begin typing *Na*.)
9. Press the Tab key and then type Namibia.
10. Click the Add button.
11. With the insertion point positioned in the *Replace* text box, type vf.
12. Press the Tab key and then type Victoria Falls.
13. Click the Add button.

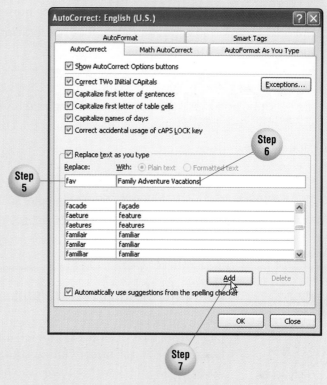

14. With the insertion point positioned in the *Replace* text box, type fct.
15. Press the Tab key and then type First Choice Travel.
16. Click the Add button.
17. Click OK to close the AutoCorrect dialog box and then click OK to close the Word Options dialog box.
18. Open **WordFCTLetterhead.docx** and then save the document and name it **WordL2_C3_P1**.
19. Press Ctrl + End and then type the text shown in Figure 3.2. Type the text exactly as shown. AutoCorrect will correct words as you type.
20. Save **WordL2_C3_P1.docx**.

Figure 3.2 Project 1a

fav

Na and vf Adventure

fct is partnering with fav(r) to provide adventurous and thrilling family vacations. Our first joint adventure is a holiday trip to Na. Na is one of the most fascinating holiday destinations in Africa and offers comfortable facilities, great food, cultural interaction, abundant wildlife, and a wide variety of activities to interest people of all ages.

During the 12-day trip, you and your family will travel across Na through national parks, enjoying the beautiful and exotic scenery and watching wildlife in natural habitats. You will cruise along the Kwando and Chobe rivers and spend time at the Okapuka Lodge located near Windhoek, the capital of Na.

fct and fav are offering a 15 percent discount if you sign up for this once-in-a-lifetime trip to Na. This exciting adventure is limited to twenty people, so don't wait to sign up!

Using the AutoCorrect Options Button

AutoCorrect Options

When AutoCorrect corrects text, rest the mouse pointer near the text and a small blue box displays below the corrected text. Move the mouse pointer to this blue box and the AutoCorrect Options button displays. Click this button and a drop-down list displays with options to change back to the original spelling, stop automatically correcting the specific text, and display the AutoCorrect dialog box.

Project 1b Using the AutoCorrect Options Button

1. With **WordL2_C3_P1.docx** open, select and then delete the last paragraph.
2. With the insertion point positioned below the second paragraph of text, type the text shown in Figure 3.3 (AutoCorrect will automatically change *Ameria* to *America*. You will change this in the next step.)
3. Change the spelling of *America* back to *Ameria* by completing the following steps:
   a. Position the mouse pointer over *America* until a blue box displays below the word.
   b. Position the mouse pointer on the blue box until the AutoCorrect Options button displays.
   c. Click the AutoCorrect Options button and then click the *Change back to "Ameria"* option.
4. Save and then print **WordL2_C3_P1.docx**.

Step 3c

> Through the sponsorship of America Resorts® we are able to offer you a 15 percent discount for groups of 20 or more people ⚡▾
>
> 🔄 Change back to "Ameria"
> Stop Automatically Correcting "Ameria"
> ⚡ Control AutoCorrect Options...

Figure 3.3 **Project 1b**

Through the sponsorship of Ameria Resorts(r) we are able to offer you a 15 percent discount for groups of 20 or more people.

Deleting AutoCorrect Text

You can delete text from the AutoCorrect dialog box. To do this, display the dialog box, click the desired word or words in the list box, and then click the Delete button.

Project 1c Deleting Text from AutoCorrect

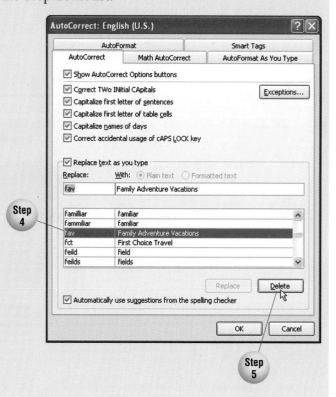

1. With **WordL2_C3_P1.docx** open, click the Office button and then click the Word Options button that displays at the bottom of the drop-down list.
2. At the Word Options dialog box, click *Proofing* in the left panel.
3. Click the AutoCorrect Options button in the *AutoCorrect options* section.
4. At the AutoCorrect dialog box, click *fav* in the list box. (You will need to scroll down the list box to display *fav*.)
5. Click the Delete button.
6. Click the *fct* option in the list box.
7. Click the Delete button.
8. Click the *Na* option in the list box.
9. Click the Delete button.
10. Click the *vf* option in the list box.
11. Click the Delete button.
12. Click OK to close the AutoCorrect dialog box.
13. Click OK to close the Word Options dialog box.
14. Save and then close **WordL2_C3_P1.docx**.

Project 2 Build a Document with Predesigned and Custom Building Blocks

You will open a report document and then add elements to the document by inserting predesigned building blocks.

Inserting Quick Parts

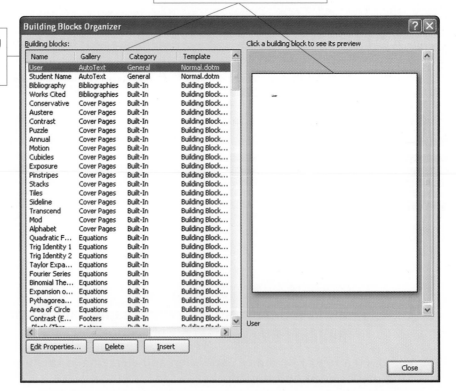

Word includes a variety of tools you can use to insert data such as text, fields, objects, and other items to help build a document. To view some of the tools available, click the Quick Parts button in the Text group in the Insert tab. This displays a drop-down list of choices for inserting document properties, fields, building blocks, connecting to the Microsoft Online site for additional content, and an option for saving selected data to the Quick Parts gallery.

Inserting Building Blocks

Building blocks are new tools you can use to develop or "build" a document. Word provides a number of building blocks you can insert in a document or you can create your own. To insert a building block into a document, click the Insert tab, click the Quick Parts button in the Text group, and then click *Building Blocks Organizer* at the drop-down list. This displays the Building Blocks Organizer dialog box shown in Figure 3.4. The dialog box displays columns of information about the building blocks. The columns in the dialog box display the building block name, the gallery that contains the building block, the template in which the building block is stored, the behavior of the building block, as well as a brief description.

Figure 3.4 Building Blocks Organizer Dialog Box

Click the desired building block in the list box and then preview the building block in the preview area.

Click a column heading to sort column entries alphabetically.

The Building Blocks Organizer dialog box is a central location where you can view all of the predesigned building blocks available in Word. You have been using some of the building blocks in previous chapters when you inserted a predesigned header or footer, cover page, page number, or watermark. The Building Blocks Organizer dialog box provides a convenient location for viewing and inserting building blocks.

Sorting Building Blocks

When you open the Building Blocks Organizer dialog box, the building blocks display in the list box sorted by the Gallery column. You can sort the building blocks by other columns by clicking the column heading. For example, to sort building blocks alphabetically by name click the *Name* column heading.

QUICK STEPS

Insert Building Block
1. Click Insert tab.
2. Click Quick Parts button.
3. Click *Building Blocks Organizer* at drop-down list.
4. Click desired building block.
5. Click Insert button.
6. Click Close.

Sort Building Blocks
1. Click Insert tab.
2. Click Quick Parts button.
3. Click *Building Blocks Organizer* at drop-down list.
4. Click desired column heading.

Project 2 — Inserting Predesigned Building Blocks

1. Open **WordReport11.docx** and then save the document and name it **WordL2_C3_P2**.
2. Make the following changes to the document:
   a. Insert a continuous section break at the beginning of the first paragraph below the title *CHAPTER 1: COMPUTER VIRUSES*.
   b. Insert a section break that begins a new page at the beginning of the title *CHAPTER 2: SECURITY RISKS* located in the middle of the third page.
   c. Insert a continuous section break at the beginning of the first paragraph below the title *CHAPTER 2: SECURITY RISKS*.
   d. Change the line spacing to 1.15 for the entire document.
   e. Format the section below the first title *CHAPTER 1: COMPUTER VIRUSES* into two columns of equal width.
   f. Balance the columns of text on the second page.
   g. Format the section below the second title *CHAPTER 2: SECURITY RISKS* into two equally spaced columns.
3. Sort the building blocks and then insert a table of contents building block by completing the following steps:
   a. Press Ctrl + Home, press Ctrl + Enter to insert a page break, and then press Ctrl + Home to move the insertion point back to the beginning of the document.

b. Click the Insert tab.

c. Click the Quick Parts button and then click *Building Blocks Organizer* at the drop-down list.

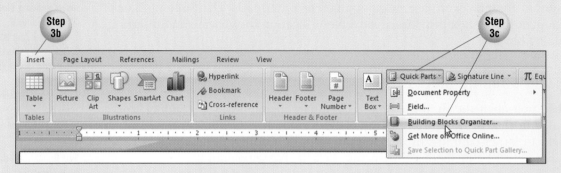

Step
3b

Step
3c

d. At the Building Blocks Organizer dialog box, notice the arrangement of building blocks in the list box. (More than likely, the building blocks are organized alphabetically by Gallery.)

e. Click the *Name* column heading. (This sorts the building blocks alphabetically by name. However, some blank building blocks may display at the beginning of the list box.)

Step
3e

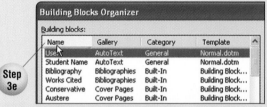

f. Scroll down the list box and then click *Automatic Table 1*. (You may see only a portion of the name. Click the name and the full name as well as a description display in the dialog box below the preview of the table of contents building block.)

g. Click the Insert button that displays toward the bottom of the dialog box. (This inserts a Contents page at the beginning of the page and uses the heading styles applied to the titles and headings in the document to create the table of contents.)

Step
3f

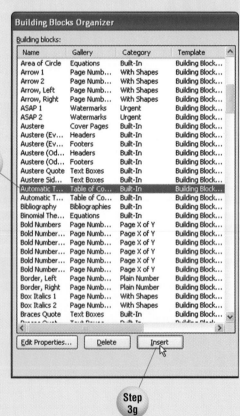

4. Apply the Heading 1 style to the title *CONTENTS* by completing the following steps:

a. Click on any character in the title *CONTENTS*.

b. Click the Home tab.

c. Click the *Heading 1* style in the Styles group.

5. Insert a sidebar building block by completing the following steps:

a. Position the insertion point at the beginning of the title *CHAPTER 1: COMPUTER VIRUSES*.

b. Click the Insert tab.

c. Click the Quick Parts button in the Text group.

d. Click *Building Blocks Organizer* at the drop-down list.

Step
3g

e. At the Building Blocks Organizer dialog box, scroll down the list box and then click *Tiles Sidebar* in the *Name* column. (This displays the sidebar in the preview section of the dialog box.)

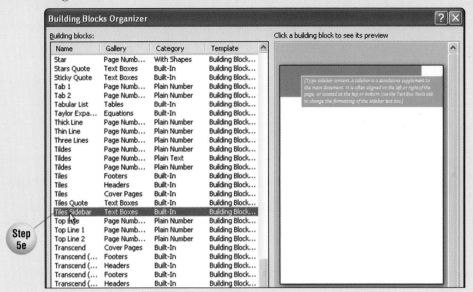

Step 5e

f. Click the Insert button that displays toward the bottom of the dialog box.
g. With the pull quote placeholder text selected, type "Although accurate estimates are difficult to pinpoint, businesses certainly lose millions of dollars a year in stolen computer hardware and software."
h. Select the text you just typed, change the font size to 14 points, and then deselect the text.
6. Insert a footer building block by completing the following steps:
   a. Click the Insert tab, click the Quick Parts button, and then click *Building Blocks Organizer*.
   b. Scroll down the Building Blocks Organizer list box, click the *Tiles* footer, and then click the Insert button.
   c. Click the placeholder text *[Type the company address]* and then type Northland Security Systems.

Step 6c

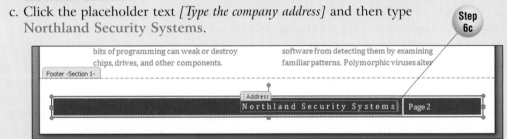

   d. Double-click in the document.
7. Insert a cover page building block by completing the following steps:
   a. Press Ctrl + Home to move the insertion point to the beginning of the document.
   b. Click the Insert tab, click the Quick Parts button, and then click *Building Blocks Organizer*.
   c. Scroll down the Building Blocks Organizer list box, click the *Tiles* cover page, and then click the Insert button.
   d. Click the placeholder text *[TYPE THE COMPANY NAME]* and then type Northland Security Systems.
   e. Click the placeholder text *[Type the document title]* and then type Computer Security.
   f. Click the placeholder text *[Type the document subtitle]* and then type Computer Viruses and Security Risks.

g. Click the placeholder text *[Type the author name]* and then type your first and last names.

h. Click the placeholder text *[Year]* and then type the current year.

8. Scroll through the document and look at each page in the document. The sidebar, footer, and cover page building blocks you inserted have similar formatting and are part of the *Tiles* group. Using building blocks from the same group provides consistency in the document and gives the document a polished and professional appearance. If the title *METHODS OF VIRUS OPERATION* displays at the beginning of the second column, remove the 20 points of spacing before the title.

9. Save, print, and then close **WordL2_C3_P2.docx**.

Project ③ Create a Letter Document Using Custom Building Blocks

You will create custom building blocks and then use those building blocks to prepare a business letter.

Saving Content to the Quick Part Gallery

Save Content to Quick Part Gallery
1. Select desired data.
2. Click Insert tab.
3. Click Quick Parts button.
4. Click *Save Selection to Quick Part Gallery* at drop-down list.
5. Type name and description of building block.
6. Click OK.

HINT
When selecting content to save as a building block, you may want to turn on the display of nonprinting characters by clicking the Show/Hide ¶ button in the Insert tab.

If you find yourself typing and formatting the same data on a regular basis, consider saving the data as a building block. Saving commonly created data as a building block saves you time and reduces errors that might occur each time you type data or apply formatting. When you save data as a building block it becomes available in the Building Blocks Organizer dialog box as well as the Quick Parts drop-down gallery. Before you create your own building blocks, clicking the Quick Parts button in the Insert group will display a drop-down list of choices. Create your own building block and then click the Quick Parts button, and your building blocks display at the beginning of the drop-down gallery.

To save data as a building block, select the desired data, click the Quick Parts button, and then click the *Save Selection to Quick Part Gallery* option at the drop-down list. This displays the Create New Building Block dialog box similar to the one shown in Figure 3.5. You can also display this dialog box by selecting the desired data and then pressing Alt + F3. At the Create New Building Block dialog box, type a name for the building block, decide whether to insert the building block in the General category or create a new category, provide a description, identify where to save the building block, and specify if you want only the content inserted in a document or the building block inserted in its own paragraph or page.

Figure 3.5 Create New Building Block Dialog Box

At this dialog box, type the building block name, specify the gallery and category, and write a description of the building block.

By default, building blocks you create are saved in the *Building Blocks.dotx* template. Click the down-pointing arrow at the right side of the *Save in* option and a drop-down list displays with the default choice of *Building Blocks.dotx* as well as *Normal.dotm*. Saving a building block in one of these templates makes it available each time you open Word. In a public environment such as a school, you may not be able to save data to a template. Before completing Project 3, check with your instructor to determine if you can save your building blocks. At the completion of Project 4, you will be instructed to delete the building blocks you create.

Project ③ₐ Creating a Building Block from Existing Files

1. As an employee of First Choice Travel, you type letters on a regular basis and decide that saving the letterhead as a building block will help you "build" a letter more efficiently. Complete the following steps to save the letterhead as a building block:
   a. Open **WordFCTLetterhead.docx**.
   b. Press Ctrl + A to select the entire document (picture image, text, and border line).
   c. Click the Insert tab.
   d. Click the Quick Parts button and then click *Save Selection to Quick Part Gallery* at the drop-down list.
   e. At the Create New Building Block dialog box, type your last name and then type FCT.
   f. Click OK to close the dialog box.

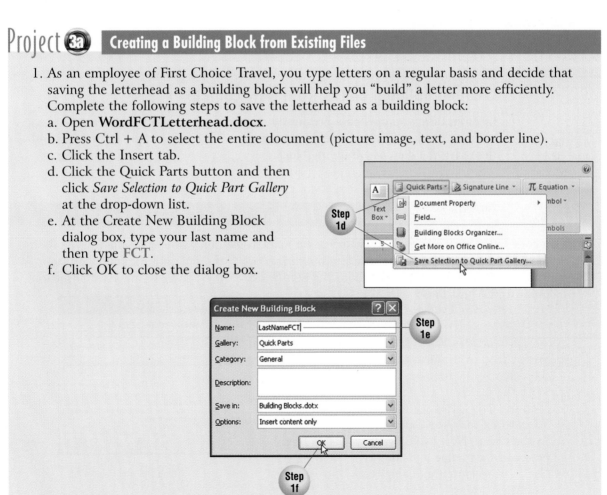

2. Click the Quick Parts button in the Text group and notice the letterhead that appears in the drop-down gallery.

3. Click in the document screen to remove the drop-down gallery.

4. Close **WordFCTLetterhead.docx** without saving it.

5. For many documents you create at First Choice Travel, you generally insert footer information. Since you are going to use the information on a regular basis you decide to save it as a building block by completing the following steps:

   a. Open **WordFCTFooter.docx**.

   b. Select the entire document and then press Alt + F3.

   c. At the Create New Building Block dialog box, type your last name and then type FCTFooter.

   d. Click OK to close the dialog box.

6. Click the Quick Parts button in the Text group and notice the letterhead and footer that appear in the drop-down gallery.

7. Click in the document screen to remove the gallery.

8. Close **WordFCTFooter.docx** without saving it.

Creating Building Blocks from New Content

In Project 3a, you opened a previously created document and then saved it as a building block. You can also type text, insert objects, and apply formatting and then save the data as a building block.

Project 3b · **Typing Text and Saving as a Building Block**

1. You correspond on a regular basis with Pacific Sky Cruise Lines so you decide to type their name and address and save the text as a building block by completing the following steps:

   a. At a blank document, type the following text (press Shift + Enter to move the insertion point to the next line):

      Pacific Sky Cruise Lines
      120 Montgomery Boulevard
      Los Angeles, CA 97032

   b. Press Ctrl + A to select the entire document and then change the font to 11-point Candara.

   c. With the text still selected, click the Insert tab, click the Quick Parts button, and then click *Save Selection to Quick Part Gallery*.

   d. At the Create New Building Block dialog box, type your last name and then type PacificSky.

   e. Click OK to close the dialog box.

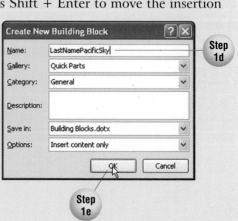

2. Create a building block with your name and company title by completing the following steps:
   a. Press Ctrl + End to move the insertion point to the end of the document.
   b. Press the Enter key.
   c. Type your first and last names.
   d. Press Shift + Enter to move the insertion point to the next line.
   e. Type Travel Consultant. (Make sure your name and title are set in 11-point Candara.)
   f. Select your name and the title, click the Insert tab, click the Quick Parts button, and then click *Save Selection to Quick Part Gallery*.
   g. At the Create New Building Block dialog box, type your last name and then type Title.
   h. Click OK to close the dialog box.
3. Close the document without saving it.

QUICK STEPS

Edit Building Blocks
1. Click Insert tab.
2. Click Quick Parts button, *Building Blocks Organizer*.
3. Click desired building block.
4. Click Edit Properties button.
5. Make desired changes.
6. Click OK.
OR
1. Click Insert tab.
2. Click Quick Parts button.
3. Right-click desired building block.
4. Click *Edit Properties*.
5. Make desired changes.
6. Click OK.

Editing Building Block Properties

You can make changes to the properties of a building block with options at the Modify Building Block dialog box. This dialog box contains the same options as the Create New Building Block dialog box. Display the Modify Building Block dialog box by opening the Building Blocks Organizer dialog box, clicking the desired building block in the list box, and then clicking the Edit Properties button. You can also display this dialog box for a building block that displays in the drop-down gallery. To do this, click the Quick Parts button, right-click on the building block that displays in the drop-down gallery, and then click *Edit Properties* at the shortcut menu.

Make desired changes to the options in the Modify Building Block dialog box and then click OK. At the message that displays asking if you want to redefine the building block entry, click Yes.

Project **3c** | **Editing Building Block Properties**

1. At a blank document, click the Insert tab, click the Quick Parts button, and then click *Building Blocks Organizer* at the drop-down list.
2. At the Building Blocks Organizer dialog box, make sure the building blocks display in the list box in alphabetical order by name. (If not, click the *Name* column heading.)
3. Scroll down to the location of the four building blocks you created that begin with your last name.

4. As you look at the building blocks, you realize that the letterhead building block name is *FCT* and does not provide information on what is in the building block. Edit the building block properties by completing the following steps:
   a. Click the building block that begins with your last name followed by FCT.
   b. Click the Edit Properties button located at the bottom of the dialog box.
   c. At the Modify Document Properties dialog box, click in the *Name* text box and then add *Letterhead* to the end of the name.
   d. Click in the *Description* text box and then type Inserts the First Choice Travel letterhead including the company name and address.
   e. Click OK to close the dialog box.

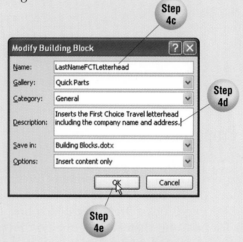

Step 4c

Step 4d

Step 4e

f. At the message asking if you want to redefine the building blocks entry, click Yes.
5. Edit the building block that begins with your last name followed by *PacificSky* and then insert the following text in the *Description* text box: Inserts Pacific Sky Cruise Lines name and address.
6. Close the Building Blocks Organizer dialog box.

QUICK STEPS

Inserting Custom Building Blocks

Insert Custom Building Block
1. Click Insert tab.
2. Click Quick Parts button.
3. Click desired building block at drop-down gallery.
OR
1. Click Insert tab.
2. Click Quick Parts button, *Building Blocks Organizer.*
3. Click desired building block.
4. Click Insert button.

A building block you create is available at the Building Blocks Organizer dialog box as well as the Quick Parts drop-down gallery. Insert your building block by clicking the Quick Parts button and then clicking the building block at the drop-down gallery or by displaying the Building Blocks Organizer dialog box, clicking the desired building block, and then clicking the Insert button.

You can specify where you want the building block inserted by clicking the Quick Parts button, right-clicking the building block in the drop-down gallery, and then choosing the desired location at the shortcut menu similar to the one shown in Figure 3.6.

Figure 3.6 Quick Parts Button Drop-down Gallery Shortcut Menu

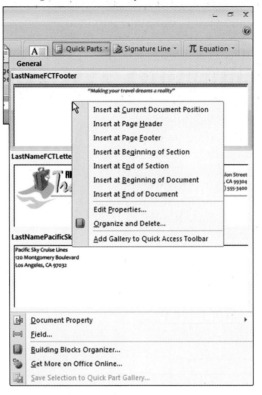

Right-click the desired building block at the Quick Parts drop-down gallery and then click the location for inserting the building block at the shortcut menu.

Project 3d **Inserting Custom Building Blocks**

1. At a blank document, insert the letterhead building block you created by clicking the Insert tab, clicking the Quick Parts button, and then clicking the First Choice Travel letterhead at the drop-down gallery.
2. Type today's date and then press the Enter key twice.
3. Type **Mrs. Jody Lancaster** and then press Shift + Enter.
4. Insert the Pacific Sky Cruise Lines company name and address building block by clicking the Quick Parts button and then clicking the building block at the drop-down gallery.
5. Make sure the insertion point is positioned on the line below the address.
6. Insert a letter document by completing the following steps:
   a. Make sure the Insert tab is selected
   b. Click the Object button arrow and then click *Text from File.*

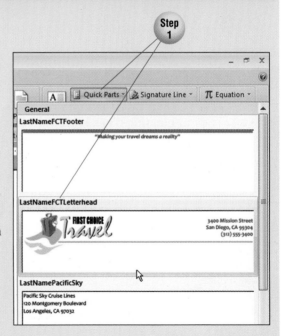

Step 1

c. At the Insert File dialog box, navigate to the Word2007L2C3 folder and then double-click *WordPacificSkyLetter01.docx*.

d. Press Ctrl + End to move the insertion point to the end of the document, type Sincerely, and then press the Enter key twice.

7. Insert your name and title building block by clicking the Quick Parts button and then clicking your name in the drop-down gallery.

8. Insert the footer building block you created by clicking the Quick Parts button, right-clicking the footer building block, and then clicking *Insert at Page Footer* in the shortcut menu.

9. Select the text in the document (excluding the text in the letterhead and footer) and then change the font to 11-point Candara.

10. Save the completed letter and name it **WordL2_C3_P3**.

11. Print and then close **WordL2_C3_P3.docx**.

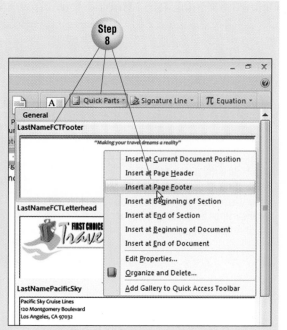

Project 4 Create a Letter Document with Modified Building Blocks

You will modify your custom building blocks and then use the building blocks to prepare a business letter. You will then delete your custom building blocks.

Modify a Building Block
1. Insert desired building block.
2. Make corrections or changes.
3. Select modified building block.
4. Click Insert tab.
5. Click Quick Parts button, *Save Selection to Quick Part Gallery*.
6. Type original name, category, and gallery for building block.
7. Click OK.
8. Click Yes.

Modifying a Building Block

You can insert a building block in a document, make corrections or changes, and then save the building block with the same name or a different name. Save a building block with the same name when you want to update the building block to reflect any changes. Save the building block with a new name if you want to use an existing building block as a beginning to creating a new building block.

To save a modified building block with the same name, insert the building block in the document and then make the desired modifications. Select the building block data, click the Insert tab, click the Quick Parts button, and then click *Save Selection to Quick Part Gallery*. At the Create New Building Block dialog box, type the original name, category, and gallery for the building block and then click OK. At the message asking if you want to redefine the building block entry, click Yes.

Project 4a Modifying Building Blocks

1. As a travel consultant at First Choice Travel, you have been given a promotion and are now a senior travel consultant. You decide to modify your name and title building block by completing the following steps:
   a. At a blank document, click the Insert tab, click the Quick Parts button, and then click your name and title building block in the drop-down gallery.
   b. Edit your title so it displays as *Senior Travel Consultant*.
   c. Select your name and title, click the Quick Parts button, and then click *Save Selection to Quick Part Gallery* option.
   d. At the Create New Building Block dialog box, type the original name (your last name followed by *Title*).
   e. Click OK.
   f. At the message asking if you want to redefine the building block entry, click Yes.

Step 1d

Step 1e

2. Since most of the correspondences you send to Pacific Sky Cruise Lines are addressed to Jody Lancaster, you decide to include her name at the beginning of the company name and address by completing the following steps:
   a. Click the Insert tab, click the Quick Parts button, and then click the Pacific Sky Cruise Lines name and address building block at the drop-down gallery.
   b. Insert the name *Mrs. Jody Lancaster* above the name of the cruise line.
   c. Select the name, company name, and address.
   d. Click the Quick Parts button and then click *Save Selection to Quick Part Gallery* option.
   e. At the Create New Building Block dialog box, type the original name (your last name followed by *PacificSky*).
   f. Click OK.
   g. At the message asking if you want to redefine the building block entry, click Yes.

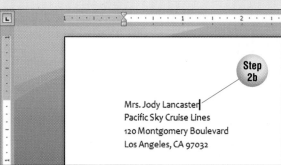

Step 2b

3. Close the document without saving it.
4. Create a business letter by completing the following steps:
   a. Click the New button on the Quick Access toolbar (or press Ctrl + N).
   b. At the blank document, insert the First Choice Travel letterhead building block.
   c. Type today's date and then press the Enter key twice.
   d. Insert the building block that includes Jody Lancaster's name as well as the cruise line name and address.
   e. Insert the file named **WordPacificSkyLetter02.docx** located in the Word2007L2C3 folder on your storage medium. ***Hint: Do this with the Object button in the Text group in the Insert tab.***
   f. Type Sincerely, and then press the Enter key twice.
   g. Insert the building block that contains your name and title.
   h. Insert the footer building block you created by clicking the Quick Parts button, right-clicking the footer building block, and then clicking *Insert at Page Footer* in the shortcut list.

5. Select the text in the document (excluding the text in the letterhead and footer) and then change the font to 11-point Candara.
6. Save the completed letter and name it **WordL2_C3_P4**.
7. Print and then close **WordL2_C3_P4.docx**.

QUICK STEPS

Delete Building Block
1. Click Insert tab.
2. Click Quick Parts button, *Building Blocks Organizer*.
3. Click desired building block.
4. Click Delete button.
5. Click Yes.
6. Click Close.
OR
1. Click Insert tab.
2. Click Quick Parts button.
3. Right-click desired building block in drop-down gallery.
4. Click *Organize and Delete* at shortcut menu.
5. Click Delete button.
6. Click Yes.
7. Click Close.

Deleting Building Blocks

If you no longer use a building block you created, consider deleting it. To do this, display the Building Blocks Organizer dialog box, click the building block you want to delete, and then click the Delete button. At the message asking if you are sure you want to delete the selected building block, click Yes.

You can display the Building Blocks Organizer dialog box by clicking the Quick Parts button and then clicking *Building Blocks Organizer* at the drop-down list. You can also display the dialog box with the building block you want to delete selected by clicking the Quick Parts button, right-clicking the building block, and then clicking *Organize and Delete* at the shortcut menu. This displays the Building Blocks Organizer dialog box with the building block selected. Click the Delete button and then answer yes to the confirmation question.

Project 4b   Deleting Building Blocks

1. At a blank document, delete the FCTLetterhead building block (that is preceded by your last name) by completing the following steps:
   a. Click the Insert tab and then click the Quick Parts button.
   b. Right-click the FCTLetterhead building block (preceded by your last name) and then click *Organize and Delete*.
   c. At the Building Blocks Organizer dialog box with the building block selected, click the Delete button.
   d. At the message that displays asking if you are sure you want to delete the selected building block, click Yes.
2. Close the Building Blocks Organizer dialog box.
3. Complete steps similar to those in Step 1 to delete the three other building blocks you created (the FCTFooter, PacificSky, and Title that are all preceded by your last name).

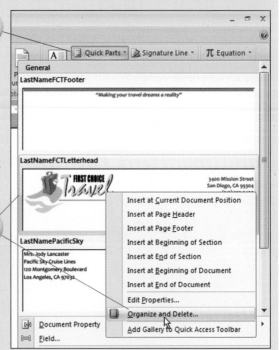

Project 5 Navigate and Insert Hyperlinks in a Computer Viruses Report

You will open a report containing information on computer viruses and navigate in the document using Document Map, Thumbnails, bookmarks, hyperlinks, and cross-references.

Navigating in a Document

Word offers a number of methods you can use to navigate to specific locations in a document. Navigating is particularly useful in lengthy, multiple-paged documents. Some navigating methods include Document Map, Thumbnails, bookmarks, hyperlinks, and cross-references.

In a previous chapter, you learned about the Document Map and Thumbnails features. Turn on the Document Map feature by clicking the View tab and then clicking the *Document Map* check box. This displays the Document Map navigation pane at the left side of the screen. The navigation pane displays any headings that are formatted with heading styles. If no headings are formatted with heading styles, Document Map searches for paragraphs that look like headings, such as short lines set in a larger type size. To navigate in the document, click the desired heading in the navigation pane. Click the *Thumbnails* check box in the View tab and miniature page thumbnails display in the navigation pane. Click a thumbnail and that page displays in the document screen.

QUICK STEPS

Navigate in Document
1. Click View tab.
2. Click *Document Map* check box.
3. Click desired heading in navigation pane.
OR
1. Click View tab.
2. Click *Thumbnails* check box.
3. Click miniature page thumbnails in navigation pane.

1. Open **WordReport11.docx** and then save the document and name it **WordL2_C4_P5**.
2. Insert a file by completing the following steps:
   a. Press Ctrl + End to move the insertion point to the end of the document.
   b. Press Ctrl + Enter to insert a page break.
   c. Click the Insert tab.
   d. Click the Object button arrow and then click *Text from File*.
   e. At the Insert File dialog box, navigate to the Word2007L2C4 folder on your storage medium and then double-click **WordReport13.docx**.
   f. Select the entire document and then change the line spacing to 1.5.
3. Move the insertion point to the beginning of the *CHAPTER 2: SECURITY RISKS* title and then press Ctrl + Enter to insert a page break.
4. Since this document has title and heading styles applied you can easily navigate in the document with the Document Map feature by completing the following steps:
   a. Click the View tab.
   b. Click the *Document Map* check box.
   c. Click the Chapter 1 heading in the Document Map navigation pane. (This displays the beginning of the document.)

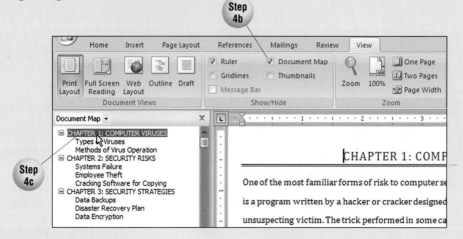

d. Click the Employee Theft heading in the navigation pane.
5. Click the *Thumbnails* check box in the Show/Hide group in the View tab.
6. Click the page 1 thumbnail to view the beginning of the document.
7. Click the page 3 thumbnail.
8. Click the *Thumbnails* check box to remove the check mark and close the navigation pane.
9. Save **WordL2_C4_P5.docx**,

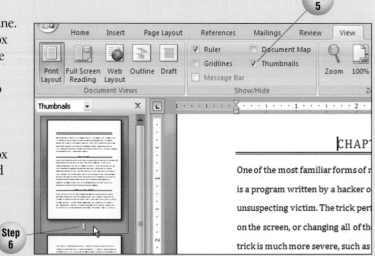

Navigating with Bookmarks

In a long document, you may find marking a location in the document useful so you can quickly move the insertion point to the location. Create bookmarks for locations in a document at the Bookmark dialog box. To create a bookmark, position the insertion point at the desired location, click the Insert tab, and then click the Bookmark button in the Links group. This displays the Bookmark dialog box shown in Figure 4.8. Type a name for the bookmark in the *Bookmark name* text box and then click the Add button. Repeat these steps as many times as needed to insert the desired bookmarks. Give each bookmark a unique name. A bookmark must begin with a letter and it can contain numbers but not spaces. Use the underscore character if you want to separate words in a bookmark name.

By default, bookmarks you insert are not visible in the document. Turn on the display of bookmarks at the Word Options dialog box with *Advanced* selected. Display this dialog box by clicking the Office button and then clicking the Word Options button. At the Word Options dialog box, click the *Advanced* option in the left panel. Click the *Show bookmarks* check box in the *Show document content* section to insert a check mark. Complete similar steps to turn off the display of bookmarks. A bookmark displays in the document as an I-beam marker.

You can also create a bookmark for selected text. To do this, select the text first and then complete the steps to create a bookmark. When you create a bookmark for selected text, a left bracket ([) indicates the beginning of the selected text and a right bracket (]) indicates the end of selected text.

Create a Bookmark
1. Position insertion point at desired location.
2. Click Insert tab.
3. Click Bookmark button.
4. Type name for bookmark.
5. Click Add button.

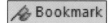

HINT
Bookmark brackets do not print.

Figure 4.8 Bookmark Dialog Box

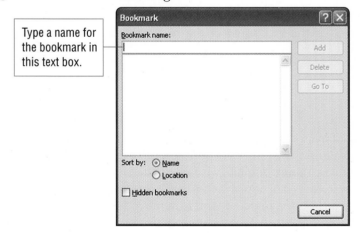

Type a name for the bookmark in this text box.

1. With **WordL2_C4_P5.docx** open, turn on the display of bookmarks by completing the following steps:
   a. Click the Office button and then click the Word Options button that displays at the bottom of the drop-down list.
   b. At the Word Options dialog box, click *Advanced* in the left panel.
   c. Click the *Show bookmarks* check box in the *Show document content* section to insert a check mark.
   d. Click OK to close the dialog box.
2. Insert a bookmark by completing the following steps:
   a. Move the insertion point to the beginning of the *TYPES OF VIRUSES* section (the paragraph that begins *Viruses can be categorized . . .*).
   b. Click the Insert tab.
   c. Click the Bookmark button in the Links group.
   d. At the Bookmark dialog box, type **Viruses** in the *Bookmark name* text box.
   e. Click the Add button.

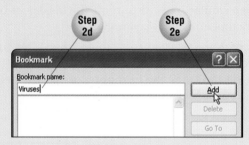

3. Insert a bookmark named *Electrical* at the beginning of the paragraph in the *SYSTEMS FAILURE* section.
4. Insert a bookmark named *Strategies* at the beginning of the first paragraph in the *CHAPTER 3: SECURITY STRATEGIES* section.
5. Save **WordL2_C4_P5.docx**.

QUICK STEPS

Navigate with Bookmarks
1. Click Insert tab.
2. Click Bookmark button.
3. Double-click desired bookmark name.

After you insert bookmarks in a document, you can move the insertion point to a specific bookmark. To do this, display the Bookmark dialog box, and then double-click the bookmark name. You can also click the Bookmark name and then click the Go To button. When Word stops at the location of the bookmark, click the Close button to close the dialog box. If you move the insertion point to a bookmark created with selected text, Word moves the insertion point to the bookmark and selects the text. Delete bookmarks in the Bookmark dialog box by clicking the bookmark name in the list box and then clicking the Delete button.

Project 5C — Navigating Using Bookmarks and Deleting Bookmarks

1. With **WordL2_C4_P5.docx** open, navigate to the Viruses bookmark by completing the following steps:
   a. If necessary, click the Insert tab.
   b. Click the Bookmark button in the Links group.
   c. At the Bookmark dialog box, click *Viruses* in the list box.
   d. Click the Go To button.

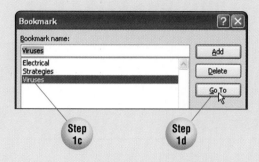

Step 1c

Step 1d

2. With the Bookmark dialog box open, navigate to the Strategies bookmark by double-clicking *Strategies* in the list box.
3. With the Bookmark dialog box open, delete the *Electrical* bookmark by clicking *Electrical* in the list box and then clicking the Delete button.
4. Click the Close button to close the Bookmark dialog box.
5. Save **WordL2_C4_P5.docx**.

Inserting Hyperlinks

You can insert a hyperlink in a document that you can click to navigate to a specific location in the document, display a different document, open a file in a different program, create a new document, or link to an e-mail address. Click the Hyperlink button in the Links group in the Insert tab and the Insert Hyperlink dialog box displays similar to what you see in Figure 4.9. At this dialog box, identify where you want to link, the location of the link, a location for the link, and to customize the hyperlink ScreenTip. You can also display the Insert Hyperlink dialog box by pressing Ctrl + K.

Insert Hyperlink
1. Click Insert tab.
2. Click Hyperlink button.
3. Make desired changes at the Insert Hyperlink dialog box.
4. Click OK.

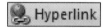

Figure 4.9 Insert Hyperlink Dialog Box

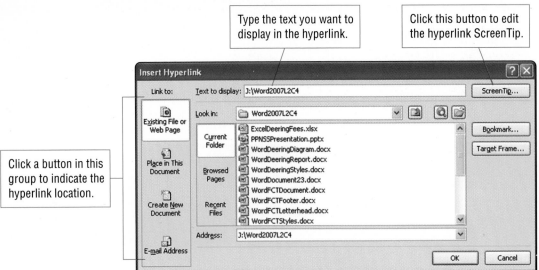

Type the text you want to display in the hyperlink.

Click this button to edit the hyperlink ScreenTip.

Click a button in this group to indicate the hyperlink location.

Linking to a Place in the Document

To create a hyperlink to another location in the document, you need to mark the location by either applying heading styles to text or inserting bookmarks. To hyperlink to a heading or bookmark in a document, display the Insert Hyperlink dialog box and then click the Place in This Document button in the *Link to* group. This displays any text with heading styles applied as well as bookmarks in the *Select a place in this document* list box. Click the desired heading style or bookmark name and the heading or bookmark name displays in the *Text to display* text box. You can leave the text as displayed or you can select the text and then type the text you want to appear in the document.

Navigate to a hyperlink by hovering the mouse over the hyperlink text, holding down the Ctrl key, and then clicking the left mouse button. When you hover the mouse over hyperlink text, a ScreenTip displays with the name of the heading or bookmark. If you want specific information to display in the ScreenTip, click the ScreenTip button in the Insert Hyperlink dialog box, type the desired text in the Set Hyperlink ScreenTip dialog box, and then click OK.

Project **5** | **Inserting a Hyperlink to a Location in the Document**

1. With **WordL2_C4_P5.docx** open, insert a hyperlink to a location in the document by completing the following steps:
   a. Position the insertion point immediately right of the period that ends the first paragraph of text in the *CHAPTER 1: COMPUTER VIRUSES* section.
   b. Press the spacebar once.
   c. If necessary, click the Insert tab.
   d. Click the Hyperlink button.
   e. At the Insert Hyperlink dialog box, click the Place in This Document button in the *Link to* group.

f. Scroll down the *Select a place in this document* list box and then click *Strategies* that displays below *Bookmarks* in the list box.

g. Select the text that displays in the *Text to display* text box and then type Click to view strategies.

h. Click the ScreenTip button located in the upper right corner of the dialog box. At the Set Hyperlink ScreenTip dialog box, type View computer security strategies and then click OK.

i. Click OK to close the Insert Hyperlink dialog box.

2. Navigate to the hyperlinked location by hovering the mouse over the *Click to view strategies* hyperlink, holding down the Ctrl key, and then clicking the left mouse button.

3. Save **WordL2_C4_P5.docx**.

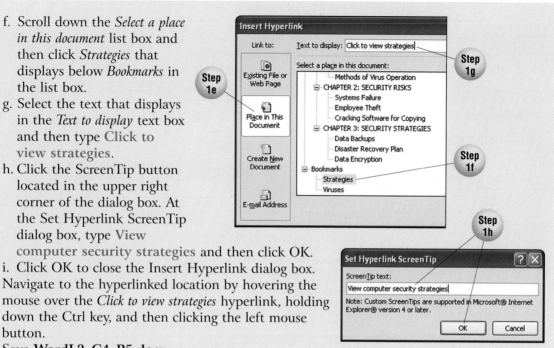

Linking to a File in Another Program

In some situations, you may want to provide information to your readers from a variety of locations. You may want to provide information in a Word document, an Excel spreadsheet, as well as a PowerPoint presentation. To link a Word document to a file in another application, display the Insert Hyperlink dialog box and then click the Existing File or Web Page button in the *Link to* group. Use the *Look in* option to navigate to the folder containing the desired file and then click the file. Make other changes in the Insert Hyperlink dialog box as needed and then click OK.

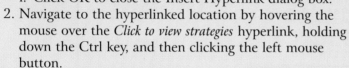
Project 5e · **Inserting a Hyperlink to a PowerPoint Presentation**

1. The **WordL2_C4_P5.docx** contains information used by Northland Security Systems and the company also has a PowerPoint presentation with similar information. You decide to link the document with the presentation by completing the following steps:

a. Press Ctrl + End to move the insertion point to the end of the document.

b. If necessary, click the Insert tab.

c. Click the Hyperlink button in the Links group.

d. Click the Existing File or Web Page button in the *Link to* group.
e. Click the down-pointing arrow at the right side of the *Look in* list box and then navigate to the Word2007L2C4 folder on your storage medium.
f. Click the presentation named **PPNSSPresentation.pptx** in the list box.
g. Select the text in the *Text to display* text box in the dialog box and then type Computer Viruses Presentation.
h. Click OK to close the Insert Hyperlink dialog box.

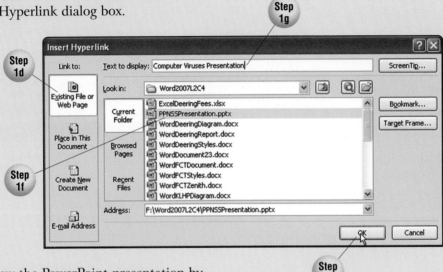

2. View the PowerPoint presentation by completing the following steps:
   a. Position the mouse pointer over the *Computer Viruses Presentation* hyperlink, hold down the Ctrl key, and then click the left mouse button.
   b. At the PowerPoint presentation, click the Slide Show button in the View area on the Status bar.
   c. Click the left mouse button to advance each slide.
   d. Click the left mouse button at the black screen that displays the message *End of slide show, click to exit*.
   e. Close the presentation and PowerPoint by clicking the Close button (contains an X) that displays in the upper right corner of the screen.
3. Save **WordL2_C4_P5.docx**.

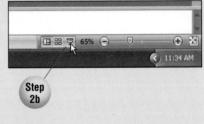

Creating a Cross-Reference

A cross-reference in a Word document refers the reader to another location within the document. This feature is useful in a long document or a document containing related information. You can insert a reference to an item such as a heading, figure, or table. For example, you can insert a cross-reference that refers readers to another location with more information about the topic, refers readers to a specific table, or refers readers to a specific page. Cross-references are inserted in a document as hyperlinks.

To insert a cross-reference, type introductory text, click the Insert tab, and then click the Cross-reference button in the Links group. This displays the Cross-reference dialog box similar to the one shown in Figure 4.10. At the Cross-reference dialog box, identify the reference type, where to refer, and the specific text.

The reference identified in the Cross-reference dialog box displays immediately after the introductory text. To move to the specified reference, hold down the Ctrl key, position the mouse pointer over the introductory text (pointer turns into a hand), and then click the left mouse button.

QUICK STEPS

Insert a Cross-reference
1. Type introductory text.
2. Click Insert tab.
3. Click Cross-reference button.
4. Identify reference type, where to refer, and specific text.
5. Click Insert.
6. Click Close.

Figure 4.10 Cross-reference Dialog Box

At this dialog box, identify the reference type, where to refer, and the specific reference text.

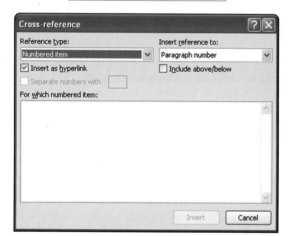

Project ⑤   **Inserting and Navigating with Cross-references**

1. With **WordL2_C4_P5.docx** open, insert a cross-reference in the document by completing the following steps:
   a. Move the insertion point so it is positioned immediately right of the period that ends the paragraph in the *TYPES OF VIRUSES* section.
   b. Press the spacebar once and then type (For more information, refer to.
   c. Press the spacebar once.
   d. If necessary, click the Insert tab.
   e. Click the Cross-reference button in the Links group.

f. At the Cross-reference dialog box, click the down-pointing arrow at the right side of the *Reference type* list box and then click *Heading* at the drop-down list.

g. Click *Data Backups* in the *For which heading* list box.

h. Click the Insert button.

i. Click the Close button to close the dialog box.

j. At the document, type a period followed by the right parenthesis.

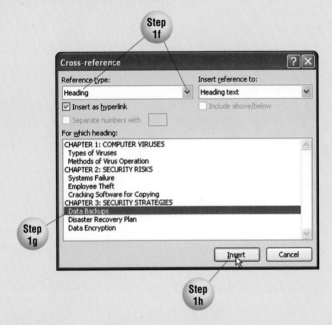

2. Move to the reference text by holding down the Ctrl key, positioning the mouse pointer over *Data Backups* until the pointer turns into a hand, and then clicking the left mouse button.

3. Save **WordL2_C4_P5.docx**.

4. Print page 1 and page 6 of the document.

5. Turn off the display of bookmarks by completing the following steps:

   a. Click the Office button and then click the Word Options button that displays at the bottom of the drop-down list.

   b. At the Word Options dialog box, click *Advanced* in the left panel.

   c. Click the *Show bookmarks* check box in the *Show document content* section to remove the check mark.

   d. Click OK to close the dialog box.

6. Close **WordL2_C4_P5.docx**.

CHAPTER 5

Inserting Special Features and References

PERFORMANCE OBJECTIVES

Upon successful completion of Chapter 5, you will be able to:

- Sort text in paragraphs, columns, and tables
- Sort records in a data source file
- Select specific records in a data source file for merging
- Insert nonbreaking spaces
- Find and replace special characters
- Create and use a specialized template
- Create footnotes and endnotes
- Insert and modify sources and citations
- Insert, modify, and format bibliographies

Tutorial 5.1
Sorting and Selecting Text
Tutorial 5.2
Working with Footnotes and Endnotes
Tutorial 5.3
Using Sources, Citations, and Bibliographies

In Word, you can sort text in paragraphs, columns, and tables and sort records in a data source file. You can also select specific records in a data source file for merging with a main document. If you want to control the line break within text, consider inserting nonbreaking spaces and use the find and replace feature to search for special characters in a document such as nonprinting characters. You can use the default template provided by Word or you can create and use your own specialized template.

When you prepare research papers and reports, citing information sources properly is important. In this chapter, you will learn to reference documents and acknowledge sources using footnotes, endnotes, citations, and bibliographies.

Note: Before beginning computer projects, copy to your storage medium the Word2007L2C5 subfolder from the Word2007L2 folder on the CD that accompanies this textbook and then make Word2007L2C5 the active folder.

Project ① Sort Company Information

You will open a document containing information on company employees and then sort data in paragraphs, columns, and tables. You will also create a document and insert nonbreaking spaces within keyboard shortcuts.

Sorting Text in Paragraphs

Sort Text in Paragraph
1. Click Sort button.
2. Make any needed changes at the Sort Text dialog box.
3. Click OK.

Display Sort Options Dialog Box
1. Click Sort button.
2. Click Options button.

Sort

You can sort paragraphs of text in a document alphanumerically, numerically, or by date. For example, you might want to sort a list of company employees to create an internal telephone directory or to create a list for a company-wide mailing. Other situations in which sorting a Word document is an effective problem-solving method are times when you need to organize a list of customers by ZIP Code or by product purchased (product number).

In an alphanumeric sort, punctuation marks or special symbols are sorted first, followed by numbers, and then text. If you sort paragraphs either alphanumerically or numerically, dates are treated as regular text. Also be aware that during a paragraph sort, any blank lines in a document are moved to the beginning of the document.

To sort text, select the text and then click the Sort button in the Paragraph group in the Home tab. This displays the Sort Text dialog box containing sorting options. The *Sort by* option has a default setting of *Paragraphs*. This default setting changes depending on the text in the document. For example, if you are sorting a table, the *Sort by* option has a default setting of *Column 1*. The *Sort by* options will also vary depending on selections at the Sort Options dialog box shown in Figure 5.1. To display this dialog box, click the Options button in the Sort Text dialog box. At the Sort Options dialog box, specify how fields are separated.

Figure 5.1 Sort Options Dialog Box

In this section, specify how fields are separated.

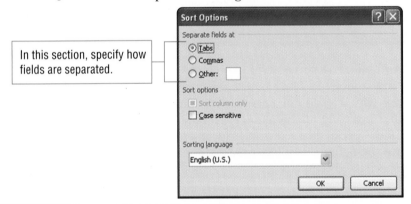

Project 1a Sorting by First and Last Names

1. Open **WordSort01.docx** and then save the document and name it **WordL2_C5_P1**.
2. Sort the text alphabetically by first name by completing the following steps:
   a. Select the eight lines of text at the beginning of the document.
   b. Click the Sort button in the Paragraph group in the Home tab.

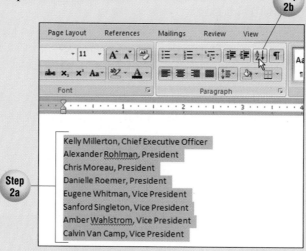

Step 2b

Step 2a

c. At the Sort Text dialog box, click OK.
3. Sort the text by last name by completing the following steps:
   a. With the eight lines of text still selected, click the Sort button.
   b. At the Sort Text dialog box, click the Options button.
   c. At the Sort Options dialog box, click *Other* and then press the spacebar. (This indicates the first and last names are separated by a space.)
   d. Click OK.
   e. At the Sort Text dialog box, click the down-pointing arrow at the right side of the *Sort by* and then click *Word 2* at the drop-down list.
   f. Click OK.
4. Save **WordL2_C5_P1.docx**.

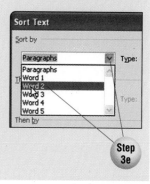

Step 3e

Sorting Text in Columns

To sort text set in columns, the text must be separated with tabs. When sorting text in columns, Word considers the left margin *Field 1*, text typed at the first tab is considered *Field 2*, and so on. When sorting text in columns, make sure columns of text are separated by only one tab. If you press the Tab key more than once between columns, Word recognizes each tab as a separate column. Thus pressing the Tab key more than once may result in a field number that corresponds to an empty column rather than the desired column.

QUICK STEPS

Sort Text in Columns
1. Select specific text.
2. Click Sort button.
3. Click Options button.
4. Specify *Tabs* as separator.
5. Click OK.
6. Make any needed changes at Sort Text dialog box.
7. Click OK.

Project 1b Sorting Text in Columns

1. With **WordL2_C5_P1.docx** open, sort text in columns by completing the following steps:
   a. Select the seven lines of text set in columns.
   b. Click the Sort button in the Paragraph group in the Home tab.
   c. Click the Options button.
   d. At the Sort Options dialog box, make sure the *Separate fields at* option is set at *Tabs* and then click OK to close the dialog box.

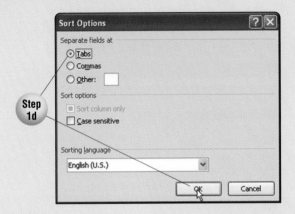

Step 1d

   e. At the Sort Text dialog box, click the down-pointing arrow at the right side of the *Sort by* option and then click *Employee* at the drop-down list.
   f. Click OK.
2. With the columns of text still selected, sort the third column of text numerically by completing the following steps:
   a. Click the Sort button.
   b. Click the down-pointing arrow at the right side of the *Sort by* option and then click *Ext.* at the drop-down list.
   c. Click OK.
3. Save **WordL2_C5_P1.docx**.

Sorting on More Than One Field

HINT

When sorting on two fields, Word sorts on the first field and then sorts the second field within the first.

When sorting text, you can sort on more than one field. For example, in Project 1c you will sort the department entries alphabetically and then sort the employee names alphabetically within the departments. To do this, you specify the department column in the *Sort by* option and then specify the employee column in the *Then by* option. If a document contains columns with heading text, click the *Header row* option in the *My list has* section.

Project 1c — Sorting on Two Fields

1. With **WordL2_C5_P1.docx** open, sort two columns by completing the following steps:
   a. Make sure the seven lines of text set in columns are still selected.
   b. Click the Sort button.
   c. At the Sort Text dialog box, if necessary, click the *Header row* option in the *My list has* section of the dialog box.
   d. Click the down-pointing arrow at the right side of the *Sort by* option and then click *Department*.
   e. Click the down-pointing arrow at the right side of the *Then by* option and then click *Employee* at the drop-down list.
   f. Click OK.
2. Save **WordL2_C5_P1.docx**.

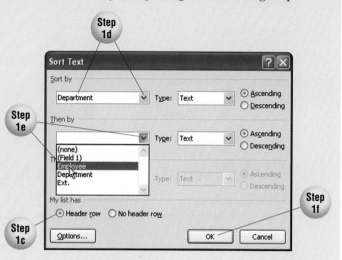

Sorting Text in Tables

Sorting text in columns within tables is similar to sorting columns of text separated by tabs. If a table contains a header, you can tell Word not to include the header row when sorting by clicking the *Header row* option at the Sort dialog box. The Sort Text dialog box becomes the Sort dialog box when sorting a table. If you want to sort only specific cells in a table, select the cells and then complete the sort.

QUICK STEPS

Sort Text in Table
1. Position insertion point in table.
2. Click Sort button.
3. Make any needed changes at Sort dialog box.
4. Click OK.

Project 1d — Sorting Text in a Table

1. With **WordL2_C5_P1.docx** open, sort text in the first column in the table by completing the following steps:
   a. Position the insertion point in any cell in the table.
   b. Click the Sort button.
   c. At the Sort dialog box, make sure the *Header row* option is selected in the *My list has* section.
   d. Click the down-pointing arrow at the right side of the *Sort by* option and then click *Sales, First Half* at the drop-down list.
   e. Click OK.
2. Sort the numbers in the third column in descending order by completing the following steps:
   a. Select all of the cells in the table except the cells in the first row.
   b. Click the Sort button.

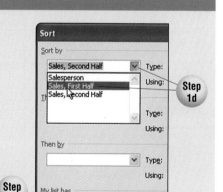

c. Click the down-pointing arrow at the right side of the *Sort by* option and then click *Column 3* at the drop-down list.
d. Click *Descending*.
e. Click OK.

3. Save, print, and then close **WordL2_C5_P1.docx**.

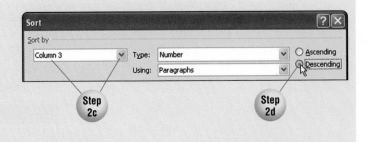

Project ② **Sort and Select Records in a Data Source File**

You will sort data in a data source file and then create labels and select specific records in a data source file and then create labels.

Sorting Records in a Data Source

When you are working on a project that requires sorting data and merging documents, consider the order in which you want your merged documents printed and then sort the data before merging. To sort records in a data source, click the Mailings tab, click the Select Recipients button, and then click *Use Existing List*. At the Select Data Source dialog box, navigate to the folder containing the data source file and then double-click the file. Click the Edit Recipient List button in the Start Mail Merge group in the Mailings tab and the Mail Merge Recipients dialog box displays similar to the one shown in Figure 5.2.

Figure 5.2 Mail Merge Recipients Dialog Box

To sort on a specific field, click on the column heading.

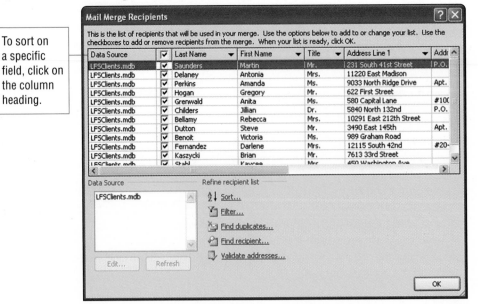

Click the column heading to sort data in a specific column in ascending order. To perform additional sorts, click the down-pointing arrow at the right side of the column heading and then click the desired sort order. You can also click the *Sort* hyperlink located in the *Refine recipient list* section of the Mail Merge Recipients dialog box. Clicking this hyperlink displays the Filter and Sort dialog box with the Sort Records tab selected as shown in Figure 5.3. The options at the dialog box are similar to the options available at the Sort Text (and Sort) dialog box.

Figure 5.3 Filter and Sort Dialog Box with Sort Records Tab Selected

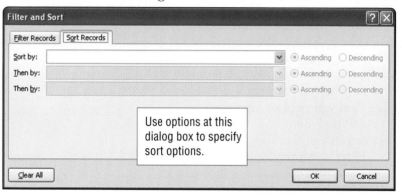

Project 2a Sorting Data in a Data Source

1. At a blank document, click the Mailings tab, click the Start Mail Merge button in the Start Mail Merge group, and then click *Labels* at the drop-down list.
2. At the Label Options dialog box, click the down-pointing arrow at the right side of the *Label vendors* option and then click *Avery US Letter* at the drop-down list. Scroll down the *Product number* list box, click *5160* in the *Product number* list box, and then click OK.
3. Click the Select Recipients button in the Start Mail Merge group and then click *Use Existing List* at the drop-down list.

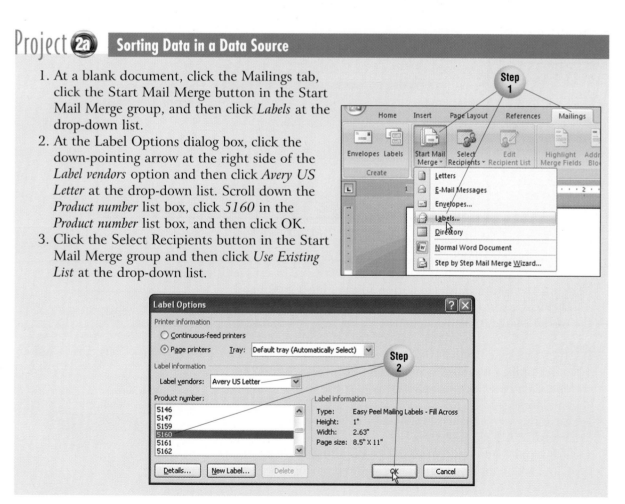

4. At the Select Data Source dialog box, navigate to the Word2007L2C5 folder on your storage medium and then double-click the data source file named **LFSClients.mdb**.
5. Click the Edit Recipient List button.
6. At the Mail Merge Recipients dialog box, click the *Last Name* column heading. (This sorts the last names in ascending alphabetical order.)

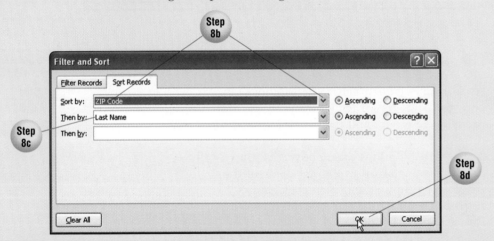

7. Scroll to the right to display the *City* field and then click the *City* column heading.
8. Sort records by ZIP Codes and then by last name by completing the following steps:
   a. Click the <u>Sort</u> hyperlink located in the *Refine recipient list* section of the Mail Merge Recipients dialog box.
   b. At the Filter and Sort dialog box with the Sort Records tab selected, click the down-pointing arrow at the right side of the *Sort by* option box and then click *ZIP Code* at the drop-down list. (You will need to scroll down the list to display the *ZIP Code* field.)
   c. Make sure *Last Name* displays in the *Then by* option box.
   d. Click OK to close the Filter and Sort dialog box.
   e. Click OK to close the Mail Merge Recipients dialog box.

9. At the labels document, click the Address Block button in the Write & Insert Fields group.
10. At the Insert Address Block dialog box, click the OK button.
11. Click the Update Labels button in the Write & Insert Fields group.
12. Click the Finish & Merge button in the Finish group and then click *Edit Individual Documents* at the drop-down list.

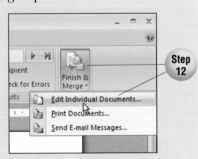

13. At the Merge to New Document dialog box, make sure *All* is selected, and then click OK. (If the labels display with 1.15 line spacing and 10 points of spacing after paragraphs, press Ctrl + A to select the entire document and then click the No Spacing style in the Styles group in the Home tab.)
14. Save the merged labels and name the document **WordL2_C5_P2_Lbls01**.
15. Print and then close **WordL2_C5_P2_Lbls01.docx**.
16. Close the main labels document without saving it.

Selecting Records

If you have a data source file with numerous records, situations may arise where you want to merge the main document with only specific records in the data source. For example, you may want to send a letter to customers with a specific ZIP code or who live in a particular city. One method for selecting specific records is to display the Mail Merge Recipients dialog box and then insert or remove check marks from specific records.

Using check boxes to select specific records is useful in a data source containing a limited number of records, but may not be practical in a data source containing many records. In a large data source, use options at the Filter and Sort dialog box with the Filter Records tab selected as shown in Figure 5.4. To display this dialog box, click the <u>Filter</u> hyperlink that displays in the *Refine recipient list* section of the Mail Merge Recipients dialog box.

HINT

Including or excluding certain records from the merge is referred to as *filtering*.

Figure 5.4 Filter and Sort Dialog Box with Filter Records Tab Selected

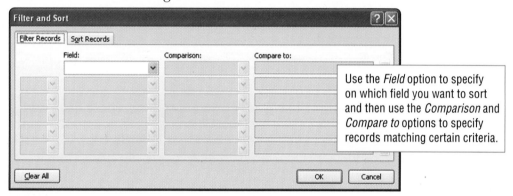

Use the *Field* option to specify on which field you want to sort and then use the *Comparison* and *Compare to* options to specify records matching certain criteria.

When you select a field from the *Field* drop-down list, Word automatically insets *Equal to* in the *Comparison* option box. You can make other comparisons. Clicking the down-pointing arrow to the right of the *Comparison* option box causes a drop-down list to display with these additional options: *Not equal to, Less than, Greater than, Less than or equal, Greater than or equal, Is blank,* and *Is not blank.* Use one of these options to create a select equation.

Project 2b   Selecting Records

1. At a blank document, click the Mailings tab, click the Start Mail Merge button in the Start Mail Merge group, and then click *Labels* at the drop-down list.
2. At the Label Options dialog box, make sure *Avery US Letter* displays in the *Label products* option box and *5160* displays in the *Product number* list box and then click OK.
3. Click the Select Recipients button in the Start Mail Merge group and then click *Use Existing List* at the drop-down list.
4. At the Select Data Source dialog box, navigate to the Word2007L2C5 folder on your storage medium and then double-click the data source file named **LFSClients.mdb**.
5. Click the Edit Recipient List button.
6. At the Mail Merge Recipients dialog box, click the <u>Filter</u> hyperlink in the *Refine recipient list* section of the dialog box.

7. At the Filter and Sort dialog box with the Filter Records tab selected, click the down-pointing arrow at the right side of the *Field* option and then click *ZIP Code* at the drop-down list. (You will need to scroll down the list to display *ZIP Code*. When *ZIP Code* is inserted in the *Field* option box, *Equal to* is inserted in the *Comparison* option box and the insertion point is positioned in the *Compare to* text box.)
8. Type **21000** in the *Compare to* text box.
9. Click the down-pointing arrow at the right side of the *Comparison* option box and then click *Greater than* at the drop-down list.

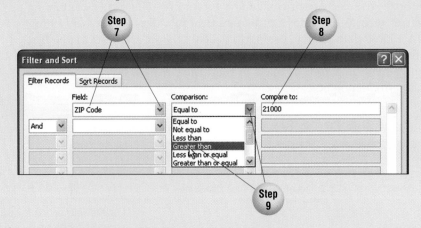

10. Click OK to close the Filter and Sort dialog box.
11. Click OK to close the Mail Merge Recipients dialog box.
12. At the labels document, click the Address Block button in the Write & Insert Fields group and then click OK at the Insert Address Block dialog box.
13. Click the Update Labels button in the Write & Insert Fields group.
14. Click the Finish & Merge button in the Finish group and then click *Edit Individual Documents* at the drop-down list.
15. At the Merge to New Document dialog box, make sure *All* is selected, and then click OK. (If the labels display with 1.15 line spacing and 10 points of spacing after paragraphs, press Ctrl + A to select the entire document and then click the No Spacing style in the Styles group in the Home tab.)
16. Save the merged labels and name the document **WordL2_C5_P2_Lbls02**.
17. Print and then close **WordL2_C5_P2_Lbls02.docx**.
18. Close the main labels document without saving it.

When a field is selected from the *Field* option box, Word automatically inserts *And* in the first box at the left side of the dialog box. You can change this, if needed, to *Or*. With the *And* and *Or* options, you can specify more than one condition for selecting records. For example, in Project 2c, you will select all records of clients living in the cities of Rosedale or Towson. If the data source file contained another field such as a specific financial plan for each customer, you could select all customers in a specific city that subscribe to a specific financial plan. For this situation, you would use the *And* option.

If you want to clear the current options at the Filter and Sort dialog box with the Filter Records tab selected, click the Clear All button. This clears any text from text boxes and leaves the dialog box on the screen. Click the Cancel button if you want to close the Filter and Sort dialog box without specifying any records.

1. At a blank document, click the Mailings tab, click the Start Mail Merge button in the Start Mail Merge group, and then click *Labels* at the drop-down list.
2. At the Label Options dialog box, make sure *Avery US Letter* displays in the *Label products* option box and *5160* displays in the *Product number* list box and then click OK.
3. Click the Select Recipients button in the Start Mail Merge group and then click *Use Existing List* at the drop-down list.
4. At the Select Data Source dialog box, navigate to the Word2007L2C5 folder on your storage medium and then double-click the data source file named *LFSClients.mdb*.
5. Click the Edit Recipient List button.
6. At the Mail Merge Recipients dialog box, click the <u>Filter</u> hyperlink in the *Refine recipient list* section of the dialog box.
7. At the Filter and Sort dialog box with the Filter Records tab selected, click the down-pointing arrow at the right side of the *Field* option and then click *City* at the drop-down list. (You will need to scroll down the list to display this field.)
8. Type Rosedale in the *Compare to* text box.
9. Click the down-pointing arrow to the right of the option box containing the word *And* (at the left side of the dialog box) and then click *Or* at the drop-down list.
10. Click the down-pointing arrow at the right side of the second *Field* option box, and then click *City* at the drop-down list.
    (You will need to scroll down the list to display this field.)
11. With the insertion point positioned in the second *Compare to* text box (the one below the box containing *Rosedale*), type Towson.
12. Click OK to close the Filter and Sort dialog box.
13. Click OK to close the Mail Merge Recipients dialog box.

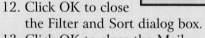

14. At the labels document, click the Address Block button in the Write & Insert Fields group and then click OK at the Insert Address Block dialog box.
15. Click the Update Labels button in the Write & Insert Fields group.
16. Click the Finish & Merge button in the Finish group and then click *Edit Individual Documents* at the drop-down list.
17. At the Merge to New Document dialog box, make sure *All* is selected and then click OK. (If the labels display with 1.15 line spacing and 10 points of spacing after paragraphs, press Ctrl + A to select the entire document and then click the No Spacing style in the Styles group in the Home tab.)
18. Save the merged labels and name the document **WordL2_C5_P2_Lbls03**.
19. Print and then close **WordL2_C5_P2_Lbls03.docx**.
20. Close the main labels document without saving it.

Project ③ Type a Keyboard Shortcut Document

You will type a document with information on keyboard shortcuts and use nonbreaking spaces within the shortcuts to keep them from being split between two lines of text. You will then use the find and replace feature to search for all nonbreaking spaces and replace them with regular spaces.

Inserting a Nonbreaking Space

HINT
You can insert a nonbreaking space at the Symbol dialog box with the (normal text) font selected.

As you type text in a document, Word makes line-end decisions and automatically wraps text to the next line. In some situations, word wrap may break up words or phrases on separates lines that should remain together. To control where text is wrapped to the next line, consider inserting a nonbreaking space between words. Press Ctrl + Shift + spacebar to insert a nonbreaking space. With the display of nonprinting characters turned on, a normal space displays as a dot and a nonbreaking space displays as a degree symbol.

Project ③a   Inserting Nonbreaking Spaces

1. At a blank document, turn on the display of nonprinting characters by clicking the Show/Hide ¶ button in the Paragraph group in the Home tab.
2. Type the text shown in Figure 5.5 and insert nonbreaking spaces in keyboard shortcuts by pressing Ctrl + Shift + spacebar before and after the plus symbol in the keyboard shortcuts.
3. Turn off the display of nonprinting characters.
4. Save the document and name it **WordL2_C5_P3**.

Figure 5.5 Project 3a

KEYBOARD SHORTCUTS

Microsoft Word includes a number of keyboard shortcuts you can use to access features and commands. The ScreenTip for some buttons displays the keyboard shortcut you can use to access the command. For example, hover the mouse over the Font button and the ScreenTip displays Ctrl + Shift + F as the keyboard shortcut. Additional Home tab Font group keyboard shortcuts include Ctrl + B to bold text, Ctrl + I to italicize text, and Ctrl + U to underline text. You can also press Ctrl + Shift + + to turn on superscript and press Ctrl + = to turn on subscript.

Buttons in the Clipboard group include keyboard shortcuts. For example, to cut selected text press Ctrl + X, press Ctrl + C to copy selected text, and use the keyboard shortcut Ctrl + V to insert text. Ctrl + Shift + C is the keyboard command to turn on and off the Format Painter feature.

Finding and Replacing Special Characters

You can use the find feature to find special text and the find and replace feature to find specific text and replace with other text. You can also use these features to find special formatting, characters, or nonprinting elements in a document. To display a list of special characters and nonprinting elements, display the Find and Replace dialog box with either the Find or Replace tab selected, expand the dialog box, and then click the Special button. This displays a pop-up list similar to the one shown in Figure 5.6.

If you are not sure about the name of the special character you want to find or if the names of the special characters in the Special button pop-up list are unclear, you can access Word's list of special characters to see the characters and their names. Click the Symbol button in the Symbols group in the Insert tab and a short list of symbols displays. Click the More Symbols option at the drop-down list and the Symbol dialog box displays. Click the Special Characters tab to see a list of characters and their names. For example, many users may not know the difference between an Em dash (—) and an En dash (–). The Special Characters listing shows each type of dash.

QUICK STEPS

Find and Replace Special Character
1. Click Replace button.
2. Click More button.
3. Click Special button.
4. Click desired character.
5. Click in *Replace with* text box.
6. Click Special button.
7. Click desired character.
8. Click Replace All.

HINT
Press Ctrl + H to display the Find and Replace dialog box with the Replace tab selected.

Figure 5.6 Special Button Pop-up List

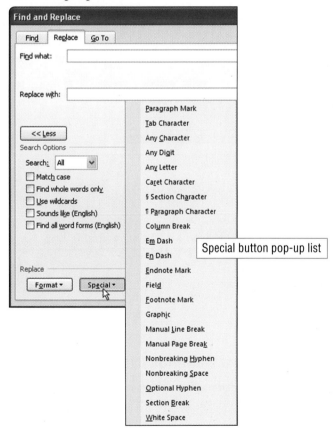

Project 3b | **Finding and Replacing Nonbreaking Spaces**

1. With **WordL2_C5_P3.docx** open, find all occurrences of nonbreaking spaces and replace with regular spaces by completing the following steps:
   a. Click the Replace button in the Editing group in the Home tab.
   b. At the Find and Replace dialog box with the Replace tab selected, click the More button.
   c. With the insertion point positioned in the *Find what* text box, click the Special button that displays toward the bottom of the dialog box.
   d. At the pop-up list that displays, click *Nonbreaking Space*. (This inserts ^s in the *Find what* text box.)
   e. Click in the *Replace with* text box (make sure the text box does not contain any text) and then press the spacebar once. (This tells the Find and Replace feature to find a nonbreaking space and replace it with a regular space.)
   f. Click the Replace All button.
   g. At the message telling you that Word completed the search and made the replacements, click OK.

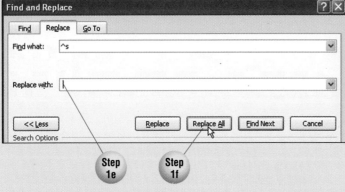

Step 1c

Step 1d

Step 1e

Step 1f

   h. Click the Less button.
   i. Click the Close button to close the Find and Replace dialog box.
2. Save, print, and then close **WordL2_C5_P3.docx**.

Project 4 Create and Use a Summons Template

You will open a Summons legal document, save it as a template, and then use it to create other Summonses.

Creating a Template

If you use the contents of a document to create other documents, consider saving the document as a template. To save a document as a template, display the Save As dialog box. At the Save As dialog box, click the Trusted Templates button located toward the upper left corner of the dialog box. At the Save As dialog box with the Templates folder selected, change the *Save as type* option to *Word Template (*.dotx)*, type a name for the template, and then press Enter. Word template documents are saved with the *.dotx* file extension. You can also save a template as a Word Macro-Enabled Template with the file extension *.dotm*.

Project 4a — Creating a Specialized Template

1. Open **WordLegal01.docx**.
2. Save the document as a specialized template named Summons in the Templates folder by completing the following steps:
   a. Click the Office button and then click Save As.
   b. At the Save As dialog box, click the *Trusted Templates* button located toward the upper left corner of the dialog box.
   c. Click the down-pointing arrow at the right side of the *Save as type* option box and then click *Word Template (*.dotx)*.
   d. Select the name in the *File name* text box and then type your last name followed by *Summons*.
   e. Press Enter or click the Save button.
3. Close the Summons template.

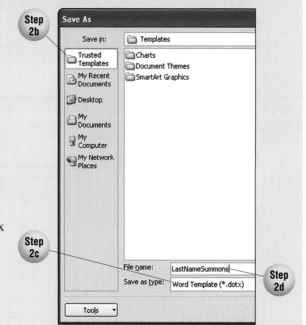

Step 2b

Step 2c

Step 2d

Creating a Document Using a Specialized Template

If you have created specialized template documents, create a document based on the template by opening the template, making edits and changes to the document and then saving it as a normal Word document. To open a specialized template, click the Office button and then click *New* at the drop-down list. At the New Document dialog box, click the *My templates* option in the *Templates* section of the dialog box. At the New dialog box similar to the one shown in Figure 5.7, click the desired template in the list box and then click OK. To create structured and complex templates, consider using the forms creation program, Microsoft Office InfoPath 2007.

Figure 5.7 New Dialog Box

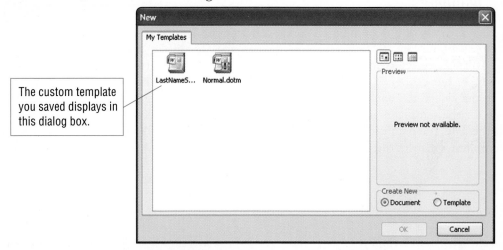

The custom template you saved displays in this dialog box.

Project 4b   Creating a Document Based on a Specialized Template

1. Open the Summons template by completing the following steps:
   a. Click the Office button and then click *New* at the drop-down list.
   b. At the New Document dialog box, click the *My templates* option in the *Templates* section of the dialog box.
   c. At the New dialog box, click the Summons template that is preceded by your last name.
   d. Click OK.

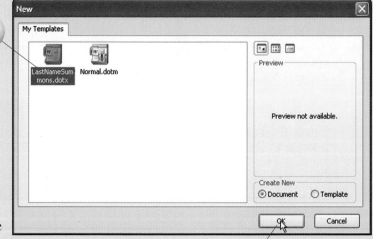

2. With the Summons template document open, make the following find and replaces:
   a. Find *NAME1* and replace with *AMY GARCIA*.
   b. Find *NAME2* and replace with *NEIL CARLIN*.
   c. Find *NUMBER* and replace with *C-98002*.
3. Save the document in the Word2007L2C5 folder on your storage medium and name it **WordL2_C5_P4**.
4. Print and then close **WordL2_C5_P4.docx**.
5. Delete the Summons template by completing the following steps:
   a. At a blank document, click the Office button and then click *Save As*.
   b. At the Save As dialog box, click the Trusted Templates button.
   c. Click the down-pointing arrow at the right side of the *Save as type* option box and then click *Word Template (*.dotx)*.
   d. Click the Summons template that is named beginning with your last name.
   e. Click the Delete button on the dialog box toolbar.
   f. At the message asking if you are sure you want to send the template to the Recycle Bin, click Yes.
6. Close the Save As dialog box.

Project 5 Insert Footnotes and Endnotes in Reports

You will open a report on artificial intelligence and then insert, format, and modify footnotes. You will also open a report on the future of the Internet and then insert endnotes.

Creating Footnotes and Endnotes

A research paper or report contains information from a variety of sources. To give credit to those sources, you can insert a footnote or endnote in a document. A footnote is an explanatory note or reference that is printed at the bottom of the page where it is referenced. An endnote is also an explanatory note or reference, but it prints at the end of the document.

Two steps are involved in creating a footnote or endnote. First, the note reference number is inserted in the document at the location where the note is referenced. The second step is to type the note entry text. Footnotes and endnotes are created in a similar manner. To create a footnote, position the insertion point at the location where the reference number is to appear, click the References tab, and then click the Insert Footnote button in the Footnotes group. This inserts a number in the document and also inserts a separator line at the bottom of the page with a superscript number below. With the insertion point positioned immediately right of the superscript number, type the footnote entry text. Word automatically numbers footnotes with superscript Arabic numbers and endnotes with superscript lowercase Roman numerals.

QUICK STEPS

Insert Footnote
1. Click References tab.
2. Click Insert Footnote button.
3. Type footnote text.

Insert Endnote
1. Click References tab.
2. Click Insert Endnote button.
3. Type endnote text.

HINT
Ctrl + Alt + F is the keyboard shortcut to insert a footnote.

Insert Endnote

Project 5a Creating Footnotes

1. Open **WordReport01.docx** and then save the document and name it **WordL2_C5_P5a**.
2. Create the first footnote shown in Figure 5.8 by completing the following steps:
   a. Position the insertion point at the end of the first paragraph of text in the document.
   b. Click the References tab.
   c. Click the Insert Footnote button in the Footnotes group.

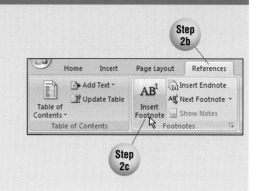

Step 2b

Step 2c

d. With the insertion point positioned at the bottom of the page immediately following the superscript number, type the first footnote shown in Figure 5.8.

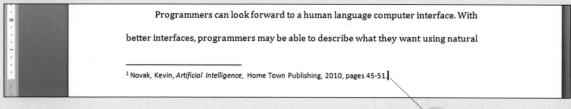

Programmers can look forward to a human language computer interface. With

better interfaces, programmers may be able to describe what they want using natural

_____

[1] Novak, Kevin, *Artificial Intelligence*, Home Town Publishing, 2010, pages 45-51.

Step 2d

3. Move the insertion point to the end of the paragraph in the *Speech Recognition* section and then create the second footnote shown in Figure 5.8.
4. Move the insertion point to the end of the second paragraph in the *Natural-Language Interface* section and then create the third footnote shown in Figure 5.8.
5. Move the insertion point to the end of the paragraph in the *Virtual Reality* section and then create the fourth footnote shown in Figure 5.8.
6. Move the insertion point to the end of the last paragraph in the document and then create the fifth footnote shown in Figure 5.8.
7. Save and then close **WordL2_C5_P5a.docx**.

Figure 5.8 Project 5a

Novak, Kevin, *Artificial Intelligence*, Home Town Publishing, 2010, pages 45-51.

Everson, Heather and Nicolas Reyes, "Integrating Speech Recognition," *Design Technologies*, January/February 2010, pages 24-26.

Glenovich, James, "Language Interfaces," *Corporate Computing*, November 2009, pages 8-12.

Curtis, William, *Virtual Reality Worlds*, Lilly-Harris Publishers, 2010, pages 53-68.

Beal, Marilyn, "Challenges of Artificial Intelligence," *Interface Designs*, April 2010, pages 10-18.

Printing Footnotes and Endnotes

HINT

Ctrl + Alt + D is the keyboard shortcut to insert an endnote.

When you print a document containing footnotes, Word automatically reduces the number of text lines on a page by the number of lines in the footnote plus the separator line. If the page does not contain enough space, the footnote number and footnote entry text are taken to the next page. Word separates the footnotes from the text with a 2-inch separator line that begins at the left margin. When endnotes are created in a document, Word prints all endnote references at the end of the document separated from the text by a 2-inch separator line.

Project 5b | **Creating Endnotes**

1. Open **WordReport02.docx** and then save the document and name it **WordL2_C5_P5b**.
2. Apply the *Simple* Quick Styles set.
3. Create the first endnote shown in Figure 5.9 by completing the following steps:
   a. Position the insertion point at the end of the paragraph in the *Satellite Internet Connections* section.
   b. Click the References tab.
   c. Click the Insert Endnote button.
   d. Type the first endnote shown in Figure 5.9.
4. Move the insertion point to the end of the second paragraph in the *Second Internet* section and then create the second endnote shown in Figure 5.9.
5. Move the insertion point to the end of the paragraph in the *Internet Services for a Fee* section and then create the third endnote shown in Figure 5.9.
6. Save, print, and then close **WordL2_C5_P5b.docx**.

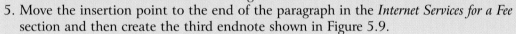

Figure 5.9 **Project 5b**

Clements, Aileen, *Satellite Systems*, Robison Publishing House, 2010, pages 23-51.

Ventrella, Terry, "Future of the Internet," *Computing Today*, October 2010, pages 29-33.

Campbell, Jolene, "Fee-Based Internet Services," *Connections*, March/April 2010, pages 5-8.

Viewing and Showing Footnotes and Endnotes

To view footnotes in a document, click the Next Footnote button in the Footnotes group in the References tab. This moves the insertion point to the location in the document where the footnote reference number is located. Click the Next Footnote button arrow and a drop-down list displays with options for viewing the previous footnote and viewing endnotes.

You can move the insertion point to specific footnote text with the Show Notes button. Click the Next Footnote button to move the insertion point to the next footnote reference number and then click the Show Notes button. This moves the insertion point to the specific footnote text at the bottom of the page. Click the Show Notes button again and the insertion point is moved back to the footnote reference number.

HINT
Position the mouse pointer on a footnote or endnote reference mark, and the footnote or endnote text displays in a box above the mark.

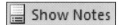

Moving, Copying, and Deleting Footnotes or Endnotes

You can move, copy, or delete footnote or endnote reference numbers. If a footnote or endnote reference is moved, copied, or deleted, all footnotes or endnotes remaining in the document are automatically renumbered. To move a footnote or endnote, select the reference number and then click the Cut button in the Clipboard group in the Home tab. Position the insertion point at the location where you want the footnote or endnote inserted and then click the Paste button. Complete similar steps to copy and paste footnotes or endnotes. To delete a footnote or endnote, select the reference number and then press the Delete key. When the reference number is deleted, the entry text is also deleted.

Project 5c | Editing and Deleting Footnotes

1. Open **WordL2_C5_P5a.docx** and navigate to footnote reference numbers and footnote text by completing the following steps:

   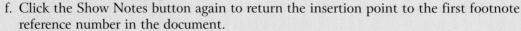

   a. Click the References tab.
   b. Click the Next Footnote button.
   c. Click the Next Footnote button again.
   d. Click the Next Footnote button arrow and then click *Previous Footnote* at the drop-down list.
   e. Click the Show Notes button to display the first footnote text located at the bottom of the page.
   f. Click the Show Notes button again to return the insertion point to the first footnote reference number in the document.

2. Select the entire document and then change the font to Constantia. (Footnote text is not selected.)

3. Change the font for the footnotes by completing the following steps:
   a. Press Ctrl + Home.
   b. Click the References tab, click the Next Footnote button, and then click the Show Notes button.
   c. Press Ctrl + A. (This selects all footnote entry text on every page.)
   d. Change the font to Constantia.
   e. Click in the document to deselect the text.

4. Delete the fourth footnote by completing the following steps:
   a. Press Ctrl + Home.
   b. Click the Next Footnote button four times.
   c. Select the fourth footnote reference number (superscript number).
   d. Press the Delete key.

5. Save, print, and then close **WordL2_C5_P5a.docx**.

Project 6 | Cite References in an Internet Report

You will open a report on the development of the Internet, add additional information and then insert citations and a bibliography, and then modify and customize citation styles.

Creating Citations and Bibliographies

When preparing a student research paper or manuscript, consider inserting citations and a bibliography to give credit to the sources of words, ideas, and any material borrowed or summarized. Citing a source shows readers that you are borrowing information from another source rather than plagiarizing (stealing) the ideas.

Word includes some common reference styles for citing and referencing research papers and reports. The American Psychological Association (APA) reference style is generally used in science and research fields. Students in humanities and English generally use the Modern Language Association (MLA) style and the Chicago Manual of Style (CMS) is used both in humanities and social sciences and is considered more complex than APA or MLA styles.

When preparing a research paper or report in the APA or MLA styles, format your document with the following general guidelines. Use standard-sized paper (8.5 × 11 inches); set one-inch top, bottom, left, and right margins; double-space text; indent the first line of each paragraph one-half inch; and insert page numbers in the upper right corner of pages.

Inserting Sources and Citations

As you are typing your paper, you will need to insert a citation identifying the source of the information. While creating a citation, Word requires you to fill in the source information in the required fields in the Create Source dialog box.

To insert a citation in a Word document, click the References tab, click the Insert Citation button in the Citations & Bibliography group, and then click *Add New Source* at the drop-down list. At the Create Source dialog box shown in Figure 5.10, select the type of reference you want to cite such as a book, journal article, or report and then insert bibliography information in the required fields. If you would like to include more information than the displayed fields, click the *Show All Bibliography Fields* check box to insert a check mark and then insert bibliography information in the extra fields. After filling in the necessary source information, click OK and the citation will automatically be inserted in the document where the insertion point is located.

QUICK STEPS

Insert Citation
1. Click References tab.
2. Click Insert Citation button.
3. Click *Add New Source* at drop-down list.
4. Type necessary reference information.
5. Click OK.

HINT
Each new source you save is saved on your computer so you can use it at any time.

Figure 5.10 Create Source Dialog Box

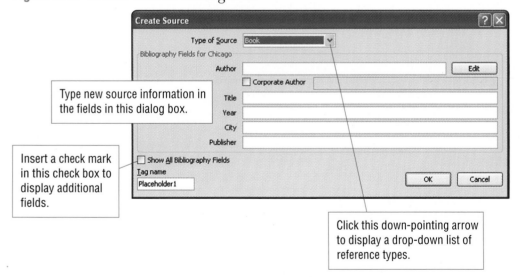

Type new source information in the fields in this dialog box.

Insert a check mark in this check box to display additional fields.

Click this down-pointing arrow to display a drop-down list of reference types.

HINT

Find additional sources or information about sources by clicking the Insert Citations button and then clicking *Search Libraries*.

If you include a direct quote from another source, you will want to include quotation marks around all of the text borrowed from another source and then insert the page number of the source containing the borrowed quote. To insert specific page numbers into a citation, click the citation in the document and this selects the citation placeholder. Click the Citation Options arrow, and then click *Edit Citation* at the drop-down list. At the Edit Citation dialog box, type in the page or page numbers of the source where the quote was borrowed.

Project 6a Inserting Sources and Citations

1. Open **WordReference01.docx** and then save the document and name it **WordL2_C5_P6**.
2. Press Ctrl + End to move the insertion point to the end of the document and then type the text shown in Figure 5.11 up to the first citation (the text *(Alexander, 2010)*). To insert the citation, complete these steps:
   a. Click the References tab.
   b. Click the Insert Citation button in the Citations & Bibliography group and then click *Add New Source* at the drop-down list.
   c. At the Create Source dialog box, click the down-pointing arrow at the right of the *Type of Source* option and then click *Journal Article* at the drop-down list.
   d. Type Olivia Alexander in the *Author* text box.
   e. Type Future Computer-Related Technology Jobs in the *Title* text box.
   f. Type Computer Education in the *Journal Name* text box.
   g. Type 2010 in the *Year* text box.
   h. Type 12-32 in the *Pages* text box.
   i. Click OK.

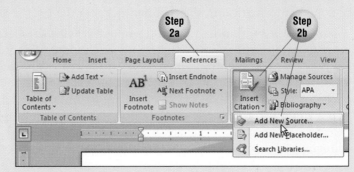

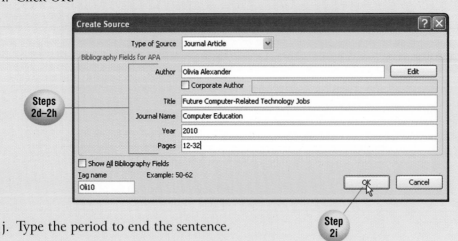

   j. Type the period to end the sentence.

3. Continue typing the text up to the next citation (the text *(Miraldi, 2010)*) and insert the following source information from a book (make sure you change the *Type of Source* option to Book):

> *Author* = Allen Miraldi
> *Title* = Exploring Advancements in Technology
> *Year* = 2010
> *City* = Madison
> *Publisher* = Great Lakes Publishing House

4. Continue typing the text up to the next citation (the text *(Suong, 2009)*) and insert the following source information from a journal article (make sure you change the *Type of Source* option to Journal Article):

> *Author* = Chay Suong
> *Title* = Computers and Publishing
> *Journal Name* = Technology Times
> *Year* = 2009
> *Pages* = 20-28
> *Volume* = 8 (Display the *Volume* field by clicking the *Show All Bibliography Fields* check box and then scrolling down the options list.)

5. Continue typing the text up to the next citation (the second occurrence of the text *(Alexander, 2010)*) and then insert a citation from an existing source by completing the following steps:
   a. Click the Insert Citation button in the Citations & Bibliography group.
   b. Click the Olivia Alexander reference in the drop-down gallery.

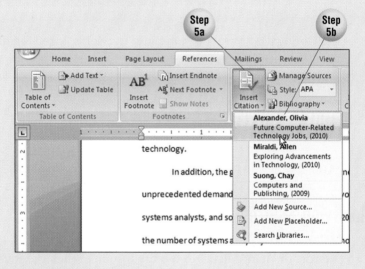

6. Type the remaining text in Figure 5.11.
7. Save and then print **WordL2_C5_P6.docx**.

Figure 5.11 Project 6a

In addition, the growth of computer- and Internet-related businesses has created an

unprecedented demand for highly skilled technology workers, particularly computer

programmers, systems analysts, and software engineers (Alexander, 2010). According to the U.S.

Department of Labor, the number of systems analysts jobs added to the economy will continue to

grow in the near future.

Similarly, the number of computer engineer and computer support specialist jobs will

grow by 108 percent and 102 percent, respectively (Miraldi, 2010). In the year 2000 alone, some

300,000 high-tech jobs remained unfilled. In response to this high demand and the lack of

enough workers to fill the positions, Congress passed a bill in the fall of 2000 to increase the

number of annual visas for skilled foreign workers from 115,000 to 195,000 (Suong, 2009).

What is the Internet?

The Internet is a worldwide network of computer networks linked together via

communications software and media, such as telephone lines, for the purpose of sharing

information (Alexander, 2010). Any properly equipped computer can be connected to the

Internet.

Modifying Sources

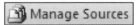

After inserting sources into a document, you may need to modify a citation to correct errors or change data. To modify a source, click the References tab and then click the Manage Sources button in the Citations & Bibliography group. This displays the Source Manager dialog box as shown in Figure 5.12. The Source Manager dialog box displays in the *Master List* section all of the citations you have created in Word. The *Current List* section of the dialog box displays all of the citations included in the currently open document. At the Source Manager dialog box, click the desired source in the *Current List* section. Click the Edit button that displays between the list boxes and then make any desired changes at the Edit Source dialog box. The Edit Source dialog box contains the same options as the Create Source dialog box. You can also edit a source by clicking the desired citation, clicking the Citation Options arrow, and then clicking *Edit Source* at the drop-down list.

Figure 5.12 Source Manager Dialog Box

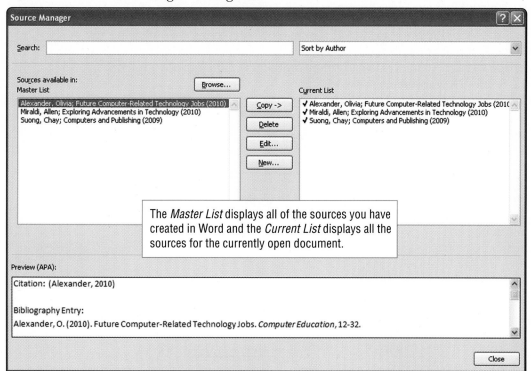

Usually, you will be adding sources as you create citations. However, at times you may want to create a new source without adding a related footnote or endnote immediately. This situation could occur when you are writing the first draft of a report and you remember another valuable information source that you could cite later, when you revise your draft. To insert a new source, click the New button at the Source Manager dialog, and then insert the source information in the required fields. You can also delete existing sources. To delete a source from a document, click the source you wish to delete in the *Current List* section and then click the Delete button.

QUICK STEPS

Modify Sources
1. Click References tab.
2. Click Manage Sources button.
3. Edit, add, and/or delete references.
4. Click Close.

HINT
Click the Browse button in the Source Manager dialog box to select another master list.

1. With **WordL2_C5_P6.docx** open, edit a source by completing the following steps:
   a. Click the References tab.
   b. Click the Manage Sources button in the Citations & Bibliography group.
   c. At the Source Manager dialog
      box, click the source entry for
      Allen Miraldi in the *Master List*
      section.
   d. Click the Edit button.
   e. At the Edit Source dialog box,
      delete the text in the *Year* text
      box and then type 2009.
   f. Click OK to close the Edit
      Source dialog box.
   g. At the message asking if you
      want to update both the master
      list and the current list with the
      changes, click Yes.
   h. Click the Close button to close
      the Source Manager dialog box.
      (Notice the year has changed in the Miraldi citation to reflect the edit.)

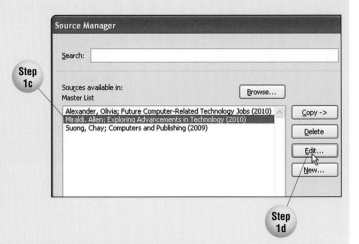

Step 1c

Step 1d

2. Delete a source by completing the following steps:
   a. Select and then delete the last sentence in the third paragraph in the document,
      including the citation (the sentence that begins *In response to this high demand . . .*).
   b. Click the Manage Sources button in the Citations & Bibliography group in the
      References tab.
   c. At the Source Manager dialog box, click the Chay Suong entry in the *Current List*
      section. (This entry in the list will not contain a check mark because you deleted the
      citation from the document.)
   d. Click the Delete button.

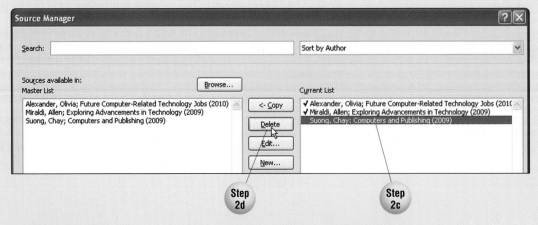

Step 2d

Step 2c

   e. Click the Close button to close the Source Manager dialog box.
3. Create and insert a new source in the document by completing the following steps:
   a. Click the Manage Sources button in the Citations & Bibliography group in the
      References tab.
   b. Click the New button in the Source Manager dialog box.

c. Type the following report information in the Create Source dialog box:
   Author = Susan Mancini
   Title = The Future of Internet Computing Technologies
   Year = 2008
   Publisher = Central Avenue Publishing House
   City = Los Angeles
d. Click OK to close the Create Source dialog box.
e. Click the Close button to close the Source Manager dialog box.
f. Press Ctrl + End to move the insertion point to the end of the document, press the spacebar once, and then type the sentence "A personal computer, a school's mainframe computer system, and NASA's supercomputers can all be connected to the Internet at the same time". (Press the spacebar after typing *time*".)
g. Insert a citation at the end of the sentence for Susan Mancini by clicking the Insert Citation button in the Citations & Bibliography group and then clicking the Susan Mancini reference at the drop-down gallery.
h. Type the period to end the sentence.

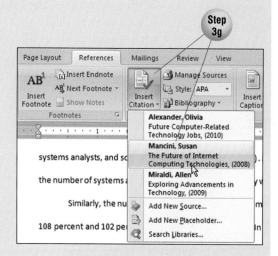

4. Because you inserted a direct quote from Susan Mancini, you will need to include the page number of the report where you found the quote. Insert the page number within the citation by completing the following steps:
   a. Click on any character in the Mancini citation. (This displays the citation placeholder.)
   b. Click the Citation Options arrow that displays at the right side of the citations placeholder and then click *Edit Citation* at the drop-down list.
   c. At the Edit Citation dialog box, type 4 in the *Pages* text box.
   d. Click OK.
5. Save **WordL2_C5_P6.docx**.

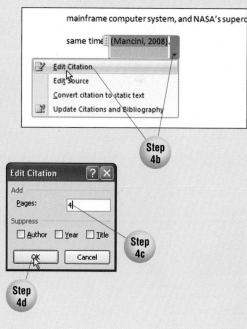

Inserting and Modifying Bibliographies

QUICK STEPS

Insert Bibliography
1. Click References tab.
2. Click Bibliography button.
3. Click predesigned bibliography at drop-down gallery.

Update Bibliography
1. Click on any character in the bibliography.
2. Click Update Citations and Bibliography tab.

Once you include citations in a report or research paper, you need to insert a bibliography or works cited page at the end of the document on a separate page. A bibliography or works cited page is an alphabetic list of the books, journal articles, reports, or any other sources referenced in the document. When you typed the source information for the citations, Word automatically saved all of the field information into a bibliography and works cited list in alphabetical order. To insert a bibliography, click the References tab and then click the Bibliography button in the Citations & Bibliography group. At the Bibliography drop-down gallery, click a predesigned built-in bibliography.

If you insert a new source at the Source Manager dialog box or modify an existing source, Word automatically inserts the source information in the bibliography. If you insert a new citation, which requires you to add a new source, Word will not automatically update the bibliography. To update the bibliography, click anywhere in the bibliography and then click the Update Citations and Bibliography tab. The updated bibliography will reflect any changes made to the citations and source information in the document.

Project 6c   Inserting and Modifying Bibliographies

1. With **WordL2_C5_P6.docx** open, insert a bibliography at the end of the document by completing these steps:
   a. Press Ctrl + End to move the insertion point to the end of the document.
   b. Press Ctrl + Enter to insert a hard page break.
   c. Click the References tab.
   d. Click the Bibliography button located in the Citations & Bibliography group.
   e. Click the *Bibliography* option in the *Built-In* section of the drop-down gallery.

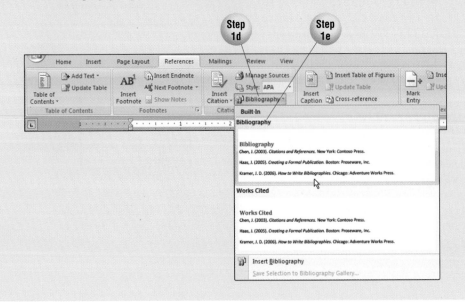

2. Create a new source and citation by completing the following steps:
   a. Position the insertion point immediately left of the period that ends the last sentence in the first paragraph of the document.
   b. Press the spacebar once.
   c. Click the References tab.
   d. Click the Insert Citation button in the Citations & Bibliography group and then click *Add New Source* at the drop-down list.
   e. At the Create Source dialog box, insert the following source information from a book:
      Author = Barbara Schroeder
      Title = Computers in the Business World
      Year = 2009
      City = Dallas
      Publisher = Rio Grande Publishing
   f. Click OK to close the Create Source dialog box.
3. Update the bibliography to include the new source by completing the following steps:
   a. Click on any character in the bibliography text.
   b. Click the Update Citations and Bibliography tab. (Notice that the updated bibliography includes the Schroeder reference.)

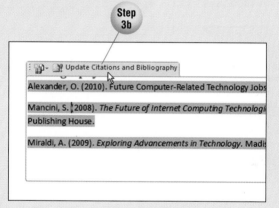

4. Save **WordL2_C5_P6.docx**.

Formatting Bibliographies

Reference styles have specific formatting guidelines. The formatting applied by Word to the bibliography or works cited page may need to be changed to meet specific guidelines of the APA, MLA, or Chicago style. For example, APA and MLA styles require the following formatting guidelines for the bibliography or works cited page:

- Begin bibliography or work cited on a separate page after the text of the report.
- Include the title "Bibliography" or "Works Cited" and center the title.
- Double-space between and within entries.
- Begin each entry at the left margin and hang indent second and subsequent lines in each entry.
- Alphabetize the entries.

The general formatting requirements for the Chicago style are similar except entries are single-spaced within and double-spaced between.

Project 6d Formatting the Bibliography

1. With **WordL2_C5_P6.docx** open, make the following formatting changes to the bibliography:

   a. Click on any character in the title *Bibliography* (the placeholder tab will display over the title) and then press Ctrl + E to center the title.

   b. Select the Bibliography heading and the entries below the heading.

   c. Click the Home tab.

   d. Click the Line spacing button in the Paragraph group and then click *2.0* at the drop-down list.

   e. Click the Page Layout tab.

   f. Click once on the down-pointing arrow at the right side of the *After* option box. (This inserts *0 pt* in the option box.)

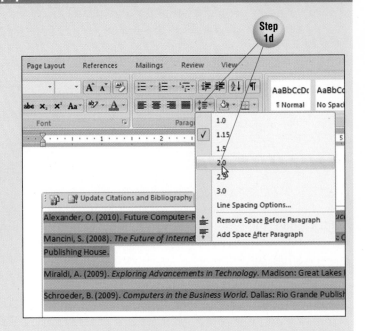

Step 1d

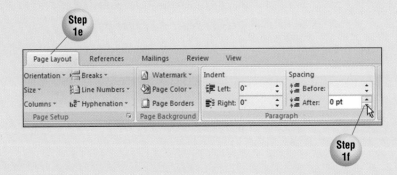

Step 1e

Step 1f

   g. Select only the bibliography entries and then press Ctrl + T. (This hang indents the entries.)

2. Save and then print **WordL2_C5_P6.docx**.

QUICK STEPS

Change Citation Style
1. Click References tab.
2. Click down-pointing arrow at right of *Style* option.
3. Click desired style.

Choosing a Citation Style

Instructors or professors may require different forms of citation and reference styles. You can change the citation and reference style before beginning a new document or in an existing document. To do this, click the References tab, click the down-pointing arrow at the right side of the *Style* option box, and then click the desired style at the drop-down list.

Project 6e Choosing Citation Styles

1. With **WordL2_C5_P6.docx** open, change the document and bibliography from APA style to MLA style by completing the following steps:
   a. Press Ctrl + Home to move the insertion point to the beginning of the document.
   b. Click the References tab.
   c. Click the down-pointing arrow at the right side of the *Style* option in the Citations & Bibliography group and then click *MLA* at the drop-down list. (Notice the changes in the style of the citations and the bibliography.)

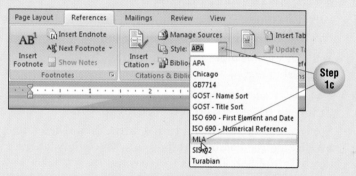

2. Save and then print page 2 of **WordL2_C5_P6.docx**.
3. Change the document and bibliography style to Chicago by clicking the down-pointing arrow at the right side of the *Style* option and then clicking *Chicago* in the drop-down list.
4. Print page 2 of **WordL2_C5_P6.docx**.
5. Change the document and bibliography style to APA.
6. Save and then close the document.

CHAPTER summary

- You can sort text in paragraphs, columns, and tables and sort records in a data source file. You can also select specific records in a data source file for merging with a main document.

- Use the Sort button in the Paragraph group in the Home tab to sort text in paragraphs, columns, and tables.

- When sorting text set in columns, Word considers the left margin *Field 1*, text typed at the first tab *Field 2*, and so on.

- You can sort on more than one field with the *Sort by* and *Then by* options at the Sort dialog box.

- Use the *Header row* option in the *My list has* section in the Sort Text dialog box to sort all text in columns except the first row.

- Sort records in a data source file at the Mail Merge Recipients dialog box. Sort by clicking the column heading or with options at the Filter and Sort dialog box with the Sort Records tab selected.

- Select specific records in a data source file with options at the Filter and Sort dialog box with the Filter Records tab selected.

- When a nonbreaking space is inserted between words, Word considers these words as one unit and will not divide them when wrapping text to the next line. Insert a nonbreaking space with the keyboard shortcut, Ctrl + Shift + spacebar.

- Use the find and replace feature to find special formatting, characters, or nonprinting elements, and replace with nothing or other special text.

- Save a document as a template by changing the *Save as type* option at the Save As dialog box to *Word Template (*.dotx)* and then saving the template in the Templates folder.

- Word adds the extension *.dotx* to a template.

- Display the Templates folder by clicking the Trusted Templates button in the Save As dialog box.

- Open a template by clicking the desired template at the New dialog box. Display this dialog box by clicking the Office button, clicking the *New* option, and then clicking the *My templates* option in the *Templates* section of the New Document dialog box.

- Footnotes and endnotes are explanatory notes or references. Footnotes are inserted and printed at the bottom of the page and endnotes are printed at the end of the document. Type footnote/endnote text at the footnote or endnote pane.

- By default, footnotes are numbered with Arabic numbers and endnotes are numbered with lowercase Roman numerals.

- Move, copy, or delete a reference number in a document and all other footnotes or endnotes are automatically renumbered.

- Delete a footnote or endnote by selecting the reference number and then pressing the Delete key.

- Consider using citation and reference styles to acknowledge sources in a paper. Common styles include American Psychological Association (APA), Modern Language Association (MLA), and Chicago Manual of Style (CMS).

- Use the Insert Citation button in the Citations & Bibliography group in the References tab to insert a citation. Specify source information at the Create Source dialog box.

- To modify a source, click the References tab, click the Manage Sources button, click the source you want to modify in the Source Manager dialog box, click the Edit button, and then make any desired changes at the Edit Source dialog box.

- To insert a new source, click the New button at the Source Manager dialog box and then insert the information in the required fields. To delete a source, click the source in the *Current List* section in the Source Manager dialog box and then click the Delete button.

- After including citations in a report or paper, insert a bibliography or works cited page at the end of the document on a separate page. Insert a bibliography or works cited page with the Bibliography button in the Citations & Bibliography group in the References tab.

- To update a bibliography, click in the bibliography and then click the Update Citations and Bibliography tab.

COMMANDS review

FEATURE	RIBBON TAB, GROUP	BUTTON, OPTION	KEYBOARD SHORTCUT
Sort Text dialog box	Home, Paragraph		
Sort Options dialog box	Home, Paragraph	, Options	
Filter and Sort dialog box with Sort Records tab selected	Mailings, Start Mail Merge	, Sort	
Filter and Sort dialog box with Select Records tab selected	Mailings, Start Mail Merge	, Filter	
Nonbreaking space			Ctrl + Shift + Spacebar
Find and Replace dialog box	Home, Editing	Replace	Ctrl + H
Footnote	References, Footnotes	AB¹	Alt + Ctrl + F
Endnote	References, Footnotes	Insert Endnote	Alt + Ctrl + D
Hide/Display Notes	References, Footnotes	Show Notes	
Create Source dialog box	References, Citations & Bibliography		
Source Manager dialog box	References, Citations & Bibliography	Manage Sources	
Bibliography	References, Citations & Bibliography	Bibliography	
Style	References, Citations & Bibliography	Style: APA	

CONCEPTS check

Test Your Knowledge

Completion: In the space provided at the right, indicate the correct term, symbol, or command.

1. The Sort button is located in this group in the Home tab.

2. When sorting text in columns, Word considers the first tab this field number.

3. Click this option at the Sort Text dialog box to tell Word not to include the column headings in the sort.

4. Click the Filter hyperlink at this dialog box to display the Filter and Sort dialog box with the Filter Records tab selected.

5. This is the keyboard shortcut to insert a nonbreaking space.

6. Click this button at the expanded Find and Replace dialog box to display a pop-up list of special characters and nonprinting elements.

7. Word saves template documents with this file extension.

8. Click this button in the Save As dialog box to display the Templates folder.

9. Click the *My templates* option at the New Document dialog box and this dialog box displays.

10. Word numbers footnotes with this type of number.

11. Word numbers endnotes with this type of number.

12. Two of the most popular styles for preparing a report are APA (American Psychological Association) and this.

13. Click this tab to display the Citations & Bibliography group.

14. To modify a source, click this button in the Citations & Bibliography group.

15. To update a bibliography, click anywhere in the bibliography and then click this tab.

SKILLS check
Demonstrate Your Proficiency

Assessment

1 CREATE KEYBOARD SHORTCUTS WITH NONBREAKING SPACES

1. Open **WordSort02.docx** and save the document and name it **WordL2_C5_A1**.
2. Select the nine lines of text below the *Executive Team* heading and then sort the text alphabetically by last name.
3. Sort the three columns of text below the title *New Employees* by the date of hire in ascending order.
4. Sort the text in the First Qtr. column in the table numerically in descending order.
5. Press Ctrl + End to move the insertion point to the end of the document and then type the text shown in Figure 5.13. Insert nonbreaking spaces within keyboard shortcuts.
6. Save, print, and then close **WordL2_C5_A1.docx**.

Figure 5.13 Assessment 1

Keyboard Shortcuts

Word includes keyboard shortcuts you can use for creating, viewing, and saving documents. Press Ctrl + N to display a new blank document or press Ctrl + O to open a document. Use the shortcut Ctrl + W to close the currently open document. Additional keyboard shortcuts include pressing Alt + Ctrl + S to split the document window and pressing Alt + Shift + C to remove the document window split.

Assessment

2 INSERT FOOTNOTES IN DESIGNING A NEWSLETTER REPORT

1. Open **WordReport14.docx** and then save the document and name it **WordL2_C5_A2**.
2. Create the first footnote shown in Figure 5.14 at the end of the first paragraph in the *Applying Guidelines* section.
3. Create the second footnote shown in Figure 5.14 at the end of the third paragraph in the *Applying Guidelines* section.
4. Create the third footnote shown in Figure 5.14 at the end of the last paragraph in the *Applying Guidelines* section.
5. Create the fourth footnote shown in Figure 5.14 at the end of the only paragraph in the *Choosing Paper Size and Type* section.

6. Create the fifth footnote shown in Figure 5.14 at the end of the only paragraph in the *Choosing Paper Weight* section.
7. Save and then print **WordL2_C5_A2.docx**.
8. Select the entire document and then change the font to Constantia.
9. Select all of the footnotes and change the font to Constantia.
10. Delete the third footnote.
11. Save, print, and then close **WordL2_C5_A2.docx**.

Figure 5.14 Assessment 2

Habermann, James, "Designing a Newsletter," *Desktop Designs*, January/February 2010, pages 23-29.

Pilante, Shirley G., "Adding Pizzazz to Your Newsletter," *Desktop Publisher*, September 2009, pages 32-39.

Maddock, Arlita G., "Guidelines for a Better Newsletter," *Business Computing*, June 2010, pages 9-14.

Alverso, Monica, "Paper Styles for Newsletters," *Design Technologies*, March 14, 2009, pages 45-51.

Sutton, Keith, "Choosing Paper Styles," *Design Techniques*, March/April, 2009, pages 8-11.

Assessment

3 INSERT CITATIONS AND BIBLIOGRAPHY IN A PRIVACY RIGHTS REPORT

1. Open **WordReference02.docx** and then save the document and name it **WordL2_C5_A3**.
2. Press Ctrl + End to move the insertion point to the end of the document and then type the text shown in Figure 5.15 up to the first citation (the text *(Hartley, 2008)*). Insert the source information from a journal article written by Kenneth Hartley using the following information:
   Author = Kenneth Hartley
   Title = Privacy Laws
   Journal Name = Business World
   Year = 2008
   Pages = 24-46
   Volume = 12

3. Continue typing the text up to the next citation (the text *(Ferraro, 2010)*) and insert the following source information from a book:

    Author = Ramona Ferraro
    Title = Business Employee Rights
    Year = 2010
    City = Tallahassee
    Publisher = Everglades Publishing House

4. Continue typing the text up to the next citation (the text *(Aldrich, 2010)*) and insert the following information from a periodical article:

    Author = Nadine Aldrich
    Title = Do Employers Have the Right?
    Periodical Title = Great Plains Times
    Year = 2008
    Month = May
    Day = 6
    Pages = 18-22

5. Insert the page number in the citation by Nadine Aldrich using the Edit Citation dialog box.
6. Type the remaining text in Figure 5.15.
7. Edit the Kenneth Hartley source title to read *Small Business Privacy Laws* in the *Master List* section of the Source Manager dialog box.
8. Select and delete the last two sentences in the second paragraph and then delete the Ramona Ferraro source in the *Current List* section of the Source Manager dialog box.
9. Insert a bibliography at the end of the document on a separate page.
10. Create a new source in the document using the Source Manager dialog box and include the following source information for an article at a Web site:

    Author = Rom Farooq
    Name of Webpage = Small Business Policies and Procedures
    Name of Website = Small Business Administration
    Year = 2009
    Month = December
    Day = 12
    Year Accessed = (type current year)
    Month Accessed = (type current month)
    Day Accessed = (type current day)
    URL = www.emcp.org

11. Insert a citation for Rom Farooq at the end of the last sentence in the first paragraph.
12. Update the bibliography.
13. Format the bibliography to meet APA requirements with the following changes:
    a. Center the title *Bibliography*.
    b. Select the *Bibliography* title and the entries below the title and change the line spacing to 2.0.
    c. Change the spacing after to *0 pt*.
    d. Hang indent the bibliography entries.
14. Save and then print **WordL2_C5_A3.docx**.
15. Change the document and bibliography from APA style to MLA style.
16. Save, print page 2, and then close **WordL2_C5_A3.docx**.

Figure 5.15 **Assessment 3**

An exception to the ability of companies to monitor their employees does

exist. If the company has pledged to respect any aspect of employee privacy, it must

keep that pledge. For example, if a business states that it will not monitor employee

e-mail or phone calls, by law, it must follow this stated policy (Hartley, 2008).

However, no legal requirement exists mandating that companies notify their

employees when and if monitoring takes place (Ferraro, 2010). Therefore,

employees should assume they are always monitored and act accordingly.

Privacy advocates are calling for this situation to change. "They acknowledge

that employers have the right to ensure that their employees are doing their jobs,

but they question the need to monitor employees without warning and without

limit" (Aldrich, 2008, p. 18). The American Civil Liberties Union has, in fact, proposed

a Fair Electronic Monitoring Policy to prevent abuses of employee privacy.

Assessment

4 **CONVERT FOOTNOTES TO ENDNOTES IN DESIGNING A NEWSLETTER REPORT**

1. Using the Help files, learn how to convert footnotes to endnotes.
2. Open **WordL2_C5_A2.docx** and then save the document and name it **WordL2_C5_A4**.
3. Convert the footnotes to endnotes.
4. Save, print, and then close **WordL2_C5_A4.docx**.

CASE study

Apply Your Skills

Part 1

You are the office manager for Lincoln Freelance Services. You have been compiling information on keyboard shortcuts for an employee training manual. Using the Help feature, find information on keyboard shortcuts for finding, replacing, and browsing through text as well as keyboard shortcuts for references, footnotes, and endnotes. Type the information you find on the keyboard shortcuts in a Word document. Use nonbreaking spaces within keyboard shortcuts. Provide a title for the document and insert any other formatting to improve the visual appeal of the document. Save the document and name it **WordL2_C5_CS_P1**. Print and then close the document.

Part 2

Lincoln Freelance Services provides freelance employees for businesses in Baltimore and surrounding communities. A new industrial park has opened in Baltimore and you need to fill a number of temporary positions. You decide to send a letter to current clients living in Baltimore to let them know about the new industrial park and the temporary jobs that are available. Create a letter main document and include in the letter, the information that a new industrial park is opening in a few months, the location of the park (you determine a location), and that Lincoln Freelance Services will be providing temporary employees for many of the technology jobs. Include a list of at least five technology jobs (find job titles on the Internet) for which you will be placing employees. Include any additional information in the letter. Merge the letter main document with only those clients in the **LFSClients.mdb** data source file living in Baltimore. Save the merged letters and name the document **WordL2_C5_CS_P2**. Print and then close **WordL2_C5_CS_P2.docx**. Save the letter main document and name it **WordL2_C5_CS_P2_MD** and then close the document.

Part 3

Your supervisor has given you a report on newsletter guidelines and asked you to reformat it into the APA reference style. Open the **WordL2_C5_A2.docx** document and then save it and name it **WordL2_C5_CS_P3**. Change the title to *DESIGNING A NEWSLETTER* and remove the title *SECTION 2: CREATING NEWSLETTER LAYOUT*. Remove the footnotes and instead insert the information as citations and insert a bibliography on a separate page. Save **WordL2_C5_CS_P3.docx**.

Part 4

Your supervisor has asked you to include some additional information on newsletter guidelines. Using the Internet, look for sites that provide information on desktop publishing and/or newsletter design guidelines. Include in the **WordL2_C5_CS_P3.docx** report document at least one additional paragraph with information you found on the Internet and include a citation to the source(s). Save, print, and then close the report.

Working with Shared Documents

PERFORMANCE OBJECTIVES

Upon successful completion of Chapter 7, you will be able to:

- Insert, edit, and delete comments
- Track changes to a document and customize tracking
- Compare documents
- Combine documents

word Chapter 7

SNAP

Tutorial 7.1
Working with Shared Documents

In a company environment, you may work with other employees and you may need to share and distribute documents to members of the company. You may be part of a workgroup in a company, which is a networked collection of computers sharing files, printers, and other resources. As a member of a workgroup, you can collaborate with other members of the workgroup and distribute documents for review and/or revision. In this chapter, you will perform workgroup activities such as inserting comments, tracking changes in a document from multiple users, comparing documents, and combining documents from multiple users.

Note: Before beginning computer projects, copy to your storage medium the Word2007L2C7 subfolder from the Word2007L2 folder on the CD that accompanies this textbook and then make Word2007L2C7 the active folder.

Project 1 Insert Comments in a Computers Report

You will open a report on computers in communications and entertainment and then insert and edit comments from multiple users.

Inserting Comments

If you want to make comments in a document, or if a reviewer wants to make comments in a document written by someone else, insert a comment. To create a comment, select the text or item on which you want to comment or position the insertion point at the end of the text, click the Review tab, and then click the New Comment button in the Comments group. This displays a Comment balloon at the right margin as shown in Figure 7.1.

Depending on any previous settings applied, clicking the New Comment button may cause the Reviewing pane to display at the left side of the document rather than the Comment balloon. If this happens, click the Balloons button in the Tracking group in the Review tab and then click *Show Only Comments and Formatting in Balloons* at the drop-down list.

HINT
Use comments to add notes, suggestions, or explanations, or add a comment to communicate with other members in your workgroup.

HINT
If your computer has a sound card and a microphone, you can record voice comments.

Figure 7.1 Comment Balloon

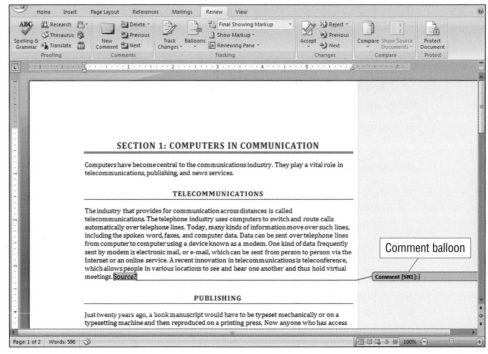

Project 1a Inserting Comments

1. Open **WordReport06.docx** and then save the document and name it **WordL2_C7_P1**.
2. Insert a comment by completing the following steps:
   a. Position the insertion point at the end of the paragraph in the *TELECOMMUNICATIONS* section.
   b. Press the spacebar once and then type Source?.
   c. Select *Source?*.
   d. Click the Review tab.
   e. Click the New Comment button in the Comments group.
   f. Type Please add the source for the information in this paragraph. in the Comment balloon.

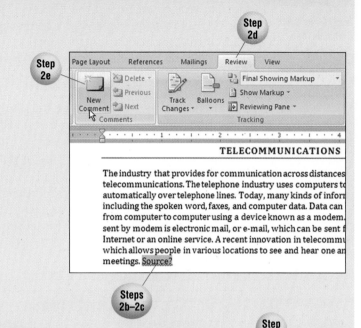

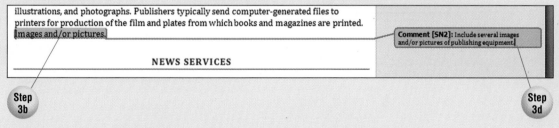

3. Insert another comment by completing the following steps:
   a. Move the insertion point to the end of the paragraph in the *Publishing* section.
   b. Press the spacebar once, type Images and/or pictures., and then select *Images and/or pictures*.
   c. Click the New Comment button in the Comments group.
   d. Type Include several images and/or pictures of publishing equipment. in the Comment balloon.

illustrations, and photographs. Publishers typically send computer-generated files to printers for production of the film and plates from which books and magazines are printed. Images and/or pictures.

NEWS SERVICES

Comment [SN2]: Include several images and/or pictures of publishing equipment.

Step 3b

Step 3d

4. Save **WordL2_C7_P1.docx**.

Inserting Comments in the Reviewing Pane

You can type comments in the Reviewing pane rather than a Comment balloon. The Reviewing pane displays any comments inserted in the document as well as tracked changes made to the document. To insert a comment in the Reviewing pane, click the Balloons button in the Tracking group in the Review tab and then click *Show All Revisions Inline* at the drop-down list. The Reviewing pane displays at the left side of the screen as shown in Figure 7.2. (The Reviewing pane might also display along the bottom of the screen. To specify the location, click the Reviewing pane button arrow in the Tracking group in the Review tab and then click *Reviewing Pane Vertical* or *Reviewing Pane Horizontal*.)

The summary section at the top of the Reviewing pane displays information about the number of comments and changes made to the document. Type your comment in the Reviewing pane and then click the Reviewing Pane button in the Review tab to remove the pane or click the Close button (contains an X) located in the upper right corner of the Reviewing pane.

Figure 7.2 Vertical Reviewing Pane

Comments inserted into a document display in the Reviewing pane.

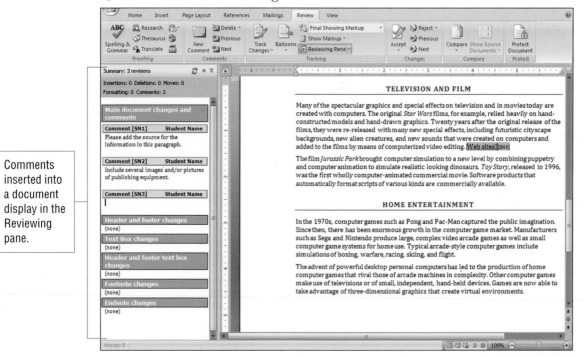

Project 1b — Inserting a Comment in the Reviewing Pane

1. With **WordL2_C7_P1.docx** open, show comments in the Reviewing Pane rather than in Comment balloons by completing the following steps:
   a. If necessary, click the Review tab.
   b. Click the Balloons button.
   c. Click *Show All Revisions Inline* at the drop-down list.

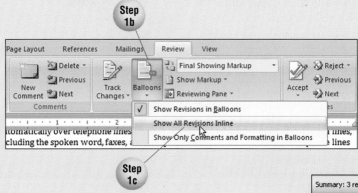

Step 1b

Step 1c

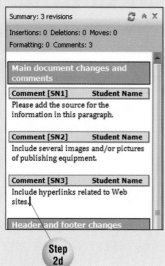

2. Insert a comment by completing the following steps:
   a. Move the insertion point to the end of the first paragraph of text in the *Television and Film* section.
   b. Press the spacebar once, type Web sites?, and then select *Web sites?*
   c. Click the New Comment button in the Comments group in the Review tab.
   d. With the insertion point positioned in the Reviewing pane, type Include hyperlinks related to Web sites.
3. Click the Reviewing Pane button in the Tracking group to turn off the display of the Reviewing pane.

Step 2d

Navigating to Comments

In a long document with many comments, the Previous and Next buttons in the Comments group in the Review tab are useful. Click the Next button in the Comments group to navigate to the next comment or click the Previous button to move the insertion point to the previous comment in the document.

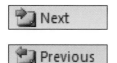

QUICK STEPS

Edit a Comment
1. Click Review tab.
2. Click the Reviewing Pane button.
3. Click in desired comment in pane.
4. Make desired changes.
OR
1. Click Review tab.
2. Turn on display of Comment balloons.
3. Click in Comment balloon.
4. Make desired changes.

Editing a Comment

To edit a comment in the Reviewing pane, click the Reviewing Pane button to turn it on and then click in the comment in the pane. Make desired changes to the comment and then click the Reviewing Pane button to remove it. To edit a comment in a Comment balloon, turn on the display of Comment balloons, click in the Comment balloon, and then make desired changes. You can respond directly to another user's comments by clicking in the Comment balloon, adding your initials so the source is clear, and then typing your response.

Project 1c   Editing Comments

1. With **WordL2_C7_P1.docx** open, navigate to comments by completing the following steps:
   a. Press Ctrl + Home to move the insertion point to the beginning of the document.
   b. If necessary, click the Review tab.
   c. Click the Next button in the Comments group. (This moves the insertion point to the first comment reference, opens the Reviewing pane, and inserts the insertion point in the pane.)

Step 1c

   d. Click the Next button to display the second comment.
   e. Click the Next button to display the third comment.
   f. Click the Previous button to display the second comment.
2. With the insertion point positioned in the Reviewing pane, edit the second comment so it displays as *Include several clip art, photos, or other images of publishing equipment.*
3. Click the Reviewing Pane button to remove the pane.
4. Edit a comment in a Comment balloon by completing the following steps:
   a. Click the Balloons button in the Tracking group and then click *Show Only Comments and Formatting in Balloons* at the drop-down list.
   b. Move the insertion point to the first paragraph in the *Television and Film* paragraph and then click in the Comment balloon that displays at the right.
   c. Move the insertion point immediately left of the period at the end of the sentence and then type and include any pertinent Web sites.

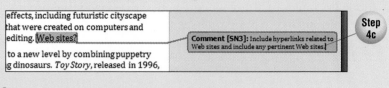

Step 4c

   d. Click in the document.
   e. Click the Balloons button and then click *Show All Revisions Inline*.
5. Save **WordL2_C7_P1.docx**.

Inserting Comments from Other Users

More than one user can make comments in a document. Word distinguishes comments from users by color. Comments from the first person are inserted in red and comments from the second person are inserted in blue. You can.change the user name and initials at the Word Options dialog box with *Popular* selected at the left as shown in Figure 7.3. To change the user name, select the current name in the *User name* text box and then type the desired name. Complete similar steps to change the user initials in the *Initials* text box.

Printing Comments

Print a document with the comments or print just the comments and not the document. To print a document and comments, display the Print dialog box, click the down-pointing arrow at the right side of the *Print what* option, and then click *Document showing markup* at the drop-down list. To print only comments, display the Print dialog box, click the down-pointing arrow at the right side of the *Print what* option, and then click *List of markup* at the drop-down list. This prints the contents of the Reviewing pane including comments as well as any tracked changes or changes to headers, footers, text boxes, footnotes, or endnotes.

QUICK STEPS

Change User Name and Initials
1. Click Office button, Word Options.
2. Type desired name in *User name* text box.
3. Type desired initials in *Initials* text box.
4. Click OK.

Print Comments
1. Click Office button, *Print*.
2. Click down-pointing arrow at right of *Print what* option.
3. Click *Document showing markup* at drop-down list.
4. Click OK.

Figure 7.3 Word Options Dialog Box with Popular Selected

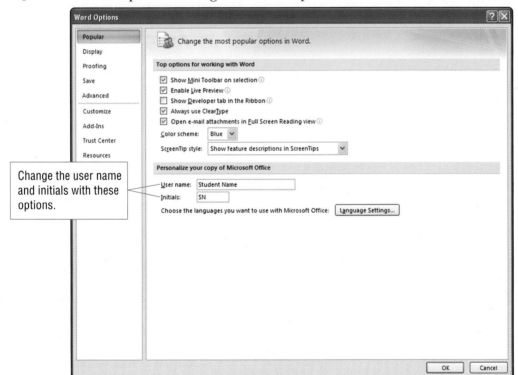

Change the user name and initials with these options.

Deleting a Comment

Delete a comment by clicking the Next button in the Comments group in the Review tab and then clicking the Delete button. If you want to delete all comments in a document, click the Delete button arrow and then click *Delete All Comments in Document* at the drop-down list.

Project 1d Changing User Information; Inserting and Deleting Comments

1. With **WordL2_C7_P1.docx** open, change the user information by completing the following steps:
   a. Click the Office button.
   b. Click the Word Options button that displays toward the bottom of the drop-down list.
   c. At the Word Options dialog box, make sure *Popular* is selected in the left panel.
   d. Make a note of the current name and initials in the *Personalize your copy of Microsoft Office* section.
   e. Select the current name in the *User name* text box and then type Olivia Stanton.
   f. Select the current initials in the *Initials* text box and then type OS.
   g. Click OK to close the Word Options dialog box.

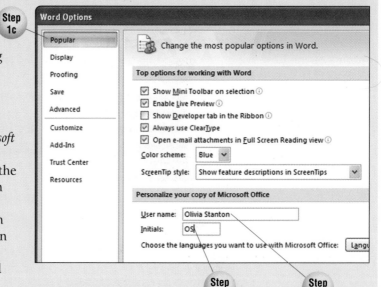

2. Insert a comment by completing the following steps:
   a. Move the insertion point to the end of the first paragraph of text in the *HOME ENTERTAINMENT* section.
   b. Press the spacebar once and then type Examples?.
   c. Make sure the Review tab is active and then select *Examples?*
   d. Click the New Comment button in the Comments groups.
   e. Type Provide pictures of gaming systems. in the Reviewing pane.
   f. Click the Reviewing Pane button to remove the pane.

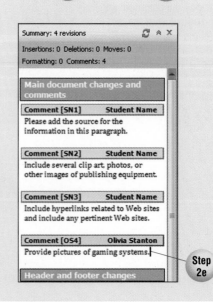

3. Print only the information in the Reviewing pane by completing the following steps:
   a. Press Ctrl + P to display the Print dialog box.
   b. At the Print dialog box, click the down-pointing arrow at the right side of the *Print what* option and then click *List of markup* at the drop-down list.
   c. Click OK.
4. Delete a comment by completing the following steps:
   a. Press Ctrl + Home.
   b. If necessary, click the Review tab.
   c. Click the Next button in the Comments group.
   d. Click the Next button again.
   e. Click the Delete button in the Comments group.
5. Print only the information in the Reviewing pane by completing Step 3.
6. Click the Reviewing Pane button to remove the pane.
7. Change the user information back to the default by completing the following steps:
   a. Click the Office button and then click the Word Options button at the bottom of the drop-down list.
   b. At the Word Options dialog box with *Popular* selected, select *Olivia Stanton* that displays in the *User name* text box and then type original name.
   c. Select the initials *OS* in the *Initials* text box and then type the original initials.
   d. Click OK to close the dialog box.
8. Save and then close **WordL2_C7_P1.docx**.

Step 3b

 roject ② **Track Changes in a Building Construction Agreement**

You will open a building construction agreement, turn on tracking, and then make changes to the document. You will also customize tracking and accept and reject changes.

Tracking Changes to a Document

If more than one person in a workgroup needs to review and edit a document, consider using the tracking feature. When tracking is turned on, Word tracks each deletion, insertion, or formatting change made to the document. For example, deleted text is not removed from the document but instead displays with a line through it and in a different color. Word uses a different color (up to eight) for each person making changes to the document. In this way, the person looking at the document can identify which author made what change.

Turn on tracking by clicking the Review tab and then clicking the Track Changes button in the Tracking group. You can also press Ctrl + Shift + E to turn on tracking. Turn off tracking by completing the same steps. By default, some changes such as deleting and inserting text display in the document. If you make changes to formatting such as changing the font or font size, Word inserts a vertical line at the left margin indicating a change was made to text.

QUICK STEPS

Turn on Tracking
1. Click Review tab.
2. Click the Track Changes button.
OR
Press Ctrl + Shift + E.

Track Changes

You can specify what tracking information displays in the document with options at the Balloons button drop-down list. To show all revisions in the document in balloons at the right margin, click the *Show Revisions in Balloons* option at the Balloons button drop-down list. Click the *Show Only Comments and Formatting in Balloons* option at the drop-down list and insertions and deletions display in the text while comments and formatting changes display in balloons at the right margin. Remember that the Reviewing Pane displays the total number of changes made to the document as well as the number of changes of each type.

Project 2a   Tracking Changes in a Document

1. Open **WordContract03.docx** and then save the document and name it **WordL2_C7_P2**.
2. Turn on tracking by clicking the Review tab and then clicking the Track Changes button in the Tracking group.
3. Type the word **BUILDING** between the words *THIS* and *AGREEMENT* in the first paragraph of text in the document. (The text you type displays in the document underlined and in red.)
4. Delete *thirty (30)* in the second paragraph. (The deleted text displays as strikethrough text in the document.)
5. Type *sixty (60)*.

Step 3

BUILDING CONSTRUCTION AGREEMENT

THIS BUILDING AGREEMENT made this _____ day of_____, 20____ by and between
_____, hereinafter referred to as "builder," and
_____, hereinafter referred to as "owner," the builder and the owner, for the considerations hereinafter named, agrees as follows:

Construction Loan and Financing Arrangements: The owner either has or will obtain a construction loan to finance the work to be performed under this Agreement. If adequate financing has not been arranged within thirty (30) sixty (60) days of the date of this Agreement, or the owner cannot provide evidence to the builder of other financial ability to pay the full amount of the contract, then the builder at his option may treat this Agreement as null and void, and retain the down payment made on the execution of this Agreement.

Step 4   **Step 5**

6. Move a paragraph of text by completing the following steps:
   a. Select the paragraph of text that begins with *Supervision of Work:* including the blank line below the paragraph.
   b. Press Ctrl + X to cut the text. (The text stays in the document and displays in red with strikethrough characters.)
   c. Position the insertion point at the beginning of the word *Start* (in the paragraph that begins *Start of Construction and Completion:*).
   d. Press Ctrl + V to insert the cut text. (This inserts the text in green and double underlined in the new location and also changes the text in the original location to green with double-strikethrough characters.)
7. Turn off tracking by clicking the Track Changes button in the Tracking group.
8. Display revisions in balloons by clicking the Balloons button in the Tracking group and then clicking *Show Revisions in Balloons* at the drop-down list.
9. After looking at the revisions in balloons, click the Balloons button and then click *Show All Revisions Inline* at the drop-down list.
10. Save **WordL2_C7_P2.docx**

Display information on tracking changes by positioning the mouse pointer on a change. After approximately one second, a box displays above the change containing the author's name, date, time, and the type of change (for example, whether it was a deletion or insertion). You can also display information on tracking changes by displaying the Reviewing pane. Each change is listed separately in the Reviewing pane. Use the arrow keys at the right side of the Reviewing pane to scroll through the pane and view each change.

Changing User Information

If more than one person makes tracked changes in a document, the revisions display in a different color. In the Comments section in this chapter, you learned how to change the user name and initials at the Word Options dialog box. You can also display the Word Options dialog box with *Popular* selected by clicking the Track Changes button arrow and then clicking *Change User Name* at the drop-down list.

QUICK STEPS

Change User Information
1. Click Review tab.
2. Click the Track Changes button arrow.
3. Click *Change User Name* at drop-down list.
4. Type desired name in *User name* text box.
5. Type desired initials in *Initials* text box.

Project 2b Changing User Information and Tracking Changes

1. With **WordL2_C7_P2.docx** open, change the user information by completing the following steps:
   a. If necessary, click the Review tab.
   b. Click the Track Changes button arrow and then click *Change User Name*.
   c. At the Word Options dialog box with *Popular* selected, select the current name in the *User name* text box and then type Julia Moore.
   d. Select the initials in the *Initials* text box and then type JM.
   e. Click OK to close the dialog box.
2. Make additional changes to the contract and track the changes by completing the following steps:
   a. Click the Track Changes button to turn on tracking.
   b. Select the title *BUILDING CONSTRUCTION AGREEMENT* and then change the font size to 14.
   c. Delete the text *at his option* located in the second sentence in the second paragraph.
   d. Delete the text *and Completion* that displays in the beginning text in the fourth paragraph.

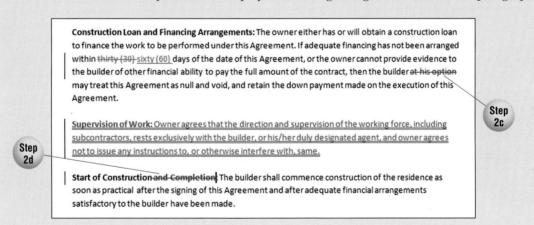

Construction Loan and Financing Arrangements: The owner either has or will obtain a construction loan to finance the work to be performed under this Agreement. If adequate financing has not been arranged within ~~thirty (30)~~ _sixty (60)_ days of the date of this Agreement, or the owner cannot provide evidence to the builder of other financial ability to pay the full amount of the contract, then the builder ~~at his option~~ may treat this Agreement as null and void, and retain the down payment made on the execution of this Agreement.

Supervision of Work: Owner agrees that the direction and supervision of the working force, including subcontractors, rests exclusively with the builder, or his/her duly designated agent, and owner agrees not to issue any instructions to, or otherwise interfere with, same.

Start of Construction ~~and Completion~~ The builder shall commence construction of the residence as soon as practical after the signing of this Agreement and after adequate financial arrangements satisfactory to the builder have been made.

e. Delete *thirty (30)* in the paragraph that begins *Builder's Right to Terminate the Contract:* (located on the second page).

f. Type *sixty (60)*.

g. Select the text *IN WITNESS WHEREOF* that displays toward the bottom of the document and then turn on bold.

3. Click the Review tab and then click the Track Changes button to turn off tracking.

4. Click the Reviewing Pane button to turn on the display of the pane and then use the up- and down-pointing arrow at the right side of the Reviewing pane to review the changes.

5. View the changes in balloons by clicking the Balloons button and then clicking *Show Revisions in Balloons*.

6. Click the Reviewing Pane button to turn off the display of the pane. Scroll through the document and view the changes in the balloons.

7. Click the Balloons button and then click *Show All Revisions Inline* at the drop-down list.

8. Change the user information back to the information that displayed before you typed *Julia Moore* and the initials *JM* by completing the following steps:

a. Click the Track Changes button arrow and then click *Change User Name*.

b. At the Word Options dialog box, select *Julia Moore* in the *User name* text box and then type the original name.

c. Select the initials *JM* in the *Initials* text box and then type the original initials.

d. Click OK to close the dialog box.

9. Print the document with the markups by completing the following steps:

a. Press Ctrl + P to display the Print dialog box.

b. At the Print dialog box, make sure the *Print what* option displays as *Document showing markup* and then click OK.

10. Save **WordL2_C7_P2.docx**.

Displaying for Review

Word displays all tracked changes and comments in a document by default. You can change this default with options at the Display for Review button drop-down list. The default setting is *Final Showing Markup*. You can change this to *Final*, which displays the document with all changes included, *Original Showing Markup*, which displays the original document with changes, or *Original*, which displays the original document without the changes.

Showing Markup

You can customize what tracked changes display with options at the Show Markup drop-down list. If you want to show only one particular type of tracked change, remove the check marks before all options except the desired one. For example, if you want to view only formatting changes and not other types of changes such as insertions and deletions, remove the check mark before each option except *Formatting*. If more than one reviewer has made tracked changes in a document, you can show only those changes from a particular reviewer. To do this, click the Show Markup button, point to *Reviewer* at the bottom of the drop-down list, and then click the *All Reviewer* check box to remove the check mark. Click the Show Markup button, point to *Reviewers*, and then click the check box before the desired reviewer.

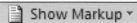

Project 2c | Changing the Display for Review and Showing Markup

1. With **WordL2_C7_P2.docx** open, change the display for review by completing the following steps:
   a. If necessary, click the Review tab.
   b. Click the Display for Review button arrow and then click *Final*. (This displays the document with the changes included.)
   c. Click the Display for Review button and then click *Original*. (This displays the original document before changes.)
   d. Click the Display for Review button and then click *Final Showing Markup*.
2. Display only those changes made by Julia Moore by completing the following steps:
   a. Click the Show Markup button in the Tracking group and then point to *Reviewers*.
   b. Click the *All Reviewers* check box to remove the check mark. (This also removes the drop-down list.)
   c. Click the Show Markup button, point to *Reviewers*, and then click *Julia Moore*.
   d. Scroll through the document and notice that only changes made by Julia Moore display in the document.
   e. Return the display to all reviewers by clicking the Show Markup button, pointing to *Reviewers*, and then clicking *All Reviewers*.
3. Save **WordL2_C7_P2.docx**.

Customizing Track Changing Options

The track changes feature uses default settings when displaying changes to a document. For example, inserted text displays in red with an underline below the text and deleted text displays in red with strikethrough characters. Moved text displays in the original location in green with double strikethrough characters and the text in the new location displays in green with double-underline below the text. You can customize these options along with others at the Track Changes Options dialog box shown in Figure 7.4. With options at this dialog box, you can customize the displays of markup text, moved text, table cell highlighting, formatting, and balloons.

Figure 7.4 Track Changes Options Dialog Box

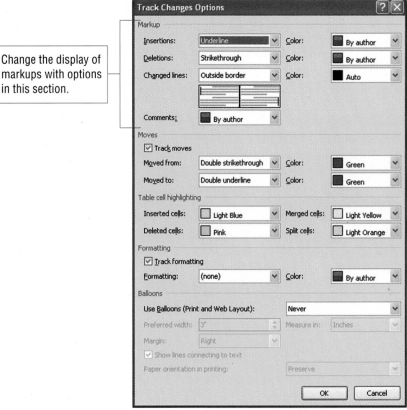

Change the display of markups with options in this section.

Project 2d   Customizing Track Changing Options

1. With **WordL2_C7_P2.docx** open, customize the track changes options by completing the following steps:

   a. If necessary, click the Review tab.

   b. Click the Track Changes button arrow and then click *Change Tracking Options*.

   c. At the Track Changes Options dialog box, click the down-pointing arrow at the right side of the *Insertions* option and then click *Double underline* at the drop-down list.

   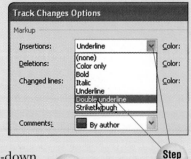

   d. Click the down-pointing arrow at the right side of the *Insertions* color option box and then click *Green* at the drop-down list. (You will need to scroll down the list to display this color.)

   e. Click the down-pointing arrow at the right side of the *Moved from* color option box and then click the *Dark Blue* color at the drop-down list.

   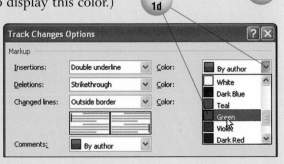

   f. Click the down-pointing arrow at the right side of the *Moved to* color option box and then click the *Violet* color at the drop-down list. (You will need to scroll down the list to display this color.)

   g. Click OK to close the dialog box.

2. Save **WordL2_C7_P2.docx**.

Step 1c

Step 1d

Navigating to Revisions

Navigate to revisions in a document using the Next and Previous buttons in the Changes group in the Review tab. Click the Next button and Word selects the next revision in the document or click the Previous button to select the previous revision. If you turn on tracked changes and then move text, revision balloons will display a small Go button in the lower right corner of the balloon identifying the deleted (cut) text and the balloon identifying the inserted (pasted) text. Click the Go button in one of the balloons to move the insertion point to the other balloon.

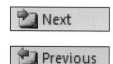

Accepting/Rejecting Revisions

You can accept or reject changes made to a document. Click the Accept button to accept the change and move to the next change. Click the Reject button to reject the change and move to the next. Click the Reject button arrow and a drop-down list displays with options to reject the change and move to the next change, reject the change, reject all changes shown, and reject all changes in the document. Similar options are available at the Accept button arrow drop-down list.

Project **2e** **Accepting/Rejecting Changes**

1. With **WordL2_C7_P2.docx** open, display all tracked changes *except* formatting changes by completing the following steps:
   a. Click the Show Markup button and then click *Formatting* at the drop-down list.
   b. Scroll through the document and notice that the vertical line at the left side of the formatting locations is removed.
   c. Click the Show Markup button and then click *Formatting* at the drop-down list. (This inserts a check mark in the check box.)
2. Navigate to tracked changes by completing the following steps:
   a. Press Ctrl + Home to move the insertion point to the beginning of the document.
   b. Click the Next button in the Changes group to select the first change.
   c. Click the Next button again to select the second change.
   d. Click the Previous button to select the first change.
3. Navigate between the original location of the moved text and the new location by completing the following step:
   a. Press Ctrl + Home to move the insertion point to the beginning of the document.
   b. Click the Balloons button and then click *Show Revisions in Balloons*.
   c. Scroll to the right to display the right edge of the balloons and then click the Go button that displays in the lower right corner of the Moved balloon. (This selects the text in the Moved up balloon.)

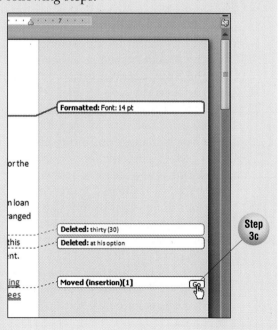

d. Click the Go button in the lower right corner of the Moved up balloon. (This selects the text in the Moved balloon.)

e. Click the Balloons button and then click *Show All Revisions Inline*.

4. Press Ctrl + Home to move the insertion point to the beginning of the document.

5. Display and then accept only formatting changes by completing the following steps:

a. Click the Show Markup button in the Tracking group and then click *Comments* at the drop-down list. (This removes the check mark and the drop-down list.)

b. Click the Show Markup button and then click *Ink*.

c. Click the Show Markup button and then click *Insertions and Deletions*.

d. Click the Show Markup button and then click *Markup Area Highlight* (*Formatting* is now the only option containing a check mark.)

e. Click the Accept button arrow and then click *Accept All Changes Shown* at the drop-down list. (This accepts only the formatting changes in the document since those are the only changes showing.)

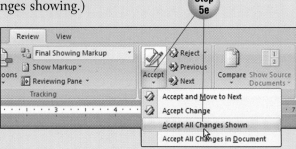

6. Display all changes by completing the following steps:

a. Click the Show Markup button and then click *Comments* at the drop-down list.

b. Click the Show Markup button and then click *Ink*.

c. Click the Show Markup button and then click *Insertions and Deletions*.

d. Click the Show Markup button and then click *Markup Area Highlight*.

7. Press Ctrl + Home to move the insertion point to the beginning of the document.

8. Reject the change inserting the word *BUILDING* by clicking the Next button in the Changes group and then clicking the Reject button. (This rejects the change and moves to the next revision in the document.)

9. Click the Accept button to accept the change deleting *thirty (30)*.

10. Click the Accept button to accept the change inserting *sixty (60)*.

11. Click the Reject button to reject the change deleting the words *at his option*.

12. Accept all remaining changes by clicking the Accept button arrow and then clicking *Accept All Changes in Document* at the drop-down list.

13. Return track changes options to the default settings by completing the following steps:

a. If necessary, click the Review tab.

b. Click the Track Changes button arrow and then click *Change Tracking Options*.

c. At the Track Changes Options dialog box, click the down-pointing arrow at the right side of the *Insertions* option and then click *Underline* at the drop-down list.

d. Click the down-pointing arrow at the right side of the *Insertions* color option box and then click *By author* at the drop-down list. (You will need to scroll up the list to display this color.)

e. Click the down-pointing arrow at the right side of the *Moved from* color option box and then click the *Green* color at the drop-down list. (You may need to scroll down the list to display this color.)

f. Click the down-pointing arrow at the right side of the *Moved to* color option box and then click the *Green* color at the drop-down list.

g. Click OK to close the dialog box.

14. Check to make sure all tracking changes are accepted or rejected by completing the following steps:

a. Click the Reviewing Pane button in the Tracking group.

b. Check the summary information that displays at the top of the Reviewing pane and make sure that a zero follows all of the options.

c. Click the Reviewing Pane button.

15. Save, print, and then close **WordL2_C7_P2.docx**.

Project 3 Compare Lease Agreement Documents

You will compare the contents of a lease agreement and an edited version of the lease agreement. You will then customize compare options and then compare the documents again.

Comparing Documents

Word contains a legal blackline option you can use to compare two documents and display the differences as tracked changes in a third document. To use this option, click the Review tab, click the Compare button in the Compare group, and then click *Compare* at the drop-down list. This displays the Compare Documents dialog box shown in Figure 7.5. At this dialog box, click the Browse for Original button and then, at the Open dialog box, navigate to the folder containing the desired document and then double-click the document. Click the Browse for Revised button in the Compare Documents dialog box, navigate to the folder containing the desired document, and then double-click the document.

Compare Documents
1. Click Review tab.
2. Click the Compare button.
3. Click *Compare* at drop-down list.
4. Click the Browse for Original button.
5. Double-click desired document.
6. Click the Browse for Revised button.
7. Double-click desired document.

Figure 7.5 Compare Documents Dialog Box

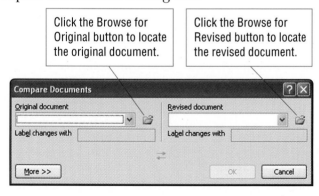

Click the Browse for Original button to locate the original document.

Click the Browse for Revised button to locate the revised document.

HINT
Word does not change the documents you are comparing.

Differences between the original and revised documents display in a new document as tracked changes. (This display may vary depending on the selected option at the Show Source Documents button drop-down list.) You can accept and/or reject changes with the Accept and Reject buttons in the Changes group in the Review tab.

1. Close any open documents.
2. Click the Review tab.
3. Click the Compare button and then click *Compare* at the drop-down list.
4. At the Compare Documents dialog box, click the Browse for Original button.

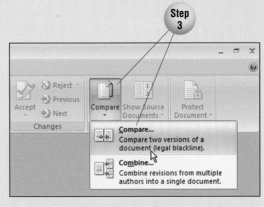

Step 3

Step 4

5. At the Open dialog box, navigate to the Word2007L2C7 folder on your storage medium and then double-click **WordLease02.docx**.
6. At the Compare Documents dialog box, click the Browse for Revised button.
7. At the Open dialog box, double-click **WordEditedLease02.docx**.

Step 6

8. Click the OK button. (This displays a new document with tracked changes identifying the differences between the two documents. If multiple windows display, click the Show Source Documents button in the Compare group and then click Hide Source Documents in the drop-down list.)
9. Click the Quick Print button on the Quick Access toolbar to print the document showing markups.
10. Close the document without saving it.

Customizing Compare Options

H I N T

Changes you make to options in the expanded Compare Documents dialog box will be the default the next time you open the dialog box.

By default, Word compares the original document with the revised document and displays the differences as tracked changes in a third document. You can change this default along with others by expanding the Compare Documents dialog box. Expand the dialog box by clicking the More button and additional options display as shown in Figure 7.6.

Control what types of comparisons are made to the original and revised document with options in the *Comparison settings* section of the dialog box. The *Show changes at* option in the *Show changes* section of the dialog box has a default setting of *Word level*. At this setting, Word shows changes to whole words rather than individual characters within the word. For example, if you deleted the letters *ed* from the end of a word, Word would display the entire word as a change rather than just the *ed*. If you want to show changes by character, click the *Character level* option.

By default, Word displays differences between compared documents in a new document. With options in the *Show changes* section, you can change this to *Original document* or *Revised document*.

Figure 7.6 Expanded Compare Documents Dialog Box

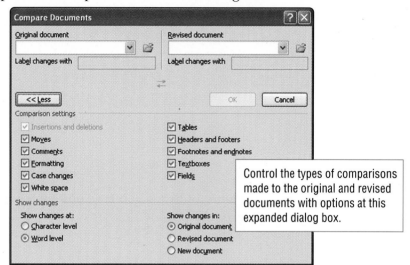

Control the types of comparisons made to the original and revised documents with options at this expanded dialog box.

Project ③ⓓ Customizing Compare Options and Then Comparing Documents

1. Close any open documents.
2. Click the Review tab.
3. Click the Compare button and then click *Compare* at the drop-down list.
4. At the Compare Documents dialog box, click the Browse for Original button.
5. At the Open dialog box, navigate to the Word2007L2C7 folder on your storage medium and then double-click *WordLease02.docx*.
6. At the Compare Documents dialog box, click the Browse for Revised button.
7. At the Open dialog box, double-click *WordEditedLease02.docx*.
8. At the Compare Documents dialog box, click the More button.
9. Click the *Moves* check box and then click the *Formatting* check box to remove the check marks.
10. Click the OK button.
11. Click the Quick Print button on the Quick Access toolbar to print the document showing markups.
12. Close the document without saving it.
13. Return the options to the default settings by completing the following steps:
    a. Close any open documents.
    b. Click the Review tab.
    c. Click the Compare button and then click *Compare* at the drop-down list.
    d. At the Compare Documents dialog box, click the Browse for Original button.
    e. At the Open dialog box, double-click *WordLease02.docx*.
    f. At the Compare Documents dialog box, click the Browse for Revised button.
    g. At the Open dialog box, double-click *WordEditedLease02.docx*.
    h. At the Compare Documents dialog box, click the *Moves* check box to insert a check mark and then click the *Formatting* check box to insert a check mark.

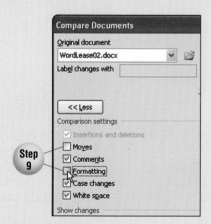

Step 9

i. Click the Less button.
j. Click the OK button.
14. At the new document, accept all of the changes.
15. Save the document and name it **WordL2_C7_P3**.
16. Print and then close the document.

P roject ④ Combine Documents

You will open a lease agreement document and then combine edited versions of the agreement into the original document.

Combine Multiple Versions of a Document
1. Click Review tab.
2. Click the Compare button.
3. Click *Combine* at drop-down list.
4. Click the Browse for Original button.
5. Double-click desired document.
6. Click the Browse for Revised button.
7. Double-click desired document.

Combining Documents

If you send a document for reviewing to several people, you can combine changes made by each person into the original document. You can combine each document with the original until you have incorporated all changes in the original document. To do this, click the Compare button in the Review tab and then click *Combine* at the drop-down list. This displays the Combine Documents dialog box as shown in Figure 7.7. The Combine Documents dialog box contains many of the same options as the Compare Documents dialog box.

Figure 7.7 Combine Documents Dialog Box

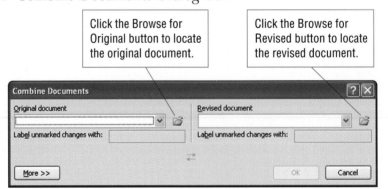

Click the Browse for Original button to locate the original document.

Click the Browse for Revised button to locate the revised document.

Click the Browse for Original button, navigate to the desired folder, and then double-click the original document. Click the Browse for Revised button, navigate to the desired folder, and then double-click one of the documents containing revisions. You can also click the down-pointing arrow at the right side of the *Original document* text box or the *Revised document* text box and a drop-down list displays with the most recently selected documents.

Control how changes are combined with options in the expanded Combine Document dialog box. This document contains many of the same options as the expanded Compare Documents dialog box. By default, Word combines the changes in the revised document into the original document. You can change this default setting with options in the *Show changes in* section. You can choose to combine changes in the revised document or combine changes into a new document.

Project **4a**   **Combining Documents**

1. Close all open documents.
2. Click the Review tab.
3. Click the Compare button in the Compare group and then click *Combine* at the drop-down list.
4. At the Combine Documents dialog box, click the More button to expand the Combine Documents dialog box.
5. Click the *Original Document* option in the *Show changes in* section.
6. Click the Browse for Original button.
7. At the Open dialog box, navigate to the Word2007L2C7 folder on your storage medium and then double-click *WordOriginalLease.docx*.
8. At the Combine Documents dialog box, click the Browse for Revised button.
9. At the Open dialog box, double-click *WordLeaseReviewer1.docx*.
10. Click the OK button.
11. At the message that displays telling you that Word can only store one set of formatting changes in the final, merged document, make sure *Your document (WordOriginalLease.docx)* is selected, and then click the Continue with Merge button.
12. Save the document with Save As and name it **WordL2_C7_P4**.

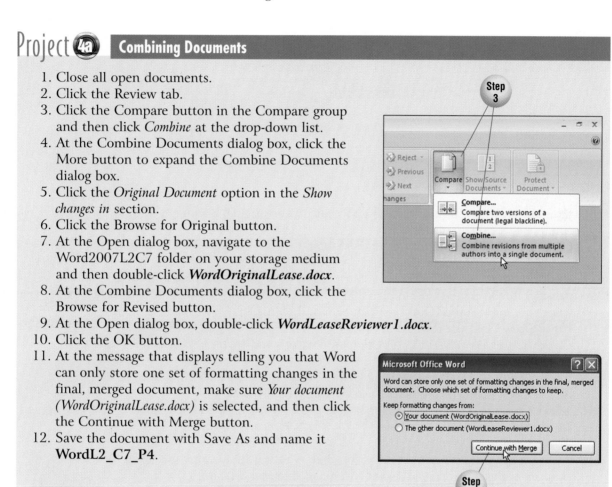

Showing Source Documents

With the Show Source Documents button in the Compare group in the Review tab, you can specify which source documents to display. Click this button and a drop-down list displays with the options *Hide Source Documents*, *Show Original*, *Show Revised*, and *Show Both*. With the *Hide Source Documents* option selected, the original and revised documents do not display on the screen, only the combined document. If you choose the *Show Original* option, the original document displays in a side panel at the right side of the document. Synchronous scrolling is selected so if you scroll in one document the other also scrolls. Choose the *Show Revised* option and the revised document displays in the panel at the right. Choose the *Show Both* option to display the original document in a panel at the right side of the screen and the revised document in a panel below the original document panel.

Project 4b Combining and Showing Documents

1. With **WordL2_C7_P4.docx** open, click the Show Source Documents button in the Compare group and then click *Show Original*. (This displays the original document in a panel at the right side of the screen.)

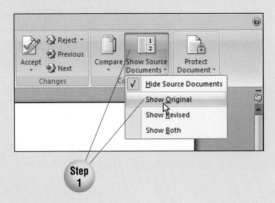

Step 1

2. Drag the scroll box on the vertical scroll bar for the original document and notice how the combined document also scrolls.
3. Click the Show Source Documents button and then click *Show Revised*. Scroll through the combined and revised documents.
4. Click the Show Source Documents button and then click *Show Both* and then scroll through the documents and notice that all three documents scroll simultaneously.
5. Click the Show Source Documents button and then click *Hide Source Documents*.
6. If necessary, close the Reviewing Pane.
7. Click the Review tab, click the Compare button, and then click *Combine* at the drop-down list.
8. At the Combine Documents dialog box, click the Browse for Original button.
9. At the Open dialog box, double-click ***WordL2_C7_P4.docx***.
10. At the Combine Documents dialog box, click the Browse for Revised button.
11. At the Open dialog box, double-click ***WordLeaseReviewer2.docx***.
12. At the Combine Documents dialog box, click the OK button.
13. At the message that displays telling you that Word can only store one set of formatting changes in the final, merged document, make sure *Your document (WordL2_C7_P4.docx)* is selected, and then click the Continue with Merge button.
14. Save **WordL2_C7_P4.docx**.
15. Print the document showing markups.
16. Accept all changes to the document.
17. Save, print, and then close **WordL2_C7_P4.docx**.

CHAPTER summary

- Insert a comment in a document by clicking the New Comment button in the Comments group in the Review tab. When you click the New Comment button, the Reviewing pane displays at the left side of the screen.

- Turn on/off the display of the Reviewing pane with the Reviewing Pane button in the Tracking group in the Review tab.

- You can insert comments in the Reviewing pane or in a Comment balloon. Insert comments in a balloon by clicking the Balloons button in the Tracking group in the Review tab.

- Navigate through comments using the Previous and Next buttons in the Comments group in the Review tab.

- Edit a comment in the Reviewing pane by displaying the Reviewing pane and then making desired changes to the comment. Edit comments in a Comment balloon by turning on the display of balloons, clicking in the desired Comment balloon, and then making desired changes.

- Display information on tracking changes such as author's name, date, time, and the type of change by positioning the mouse pointer on a change. After approximately one second, a box displays with the information. You can also display information on tracking changes by displaying the Reviewing pane.

- If changes are made to a document by another person with different user information, the changes display in a different color. Change user name and initials at the Word Options dialog box with *Popular* selected.

- Print a document containing comments with the comments or choose to print just the comments and not the document.

- Delete a comment by clicking the Next button in the Comments group in the Review tab until the desired comment is selected and then clicking the Delete button in the Comments group.

- Use the tracking feature when more than one person is reviewing a document and making editing changes. Turn on tracking by clicking the Track Changes button in the Tracking group in the Review tab.

- Control how editing markings display in a document with the Display for Review button in the Tracking group in the Review tab. Control the marking changes that Word displays in a document with options at the Show Markup button drop-down list.

- Change tracking default settings with options at the Track Changes Options dialog box. Display this dialog box by clicking the Track Changes button arrow in the Tracking group and then clicking *Change Tracking Options* at the drop-down list.

- Move to the next change in a document by clicking the Next button in the Changes group in the Review tab or click the Previous button to move to the previous change.

- Use the Accept and Reject buttons in the Changes group in the Review tab to accept or reject revisions made in a document.

- Use the Compare button in the Compare group in the Review tab to compare two documents and display the differences between the documents as tracked changes.
- Customize compare document options at the expanded Compare Documents dialog box. Click the More button to expand the dialog box.
- If you send a document for reviewing to several people, you can combine changes made by each person with the original document until all changes are incorporated in the original document. Combine documents with options at the Combine Documents dialog box.
- Customize combining options at the expanded Combine Documents dialog box. Click the More button to expand the dialog box.
- Specify which source documents to display by clicking the Show Source Documents button arrow in the Compare group in the Review tab and then clicking the desired option at the drop-down list.

COMMANDS review

FEATURE	RIBBON TAB, GROUP	BUTTON, OPTION	KEYBOARD SHORTCUT
Comment	Review, Comments		
Reviewing pane	Review, Tracking	Reviewing Pane ▾	
Balloons	Review, Tracking		
Delete comment	Review, Comments	✕ Delete ▾	
Next comment	Review, Comments	Next	
Previous comment	Review, Comments	Previous	
Track changes	Review, Tracking		Ctrl + Shift + E
Display for review	Review, Tracking	Final Showing Markup ▾	
Show markup	Review, Tracking	Show Markup ▾	
Track Changes Options dialog box	Review, Tracking	, Change Tracking Options	
Next revision	Review, Changes	Next	
Previous revision	Review, Changes	Previous	
Accept changes	Review, Changes		
Reject changes	Review, Changes	Reject ▾	
Compare Documents dialog box	Review, Compare	, Compare	
Combine Documents dialog box	Review, Compare	, Combine	
Show source documents	Review, Compare		

CONCEPTS check

Test Your Knowledge

Completion: In the space provided at the right, indicate the correct term, command, or number.

1. Insert a comment into a document by clicking this button in the Comments group in the Review tab.

   _____

2. Navigate to comments by using these two buttons in the Comments group in the Review tab.

   _____

3. If a document contains comments, print only the comments by choosing this option at the Print dialog box *Print what* drop-down list.

   _____

4. Display information on tracking changes in this pane.

   _____

5. Change user information with options at this dialog box.

   _____

6. Turn on the tracking feature by clicking the Track Changes button in this group in the Review tab.

   _____

7. Change tracking default settings with options at this dialog box.

   _____

8. This is the keyboard shortcut to turn on tracking.

   _____

9. This is the default setting for the Display for Review button.

   _____

10. With track changes on, moved text displays in this color by default.

    _____

11. Customize tracking options at this dialog box.

    _____

12. Click the *Combine* option at the Compare button drop-down list and this dialog box displays.

    _____

13. Specify which source document to display with options at this button's drop-down list.

    _____

SKILLS check
Demonstrate Your Proficiency

Assessment

1 INSERT COMMENTS AND TRACK CHANGES IN COMPUTER VIRUSES REPORT

1. Open **WordReport11.docx** and then save the document and name it **WordL2_C7_A1**.
2. Insert a comment at the end of the paragraph in the *TYPES OF VIRUSES* section. To do this, type the word Update, select it, and then create a comment with the following text: *Insert information on the latest virus.*
3. Insert a comment at the end of the last paragraph in the *METHODS OF VIRUS OPERATION* section. To do this, type the words Company Example, select the words, and then create a comment with the following text: *Include information on the latest virus to affect our company.*
4. Insert a comment at the end of the last paragraph in the document. To do this, type the word Information, select it, and then create a comment with the following text: *Include information about laws related to copying software.*
5. Turn on tracking and then make the following changes:
    a. Edit the first sentence in the document so it displays as *The computer virus is one of the most familiar forms of risk to computer security.*
    b. Insert the word computer's between *the* and *motherboard* in the last sentence in the first paragraph of the document.
    c. Delete the word *real* in the second sentence of the *TYPES OF VIRUSES* section and then type significant.
    d. Select and then delete the last sentence in the *Methods of Virus Operation* section (the sentence that begins *A famous logic bomb was the . . .*).
    e. Turn off tracking.
6. Display the Word Options dialog box with *Popular* selected and then change the *User name* to Stacey Phillips and the *Initials* to SP.
7. Turn on tracking and then make the following changes:
    a. Delete the words *or cracker* located in the seventh sentence in the *TYPES OF VIRUSES* section.
    b. Delete the word *garner* in the first sentence in the CHAPTER 2: SECURITY RISKS section and then type generate.
    c. Select and then move the *EMPLOYEE THEFT* section below the *CRACKING SOFTWARE FOR COPYING* section.
    d. Turn off tracking.
8. Display the Word Options dialog box with *Popular* selected and then change the *User name* back to the original name and *Initials* back to the original initials.
9. Accept all of the changes in the document *except* the change moving the *EMPLOYEE THEFT* section below the *CRACKING SOFTWARE FOR COPYING* section.
10. Save, print, and then close **WordL2_C7_A1.docx**.

Assessment

2 COMPARE ORIGINAL AND REVISED DISASTER RECOVERY PLAN REPORT

1. Compare **WordReport13.docx** with **WordEditedReport13.docx** and insert the changes into a new document.
2. Save the compared document and name it **WordL2_C7_A2**.
3. Print only the markups.
4. Reject the changes made to the bulleted text and the changes made to the last paragraph in the *DISASTER RECOVERY PLAN* section and accept all other changes.
5. Number the pages at the bottom center of each page.
6. Insert a table of contents. (Apply the Heading 1 style to the title of the table of contents.)
7. Number the table of contents page at the bottom center of the page. (Change the number to a lowercase Roman numeral. Make sure the table of contents reflects the correct page numbers.)
8. Save **WordL2_C7_A2.docx** and then print the table of contents page.
9. Insert a page break at the beginning of the title *DISASTER RECOVERY PLAN* heading.
10. Update the table of contents.
11. Save, print, and then close **WordL2_C7_A2.docx**.

Assessment

3 COMBINE ORIGINAL AND REVISED LEGAL DOCUMENTS

1. Open **WordLegal01.docx** and then save the document and name it **WordL2_C7_A3**.
2. Close **WordL2_C7_A3.docx**.
3. At a blank screen, combine **WordL2_C7_A3.docx** (the original document) with **WordLegal01Reviewer1.docx** (the revised document) into the original document.
4. Save **WordL2_C7_A3.docx**.
5. Combine **WordL2_C7_A3.docx** (the original document) with **WordLegal01Reviewer2.docx** (the revised document) into the original document.
6. Save **WordL2_C7_A3.docx**.
7. Print the document showing markups.
8. Accept all changes to the document.
9. Save, print, and then close **WordL2_C7_A3.docx**.

Assessment

4 TRACK CHANGES IN A TABLE

1. Open **WordSales.docx** and then save the document and name it **WordL2_C7_A4**.
2. You can track changes made to a table and customize the track changes options for table. Display the Track Changes Options dialog box and experiment with the options in the *Table Cell Highlighting* section and then make the following changes:

a. Change the color for inserted cells to light purple.

b. Change the color for deleted cells to light green.

3. Turn on track changes and then make the following changes:

   a. Insert a new row at the beginning of the table.

   b. Merge the cells in the new row.

   c. Type Clearline Manufacturing in the merged cell.

   d. Delete the *Fanning, Andrew* row.

   e. Insert a new row below *Barnett, Jacqueline* and then type Montano, Neil in the first cell, $530,678 in the second cell, and type $550,377 in the third cell.

   f. Turn off track changes.

4. Save and then print the document with markups.

5. Accept all of the changes.

6. Display the Track Changes Options dialog box and then return the inserted cells color back to *Light Blue* and the deleted cells color back to *Pink*.

7. Save, print, and then close **WordL2_C7_A4.docx**.

Assessment

5 INSERT COMMENTS AND TRACK CHANGES IN A TRAVEL DOCUMENT

1. Open **WordFCTDocument.docx** and then save the document and name it **WordL2_C7_A5**.

2. Display the Track Changes Options dialog box, change the *Use Balloons (Print and Web Layout)* option to *Always* and then make the following changes:

   a. Change the balloon width to 2 inches.

   b. Display balloons at the left margin.

   c. Change the paper orientation to forced landscape.

3. Insert the following comments:

   a. Type the text Country names at the end of the paragraph in the *African Study Adventure* section, select the text, and then insert the comment Ask Jan if she wants to include specific country names.

   b. Type the word Examples at the end of the paragraph in the *Custom Groups* section, select the word, and then insert the comment Please provide custom program examples.

4. Turn on tracking and then make the following changes:

   a. Insert the word *Travel* between *Comprehensive* and *Itineraries* in the *Comprehensive Itineraries* heading.

   b. Change the number *25* in the *Small Groups* section to *20*.

   c. Delete the words *make sure* in the *Accommodations and Meals* section and then type ensure.

   d. Turn off tracking.

5. Save and then print the document with markups.

6. Accept the changes.

7. Return the options at the Track Changes Option dialog box back to the default settings.

8. Save, print, and then close **WordL2_C7_A5.docx**.

CASE study

Apply Your Skills

Part 1

You work in the Training Department at Hart International. Your department is responsible for preparing training material and for training employees on how to use software applications within the company. Your supervisor, Nicole Sweeney, has asked you to help her prepare a Microsoft Word training manual. She has written a portion of the manual and has had two employees, Terry Oberman and Gina Singh, review the contents and make tracked changes. She has asked you to combine the two reviewers' changes into the original document. Combine **WordHIWordTraining.docx** with **WordHIWordTrainingTO.docx** and then combine **WordHIWordTraining.docx** with **WordHIWordTrainingGS.docx**. Go through the original document with the tracked changes and accept and/or reject revisions. Not all revisions made by Terry Oberman or Gina Singh are correct so check each revision before accepting it. Save the combined document with Save As and name it **WordL2_C7_CS_P1**.

Part 2

Ms. Sweeney has asked you to prepare training materials on how to check the spelling and grammar in a document and how to customize spelling and grammar options. Using the **WordL2_C7_CS_P1.docx** document as a guideline, write information (including steps) on how to complete a spelling and grammar check in a document and how to change spelling and grammar options at the Word Options dialog box with *Proofing* selected. Include in the document a table that presents the names of the buttons available at the Spelling and Grammar dialog box and a brief description of what tasks the buttons complete. Save the completed document and name it **WordL2_C7_CS_P2**.

Part 3

If possible, send a copy of your document to one or two classmates and have him or her edit the document with track changes turned on. Combine the edited documents with your original **WordL2_C7_CS_P2.docx** document. Save, print, and then close the document.

Part 4

Open **WordL2_C7_CS_P1.docx**, move the insertion point to the end of the document, and then insert **WordL2_C7_CS_P2.docx**. Apply at least the following to the document:

- Heading styles
- Quick Styles set
- Theme
- Table of contents
- Page numbering
- Cover page

Save the completed document with Save As and name it **WordL2_C7_CS_P4**. Save, print, and then close the document.

Advanced Formatting Techniques

PERFORMANCE OBJECTIVES

Upon successful completion of Chapter 1, you will be able to:

- Apply conditional formatting by entering parameters for a rule
- Apply conditional formatting using a predefined rule
- Create and apply a new rule for conditional formatting
- Edit and delete a conditional formatting rule
- Apply conditional formatting using an icon set, data bars, and color scale
- Apply fraction and scientific formatting
- Apply a special format for a number
- Create a custom number format
- Apply wrap text and shrink to fit text control options
- Filter a worksheet using a custom AutoFilter
- Filter and sort a worksheet using conditional formatting
- Filter and sort a worksheet using cell attributes

excel Chapter 1

Tutorial 1.1
Formatting an Excel Worksheet

Although many worksheets can be formatted using buttons available in the Font, Alignment, and Number groups in the Home tab of the ribbon or in the Mini toolbar, some situations require format categories that are not represented with a button. In other worksheets you may want to make use of Excel's advanced formatting techniques to format based on a condition. In this chapter you will learn how to apply advanced formatting and filtering techniques.

Note: Before beginning computer projects, copy to your storage medium the Excel2007L2C1 subfolder from the Excel2007L2 folder on the CD that accompanies this textbook and make Excel2007L2C1 the active folder. Steps on how to copy a folder are presented on the inside of the back cover of this textbook. Do this every time you start a chapter's projects.

 roject **1** Format Cells Based on Values

Working with a payroll worksheet, you will change the appearance of cells based on criteria related to overtime hours and gross pay.

Conditional Formatting

QUICK STEPS

Apply Conditional Formatting Using Predefined Rule
1. Select desired range.
2. Click Conditional Formatting button.
3. Point to desired rule category.
4. Click desired rule.
5. If necessary, enter parameter value.
6. If necessary, change format options.
7. Click OK.

Conditional formatting applies format changes to a range of cells for those cells within the selection that meet a condition. Cells that do not meet the condition remain unformatted. Changing the appearance of a cell based on a condition allows you to quickly identify values that are high, low, or that represent a trend. Formatting can be applied based on a specific value, a value that falls within a range, or by using a comparison operator such as equals (=), greater than (>), or less than (<). Conditional formats can also be based on date, text entries, or duplicated values. Consider using conditional formatting to analyze a question such as *Which store locations earned sales above their target?* Using a different color and/or shading the cells that exceeded a sales target easily identifies the top performers. Excel 2007 provides predefined conditional formatting rules accessed from the Conditional Formatting drop-down list shown in Figure 1.1. You can also create your own conditional formatting rules.

Figure 1.1 Conditional Formatting Drop-down List

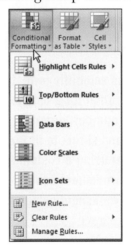

Project 1a   Formatting Cells Based on a Value Comparison

1. Start Excel.
2. Open **VantagePayroll-Oct24.xlsx**. (This workbook is located in the Excel2007L2C1 folder you copied to your storage medium.)
3. Save the workbook with Save As and name it **ExcelL2_C1_P1**.
4. Apply conditional formatting to highlight overtime hours that exceeded 5 for the week by completing the following steps:
   a. Select K6:K23.
   b. Click the Conditional Formatting button in the Styles group of the Home tab.
   c. Point to *Highlight Cells Rules* and then click *Greater Than* at the drop-down list.
   d. At the Greater Than dialog box, with the text already selected in the *Format cells that are GREATER THAN* text box, type 5.

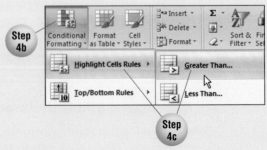

e. Click the down-pointing arrow next to the list box to the right of *with* (currently displays *Light Red Fill with Dark Red Text*) and then click *Red Text* at the drop-down list.

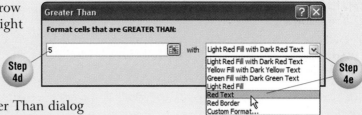

Step 4d

Step 4e

f. Click OK to close the Greater Than dialog box and apply the conditional format.
g. Click in any cell to deselect the range.
h. Review the cells that have been conditionally formatted. Notice that cells with overtime hours greater than 5 are formatted with red text.
5. Save **ExcelL2_C1_P1.xlsx**.

Using the Top/Bottom Rules list you can elect to highlight cells based on a top ten or bottom ten value or percent, or by above average or below average values.

Project 1b   **Formatting Cells Based on Top/Bottom Rules**

1. With **ExcelL2_C1_P1.xlsx** open, apply conditional formatting to the Gross Pay values to identify employees who earned above average wages for the week by completing the following steps:
   a. Select M6:M23.
   b. Click the Conditional Formatting button in the Styles group of the Home tab.
   c. Point to *Top/Bottom Rules* and then click *Above Average* at the drop-down list.
   d. At the Above Average dialog box, with *Light Red Fill with Dark Red Text* selected in the *Format cells that are ABOVE AVERAGE* list box, click OK.

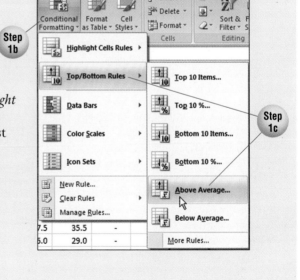

Step 1b

Step 1c

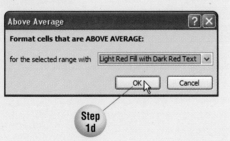

Step 1d

   e. Click in any cell to deselect the range.
   f. Review the cells that have been conditionally formatted.
2. Change the page orientation to landscape and print the worksheet.
3. Save and then close **ExcelL2_C1_P1.xlsx**.

Project ② Apply Conditional Formatting to Insurance Policy Data

In an insurance claims worksheet you will format cells by creating, editing, and deleting conditional formatting rules and classify the number of cars into categories using an icon set.

QUICK STEPS

Create and Apply New Formatting Rule
1. Select desired range.
2. Click Conditional Formatting button.
3. Click *Manage Rules.*
4. Click New Rule button.
5. Click desired rule type.
6. Add criteria as required.
7. Click Format button.
8. Select desired formatting attributes.
9. Click OK to close Format Cells dialog box.
10. Click OK to close New Formatting Rule dialog box.
11. Click Apply button.
12. Click OK.

HINT

You can create a rule to format cells based on cell values, specific text, dates, blank, or error values.

Creating a New Formatting Rule

Cells are conditionally formatted based on a rule that defines the criterion by which the cell is selected for formatting and includes the formatting attributes that are applied to the cells that meet the conditional test. The predefined rules that you used in Project 1a and Project 1b allowed you to use the feature without having to specify each component in the rule's parameters. At the New Formatting Rule dialog box shown in Figure 1.2, you can create your own custom conditional formatting rule in which you define all parts of the criterion and the formatting. The *Edit the Rule Description* section of the dialog box varies depending on the active option in the *Select a Rule Type* section.

Figure 1.2 New Formatting Rule Dialog Box

Begin creating a new rule by choosing the type of condition you want Excel to check before formatting.

This section varies depending on the option selected in the *Select a Rule Type* section.

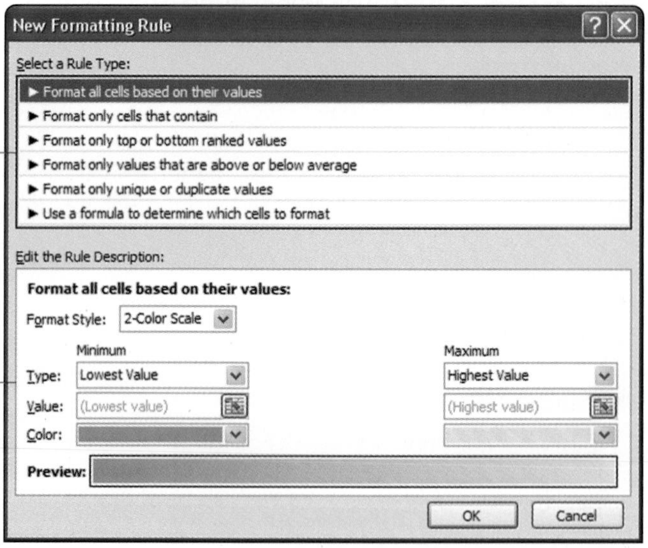

Project 2a — Creating and Applying New Formatting Rules

1. Open **AllClaims-Policies.xlsx**.
2. Save the workbook with Save As and name it **ExcelL2_C1_P2**.
3. The owner of AllClaims Insurance Brokers is considering changing the discount plan for those customers with no claims or with only one claim. The owner would like to see the two claim criteria formatted in color to provide a reference for how many customers this discount would affect. Create a formatting rule that will change the appearance of cells in the claims columns for those values that equal 0 by completing the following steps:

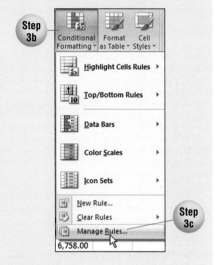

   a. Select H4:H20.
   b. Click the Conditional Formatting button.
   c. Click *Manage Rules* at the drop-down list.
   d. At the Conditional Formatting Rules Manager dialog box, click the New Rule button.
   e. At the New Formatting Rule dialog box, click *Format only cells that contain* in the *Select a Rule Type* section.

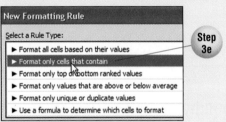

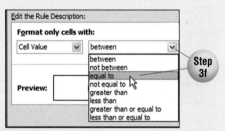

   f. Click the down-pointing arrow located at the right of the second list box from the left in the *Format only cells with* section (currently displays *between*) and then click *equal to* at the drop-down list.
   g. Click in the blank text box next to *equal to* and then type 0.
   h. Click the Format button in the *Preview* section.

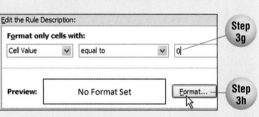

   i. At the Format Cells dialog box with the Font tab selected, change the *Color* to *Dark Red*, turn on bold, and then click OK.
   j. Click OK at the New Formatting Rule dialog box.
4. Create a second formatting rule that will change the appearance of cells in the claims columns for those values that equal 1 by completing the following steps:
   a. At the Conditional Formatting Rules Manager dialog box, click the New Rule button.
   b. At the New Formatting Rule dialog box, click *Format only cells that contain* in the *Select a Rule Type* section.
   c. Click the down-pointing arrow located at the right end of the second list box from the left in the *Format only cells with* section (currently displays *between*) and then click *equal to* at the drop-down list.
   d. Click in the blank text box next to *equal to* and then type 1.
   e. Click the Format button.
   f. At the Format Cells dialog box with the Font tab selected, change the *Color* to *Red*, turn on bold, and then click OK.

g. Click OK at the New Formatting Rule dialog box.
5. At the Conditional Formatting Rules Manager dialog box, click the Apply button to apply the rules to the selected range.

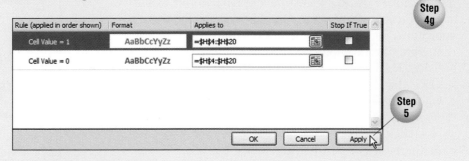

6. Click OK to close the Conditional Formatting Rules Manager dialog box.
7. Click in any cell to deselect the range.
8. Save **ExcelL2_C1_P2.xlsx**.

QUICK STEPS

Edit Formatting Rule
1. Select range.
2. Click Conditional Formatting button.
3. Click *Manage Rules*.
4. Click desired rule.
5. Click Edit Rule button.
6. Make desired changes to parameters and/or formatting options.
7. Click OK twice.

Delete Formatting Rule
1. Click Conditional Formatting button.
2. Click *Manage Rules*.
3. Change *Show formatting rules for* to *This Worksheet*.
4. Click desired rule.
5. Click Delete Rule button.
6. Click OK.

Editing and Deleting Conditional Formatting Rules

Edit the comparison rule criteria and/or formatting options for a conditional formatting rule by opening the Conditional Formatting Rules Manager dialog box. Click to select the rule that you want to change and then click the Edit Rule button. At the Edit Formatting Rule dialog box, make the desired changes and then click OK twice. By default, *Show formatting rules for* is set to *Current Selection* when you open the Conditional Formatting Rules Manager. If necessary, click the down-pointing arrow to the right of the list box and select *This Worksheet* to show all formatting rules in the current sheet.

To remove conditional formatting from a range, select the range, click the Conditional Formatting button, point to *Clear Rules* at the drop-down list, and then click either *Clear Rules from Selected Cells* or *Clear Rules from Entire Sheet*. You can also delete a custom rule at the Conditional Formatting Rules Manager dialog box. Formatting options applied to the cells by the rule that was deleted are removed.

Project 2h — Creating, Editing, and Deleting a Formatting Rule

1. With **ExcelL2_C2_P2.xlsx** open, create a new formatting rule to add a fill color to the cells in the *No. of Autos* column for those policies that have more than two cars by completing the following steps:
   a. Select C4:C20.
   b. Click the Conditional Formatting button and then click *New Rule* at the drop-down list.
   c. Click *Format only cells that contain* in the *Select a Rule Type* section of the New Formatting Rule dialog box.
   d. In the *Edit the Rule Description* section, change the rule's parameters to format only cells with a *Cell Value greater than 2*.
   e. Click the Format button and then click the Fill tab at the Format Cells dialog box.
   f. Click the *Yellow* color square (fourth from left in last row) in the *Background Color* palette and then click OK.
   g. Click OK to close the New Formatting Rule dialog box and apply the rule to the selected cells.

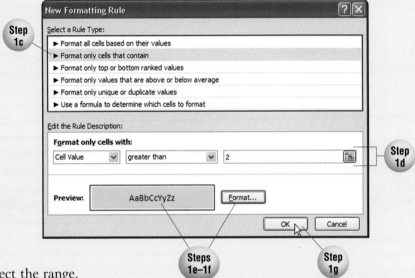

h. Deselect the range.
2. After reviewing the formatted cells, you decide that cells should be formatted for all policies with 2 or more cars. Edit the formatting rule by completing the following steps:
   a. Select C4:C20.
   b. Click the Conditional Formatting button and then click *Manage Rules* at the drop-down list.
   c. Click to select *Cell Value > 2* in the Conditional Formatting Rules Manager dialog box and then click the Edit Rule button.

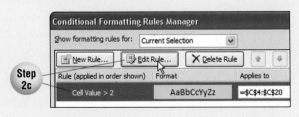

Customer ID	Policy ID	No. of Autos
C-025	6512485	2
C-055	6123584	1
C-072	6583157	2
C-085	6124893	3
C-094	3481274	1
C-114	4956875	2
C-124	3354867	1
C-131	6598642	3
C-148	4668457	3
C-155	8512475	4
C-168	6984563	2
C-171	4856972	1
C-184	5124876	1
C-190	6845962	1
C-199	8457326	1
C-201	4968532	2
C-212	2698715	2

Formatting applied to cell values greater than 2.

d. Click the down-pointing arrow next to the second list box (currently displays *greater than*) and then click *greater than or equal to* at the drop-down list.

e. Click OK.

f. Click OK to close the Conditional Formatting Rules Manager dialog box and apply the revised rule to the selected cells.

g. Deselect the range.

3. Save and print the worksheet.

4. After reviewing the printed copy of the formatted worksheet, you decide to experiment with another method of formatting the data that classifies the policies by the number of cars. You will do this in the next project. In preparation for the next project, save the revised worksheet under a new name and then delete the formatting rule in the original worksheet by completing the following steps:

a. Use Save As to name the workbook **ExcelL2_C1_P2-Autos2+**. By saving the workbook under a new name you will have a copy of the conditional formatting applied in this project.

b. Close **ExcelL2_C1_P2-Autos2+.xlsx**.

c. Open **ExcelL2_C1_P2.xlsx**.

d. Click the Conditional Formatting button and then click *Manage Rules* at the drop-down list.

e. Click the down-pointing arrow next to the *Show formatting rules for* list box and then click *This Worksheet*.

f. Click to select *Cell Value >= 2* and then click the Delete Rule button.

g. Click OK to close the Conditional Formatting Rules Manager dialog box. Notice the formatting has been removed from the cells in column C.

5. Save **ExcelL2_C1_P2.xlsx**.

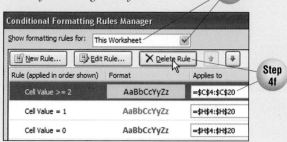

Conditional Formatting Using Icon Sets

Format a range of values using an icon set to classify data into three to five categories. Icons are assigned to cells based on threshold values for the selected range. For example, if you choose the *3 Arrows (Colored)* icon set, icons are assigned as follows:

- Green up arrow for higher values
- Red down arrow for lower values
- Yellow sideways arrow for middle values

The available icon sets are shown in Figure 1.3. Choose the icon set that best represents the number of different categories within the range and the desired symbol type such as flags, arrows, traffic lights, and so on. To create your own icon set where you can set the threshold values, open the Manage Rules dialog box and add a new rule.

Figure 1.3 Conditional Formatting Icon Sets Gallery

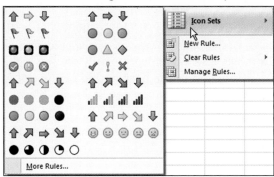

Project 2c   Conditionally Formatting Using an Icon Set

1. With **ExcelL2_C1_P2.xlsx** open, select C4:C20.
2. Classify the number of automobiles into categories using an icon set by completing the following steps:
   a. Click the Conditional Formatting button.
   b. Point to *Icon Sets*.
   c. Click *Red To Black* at the Icon Sets drop-down gallery (sixth from the top in the left column).

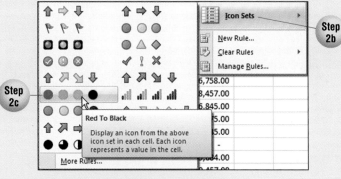

    d. Click in any cell to deselect the range. Notice that Excel assigns an icon to each cell that correlates the icon with the value group. For example, all cells containing the value 1 have the same icon, all cells containing the value 2 have the same icon, and so on.
3. Save, print, and then close **ExcelL2_C1_P2.xlsx**.

Conditional Formatting Using Data Bars and Color Scales

Excel 2007 also provides the ability to conditionally format cells using two-color scales, three-color scales, or data bars to provide visual guides to identify distributions or variations within a range. Use a data bar to easily see the higher and lower values within the range. A bar is added to the background of the cell with the length of the bar dependent on the value within the cell. A longer bar represents a higher value within the range and a shorter bar represents a lower value within the range.

Color scales format the range using either a two-color or three-color palette. The gradation of color applied to a cell illustrates the cell's value in comparison to higher or lower values within the range. Color scales are useful to view the distribution of the data. In a two-color scale, you specify the shade of color that represents higher and lower values. In a three-color scale you specify the shade of color that represents higher, middle, or lower values. Figure 1.4 displays the payroll worksheet for Vantage Video Rentals with data bar and color scale conditional formatting applied. In column M, data bars depict the gross pay distribution. Notice the length of the colored bars in the background of the cells for various gross pay amounts. In column J, the Green-Yellow two-color scale has been applied to show the distribution of total hours. Cells with higher values are displayed in gradations of green, while cells with lower values are displayed in gradations of yellow.

Figure 1.4 Data Bar and Color Scale Conditional Formatting Applied to Payroll Worksheet

		Sun	Mon	Tue	Wed	Thu	Fri	Sat	Total Hours	Overtime Hours	Pay Rate	Gross Pay
Vantage Video Rentals — Payroll — Week Ended: October 24, 2009												
Andrew	Gridzak	-	5.0	7.0	8.0	8.0	9.0	9.5	46.5	6.5	8.35	415.41
Derrick	MacLean	8.0	-	6.5	8.0	8.0	8.5	9.0	48.0	8.0	9.25	481.00
Priya	Bhardwaj	8.0	-	4.0	8.0	8.0	8.5	6.5	43.0	3.0	8.25	367.13
Emil	Cehajic	8.0	8.0	8.0	5.5	8.0	-	8.0	45.5	5.5	9.75	470.44
Dana	Sparling	-	6.0	7.5	8.0	8.0	-	8.0	37.5	-	8.25	309.38
Irene	O'Rourke	4.0	-	8.0	-	6.5	9.5	7.5	35.5	-	8.25	292.88
Ruthann	Goldstein	3.5	-	8.0	-	4.0	7.5	6.0	29.0	-	9.25	268.25
Stefan	Kominek	-	6.0	8.0	-	8.0	8.5	4.5	35.0	-	8.35	292.25
Alex	Spivak	-	5.0	8.0	8.5	7.5	9.0	8.0	46.0	6.0	8.35	409.15
Erica	Wilkins	-	7.0	-	6.0	-	6.0	6.4	25.4	-	8.25	209.55
Carmon	Vanderhoek	8.0	7.0	-	8.0	-	5.5	5.0	33.5	-	8.25	276.38
Ashley	Castillo	4.0	8.0	-	7.5	8.0	4.0	8.5	40.0	-	8.25	330.00
Susan	Anez	-	3.0	5.5	-	-	7.0	7.0	22.5	-	9.25	208.13
Dana	Ivanowski	-	4.0	6.0	-	8.5	6.8	-	25.3	-	9.25	234.03
Linda	Lanczos	-	7.0	4.5	-	7.5	7.5	-	26.5	-	8.25	218.63
Gilbert	Yee	9.0	-	9.0	8.0	7.5	8.0	-	41.5	1.5	8.25	348.56
Annette	Frishette	8.0	-	-	6.5	5.0	7.5	7.0	34.0	-	8.35	283.90
Randy	Brown	4.0	-	-	5.5	4.0	6.0	4.0	23.5	-	9.25	217.38
TOTAL		64.5	66.0	90.0	87.5	106.5	118.8	104.9	638.2	30.5		5,632.41

Gross Pay column with data bar conditional formatting applied.

Total Hours column with *Green-Yellow* color scale conditional formatting applied.

Project ② Populate Cells by Looking Up Data

You will use a lookup formula to automatically enter discounts for containers and then calculate net prices.

Lookup Functions

The Lookup & Reference category of functions provides formulas that can be used to look up values in a range. For example, in a grades worksheet, the final numerical score for a student can be looked up in a range of cells that contain the letter grades with corresponding numerical scores for each grade. The letter grade can be returned in the formula cell by looking up the student's score. The ability to look up a value automates data entry in large worksheets and when used properly can avoid inaccuracies from data entry errors. Excel provides two lookup functions: VLOOKUP and HLOOKUP which refer to a vertical or horizontal lookup. The layout of the lookup range (referred to as a lookup table) determines whether to use VLOOKUP or HLOOKUP. VLOOKUP is more commonly used since most lookup tables are arranged with comparison data in columns which means Excel searches for the lookup value in a vertical order. HLOOKUP is used when the lookup range has placed comparison data in rows and Excel searches for the lookup value in a horizontal pattern.

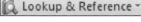

VLOOKUP

QUICK STEPS

Create VLOOKUP formula
1. Make desired cell active.
2. Click Formulas tab.
3. Click Lookup & Reference button.
4. Click *VLOOKUP*.
5. Enter cell address or value in *Lookup_value* text box.
6. Enter range or range name in *Table_array* text box.
7. Type column number to return values from in *Col_index_num* text box.
8. Type FALSE or leave blank for *TRUE* in *Range_lookup* text box.
9. Click OK.

The structure of a VLOOKUP formula is =*VLOOKUP(lookup_value,table_array,col_index_num,range_lookup)*. Table 2.2 explains each section of the VLOOKUP argument.

VLOOKUP is easier to understand using an example. In the worksheet shown in Figure 2.6, VLOOKUP is used to return the starting salary for new hires. Each new hire is assigned a salary grid number that places his or her starting salary depending on their education and years of work experience. The lookup table contains the grid numbers with the corresponding starting salary. VLOOKUP formulas in column E automatically insert the starting salary for each new employee based on the employee's grid number in column D.

Table 2.2 VLOOKUP Argument Parameters

Argument parameter	*Description*
Lookup_value	The value that you want Excel to search for in the lookup table. You can enter a value or a cell reference to a value.
Table_array	The range address or range name for the lookup table that you want Excel to search. The first column of the table is the column Excel compares with the lookup_value.
Col_index_num	The column number from the lookup table that contains the data you want placed in the formula cell.
Range_lookup	Enter TRUE or FALSE to instruct Excel to find an exact match for the lookup value or an approximate match. If this parameter is left out of the formula, Excel assumes TRUE, which means if an exact match is not found, Excel returns the value for the next largest number that is less than the lookup value. For the formula to work properly, the first column of the lookup table must be sorted in ascending order. Enter FALSE to instruct Excel to return only exact matches to the lookup value.

Figure 2.6 VLOOKUP Example

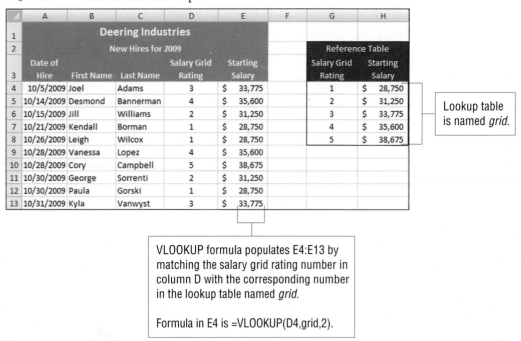

Lookup table is named *grid*.

VLOOKUP formula populates E4:E13 by matching the salary grid rating number in column D with the corresponding number in the lookup table named *grid*.

Formula in E4 is =VLOOKUP(D4,grid,2).

1. Open **Precision-BulkPriceList.xlsx**.
2. Save the workbook with Save As and name it **ExcelL2_C2_P2**.
3. Create a VLOOKUP formula to find the correct discount values for each product by completing the following steps:

   a. Make E4 the active cell.
   b. Click the Formulas tab.
   c. Click the Lookup & Reference button in the Function Library group.
   d. Click *VLOOKUP* at the drop-down list.
   e. If necessary, drag the Function Arguments dialog box down so that you can see the first few rows of the product list and the Discount Table data.
   f. With the insertion point positioned in the *Lookup_value* text box, type c4 and then press Tab. Product discounts are categorized by letter codes. To find the correct discount, you need Excel to look for the matching category letter code for the product within the first column of the Discount table. Notice the letter codes in the Discount table are listed in ascending order.
   g. Type Discount_Table in the *Table_array* text box and then press Tab. The worksheet has the range name *Discount_Table* created, which references the cells $H$4:$I$8. Using a range name for a reference table is a good idea since the formula will be copied and absolute references are needed.
   h. Type 2 in the *Col_index_num* text box and then press Tab.
   i. Type false in the *Range_lookup* text box and then click OK. By typing *false*, you are instructing Excel to return a value for exact matches only. Should a discount category be typed into a cell in column C for which no entry exists in the Discount Table, Excel will return *#N/A* in the formula cell, which will alert you that an error has occurred in the data entry.

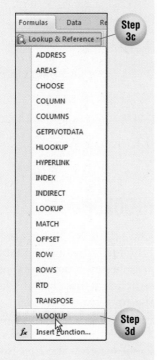

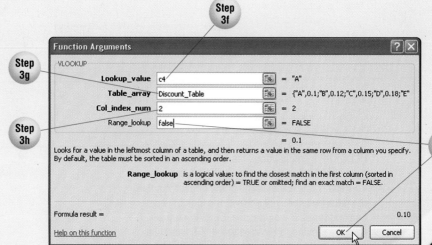

4. Look at the formula in the Formula bar =*VLOOKUP(C4,Discount_Table*
5. Format E4 to Percent Style.

6. Make F4 the active cell, type the formula =d4-(d4*e4), and then press Enter.
7. Select E4:F4 and then drag the fill handle down to row 21.
8. Deselect the range.
9. Print the worksheet. *Note: The worksheet will print in landscape orientation.*
10. Save and then close **ExcelL2_C2_P2.xlsx**.

C	D	E	F	G	H	I
Packaging						
ts Price List					Discount Table	
Discount Category	List Price	Discount	Net Price		Discount Category	Discount Percent
A	18.67	10%	=d4-(d4*e4)		A	10%
C	22.50				B	12%
B	14.53				C	15%
D	5.25				D	18%
A	18.54				E	20%

Step 6

HLOOKUP

The HLOOKUP function uses the same argument parameters as VLOOKUP. Use HLOOKUP when the table in which you want to search for a comparison value is arranged in a horizontal arrangement similar to the one shown in Figure 2.7. Excel searches across the table in the first row for a matching value and then returns to the formula cell the value from the same column. The structure of an HLOOKUP formula is =*HLOOKUP(lookup_value,table_array,row_index_num,range_lookup)*. The argument parameters are similar to VLOOKUP's parameters described in Table 2.1. Excel searches the first row of the table for the lookup value. When a match is found, Excel returns the value from the same column in the row number specified in the *row_index_num* argument.

Figure 2.7 HLOOKUP Example

	A	B	C	D	E	F	G	H	I	J	K	L	M	N	O
1	Math by Janelle Tutoring Service														
2	Student Grade Report														
3	Student Name	Test1	Test2	Test3	Test4	Total	Grade		Score	0	50	60	70	80	90
4	Matthew Bilinksi	55	62	60	72	62.3	C		Grade	F	D	C	B	A	A+
5	Heather Denfield	82	83	80	74	79.8	B								
6	Jennifer Graham	75	72	71	70	72.0	B								
7	Paul Rubin	66	68	65	72	67.8	C			Lookup table is named					
8	Jacob Tylerman	88	82	80	75	81.3	A			*Grade_Table.*					
9	Quenton Gabriel	42	50	52	62	51.5	D								

HLOOKUP formula populates G4:G9 by looking up the total value in column F with the first row in Grade_Table. Excel stops at the largest value in the table that does not go over the lookup value. Looking for 62.3 would cause Excel to stop at 60 because moving to the next value, 70, would be over the lookup value.

rmula in G4 is =HLOOKUP(F4,Grade_Table,2).

Project ② Creating a VLOOKUP Function

1. Open **Precision-BulkPriceList.xlsx**.
2. Save the workbook with Save As and name it **ExcelL2_C2_P2**.
3. Create a VLOOKUP formula to find the correct discount values for each product by completing the following steps:

   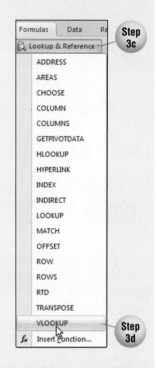

   a. Make E4 the active cell.
   b. Click the Formulas tab.
   c. Click the Lookup & Reference button in the Function Library group.
   d. Click *VLOOKUP* at the drop-down list.
   e. If necessary, drag the Function Arguments dialog box down so that you can see the first few rows of the product list and the Discount Table data.
   f. With the insertion point positioned in the *Lookup_value* text box, type **c4** and then press Tab. Product discounts are categorized by letter codes. To find the correct discount, you need Excel to look for the matching category letter code for the product within the first column of the Discount table. Notice the letter codes in the Discount table are listed in ascending order.
   g. Type **Discount_Table** in the *Table_array* text box and then press Tab. The worksheet has the range name *Discount_Table* created, which references the cells $H$4:$I$8. Using a range name for a reference table is a good idea since the formula will be copied and absolute references are needed.
   h. Type **2** in the *Col_index_num* text box and then press Tab.
   i. Type **false** in the *Range_lookup* text box and then click OK. By typing *false*, you are instructing Excel to return a value for exact matches only. Should a discount category be typed into a cell in column C for which no entry exists in the Discount Table, Excel will return *#N/A* in the formula cell, which will alert you that an error has occurred in the data entry.

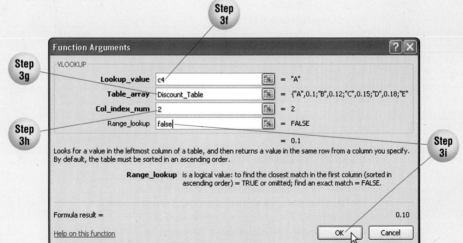

4. Look at the formula in the Formula bar *=VLOOKUP(C4,Discount_Table,2,FALSE)*.
5. Format E4 to Percent Style.

6. Make F4 the active cell, type the formula =d4-(d4*e4), and then press Enter.
7. Select E4:F4 and then drag the fill handle down to row 21.
8. Deselect the range.
9. Print the worksheet. *Note: The worksheet will print in landscape orientation.*
10. Save and then close **ExcelL2_C2_P2.xlsx**.

	C	D	E	F	G	H	I
	Packaging						
	ts Price List					Discount Table	
	Discount Category	List Price	Discount	Net Price		Discount Category	Discount Percent
	A	18.67	10%	=d4-(d4*e4)		A	10%
	C	22.50				B	12%
	B	14.53				C	15%
	D	5.25				D	18%
	A	18.54				E	20%

Step 6

HLOOKUP

The HLOOKUP function uses the same argument parameters as VLOOKUP. Use HLOOKUP when the table in which you want to search for a comparison value is arranged in a horizontal arrangement similar to the one shown in Figure 2.7. Excel searches across the table in the first row for a matching value and then returns to the formula cell the value from the same column. The structure of an HLOOKUP formula is *=HLOOKUP(lookup_value,table_array,row_index_num,range_lookup)*. The argument parameters are similar to VLOOKUP's parameters described in Table 2.1. Excel searches the first row of the table for the lookup value. When a match is found, Excel returns the value from the same column in the row number specified in the *row_index_num* argument.

Figure 2.7 HLOOKUP Example

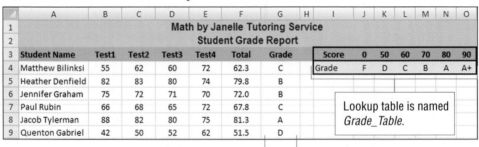

	A	B	C	D	E	F	G	H	I	J	K	L	M	N	O
1				Math by Janelle Tutoring Service											
2				Student Grade Report											
3	Student Name	Test1	Test2	Test3	Test4	Total	Grade		Score	0	50	60	70	80	90
4	Matthew Bilinksi	55	62	60	72	62.3	C		Grade	F	D	C	B	A	A+
5	Heather Denfield	82	83	80	74	79.8	B								
6	Jennifer Graham	75	72	71	70	72.0	B								
7	Paul Rubin	66	68	65	72	67.8	C			Lookup table is named *Grade_Table*.					
8	Jacob Tylerman	88	82	80	75	81.3	A								
9	Quenton Gabriel	42	50	52	62	51.5	D								

HLOOKUP formula populates G4:G9 by looking up the total value in column F with the first row in Grade_Table. Excel stops at the largest value in the table that does not go over the lookup value. Looking for 62.3 would cause Excel to stop at 60 because moving to the next value, 70, would be over the lookup value.

Formula in G4 is =HLOOKUP(F4,Grade_Table,2).

Project ④ Calculate Benefit Costs Using Conditional Logic

You will create formulas to calculate the employee benefit costs for Vantage Video Rentals using logical functions to test multiple conditions.

Create IF Formula
1. Make desired cell active.
2. Click Formulas tab.
3. Click Logical button.
4. Click *IF*.
5. Type conditional test argument in *Logical_test* text box.
6. Press Tab.
7. Type argument in *Value_if_true* text box.
8. Press Tab.
9. Type argument in *Value_if_false* text box.
10. Click OK.

Logical Functions

Conditional logic in formulas requires Excel to perform a calculation based on the outcome of a conditional test where one calculation is performed if the test proves true and another calculation is performed if the test proves false. For example, an IF statement to calculate a sales bonus if sales exceed a target could be created similar to the following: *=IF(Sales>Target,Bonus,0)*. Excel first tests the value in the cell named Sales to see if the value is greater than the value in the cell named Target. If the condition proves true, Excel returns the value in the cell named Bonus; if Sales are not greater than Target the condition proves false and Excel places a 0 in the cell. The structure of the IF statement is *=IF(condition,value_if_true,value_if_false)*.

AND, OR, and NOT

Other logic functions offered in Excel include AND, OR, and NOT. These functions use Boolean logic to construct a conditional test in a formula. Table 2.3 describes how the three functions work to test a statement and provides an example for each.

Table 2.3 AND, OR, and NOT Logical Functions

Logical Function	Description	Example
AND	Excel returns *True* if all conditions test true. Excel returns *False* if any one of the conditions test false.	=AND(Sales>Target,NewClients>5) Returns *True* if both test true. If Sales>Target but NewClients<5, returns *False*. If Sales<Target but NewClients>5, returns *False*.
OR	Excel returns *True* if any condition tests true. Excel returns *False* if all conditions test false.	=OR(Sales>Target,NewClients>5) Returns *True* if either Sales>Target or NewClients>5. Returns *False* only if both Sales is not greater than Target and NewClients is not greater than 5.
NOT	Performs reverse logic. If the condition tests true, Excel returns *False* in the cell. If the condition tests false, Excel returns *True* in the cell.	=NOT(Age>65) If Age is 70, returns *False*. If Age is 60, returns *True*. If Age is 65, returns *True*.

Create AND Formula
1. Make desired cell active OR nest formula in IF statement *Logical_test* text box.
2. Type =AND(OR AND(if nesting in IF statement.
3. Type first conditional test argument.
4. Type ,.
5. Type second conditional test argument.
6. Repeat Steps 4–5 for remaining conditions.
7. Type).

Create OR Formula
1. Make desired cell active OR nest formula in IF statement *Logical_test* text box.
2. Type =OR(OR OR(if nesting in IF statement.
3. Type first conditional test argument.
4. Type ,.
5. Type second conditional test argument.
6. Repeat Steps 4–5 for remaining conditions.
7. Type).

Create NOT Formula
1. Make desired cell active.
2. Type =NOT(.
3. Type argument or value to test.
4. Type).
5. Press Enter.

HINT

You can nest an AND, OR, or NOT function with an IF function to test multiple conditions.

1. Open **VantageSalary&Benefits.xlsx**.
2. Save the workbook with Save As and name it **ExcelL2_C2_P4**.
3. Vantage Video Rentals contributes 5% of an employee's salary into a privately managed company retirement account if the employee is full-time and earns more than $45 thousand in salary. Calculate the pension benefit cost for eligible employees by completing the following steps:
   a. Make H6 the active cell.
   b. Click the Formulas tab.
   c. Click the Logical button in the Function Library group and then click *IF* at the drop-down list.
   d. If necessary, drag the Function Arguments dialog box down until you can see all of row 6 in the worksheet.
   e. With the insertion point positioned in the *Logical_test* text box, type **and(c6="FT",g6>45000)** and then press Tab. An AND function is required since both conditions must be true for the company to contribute to the pension plan. ***Note: Excel requires quotation symbols around text when used in a conditional test formula***.
   f. Type **g6*5%** in the *Value_if_true* text box and then press Tab.
   g. Type **0** in the *Value_if_false* text box and then click OK.

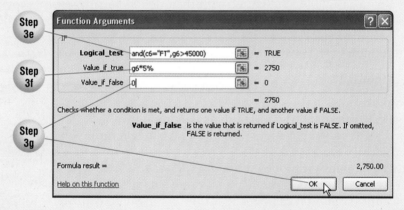

h. Look at the formula *=IF(AND(C6="FT",G6>45000),G6*5%,0)* in the Formula bar. Notice the AND function is nested within the IF function. Since both conditions for the first employee tested true, the pension cost is calculated.
i. Copy the formula in H6 to H7:H14 without copying the border formatting by completing the following steps:
   1) With H6 the active cell, click the Home tab and then click the Copy button in the Clipboard group.
   2) Select H7:H14.
   3) Click the Paste button arrow in the Clipboard group and then click *No Borders* at the drop-down list.
   4) Press the Esc key to remove the moving marquee from H6.
   5) Deselect the range.
4. Save **ExcelL2_C2_P4.xlsx**.

1. With **ExcelL2_C2_P4.xlsx** open, make I6 the active cell.
2. Vantage Video Rentals offers to pay the annual health premiums for employees who are not covered by any other medical plan. The company pays $2,100 per year per employee for family coverage and $1,380 per year for single coverage. Calculate the cost of the health benefit for those employees who opted into the plan by completing the following steps:
   a. This formula requires a nested IF statement since the result will be either *$2,180* or *$1,380* depending on the contents in cell D6. Type the formula shown below in I6 and then press Enter. (An OR statement will not work for this formula since two different values are used.)
      =if(d6="Family",2100,if(d6="Single",1380,0))

	BENEFIT COSTS		Total	Salary +	
Pension	Health	Dental	Benefits	Benefits	
2,750.00	=if(d6="Family",2100,if(d6="Single",1380,0))				Step 2a
2,475.00			2,475.00	51,975.00	

   b. Copy the formula in I6 to I7:I14. Notice the cells for which no value is entered. In column D, these employees show the text *Declined*. Excel returned zero since both conditions *D6="Family"* and *D6="Single"* proved false.
3. Vantage Video Rentals negotiated a flat fee with their dental benefit service provider. The company pays the same rate of $1,500 per year for all employees regardless of the type of coverage. The service provider requires Vantage to report each person's coverage as *Family* or *Single* for audit purposes. The dental plan is optional and some employees have declined the coverage. Calculate the dental plan cost by completing the following steps:
   a. Make J6 the active cell.
   b. Click the Formulas tab.
   c. Click the Logical button and then click *IF* at the drop-down list.
   d. If necessary, drag the Function Arguments dialog box down until you can see all of row 6 in the worksheet.
   e. With the insertion point positioned in the *Logical_test* text box, type or(e6="Family",e6="Single") and then press Tab. An OR function is suited to this benefit since either condition can be true for the company to contribute to the dental plan.
   f. Type 1500 in the *Value_if_true* text box and then press Tab.
   g. Type 0 in the *Value_if_false* text box and then click OK.

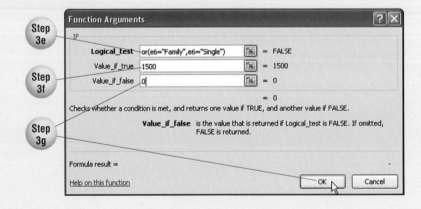

h. Look at the formula *=IF(OR(E6="Family",E6="Single"),1500,0)* in the Formula bar. Notice the OR function is nested within the IF function. Since E6 contained neither *Family* or *Single*, the OR statement tested false and the result of *0* is returned in J6.

i. Copy the formula in J6 and paste to J7:J14 without pasting the border formatting by completing the following steps:

    1) With J6 the active cell, click the Home tab and then click the Copy button in the Clipboard group.

    2) Select J7:J14.

    3) Click the Paste button arrow in the Clipboard group and then click *No Borders* at the drop-down list.

    4) Press the Esc key to remove the moving marquee from J6.

    5) Deselect the range.

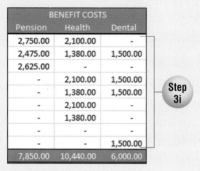

BENEFIT COSTS		
Pension	Health	Dental
2,750.00	2,100.00	-
2,475.00	1,380.00	1,500.00
2,625.00	-	-
-	2,100.00	1,500.00
-	1,380.00	1,500.00
-	2,100.00	-
-	1,380.00	-
-	-	-
-	-	1,500.00
7,850.00	10,440.00	6,000.00

Step 3i

4. Save **ExcelL2_C2_P4.xlsx**.

5. Print and then close **ExcelL2_C2_P4.xlsx**. *Note: The worksheet will print in landscape orientation.*

CHAPTER
3

Working with Tables and Data Features

PERFORMANCE OBJECTIVES

Upon successful completion of Chapter 3, you will be able to:

- Create a table in a worksheet
- Expand a table to include new rows and columns
- Add a calculated column in a table
- Format a table by applying table styles and table style options
- Add a total row to a table and add formulas to total cells
- Sort and filter a table
- Split contents of a cell into separate columns
- Remove duplicate records
- Restrict data entry by creating validation criteria
- Convert a table to a normal range
- Create subtotals in groups of related data
- Ungroup data
- Summarize data using database functions DSUM and DAVERAGE
- Summarize data using the SUBTOTAL function formula

Tutorial 3.1
Working with Tables and
Extensive Data

In Excel 2007, the List feature from earlier versions was renamed *Table*. A table can be managed separately from other rows and columns in the worksheet so that you can sort, filter, calculate, and total data as a separate unit. A worksheet can contain more than one table so that multiple groups of data can be managed separately within the same workbook. While working with the table feature you will also use data tools such as validation, duplicate records, and converting text to a table. A table that no longer needs to be managed independently can be converted back to a normal range and data tools such as grouping related records, calculating subtotals, and database functions applied to the data.

Note: Before beginning computer projects, copy to your storage medium the Excel2007L2C3 subfolder from the Excel2007L2 folder on the CD that accompanies this textbook and then make Excel2007L2C3 the active folder.

Project ① Create and Modify a Table

You will convert data in a billing summary worksheet to a table and then modify the table by applying Table Style options and sorting and filtering the data.

QUICK STEPS

Create Table
1. Open worksheet.
2. Select range.
3. Click Insert tab.
4. Click Table button.
5. Click OK.
6. Deselect range.

Table

Creating Tables

A table in Excel is similar in structure to a database. Columns are called *fields* and are used to store a single unit of information about a person, place, or object. The first row of the table contains column headings and is called the *field names row* or *header row*. Each column heading in the table should be unique. Below the field names, data entered in rows are called *records*. A record contains all of the field values related to one person, place, or object that is the topic of the table. No blank rows exist within the table as shown in Figure 3.1. To create a table in Excel, enter the data in the worksheet and then define the range as a table using the Table button in the Tables group of the Insert tab. Before converting a range to a table, delete any blank rows between column headings and data or within the data range.

Figure 3.1 Excel Table

A row in a table is called a record.

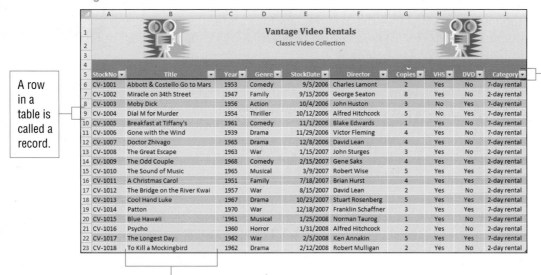

The first row of a table contains field names and is called a header row.

A column in a table contains a single unit of information and is called a field.

Project 1a Converting a Range to a Table

1. Open **O'Donovan&Sullivan-Billing.xlsx**.
2. Save the workbook with Save As and name it **ExcelL2_C3_P1**.
3. Convert the billing summary data to a table by completing the following steps:
   a. Select A4:I24.
   b. Click the Insert tab.
   c. Click the Table button in the Tables group.
   d. At the Create Table dialog box with *$A$4:$I$24* selected in the *Where is the data for your table?* text box and the *My table has headers* check box selected, click OK.
   e. Deselect the range.
4. Double-click each column boundary to AutoFit each column's width.
5. Save **ExcelL2_C3_P1**.

Step 3b

Step 3c

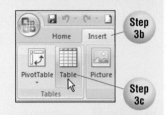

Step 3d

Modifying a Table

Once a table has been defined, typing new data in the row immediately below the last row of the table, or in the column immediately right of the last column causes the table to automatically expand to include the new entries. Excel displays the AutoCorrect Options button when the table is expanded. Click the button to display a drop-down list with the options *Undo Table AutoExpansion* and *Stop Automatically Expanding Tables*. If you need to add data near a table without having the table expand, leave a blank column or row between the table and the new data.

Typing a formula in the first row of a new table column creates a calculated column. In a calculated column, Excel copies the formula from the first cell to the remaining cells in the column automatically. The AutoCorrect Options button appears when Excel converts a column to a calculated column with the options *Undo Calculated Column* and *Stop Automatically Creating Calculated Columns* available in the drop-down list.

QUICK STEPS

Add Rows or Columns to Table
Type data in first row below table or first column to right of table.

Add Calculated Column
1. Type formula in first record in column.
2. Press Enter.

Project 1b Adding a Row and a Calculated Column to a Table

1. With **ExcelL2_C3_P1.xlsx** open, add a new record to the table by completing the following steps:
   a. Make A25 the active cell, type **RE-522**, and then press Enter. Excel automatically expands the table to include the new row and displays the AutoCorrect Options button.
   b. Make B25 the active cell and then type the remainder of the record as follows:

ClientID	10512
Date	10/09/2009
Last_Name	Melanson
First_Name	Connie

Step 1a

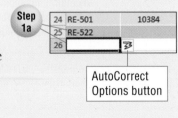

AutoCorrect Options button

Attorney	Kyle Williams
Area	Real Estate
Billable_Hrs	2.5
Rate	75.00

2. Add a calculated column to calculate Billable_Hrs times Rate by completing the following steps:
   a. Make J4 the active cell.
   b. Type **Fees_Due** and then press Enter. Excel automatically expands the table to include the new column.
   c. With J5 the active cell, type **=h5*i5** and then press Enter. Excel creates a calculated column and copies the formula to the rest of the rows in the table.
   d. Double-click the column J boundary to AutoFit the column.
3. Adjust the centering and fill color of the titles across the top of the table by completing the following steps:
   a. Make A1 the active cell.
   b. Click the Merge & Center button in the Alignment group in the Home tab to unmerge A1:I1.
   c. Select A1:J1 and then click the Merge & Center button.
   d. Make A2 the active cell and then repeat Steps 3b–3c to merge and center row 2 across columns A through J.
   e. Make A3 the active cell and then repeat Steps 3b–3c to merge and center row 3 across columns A through J.
4. Save **ExcelL2_C3_P1.xlsx**.

Rate	Fees_D
85.00	573.75
55.00	178.75
75.00	393.75
100.00	425.00
65.00	211.25
75.00	206.25
75.00	393.75
75.00	318.75
100.00	500.00
75.00	243.75
65.00	292.50
85.00	318.75
100.00	450.00
55.00	192.50
65.00	341.25
75.00	393.75
75.00	262.50
100.00	425.00
100.00	375.00
75.00	337.50
75.00	187.50

Steps 2a–2b

Step 2c

QUICK STEPS

Change Table Style
1. Make cell active within table.
2. If necessary, click Table Tools Design tab.
3. Click More button in Table Styles gallery.
4. Click desired style

Add Total Row
1. Make cell active within table.
2. If necessary, click Table Tools Design tab.
3. Click *Total Row* check box.
4. Click in total row in column to add function.
5. Click desired function.

Table Styles and Table Style Options

The contextual Table Tools Design tab shown in Figure 3.2 contains options for formatting the table. Apply a different visual style to the table using the Table Styles gallery. Excel provides several table styles categorized by Light, Medium, and Dark color themes. By default, Excel bands the rows within the table, which means that even rows are formatted differently than odd rows. Banding rows or columns makes the task of reading data across a row or down a column in a large table easier. You can remove the banding from the rows and/or add banding to the columns. Use the *First Column* and *Last Column* check boxes in the Table Style Options group to add emphasis to the first or last column in the table by formatting the column separately from the rest of the table. The *Header Row* check box is used to show or hide the column headings row in the table.

Adding a total row to the table causes Excel to add the word *Total* in a new row at the bottom of the table in the leftmost cell. A Sum function is added automatically to the last numeric column in the table. Click in a cell in the total row to display a down-pointing arrow from which you can select a function formula in a pop-up list.

Figure 3.2 Table Tools Design Tab

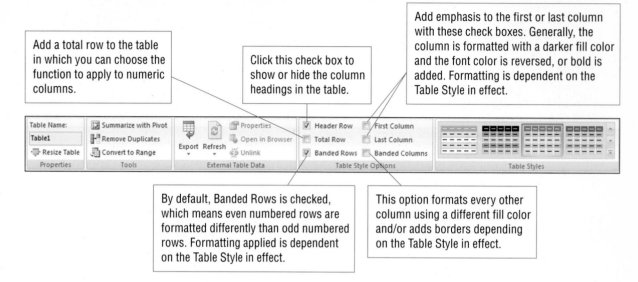

Add a total row to the table in which you can choose the function to apply to numeric columns.

Click this check box to show or hide the column headings in the table.

Add emphasis to the first or last column with these check boxes. Generally, the column is formatted with a darker fill color and the font color is reversed, or bold is added. Formatting is dependent on the Table Style in effect.

By default, Banded Rows is checked, which means even numbered rows are formatted differently than odd numbered rows. Formatting applied is dependent on the Table Style in effect.

This option formats every other column using a different fill color and/or adds borders depending on the Table Style in effect.

Project 1c Formatting a Table and Adding a Total Row

1. With **ExcelL2_C3_P1.xlsx** open, change the table style by completing the following steps:
   a. Click any cell within the table to activate the table and the contextual Table Tools Design tab.
   b. Click the Table Tools Design tab.
   c. Click the More button located at the bottom of the vertical scroll bar in the Table Styles gallery.
   d. Click *Table Style Medium 14* at the drop-down gallery (last option in second row in *Medium* section).

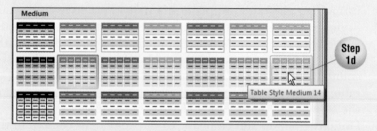

Step 1d

Table Style Medium 14

2. Change the Table Style options to remove the row banding, insert column banding, and emphasize the first column in the table by completing the following steps:
   a. Click the *Banded Rows* check box in the Table Style Options group in the Table Tools Design tab to clear the box. All of the rows in the table are now formatted the same.
   b. Click the *Banded Columns* check box in the Table Style Options group to insert a check mark. Every other column in the table is now formatted differently.
   c. Click the *First Column* check box in the Table Style Options group. Notice the first column has a darker fill color and reverse font color applied.

Step 2c

Step 2a

Step 2b

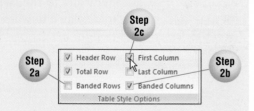

d. Click the *Header Row* check box in the Table Style Options group to clear the box. Notice the first row of the table containing the column headings disappears and is replaced with empty cells. The row is also removed from the table range definition.

e. Click the *Header Row* check box to insert a check mark and redisplay the column headings.

3. Add a total row and add function formulas to numeric columns by completing the following steps:

a. Click the *Total Row* check box in the Table Style Options group to add a total row to the bottom of the table. Excel formats row 26 as a total row, adds the label *Total* in A26, and automatically creates a Sum function in J26.

b. Make H26 the active cell.

c. Click the down-pointing arrow that appears in H26 and then click *Sum* at the pop-up list.

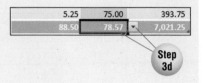

Fees_Due column totaled automatically when Total Row added to table in Step 3a.

d. Make I26 the active cell, click the down-pointing arrow that appears, and then click *Average* at the pop-up list.

4. Click the Page Layout tab and scale the worksheet to 1 page width.

5. Preview and then print the worksheet. ***Note: The worksheet will print in landscape orientation.***

6. Save **ExcelL2_C3_P1.xlsx**.

Sorting and Filtering a Table

QUICK STEPS

Filter Table
1. Click desired filter arrow button.
2. Click desired filter options.
3. Click OK.

Sort Table
1. Click desired filter arrow button.
2. Click desired sort order.
OR
1. Click Sort & Filter button.
2. Click Custom Sort.
3. Define sort levels.
4. Click OK.

By default, Excel displays a filter arrow button next to each label in the table header row. Click the filter arrow button to display a drop-down list with the same sort and filter options you used in Chapter 1.

Project 1d Sorting and Filtering a Table

1. With **ExcelL2_C3_P1.xlsx** open, filter the table by attorney name to print a list of billable hours for Marty O'Donovan by completing the following steps:

   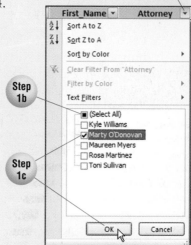

   Step 1a

   a. Click the filter arrow button located next to *Attorney* in F4.
   b. Click the *(Select All)* check box to clear the check mark from the box.
   c. Click the *Marty O'Donovan* check box to insert a check mark and then click OK. The table is filtered to display only those records with *Marty O'Donovan* in the *Attorney* field. The sum functions in columns H and J reflect the totals for the filtered records only.

   Step 1b

   Step 1c

   d. Print the filtered worksheet.
2. Redisplay all records by clicking the Attorney filter arrow button and then clicking *Clear Filter From "Attorney"* at the drop-down list.
3. Sort the table first by the attorney name, then by the area of law, and then by the client last name using the Sort dialog box by completing the following steps:

   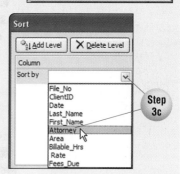

   Step 3c

   a. With the active cell positioned anywhere within the table, click the Home tab.
   b. Click the Sort & Filter button in the Editing group and then click *Custom Sort* at the drop-down list.
   c. At the Sort dialog box, click the down-pointing arrow next to the *Sort by* list box in the *Column* section and then click *Attorney* at the drop-down list. The default options for *Sort On* and *Order* are correct since you want to sort by the column values in ascending order.
   d. Click the Add Level button.
   e. Click the down-pointing arrow next to the *Then by* list box and then click *Area* at the drop-down list.
   f. Click the Add Level button.
   g. Click the down-pointing arrow next to the second *Then by* list box and then click *Last_Name* at the drop-down list.
   h. Click OK.

   Steps 3d & 3f

   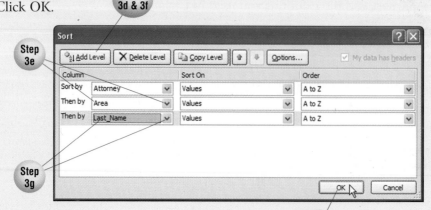

   Step 3e

   Step 3g

4. Print the sorted table.
5. Save and then close **ExcelL2_C3_P1.xlsx**.

   Step 3h

Project ② Use Data Tools to Split Data and Ensure Data Integrity

You will use Excel's data tools to split the attorney first and last names into two separate columns, remove duplicate records, and restrict the type of data that can be entered into a field.

QUICK STEPS

Split Text into Multiple Columns
1. Insert blank column(s) next to source data.
2. Select data to be split.
3. Click Data tab.
4. Click Text to Columns button.
5. Click Next at first dialog box.
6. Select delimiter check box for character that separates data.
7. Click Next.
8. Click Finish.
9. Deselect range.

Data Tools

The Data Tools group in the Data tab shown in Figure 3.3 includes features useful for working with data in tables. A worksheet that has a column in which multiple data have been entered into the same column can be separated into multiple columns using the Text to Columns feature. For example, a worksheet with a column that has first and last names entered into the same cell can have the first name split into one column and the last name split into a separate column. Breaking up the data into separate columns facilitates sorting and other data management functions. Before using the Text to Columns feature, insert the number of blank columns you will need to separate the data immediately right of the column to be split. Next, select the column containing multiple data and then click the Text to Columns button to start the Convert Text to Columns Wizard. The wizard contains three dialog boxes to guide you through the steps of separating the data.

Figure 3.3 Data Tools Group in Data Tab

Project ②a Separating Attorney Names into Two Columns

1. Open **ExcelL2_C3_P1.xlsx**.
2. Save the workbook with Save As and name it **ExcelL2_C3_P2**.
3. Position the active cell anywhere within the table, click the Sort & Filter button in the Editing group of the Home tab, and then click *Clear* at the drop-down list to clear the existing sort criteria.
4. Create a custom sort to sort the table first by *Date* (Oldest to Newest) and then by *ClientID* (Smallest to Largest). Refer to Project 1d, Step 3 if you need assistance with this step.
5. Split the attorney first and last names in column F into two columns by completing the following steps:
   a. Right-click column letter G at the top of the worksheet area and then click *Insert* at the shortcut menu to insert a blank column between the *Attorney* and *Area* columns in the table.
   b. Select F5:F25.
   c. Click the Data tab.

d. Click the Text to Columns button 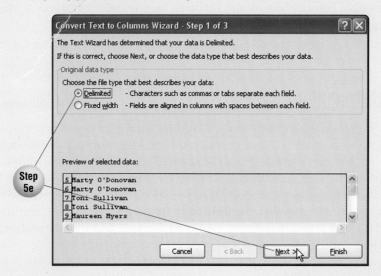 in the Data Tools group.
e. At the Convert Text to Columns Wizard - Step 1 of 3 dialog box, with *Delimited* selected in the *Choose the file type that best describes your data* section, click Next.

Convert Text to Columns Wizard - Step 1 of 3

The Text Wizard has determined that your data is Delimited.

If this is correct, choose Next, or choose the data type that best describes your data.

Original data type

Choose the file type that best describes your data:
- ⦿ Delimited - Characters such as commas or tabs separate each field.
- ○ Fixed width - Fields are aligned in columns with spaces between each field.

Preview of selected data:

```
5 Marty O'Donovan
6 Marty O'Donovan
7 Toni Sullivan
8 Toni Sullivan
9 Maureen Myers
```

Step 5e

Cancel < Back Next > Finish

f. At the Convert Text to Columns Wizard - Step 2 of 3 dialog box, click the *Space* check box in the *Delimiters* section and then click Next. The *Data preview* section of the dialog box updates after you click the *Space* check box to show the names split into two columns.

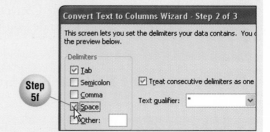

Convert Text to Columns Wizard - Step 2 of 3

This screen lets you set the delimiters your data contains. You the preview below.

Delimiters
- ☑ Tab
- ☐ Semicolon   ☑ Treat consecutive delimiters as one
- ☐ Comma
- ☑ Space   Text qualifier: "
- ☐ Other:

Step 5f

g. Click Finish at the last Convert Text to Columns Wizard dialog box to accept the default *General* data format for both columns.
h. Deselect the range.
6. Make F4 the active cell, edit the label to Attorney_FName, and then AutoFit the column width.
7. Make G4 the active cell, edit the label to Attorney_LName, and then AutoFit the column width.
8. Save **ExcelL2_C3_P2.xlsx**.

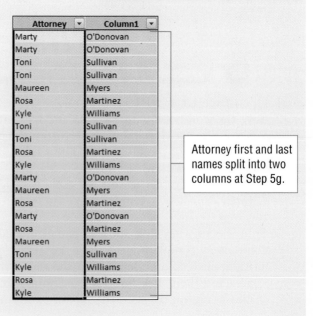

Attorney	Column1
Marty	O'Donovan
Marty	O'Donovan
Toni	Sullivan
Toni	Sullivan
Maureen	Myers
Rosa	Martinez
Kyle	Williams
Toni	Sullivan
Toni	Sullivan
Rosa	Martinez
Kyle	Williams
Marty	O'Donovan
Maureen	Myers
Rosa	Martinez
Marty	O'Donovan
Rosa	Martinez
Maureen	Myers
Toni	Sullivan
Kyle	Williams
Rosa	Martinez
Kyle	Williams

Attorney first and last names split into two columns at Step 5g.

QUICK STEPS

Remove Duplicate Rows
1. Select range or make cell active in table.
2. Click Data tab.
3. Click Remove Duplicates button.
4. Select columns to compare.
5. Click OK.
6. Click OK

Remove Duplicates

Removing Duplicate Records

Excel can compare records within a worksheet and automatically delete duplicate rows based on the columns you select that might contain duplicate values. At the Remove Duplicates dialog box shown in Figure 3.4, by default all columns are selected when the dialog box is opened. Click the Unselect All button to remove the check marks from each column and then click the individual columns you want to compare if you do not want Excel to check for duplicates in every column. When you click OK, Excel performs an automatic deletion of rows containing duplicate values and displays a message box when the operation is completed informing you of the number of rows that were removed from the worksheet or table and the number of unique values that remain. Consider conditionally formatting duplicate values first to view the records that will be deleted. Use the *Duplicate Values* option in *Highlight Cells Rules* from the Conditional Formatting drop-down list. (Display the Conditional Formatting drop-down list by clicking the Conditional Formatting button in the Styles group in the Home tab.)

Excel includes the Remove Duplicates button in the Data Tools group in the Data tab and in the Tools group in the Table Tools Design tab. Click Undo if you remove duplicate rows by mistake.

Figure 3.4 Remove Duplicates Dialog Box

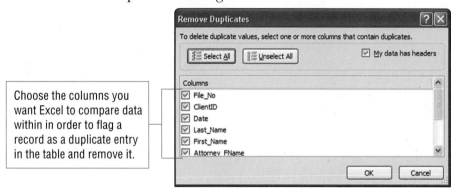

Choose the columns you want Excel to compare data within in order to flag a record as a duplicate entry in the table and remove it.

1. With **ExcelL2_C3_P2.xlsx** open, remove duplicate rows in the billing summary table by completing the following steps:
   a. With the active cell positioned anywhere within the table, click the Remove Duplicates button in the Data Tools group in the Data tab.
   b. At the Remove Duplicates dialog box with all columns selected in the *Columns* list box, click the Unselect All button.
   c. The billing summary table should have only one record per file per client per date since attorneys record once per day the total hours spent on each file. A record is a duplicate if the same values exist in the three columns that store the file number, client number, and date. Click the *File_No* check box to insert a check mark.
   d. Click the *ClientID* check box to insert a check mark.
   e. Click the *Date* check box to insert a check mark and then click OK.
   f. Click OK at the Microsoft Office Excel message box that says 1 duplicate value was found and removed and 20 unique values remain.
2. Scroll the worksheet to view the total in K25. Compare the total with your printout from Project 1d, Step 4. Notice the total in *Fees_Due* is now *6,627.50* compared to *7,021.25* in the printout.
3. Save **ExcelL2_C3_P2.xlsx**.

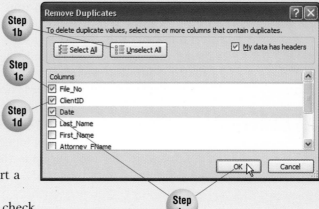

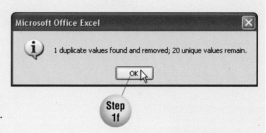

Validating and Restricting Data Entry

Excel's data validation feature allows you to control the type of data that is accepted for entry in a cell. You can specify the type of data that is allowed as well as parameters that validate whether the entry is within a certain range of acceptable values, dates, times, or text length. You can also set up a list of values that display in a drop-down list when the cell is made active. At the Data Validation dialog box shown in Figure 3.5, begin by choosing the type of data you want to validate in the *Allow* list box in the Settings tab. Additional list or text boxes appear in the dialog box depending on the option chosen in the *Allow* list.

As well as defining acceptable data entry parameters, you have the option of adding an input message and an error alert message to the range. You define the text that appears in these messages. The input message displays when the cell is made active for which data validation rules apply. These messages are informational in nature. Error alerts are messages that appear if incorrect data is entered in the cell. Three styles of error alerts are available. A description and example for each type of alert is described in Table 3.1.

Figure 3.5 Data Validation Dialog Box with Settings Tab Selected

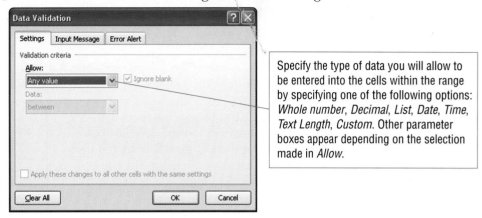

Specify the type of data you will allow to be entered into the cells within the range by specifying one of the following options: *Whole number, Decimal, List, Date, Time, Text Length, Custom.* Other parameter boxes appear depending on the selection made in *Allow.*

Table 3.1 Data Validation Error Alert Message Styles

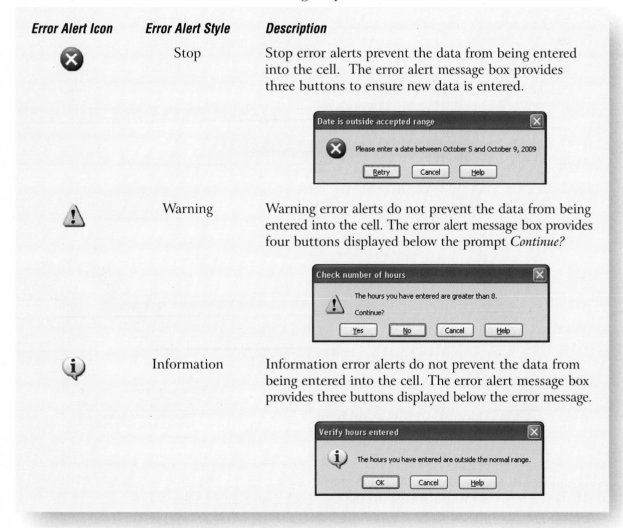

Error Alert Icon	Error Alert Style	Description
⊗	Stop	Stop error alerts prevent the data from being entered into the cell. The error alert message box provides three buttons to ensure new data is entered.
⚠	Warning	Warning error alerts do not prevent the data from being entered into the cell. The error alert message box provides four buttons displayed below the prompt *Continue?*
ⓘ	Information	Information error alerts do not prevent the data from being entered into the cell. The error alert message box provides three buttons displayed below the error message.

If an error alert message has not been defined, Excel displays the Stop error alert with a default error message of *The value you entered is not valid. A user has restricted values that can be entered into this cell.*

1. With **ExcelL2_C3_P2.xlsx** open, create a validation rule, input message, and error alert for dates in the billing summary worksheet by completing the following steps:
   a. Select C5:C24.
   b. Click the Data Validation button in the Data Tools group in the Data tab.
   c. With Settings the active tab at the Data Validation dialog box, click the down-pointing arrow next to the *Allow* list box (currently displays *Any value*) and then click *Date* at the drop-down list. Validation options are dependent on the *Allow* setting. When you choose *Date*, Excel adds *Start date* and *End date* text boxes to the *Validation criteria* section.
   d. With *between* automatically selected in the *Data* list box, click in the *Start date* text box and then type 10/05/2009.
   e. Click in the *End date* text box and then type 10/09/2009. Since the billing summary worksheet is for the week of October 5 to 9, 2009, entering this validation criteria will ensure that only dates between the start date and end date are accepted.
   f. Click the Input Message tab.
   g. Click in the *Title* text box and then type Billing Date.
   h. Click in the *Input message* text box and then type This worksheet is for the week of October 5 to October 9, 2009 only.
   i. Click the Error Alert tab.

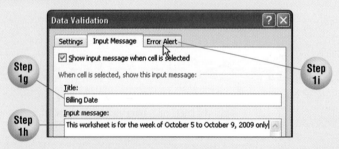

   j. With *Stop* selected in the *Style* list box, click in the *Title* text box and then type Date is outside accepted range.
   k. Click in the *Error message* text box and then type Please enter a date between October 5 and October 9, 2009.
   l. Click OK. Since the range is active for which the data validation rules apply, the input message box appears.
   m. Deselect the range.
2. Add a new record to the table to test the date validation rule by completing the following steps:
   a. Right-click row number 25 and then click *Insert* at the shortcut menu to insert a new row into the table.

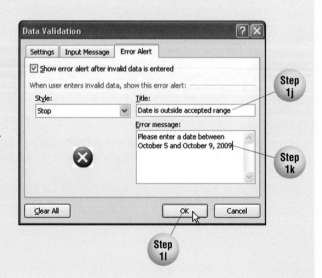

b. Make A25 the active cell, type **PL-348**, and then press Tab.

c. Type **10420** in *ClientID* and then press Tab. The input message title and text appear when the *Date* column is made active.

d. Type **10/12/2009** and then press Enter. Since the date entered is invalid, the error alert message box appears.

e. Click the Retry button.

f. Type **10/09/2009** and then press Tab.

g. Enter the data in the remaining fields as follows. Press Tab to move from column to column in the table.

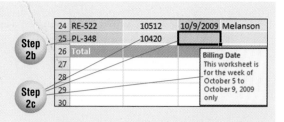

Step 2b

Step 2c

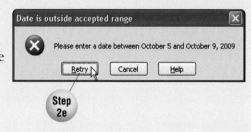

Step 2e

Last_Name	Torrez
First_Name	Alexander
Attorney_FName	Rosa
Attorney_LName	Martinez
Area	Patent
Billable_Hrs	2.25
Rate	100.00

3. Save **ExcelL2_C3_P2.xlsx**.

Project ❷ᵈ   Restricting Data Entry to Values Within a List

1. With **ExcelL2_C3_P2.xlsx** open, create a list of values that are allowed in a cell by completing the following steps:

   a. Select J5:J25.

   b. Click the Data Validation button in the Data Tools group.

   c. If necessary, click the Settings tab.

   d. Click the down-pointing arrow next to the *Allow* list box and then click *List* at the drop-down list.

   e. Click in the *Source* text box and then type 55.00,65.00,75.00,85.00,100.00.

   f. Click OK.

   g. Deselect the range.

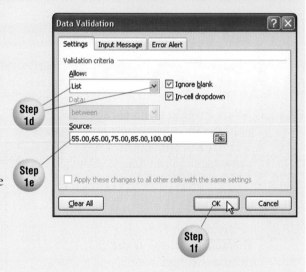

Step 1d

Step 1e

Step 1f

2. Add a new record to the table to test the rate validation list by completing the following steps:

   a. Right-click row number 26 and then click *Insert* at the shortcut menu to insert a new row into the table.

b. Make A26 the active cell and then type data in the fields as follows. Press Tab to move from column to column in the table.

File_No	IN-745
ClientID	10210
Date	10/09/2009
Last_Name	Boscovic
First_Name	Victor
Attorney_FName	Maureen
Attorney_LName	Myers
Area	Insurance
Billable_Hrs	1.75

c. At the *Rate* field, the validation list becomes active and a down-pointing arrow appears at the field. Type *125.00* and then press Tab to test the validation rule. Since no error alert message was entered, the default message appears.

d. Click the Cancel button. The value is cleared from the field.

e. Click the down-pointing arrow at the end of the field, click *100.00* at the drop-down list, and then press Tab.

3. Save **ExcelL2_C3_P2.xlsx**.

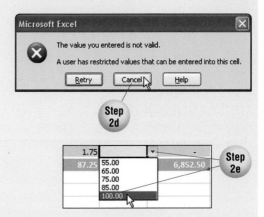

Step 2d

Step 2e

Project **2e** **Ensuring Data Entered Is a Specified Text Length**

1. With **ExcelL2_C3_P2.xlsx** open, create a validation rule to ensure that all client identification numbers are five characters in length to coincide with the firm's accounting system by completing the following steps:

a. Select B5:B26 and click the Data Validation button.

b. Click the down-pointing arrow next to the *Allow* list box and then click *Text length* at the drop-down list.

c. Click the down-pointing arrow next to *Data* and then click *equal to* at the drop-down list.

d. Click in the *Length* text box, type *5*, and then click OK.

e. Deselect the range.

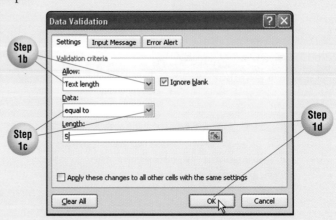

Step 1b

Step 1c

Step 1d

2. Add a new record to the table to test the client identification validation rule by completing the following steps:

a. Right-click row number 27 and then click *Insert* at the shortcut menu.

b. Make A27 the active cell, type FL-325, and then press Tab.

c. Type 1010411 in B27 and then press Tab. Since this value is greater than the specified number of characters allowed in the cell, the default error message appears.

d. Click the Retry button.

e. Delete the selected text, type 1010, and then press Tab. Since this value is less than the specified text length, the default error message appears again. Using a Text Length validation rule ensures that all entries in the range have the same number of characters. This rule is useful to validate customer numbers, employee numbers, inventory numbers, or any other data that requires a consistent number of characters.

f. Click the Cancel button, type 10104, and then press Tab. Since this entry is five characters in length, Excel moves to the next field.

g. Enter the remaining fields as follows:

Date	10/09/2009
Last_Name	Ferreira
First_Name	Joseph
Attorney_FName	Marty
Attorney_LName	O'Donovan
Area	Divorce
Billable_Hrs	5.75
Rate	85.00

3. Save, print, and then close **ExcelL2_C3_P2.xlsx**.

Project ② Calculate a Target Test Score

Using a grades worksheet for a student, you will determine the score a student needs to earn on a final test in order to achieve a specified final average grade.

Using Goal Seek to Populate a Cell

Excel's Goal Seek feature returns a value based upon a target that you want to achieve in another cell that is dependent on the cell you want Goal Seek to populate. For example, the worksheet shown in Figure 5.3 shows Whitney's grades on the first four tutoring assessments. The value in B11 (average grade) is calculated as the average of the five values in B5:B9. Note that the final test is showing a grade of zero although the test has not yet occurred. Once the final test grade is entered, the value in B11 will update to reflect the average of all five scores. Suppose Whitney wants to achieve a final grade of 76% in her course. Using Goal Seek, you can determine the score she needs to earn on the final test in order to achieve the 76% average.

In Project 2 you will return a value in B9 that the Goal Seek feature will calculate based on the target value you will set in B11. Goal Seek causes Excel to calculate in reverse—you specify the ending value and Excel figures out the input numbers that will achieve the end result you want. Note that the cell in which you want Excel to calculate the target value must be referenced by a formula in the *Set cell* box. Goal Seek is useful for any situation where you know the result you want to achieve but are not sure what value will get you there.

QUICK STEPS

Use Goal Seek to Return a Value
1. Make desired cell active.
2. Click Data tab.
3. Click What-If Analysis button.
4. Click *Goal Seek*.
5. Enter desired cell address in *Set cell* text box.
6. Enter desired target value in *To value* text box.
7. Enter dependent cell address in *By changing cell* text box.
8. Click OK.
9. Click OK or Cancel to accept or reject results.

HINT
The cell in which you want Excel to calculate the target value must be referenced by a formula in the *Set cell* box.

What-If Analysis ▾

Figure 5.3 Project 2 Worksheet

	A	B	C
1	Math by Janelle Tutoring Service		
2	Student Assessment Report		
3	Whitney Orlowicz		
4	Assessments	100	Session
5	Objective test	64.5	1
6	Performance test	72.0	6
7	Problem-solving test	83.5	10
8	Comprehensive test	78.5	15
9	Final test	0.0	20
10			
11	Average grade	59.7	

Goal Seek can determine the value that needs to be entered for the final test in order to achieve an average grade that you specify in B11.

Project ② Using Goal Seek to Return a Target Value

1. Open **JanelleTutoring-OrlowiczRpt.xlsx**.
2. Save the workbook with Save As and name it **ExcelL2_C5_P2**.
3. Use Goal Seek to find the score Whitney needs to earn on the final test to achieve a 76% average grade by completing the following steps:
   a. Make B11 the active cell.
   b. Click the Data tab.
   c. Click the What-If Analysis button in the Data Tools group and then click *Goal Seek* at the drop-down list.

 Step 3c

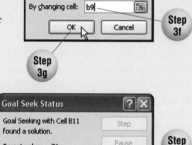 Step 3e / Step 3f / Step 3g

   d. If necessary, drag the Goal Seek dialog box to the right of the worksheet so that you can see all of the values in column B.
   e. With *B11* already entered in the *Set cell* text box, click in the *To value* text box and then type **76**.
   f. Press Tab and then type **b9** in the *By changing cell* text box.
   g. Click OK.
   h. Click OK at the Goal Seek Status dialog box that shows Excel found a solution.

Step 3h

4. Notice that Excel entered the value *81.5* in B9. This is the score Whitney must earn in order to achieve a final average grade of 76%.
5. Print the worksheet.
6. Assume that Whitney wants to achieve a final average grade of 80%. Use Goal Seek to find the value that she will need to earn on the final test to accomplish the new target by completing the following steps:
   a. Click the What-If Analysis button in the Data Tools group and then click *Goal Seek* at the drop-down list.
   b. Click in the *To value* text box, type **80**, and then press Tab.
   c. Type **b9** in the *By changing cell* text box and then click OK.
   d. Click OK.
   e. Notice that the value returned in B9 is 101.5. This is the new value Excel has calculated Whitney needs on the final test in order to earn an 80% final average grade.
   f. Click the Cancel button at the Goal Seek Status dialog box to restore the previous values.

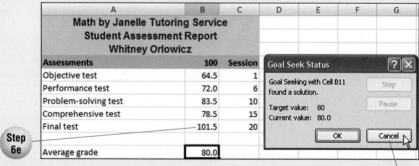

Step 6e

Step 6f

7. Save and then close **ExcelL2_C5_P2.xlsx**.

Project ① Import Data from External Sources to Excel

You will import U.S. Census Bureau data related to a market research project from an Access database, from the U.S. Census Bureau's Web site, and from a text file previously downloaded from the Census Bureau.

QUICK STEPS

Import Access Table
1. Make active cell at which to begin import.
2. Click Data tab.
3. Click From Access button.
4. Navigate to drive and/or folder.
5. Double-click source database file name.
6. If necessary, click desired table name and OK.
7. Select desired view format.
8. Click OK.

Importing Data into Excel

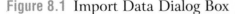

The Get External Data group in the Data tab contains buttons used to import data from external sources into an Excel worksheet. Make the cell active at which you want the import to begin and click the button representing the source application, or click the Other Sources button to select the source from a drop-down list. A connection can be established to an external data source to avoid having to repeat the import process each time you need to analyze the data in Excel. Once a connection has been created, you can repeat the import in another worksheet by simply clicking the connection file in the Existing Connections dialog box.

Importing Data from Access

Exchanging data between Access and Excel is a seamless process since data in an Access datasheet is structured in the same row and column format as an Excel worksheet. You can import the Access data as an Excel table, a PivotTable Report, or as a PivotChart and a PivotTable report. The imported data can be placed in a cell you identify in the active worksheet or in a new worksheet. To import an Access table, click the Data tab and then click the From Access button in the Get External Data group. At the Select Data Source dialog box, navigate to the drive and/or folder in which the source database resides and then double-click the Access database file name in the file list. If the source database contains more than one table, the Select Table dialog box opens in which you choose the table containing the data you want to import. If the source database contains only one table you are not prompted to select a table name. Once the table is identified, the Import Data dialog box shown in Figure 8.1 appears. Choose how you want to view the data and the location to begin the import and click OK.

HINT

Only one table can be imported at a time. To import all of the tables in the source database, repeat the Import process for each table.

🗎 From Access

Figure 8.1 Import Data Dialog Box

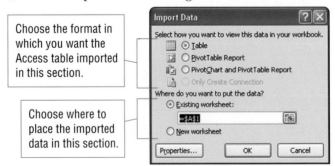

Choose the format in which you want the Access table imported in this section.

Choose where to place the imported data in this section.

Project 1a   Importing Data from an Access Database

1. Open **NuTrendsMktRsrch-CensusData.xlsx**.
2. Save the workbook with Save As and name it **ExcelL2_C8_P1**.
3. Import four years of U.S. state population estimates compiled by the U.S. Census Bureau that are stored in an Access database by completing the following steps:
   a. With PopulationEstimates the active worksheet, make A5 the active cell.
   b. Click the Data tab.
   c. Click the From Access button in the Get External Data group.
   d. At the Select Data Source dialog box, navigate to the Excel2007L2C8 folder on your storage medium and then double-click **NuTrendsMktRsrch-CensusData.accdb**.

   e. Since the source database contains more than one table, the Select Table dialog box appears. Click *PopulationByState* in the *Name* column and then click OK.

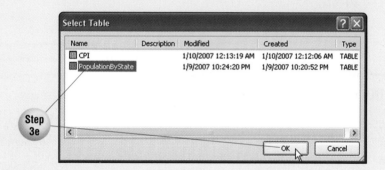

   f. At the Import Data dialog box with *Table* selected in the *Select how you want to view this data in your workbook* section and *=$A$5* in the *Existing worksheet* text box in the *Where do you want to put the data?* section, click OK.

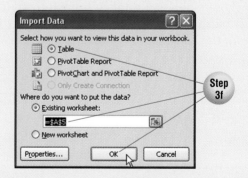

4. Scroll down the imported table data. Notice the data is formatted as a table with filter arrow buttons.

5. Make the following changes to the worksheet:
   a. The clip art image at the top of the worksheet became skewed when the columns were automatically widened upon import. Display the sizing handles on the image and decrease the width to the approximate width shown.
   b. Remove the filter arrow buttons.
   c. Change the table style to Table Style Medium 1 (first from left in *Medium* section) at the Format as Table drop-down gallery.
   d. Format all of the values to display a comma in the thousands and zero decimals.

	A	B	C	D	E	F	
1			NuTrends Market Research				
2			U.S. Population Estimates by State				
3							
4	Source: U.S. Census Bureau						
5	ID	State	Pop_July1_06	Pop_July1_05	Pop_July1_04	Pop_Jul1_03	
6	1	Alabama	4,599,030	4,548,327	4,517,442	4,495,089	
7	2	Alaska	670,053	663,253	656,834	647,747	
8	3	Arizona	6,166,318	5,953,007	5,745,674	5,582,252	
9	4	Arkansas	2,810,872	2,775,708	2,746,823	2,723,645	
10	5	California	36,457,549	36,154,147	35,841,254	35,466,365	

Steps 5a–5d

6. Print the PopulationEstimates worksheet scaled to fit 1 page in width and height.
7. Save **ExcelL2_C8_P1.xlsx**.

Importing Data from a Web Site

Import Data from Web Page
1. Make active cell at which to begin import.
2. Click Data tab.
3. Click From Web button.
4. Navigate to desired Web page.
5. Click arrows next to tables to import.
6. Click Import button.
7. Click OK.

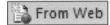
From Web

Tables in a Web site can be downloaded directly from the Web source using the New Web Query dialog box shown in Figure 8.2. Make active the cell at which you want to begin the import, click the Data tab, and then click the From Web button in the Get External Data group. Use the Address bar and Web navigation buttons to go to the page containing the data you want to use in Excel. At the desired page, Excel displays black right-pointing arrows inside yellow boxes next to elements on the page that contain importable tables. Point to an arrow and a blue border surrounds the data Excel will capture if you click the arrow. Click the arrow for those tables you want to bring into your Excel worksheet and then click the Import button. In Project 1b, you will import multiple sections of data about Florida from the U.S. Census Bureau QuickFacts Web page.

Figure 8.2 New Web Query Dialog Box

Navigate to the desired Web site as you would in a browser window.

Point to an arrow in a yellow box to display a blue border around a table on the Web page. Click the arrow to select the table and then click the Import button to copy the data into the active cell.

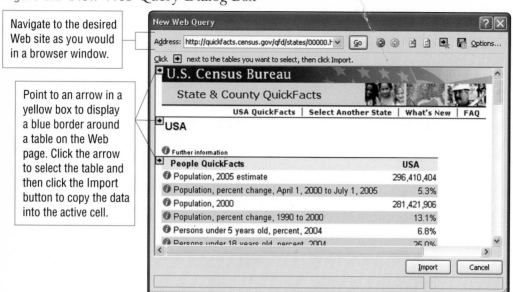

Project 1b Importing a Table from a Web Page

1. With **ExcelL2_C8_P1.xlsx** open, make FloridaGeographicData the active worksheet.
2. Import statistics related to Florida from the U.S. Census Bureau QuickFacts Web page by completing the following steps:
   a. Make A6 the active cell.
   b. Click the From Web button in the Get External Data group of the Data tab.
   c. At the New Web Query dialog box, select the current entry in the *Address* text box, type http://www.census.gov and press Enter.
   d. Click the Data Tools link located near the top left of the Web page.
   e. At the Data Access Tools page, scroll down the page if necessary and then click the QuickFacts link in the Interactive Internet Tools section.
   f. At the State & County QuickFacts page, resize the New Web Query dialog box until you can see the entire map of the USA.

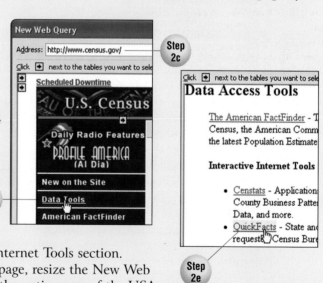

g. Click on the state of Florida in the map.

h. At the Florida QuickFacts page, notice the black right-pointing arrows inside yellow boxes along the left edge of the page. Point to one of the arrows to see the blue border that surrounds a section of data; the border indicates the data that will be imported into Excel if you click the arrow.

Step 2g

i. Scroll down the page to the section titled *Business QuickFacts*.

j. Click the black right-pointing arrow inside the yellow box next to *Business QuickFacts* to select the table. The arrow changes to a check mark inside a green box when the table is selected for import.

k. Click the arrow next to *Geography QuickFacts* to select the table.

l. Click the Import button.

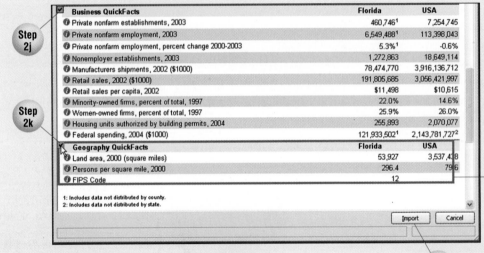

Step 2j

Step 2k

A blue border displays around the data that will be imported to Excel if the table is selected.

Business QuickFacts	Florida	USA
ⓘ Private nonfarm establishments, 2003	460,746[1]	7,254,745
ⓘ Private nonfarm employment, 2003	6,549,488[1]	113,398,043
ⓘ Private nonfarm employment, percent change 2000-2003	5.3%[1]	-0.6%
ⓘ Nonemployer establishments, 2003	1,272,863	18,649,114
ⓘ Manufacturers shipments, 2002 ($1000)	78,474,770	3,916,136,712
ⓘ Retail sales, 2002 ($1000)	191,805,685	3,056,421,997
ⓘ Retail sales per capita, 2002	$11,498	$10,615
ⓘ Minority-owned firms, percent of total, 1997	22.0%	14.6%
ⓘ Women-owned firms, percent of total, 1997	25.9%	26.0%
ⓘ Housing units authorized by building permits, 2004	255,893	2,070,077
ⓘ Federal spending, 2004 ($1000)	121,933,502[1]	2,143,781,727[2]
Geography QuickFacts	Florida	USA
ⓘ Land area, 2000 (square miles)	53,927	3,537,438
ⓘ Persons per square mile, 2000	296.4	79.6
ⓘ FIPS Code	12	

1: Includes data not distributed by county.
2: Includes data not distributed by state.

Import   Cancel

Step 2l

Step 2m

m. At the Import Data dialog box with =$A$6 in the *Existing worksheet* text box in the *Where do you want to put the data?* section, click OK. Excel imports the data from the Web page into the Excel worksheet starting in A6.

3. Make the following changes to the worksheet:

a. Move the clip art image to approximately center it horizontally and vertically within the range C1:D5.

b. Select the cells in Column A that contain imported text, click the Home tab, and then click the Wrap Text button in the Alignment group.

c. Decrease the width of column A to 35.00 (250 pixels).

Import Data [?][X]

Where do you want to put the data?
- ⊙ Existing worksheet:
  - =$A$6
- ○ New worksheet

Properties...   OK   Cancel

    d. AutoFit the height of A6:A22.

    e. Align the text in C6:D6 at the center.

    f. Change the page orientation to landscape and scale to fit one page width by one page height.

4. Print the FloridaGeographicData worksheet.

5. Save **ExcelL2_C8_P1.xlsx**.

Importing Data from a Text File

A text file is often used to exchange data between dissimilar programs since the file format is recognized by nearly all applications. Text files contain no formatting and consist of letters, numbers, punctuation symbols, and a few control characters only. Two commonly used text file formats separate fields with either a tab character (delimited file format) or a comma (comma separated file format). The text file you will use in Project 1c is shown in a Notepad window in Figure 8.3. If necessary, you can view and edit a text file in Notepad prior to importing.

Figure 8.3 Project 1c Text File Contents

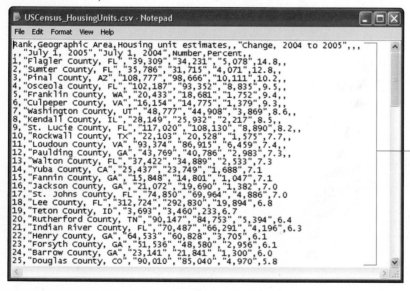

Text files contain no formatting codes. A comma separated file (.csv) contains a comma separating each field. During the import, Excel starts a new column at each comma. Notice also that quotes surround text data. Excel strips the quotes from the data upon importing.

      To import a text file into Excel, use the From Text button in the Get External Data group of the Data tab and then select the source file at the Import Text File dialog box. Excel displays in the file list any file in the active folder that ends with a text file extension *.prn*, *.txt*, or *.csv*. Once the source file is selected, Excel begins the Text Import Wizard, which guides you through the import process through three dialog boxes.

QUICK STEPS

Import Data from Comma Separated Text File

1. Make active cell at which to begin import.
2. Click Data tab.
3. Click From Text button.
4. Double-click .csv file name.
5. Click Next.
6. Click *Comma* check box.
7. Click Next.
8. Click Finish.
9. Click OK.

From Text

HINT

Most programs can export data in a text file. If you need to use data from a program that is not compatible with Excel, check the source program's export options for a text file format.

Project 1C Importing Data from a Comma Separated Text File

1. With **ExcelL2_C8_P1.xlsx** open, make HousingUnitData the active worksheet.
2. Import statistics related to the top-growing U.S. counties based on changes in housing units downloaded from the U. S. Census Bureau Web site in a text file by completing the following steps:
   a. Make A7 the active cell.
   b. Click the Data tab.
   c. Click the From Text button in the Get External Data group.
   d. At the Import Text File dialog box, double-click the file named **USCensus_HousingUnits.csv** in the file list.
   e. At the Text Import Wizard - Step 1 of 3 dialog box, with *Delimited* selected in the *Original data type* section, click Next. Notice the preview window in the lower half of the dialog box displays a sample of the data in the source text file. Delimited files use commas or tabs as separators, while fixed-width files use spaces.

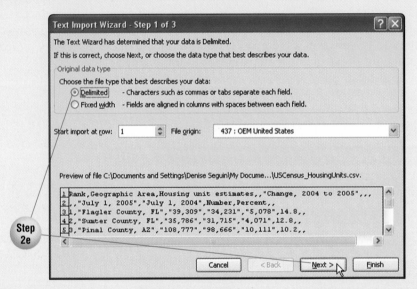

Step 2e

f. At the Text Import Wizard - Step 2 of 3 dialog box, click the *Comma* check box in the *Delimiters* section to insert a check mark and then click Next. Notice after you select the comma as the delimiter character, the data in the *Data preview* section updates to show the imported data arranged in Excel columns.

Step 2f

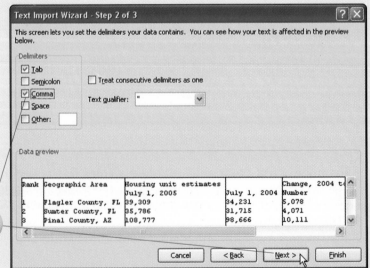

g. Click Finish at the Text Import Wizard - Step 3 of 3 dialog box to import all of the columns using the default *General* format. Formatting can be applied after the data has been imported into the worksheet.

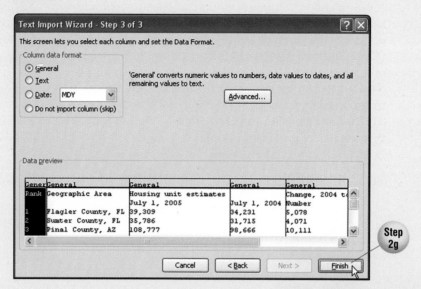

h. At the Import Data dialog box with *=$A$7* in the *Existing worksheet* text box in the *Where do you want to put the data?* section, click OK.

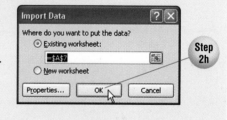

3. Scroll down the worksheet and view the imported data. The text file contained the top 100 counties in the United States ranked by change in housing units from 2004 to 2005. The number of housing units and the percent change are included.
4. Make the following changes to the data:
   a. Select C7:D7, click the Home tab, and then click the Merge & Center button in the Alignment group.
   b. Merge and center E7:F7.
   c. Align the text in E8 at the right.
   d. Change the width of columns C, D, and E to 14.00 (103 pixels).
5. Print the HousingUnitData worksheet.
6. Save and then close **ExcelL2_C8_P1.xlsx**.

Project 2 Export Data in Excel

You will copy and paste data related to car inventory from an Excel worksheet to integrate with an Access database, a Word report, and a PowerPoint presentation. You will also save a worksheet as a comma separated text file for use in a non-Microsoft program.

Append Excel Data to Access Table
1. Open Excel workbook.
2. Select cells.
3. Click Copy button.
4. Start Access.
5. Open database.
6. Open table in Datasheet view.
7. Click Paste button arrow.
8. Click *Paste Append*.
9. Click Yes.
10. Deselect pasted range.

Exporting Data from Excel

Excel data can be exported for use in other programs by copying the cells to the clipboard and pasting into the destination document or by saving the worksheet as a separate file in another file format. To use Excel data in Word, PowerPoint, or Access, use the copy and paste routine since the programs within the Microsoft Office Suite are designed for integration. To export the Excel data for use in other programs, open the Save As dialog box and change the *Save as type* option to the desired file format. If the file format for the destination program that you want to use does not appear in the *Save as type* list, you can try copying and pasting the data or go to the Microsoft Office Online Web site and search for a file format converter that you can download and install.

Copying and Pasting Worksheet Data to an Access Table

Data in an Excel worksheet can be copied and pasted to an Access table datasheet, query, or form using the clipboard. To paste data into a table datasheet, make sure that the column structure in the two programs match. If the Access datasheet already contains records, you can choose to replace the existing records or append the Excel data to the end of the table. If you want to export Excel data to an Access database that does not have an existing table in which to receive the data, perform an import routine from Access. Start Access, click the External Data tab, and then click the Import Excel spreadsheet button.

Project 2a Copying and Pasting Excel Data to an Access Datasheet

1. Open **CutRate-Inventory.xlsx**.
2. Copy and paste the rows in the NewInventory worksheet to the bottom of an Access table by completing the following steps:
   a. Make sure NewInventory is the active worksheet.
   b. Select A2:G30 and click the Copy button in the Clipboard group in the Home tab.
   c. Start Microsoft Office Access 2007.
   d. At the Getting Started with Microsoft Office Access screen, click the Office button and then click *Open* at the drop-down list.
   e. At the Open dialog box, navigate to the Excel2007L2C8 folder on your storage medium and then double-click the database named **CutRate-CarInventory.accdb**.
   f. Double-click the object named *CarPurchaseInventory : Table* in the Navigation pane at the left side of the Access window. This opens the CarPurchaseInventory table in Datasheet view. Notice the structure of the columns in the datasheet is the same as the source worksheet in Excel.

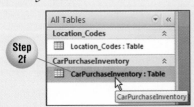

Step 2f

g. With the table open in Datasheet view, click the down-pointing arrow on the Paste button in the Clipboard group and then click *Paste Append* at the drop-down list.

Step 2g

h. At the Microsoft Office Access message box informing you that you are about to paste 29 records and asking if you are sure, click Yes.

Step 2h

i. Click any cell within the datasheet to deselect the pasted records.

3. Print the datasheet in Access in landscape orientation by completing the following steps:
   a. Click the Office button, point to *Print*, and then click *Print Preview*.
   b. Click the Landscape button in the Page Layout group in the Print Preview tab.

Step 3b

c. Click the Print button in the Print group and then click OK at the Print dialog box.
   d. Click the Close Print Preview button in the Close Preview group.

4. Click the Close button located at the top right of the datasheet to close the CarPurchaseInventory datasheet.

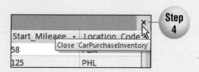

Step 4

5. Click the Office button and then click the Exit Access button located at the bottom right of the drop-down list.

6. Click any cell to deselect the range in the NewInventory worksheet and press the Esc key to remove the moving marquee.

Copying and Pasting Worksheet Data to a Word Document

QUICK STEPS

Embed Excel Data in Word Document
1. Open Excel workbook.
2. Select cells.
3. Click Copy button.
4. Start Word.
5. Open document.
6. Position insertion point at desired location.
7. Click Paste button arrow.
8. Click *Paste Special.*
9. Click *Microsoft Office Excel Worksheet Object.*
10. Click OK.
11. Save and close Word document.
12. Deselect range.

Link Excel Data in Word Document
1. Open Excel workbook.
2. Select cells.
3. Click Copy button.
4. Start Word.
5. Open document.
6. Position insertion point at desired location.
7. Click Paste button arrow.
8. Click *Paste Special.*
9. Click *Microsoft Office Excel Worksheet Object.*
10. Click *Paste link.*
11. Click OK.
12. Save and close Word document.
13. Deselect range.

Using a process similar to the one in Project 2a, you can copy and paste Excel data, copy and embed Excel data as an object, or copy and link Excel data as an object in a Word document. Use the copy and paste method if the data being brought into Word is not likely to be updated or require editing once the source cells are pasted in the Word document. Copy and embed the data if you want to have the ability to edit the data once it is inserted in Word using Excel's editing tools and features. Copy and link the data if the information being pasted into Word is likely to be changed in the future and you want the document in Word updated if the data in the source file changes.

Embedding Excel Data into Word

To embed copied Excel data into a Word document, open the desired Word document, move the insertion point to the location at which you want to insert the copied Excel data, and then open the Paste Special dialog box. At the Paste Special dialog box, click *Microsoft Office Excel Worksheet Object* in the *As* list box and then click OK.

To edit an embedded Excel object in Word, double-click over the embedded cells to open the cells for editing in a worksheet. Word's ribbon is temporarily replaced with Excel's ribbon. Click outside the embedded object to restore Word's ribbon and close the worksheet object in Word.

Linking Excel Data into Word

Linking Excel data to a Word document means that the source data exists only in Excel. Word places a shortcut to the source data file name and range in the Word document. When you open a Word document containing a link, Word prompts you to update the links. Since the data resides in the Excel workbook only, be careful not to move or rename the original workbook from which you copied the cells or the link will no longer work.

To paste copied Excel data as a link in a Word document, open the desired Word document, move the insertion point to the location at which you want to link the cells, open the Paste Special dialog box, click *Microsoft Office Excel Worksheet Object* in the *As* list box, click *Paste link*, and then click OK.

Project 2b   Embedding Excel Data in a Word Document

1. With **CutRate-Inventory.xlsx** open, copy and embed the data in the CarCosts worksheet to a Word document by completing the following steps:
   a. Make CarCosts the active worksheet.
   b. Select A4:F9.
   c. Click the Copy button in the Clipboard group.

d. Start Microsoft Office Word 2007.

e. Open **CutRate-CarReport.docx**.

f. Save the document with Save As and name it **ExcelL2_C8_P2**.

g. Press Ctrl + End to move the insertion point to the end of the document.

h. Click the down-pointing arrow on the Paste button and then click *Paste Special* at the drop-down list.

i. At the Paste Special dialog box, click *Microsoft Office Excel Worksheet Object* in the *As* list box and then click OK.

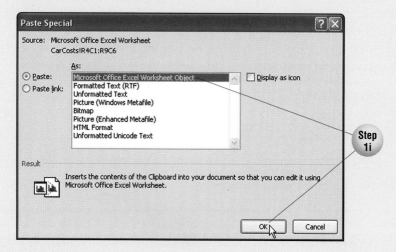

2. Save **ExcelL2_C8_P2.docx**.

3. When you use Paste Special, the copied cells are embedded as an object in the Word document. Edit the embedded object using Excel's editing tools by completing the following steps:

   a. Double-click over any cell in the embedded worksheet object. The object is surrounded with a border and Excel's column and row headers appear with the cells. Word's ribbon is temporarily replaced with Excel's ribbon.

   b. Select B5:F9 and then click the Accounting Number Format button in the Number group.

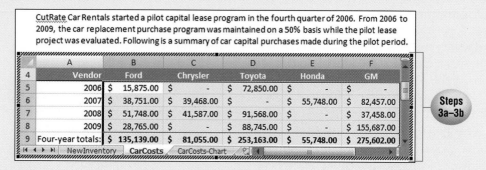

   c. Click in the document outside the embedded object to close the object and restore Word's ribbon.

4. Save, print, and then close **ExcelL2_C8_P2.docx**.

5. Click the Office button and then click the Exit Word button.

6. Click any cell to deselect the range in the CarCosts worksheet.

1. With **CutRate-Inventory.xlsx** open, copy and link the data in the CarCosts worksheet to a Word document by completing the following steps:
   a. With CarCosts the active worksheet, select A4:F9 and click the Copy button.
   b. Start Microsoft Office Word 2007.
   c. Open **CutRate-CarReport.docx**.
   d. Save the document with Save As and name it **ExcelL2_C8_P2-Linked**.
   e. Press Ctrl + End to move the insertion point to the end of the document.
   f. Click the down-pointing arrow on the Paste button and then click *Paste Special* at the drop-down list.
   g. At the Paste Special dialog box, click *Microsoft Office Excel Worksheet Object* in the *As* list box and then click *Paste link*.
   h. Click OK.

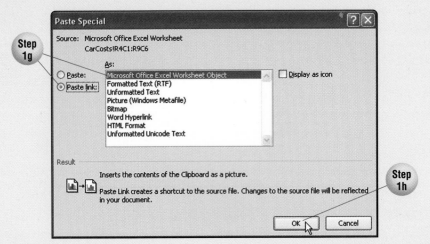

2. Save and then close **ExcelL2_C8_P2-Linked.docx**. When data is linked, the data exists only in the source program. In the destination document, Word inserted a shortcut to the source range. Edit the source range and view the update to the Word document by completing the following steps:
   a. Click the button on the Taskbar representing the Excel file named **CutRate-Inventory.xlsx**.
   b. With CarCosts the active worksheet, press the ESC key to remove the moving marquee from the source range and then make E5 the active cell.
   c. Type *85000* and press Enter.
   d. Click the button on the Taskbar representing Word.
   e. Open **ExcelL2_C8_P2-Linked.docx**.
   f. At the Microsoft Office Word message box asking if you want to update the document with data from the linked files, click Yes.

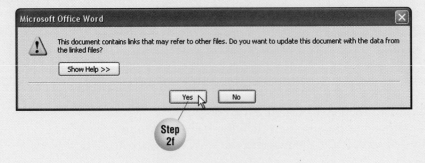

3. Notice the data inserted in the Excel worksheet is also shown in the linked Word document.
4. Save and then print **ExcelL2_C8_P2-Linked.docx**.
5. Exit Word.
6. With CarCosts the active worksheet in **CutRate-Inventory.xlsx**, delete the contents of E5.

Breaking a Link to an Excel Object

If you linked Excel data to a Word document and later decide you no longer need to maintain the link, you can break the connection between the source and destination files so that you are not prompted to update the object each time you open the document. Breaking the link means that the data in the Word document will no longer be connected to the data in the Excel workbook. If you make a change to the original source in Excel, the Word document will not reflect the updated information. To break a link, open the document, right-click over the linked object, point to *Linked Worksheet Object* and click *Links* at the shortcut menu. This opens the Links dialog box. If more than one linked object exists in the document, click the source object for the link you want to break and then click the Break Link button. Click Yes to confirm you want to break the link at the message box that appears.

QUICK STEPS

Break Link to Excel Object
1. Open document.
2. Right-click linked object.
3. Point to *Linked Worksheet Object*.
4. Click *Links*.
5. Click Break Link button.
6. Click Yes.
7. Save and close document.

Project **2d**   **Breaking a Link**

1. Start Word and open **ExcelL2_C8_P2-Linked.docx**.
2. At the message asking if you want to update links, click Yes.
3. Break the link between the Excel workbook and the linked object by completing the following steps:
   a. Right-click over the linked Excel worksheet object.
   b. Point to *Linked Worksheet Object* and then click *Links* at the shortcut menu.
   c. At the Links dialog box, with the linked object file name selected in the Source file list box, click the Break Link button.

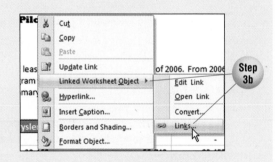

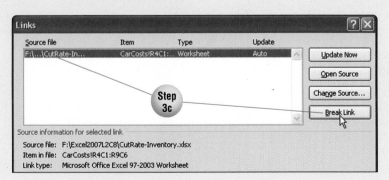

d. At the Microsoft Office Word dialog box asking if you are sure you want to break the selected link, click Yes.

4. Save **ExcelL2_C8_P2-Linked.docx** and then exit Word.

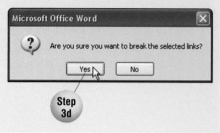

Step 3d

Embed Excel Data in PowerPoint Presentation

1. Open Excel workbook.
2. Select cells.
3. Click Copy button.
4. Start PowerPoint.
5. Open presentation.
6. Make desired slide active.
7. Click Paste button arrow.
8. Click *Paste Special.*
9. Make sure *Microsoft Office Excel Worksheet Object* is selected in *As* list box.
10. Click OK.
11. Save and close PowerPoint presentation.
12. Deselect range.

Copying and Pasting Worksheet Data to a PowerPoint Presentation

As with Word, you can copy and paste, copy and embed, or copy and link Excel data to slides in a PowerPoint presentation. Although you can create tables and charts in a PowerPoint slide, some people prefer to use Excel for these tasks and then copy and paste the data to PowerPoint. Presentations often incorporate charts to visually depict numerical data in a graph format that is easy to understand. In the Office 2007 suite, the charting system is fully integrated within Word, Excel, and PowerPoint. A chart inserted in a Word document or PowerPoint presentation is created as an embedded object with the source data used to generate the chart stored in an Excel worksheet; the Excel worksheet with the source data becomes part of the document or presentation file.

Since the chart feature is fully integrated within Word, Excel, and PowerPoint, you can edit a chart in a PowerPoint presentation using the same techniques you learned to edit a chart in Excel. Clicking a chart on a PowerPoint slide causes the contextual Chart Tools Design, Chart Tools Layout, and Chart Tools Format tabs to become active with the same groups and buttons available in Excel.

Project **2e** | **Embedding Excel Data in a PowerPoint Presentation**

1. With **CutRate-Inventory.xlsx** open, copy and embed the chart in the CarCosts-Chart worksheet to a slide in a PowerPoint presentation by completing the following steps:
   a. Make CarCosts-Chart the active worksheet.
   b. Click in a blank area around the chart to select the chart object.
   c. Click the Home tab and then click the Copy button.
   d. Start Microsoft Office PowerPoint 2007.
   e. Open **CutRate-CarReport.pptx**.
   f. Save the presentation with Save As and name it **ExcelL2_C8_P2**.

g. Click slide 3 in the Slides pane.
h. Click the Paste button in the Clipboard group. Since all charts are embedded by default, you do not need to use Paste Special.
2. Resize the chart to the approximate height and width shown and position the chart in the center of the slide horizontally.

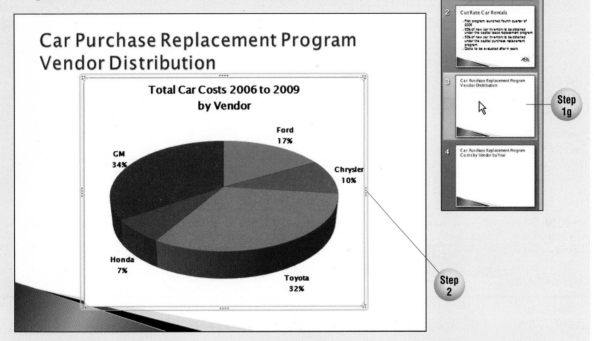

3. Copy and embed the table used to generate the chart in the CarCosts worksheet to the next slide in the PowerPoint presentation by completing the following steps:
   a. Click slide 4 in the Slides pane.
   b. Click the button on the Taskbar representing the Excel workbook **CutRate-Inventory.xlsx**.
   c. Make CarCosts the active worksheet, select A1:F9 and click the Copy button.
   d. Click the button on the taskbar representing the PowerPoint presentation **ExcelL2_C8_P2.pptx**.
   e. Click the down-pointing arrow on the Paste button and then click *Paste Special* at the drop-down list.
   f. With *Microsoft Office Excel Worksheet Object* selected in the *As* list box, click OK.

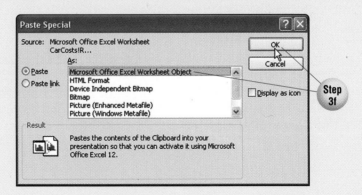

4. Resize and position the embedded table to the approximate height, width, and position shown.

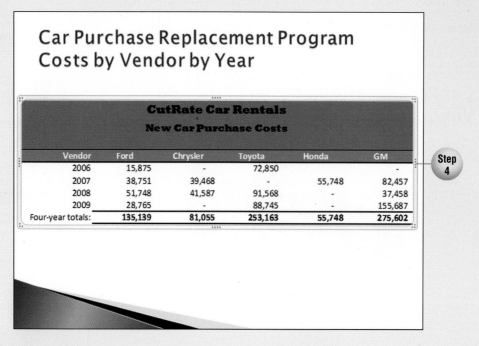

5. Click the Office button and then click *Print*. Change *Print what* to *Handouts*. Make sure *Slides per page* is *6*, and then click OK.
6. Save and close **ExcelL2_C8_P2.pptx** and then exit PowerPoint.
7. Press the ESC key to remove the moving marquee and then click any cell to deselect the range in the CarCosts worksheet.

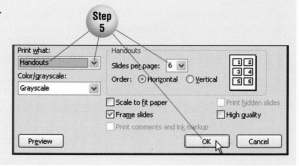

QUICK STEPS

Export Worksheet as Text File
1. Open workbook.
2. Make desired sheet active.
3. Click Office button.
4. Click *Save As*.
5. Type file name.
6. Change *Save as type* to desired text file format.
7. Click Save button.
8. Click OK.
9. Click Yes.

Exporting Excel Data as a Text File

If you need to exchange Excel data with a person who is not able to import a Microsoft Excel worksheet or cannot copy and paste using the clipboard, you can save the data as a text file. Excel provides several text file options including file formats suitable for computers that use the Macintosh operating system as shown in Table 8.1. To save a worksheet as a text file, open the Save As dialog box and change *Save as type* to the desired option. Type a file name for the text file and then click the Save button. Click OK at the message box that informs you that only the active worksheet is saved and then click Yes at the next message box to confirm you want to save the data as a text file.

Table 8.1 Supported Text File Formats for Exporting

Text File Format Option	File Extension
Text (tab delimited)	.txt
Unicode text	.txt
CSV (Comma delimited)	.csv
Formatted text (Space delimited)	.prn
Text (Macintosh)	.txt
Text (MS-DOS)	.txt
CSV (Macintosh)	.csv
CSV (MS-DOS)	.csv

HINT

Why so many text file formats? Although all systems support text files, differences occur across platforms. For example, a Macintosh computer denotes the end of a line in a text file with a carriage return character, Unix uses a linefeed character, and DOS inserts both a linefeed and a carriage return character code at the end of each line.

Project ㉑ Exporting a Worksheet as a Text File

1. With **CutRate-Inventory.xlsx** open, export the NewInventory worksheet data as a text file by completing the following steps:
   a. Make NewInventory the active worksheet.
   b. Click the Office button and then click *Save As*.
   c. Type **ExcelL2_C8_P2** in the *File name* text box.
   d. Click the down-pointing arrow to the right of the *Save as type* list box, scroll down the list, and then click *CSV (Comma delimited) (*.csv)* at the drop-down list.
   e. Click the Save button.

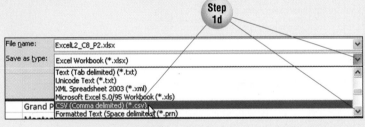

Step 1d

   f. Click OK to save only the active sheet at the Microsoft Office Excel message box that informs you the selected file type does not support workbooks that contain multiple worksheets.

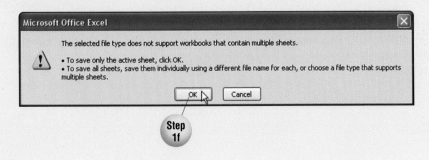

Step 1f

g. Click Yes to save the workbook in this format at the next message box that informs you Excel_L2_C8.csv may contain features that are not compatible with CSV (Comma delimited).

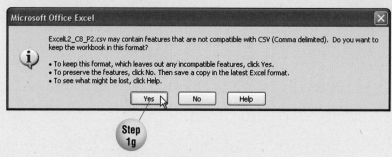

Step 1g

2. Close **ExcelL2_C8_P2.csv**. Click No when prompted to save changes.
3. Open Notepad and view the text file created in Step 1 by completing the following steps:
   a. Click the Start button, point to *All Programs*, point to *Accessories*, and then click *Notepad*.
   b. Click File on the Notepad Menu bar and then click *Open*.
   c. Navigate to the Excel2007L2C8 folder on your storage medium.
   d. Click the down-pointing arrow next to *Files of type* and then click *All Files* at the drop-down list.
   e. Double-click **ExcelL2_C8_P2.csv**.
   f. Scroll down to view all of the data in the text file. Notice that a comma has been inserted between each column's data.

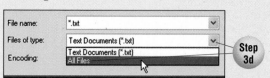

Step 3d

A comma is inserted at each column change in a csv text file.

Step 3f

4. Click File on the Notepad Menu bar and then click *Print*. Click the Print button at the Print dialog box.
5. Exit Notepad.

Word 2007 Quick Reference

Word 2007 Feature	Ribbon Tab, Group	Button	Quick Access Toolbar	Office Button Drop-down List	Keyboard Shortcut
Align Text Left	Home, Paragraph	[button]			Ctrl + L
Align Text Right	Home, Paragraph	[button]			Ctrl + R
Bold	Home, Font	B			Ctrl + B
Bullets	Home, Paragraph	[button]			
Center	Home, Paragraph	[button]			Ctrl + E
Change Styles	Home, Styles	[button]			
Clip Art	Insert, Illustrations	[button]			
Close				Close	Ctrl + F4
Columns	Page Layout, Page Setup	[button]			
Copy selected text	Home, Clipboard	[button]			Ctrl + C
Cut selected text	Home, Clipboard	[button]			Ctrl + X
Double line spacing	Home, Paragraph	[button]			Ctrl + 2
Drop cap	Insert, Text	Drop Cap			
Envelopes and Labels	Mailings, Create	[button]			
Exit Word				Exit Word	
Find and Replace	Home, Editing	[button]			Ctrl + F
Font	Home, Font	Calibri (Body)			Ctrl + Shift + F
Footer	Insert, Header & Footer	[button]			
Header	Insert, Header & Footer	[button]			
Help		[button]			F1
Hyperlink	Insert, Links	Hyperlink			Ctrl + K
New document			[button]	New, Blank document	Ctrl + N
Page break	Insert, Pages	Page Break			Ctrl + Enter
Page number	Insert, Header & Footer	[button]			
Page Setup dialog box	Page Layout, Page Setup	[button]			
Paste selected text	Home, Clipboard	[button]			Ctrl + V
Picture	Insert, Illustrations	[button]			
Print			[button]		
Quick Parts	Insert, Text	Quick Parts			
Save			[button]		Ctrl + S
Save As				Save As	F12
Section break	Page Layout, Page Setup	Breaks			
Single line spacing	Home, Paragraph	[button]			Ctrl + 1
SmartArt	Insert, Illustrations	[button]			
Spelling & Grammar	Review, Proofing	[button]			F7
Table	Insert, Tables	[button]			
Text box	Insert, Text	[button]			
Theme	Page Layout, Themes	[button]			
Underline	Home, Font	U			Ctrl + U
WordArt	Insert, Text	WordArt			

Excel 2007 Quick Reference

Excel 2007 Feature	Ribbon Tab, Group	Button	Quick Access Toolbar	Office Button Drop-down List	Keyboard Shortcut
Accounting Number Format	Home, Number	$			
Align Text Left	Home, Alignment	[button]			
Align Text Right	Home, Alignment	[button]			
Apply worksheet theme	Page Layout, Themes	[button]			
Bold	Home, Font	B			Ctrl + B
Borders	Home, Font	[button]			
Cell Styles	Home, Styles	[button]			
Center	Home, Alignment	[button]			
Column Width or Row Height	Home, Cells	Format			
Copy	Home, Clipboard	[button]			Ctrl + C
Create a column chart	Insert, Charts	[button]			F11
Cut	Home, Clipboard	[button]			Ctrl + X
Delete Cell, Column, Row, or worksheet	Home, Cells	Delete			
Draw a text box	Insert, Text	[button]			
Fill Color	Home, Font	[button]			
Filter table	Home, Editing	[button]			
Font Color	Home, Font	[button]			
Format Painter	Home, Clipboard	[button]			
Format as table	Home, Styles	[button]			
Format, Move, Copy, or Rename worksheet	Home, Cells	Format			
Freeze Panes	View, Window	Freeze Panes			
Increase Decimal	Home, Number	[button]			
Insert Cell, Column, Row, or worksheet	Home, Cells	Insert			
Insert comment	Review, Comments	[button]			
Insert function	Formulas, Function Library	[button]			
Insert header or footer	Insert, Text	[button]			
Merge & Center	Home, Alignment	[button]			
New blank workbook			[button]	New	Ctrl + N
Open			[button]	Open	Ctrl + O
Page Layout view	View, Workbook Views	[button] OR [button]			
Paste	Home, Clipboard	[button]			Ctrl + V
Percent Style	Home, Number	%			Ctrl + Shift + %
Print Preview				Print, Print Preview	Ctrl + F2
Print using Print dialog				Print	Ctrl + P
Save			[button]	Save	
Save As				Save As	F12
Scale page width and/or height	Page Layout, Scale to Fit	[button]			
Sort	Home, Editing	[button]			
SUM function	Home, Editing	[button]			Alt + =